Dedicated to the females
in my life. . .

Lauren, Jessica and Spring
''Buffy'' ''Cossette'' and ''Molly''

Library of Congress No. 90-190086
©Copyright 1/90 Artco, Boston, MA.
Second Printing 8/91
Third Printing 7/92
Fourth Printing 9/93
Fifth Printing 1/95
Sixth Printing 1/96

Artco Publishing
Division of
Artco Offset, Inc.
12 Channel Street
Boston, MA 02210

Dear Reader,

One of life's greatest joys is the bond that develops between you and your pet. The unconditional love that your pet gives is based on the companionship, trust, dependence and love you both share.

Recently my family was extended to include "Buffy", a bundle of joy and love who doesn't like being left at home, or worse, in a kennel. I was flabbergasted to learn that it is next to impossible to find a hotel that would accept my recent family member. I set out right away to make life easier for me and my fellow pet owners! I hope you find this directory useful, and that it saves you the long distance calling I did.

All of the hotels listed were contacted individually, as my office staff can vouch. If you find any of the information to be incorrect, or if you know of another lodging that accepts pets, please write and let me know.

I hope you and your pet enjoy the trip! Send me a postcard.

Sincerely,

Arthur Frank, Publisher

Front Cover Photo: Buffy and I

Publisher Notes:
How to Use Directory

States are listed alphabetically

Cities are listed alphabetically, only when we have a listed lodging. If there is no lodging that we could find the city will not appear in this book.

Lodgings are listed alphabetically
- —Restrictions on pets if any
- —Unattended pet in room policy, if any
- —Exercise area listed where available
- —Activities allowing pets listed when known
- —Room rates are guides only and are subject to change

Veterinarians
- —Animal Hospitals where available are listed first due to longer hours and greater availability of personnel.
- —Veterinarians listed where possible, if more than three in a town, we randomly selected three names. We supply these names with no prejudice or recommendation.

We have tried to be as accurate as we could when compiling this directory. All of the lodgings were called and asked the listed information. Of course, management of these accommodations are always changing and their pet policies may change at whim as well. We take no responsibility for any information listed in this directory. Please always call ahead to avoid surprises and disappointments.

Airline Travel Tips

If you and your pet plan to travel by air, be sure to check with the airline in advance to find out their pet requirements and avoid last minute disappointment or problems. Here are some other tips for flying:

1. Whenever possible, take direct flights and avoid connections. This will eliminate possible missed baggage connections. You don't want your pet in Boston if you are going to Chicago. Also in extreme weather conditions, either cold or hot, you want to eliminate the time your pet is in an outside area.

2. On some flights, many airlines will allow at least one pet in coach and one in first class, with some provisions. Your pet must be in a standard cage which will fit under your seat. And your pet must be quiet and not create an annoyance to other passengers.

3. Make sure your pet has seen a vet before travelling, and that you have all necessary health certification papers with you. Make sure all vaccinations are up to date.

4. Whenever possible, use airlines that will hand carry your pet (inside the required cage) to and from the aircraft. Otherwise the cage could be placed on a conveyor belt and your pet may experience a bumpy ride which no one would want!

5. Do not feed your pet for six hours before the flight, but do allow water up until flight time. Make sure water is always available in the cage during travel, and give your pet fresh water upon arrival.

6. Try to avoid the busiest travel times, so airline personnel will have a little extra time to give special handling to your pet.

7. **Do Not Tranquilize** your pet without first discussing with your vet.

8. Make sure your cage has specific feeding and identification labels permanently attached!

Choosing the Right Travel Cage for Your Pet

Your pet's travel cage will be his "home away from home" for much of your trip. That's why it's important to choose the right type of cage for your pet. Here are some helpful guidelines:

Size: Make sure the cage you choose is large enough for your pet to stand up in, and turn around freely. ***This is important — don't skimp!*** It is the law.

Strength: All walls must be strong and waterproof! This will prevent crushing in case of baggage travel, as well as prevent waste leakage.

Ventilation: There must be adequate ventilation, on at least three sides of the cage, better still, on the top also.

Handles: If you are travelling by public carrier, the cage must have sturdy handles for baggage personnel to use. Repair or replace broken handles before your trip.

Feeding: Attach specific feeding instructions to the outside of the cage. The best type of cage will also have a water tray which is accessible from the outside, so water can be easily added if needed.

Sanitation: Make sure you cover the bottom of the cage with an absortive covering. Cardboard, newspapers, etc. will work fine.

Most pet stores, breeders and kennels can sell you a cage which meets these requirements. Some airlines will also be able to sell you one which they may prefer to use. It would be a good idea to check with the airline or carrier you will be using in advance to see if they have other requirements beyond the ones I have mentioned.

One final bit of advice. . . try to get your pet used to his travel cage *before* you leave for your trip. Throw treats or toys into the cage and let your pet play inside with the door both open and closed. This will help eliminate some of your pet's stress from the trip, which is bound to be stressful enough!

Hotel Etiquette for Pets

1. Be wise — call ahead before you arrive to let the hotel know you are bringing your pet. This will eliminate any "surprise" at the front desk.

2. Bring your pet's cage in and set it up in the bathroom or other secure non-carpeted area.

3. If possible, have your pet sleep in his cage. Otherwise, bring a sheet or other bedding and let him sleep on your covering. This will help to eliminate pet hairs left on hotel beds or carpeting after you leave.

4. If the lodging will permit you to leave your pet unattended in your room, try to restrict her movements (and avoid possible damage to hotel property). Some suggestions. . .either leave your pet in the bathroom with food and water (don't forget the litterbox for your cat!) or keep her in the cage with water where this is possible. Don't forget to put the "Do Not Disturb" sign on the outside door and let housekeeping know that you have an unattended pet. This should eliminate any disturbance by housekeeping, and possible escape of your pet from the room.

5. Clean up after your pet! Shed hair, empty food cans, spills, accidents, etc. should be attended to promptly, and not left behind for the hotel staff.

6. Remember: the better we are with our pets, the more likely hotel management will continue to allow us to bring our pets along. Be a good guest!

7. If circumstances require it, don't neglect to leave an extra service gratuity!

Loss Prevention

What could be more disastrous than the loss of your pet? Here are some common sense rules that will keep your special travelling companion safe and sound!

1. Make sure your pet wears a collar with an identification tag securely fastened. The tag should have your name, address and phone number.

2. Always travel with a leash for your dog and a leash-harness setup for your cat. Make sure you and your pet are familiar with the use of this leash before the trip!

3. Attach your pet's leash or harness while he is still inside the cage. Don't let him out first and then try to attach the leash. A frightened or disoriented pet could run off before you have a chance to fasten the leash!

4. If you leave your pet unattended in lodging rooms, make sure there is no opportunity for her to escape. Leave her in her cage or in the bathroom, always with adequate food and water. Be sure to inform housekeeping personnel of your pet, and ask that they wait until you return before entering the room. Use ''Do Not Disturb'' signs when available.

5. If you travel by car and make ''pit stops'', be sure to attach your pet's leash or harness inside the car before stepping out. Once your pet is outside the car, he may become disoriented by the strange surroundings and run off. Pets should not be left unattended in the car. If you must, leave windows open, make water available, and park in the shade — Protect your pet!

6. Should your pet get lost, contact the local animal control officer first!

ALABAMA — HOTELS

ANNISTON
Hampton Inn-Anniston/Oxford
Highway 21S
Anniston, AL 36203
Phone: (205) 835-1492

Pet Restrictions: Up to a week
Pet left unattended in room: Yes
Exercise Area for Pets: Yes
Activities: Oxford Lake
Rates: $36 to $49

ATHENS
Welcome Inn
P.O. Box 1125
Athens, AL 35611
Phone: (205) 232-6944

Pet Restrictions: Left only 2 hours
    or less
Pet left unattended in room: Yes
Exercise Area for Pets: Yes
Rates: $27.95 to $33.50

VETERINARIANS
Limestone Veterinary Clinic
1701 Highway 72E. 35611
(205) 233-1515

Hammons, John R.
521 13th St. 35611
(205) 232-0698

ATTALIA
Holiday Inn
801 Cleveland Ave.
Attalia, AL 35954
Phone: (205) 538-7861

Pet Restrictions: None
Pet left unattended in room: Yes
Exercise Area for Pets: Yes
Rates: $50 to $52

BIRMINGHAM
Hampton Inn-S
1466 Montgomery
Birmingham, AL 35216
Phone: (205) 822-2224

Pet Restrictions: None
Pet left unattended in room: Yes
Exercise Area for Pets: Yes
Activities: Botanical Gardens and
    Zoo 4 miles from motel
Rates: $57 to $59

Holiday Inn-Airport
5000 10th Ave. N
Birmingham, AL 35212
Phone: (205) 591-6900

Pet Restrictions: None
Exercise Area for Pets: Yes
Rates: $44.95 to $69

Howard Johnsons
1485 Montgomery Hwy
Birmingham, AL 35216
Phone: (205) 823-4300

Pet Restrictions: None
Pet left unattended in room: Yes
Rates: $42 to $47

Ramada Inn-Airport
5216 Airport Hwy
Birmingham, AL 35212
Phone: (205) 591-7900

Pet Restrictions: $25 deposit
Pet left unattended in room: Yes
Exercise Area for Pets: Yes
Activities: Zoo, Botanical Gardens
Rates: $67 to $71

Red Roof Inn
151 Velicon Rd.
Birmingham, AL 35209
Phone: (205) 942-9414

Pet Restrictions: Guest responsible
    for damages. No housekeeping
Pet left unattended in room: Yes
Exercise Area for Pets: Yes
Rates: $35 to $47.99

The Residence Inn
3 Green Hill Pkwy at U.S. 280
Birmingham, AL 35242
Phone: (205) 991-8686

Pet Restrictions: None
Pet left unattended in room: Yes
Exercise Area for Pets: Yes
Rates: $89 to $119

Rime Garden Suites Hotel
5320 Beacon Dr.
Birmingham, AL 35210
Phone: (205) 951-2900

Pet Restrictions: $25 fee
Exercise Area for Pets: Yes
Activities: Park
Rates: $49 to $120

Roebuck Econo Lodge
9225 Parkway E.
Birmingham, AL 35206
Phone: (205) 836-5400
Pet Restrictions: None, notify desk
Pet left unattended in room: Yes
Exercise Area for Pets: Yes
Rates: $35 to $49

VETERINARIANS
Center Point Animal Clinic
1704 Center Point Road 35215
(205) 853-3340

Valleydale Animal Clinic
4680 Valleydale Road 35242
(205) 991-5416

Forestdale Veterinary Clinic
1320 Forestdale Blvd. 35214
(205) 798-2428

CLANTON
Holiday Inn
P.O. Box 2010
Clanton, AL 35045
Phone: (205) 755-0510
Pet Restrictions: None
Pet left unattended in room: Yes
Exercise Area for Pets: Yes
Rates: $39 to $48

CULLMAN
Days Inn
1841 4th St. SW
Cullman, AL 35055
Phone: (205) 739-3800
Pet Restrictions: $3 charge
Rates: $38 to $44

VETERINARIANS
East Point Vet Hospital Inc.
Route 8/Box 20 35055
(205) 734-0712

DALEVILLE
Green House Inn Lodge
501 S. Daleville Ave.
Daleville, AL 36332
Phone: (205) 598-1475
Pet Restrictions: $2/day/pet
    If mean dog, let maids know
Pet left unattended in room: Yes
Exercise Area for Pets: Yes
Rates: $29.95 to $41.95

DECATUR
Holiday Inn-Downtown
1101 6th Ave. NE
Decatur, AL 35601
Phone: (205) 355-3150
Pet Restrictions: None. Must be
    present during housekeeping
Pet left unattended in room: Yes
Exercise Area for Pets: Nearby
Rates: $60 to $75

Ramada Inn
1317 E. Highway 67
Decatur, AL 35601
Phone: (205) 353-0333
Pet Restrictions: None, must be quiet
Pet left unattended in room: Yes
Exercise Area for Pets: Yes
Activities: Point Mallard — water
    slides, picnic area, beach —
    pets on leash
Rates: $43 to $48

DOTHAN
Days Inn
2841 Ross Clark Circle SW
Dothan, AL 36301
Phone: (205) 793-2550
Pet Restrictions: $2/day/pet, must
    be quiet
Pet left unattended in room: Yes
Activities: Westgate Park
Rates: $22.95 to $33.80

Econo Lodge
2901 Ross Clark Circle SW
Dothan, AL 36301
Phone: (205) 793-5200
Pet Restrictions: None, inform
    housekeeping
Pet left unattended in room: Yes
Exercise Area for Pets: Yes
Rates: $22 to $47

Holiday Inn
3053 Ross Clark Circle
Dothan, AL 36301
Phone: (205) 794-6601
Pet Restrictions: Small to medium
    sized, inform management
Pet left unattended in room: Yes
Exercise Area for Pets: Yes
Rates: $39 to $60

ALABAMA — HOTELS (continued)

Holiday Inn
2195 Ross Clark Circle SE
Dothan, AL 36301
Phone: (205) 794-8711
Pet Restrictions: Yes, small pets
   only
Pet left unattended in room: Yes
Exercise Area for Pets: Yes
Rates: $46 to $66

Olympian Motel & Conf. Ctr.
P.O. Box 6108
Dothan, AL 36302
Phone: (205) 677-3321
Pet Restrictions: $2.50/day/pet
Pet left unattended in room: Yes,
   with Do Not Disturb sign
Rates: $39.50

VETERINARIANS:

Bullard Vet. Hospital
2505 W. Main St. 36301
(205) 793-0072

Garrett-Kennington Inc.
1342 S. Oates 36301
(205) 793-9779

Southeast Alabama Vet. Hosp.
2422 Montgomery Hwy 36303
(205) 793-3535

ENTERPRISE

Comfort Inn
615 Hwy 84 Bypass
Enterprise, AL 36330
Phone: (205) 393-2304
Pet Restrictions: None, $5.30 fee,
   no housekeeping unless present
Pet left unattended in room: Yes
Exercise Area for Pets: Yes
Activities: Aviation Museum —
   allows pets outside only
Rates: $40 to $45

EVERGREEN

Econo Lodge
P.O. Box 564
Evergreen, AL 36401
Phone: (205) 578-4701
Pet Restrictions: $4 for large animal,
   $2 for small animal
Pet left unattended in room: Yes
Exercise Area for Pets: Yes
Rates: $35 to $45

GADSDEN

Days Inn
1600 Rainbow Dr
Gadsden, AL 35901
Phone: (205) 543-1105
Pet Restrictions: $10 fee if caged
Pet left unattended in room: Yes
Exercise Area for Pets: Yes
Rates: $48 to $52

HOPE HULL

Days Inn
7725 Mobile Hwy
Hope Hull, AL 36043
Phone: (205) 281-7151
Pet Restrictions: None
Pet left unattended in room: Yes
Exercise Area for Pets: Yes
Rates: $35.95 to $39.95

HOOVER

Days Inn - South
1535 Montgomery Hwy.
Hoover, AL 35216
Phone: (205) 822-6030
Pet Restrictions: Under 5 lbs.
Exercise Area for Pets: Yes
Rates: $36 to $125

HUNTSVILLE

Days Inn
102 Arlington Dr.
Huntsville, AL 35758
Phone: (205) 772-9550
Pet Restrictions: $5 fee/day
Pet left unattended in room: Yes
Exercise Area for Pets: Yes
Rates: $36 to $46

Villager Lodge
3100 University Dr.
Huntsville, AL 35816
Phone: (205) 533-0610
Pet Restrictions: Under 25 lbs.
Pet left unattended in room: Yes
Exercise Area for Pets: Yes
Rates: $25.95 to $30.95

VETERINARIANS:

Horton, Charles R.
931 Cook Ave. NW 35801
(205) 539-9841

McManus, Wilson W.
7604 S. Memorial Pkwy 35802
(205) 881-4862

Nelson, Troy J.
4296 University Dr. NW 35816
(205) 837-9700

MADISON
Ramada Inn-Huntsville Airport
8716 Hwy 20W
Madison, AL 35758
Phone: (205) 772-0701
Pet Restrictions: None
Pet left unattended in room: Yes
Exercise Area for Pets: Yes
Rates: $36 to $50

VETERINARIANS:
Whitworth Animal Clinic
106 Rainbow Dr. 35758
(205) 830-1503

MILLBROOK
Holiday Inn
P.O. Box A
Millbrook, AL 36054
Phone: (205) 285-3420
Pet Restrictions: None
Exercise Area for Pets: Nearby
Rates: $43 to $53

VETERINARIANS:
Parker, Robert H.
4220 Highway 14 36054
(205) 285-4210

MOBILE
Econo Lodge
I-65 Dawphin St. Exit
1 South Beltline Hwy
Mobile, AL 36606
Phone: (205) 479-5333
Pet Restrictions: Small pets
Pet left unattended in room: Yes
Exercise Area for Pets: Yes
Rates: $34.95 to $41.95

Econo Lodge Resort & Conf. Ctr.
Historic Battleship Pkwy, Box 1626
Mobile, AL 36633
Phone: (205) 626-7200
Pet Restrictions: None
Pet left unattended in room: Yes
Exercise Area for Pets: Yes
Activities: U.S.S. Alabama has kennel
Rates: $39 to $54

Hampton Inn
930 S. Beltway
Mobile, AL 36609
Phone: (205) 344-4942
Pet Restrictions: Small pets
Pet left unattended in room: Yes
Exercise Area for Pets: Yes
Rates: $39 to $50

Holiday Inn I-65
850 S. Beltline Hwy
Mobile, AL 36616
Phone: (205) 342-3220
Pet Restrictions: Small pets, if trained
Pet left unattended in room: Yes
Exercise Area for Pets: Yes
Activities: Many parks in area; dogs
  must be leashed
Rates: $48 to $71

Motel 6
400 S. Beltline Hwy
Mobile, AL 36608
Phone: (205) 343-8448
Pet Restrictions: Small pets, if quiet
Pet left unattended in room: Yes
Exercise Area for Pets: Yes
Rates: $25.95 to $6.60/person

Red Roof Inn
5380 Coca Cola Rd.
Mobile, AL 36619
Phone: (205) 666-1044
Pet Restrictions: Smoking rooms
  only
Pet left unattended in room: Yes, no
  maid service
Exercise Area for Pets: Yes
Rates: $32 to $43

Red Roof Inn
33 South Beltline Hwy
Mobile, AL 36606
Phone: (205) 476-2004
Pet Restrictions: Small pets only
Pet left unattended in room: Yes
Exercise Area for Pets: Yes
Rates: $32.99 to $43.99

VETERINARIANS
Rehm Animal Clinic PC
951 Hillcrest Rd. 36609
(205) 639-9120

Simpson, Leann
1015 Highpoint Blvd. 36608
(205) 344-8738

Willard, G.P.
1957 Hurtel St. 36605
(205) 479-4566

MONTGOMERY

Budgetel
5225 Carmichael Blvd.
Montgomery, AL 36106
Phone: (205) 277-6000

Pet Restrictions: Small animals
Pet left unattended in room: Yes
Exercise Area for Pets: Yes
Rates: $32.95 to $50.95

Comfort Inn
5175 Carmichael Blvd.
Montgomery, AL 36106
Phone: (205) 277-1919

Pet Restrictions: Small-medium sized
  but no housekeeping, please notify
Pet left unattended in room: Yes
Exercise Area for Pets: Yes
Rates: $41.95 to $47.95

Hampton Inn
1401 Eastern Blvd.
Montgomery, AL 36117
Phone: (205) 277-2400

Pet Restrictions: None, notify desk
Pet left unattended in room: Yes
Exercise Area for Pets: Nearby
Activities: Park behind hotel
Rates: $40 to $50

Riverfront Station
200 Coosa St.
Montgomery, AL 36104
Phone: (205) 834-4300

Pet Restrictions: Small pets
Exercise Area for Pets: Nearby
Rates: $48 to $57

Statehouse Inn
924 Madison Ave.
Montgomery, AL 36104
Phone: (205) 265-0741

Pet Restrictions: Small pets but no
  housekeeping
Pets left unattended in room: Yes
Exercise Area for Pets: Yes
Rates: $48 to $60

VETERINARIANS
Capital Plaza Veterinary Clinic
2200 E. South Blvd. 36111
(205) 281-5400

Carriage Hills Animal Clinic
3200 E. Blvd. 36116
(205) 277-2867

The Animal Clinic
3505 McGehee Rd. 36111
(205) 281-6100

OXFORD

Save Inn Oxford/Anniston
25 Elm St.
Oxford, AL 36203
Phone: (800) 282-1152
Fax: (205) 831-1970

Pet Restrictions: Applies to cats,
  dogs and caged birds
Pet left unattended in room: No
  unless pet is in cage
Exercise Area for Pets: Yes
Rates: $24.95 to $29.95
  $5.00 extra for pet

OZARK

Best Western Ozark Inn
P.O. Box 1396, US 231 at Deese Rd.
Ozark, AL 36361
Phone: (205) 774-5166

Pet Restrictions: None, notify desk
Pet left unattended in room: Yes
Exercise Area for Pets: Yes
Rates: $31 to $44

Holiday Inn
151 US 231N
Ozark, AL 36360
Phone: (205) 774-7300

Pet Restrictions: None
Pet left unattended in room: Yes
Exercise Area for Pets: Yes
Rates: $46 to $48

PRATTVILLE

Ramada Inn - Prattville
P.O. Box 388
Prattville, AL 36067
Phone: (205) 365-3311

Pet Restrictions: $6 fee
Pet left unattended in room: Yes
Exercise Area for Pets: Yes
Rates: $44 for double

VETERINARIANS
Animal Medical Clinic
407 E. Main St. 36067
(205) 365-7543

TILLMAN'S CORNER
Shoney's Inn of Mobile
6556 US 90
Tillman's Corner, AL 36619
Phone: (205) 660-1520

Pet Restrictions: $5 deposit, for
    short time
Pet left unattended in room: Yes
Exercise Area for Pets: Yes
Rates: $42 to $48

TROY
Holiday Inn of Troy
Hwy 231N, P.O. Box 564
Troy, AL 36081
Phone: (205) 566-1150

Pet Restrictions: 10 lbs. or less
Pet left unattended in room: Yes
Exercise Area for Pets: Yes
Rates: $41 to $51

TUSCALOOSA
Days Inn
3600 McFarland Blvd
Tuscaloosa, AL 35405
Phone: (205) 556-2010

Pet Restrictions: None
Exercise Area for Pets: Yes
Rates: Vary

VETERINARIANS
May Veterinary Hospital
3509 Greensboro Ave. 35401
(205) 752-1564

Jordan, Loy
2211 Paul W. Bryant Dr. 35401
(205) 758-5520

ALASKA — HOTELS

ANCHORAGE

Days Inn
321 E. 5th Ave.
Anchorage AK 99501
Phone: (907) 276-7226

Pet Restrictions: None
Pet left unattended in room: Yes
Exercise Area for Pets: Yes
Rates: $59 to $129

Regal Alaskan Hotel
4800 Spenard Rd.
Anchorage, AK 99517
Phone: (907) 243-2300

Pet Restrictions: $50 deposit, must
    be locked up for housekeeping
Pet left unattended in room: Yes
Exercise Area for Pets: Yes
Rates: $134 to $210

VETERINARIANS

Alaska Veterinary Clinic
300 E. Firewood Lane 99503
(907) 277-3224

College Village Annual Clinic
2036 E. Northern Lights 99508
(907) 274-5623

Northern Lights Animal Clinic
2002 W. Benson Blvd 99517
(907) 276-2340

HAINES

Captains Choice Motel
Second and Dalton Sts.
Haines, AK 99827
Phone: (907) 766-3111

Pet Restrictions: $5/day
Exercise Area for Pets: Yes
Rates: $60 to $127

Eagle's Nest Motel
1 Mile Haines Hwy.
Haines, AK 99827
Phone: (907) 766-2891

Pet Restrictions: None
Exercise Area for Pets: Yes
Rates: $60 to $87

KETCHIKAN

The Landing Best Western
3434 Tongass Ave.
Ketchiman, AK 99901
Phone: (907) 225-5166

Pet Restrictions: $10/night, $20 for
    room cleaning is kept, $50 deposit
Pet left unattended in room: Yes
    except when housekeeping
Exercise Area for Pets: Yes
Rates: $68 to $80

VETERINARIANS

Starks, Vern R.
Route 1, Box 863 99901
Phone: (907) 247-2620

KODIAK

Kodiak Buskin River Inn
1395 Airport Way
Kodiak, AK 99615
Phone: (907) 487-2700

Pet Restrictions: $25 per night
Pet left unattended in room: Yes
Exercise Area for Pets: Yes
Rates $100 to $150

ARIZONA — HOTELS

APACHE JUNCTION

Apache Junction
1680 W. Apache Trail
Apache Junction, AZ 85220
Phone: (602) 982-7702

Pet Restrictions: Small dogs
Exercise Area for Pets: Yes
Rates: $25 to $62

VETERINARIANS

Schmidt, Marc L.
P.O. Box 1217 85220
Phone: (602) 984-2114

BISBEE

The Bisbee Inn
45 Oak St.
Bisbee, AZ 85603
Phone: (602) 432-5131

Pet Restrictions: Rooms on lower
level
Rates: $32 to $72

CAREFREE

The Boulders
34631 N. Tom Darlington
P.O. Box 2090
Carefree, AZ 85377
Phone: (602) 488-9009

Pet Restrictions: $50 non-
refundable, only small
Pet left unattended in room: Yes in
carrier
Exercise Area for Pets: Yes
Rates: $525 incl. breakfast & dinner

CHAMBERS

Best Western Chieftan Motel
P.O. Box 39
Chambers, AZ 86502
Phone: (602) 688-2754

Pet Restrictions: Small pets
Pet left unattended in room: Yes
Exercise Area for Pets: Yes
Rates: $50 to $53

DOUGLAS

Price Canyon Ranch
P.O. Box 1065
Douglas, AZ 85607
Phone: (602) 558-2383

Pet Restrictions: None
Pet left unattended in room: Yes
Exercise Area for Pets: Yes
Rates: $85 to $170

VETERINARIANS

Ames, Michael J.
2017 Rogers Avenue 85608
Phone: (602) 364-3403

ELOY

Super 8
3945 W. Houser Rd.
Eloy, Arizona 85231
Phone: (602) 466-7804

Pet Restrictions: Small pets
Exercise Area for Pets: Yes
Rates: $41 to $50

FLAGSTAFF

Flagstaff Inn
2285 E. Butler Ave.
Flagstaff, AZ 86004
Phone: (602) 774-1821

Pet Restrictions: $5/pet if quiet
Pet left unattended in room: Yes
Exercise Area for Pets: Yes
Rates: $34 to $45

Quality Inn
2000 S. Milton Rd.
Flagstaff, AZ 86001
Phone: (602) 774-8771

Pet Restrictions: None
Exercise Area for Pets: Yes
Rates: $72 to $85

VETERINARIANS

Canyon Pet Hospital
12 Mike's Pike 86001
Phone: (602) 774-5197

Howerton, Cheryl L.
4416 S. Kathy Rd. 86001
Phone: (602) 779-5770

Westover, William C.
Route 11, Box 17 86004
Phone: (602) 526-2423

GRAND CANYON NATIONAL PARK

Grand Canyon Lodges
P.O. Box 699
Grand Canyon Nat'l Park, AZ 86023
Phone: (602) 638-2631

Pet Restrictions: Must be kept in
kennel
Exercise Area for Pets: Yes
Rates: Call for rates

KINGMAN

Days Inn
3381 E. Andy Devine
Kingman, AZ 86401
Phone: (602) 757-7337

Pet Restrictions: $3 fee
Pet left unattended in room: Yes
Exercise Area for Pets: Yes
Rates: $32 to $45

Holiday Inn
3100 E. Andy Devine
Kingman, AZ 86401
Phone: (602) 753-6262

Pet Restrictions: None, if well
    behaved
Pet left unattended in room: Yes
Exercise Area for Pets: Yes
Rates: $49 to $69

VETERINARIANS

Koski, Dawn C.
3755 Stirrup Dr. 86401

Zitterkopf, Jerry L.
2323 E. Detroit Ave. 86401
Phone: (602) 753-6138

LAKE HAVASU CITY

E-Z 8 Motel - Lake Havasu
41 S. Acoma Blvd.
Lake Havasu City, AZ 86403
Phone: (602) 855-4023

Pet Restrictions: Dogs must be on
    leash while walking on premises
    Pet deposit for large dogs
Pet left unattended in room: No
Exercise Area for Pets: Nearby
    around lake and on the river
Rates: $21.88 to $34.88

Holiday Inn
245 London Bridge Rd.
Lake Havasu City, AZ 86403
Phone: (602) 855-4071

Pet Restrictions: Small pets
Exercise Area for Pets: Yes
Rates: $45 to $135

VETERINARIANS

Arnold, Jean ED
800 Havasupai 86403
Phone: (602) 768-3108

LITCHFIELD PARK

The Wigwam
Litchfield Park
Litchfield Park, AZ 85340
Phone: (602) 935-3811

Pet Restrictions: $50 deposit ½
    non-refundable, small pets
Pet left unattended in room: Yes, let
    maid know
Exercise Area for Pets: Yes
Rates: $230 to $400

MESA

Arizona Golf Resort & Conf. Ctr.
425 Power Rd.
Mesa, AZ 85206
Phone: (602) 832-3202

Pet Restrictions: None
Pet left unattended in room: Yes
Exercise Area for Pets: Yes
Rates: $69 to $155

Days Inn
333 W. Juanita
Mesa, AZ 85210
Phone: (602) 844-8900

Pet Restrictions: Prefer under 15 lbs.
Exercise Area for Pets: Yes
Rates: $49 to $54

Hampton Inn
1563 S. Gilbert Rd.
Mesa, AZ 85204
Phone: (602) 926-3600

Pet Restrictions: None, $100
    refundable deposit
Pet left unattended in room: Yes
Exercise Area for Pets: Nearby
Rates: $59 to $84

VETERINARIANS

Mesa Verde Animal Hospital
820 E. Southern 852
Phone: (602) 969-3761

Mesa Veterinary Hospital
858 N. Country Club Dr. 85201
Phone: (602) 833-7330

Kern, Virginia A.
2752 E. Birchwood Ave. 85204
Phone: (602) 833-8562

ARIZONA — HOTELS (continued)

NOZALES
Best Western Motel Time
921 N. Grand Ave.
Nozales, AZ 85621
Phone: (602) 287-4627

Pet Restrictions: Small, trained, if quiet
Pet left unattended in room: Yes
Exercise Area for Pets: Yes
Rates: $41 to $46

Super 8
547 Mariposa Rd.
Nozales, AZ 85621
Phone: (602) 281-2242

Pet Restrictions: None, $5 fee
Exercise Area for Pets: Yes
Rates: $37.80 to $53.88

PARKER
Holiday Kasbah
604 California Ave.
Parker, AZ 85344
Phone: (602) 669-2133

Pet Restrictions: $5/week/pet
Exercise Area for Pets: Yes
Rates: $33 to $89

PHOENIX
Best Western Bell Motel
17211 N. Black Canyon Hwy.
Phoenix, AZ 85023
Phone: (602) 993-8300

Pet Restrictions: $10 small dogs
Exercise Area for Pets: Yes
Rates: $59.50 to $64.50

Best Western Grace Inn Ahwatukee
10831 S. 51st St.
Phoenix, AZ 85044
Phone: (602) 893-3000

Pet Restrictions: Small pet, $50 deposit ½ refundable
Exercise Area for Pets: Yes
Rates: $95 to $105

Best Western Phoenix Northern Inn Suites
1615 E. Northern Ave.
Phoenix, AZ 85020
Phone: (602) 997-6285

Pet Restrictions: Small pets
Pet left unattended in room: Yes, notify housekeeping
Exercise Area for Pets: Yes
Rates: $72 to $129

Days Inn - Camelback
502 W. Camelback
Phoenix, AZ 85013
Phone: (602) 264-9290

Pet Restrictions: None, $10 fee
Pet left unattended in room: Yes
Exercise Area for Pets: Yes
Rates: $35 to $77

Embassy Suites - Thomas Rd.
2333 E. Thomas Rd.
Phoenix, AZ 85016
Phone: (602) 957-1910

Pet Restrictions: $3/day, well behaved
Pet left unattended in room: Yes
Exercise Area for Pets: Yes
Rates: $129 to $139

Embassy Suites - Westside
3210 N.W. Grand Ave.
Phoenix, AZ 85017
Phone: (602) 279-3211

Pet Restrictions: Small pets
Exercise Area for Pets: Yes
Rates: $92 to $102

E-Z 8 Motel - Airporter
1820 S. 7th St.
Phoenix, AZ 85034
Phone: (602) 254-9787

Pet Restrictions: Dogs must be on leash while walking on premises Pet deposit may be required
Pet left unattended in room: No
Exercise Area for Pets: Nearby
Rates: $24.88 to $34.88

Fountains Suite Hotel
2577 W. Greenway Rd.
Phoenix, AZ 85023
Phone: (602) 375-1777

Pet Restrictions: $100 nonrefundable
Pet left unattended in room: Yes
Exercise Area for Pets: Yes
Rates: $125 to $145

Hampton Inn
8101 Black Canyon Hwy
Phoenix, AZ 85021
Phone: (602) 864-6233

Pet Restrictions: Notify desk
Pet left unattended in room: Yes
Exercise Area for Pets: Yes
Rates: $65 to $71

Holiday Inn & Holidome - Phoenix Corp. Center
2532 W. Georgia Ave.
Phoenix, AZ 85029
Phone: (602) 943-2341

Pet Restrictions: Yes, small-medium, if quiet
Pet left unattended in room: Yes
Exercise Area for Pets: Yes
Rates: $79 to $89

Holiday Inn Phoenix West
1500 N. 51st Ave.
Phoenix, AZ 85034
Phone: (602) 484-9009

Pet Restrictions: Yes, small
Exercise Area for Pets: Yes
Rates: $60 to $85

Howard Johnson
124 S. 24th St.
Phoenix, AZ 85034
Phone: (602) 244-8221

Pet Restrictions: $25 deposit
Rates: $49 to $89

Knights Inn (Airport)
2201 S. 24th St.
Phoenix, AZ 85034
Phone: (602) 267-0611

Pet Restrictions: $10 fee
Pet left unattended in room: Yes
Exercise Area for Pets: Yes
Activities: Park
Rates: $45 to $50

La Quinta Motor Inn
2725 N. Black Canyon Hwy
Phoenix, AZ 85009
Phone: (602) 258-6271

Pet Restrictions: Small pets
Exercise Area for Pets: Yes
Rates: $69 to $76

Premier Inn
10402 Black Canyon Fwy (I17)
Phoenix, AZ 85051
Phone: (602) 943-2371
Fax: (602) 943-5847

Pet Restrictions: Dogs must be on leash while on premises
    Pet deposit may be required
Pet left unattended in room: No
Exercise Area for Pets: Nearby
Rates: $29.95 to $75.95

Quality Inn - Desert Sky
3541 E. Van Buren St.
Phoenix, AZ 85008
Phone: (602) 273-7121

Pet Restrictions: None, deposit
Exercise Area for Pets: Yes
Rates: $35 to $59

Quality Inn Financial Center
3600 N. 2nd Ave. at Osborn
Phoenix, AZ 85013
Phone: (602) 248-0222

Pet Restrictions: None
Pet left unattended in room: Yes
Exercise Area for Pets: Nearby
Rates: $76 to $84

Quality Inn Southeast
5121 E. La Puente Ave.
Phoenix, AZ 85044
Phone: (602) 893-3900

Pet Restrictions: $25 deposit, no housekeeping
Pet left unattended in room: Yes
Rates: $69 to $79

Radisson - Airport
3333 E. University Dr.
Phoenix, AZ 85034
Phone: (602) 437-8400

Pet Restrictions: Under 20 lbs.
Rates: $119 to $139

Ramada Inn Metro Center
12027 N. 28th Dr.
Phoenix, AZ 85029
Phone: (602) 866-7000

Pet Restrictions: $25 deposit, if well trained
Pet left unattended in room: Yes
Exercise Area for Pets: Yes
Rates: $80

Rodeway Inn - Airport
1202 S. 24th St. at Buckeye Rd.
Phoenix, AZ 85034
Phone: (602) 273-1211

Pet Restrictions: None, no housekeeping
Pet left unattended in room: Yes
Exercise Area for Pets: Yes
Rates: $60 to $66

Rodeway Inn - Grand Ave.
3400 Grand Ave.
Phoenix, AZ 85017
Phone: (602) 264-9164
Pet Restrictions: $5 fee
Pet left unattended in room: Yes
Exercise Area for Pets: Yes
Rates: $45 to $49

Royal Palms Inn
5200 E. Camelback Rd.
Phoenix, AZ 85018
Phone: (602) 840-3610
Pet Restrictions: None, if
    well-behaved
Pet left unattended in room: Yes
Exercise Area for Pets: Yes
Rates: $150 to $220

Sheraton Greenway Inn
2510 W. Greenway Rd.
Phoenix, AZ 85023
Phone: (602) 993-0800
Pet Restrictions: $25 fee, if well
    trained
Pet left unattended in room: Yes
Exercise Area for Pets: Nearby
Rates: $59 to $109

Travel Lodge - Metro
8617 N. Black Canyon Hwy
Phoenix, AZ 85020
Phone: (602) 995-9500
Pet Restrictions: $50 deposit
Pet left unattended in room: Yes
Exercise Area for Pets: Yes
Rates: $51 to $58

VETERINARIANS
American Pet Center
350 E. Bell Rd. 85022
(602) 942-9411

Northern Animal Hospital, Inc.
2609 W. Northern Ave. 85051
(602) 995-0460

Village Plaza Animal Hospital
12621 N. Tatum Blvd 85032
(602) 996-8300

PINETOP
Buck Springs Resort
P.O. Box 130
Pinetop, AZ 85935
Phone: (602) 369-3554
Pet Restrictions: $6 per night
Exercise Area for Pets: Yes
Rates: $48 to $65

VETERINARIANS
McSpadden, Mathew C.
HC 62 Box 2695   85935
(602) 367-3951

PRESCOTT
Sierra Inn
809 White Spar Rd.
Prescott, AZ 86303
Phone: (602) 445-1250
Pet Restrictions: Under 7 lbs., notify
    office, pay for damages
Pet left unattended in room: Yes
Exercise Area for Pets: Yes
Rates: $25 to $79

VETERINARIANS
**Thumb Butte Small Animal
Hospital**
1441 W. Curley St. 86301
(602) 445-2331

Dockter, Charles E.
1318 Iron Springs Rd. 86301
(602) 445-2190

SAFFORD
Best Western Desert Inn
of Safford
1391 Thatcher Blvd.
Safford, AZ 85546
Phone: (602) 428-0521
Pet Restrictions: Small,
    housebroken
Pet left unattended in room: Yes
Exercise Area for Pets: Yes
Rates: $57 to $95

SCOTTSDALE
The Adobe Resort Apt. Hotel
3635 N. 68th St.
Scottsdale, AZ 85251
Phone: (602) 945-3544
Pet Restrictions: $100 deposit
Pet left unattended in room: Yes
Exercise Area for Pets: Nearby
Rates: $54 to $89

Days Inn - Scottsdale Fashion
Square Resort
4710 N. Scottsdale Rd.
Scottsdale, AZ 85251
Phone: (602) 947-5411
Pet Restrictions: Small pets
Pet left unattended in room: Yes
Exercise Area for Pets: Yes
Rates: $98 to $105

Holiday Inn
7353 E. Indian School Rd.
Scottsdale, AZ 85251
Phone: (602) 994-9203
Pet Restrictions: Small, $150
    deposit
Exercise Area for Pets: Yes
Rates: $110 to $140

Red Lion's La Posada
4949 E. Lincoln Dr.
Scottsdale, AZ 85253
Phone: (602) 952-0420
Pet Restrictions: Small pets, must
    call ahead
Pet left unattended in room: Yes
Exercise Area for Pets: Yes
Rates: $185 to $250

The Safari-Best Western Resort
4611 N. Scottsdale Rd.
Scottsdale, AZ 85251
Phone: (602) 945-0721
Pet Restrictions: $50 deposit, notify
    housekeeping
Pet left unattended in room: Yes
Exercise Area for Pets: Yes
Activities: Park
Rates: $92 to $135

Scottsdale Embassy Suites
5001 N. Scottsdale Rd.
Scottsdale, AZ 85253
Phone: (602) 949-1414
Pet Restrictions: Small dogs if in cage
Pet left unattended in room: Yes
Exercise Area for Pets: Yes
Rates: $155

Stouffer Cottonwoods Resort
6160 N. Scottsdale Rd.
Scottsdale, AZ 85253
Phone: (602) 991-1414
Pet Restrictions: Small pets only, no
    housekeeping
Pet left unattended in room: Yes
Exercise Area for Pets: Yes
Rates: $195 to $265

Animal Hospital
3238 N. Scottsdale Rd. 85251
(602) 945-5673

Animal Hospital at McCormick Ranch
10380 N. Hayden Rd. 85258
(602) 948-3873

Kaibab Animal Hospital
3010 N. 68th St. 85251
(602) 947-8113

SEDONA

John Gardiner's Enchantment
525 Boynton Canyon Rd.
Sedona, AZ 86336
Phone: (602) 282-2900
Pet Restrictions: $45/day
    non-refundable
Pet left unattended in room: Yes
Exercise Area for Pets: Yes
Rates: $185 to $460

Quality Inn - King's Ransom Motor Hotel
P.O. Box 180
Sedona, AZ 86339
Phone: (602) 282-7151
Pet Restrictions: None
Pet left unattended in room: Yes
Exercise Area for Pets: Yes
Rates: $64 to $104

Sky Ranch Lodge
P.O. Box 2579
Sedona, AZ 86336
Phone: (602) 282-6400
Pet Restrictions: $5 per day
Exercise Area for Pets: Yes
Rates: $45 to $120

Super 8 Motel
100 Fab Ave.
Sedona, AZ 85635
Phone: (602) 459-5380
Pet Restrictions: None
Pet left unattended in room: Yes
Exercise Area for Pets: Yes
Rates: $39.88 to $46.88

SUN CITY

Best Western City Squire
Box 477, 11201 W. Grand Ave.
Sun City, AZ 85372
Phone: (602) 933-8211
Pet Restrictions: None
Exercise Area for Pets: Nearby
Rates: $34 to $62

Sun City Animal Hospital Ltd
10026 Santa Fe Dr. 85351
(602) 974-3691

SURPRISE

Winomill Inn
12545 W. Bell Rd.
Surprise, AZ 85374
Phone: (602) 583-0133

Pet Restrictions: None
Exercise Area for Pets: Yes
Rates: $95

TEMPE

Comfort Inn
5300 S. 56th St.
Tempe, AZ 85283
Phone: (602) 820-7500

Pet Restrictions: None, notify desk
Pet left unattended in room: Yes
Exercise Area for Pets: Yes
Rates: $59.95 to $74.95

Howard Johnson
225 East Apache Blvd.
Tempe, AZ 85281
Phone: (602) 967-9431

Pet Restrictions: Small pets,
    housebroken
Pet left unattended in room: Yes
Exercise Area for Pets: Yes
Rates: $62 to $79

Phoenix Airport / Tempe Best Western
1651 W. Baseline Rd.
Tempe, AZ 85283
Phone: (602) 897-7900

Pet Restrictions: None, no elephants
Pet left unattended in room: Yes
Exercise Area for Pets: Yes
Rates: $69 to $89

Tempe University Travelodge
1005 E. Apache Blvd.
Tempe, AZ 85281
Phone: (602) 968-7871

Pet Restrictions: $4/night,
    under 20 lbs.
Pet left unattended in room: Yes
Exercise Area for Pets: Yes
Rates: $42 to $65

Westcourt Inn The Buttes
2000 Westcourt Way
Tempe, AZ 85282
Phone: (602) 225-9000

Pet Restrictions: Under 20 lbs.
Exercise Area for Pets: Yes

VETERINARIANS

Countryside Veterinary Clinic
1720 E. Warner Rd. 85284
(602) 831-2600

**Tri-City Veterinary Hospital
Acacia CAT Clinic**
2332 E. Broadway Rd. 85281
(602) 968-9236

University Veterinary Hospital
925 W. Broadway 85282
(602) 968-9275

TUCSON

Best Western Exec Inn
333 W. Drachman
Tucson, AZ 85705
Phone: (602) 791-7551

Pet Restrictions: Small animals, use
    do not disturb sign
Pet left unattended in room: Yes
Exercise Area for Pets: Yes
Rates: $47 to $85

Best Western Ghost Ranch Lodge
801 W. Miracle Mile
Tucson, AZ 85705
Phone: (602) 791-7565

Pet Restrictions: Small pets, if quiet
Pet left unattended in room: Yes
Exercise Area for Pets: Yes
Rates: $68 to $106

Best Western Tucson Inn Suites
6201 N. Oracle Rd.
Tucson, AZ 85704
Phone: (602) 297-8111

Pet Restrictions: $20 deposit
Exercise Area for Pets: Yes
Rates: $79 to $150

Days Inn - Tucson Airport
3700 E. Irvington Rd.
Tucson, AZ 85714
Phone: (602) 571-1400

Pet Restrictions: None
Pet left unattended in room: Yes
Exercise Area for Pets: Yes
Rates: $48 to $60

Embassy Suites
7051 S. Tucson Blvd.
Tucson, AZ 85706
Phone: (602) 573-0700

Pet Restrictions: $50 deposit
Exercise Area for Pets: Yes
Rates: $104 to $119

E-Z 8 Motel - Tucson II
1007 S. Freeway
Tucson, AZ 85745
Phone: (602) 624-9843

Pet Restrictions: Dogs must be on
    leash while walking on premises
    Pet deposit for large dogs
Pet left unattended in room: No
Exercise Area for Pets: Nearby
Rates: $18.88 to $38.88

E-Z 8 Motel - Tucson I
720 W. 29th St.
Tucscon, AZ 85713
Phone: (602) 624-8291

Pet Restrictions: Dogs must be on
    leash while walking on premises
    Pet deposit for large dogs
Pet left unattended in room: No
Exercise Area for Pets: Nearby
Rates: $18.88 to $38.88

Flying V. Ranch
6800 N. Flying V. Ranch Rd.
Tucson, AZ 85715
Phone: (602) 299-4372

Pet Restrictions: $5/night, if trained
Pet left unattended in room: Yes
Exercise Area for Pets: Yes
Rates: $50 to $110

La Quinta Motor Inn
665 N. Freeway
Tucson, AZ 85705
Phone: (602) 622-6491

Pet Restrictions: Under 25 lbs.
Pet left unattended in room: Yes
Exercise Area for Pets: Yes
Rates: $69 to $76

The Lodge on the Desert
306 N. Alvernon Way
Tucson, AZ 85733
Phone: (602) 325-3366

Pet Restrictions: Well behaved
Exercise Area for Pets: Nearby
Rates: $51 to $171

Quality Inn - Tucson Airport
6801 S. Tucson Blvd.
Tucson, AZ 85706
Phone: (602) 746-3932

Pet Restrictions: $25 deposit
Pet left unattended in room: Yes
Exercise Area for Pets: Yes
Rates: $99 to $109

Radisson Suites Hotel-Tucson
6555 E. Speedway
Tucson, AZ 85710
Phone: (602) 721-7100

Pet Restrictions: $25 fee, house
    trained
Exercise Area for Pets: Yes
Rates: $115

Residence Inn - Marriott
6477 E. Speedway
Tucson, AZ 85710
Phone: (602) 721-0991

Pet Restrictions: Yes, $150 deposit,
    non-refundable fee depending on
    room rented
Pet left unattended in room: Yes
Exercise Area for Pets: Nearby
Rates: $74 to $99

Rodeway Inn
810 East Benson Hwy.
Tucson, AZ
Phone: (602) 884-5800

Pet Restrictions: $25, notify desk
Pet left unattended in room: Yes
Exercise Area for Pets: Yes
Rates: $37 to $42

Sheraton Pueblo Inn
350 S. Freeway
Tucson, AZ 85745
Phone: (602) 622-6611

Pet Restrictions: $3/night, notify
    housekeeping
Pet left unattended in room: Yes
Exercise Area for Pets: Yes
Rates: $68 to $76

Sheraton Tucson El Conquistador Golf & Tennis Resort
10000 N. Oracle Rd.
Tucson, AZ 85704
Phone: (602) 742-7000

Pet Restrictions: Quiet
Pet left unattended in room: Yes
Exercise Area for Pets: Yes
Rates: $180 to $250

ARIZONA — HOTELS (continued)

University Inn - Central
950 N. Stone
Tucson, AZ 85705
Phone: (602) 791-7503

Pet Restrictions: Small pets
Exercise Area for Pets: Nearby
Rates: $32 to $59

Westward Look Resort
245 E. Ina Rd.
Tucson, AZ 85704
Phone: (602) 297-1151

Pet Restrictions: $100 deposit
Pet left unattended in room: Yes
Exercise Area for Pets: Yes
Rates: $200 to $220

VETERINARIANS
Cimarron Animal Clinic
7292 E. Broadway 85710
(602) 886-1125

Sunrise Pet Clinic
5635 N. Swan Road 85718
(602) 299-5044

Valley Animal Hospital
4984 East 22nd 85711
(602) 748-0331

WICKENBERG
Best Western Rancho Grande Motor Hotel
293 Wickenberg Way
Wickenberg, AZ 85358
Phone: (602) 684-5445

Pet Restrictions: None, if well behaved
Pet left unattended in room: Yes
Exercise Area for Pets: Nearby
Rates: $49 to $74

YUMA
Best Western Yuma Inn Suites
1450 Castle Dome Rd.
Yuma, AZ 85364
Phone: (602) 783-8341

Pet Restrictions: $25 deposit, responsible for damage
Pet left unattended in room: Yes
Exercise Area for Pets: Yes
Rates: $84 to $135

Parkinn International
2600 So. 4th Ave.
Yuma, AZ 85364
Phone: (602) 726-4830

Pet Restrictions: None
Exercise Area for Pets: Yes
Rates: $67 to $106

Shilo Inn
1550 S. Castle Dome Rd.
Yuma, AZ 85365
Phone: (602) 782-9511

Pet Restrictions: $6/night
Pet left unattended in room: Yes
Exercise Area for Pets: Yes
Rates: $105 to $110

ARKANSAS — HOTELS

BLYTHEVILLE

BW Cotton Inn
P.O. Box 1229
Blytheville, AR 72315
Phone: (501) 763-5220

Pet Restrictions: No large dogs
Exercise Area for Pets: Yes
Rates: $37 to $43

Holiday Inn
P.O. Box 1408
Blytheville, AR 72315
Phone: (501) 763-5800

Pet Restrictions: None, if quiet
Pet left unattended in room: Yes
Exercise Area for Pets: Yes
Rates: $45 to $60

VETERINARIANS
East Ash Animal Hospital
402 East Ash 72315
Phone: (501) 762-5781

Palmer, Gary T.
805 South Division St. 72315
Phone: (501) 763-3101

CAMDEN

Days Inn
942 Adams Ave. SW
Camden, AR 71701
Phone: (501) 836-9372

Pet Restrictions: No really large
dogs, if trained
Pet left unattended in room: Yes
Exercise Area for Pets: Yes
Rates: $31 to $37.45

CARLISLE

BW Interstate Inn, Carlisle
P.O. Box 640
Carlisle, AR 72024
Phone: (501) 552-7566

Pet Restrictions: None
Pet left unattended in room: No
policy
Exercise Area for Pets: Yes
Rates: $36 to $44

CROSSETT

Ramada Inn
1400 Arkansas Hwy
Crossett, AR 71635
Phone: (501) 364-4101

Pet Restrictions: Notify management
Exercise Area for Pets: Yes
Rates: $59 to $66

DUMAS

Kings Inn
722 Hwy 65 S
Dumas, AR 71639
Phone: (501) 382-2707

Pet Restrictions: Responsible for
damage
Pet left unattended in room: Yes
Exercise Area for Pets: Yes
Rates: $37 to $44

EL DORADO

BW Kings Inn
1920 Junction City Rd.
El Dorado, AR 71730
Phone: (501) 862-5191

Pet Restrictions: None
Pet left unattended in room: Yes
Exercise Area for Pets: Yes
Rates: $52 to $56

Comfort Inn
2303 Junction City Hwy
El Dorado, AR 71730
Phone: (501) 863-6677

Pet Restrictions: Small pets
Pet left unattended in room: Yes
Exercise Area for Pets: Yes
Rates: $42 to $57

FORREST CITY

BW Colony Inn
2333 N. Washington
Forrest City, AR 72335
Phone: (501) 633-0870

Pet Restrictions: Small,
housebroken pets
Exercise Area for Pets: Yes
Rates: $42 to $54

Comfort Inn
115 Barrow Hill Rd.
Forrest City, AR 72335
Phone: (501) 633-0042

Pet Restrictions: Small pets, $4, if
well behaved
Pet left unattended in room: Yes
Exercise Area for Pets: Yes
Rates: $33 to $40

Holiday Inn
P.O. Box 790
Forrest City, AR 72335
Phone: (501) 633-6300

Pet Restrictions: None
Pet left unattended in room: Yes
Exercise Area for Pets: Yes
Rates: $47

VETERINARIANS
Gehring, James F.
800 East Broadway 72335

FORT SMITH
Fifth Season Inn
2219 S. Waldron Park
Fort Smith, AR 72903
Phone: (501) 452-4880

Pet Restrictions: $10/day, if in carrier
Pet left unattended in room: Yes
Exercise Area for Pets: Yes
Rates: $56 to $59

Park Inn
301 N. 11th
Fort Smith, AR 72901
Phone: (501) 783-0271

Pet Restrictions: Responsible for
    damages
Exercise Area for Pets: Nearby
Rates: $35 to $55

VETERINARIANS
Animal Care Clinic
4300 Rogers Avenue
Green Pointe Suite 33 72903
Phone: (501) 783-7387

Thames, Michael D.
4100 Kelly Highway 72904
Phone: (501) 782-1234

HELENA
Edwardian Inn
317 S. Biscoe
Helena, AR 72342
Phone: (501) 338-9155

Pet Restrictions: Small,
    housebroken, if well behaved
Pet left unattended in room: Yes
Exercise Area for Pets: Yes
Rates: $50 to $60

HETH
BW Lake Side Inn
Rt. 1
Heth, AR 72346
Phone: (501) 657-2101

Pet Restrictions: None, if well
    behaved
Pet left unattended in room: Yes
Exercise Area for Pets: Yes
Rates: $27.95 to $47.30

HOT SPRINGS NATIONAL PARK
Arlington Resort Hotel & Spa
P.O. Box 5652
Hot Springs Natl Pk., AR 71901
Phone: (501) 623-7771

Pet Restrictions: Small, under 25 lbs.
Pet left unattended in room: Yes
Exercise Area for Pets: Nearby
Rates: $51 to $90

BW Hot Springs Inn
P.O. Box CC
Hot Springs Natl Pk., AR 71902
Phone: (501) 624-4436

Pet Restrictions: None
Pet left unattended in room: Yes
Exercise Area for Pets: Yes
Rates: $19.95 to $69.95

Jonesboro BW
2901 Phillips Dr.
Hot Springs Nat'l Park, AR 72401
Phone: (501) 932-6600

Pet Restrictions: Small pets
Pet left unattended in room: Yes
Exercise Area for Pets: Yes
Rates: $37.50 to $42.50

BW Stage Coach Inn
2520 Central Ave.
Hot Springs Natl Pk., AR 71901
Phone: (501) 624-2531

Pet Restrictions: Small pets
Exercise Area for Pets: Yes
Rates: $80

Shorecrest Resort
360 Lakeland Dr.
Hot Springs Natl Pk., 71913
Phone: (501) 525-8113

Pet Restrictions: Leashed dogs, if
    behaved
Pet left unattended in room: Yes
Rates: $41 to $52

Travelin Motor Lodge
1045 E. Grand Ave.
Hot Springs Natl Pk., AR 71901
Phone: (501) 624-4681

Pet Restrictions: Housebroken
Exercise Area for Pets: Yes
Rates: $41

VETERINARIANS

Lake Hamilton Animal Hospital
1410 Airport Rd. 71913
Phone: (501) 767-8503

Cyphers, Viki F.
809 San Mateo Dr. 71913
Phone: (501) 525-5723

LAKEVIEW

Gaston's White River Resort
1 River Rd.
Lakeview, AR 72642
Phone: (501) 431-5202

Pet Restrictions: None
Pet left unattended in room: Yes
Exercise Area for Pets: Yes
Rates: $58 to $692

LITTLE ROCK

Holiday Inn City Center
617 S. Broadway
Little Rock, AR 72201
Phone: (501) 376-2071

Pet Restrictions: Small pets
Exercise Area for Pets: Nearby
Rates: $54 to $56

Holiday Inn Otter Creek
11701 I30
Little Rock AR 72209
Phone: (501) 455-2300

Pet Restrictions: Small, house
trained, inform housekeeping
Pet left unattended in room: Yes
Exercise Area for Pets: Yes
Rates: $55 to $65

La Quinta Motor Inn - Fair Park
901 Fair Park Blvd.
Little Rock, AR 72204
Phone: (501) 664-7000

Pet Restrictions: None, no
housekeeping
Pet left unattended in room: Yes
Exercise Area for Pets: Yes
Rates: $45 to $55

Red Roof Inn
7800 Scott Hamilton Dr.
Little Rock, AR 72209
Phone: (501) 562-2694

Pet Restrictions: None
Pet left uanttended in room: Yes
Exercise Area for Pets: Yes
Rates: $23.99 to $44.99

VETERINARIANS

Bellevue Animal Clinic
7824 Cantrell Rd. 72207
Phone: (501) 225-2444

Shackelford Road Veterinary Clinic
304 North Shackleford Rd. 72211
Phone: (501) 224-6998

Treasure Hill Pet Hospital
1221 Breckenridge Dr. 72205
Phone: (501) 225-8248

MT. IDA

Denby Point Lodge & Mariner
SR 1, Box 241
Mt. Ida, AR 71957
Phone: (501) 867-3651

Pet Restrictions: None
Exercise Area for Pets: Yes
Rates: $35 to $80

MOUNTAIN HOME

Blue Paradise Resort
Rt. 6, Box 379
Mountain Home, AR 72653
Phone: (501) 492-5113

Pet Restrictions: $5/day
Exercise Area for Pets: Yes
Rates: $45/night, call for week rates

Holiday Inn
1350 Hwy 62 SW
Mountain Home, AR 72653
Phone: (501) 425-5101

Pet Restrictions: Small pets
Pet left unattended in room: Yes
Exercise Area for Pets: Yes
Rates: $42 to $51

Ramada Inn
1127 Hwy 62
Mountain Home, AR 72653
Phone: (501) 425-9191

Pet Restrictions: None
Pet left unattended in room: Yes
Exercise Area for Pets: Yes
Rates: $36 to $40

Royal Motel Resort
Rt. 6, Box 500
Mountain Home, AR 72653
Phone: (501) 492-5288

Pet Restrictions: Small pets
Exercise Area for Pets: Yes
Rates: $33-$80 daily, $450/week

Teal Point Resort
Rt. 6, Box 369
Mountain Home, AR 72653
Phone: (501) 492-5145

Pet Restrictions: $5/day
Exercise Area for Pets: Yes
Rates: $49 to $99

VETERINARIANS
Animal Health Center
Route 4, Box 135A 72653
Phone: (501) 425-8272

OZARK
Ozark Budget Host Motel
1711 W. Commercial
Ozark, AR 72949
Phone: (501) 667-2166

Pet Restrictions: None
Pet left unattended in room: Yes
Exercise Area for Pets: Yes
Rates: $28 to $32

PRESCOTT
Comfort Inn
Rt. 5, Box 236
Prescott, AR 71857
Phone: (501) 887-6641

Pet Restrictions: $2 fee
Pet left unattended in room: Yes
Exercise Area for Pets: Yes
Rates: $34 to $40

RUSSELLVILLE
Budget Inn
2200 N. Arkansas Ave.
Russellville, AR 72801
Phone: (501) 968-4400

Pet Restrictions: $10 deposit
Pet left unattended in room: Yes
Exercise Area for Pets: Yes
Rates: $26.95 to $30.19

Holiday Inn
P.O. Box 460
Russellville, AR 72801
Phone: (501) 968-4300

Pet Restrictions: Small pets, if quiet
Pet left unattended in room: Yes
Exercise Area for Pets: Yes
Rates: $50 to $70

Park Motel
2615 W. Main St.
Russellville, AR 72801
Phone: (501) 968-4862

Pet Restrictions: None
Exercise Area for Pets: Yes
Rates: $23 to $33

TEXARKANA
Holiday Inn Texarkana
5100 N. State Line Ave.
Texarkana, AR 75502
Phone: (501) 774-3521

Pet Restrictions: None
Exercise Area for Pets: Yes
Rates: $67 plus $10/person

Sheraton Texarkana Hotel
5301 N. State Line Ave.
Texarkana, AR 75503-6367
Phone: (214) 792-3222

Pet Restrictions: Yes, up to 15 lbs.,
 up to $25 non-refundable deposit
Pet left unattended in room: Yes
Rates: $60.40 to $73

CALIFORNIA — HOTELS

ALTURAS

The Dunes Motel
511 N. Main St.
Alturas, CA 96101
Phone: (916) 233-3545
Pet Restrictions: Hunting dogs only
Exercise Area for Pets: Nearby
Rates: Vary

ANAHEIM

Anaheim Marriott Hotel
700 W. Convention Way
Anaheim, CA 92802
Phone: (714) 750-8000
Pet Restrictions: Special pet rooms
Pet left unattended in room: Yes, if
    caged/kennel
Rates: $89 to $160

Raffles Inn Anaheim
2040 S. Harbor Blvd.
Anaheim, CA 92802
Phone: (714) 750-6100
Pet Restrictions: Under 10 lbs., $10
    per night
Exercise Area for Pets: Yes
Rates: $69 to $139

Ana Brook Animal Hospital
335 N. Brookhurst St. 92801
(714) 772-8220

Smith, Gale D.
2307 E. Ball Rd. 92806
(714) 778-0664

Turano, Michael E.
5602 E. Santa Ana
Canyon Road 92807
(714) 637-3209

ARCATA

Arcata Super 8
4887 Valley West Blvd.
Arcata, CA 95521
Phone: (707) 822-8888
Pet Restrictions: $50 deposit, only 1
    large dog
Exercise Area for Pets: Yes
Rates: $35 to $52

Hight, James R.
900 Buttermilk Lane 95521
(707) 822-5124

ARROYO GRANDE

Econo Lodge
611 El Camino Real
Arroyo Grande, CA 93420
Phone: (805) 489-9300
Pet Restrictions: Notify desk in
    advance, limited pet rooms, no
    big dogs
Exercise Area for Pets: Yes
Rates: $40 to $79

E-Z 8 Motel - Pismo Beach
555 Camino Mercado
Arroyo Grande, CA 93420
Phone: (805) 481-4774
Pet Restrictions: Dogs must be on
    leash while walking on premises
    Pet deposit for large dogs
Pet left unattended in room: No
Exercise Area for Pets: Nearby
Rates: $28.88 to $53.88

South County Veterinary Clinic
270 N. Halcyon Rd. 93420
(805) 489-1361

AUBURN

Best Western Golden Key Motel
13450 Lincoln Way
Auburn, CA 95603
Phone: (916) 885-8611
Pet Restrictions: Sign waiver, $20
    deposit, under 20 lbs.
Pet left unattended in room: Yes
Exercise Area for Pets: Yes
Rates: $50 to $70

Companion Veterinary Clinic
1216 High St. Suite A 95603
(916) 885-3251

Traynor, Virgil R.
1055 Grass Valley Highway 95603
(916) 885-1919

BAKER

Bunboy Choya Motel
P.O. Box 130
Baker, CA 92309
Phone: (619) 733-4363
Pet Restrictions: None
Pet left unattended in room: Yes
Exercise Area for Pets: Yes
Rates: $30 to $60

BAKERSFIELD
Best Western Oak Inn
889 Oak St.
Bakersfield, CA 93304
Phone: (805) 324-9686

Pet Restrictions: $5 /night
Pet left unattended in room: Yes
Rates: $45 to $58

Econo-Lodge
2700 White Ln.
Bakersfield, CA 93304
Phone: (805) 832-3111

Pet Restrictions: None
Pet left unattended in room: Yes
Exercise Area for Pets: Yes
Rates: $29.95

E-Z 8 Motel - Bakersfield II
5200 Olive Tree Court
Bakersfield, CA 93308
Phone: (805) 392-1511

Pet Restrictions: Dogs must be on
    leash while walking on premises
    Pet deposit for large dogs
Pet left unattended in room: No
Exercise Area for Pets: Nearby
Rates: $24.88 to $34.88

E-Z 8 Motel - Bakersfield I
2604 Pierce St.
Bakersfield, CA 93308
Phone: (805) 322-1901

Pet Restrictions: Dogs must be on
    leash while walking on premises
    Pet deposit for large dogs
Pet left unattended in room: No
Rates: $24.88 to $34.88

Hill House-Vagabond Inn
700 Truxtun Ave. at S. St.
Bakersfield, CA 93301
Phone: (805) 327-4064

Pet Restrictions: $3/night
Pet left unattended in room: Yes, no
    housekeeping
Exercise Area for Pets: Yes
Rates: $47 to $50

Bakersfield Veterinary Hospital
323 Chester Ave. 93301
(805) 327-4444

Cunningham Veterinary Hosp.
2703 'M' St. 93301
(805) 327-9614

Nile Point Veterinary Hosp.
2007 Niles St. 93305
(805) 327-9516

BARSTOW
Barstow Inn
1261 E. Main St.
Barstow, CA 92311
Phone: (619) 256-7581

Pet Restrictions: None
Pet left unattended in room: Yes
Exercise Area for Pets: Yes
Rates: $35

Howard Johnson Lodge
1431 East Main
Barstow, CA 92311
Phone: (619) 256-0661,
    (800) 486-4656

Pet Restrictions: Smoking rooms
    only
Exercise Area for Pets: Yes
Rates: $55 to $75

Town & Country Motel
1230 E. Main St.
Barstow, CA 92311
Phone: (619) 256-2133

Pet Restrictions: None
Pet left unattended in room: Yes
Exercise Area for Pets: Yes
Rates: $27 to $32

Vagabond Inn
1243 E. Main St.
Barstow, CA 92311
Phone: (619) 256-5601,
    (800) 522-1555

Pet Restrictions: $3/night
Exercise Area for Pets: Yes
Rates: $41 to $51

BEAUMONT
Golden West Motel
625 E. 5th St.
Beaumont, CA 92223
Phone: (714) 845-2185

Pet Restrictions: $2/night
Exercise Area for Pets: Yes
Rates: $32 to $38

Abbey Animal Hosp.
764 East 3rd St. 92223
(714) 845-2675

CALIFORNIA — HOTELS (continued)

BIG BEAR LAKE

Cozy Hollow Lodge
40409 Big Bear Blvd., P.O. Box 1288
Big Bear Lake, CA 92315
Phone: (714) 866-8886

Pet Restrictions: $50 deposit, pet on
leash, must sign waiver
Exercise Area for Pets: Yes
Rates: $71 to $119

Grey Squirrel Resort
P.O. Box 5404
Big Bear Lake, CA 92315
Phone: (714) 866-4335

Pet Restrictions: $5 per night
Exercise Area for Pets: Yes
Rates: $62 up

Shore Acres Lodge
P.O. Box GC 4-10
Big Bear Lake, CA 92315
Phone: (714) 866-8200

Pet Restrictions: $5/night
Exercise Area for Pets: Yes
Rates: $60 to $250

Walker, Kent P.
42160 N. Shore Dr. 92314
Big Bear City
(714) 866-5828

BISHOP

Bishop Inn
805 N. Main St.
Bishop, CA 93514
Phone: (619) 873-4284

Pet Restrictions: None
Exercise Area for Pets: Nearby
Rates: $56 to $65

Sierra Foothills Motel
535 S. Main St.
Bishop, CA 93514
Phone: (619) 872-1386

Pet Restrictions: $10 deposit
Pet left unattended in room: Yes, no
housekeeping
Exercise Area for Pets: Nearby
Rates: $43 to $46

Vagabond Inn
1030 N. Main St.
Bishop, CA 93514
Phone: (619) 873-6351

Pet Restrictions: 1 pet, medium
sized, must be housebroken
Exercise Area for Pets: Yes
Rates: $50 to $61

VETERINARIANS

Bishop Veterinary Hosp.
1650 N. Sierra Hwy 93514
(714) 873-5801

BLYTHE

Best Western Sahara Motel
825 W. Hobsonway
Blythe, CA 92225
Phone: (619) 922-7105

Pet Restrictions: 2 dogs maximum
Exercise Area for Pets: Yes
Rates: $49 to $65

E-Z 8 Motel - Blythe
900 W. Rice St.
Blythe, CA 92225
Phone: (619) 922-9191

Pet Restrictions: Dogs must be on
leash while walking on premises
Pet deposit for large dogs
Pet left unattended in room: No
Exercise Area for Pets: Nearby
Rates: $24.88 to $34.88

Comfort Inn
903 W. Hobsonway
Blythe, CA 92225
Phone: (619) 922-4146

Pet Restrictions: Reserve special
room
Exercise Area for Pets: Yes
Rates: $45 to $54

BRAWLEY

Town House Lodge
135 Main St.
Brawley, CA 92227
Phone: (619) 344-5120

Pet Restrictions: None
Exercise Area for Pets: Nearby
Rates: $46 to $80

BRIDGEPORT

Best Western Ruby Inn
P.O. Box 475
Bridgeport, CA 93517
Phone: (619) 932-7241

Pet Restrictions: None
Exercise Area for Pets: Yes
Rates: $55 to $95

BURBANK

Burbank Airport Hilton
2500 Hollywood Way
Burbank, CA 91505
Phone: (818) 843-6000

Pet Restrictions: None
Pet left unattended in room: Yes,
    notify desk
Exercise Area for Pets: Yes
Rates: $84 to $156

Holiday Inn-Burbank
150 E. Angeleno
Burbank, CA 91510
Phone: (818) 841-4770

Pet Restrictions: Only on pet floor
Pet left unattended in room: Yes
Exercise Area for Pets: Yes
Rates: $81 to $106

VETERINARIANS

Rainbow Veterinary Hosp.
2321 Empire Ave. 91504
(213) 846-1166

Altman, Sheldon
2723 W. Olive Ave. 91505
(818) 845-7246

Ladley, Joseph J.
123 W. Burbank Blvd 91502
(818) 846-7743

BURLINGAME

Days Inn
779 Airport Blvd.
Burlingame, CA 94010
Phone: (415) 342-7772

Pet Restrictions: $4/night
Exercise Area for Pets: Yes
Rates: $72 to $82

Marriott Airport
1800 Old Bayshore Hwy
Burlingame, CA 94010
Phone: (415) 692-9100

Pet Restrictions: None
Pet left unattended in room: Yes
Exercise Area for Pets: Yes
Rates: $79 to $138

Raddisson
1177 Airport Blvd.
Burlingame, CA 94010
Phone: (415) 342-9200

Pet Restrictions: Caged only on pet
    floor
Pet left unattended in room: Yes
Exercise Area for Pets: Nearby
Rates: $79 to $89

Vagabond Inn - Airport
1640 Bayshore Hwy
Burlingame, CA 94010
Phone: (415) 692-4040

Pet Restrictions: $10/night
Pet left unattended in room: Yes
Exercise Area for Pets: Yes
Rates: $70 to $80

BUTTONWILLOW

Knights Inn Motel
20681 Tracy Ave.
Buttonwillow, CA 93206
Phone: (805) 764-5117

Pet Restrictions: None
Pet left unattended in room: Yes
Rates: $23 to $48

CAMERON PARK

Best Western Cameron Park
3361 Coach Ln.
Cameron Park, CA 95682
Phone: (916) 677-2203

Pet Restrictions: Under 10 lbs.
Exercise Area for Pets: Yes
Rates: $51 to $60

VETERINARIANS

Airport Pet Clinic
2995 Alhambra Dr. 95682
(916) 677-7387

CAMPBELL

Campbell Inn
675 E. Campbell Ave.
Campbell, CA 95008
Phone: (408) 374-4300,
    (800) 582-4300

Pet Restrictions: Yes
Pet left unattended in room: Yes
Exercise Area for Pets: Nearby
Rates: $75 to $100

Residence Inn San Jose
2761 S. Bascom Ave.
Campbell, CA 95008
Phone: (408) 559-1551

Pet Restrictions: $50 non-refundable
    fee, $6/day/pet
Pet left unattended in room: Yes
Exercise Area for Pets: Yes
Rates: $129 to $154

VETERINARIANS

Central Animal Hosp.
971 E. Hamilton Ave. 95008
(408) 377-4043

The Cat Hospital
163 E. Hamilton Ave. 95008
(408) 866-6188

United Emergency Animal Clinic
1657 S. Bascom Ave. 95008
(408) 371-6252

CANOGA PARK
Warner Cntr. Motor Inn
7132 De Soto Ave.
Canoga Pk., CA 91303
Phone: (818) 346-5400
Pet Restrictions: $8/night/pet, small
  pets only
Exercise Area for Pets: Nearby
Rates: $35 to $69

VETERINARIANS

Dr. Bevins & Dr. Alperin Animal Hospital
7009 Canoga Ave. 91303
(818) 340-1569

CARLSBAD
Economy Inns of Amer.
751 Raintree Dr.
Carlsbad, CA 92008
Phone: (619) 931-1185
Pet Restrictions: None
Exercise Area for Pets: Yes
Rates: $32 to $58

VETERINARIANS

Gibbs, Mary E.
2893 Sanford Lane 92008
(619) 720-0840

Wattles, Richard O.
2505 Vista Way 92008
(619) 729-2364

CARMEL
Carmel Mission Inn - Best Western
3665 Rio Rd.
Carmel, CA 93922
Phone: (408) 624-1841
Pet Restrictions: Ground floor only
Exercise Area for Pets: Yes
Rates: $99 to $149

Quail Lodge
8205 Valley Greens Dr.
Carmel, CA 93921
Phone: (408) 624-1581
Pet Restrictions: None
Pet left unattended in room: No but
  has pet sitters
Exercise Area for Pets: Yes
Rates: $225 up

Vagabond House
P.O. Box 2747, 4th and Delores Sts.
Carmel, CA 93921
Phone: (408) 624-7738
Pet Restrictions: $10 fee
Exercise Area for Pets: Nearby
Rates: $79 to $135

Valley Lodge
Carmel Valley at Ford Rd.
P.O. Box 93
Carmel Valley, CA 93924
Phone: (408) 659-2261
Pet Restrictions: $10/night
Exercise Area for Pets: Yes
Rates: $155 to $235

Wayside Inn
Corner Mission St. & 7th Ave.
P.O. Box 1900
Carmel, CT 93921
Phone: (408) 624-5336
Pet Restrictions: None
Exercise Area for Pets: Yes
Rates: $119 to $149

VETERINARIANS

Carmel by the Sea Vet Hosp.
Torres at 5th #5127 93921
(408) 624-3889

Bishop, George W.
3 The Crossroads 93923
(408) 624-0131

CARPENTERIA
Best Western
4558 Carpenteria Ave.
Carpenteria, CA 93013
Phone: (805) 684-0473
Pet Restrictions: $25 deposit
Pet left unattended in room: Yes
Exercise Area for Pets: Yes
Rates: $109 to $129

CASTAIR

Comfort Inn
31558 Castair Rd.
Castair, CA 91384
Phone: (805) 295-1100,
    (800) 221-2222
Pet Restrictions: None
Exercise Area for Pets: Nearby
Rates: $63 to $70

CHICO

Holiday Inn at Chico
586 Manzanita Ct.
Chico, CA 95926
Phone: (916) 345-2491
Pet Restrictions: None
Exercise Area for Pets: Yes
Rates: $72 to $78

Town House Motel
2231 Esplanade
Chico, CA 95926
Phone: (916) 343-1621
Pet Restrictions: Only dogs under 12″
Exercise Area for Pets: Yes
Rates: $30 to $50

VETERINARIANS

Acacia Veterinary Hosp.
479 E. Ave. 95926
(916) 345-1338

Erickson Veterinary Hosp.
11181 Midway 95926
(916) 345-5896

Mangrove Veterinary Hosp.
1900 Mangrove Ave. 95926
(916) 891-4818

CLAREMONT

Howard Johnson Lodge
721 South Indian Hill Blvd.
Claremont, CA 91711
Phone: (714) 626-2431
Pet Restrictions: $5 fee
Pet left unattended in room: Yes
Exercise Area for Pets: Yes
Rates: $45 to $60

VETERINARIANS

Chaparral Pet Hospital
421 W. 7th Street 91711
(714) 625-1561

COLUMBIA

Columbia Inn Motel
Col. State Historic Park
P.O. Box 298
Columbia, CA
Phone: (209) 533-0446
Pet Restrictions: None
Pet left unattended in room: Yes
Exercise Area for Pets: Nearby
Rates: $46 to $56

CONCORD

E-Z Motel - Concord
1581 Concord Ave.
Concord, CA 94520
Phone: (510) 674-0888
Pet Restrictions: Dogs must be on
    leash while walking on premises
    Pet deposit for large dogs
Pet left unattended in room: No
Exercise Area for Pets: Nearby
Rates: $36.88 to $50.88

Sheraton Inn
1401 Willow Paso Rd.
Concord, CA 94520
Phone: (510) 825-7700
Pet Restrictions: None
Pet left unattended in room: Yes,
    notify housekeeping
Exercise Area for Pets: Yes
Rates: $60 to $95

VETERINARIANS

Contra Costa Vet. Emergency Clinic
1410 Monument Blvd. 94520
(510) 798-2904

Four Corners Vet. Hosp.
1126 Meadow Lane 94520
(510) 685-0512

Monte Vista Vet. Hosp.
1488 Washington Blvd. 94521
(510) 672-1100

COSTA MESA

Red Lion Inn
3050 Bristol St.
Costa Mesa, CA 92626
Phone: (714) 540-7000
Pet Restrictions: None if well
    behaved/housebroken
Pet left unattended in room: Yes
Exercise Area for Pets: Yes
Rates: $79 to $99

Vagabond Inn
3205 Harbor Blvd.
Costa Mesa, CA 92626
Phone: (714) 557-8360

Pet Restrictions: $5 fee
Pet left unattended in room: Yes
Exercise Area for Pets: Yes
Rates: $39 to $49

VETERINARIANS
All Creatures Care Cottage
1912 Harbor Blvd. 92627
(714) 642-7151

Newport Harbor Animal Hosp.
125 Mesa Dr. 92627
(714) 631-1030

Maas, Marvin R.
2077 Harbor Blvd. 92627
(714) 646-1664

DELANO
Shilo Inn Delano
2231 Girard St.
Delano, CA 93215
Phone: (805) 725-7551,
   (800) 222-2244

Pet Restrictions: $6/pet/day
Exercise Area for Pets: Yes
Rates: $43 to $59.40

VETERINARIANS
Lehnhard, Kathryn
P.O. Box 998
(805) 832-7814

DESERT HOT SPRINGS
Stardust Motel
66634 5th St.
Desert Hot Springs, CA 92240
Phone: (619) 329-5443

Pet Restrictions: None
Pet left unattended in room: Yes
Exercise Area for Pets: Yes
Rates: $38 to $58

DOUGLAS CITY
Embassy Suites Hotel
8425 Firestone Blvd.
Douglas City, CA 90240
Phone: (310) 861-1900

Pet Restrictions: None
Pet left unattended in room: Yes
Exercise Area for Pets: Yes
Rates: $99 to $159

Indian Creek Lodge
P.O. Box 100 (on Trinity River)
Douglas City, CA 96024
Phone: (916) 623-6294

Pet Restrictions: No cats, never
   unattended, off furniture, quiet
   at all times
Exercise Area for Pets: Yes
Rates: $28 to $75

DUNNINGER
Best Western Country
I5 at Dunningan Exit, P.O. Box 740
Dunninger, CA 95937
Phone: (916) 724-3471

Pet Restrictions: None
Exercise Area for Pets: Yes
Rates: $50 to $60

EL SEGUNDO
Crown Sterling
1440 E. Imperial Ave.
El Segundo, CA 90245
Phone: (310) 640-3600

Pet Restrictions: $15/night
Pet left unattended in room: Yes, no
   maid service
Exercise Area for Pets: Nearby
Rates: $134 and up

EL CENTRO
E-Z 8 Motel - El Centro
455 Wake Ave.
El Centro, CA 92243
Phone: (619) 352-6620

Pet Restrictions: Dogs must be on
   leash while walking on premises
   Pet deposit for large dogs
Pet left unattended in room: No
Exercise Area for Pets: Nearby —
   large area around motel
Rates: $25.88 to $35.88

Ramada Inn
1455 Ocotillo Dr.
El Centro, CA 92243
Phone: (619) 352-5152

Pet Restrictions: None
Pet left unattended in room: Yes
Exercise Area for Pets: Yes
Rates: $48 to $60

CALIFORNIA — HOTELS (continued)

Sands Motel
611 N. Imperial Ave.
El Centro, CA 92243
Phone: (619) 352-0715

Pet Restrictions: Small pets only,
$10 deposit
Exercise Area for Pets: Yes
Rates: $33 to $54

VETERINARIANS
Valley Veterinary Clinic
485 Broadway Suite F 92243
(619) 352-1279

EUREKA
Red Lion Inn
1929 4th St.
Eureka, CA 95501
Phone: (707) 445-0844

Pet Restrictions: None
Exercise Area for Pets: Nearby
Rates: $110 to $175

VETERINARIANS
Broadway Animal Hosp.
3700 Broadway 95501
(707) 442-5717

Kelley-Day, Jeffrey
2550 Myrtle Ave. 95501
(707) 443-8686

FAIRFIELD
E-Z 8 Motel - Fairfield
3331 N. Texas St.
Fairfield, CA 94533
Phone: (707) 426-6161

Pet Restrictions: Dogs must be on
leash while walking on premises
Pet deposit for large dogs
Pet left unattended in room: No
Exercise Area for Pets: Nearby
Rates: $28.88 to $40.88

FIREBAUGH
Aprico Inn
46290 W. Panoche Rd.
Firebaugh, CA 93622
Phone: (209) 659-1444

Pet Restrictions: $3 fee
Exercise Area for Pets: Yes
Rates: $42.50 to $50

FORT BRAGG
Wishing Well Cottages
31430 Hwy 20
Fort Bragg, CA 95437
Phone: (707) 961-5450
800-362-9305
Fax: (707) 961-0285

Pet Restrictions: Well behaved,
housebroken, leashed
Pet left unattended in room: No
Exercise Area for Pets: Nearby
Other Areas: California State Parks;
Jackson Demonstration State
Forest, Ft. Bragg; Mendacino
Coast Botanical Gardens under
control on leash; Calif. Western
Railroad-Skunk Train, large dogs
on leash
Rates: $55 to $65; $250 per week
and $275/wk.

FRESNO
Best Western Tradewinds Motor Hotel
2141 N. Parkway Dr.
Fresno, CA 93705
Phone: (209) 237-1881

Pet Restrictions: None, manager's
discretion
Pet left unattended in room: Yes, no
housekeeping
Exercise Area for Pets: Yes
Rates: $41 to $60

Centre Plaza Holiday Inn
2233 Ventura St.
Fresno, CA 93709
Phone: (209) 268-1000

Pet Restrictions: None
Exercise Area for Pets: Yes
Rates: $72 to $97

Hill House Vagabond Inn
1101 N. Parkway Dr.
Fresno, CA 93728
Phone: (209) 268-6211

Pet Restrictions: $5
Pet left unattended in room: Yes, in
cage
Rates: $38 to $48

Holiday Inn - Airport
5090 E. Clinton Ave.
Fresno, CA 93727
Phone: (209) 252-3611
Pet Restrictions: None
Pet left unattended in room: Yes,
   short periods
Exercise Area for Pets: Yes
Rates: $59 to $81

La Quinta Fresno Inn
2926 Tulane St.
Fresno, CA 93721
Phone: (209) 442-1110
Pet Restrictions: None
Pet left unattended in room: Yes,
   will not clean
Exercise Area for Pets: Yes
Rates: $44.50 to $54

VETERINARIANS
Hill, Daphne T.
5139 N. Blackstone 93710
(209) 227-5575

Larsen, Robert
1119 E. Shaw Ave. 93710
(209) 222-6233

Swart, Raymond L.
66 E. Escalon #102 93710
(209) 432-3300

GILROY
Best Western Inn
360 Leavesley Rd.
Gilroy, CA 95020
Phone: (408) 848-1467
Pet Restrictions: None
Exercise Area for Pets: Nearby
Rates: $48 to $71

Leavesley Inn
8430 Murray Ave.
Gilroy, CA 95020
Phone: (408) 847-5500
Pet Restrictions: No deposit if by
   credit card, $20 if cash
Pet left unattended in room: Yes
Exercise Area for Pets: Yes
Rates: $43 to $55

VETERINARIANS
Nelson, Christopher G.
793 Lawrence Dr. 95020
(408) 842-9348

GLENDALE
Days Inn
600 N. Pacific Ave.
Glendale, CA 91203
Phone: (818) 956-0202
Pet Restrictions: 1-2 nights only
Pet left unattended in room: Yes,
   short term
Exercise Area for Pets: Nearby
Rates: $49 to $59

VETERINARIANS
Arden Animal Hosp.
407 W. Arden Ave. 91203
(818) 246-2478

Glendale Small Animal Hosp.
831 W. Milford St. 91203
(213) 241-5181

Parkview Pet Clinic
1534 Canada Blvd. 91208
(818) 244-7268

GRASS VALLEY
Alta Sierra Resort Motel
135 Tammy Way
Grass Valley, CA 95949
Phone: (916) 273-9102
Pet Restrictions: Small pets
Exercise Area for Pets: Yes
Rates: $69

Holiday Lodge
1221 E. Main St.
Grass Valley, CA 95945
Phone: (916) 273-4406
Pet Restrictions: $20 deposit
Exercise Area for Pets: Yes
Rates: $41.30 to $46.20/person

Vagabond Inn
20455 Hesperian Blvd.
Grass Valley, CA 94541
Phone: (510) 785-5480
Pet Restrictions: Pet rooms, $5
Exercise Area for Pets: Yes
Rates: $50 to $65

VETERINARIANS
Brunswick Vet. Clinic
10113 Joerschke Dr. 95945
(916) 477-2287

Fossum, Linda L.
13921 Loma Rica Dr. 95945

Mother Lode Vet. Hosp.
10113 Joerschke Dr. 95945
(916) 272-6651

HEALDSBURG

Madrona Manor
1001 Westside Rd., P.O. Box 818
Healdsburg, CA 95448
Phone: (707) 433-4231
Pet Restrictions: $20, one room for
    pets
Pet left unattended in room: Yes
Exercise Area for Pets: Yes
Rates: $135 to $225

HOLLYWOOD

Chateau Mamont
8221 Sunset Blvd.
Hollywood, CA 90046
Phone: (213) 656-1010
Pet Restrictions: None
Pet left unattended in room: Yes
Exercise Area for Pets: Yes
Rates: $150 to $650

HOPE VALLEY

Sorensen's Resort
Highway 88
Hope Valley, CA 96120
Phone: (916) 694-2203
Pet Restrictions: 2 cabins for pets
Exercise Area for Pets: Yes
Rates: $55 to $120

IRVINE

**Holiday Inn Irvine/Orange
County Airport**
17941 Von Karman
Irvine, CA 92714
Phone: (714) 863-1999
Fax: (714) 474-7236
Pet Restrictions: 25 lb. limit; pets
    not allowed in non-smoking
    rooms; pets allowed on 3rd and
    4th floors
Pet left unattended in room: No
Rates: $62 to $141

Irvine Marriott
18000 Von Karman Ave.
Irvine, CA 92715
Phone: (714) 553-0100
Pet Restrictions: None
Pet left unattended in room: Yes
Exercise Area for Pets: Yes
Rates: $49 to $160

VETERINARIANS

**Woodbridge Hosp. Animals
and Birds**
34 Creek Rd 92714
(714) 551-0304

Kobayashi, Atsuko
14130 Culver Dr., Suite A 92714
(714) 559-8972

JACKSON

Amador Motel
12408 Kennedy Flat Rd.
Jackson, CA 95642
Phone: (209) 223-0970
Pet Restrictions: No birds
Exercise Area for Pets: Yes
Rates: $27 to $45

Best Western Amador Inn
200 Hwy 495, P.O. Box 758
Jackson, CA 95642
Phone: (209) 223-0211
Pet Restrictions: $6/night/pet
Exercise Area for Pets: Yes
Rates: $42 to $84

Jackson Holiday Lodge
P.O. Box 1147
Jackson, CA 95642
Phone: (209) 223-0486
Pet Restrictions: $10 refund. deposit
Exercise Area for Pets: Yes
Rates: $33 to $63

JUNE LAKE

Gull Lake Lodge
P.O. Box 25
June Lake, CA 93529
Phone: (619) 648-7516
Pet Restrictions: Downstairs only,
    $6/night/pet
Exercise Area for Pets: Nearby
Rates: $60 to $170

June Lake Motel & Cabins
On SR 158, P.O. Box 98
June Lake, CA 93529
Phone: (619) 648-7547
Pet Restrictions: $5, no more than 2
    pets
Exercise Area for Pets: Nearby
Rates: $48 to $125

KERNVILLE

Hi Ho Resort Lodge
11901 Sierra Way, Rt. 1, Box 21
Kernville, CA 93238
Phone: (619) 376-2671

Pet Restrictions: Small dogs
Exercise Area for Pets: Yes
Rates: $60 to $80

Kern Lodge Motel
67 Valley View Corner of Sierra Way
P.O. Box 66
Kernville, CA 93238
Phone: (619) 376-2223

Pet Restrictions: $20 deposit,
    $5/day
Exercise Area for Pets: Yes
Rates: $47 to $85

KING CITY

Palm Motel
640 Broadway
King City, CA 93930
Phone: (408) 385-3248

Pet Restrictions: $7-$10/pet
Rates: $27 to $49

Sage Motel
633 Broadway
King City, CA 93930
Phone: (408) 385-3274

Pet Restrictions: None
Pet left unattended in room: Yes, in
    kennel
Exercise Area for Pets: Yes
Rates: $29

LA MESA

E-Z 8 Motel - La Mesa
7851 Fletcher Pkwy.
La Mesa, CA 91942
Phone: (619) 698-9444

Pet Restrictions: Dogs must on
    leash while walking on premises
    Pet deposit for large dogs
Pet left unattended in room: No
Exercise Area for Pets: Nearby
Rates: $26.88 to $43.88

LANCASTER

E-Z 8 Motel - Lancaster
43530 N. 17th St. West
Lancaster, CA 93534
Phone: (805) 945-9477

Pet Restrictions: Dogs must be on
    leash while walking on premises
    Pet deposit for large dogs
Pet left unattended in room: No
Exercise Area for Pets: Nearby
Rates: $28.88 to $40.88

LEMON GROVE

Value Inn
7458 Broadway
Lemon Grove, CA 91945
Phone: (619) 462-7022

Pet Restrictions: Dogs must be on
    leash while walking on premises
    Pet deposit may be required
Pet left unattended in room: No
Exercise Area for Pets: Nearby
Rates: $26.88 to $47.88

LIVERMORE

Holiday Inn - Livermore
720 Las Flores Rd.
Livermore, CA 94550
Phone: (510) 443-4950

Pet Restrictions: Ground floor only
    with 2 double beds & smoking
Exercise Area for Pets: Nearby
Rates: $49 to $71 includes breakfast

VETERINARIANS

Livermore Vet. Hosp.
2494 Railroad Ave. 94550
(415) 447-1420

Plone, Martin H.
1172 Murrieta Blvd. 94550
(415) 443-6000

LOMPOC

Quality Inn
1621 North H. St.
Lompoc, CA 93436
Phone: (805) 735-8555

Pet Restrictions: $15
Pet left unattended in room: Yes
Exercise Area for Pets: Yes
Rates: $54 to $75

CALIFORNIA — HOTELS (continued)

West Valley Vet. Clinic
123 N. V St. 93436
(805) 736-1238

Longley, Frank Ellis
510 North I St. 93436
(805) 736-5658

LONE PINE
Dow Villa Motel
310 S. Main St.
Lone Pine, CA 93545
Phone: (619) 876-5521,
    (800) 888-0017
Pet Restrictions: Small pets
Rates: $54 and up

Vagabond Inn
185 Atlantic Ave.
Lone Pine, CA 90802
Phone: (310) 435-3791
Pet Restrictions: $5 pet/day
Pet left unattended in room: Yes
Exercise Area for Pets: Nearby
Rates: $42.50 to $60, $5/extra
    person

LONG BEACH
Holiday Inn - Long Beach Airport
2640 Lakewood Blvd.
Long Beach, CA 90815
Phone: (310) 597-4401
Pet Restrictions: Specific rooms
Pet left unattended in room: Yes
Exercise Area for Pets: Yes
Rates: $105 to $115

Ramada Inn Long Beach
5325 E. Pacific Coast Hwy.
Long Beach, CA 90804
Phone: (310) 597-1341
Pet Restrictions: $125 deposit,
    inform desk
Pet left unattended in room: Yes
Exercise Area for Pets: Yes
Rates: $65 to $95

Jaymore Animal Hosp.
3449 E. Pacific Coast Hwy 90804
(310) 597-5533

Uptown Animal Hosp.
3350 Atlantic Ave. 90807
(310) 424-8541

Kennedy, Lillian L.
1775 Orizaba Ave. #E 90804
(310) 860-7747

LOS ANGELES
Best Western Hollywood
6141 Franklin Ave.
Los Angeles, CA 90028
Phone: (213) 464-5181
Pet Restrictions: $25 small, $50 big
    dogs
Pet left unattended in room: Yes
Exercise Area for Pets: Nearby
Rates: $55 to $85

Holiday Inn - Conv. Ctr
1020 S. Figueroa St. at Olympic Blvd
Los Angeles, CA 90015
Phone: (213) 748-1291
Pet Restrictions: Kennel on
    premises
Pet left unattended in room: Yes
Exercise Area for Pets: Nearby
Rates: $89 to $130

Holiday Inn - Hollywood
1755 N. Highland Ave.
Los Angeles, CA 90028
Phone: (213) 462-7181
Pet Restrictions: Small, well trained
Pet left unattended in room: Yes, no
    cleaning
Exercise Area for Pets: Nearby
Rates: $85 to $99

Holiday Inn - LA Int. Airport
9901 La Cienega Blvd.
Los Angeles, CA 90045
Phone: (310) 649-5151
Pet Restrictions: Small pets
Rates: $75 to $99

Vagabond Inn Downtown/ Figueroa
3101 S. Figueroa St.
Los Angeles, CA 90007
Phone: (213) 746-1531
Pet Restrictions: Small ones, $5 fee
Pet left unattended in room: Yes
Rates: $64 to $74

Westin Bonaventure
404 S. Figueroa St.
Los Angeles, CA 90071
Phone: (213) 624-1000
Pet Restrictions: Small, quiet
Pet left unattended in room: Yes
Exercise Area for Pets: Nearby
Rates: $157 to $222 regular rates

CALIFORNIA — HOTELS (continued)

Brentwood Pet Clinic
11718 Olympic Blvd. 90064
(213) 478-7789

Calif. Animal Hosp.
1736 Sepulveda Blvd. 90025
(213) 478-0545

Laurel Pet Hospital
7970 Santa Monica Blvd. 90046
(213) 654-7060

LOS BANOS

Bonanza Motel
349 W. Pacheco Blvd.
Los Banos, CA 93635
Phone: (209) 826-3871
Pet Restrictions: $20 fee, $20/pet
Exercise Area for Pets: Nearby

MAMMOTH LAKES

Shilo Inn Mammoth Lakes
2963 Main St., PO Box 2179
Mammoth Lakes, CA 93546
Phone: (619) 934-4500,
    (800) 222-2244
Pet Restrictions: $6/pet/day
Exercise Area for Pets: Nearby
Rates: $69 to $140

Wildwood Inn
State Hwy 203
Mammoth Lakes, CA 93546
Phone: (619) 934-6855,
    (800) 845-8764
Pet Restrictions: None
Pet left unattended in room: Yes
Exercise Area for Pets: Yes
Rates: $49 to $99

MANHATTAN BEACH

Residence Inn by Marriott
1700 N. Sepulveda Blvd.
Manhattan Beach, CA 90266
Phone: (310) 546-7627
Pet Restrictions: $250 deposit ($50
    non-refund for studio / $75 for
    penthouse), $6/day/pet, $3 add'l
    pet
Pet left unattended in room: Yes
Exercise Area for Pets: Yes
Rates: $87 to $185

Liebl, Thomas G.
1801 Sepulveda Blvd. 90266
(310) 545-6596

MARINA DEL REY

Marina Del Rey Marriott
13480 Maxella Ave.
Marina Del Rey, CA 90291
Phone: (310) 822-8555
Pet Restrictions: None
Pet left unattended in room: Yes
Exercise Area for Pets: Nearby
Rates: $79 to $129 (21 days in
    advance)

Bay Cities Veterinary Hosp.
13476 Washington Blvd. 90292
(310) 821-4967

MILBRAE

Clarion Hotel-San Francisco Airport
401 E. Milbrae Ave.
Milbrae, CA 94030
Phone: (415) 692-6363
Pet Restrictions: Travel kennel
Pet left unattended in room: Yes but
    must be present for cleaning
Exercise Area for Pets: Nearby
Rates: $69 to $109

Capuchino Veterinary Clinic
128 Park Place 94030
(415) 583-1500

MILPITAS

Economy Inns of America
270 S. Abbott Ave.
Milpitas, CA 95035
Phone: (408) 946-8889
Pet Restrictions: Notify mgmt when
    making reservation
Rates: $39.90 to $69

Jorgensen, Myron
1316 South Main 95035
(408) 262-2325

MIRANDA

Miranda Gardens Resort
P.O. Box 186
Miranda, CA 95553
Phone: (707) 943-3011
Pet Restrictions: $5/pet/night
Exercise Area for Pets: Nearby
Rates: $45 to $155

MI WUK

Mi Wuk Motor Lodge
P.O. Box 70
Mi Wuk Village, CA 95346
Phone: (209) 586-3031
Pet Restrictions: None
Exercise Area for Pets: Yes
Rates: $45 to $64 includes kitchen

MODESTO

Chalet Motel
115 Downey Ave.
Modesto, CA 95354
Phone: (209) 529-4370
Pet Restrictions: None

Vagabond Inn
1525 McHenry Ave.
Modesto, CA 95350
Phone: (209) 521-6340
Pet Restrictions: None
Exercise Area for Pets: Nearby
Rates: $35 to $58

VETERINARIANS

Crows Landing Rd-Vet. Clinic
2109 Crows Landing Rd. 95351
(209) 538-1782

Standiford Veterinary Clinic
1409 Standiford Ave. 95356
(916) 753-9436

Veterinary Medical Associates
204 W. Granger Ave. 95350
(209) 527-5855

MONROVIA

Howard Johnson Plaza-Hotel
700 West Huntington Dr.
Monrovia, CA 91016
Phone: (818) 357-5211
Pet Restrictions: $10, under 20 lbs.
Pet left unattended in room: Yes
Exercise Area for Pets: Yes
Rates: $60 to $80

VETERINARIANS

Huntington Dr. Animal Hosp.
535 W. Huntington Dr. 91016
(213) 357-2335

Monrovia Animal Hospital
1128 S. Myrtle 91016
(213) 358-1146

Santa Anita Small Animal Hosp.
245 W. Duarte Rd. 91016
(818) 359-3281

MONTECITO

San Ysidro Ranch
900 San Ysidro La.
Montecito, CA 93108
Phone: (805) 969-5046
Pet Restrictions: $45
Exercise Area for Pets: Nearby
Rates: $195 to $995

VETERINARIANS

McDonald, Gregory C.
1230A Coast Village Circle 93108
(805) 969-3225

MONTEREY

Bay Park Hotel
1525 Munras Ave.
Monterey, CA 93946
Phone: (408) 649-1020
Pet Restrictions: None
Exercise Area for Pets: Nearby
Rates: $59 to $139

Cypress Gardens Motel
1150 Munras Ave.
Monterey, CA 93940
Phone: (408) 373-2761
Pet Restrictions: None
Exercise Area for Pets: Nearby
Rates: $84 to $104

Monterey Beach Hotel-Best Western
2600 Sand Dunes Dr.
Monterey, CA 93940
Phone: (408) 394-3321,
         (800) 242-8627
Pet Restrictions: $25, 1st floor only
Exercise Area for Pets: Yes
Rates: $69 to $99

VETERINARIANS

Aguajito Veterinary Hospital
1221 Tenth St. 93940
(408) 372-8151

Monterey Animal Hosp.
725 Foam St. 93940
(408) 373-0711

MT. SHASTA

Alpine Lodge
908 S. Mt. Shasta Blvd.
Mt. Shasta, CA 96067
Phone: (916) 926-3145
Pet Restrictions: $20 refund. deposit
Exercise Area for Pets: Yes
Rates: $33 to $75

Swiss Holiday Lodge
2400 S. Mt. Shasta Blvd.
P.O. Box 335
Mt. Shasta, CA 96067
Phone: (916) 926-3446

Pet Restrictions: None
Exercise Area for Pets: Yes
Rates: $40.95 to $90

Tree House Best Western
11 Morgan Way
Mt. Shasta, CA 96067
Phone: (916) 926-3101,
(800) 545-7164

Pet Restrictions: None
Exercise Area for Pets: Nearby
Rates: $66 to $82

MOUNTAIN VIEW
Best Western Tropicana Lodge
1720 El Camino Real
Mountain View, CA 94040
Phone: (415) 961-0220

Pet Restrictions: Not left alone
unless in caged
Pet left unattended in room: Yes in
cage
Exercise Area for Pets: Yes
Rates: $55 to $85

VETERINARIANS

Alpine Animal Hosp.
2460 El Camino Real West 94040
(415) 969-8555

Grant Rd. Pet Clinic
1350 #14A Grant Rd. 94040
(415) 968-4448

Shibuya, Maremaro
1413 Grant Rd. 94040
(415) 967-5600

NAPA
Best Western Inn
100 Soscal Ave.
Napa, CA 94559
Phone: (707) 257-1930,
(800) 528-1234

Pet Restrictions: None
Rates: $75 to $149

VETERINARIANS

Silverado Veterinary Hosp.
2035 Silverado Trail 94558
(707) 224-7953

Lee, Robert M.
3131 California Blvd. 94558
(707) 255-6832

Miller, Frederick W.
2109 First St. 94559
(707) 255-0682

NATIONAL CITY
Value Inn
607 Roosevelt Ave.
National City, CA 91950
Phone: (619) 474-7502

Pet Restrictions: Dogs must be on
leash while walking on premises
Pet deposit may be required
Pet left unattended in room: No
Exercise Area for Pets: Nearby
Rates: $26.88 to $47.88

Value Inn
1700 Plaza Blvd.
National City, CA 91950
Phone: (619) 474-6491

Pet Restrictions: Dogs must be on
leash while walking on premises
Pet deposit may be required
Pet left unattended in room: No
Exercise Area for Pets: Nearby
Rates: $26.88 to $47.88

NEWARK
E-Z 8 Motel - Newark
5555 Cedar Court
Newark, CA 94560
Phone: (510) 794-7775

Pet Restrictions: Dogs must be on
leash while walking on premises
Pet deposit for large dogs
Pet left unattended in room: No
Exercise Area for Pets: Nearby
Rates: $26.88 to $41.88

NEWBURY PARK
E-Z 8 Motel - Thousand Oaks
2434 W. Hillcrest Dr.
Newbury Park, CA 91320
Phone: (805) 499-0755

Pet Restrictions: Dogs must be on
leash while walking on premises
Pet deposit for large dogs
Pet left unattended in room: No
Exercise Area for Pets: Nearby
Rates: $28.88 to $40.88

CALIFORNIA — HOTELS (continued)

NEW HALL

Hampton Inn
25259 The Old Rd.
New Hall, CA 91381
Phone: (805) 253-2400,
　　(800) HAMPTON

Pet Restrictions: $8/night, leashed
　in public, under 25 lbs.
Exercise Area for Pets: Nearby
Rates: $69 to $89

Bullock's Veterinary Hosp.
24899 San Fernando Rd. 91321
(805) 255-6483

Clark, S.H.
24639 North Arch St. 91321
(805) 259-3355

NORTH HIGHLAND

Rodeway Inn
3425 Orange Grove Ave.
North Highland, CA 95660
Phone: (916) 488-4100

Pet Restrictions: Small, no suites
Rates: $48 (2 people)

Reed, John R.
3451 Elkhorn Blvd. 95660
(916) 332-2845

NOVATO

Novato Motel
8141 Redwood Blvd.
Novato, CA 94945
Phone: (415) 897-7111,
　　(800) 854-6259

Pet Restrictions: Ground floor only,
　$10
Pet left unattended in room: Yes
Exercise Area for Pets: Yes
Rates: $39 to $59

Northbay Animal Hosp.
103 San Marin Plaza 94947
(415) 892-8387

Bottasso, Michael S.
1770 Novato Blvd. 94947
(415) 897-8200

OAKLAND

E-Z 8 Motel — Oakland
8471 Enterprise Way
Oakland, CA 94621
Phone: (510) 562-4888

Pet Restrictions: Dogs must be on
　leash while walking on premises
　Pet deposit for large dogs
Pet left unattended in room: No
Exercise Area for Pets: Nearby
Rates: $33.88 to $43.88

OJAI

Best Western Casa Ojai
1302 East Ojai Ave.
Ojai, CA 93023
Phone: (800) 255-8175

Pet Restrictions: 30 lb. max.,
　downstairs rooms only
Exercise Area for Pets: Nearby
Rates: $55 to $95

Bee, John G.
PO Box 817
(805) 646-5539

ONTARIO

Holiday Inn - Ontario
1801 East G St.
Ontario, CA 91764
Phone: (714) 983-3604,
　　(800) HOLIDAY

Pet Restrictions: None
Pet left unattended in room: Yes, no
　service
Exercise Area for Pets: Yes
Rates: $39 to $75

Red Lion Inn
222 N. Vineyard Ave.
Ontario, CA 91764
Phone: (714) 983-0909

Pet Restrictions: $50 deposit
Pet left unattended in room: Yes
Exercise Area for Pets: Nearby
Rates: $69 to $89

CALIFORNIA — HOTELS (continued)

ORANGE

The Residence Inn by Marriott
201 N. State College Blvd.
Orange, CA 92668
Phone: (714) 978-7700

Pet Restrictions: $250 deposit ($75 non-refund.), $8/day/pet
Pet left unattended in room: Yes
Exercise Area for Pets: Nearby
Rates: $95 to $129 incl. dinner & breakfast (cheaper for longer stays)

American Animal Hosp.
9 City Blvd. West #67 92668
(714) 634-8988

Tustin Avenue Veterinary Hosp.
434 S. Tustin Ave. 92666
(714) 633-3323

Villa Animal Hosp.
4250 Chapman Ave. 92669
(714) 633-9780

ORLAND

Orland Inn
1052 South St.
Orland, CA 95963
Phone: (916) 865-7632

Pet Restrictions: $5
Pet left unattended in room: Yes
Exercise Area for Pets: Yes
Rates: $28 to $38

OXNARD

Vagabond Inn
1245 N. Oxnard Blvd.
Oxnard, CA 93030
Phone: (805) 983-0251

Pet Restrictions: $5/day
Pet left unattended in room: Yes
Exercise Area for Pets: Yes
Rates: $40 to $60

Adobe Animal Hospital
1420 S. Oxnard Blvd. 93033
(805) 486-8333

Feingold, Jan
651 S. Ventura Rd. 93030
(805) 984-1850

PALMDALE

E-Z 8 Motel - Palmdale
430 West Palmdale Ave.
Palmdale, CA 93551
Phone: (805) 273-6400

Pet Restrictions: Dogs must be on leash while walking on premises Pet deposit for large dogs
Pet left unattended in room: No
Exercise Area for Pets: Nearby
Rates: $26.88 to $34.88

Vagabond Inn
130 E. Palmdale Blvd.
Palmdale, CA 93550
Phone: (805) 273-1400, (800) 522-1555

Pet Restrictions: $5/night
Pet left unattended in room: Yes
Exercise Area for Pets: Nearby
Rates: $30 to $45

Antelope Valley Animal Hosp.
1326 W. Avenue North 93551
(805) 273-1234

McEwan, Lynn Clark
38568 North 6th St. East 93550
(805) 273-1555

PARADISE

Palos Verdes Motel
5423 Skyway, P.O. Box 458
Paradise, CA 95969
Phone: (916) 877-2127

Pet Restrictions: Small pets only
Exercise Area for Pets: Nearby
Rates: $35 to $43

Clark Road Veterinary Hosp.
5799 Clark Rd. 95969
(916) 872-5111

Skyway Pet Hospital
7334 Skyway 95969
(916) 877-4153

PASADENA

Holiday Inn
303 E. Cordova St.
Pasadena, CA 91101
Phone: (818) 449-4000, (800) 457-7940

Pet Restrictions: $50 deposit
Exercise Area for Pets: Yes
Rates: $69 to $99

CALIFORNIA — HOTELS (continued)

Vagabond Inn
2863 E. Colorado Blvd.
Pasadena, CA 91107
Phone: (818) 449-3020
Pet Restrictions: $5/pet/night
Pet left unattended in room: Yes
Exercise Area for Pets: Nearby
Rates: $40 to ($400 special events)

Animal Medical Hosp.
2116 E. Colorado Blvd. 91107
(818) 796-3019

Arroyo Veterinary Hosp.
797 S. Arroyo Parkway 91105
(818) 796-9206

Foothill Veterinary Hosp.
2204 E. Foothill Blvd. 91107
(818) 792-1187

PASO ROBLES
Paso Robles Travelodge
2701 Spring St.
Paso Robles, CA 93446
Phone: (805) 238-0078
Pet Restrictions: $4/pet/night
Exercise Area for Pets: Yes
Rates: $45-$50 winter, $65-$85
   summer

Bryant, B.R.
725 Walnut Dr. 93446
(805) 238-4622

PIERCY
Hartsbrook Inn
900 Highway 101
Piercy, CA 95467
Phone: (707) 247-3305
Pet Restrictions: $5/night/pet, only
   in rooms w/o carpet
Pet left unattended in room: Yes
Exercise Area for Pets: Yes, on
   leashes
Rates: $39 to $100

PINE VALLEY
Sunrise Motel
28940 Old Hwy 80
Pine Valley, CA
Phone: (619) 473-8777
Pet Restrictions: None
Pet left unattended in room: Yes
Exercise Area for Pets: Nearby
Rates: $39.95/1 person, $45.95/2,
   $49.95/3

Pine Valley Veterinary Clinic
P.O. Box 949 92062
(619) 473-8797

PISMO BEACH
Sandcastle Inn
100 Stimson Ave.
Pismo Beach, CA 93449
Phone: (805) 773-2422
Pet Restrictions: $10/day, 5 rooms
   only
Exercise Area for Pets: Nearby
Rates: $105 to $130

PT. REYES
Thirty Nine Cypress
Bed & Breakfast
23 Cypress, PO Box 176
Pt. Reyes, CA 94956
Phone: (415) 663-1709
Pet Restrictions: Dogs subject to
   approval
Exercise Area for Pets: Yes
Rates: $100 to $125

POMONA
Shilo Inn Hotel
3200 Temple Ave.
Pomona, CA 91768
Phone: (714) 598-0073
Pet Restrictions: $6/day
Exercise Area for Pets: Yes
Rates: $85

RANCHO CUCAMONGA
Rancho Marriott Las Palmas
41-000 Bob Hope Dr.
Rancho Cucamonga, CA 92270
Phone: (619) 568-2727
Pet Restrictions: Must sign waiver,
   no poolside rooms
Exercise Area for Pets: Nearby
Rates: $79 to $99

Upland Animal Hospital
8763 Grove Avenue 91730
(714) 982-8854

RED BLUFF

Flamingo Hotel
250 S. Main St.
Red Bluff, CA 96080
Phone: (916) 527-3545
Pet Restrictions: $3/day
Exercise Area for Pets: Yes
Rates: $30 to $45

Kings Lodge
38 Antelope Blvd.
Red Bluff, CA 96080
Phone: (916) 527-6020
Pet Restrictions: None
Exercise Area for Pets: Nearby
Rates: $34.95

REDDING

Bel Air Motel
540 N. Market St.
Redding, CA 96003
Phone: (916) 243-5291
Pet Restrictions: None
Exercise Area for Pets: Nearby
Rates: $24 to $49

Days Inn-Redding
2180 Hilltop Dr.
Redding, CA 96002
Phone: (916) 221-8200
Pet Restrictions: $25 refund.
    deposit, 2 pet max.
Exercise Area for Pets: Yes
Rates: $60 to $89

Park Terrace Inn
1900 Hilltop Dr.
Redding, CA 96002
Phone: (916) 221-7500
Pet Restrictions: None
Exercise Area for Pets: Yes
Rates: $58 to $75

Red Lion Inn
1830 Hilltop Dr.
Redding, CA 96002
Phone: (916) 221-8700
Pet Restrictions: Smoking rooms
    only
Exercise Area for Pets: Nearby
Rates: $100 to $140

Vagabond Inn
536 E. Cypress Ave.
Redding, CA 96002
Phone: (916) 223-1600
Pet Restrictions: $5/day, 2 pet max.
Exercise Area for Pets: Nearby
Rates: $55 to $70

VETERINARIANS

Asher Veterinary Clinic
2824 Freebridge St. 96001
(916) 221-5536

Hilltop Veterinary Hosp.
2095 Hilltop Dr. 96002
(916) 221-6733

Stovall, Thomas L.
1800 Eureka Way 96001
(916) 241-0787

REDONDO BEACH

Vagabond Inn
6226 Pacific Coast Hwy
Redondo Beach, CA 90277
Phone: (310) 378-8555
Pet Restrictions: $3/day, 2 pet max.
Exercise Area for Pets: Nearby
Rates: $45 to $54

VETERINARIANS

Animal Medical clinic
2006 Artesia Blvd. 90278
(310) 376-0072

Bohn, Michael D.
1020 S. Pacific Coast Hwy 90277
(310) 540-5663

Schooley, Robert
240 the Village #204 90277
(310) 379-8247

REDWOOD CITY

Howard Johnson Lodge
485 Veterans Boulevard
Redwood City, CA 94063
Phone: (415) 365-5500,
    (800) 654-2000
Pet Restrictions: None
Pet left unattended in room: Yes
Exercise Area for Pets: Yes
Rates: $62 to $79

CALIFORNIA — HOTELS (continued)

VETERINARIANS

Sequoia Animal Hosp.
1409 El Camino Real 94063
(415) 369-7326

Kennedy, Edward J.
338 Lakeview Way 94062
(415) 364-5173

RIVERSIDE
Super Eight Motel
1199 University Ave.
Riverside, CA 92507
Phone: (714) 682-9011,
    (800) 800-8000
Pet Restrictions: $50 deposit
Pet left unattended in room: Yes
Exercise Area for Pets: Yes
Rates: $34.88 to $49.88

VETERINARIANS

Riverside Animal Hosp.
6162 Magnolia Ave. 92506
(714) 683-4200

Victoria Animal Hosp.
3400 Arlington Ave. 92506
(714) 683-7133

Wilds, Dennis W.
625 W. LaCadena Dr. 92501
(714) 684-2181

ROSEMEAD
Vagabond Inn-Rosemead
3633 N. Rosemead Blvd.
Rosemead, CA 91770
Phone: (818) 288-6661,
    (800) 522-1555
Pet Restrictions: $3 fee, 1 small pet
    per room/night
Exercise Area for Pets: Yes
Rates: $47 to $57

VETERINARIANS

Community Animal Hosp.
8338 Valley Blvd. 90274
(818) 573-2650

Rosemead Animal Hosp.
9639 E. Valley Blvd. 91770
(818) 444-0565

ROSEVILLE
Best Western Roseville Inn
220 Harding Blvd.
Roseville, CA 95678
Phone: (916) 782-4434,
    (800) 255-4747
Pet Restrictions: $5/pet/night, small,
    under 40 lbs.
Rates: $46 to $57

SACRAMENTO
Holiday Inn Capitol Plaza
300 J St.
Sacramento, CA 95814
Phone: (916) 446-0100,
    (800) HOLIDAY
Pet Restrictions: No large pets
Pet left unattended in room: Yes
Exercise Area for Pets: Nearby
Rates: $82 to $95

La Quinta Inn
4604 Madison Ave.
Sacramento, CA 95841
Phone: (916) 348-0900,
    (800) 531-5900
Pet Restrictions: Small
Pet left unattended in room: Yes, no
    service unless caged
Exercise Area for Pets: Nearby
Rates: $54 to $85

Motel Orleans
228 Jibboom St.
Sacramento, CA 95814
Phone: (916) 443-4811,
    (800) 626-1900
Pet Restrictions: $25 refund. deposit
Rates: $40 to $62

Red Lion Hotel
2001 Point West Way
Sacramento, CA 95815
Phone: (916) 929-8855,
    (800) 547-8010
Pet Restrictions: Small
Pet left unattended in room: Yes
Exercise Area for Pets: Nearby
Rates: $76 to $105

Sacramento Hilton Inn
2200 Howard St.
Sacramento, CA 95815
Phone: (916) 922-4700,
  (800) 344-4321

Pet Restrictions: $25 non-refund.
  deposit
Pet left unattended in room: Yes
Exercise Area for Pets: Yes
Rates: $89 to $119

Vagabond Inn
909 3rd St.
Sacramento, CA 95814
Phone: (916) 446-1481,
  (800) 522-1555

Pet Restrictions: $5/day
Pet left unattended in room: Yes
Exercise Area for Pets: Nearby
Rates: $60 to $70

VETERINARIANS

Del Paso Veterinary Clinic
924 De Paso Blvd. 95815
(916) 925-2107

Fulton Avenue Veterinary Hosp.
2173 Fulton Avenue 95825
(916) 483-8548

Sacramento Veterinary Surgical Services
9700 Business Pk Dr. #404 95827
(916) 362-3111

SAN BERNARDINO

Best Western Sands Motel
606 North H St.
San Bernardino, CA 92410
Phone: (714) 889-8391,
  (800) 331-4409

Pet Restrictions: None
Pet left unattended in room: Yes
Exercise Area for Pets: Yes
Rates: $52 to $72

E-Z 8 Motel - San Bernardino
1750 S. Waterman Ave.
San Bernardino, CA 92408
Phone: (909) 888-4827

Pet Restrictions: Dogs must be on
  leash while walking on premises
  Pet deposit for large dogs
Pet left unattended in room: No
Exercise Area for Pets: Nearby
Rates: $26.88 to $38.88

VETERINARIANS

Allard-Ward, Barbara
939 West 40th St. 92407
(714) 882-2408

SAN DIEGO

Beach Haven Inn
4740 Mission Blvd.
San Diego, CA 92109
Phone: (619) 272-3812,
  (800) 831-6323

Pet Restrictions: $50 deposit, under
  20 lbs.
Exercise Area for Pets: Nearby
Rates: $62 to $135

E-Z 8 Motel - South Bay
1010 Outer Rd.
San Diego, CA 92154
Phone: (619) 575-8808

Pet Restrictions: Dogs must be on
  leash while walking on premises
  Pet deposit for large dogs
Pet left unattended in room: No
Exercise Area for Pets: Nearby
Rates: $26.88 to $43.88

E-Z 8 Motel - Sports Arena
3333 Channel Way
San Diego, CA 92110
Phone: (619) 223-9500

Pet Restrictions: Dogs must be on
  leash while walking on premises
  Pet deposit for large dogs
Pet left unattended in room: No
Exercise Area for Pets: Nearby
Rates: $28.88 to $45.88

E-Z 8 Motel - Old Town
4747 Pacific Hwy.
San Diego, CA 92110
Phone: (619) 294-2512

Pet Restrictions: Dogs must be on
  leash while walking on premises
  Pet deposit for large dogs
Pet left unattended in room: No
Exercise Area for Pets: Nearby
Rates: $28.88 to $45.88

E-Z 8 Motel - Mission Valley
2484 Hotel Circle Place
San Diego, CA 92108
Phone: (619) 291-8252

Pet Restrictions: Dogs must be on
  leash while walking on premises
  Pet deposit for large dogs
Pet left unattended in room: No
Exercise Area for Pets: Nearby
Rates: $31.88 to $40.88

Holiday Inn Montgomery Field
8110 Aero Dr.
San Diego, CA 92123
Phone: (619) 277-8888,
    (800) 992-1441

Pet Restrictions: No non-smoking
    avail. room
Pet left unattended in room: Yes
Exercise Area for Pets: Yes
Rates: $59 to $76

Holiday Inn On the Bay
1355 N. Harbor Dr.
San Diego 92101
Phone: (619) 232-3861,
    (800) 465-4329

Pet Restrictions: Must sign waiver
Pet left unattended in room: Yes, no
    maid service
Exercise Area for Pets: Nearby
Rates: $145 to $165

Howard Johnson Lodge
4545 Waring Road
San Diego, CA 92120
Phone: (619) 286-7000

Pet Restrictions: None
Pet left unattended in room: Yes, no
    housekeeping
Exercise Area for Pets: Yes
Rates: $49 to $59

Marriott Hotel & Marina
333 W. Harbor Dr.
San Diego, CA 92101
Phone: (619) 234-1500

Pet Restrictions: None
Pet left unattended in room: Yes
Exercise Area for Pets: Yes
Rates: $149 to $179

San Diego Hilton Beach & Tennis Resort
1775 E. Mission Bay Dr.
San Diego, CA 92109
Phone: (619) 276-4010,
    (800) 445-8666 (all Hiltons)

Pet Restrictions: None; must sign
    waiver
Pet left unattended in room: Yes
Exercise Area for Pets: Nearby
Rates: $145 to $225

San Diego Princess Resort
1404 W. Vacation Rd.
San Diego, CA 92109
Phone: (619) 274-4630,
    (800) 542-6275

Pet Restrictions: Must sign waiver,
    leashed in public
Exercise Area for Pets: Yes
Rates: $150 to $345

Vagabond Inn-Mission Valley
625 Hotel Circle
San Diego, CA 92108
Phone: (619) 297-1691,
    (800) 522-1555

Pet Restrictions: $5/night
Exercise Area for Pets: Yes
Rates: $32 to $60

Vagabond Inn-Point Loma
1325 Scott St.
San Diego, CA 92106
Phone: (619) 224-3371,
    (800) 522-1555

Pet Restrictions: $5/night
Exercise Area for Pets: Nearby
Rates: $50 to $70

Value Inn
3225 Midway Dr.
San Diego, CA
Phone: (619) 224-3166

Pet Restrictions: Dogs must be on
    leash while walking on premises
    Pet deposit for large dogs
Pet left unattended in room: No
Exercise Area for Pets: Nearby
Rates: $26.88 to $47.88

VETERINARIANS

Angel Animal Clinic of North Park
3537 30th St. 92104
(619) 291-0042

Cabrillo Veterinary Clinic
4138 Voltaire St. 92107
(619) 225-9684

Turquoise Animal Hosp.
950 Turquoise St. 92109
(619) 488-0658

CALIFORNIA — HOTELS (continued)

SAN FRANCISCO

Beresford Arms
701 Post St.
San Francisco, CA 94109
Phone: (415) 673-2600,
(800) 533-6533
Pet Restrictions: None, small
Pet left unattended in room: Yes
Rates: $75 to $120

Beresford Hotel
635 Sutter St.
San Francisco, CA 94102
Phone: (415) 673-9900,
(800) 533-6533
Pet Restrictions: Small
Exercise Area for Pets: Nearby
Rates: $75 to $99

Campton Place
340 Stockton St.
San Francisco, CA 94108
Phone: (415) 781-5555
Pet Restrictions: $25
Pet left unattended in room: Yes
Exercise Area for Pets: Nearby
Rates: $185 to $320

Four Seasons-Clift Hotel
495 Geary St.
San Francisco, CA 94102
Phone: (415) 775-4700,
(800) 332-3442
Pet Restrictions: $25 deposit
Pet left unattended in room: No,
doormen may walk dogs for you
Exercise Area for Pets: Nearby
Rates: $195 to $335

Laurel Motor Inn
444 Presidio Ave.
San Francisco, CA 94115
Phone: (415) 567-8467,
(800) 552-8735
Pet Restrictions: None
Exercise Area for Pets: Nearby
Rates: $80 to $98

The Ramada Hotel
245 S. Airport Blvd.
San Francisco, CA 94080
Phone: (415) 589-7200,
(800) 452-3456
Pet Restrictions: Refund. cash
deposit if paying cash, not if
using credit card
Pet left unattended in room: Yes, no
housekeeping unless caged,
notify maids
Rates: $82 to $150

Rodeway Inn
1450 Lombard St.
San Francisco, CA 94123
Phone: (415) 673-0691,
(800) 228-2000
Pet Restrictions: Ground floor only,
$20 deposit
Pet left unattended in room: Yes, no
service
Exercise Area for Pets: Nearby
Rates: $85 to $95

San Francisco Hilton
333 O'Farrell St.
San Francisco, CA 94102
Phone: (415) 771-1400,
(800) 445-8667 (worldwide)
Pet Restrictions: $5 under 20 lbs.,
$10 over 20 lbs.
Pet left unattended in room: Yes if
caged
Exercise Area for Pets: Nearby
Rates: $145 to $235

San Francisco Drake
450 Powell St.
San Francisco, CA 94102
Phone: (415) 392-7755,
(800) 227-5480
Pet Restrictions: $75 refund. deposit
Pet left unattended in room: Yes
Rates: $95 to $135

The Westin St. Fancis
Union Sq.
San Francisco, CA 94102
Phone: (415) 397-7000
Pet Restrictions: Small dogs only
Rates: $180 to $260

VETERINARIANS
Balboa Pet Hosp.
3329 Balboa St. 94121
(415) 752-3300

CALIFORNIA — HOTELS (continued)

Ocean Avenue Vet. Hosp.
1001 Ocean Ave. 94112
(415) 586-5327

San Francisco SPCA Animal Hospital
2500 16th St. 94103
(415) 554-3030

SAN LUIS OBISPO
Howard Johnson Lodge
1585 Calle Joaquin
San Luis Obispo, CA 93401
Phone: (805) 544-5300

Pet Restrictions: 4 rooms, $10
Exercise Area for Pets: Nearby
Rates: $49 to $59 with pet

Vagabond Inn
210 Madonna Rd.
San Luis Obispo, CA 93401
Phone: (805) 544-4710

Pet Restrictions: $5/pet
Exercise Area for Pets: Nearby
Rates: $71 to $64

VETERINARIANS
Longabach, Jay O.
2404 Loomis St. 93401
(805) 543-0956

O'Connor, Betty J.
300 Higuera St. 93401
(805) 543-4615

SAN JOSE
E-Z 8 Motel - San Jose II
2050 N. First St.
San Jose, CA 95131
Phone: (408) 436-0636

Pet Restrictions: Dogs must be on
   leash while walking on premises
   Pet deposit for large dogs
Pet left unattended in room: No
Exercise Area for Pets: Nearby
Rates: $32.88 to $47.88

E-Z 8 Motel - San Jose I
1550 N. First St.
San Jose, CA 95112
Phone: (408) 453-1830

Pet Restrictions: Dogs must be on
   leash while walking on premises
   Pet deposit for large dogs
Pet left unattended in room: No
Exercise Area for Pets: Nearby
Rates: $33.88 to $48.88

Holiday Inn-Airport
1355 N. 4th St.
San Jose, CA 95112
Phone: (408) 453-5340

Pet Restrictions: None, 10 rooms
   for pets
Exercise Area for Pets: Nearby
Rates: $59 to $68

Howard Johnson Lodge
1755 North First Street
San Jose, CA 95112
Phone: (408) 453-3133

Pet Restrictions: Small, 20 lbs. pet
Exercise Area for Pets: Nearby
Rates: $49 to $89

VETERINARIANS
Blossom Hill Veterinary Clinic
955 Blossom Hill Rd. 95123
(408) 227-3717

Crocker Animal Hospital
475 N. Jackson Ave. 95133
(408) 272-1330

Sara Creek Vet. Clinic
375 S. Saratoga Ave. 95129
(408) 246-1470

SAN MARCOS
Lake San Marco's Quails Inn
1025 La Bonita Dr.
San Marcos, CA 92069
Phone: (619) 744-0120

Pet Restrictions: 5 rooms only,
   small dogs, $10/day
Exercise Area for Pets: Nearby
Rates: $85

VETERINARIANS
San Marcos Veterinary Clinic
145 S. Rancho Santa Fe 92069
(714) 744-5400

SAN RAFAEL
Holiday Inn Marin
1010 Northgate Dr.
San Rafael, CA 94903
Phone: (415) 479-8800

Pet Restrictions: $50 deposit, $10/day
Pet left unattended in room: Yes
Exercise Area for Pets: Nearby
Rates: $89 to $120

CALIFORNIA — HOTELS (continued)

VETERINARIANS
Northbay Animal Hosp.
4140 Redwood Hwy 94903
(415) 499-8387

Owens, Jerry M.
100 Circle Rd. 94903
(415) 848-5150

SANTA BARBARA
Fiss Parkers Red Lion Resort
633 E. Cabrillo Blvd.
Santa Barbara, CA 93103
Phone: (805) 564-4333
Pet Restrictions: $50 deposit
Pet left unattended in room: Yes
Exercise Area for Pets: Nearby
Rates: $185 to $255

Four Seasons Biltmore
1260 Channel Dr.
Santa Barbara, CA 93108
Phone: (805) 969-2261
Pet Restrictions: Outside cottages only
Exercise Area for Pets: Nearby
Rates: $295 to $1700

The Vagabond
3580 El Camino Real
Santa Barbara, CA 95051
Phone: (408) 241-0771
Pet Restrictions: 3-4 rooms for pets, $5/day
Pet left unattended in room: Yes
Exercise Area for Pets: Nearby
Rates: $45 to $55

Vagabond Inn
2819 State St.
Santa Barbara, CA 93105
Phone: (805) 687-6444
Pet Restrictions: $5/day
Exercise Area for Pets: Nearby
Rates: $63 to $95

VETERINARIANS
Montecito Animal Hosp.
1252 Coast Village Circle 93108
(805) 969-2213

Carl, Bonniek
101 West Mission 93101
(805) 569-2287

Mutti, David R.
1097 Via Regina 93111
(805) 963-1544

SANTA CLARA
Econo Lodge
2930 El Caminno Real, P.O. Box 2841
Santa Clara, CA 95055
Phone: (408) 241-3010
Pet Restrictions: $5/day
Pet left unattended in room: Yes
Rates: $50 to $90

E-Z 8 Motel - Santa Clara
3550 El Camino Real
Santa Clara, CA 95051
Phone: (408) 246-3119
Pet Restrictions: Dogs must be on leash while walking on premises. Pet deposit for large dogs
Pet left unattended in room: No
Exercise Area for Pets: Nearby
Rates: $33.88 to $45.88

Howard Johnson Lodge
5405 Stevens Creek Blvd.
Santa Clara, CA 95051
Phone: (408) 257-8600
Pet Restrictions: $10/day - credit card at check in
Exercise Area for Pets: Nearby
Rates: $74 to $89

VETERINARIANS
Brees, John W.
3100 El Camino Real 95051
(408) 248-3844

Freeman, Roark R.
3345 El Camino Real 95051
(408) 246-1893

SANTA CRUZ
Motel Continental
414 Ocean St.
Santa Cruz, CA 95060
Phone: (408) 429-1221
Pet Restrictions: None
Exercise Area for Pets: Nearby
Rates: $48.50 to $135

Vagabond Inn
1519 E. First St.
Santa Cruz, CA 92701
Phone: (714) 547-9426
Pet Restrictions: $5/day
Exercise Area for Pets: Yes
Rates: $38 to $48

VETERINARIANS
Animal Clinic of Santa Cruz
815 Mission St. 95062
(408) 427-3345

Santa Cruz Veterinary Clinic
2585 Soquel Dr. 95065
(408) 475-5400

SANTA MARIA

Howard Johnson Lodge
210 South Nicholson Ave.
Santa Maria, CA 93454
Phone: (805) 922-5891

Pet Restrictions: 5 rooms only
Exercise Area for Pets: Nearby
Rates: $39 to $69

VETERINARIANS

Animal Clinic of Santa Maria
2548 Santa Maria Way 93455
(805) 922-3361

Olwin, David B.
3440 Orcutt Rd. 93455
(805) 937-6341

Vale, Martin M.
230A E. Betteravia Rd. 93454
(805) 922-0305

SANTA NELLA

Best Western Andersen's Inn
12367 Hwy 338
Santa Nella, CA 95322
Phone: (209) 826-5534

Pet Restrictions: 5 per day (dog),
    $10/day
Exercise Area for Pets: Nearby
Rates: $53 to $59

Holiday Inn Missiondeoro
13070 Hwy 335
Santa Nella, CA 95322
Phone: (209) 826-4444

Pet Restrictions: None
Exercise Area for Pets: Nearby
Rates: $44.95 to $72.95

SANTA ROSA

Best Western Garden Inn
1500 Santa Rosa Ave.
Santa Rosa, CA 95404
Phone: (707) 546-4031

Pet Restrictions: $10 deposit, 2 pet
    max.
Exercise Area for Pets: Yes
Rates: $73

Los Robles Lodge
925 Edwards Ave.
Santa Rosa, CA 95401
Phone: (707) 545-6330

Pet Restrictions: None
Exercise Area for Pets: Nearby
Rates: $75 to $94

VETERINARIANS

Lakeside Pet Hospital
4331 Montgomery Dr. 95405
(707) 539-3393

Northtown Animal Hosp.
3881 Old Redwood Hwy. 95403
(707) 546-6355

Redwood Veterinary Clinic
1946 Santa Rosa Ave. 95407
(707) 542-4012

SEASIDE

Days Inn
1400 Del Monte Blvd.
Seaside, CA 93955
Phone: (408) 394-5335

Pet Restrictions: $10/day
Pet left unattended in room: Yes
Exercise Area for Pets: Nearby
Rates: $45 to $99

VETERINARIANS

Coast Veterinary Hosp.
780 Elm Ave. 93955
(408) 899-2381

Grant, Patricia
P.O. Box 1578 93955
(408) 384-6055

SHELL BEACH

Spyglass Inn
2705 Spyglass Dr.
Shell Beach, CA 93449
Phone: (800) 824-2612

Pet Restrictions: 30 lb. max.,
    downstairs rooms only
Exercise Area for Pets: Nearby
Rates: $64 to $99

SIERRA CITY

Heringtons Sierra Pines
P.O. Box 235
Sierra City, CA 96125
Phone: (916) 862-1151

Pet Restrictions: None
Exercise Area for Pets: Yes
Rates: $49 to $68

SONOMA

Best Western Sonoma Valley Inn
550 2nd St. W.
Sonoma, CA 95476
Phone: (707) 938-9200

Pet Restrictions: Small pets only,
Exercise Area for Pets: Nearby
Rates: $139 to $125

SOUTH LAKE TAHOE

Tahoe Sands Inn
P.O. Box J
South Lake Tahoe, CA 95705
Phone: (916) 544-3476

Pet Restrictions: $6/day, 2 pets
  max.
Exercise Area for Pets: Yes
Rates: $48 to $78

Tahoe Valley Motel
at Tahoe Keys Blvd., P.O. Box 7702
South Lake Tahoe, CA 95731
Phone: (916) 541-0353

Pet Restrictions: Small dogs only,
  $10/day
Exercise Area for Pets: Yes
Rates: $85 to $195

STOCKTON

Best Western Charter Way Inn
550 W. Charter Way
Stockton, CA 95206
Phone: (209) 948-0321

Pet Restrictions: None
Exercise Area for Pets: Nearby
Rates: $46 to $64

La Quinta Inn
2710 W. March La.
Stockton, CA 95207
Phone: (209) 952-7800

Pet Restrictions: Small pets only
Exercise Area for Pets: Nearby,
  scooper needed
Rates: $58 to $68

Vagabond Inn
33 N. Center St.
Stockton, CA 95202
Phone: (209) 948-6151

Pet Restrictions: $3 day, 2 pet max.
Exercise Area for Pets: Yes
Rates: $40 to $45

VETERINARIANS

Animal Clinic
7575 Pacific Ave.
(209) 477-4853

Bear Creek Veterinary Hosp.
8728 Thornton Rd. 95209
(209) 951-8911

Delph, Wilbur E.
9629 North Highway 99 95212
(209) 931-1874

SUNNYVALE

Residence Inn By Marriott
750 Lakeway Dr.
Sunnyvale, CA 94086
Phone: (408) 720-1000

Pet Restrictions: $50 cleaning fee
  ($100 penthouse), $6/day
Exercise Area for Pets: Nearby
Rates: $119 to $139

Woodfin Suites
635 E. El Camino Real
Sunnyvale, CA 94087
Phone: (408) 738-1700

Pet Restrictions: $15/pet/day, $400
  deposit ($75 non-refund.
  cleaning)
Exercise Area for Pets: Nearby
Rates: $79 to $152

VETERINARIANS

Beatty, James O.
1036 West El Camino Real 94087
(408) 736-8296

Lebo, James B.
1295 West El Camino Real 94087
(415) 961-4550

TAHOE VISTA

Tatami Cottage Resort
P.O. Box 18
Tahoe Vista, CA 96148
Phone: (916) 546-3523
Pet Restrictions: None
Pet left unattended in room: Yes
Exercise Area for Pets: Yes
Other: Enclosed pet lot
Rates: $69 to $157

THREE RIVERS

Best Western Holiday Lodge
P.O. Box 129
Three Rivers, CA 93271
Phone: (209) 561-4119
Pet Restrictions: None
Exercise Area for Pets: Nearby
Rates: $48 to $74

Buckeye Tree Lodge
46000 Sierra Dr.
Three Rivers, CA 93271
Phone: (209) 561-4611

Pet Restrictions: $4/day, on leash
Exercise Area for Pets: Yes
Rates: $52 to $60

The River Inn
45176 Sierra Dr.
Three Rivers, CA 93271
Phone: (209) 561-4367

Pet Restrictions: $3/day/pet, 3 pet max.
Exercise Area for Pets: Nearby
Rates: $38 to $61

THOUSAND OAKS

Howard Johnson Lodge
75 West Thousand Oaks Blvd.
Thousand Oaks, CA 91360-4484
Phone: (805) 497-3701

Pet Restrictions: $5 spray charge
Pet left unattended in room: Yes
Exercise Area for Pets: Yes
Rates: $49 to $69

VETERINARIANS

Camino Animal Clinic
700 North Moorpark Rd. 91360
(805) 497-0969

Conejo Valley Veterinary Clinic
1850 Thousand Oaks 91362
(805) 495-4671

TORRANCE

Howard Johnson Lodge
2880 Pacific Coast Hwy.
Torrance, CA 90505
Phone: (310) 325-0660

Pet Restrictions: $5/day, 2 pet max.
Exercise Area for Pets: Yes
Rates: $79 to $94

VETERINARIANS

Bay Cities Pet Hosp.
20447 Hawthorne Blvd. 90503
(310) 371-6508

County Hills Animal Clinic
2919 Rolling Hills Rd. 90505
(310) 539-3851

Harbor Animal Hosp.
2078 Torrance Blvd. 90501
(310) 328-3733

TRINIDAD

Bishop Pine Lodge
1481 Patricks Pt. Dr.
Trinidad, CA 95570
Phone: (707) 677-3314

Pet Restrictions: $5/day, 2 pet max.
Exercise Area for Pets: Nearby
Rates: $65 to $100

TRUCKEE

Super 8 Lodge
11506 Deerfield Dr., P.O. Box 9048
Truckee, CA 95737
Phone: (916) 587-8888

Pet Restrictions: $50 refund. deposit
Exercise Area for Pets: Nearby
Rates: $56 to $70

VETERINARIANS

Ryan, Michael T.
10038 Meadow Way 95737
(916) 587-7200

TURLOCK

The Gardens Best Western Motor Inn
1119 Pedras Rd.
Turlock CA 95380
Phone: (209) 634-9351

Pet Restrictions: Small pets only
Exercise Area for Pets: Yes
Rates: $42 to $64

Best Western Orchard Inn
5025 N. Golden State Blvd.
Turlock, CA 95380
Phone: (209) 667-2827

Pet Restrictions: None
Exercise Area for Pets: Nearby
Rates: $49 to $90

VETERINARIANS

Canal Veterinary Hosp.
2040 East Canal Dr. 95380
(209) 668-1807

First Street Veterinary Medical Center
1342 South First St. 95380
(209) 634-4974

Olive Animal Clinic
1141 N. Olive Ave. 95380
(209) 634-0023

UREKA

Thunderbird Lodge
526 S. Main St.
Ureka, CA 96097
Phone: (916) 842-4404
Pet Restrictions: 3 pet max., no
  puppies
Exercise Area for Pets: Nearby
Rates: $32 to $60

VACAVILLE

Days Inn
1571 E. Monte Vista Ave.
Vacaville, CA 95688
Phone: (707) 448-6482
Pet Restrictions: $10/day, 1 pet only
Exercise Area for Pets: Yes
Rates: $45 to $75

Animal Medical Center of Vacaville
807-B Davis St. 95688
(707) 446-8148

VALLEJO

E-Z 8 Motel - Vallejo
4 Mariposa St.
Vallejo, CA 94590
Phone: (707) 554-1840
Pet Restrictions: Dogs must be on
  leash while walking on premises
  Pet deposit for large dogs
Pet left unattended in room: No
Exercise Area for Pets: Nearby
Rates: $24.88 to $33.88

VICTORVILLE

E-Z 8 Motel - Victorville
15401 Park Avenue East
Victorville, CA 92392
Phone: (619) 241-7516
Pet Restrictions: Dogs must be on
  leash while walking on premises
  Pet deposit for large dogs
Pet left unattended in room: No
Exercise Area for Pets: Nearby
Rates: $23.88 to $33.88

Holiday Inn
15494 Palmdale Rd.
Victorville, CA 92392
Phone: (619) 245-6565
Pet Restrictions: $25 refund. deposit
  upon inspection, 50 lb. max.
Exercise Area for Pets: Yes, scooper
  needed
Rates: $51 to $125

Appleton, James D.
15028 7th Street 10 92392
(619) 245-0109

Hawley, Allen F.
14904 7th Street 92392
(619) 245-5566

McClaine, Julie G.
P.O. Box 1415 92392
(619) 245-0109

VISALIA

Holiday Inn Plaza Park
9000 W. Airport Dr.
Visalia, CA 93277
Phone: (209) 651-5000
Pet Restrictions: None
Pet left unattended in room: Yes
Exercise Area for Pets: Nearby
Rates: $59 to $86

Lindquist, Gary
1946A W. Dorothea Ave. 93277
(209) 625-8549

Migliore, John
34775 Rd. 132 93277
(209) 732-4818

VISTA

Hilltop Motor Lodge
330 Mar Vista Dr.
Vista, CA 92083
Phone: (619) 726-7010
Pet Restrictions: $5/day, $3 for
  small pet
Exercise Area for Pets: Nearby
Rates: $36 to $44

East Vista Pet Clinic
2020 E. Vista Way 92083
(619) 724-8313

WESTLEY

5 Star Inn
7144 McKraken Rd.
Westley, CA 95387
Phone: (209) 894-5500
Pet Restrictions: 5 lb. max
Exercise Area for Pets: Yes
Rates: $45 to $65

WHITTIER

Vagabond Inn
14125 E. Whittier Blvd.
Whittier, CA 90605
Phone: (310) 698-9701

Pet Restrictions: $5/day
Exercise Area for Pets: Yes
Rates: $35 to $55

VETERINARIANS

Macy and Thomas Veterinary Hosp.
13021 E. Whittier Blvd. 90602
(310) 698-7985

Washington Blvd. Animal Hosp.
12116 E. Washington Blvd. 90606
(310) 693-8233

Whittier Dog & Cat Hosp.
12124 Philadelphia St. 90601
(310) 698-0264

WILLOWS

Best Western Golden Pheasant Inn
249 N. Humboldt Ave.
Willows, CA 95988
Phone: (916) 934-4603

Pet Restrictions: None
Exercise Area for Pets: Nearby
Rates: $31 to $77

Blue Gum Motel
Rt. 2, P.O. Box 171A
Willows, CA 95988
Phone: (916) 934-5401

Pet Restrictions: $5/day, 2 pet max.
Pet left unattended in room: Yes
Exercise Area for Pets: Nearby
Rates: $26 to $36

Cross Roads West Inn
452 N. Humboldt Ave.
Willows, CA 95988
Phone: (916) 934-7026

Pet Restrictions: Only in smoking
   rooms
Exercise Area for Pets: Yes
Rates: $28 to $33

Super 8 Motel
457 N. Humboldt Ave.
Willows, CA 95988
Phone: (916) 934-2871

Pet Restrictions: $20 refund. deposit
Exercise Area for Pets: Yes
Rates: $35.90 to $37.88

WOODLAND

Cinderella Motel
99 W. Main St.
Woodland, CA 95695
Phone: (916) 662-1091

Pet Restrictions: None
Exercise Area for Pets: Yes
Rates: $38

VETERINARIANS

Bruga, Richard D.
214 5th Street 95695
(916) 666-1973

YOUNTVILLE

Vintage Inn
6541 Washington St.
Yountville, CA 94599
Phone: (707) 944-1112,
   (800) 351-1133

Pet Restrictions: $25
Pet left unattended in room: Yes
Exercise Area for Pets: Yes
Rates: $139 to $199

COLORADO — HOTELS

AURORA
La Quinta-Aurora
1011 S. Abilene St.
Aurora, CO 80012
Phone: (303) 337-0206

Pet Restrictions: Under 20 lbs.
Exercise Area for Pets: Nearby
Rates: $49 to $265

Buckeye Square Veterinary Clinic
8020 Sheridan Blvd. 80003
Phone: (303) 429-9719

Mississippi Animal Hospital
10695 E. Mississippi Ave. 80012
Phone: (303) 364-9117

AVON
Comfort Inn-Vail/Beaver Creek
P.O. Box 5510
Avon, CO 81620
Phone: (303) 949-5511

Pet Restrictions: $10 fee
Rates: $35 to $195

BOULDER
Boulder Mt. Lodge
91 Four Mile Canyon Rd.
Boulder, CO 80302
Phone: (303) 444-0882

Pet Restrictions: $50 deposit; leash
    at all times; clean up after pet
Pet left unattended in room: Yes
Rates: $50 to $85

Foot of the Mountain Motel
200 Arapahoe Ave.
Boulder, CO 80302
Pone: (303) 442-5688

Pet Restrictions: None
Exercise Area for Pets: Yes
Rates: $35 to $60

Highlander Inn Motel
970 28th St.
Boulder, CO 80303
Phone: (303) 443-7800

Pet Restrictions: None; register at
    desk; use pooper scoopers
Exercise Area for Pets: Yes
Rates: $40 to $96

Residence Inn by Marriott
30 30 Canter Green Dr.
Boulder, CO 80301
Phone: (303) 449-5545

Pet Restrictions: $5/day, add'l pet
    $3 more
Pet left unattended in room: Yes
Exercise Area for Pets: Nearby
Rates: $109 to $139

Sandy Pointe Inn
64 85 Twin Lakes Rd.
Boulder, CO 80301
Phone: (303) 530-2939

Pet Restrictions: $5/day; 1/8 of hotel
    for pets
Pet left unattended in room: Yes
Exercise Area for Pets: Nearby
Rates: $45 to $130

All Pets Clinic
5290 Manhattan Cr. 80303
Phone: (303) 499-5335

Alpine Hospital for Animals
1730 15th Street 80302
Phone: (303) 443-9661

Marshall Road Animal Clinic
1405 S. Broadway 80303
Phone: (303) 499-5505

BURLINGTON
Sloan's Motel
1901 Rose Ave.
Burlington, CO 80807
Phone: (719) 346-5333

Pet Restrictions: None
Exercise Area for Pets: Nearby
Rates: $24 to $36

BYERS
Longhorn Motel
P.O. Box 196
Byers, CO 80103
Phone: (303) 822-5205

Pet Restrictions: Claimed pets
Exercise Area for Pets: Nearby
Rates: $30 to $45

COLORADO — HOTELS (continued)

CANON CITY

Canyon Inn
3075 E. Hwy 50
Canon City, CO 81212
Phone: (719) 275-8676

Pet Restrictions: $20 deposit
    refundable if you pay in cash
Pet left unattended in room: Yes
Exercise Area for Pets: Nearby
Rates: $60 to $90

Park Lane Motel
1401 Main St.
Canon City, CO 81212
Phone: (719) 275-7240

Pet Restrictions: None
Exercise Area for Pets: Yes
Rates: $38 to $55

COLORADO CITY

Comfort Inn
8280 Hwy 83
Colorado City, CO 80920
Phone: (719) 598-6700

Pet Restrictions: Smoking rooms only
Pet left unattended in room: Yes
Exercise Area for Pets: Yes
Rates: $35 to $75

Chief Motel
1624 S. Nevada Ave.
Colorado City, CO 80906
Phone: (719) 473-5228

Pet Restrictions: $10 deposit
Exercise Area for Pets: Yes
Rates: $25 to $60

Greenhorn Mt. Resort Motel
SR 165, P.O. Box 136
Colorado City, CO 81019
Phone: (719) 676-3315

Pet Restrictions: Allowed in certain
    rooms only
Pet left unattended in room: Yes
Exercise Area for Pets: Yes
Rates: $49.25 to $44.25

Hampton Inn-North
7245 Commerce Center Dr.
Colorado City, CO 80919
Phone: (719) 593-9700

Pet Restrictions: $25 deposit
Pet left unattended in room: Yes
Exercise Area for Pets: Nearby
Rates: $45 to $72

Holiday Inn-North
3125 Sinton Rd.
Colorado City, CO 80907
Phone: (719) 633-5541

Pet Restrictions: Outside rooms only
Pet left unattended in room: Yes
Exercise Area for Pets: Yes
Rates: $35 to $85

La Quinta
4385 Sinton Rd.
Colorado City, CO 80907
Phone: (719) 528-5060

Pet Restrictions: Under 30 lbs.; in
    smoking rooms only
Exercise Area for Pets: Nearby
Rates: $80 to $115

Raintree Inn-West
2625 Ore Mill Rd.
Colorado City, CO 80904
Phone: (719) 632-4600

Pet Restrictions: None
Exercise Area for Pets: Yes
Rates: $40 to $55

Ramada Inn-Airport
520 N. Murray Blvd.
Colorado City, CO 80915
Phone: (719) 596-7660

Pet Restrictions: $15 deposit
Pet left unattended in room: Yes
Exercise Area for Pets: Yes
Rates: $41 to $85

Ramada Inn-North
4440 I 25 N
Colorado City, CO 80907
Phone: (719) 594-0700

Pet Restrictions: $35 deposit
Exercise Area for Pets: Yes
Rates: $52 to $70

Red Lion Inn
1775 E. Cheyenne Blvd.
Colorado City, CO 80906
Phone: (719) 576-8900

Pet Restrictions: Small dogs
Pet left unattended in room: Yes
Exercise Area for Pets: Yes
Rates: $89 to $119

Residence Inn by Marriott
3880 N. Academy Blvd.
Colorado City, CO 80907
Phone: (719) 574-0370
Pet Restrictions: $10/night (up to 10 nights)
Pet left unattended in room: Yes
Exercise Area for Pets: Yes
Rates: $79 to $129

Rodeway Inn
2409 E. Pikes Peak Ave.
Colorado City, CO 80909
Phone: (719) 471-0990
Pet Restrictions: None
Pet left unattended in room: Yes
Exercise Area for Pets: Yes
Rates: $40 to $55

Stagecoach Motel
1647 S. Nevada Ave.
Colorado City, CO 80906
Phone: (719) 633-3894
Pet Restrictions: Small pets
Pet left unattended in room: Yes
Exercise Area for Pets: Yes
Rates: $36 to $42

COLORADO SPRINGS
Radisson Springs
8110 Academy Blvd.
Colorado Springs, CO 80920
Phone: (719) 598-5770
Pet Restrictions: Under 25 lbs
Pet left unattended in room: Yes
Exercise Area for Pets: Yes
Rates: $110 to $70

VETERINARIANS
Bijou Animal Hospital
2502 E. Bijou 80909
Phone: (719) 471-4457

Brown Veterinary Hospital
45 E. Old Broadmor Rd. 80906
Phone: (719) 636-3341

CRAIG
A Bar Z Motel
2690 W. Hwy 40
Craig, CO 81625
Phone: (303) 824-7066
Pet Restrictions: Small; not allowed on beds
Exercise Area for Pets: Yes
Rates: $31 to $39

Best Western Inn
755 E. Victory Way
Craig, CO 81625
Phone: (303) 824-8101, (800) 528-1234
Pet Restrictions: Smoking rooms only (24)
Pet left unattended in room: Yes
Exercise Area for Pets: Yes
Rates: $26 to $59

Block Nugget Budget Host Motel
2855 W. Victory Way
Craig, CO 81625
Phone: (303) 824-8161
Pet Restrictions: $2/day; smoking rooms only
Exercise Area for Pets: Yes

Craig Motel
894 Yampa Ave.
Craig, CO 81625
Phone: (303) 824-4491
Pet Restrictions: $2/night
Pet left unattended in room: Yes
Exercise Area for Pets: Yes
Rates: $20 to $36

Holiday Inn-Craig
300 S. Hwy 13
Craig, CO 81625
Phone: (303) 824-9455
Pet Restrictions: $50 deposit; let housekeeping know if pet is alone
Pet left unattended in room: Yes
Exercise Area for Pets: Nearby
Rates: $52 to $71

DELTA
Southgate Inn
2124 S. Main St.
Delta, CO 81416
Phone: (303) 874-9726
Pet Restrictions: $5/night; dogs only
Exercise Area for Pets: Yes
Rates: $20 to $55

DENVER
BW Inn at the Mart
401 E. 58th Ave.
Denver, CO 80216
Phone: (303) 297-1717
Pet Restrictions: $25 deposit refundable in cash only
Pet left unattended in room: Yes
Exercise Area for Pets: Yes
Rates: $48 to $54

COLORADO — HOTELS (continued)

BW Landmark Inn
455 S. Colorado Blvd.
Denver, CO 80222
Phone: (303) 388-5561

Pet Restrictions: None
Exercise Area for Pets: Yes
Rates: $46 to $65

Burnsley
1000 Grant St.
Denver, CO
Phone: (303) 830-1000

Pet Restrictions: $50 deposit; 2 small
pets or less; $6/day/pet
Exercise Area for Pets: Yes
Rates: $65 to $135

Comfort Inn-Airport
7201 E. 36th Ave.
Denver, CO 80207
Phone: (303) 393-7666

Pet Restrictions: $25 refund. cash
deposit
Pet left unattended in room: Yes
Exercise Area for Pets: Nearby
Rates: $48.95 to $54.95

Days Inn - Airport
4590 Quebec St.
Denver, CO 80216
Phone: (303) 320-0260

Pet Restrictions: $10 fee; always
supervised
Exercise Area for Pets: Yes
Rates: $56 to $72

Embassy Suites
7525 E. Hampden Ave.
Denver, CO 80231
Phone: (303) 696-6644

Pet Restrictions: kennels only
Exercise Area for Pets: Nearby
Rates: $79 to $129

Hilton-Denver South
7801 E. Orchard Rd.
Denver, CO 80111
Phone: (303) 779-6161

Pet Restrictions: $50 deposit; sign
waiver
Pet left unattended in room: Yes
Exercise Area for Pets: Yes
Rates: $65 to $154

Hilton Inn-Airport
4411 Peoria St.
Denver, CO 80239
Phone: (303) 373-5730

Pet Restrictions: $10 fee
Pet left unattended in room: Yes
Exercise Area for Pets: Yes
Rates: $54 to $59

Holiday Inn-Airport
4040 Quebec St.
Denver, CO 80216
Phone: (303) 321-6666

Pet Restrictions: None
Pet left unattended in room: Yes
Exercise Area for Pets: Nearby
Rates: $69 to $79

Holiday Inn-Denver Downtown
1450 Glen Arm Pl.
Denver, CO 80202
Phone: (303) 573-1450

Pet Restrictions: $35 deposit
Exercise Area for Pets: Yes
Rates: $80 to $105

Holiday Inn-Denver-North
4849 Bannock St.
Denver, CO 80216
Phone: (303) 292-9500

Pet Restrictions: $15 fee; $50 deposit
Pet left unattended in room: Yes,
only small pets
Exercise Area for Pets: Yes
Rates: $68 to $75

Holiday Inn Denver Northglenn
10 E. 120th St.
Denver, CO 80233
Phone: (303) 452-4100

Pet Restrictions: Depends on if there
is a group of animals
Exercise Area for Pets: Yes
Rates: $65 to $80

Holiday Inn-Sports Center
1975 Bryant St.
Denver, CO 80204
Phone: (303) 433-8331

Pet Restrictions: None
Pet left unattended in room: Yes,
notify desk
Exercise Area for Pets: Nearby
Rates: $49 to $70

COLORADO — HOTELS (continued)

Howard Johnson Motor Lodge South
6300 E. Hampden Ave.
Denver, CO 80222
Phone: (303) 758-2211

Pet Restrictions: $5 fee
Exercise Area for Pets: Yes
Rates: $60 to $67

Howard Johnson Motor Lodge West
4765 Federal Blvd.
Denver, CO 80211
Phone: (303) 433-8441

Pet Restrictions: Small pets only
Exercise Area for Pets: Yes
Rates: $30 to $90

La Quinta-Central
3500 Fox St.
Denver, CO 80216
Phone: (303) 458-1222

Pet Restrictions: Downstairs rooms
Rates: $49 to $56

La Quinta Inn-South
1975 S. Colorado Blvd.
Denver, CO 80222
Phone: (303) 758-8886

Pet Restrictions: No large pets
Exercise Area for Pets: Yes
Rates: $49 to $69

La Quinta Inn-Westminster
8701 Turnpike Dr.
Denver, CO 80030
Phone: (303) 425-9099

Pet Restrictions: Smoking rooms only
Pet left unattended in room: Yes, but room won't be cleaned
Rates: $55 to $62

Marriott Southeast
6363 E. Hampden Ave.
Denver, CO 80222
Phone: (303) 758-7000

Pet Restrictions: Small pets
Pet left unattended in room: Yes
Exercise Area for Pets: Yes
Rates: $74 to $155

Motel 6
3050 W. 49th Ave.
Denver, CO 80221
Phone: (303) 455-8888

Pet Restrictions: Small pets
Exercise Area for Pets: Yes
Rates: $26.95 and up

Radisson
1550 Court St.
Denver, CO 80202
Phone: (303) 893-3333

Pet Restrictions: Small pets
Exercise Area for Pets: Nearby
Rates: $95 to $700

Ramada Inn
1150 E. Colfax Ave.
Denver, CO 80218
Phone: (303) 831-7700

Pet Restrictions: $25 deposit
Pet left unattended in room: Yes
Exercise Area for Pets: Nearby
Rates: $30 to $59.95

Ramada Inn-Airport
3737 Quebec St.
Denver, CO 80207
Phone: (303) 388-6161

Pet Restrictions: None
Exercise Area for Pets: Nearby
Rates: $49 to $89

Residence Inn Downtown
2777 N. Zuni St.
Denver, CO 80211
Phone: (303) 458-5318

Pet Restrictions: $6/day; $100/month if staying a month or more
Pet left unattended in room: Yes
Exercise Area for Pets: Nearby
Rates: $89 to $119

Rockies Lodge
4760 E. Evans Ave.
Denver, CO 80222
Phone: (303) 757-7601

Pet Restrictions: Small pets; cats must be in carrier
Pet left unattended in room: Yes
Exercise Area for Pets: Yes
Rates: $48 to $25.95

VETERINARIANS

Alameda East Veterinary Hosp.
9870 E. Alameda 80231
Phone: (303) 366-2639

Harvey Bird and Animal Hosp.
2110 South Holly St. 80222
Phone: (303) 757-6188

University Hills Animal Hosp.
4040 E. Warren Ave. 80222
Phone: (303) 757-5638

COLORADO — HOTELS (continued)

DILLON
Best Western Ptarmigan Motel
652 Lake Dillon Dr.
Dillon, CO 80435
Phone: (303) 468-2341,
   (800) 842-5939
Pet Restrictions: Yes
Exercise Area for Pets: Yes
Rates: $38 to $76

DURANGO
Adobe Inn
2178 Main St.
Durango, CO 81301
Phone: (303) 247-2743
Pet Restrictions: Under 35 lbs
Exercise Area for Pets: Nearby
Rates: $40 to $100

Caboose Motel
3363 Main Ave.
Durango, CO 81301
Phone: (303) 247-1191
Pet Restrictions: 1 pet per room
Exercise Area for Pets: Nearby
Rates: $26 to $68

Days Inn Durango
1700 CR 203
Durango, CO 81301
Phone: (303) 259-1430
Pet Restrictions: None
Exercise Area for Pets: Yes
Rates: $49 to $82

Holiday Inn
800 Canundel Rio
Durango, CO 81301
Phone: (303) 247-5393
Pet Restrictions: None
Pet left unattended in room: Yes
Exercise Area for Pets: Nearby
Rates: $60 to $109

Red Lion Inn
501 Canuno Del Rio
Durango, CO 81301
Phone: (303) 259-6580
Pet Restrictions: None
Exercise Area for Pets: Yes
Rates: $69 to $150.

Siesta Motel
3475 N. Main St.
Durango, CO 81301
Phone: (303) 247-0741
Pet Restrictions: No cats
Exercise Area for Pets: Yes
Rates: $52 to $84

Sunset Hotel
2855 N. Main St.
Durango, CO 81301
Phone: (303) 247-2653
Pet Restrictions: 1 pet/room; certain
   rooms only; limit for number of
   pets in hotel
Exercise Area for Pets: Yes
Rates: $29 to $79

VETERINARIANS
Hartney, Cathleen T.
56 Saddle Lane 81301
Phone: (303) 259-2934

Morrow, James K.
2461 N. Main Ave. 81301
Phone: (303) 247-3174

ENGLEWOOD
Motel 6
9201 E. Arapahoe Rd.
Englewood, CO 80111
Phone: (303) 790-8220
Pet Restrictions: Small pets
Exercise Area for Pets: Yes
Rates: $35.19 to $48.39

Raddison Hotel/Denver South
7007 S. Clinton St.
Englewood, CO 80112
Phone: (303) 799-6200
Pet Restrictions: Small pets only
Exercise Area for Pets: Yes
Rates: $90 to $130

Residence Inn by Marriott-South
6565 S. Yosemite
Englewood, CO 80111
Phone: (303) 740-7177
Pet Restrictions: $10/night; up to
   $150 (for extended stays)
Pet left unattended in room: Yes
Exercise Area for Pets: Yes
Rates: $68 to $130

COLORADO — HOTELS (continued)

VETERINARIANS

Belleview Animal Clinic
200 W. Lehow Ave. 80110
Phone: (303) 794-2008

Homestead Animal Hospital
6900 S. Holly Circle 80112
Phone: (303) 771-7350

Romano, Sam L.
4690 S. Broadway 80110
Phone: (303) 781-7841

EVANS
Winterset Inn of Greeley
800 31st St.
Evans, CO 80620
Phone: (303) 339-2492

Pet Restrictions: $10 deposit
Exercise Area for Pets: Yes
Rates: $25.95 to $75.95

FORT COLLINS
Fort Collins Marriott
350 E. Horsetooth Rd.
Fort Collins, CO 80525
Phone: (303) 226-5200

Pet Restrictions: Small pets; 1st
    floor only
Pet left unattended in room: Yes
Rates: $69 to $94 (varies much)

Holiday Inn I-25
3836 E. Mulberry St.
Fort Collins, CO 80524
Phone: (303) 484-4660

Pet Restrictions: In outside entrance
    rooms only
Pet left unattended in room: Yes,
    must be quiet
Exercise Area for Pets: Yes
Rates: $39 to $59

Ramada Inn
3709 E. Mulberry St.
Fort Collins, Co 80524
Phone: (303) 493-7800

Pet Restrictions: $25 deposit
Exercise Area for Pets: Yes
Rates: $48 to $52

University Park Holiday Inn
425 W. Prospect Rd.
Fort Collins, CO 80526
Phone: (303) 482-2626

Pet Restrictions: None
Exercise Area for Pets: Yes
Rates: $76.50 to $91.00

VETERINARIANS
**Colorado State University
Vetny Medical Teaching Hosp.**
300 W. Drake Rd. 80526
Phone: (303) 221-4535

Lemay Animal Hospital
816 Lemay Ave. 80524
Phone: (303) 482-9840

Raintree Village Animal Clinic
2519 S. Shields St. #1-L 80526
Phone: (303) 482-1987

FORT MORGAN
BW Park Terrace Motor Hotel
725 Main St.
Fort Morgan, CO 80701
Phone: (303) 867-8256

Pet Restrictions: $25 fee or open
    credit card
Exercise Area for Pets: Nearby
Rates: $38 to $54

Central Motel
201 W. Platte Ave.
Fort Morgan, CO 80701
Phone: (303) 867-2401

Pet Restrictions: No puppies
Exercise Area for Pets: Yes
Rates: $29.95 to $59.95

FRISCO
BW Lake Dillon Lodge
1202 Summitt Blvd., P.O. Box 552
Frisco, CO 80435
Phone: (303) 668-5094

Pet Restrictions: $50 deposit;
    smoking rooms; sign release form
Exercise Area for Pets: Yes
Rates: $87 to $199

COLORADO — HOTELS (continued)

Holiday Inn Summitt County
1129 Summitt Blvd., P.O. Box 10
Frisco, CO 80435
Phone: (303) 668-5000

Pet Restrictions: $25 cash deposit
Pet left unattended in room: Yes
Exercise Area for Pets: Yes
Rates: $49 to $165

VETERINARIANS
Animal Hosp. of the Hish Country
705 Main St. 80443
Phone: (303) 668-5544

GARFIELD
Monarch Lodge
22720 Hwy. 50
Garfield, CO 81227
Phone: (719) 539-2581

Pet Restrictions: None
Pet left unattended in room: Yes
Exercise Area for Pets: Yes
Rates: $50 to $55

GEORGETOWN
The Lodge by Georgetown
P.O. Box 278
Georgetown, CO 80444
Phone: (303) 569-3211

Pet Restrictions: $3/night
Exercise Area for Pets: Nearby
Rates: $40 to $50

GLENWOOD SPRINGS
Holiday Inn
51359 US 6 & 24
Glenwood Springs, CO 81601
Phone: (303) 945-8551

Pet Restrictions: None
Exercise Area for Pets: Nearby
Rates: $58 to $68

VETERINARIANS
Akers, James T.
2514 Grand Ave. 81601
Phone: (303) 945-5401

Niehoff, Steve
P.O. Box 1712 81602
Phone: (303) 945-6762

GOLDEN
Days Inn-West
15059 W. Colfax Ave.
Golden, CO 80401
Phone: (303) 277-0200

Pet Restrictions: $3/night
Exercise Area for Pets: Yes
Rates: $39 to $59

Denver West Holiday Inn
14707 W. Colfax Ave.
Golden, CO 80401
Phone: (303) 279-7611

Pet Restrictions: Ground floor rooms
Exercise Area for Pets: Yes
Rates: $60 to $82

La Quinta Inn-Golden
3301 Youngfield Svc. Rd.
Golden, CO 80401
Phone: (303) 279-5565

Pet Restrictions: None
Exercise Area for Pets: Yes
Rates: $49 to $65

Marriott Denver West
1717 Denver West Marriott Blvd.
Golden, CO 80401
Phone: (303) 279-9100

Pet Restrictions: Sign release form
Rates: $95 to $115

VETERINARIANS
Francis Veterinary Hospital
16199 S. Golden Rd. 80401
Phone: (303) 279-5952

Mesa Veterinary Hospital
2525 Youngfield St. 80401
Phone: (303) 237-9542

Table Mountain Vet. Clinic
15555 West 44th Ave. 80403
Phone: (303) 279-1701

GRAND JUNCTION
BW Horizon Inn
754 Horizon Dr.
Grand Junction, CO 81506
Phone: (303) 245-1410

Pet Restrictions: None
Exercise Area for Pets: Yes
Rates: $47 to $62

BW Sandman Motel
708 Horizon Dr.
Grand Junction, CO 81506
Phone: (303) 243-4150

Pet Restrictions: No cats
Exercise Area for Pets: Yes
Rates: $48 to $60

Holiday Inn
755 Horizon Dr.
Grand Junction, CO 81502
Phone: (303) 243-6790

Pet Restrictions: None
Exercise Area for Pets: Yes
Rates: $48 to $60

Howard Johnson Lodge
752 Horizon Drive
Grand Junction, CO 81506
Phone: (303) 243-5150

Pet Restrictions: $10/pet/day;
    smoking rooms only
Exercise Area for Pets: Yes
Rates: $49 to $60

Ramada Inn of Grand Junction
2790 Crossroad Blvd.
Grand Junction, CO 81506
Phone: (303) 241-8411

Pet Restrictions: None
Pet left unattended in room: Yes
Exercise Area for Pets: Yes
Rates: $49 to $99.95

Value Lodge
104 White Ave.
Grand Junction, CO 81501
Phone: (303) 242-0651

Pet Restrictions: None
Exercise Area for Pets: Nearby
Rates: $29 to $48

West Gate Inn
2210 Hwys 6 & 50
Grand Junction, CO 81505
Phone: (303) 241-3020

Pet Restrictions: None
Exercise Area for Pets: Nearby
Rates: $39 to $49

VETERINARIANS

All Pets Center
424 South Fifth St. 81501
Phone: (303) 241-1976

Animal Medical Clinic
504 Fruitvale Court 81501
Phone: (303) 434-4094

Turrou, Robert M.
2517 S. Broadway 81503
Phone: (303) 245-4060

GREELEY

Holiday Inn of Greeley
609 8th Ave.
Greeley, CO 80631
Phone: (303) 356-3000

Pet Restrictions: None
Exercise Area for Pets: Yes
Rates: $55 to $72

VETERINARIANS

West Ridge Animal Hospital
6525 West 28th St. 80631
Phone: (303) 330-7283

Freemyer, Francis G.
1825 9th St. 80631
Phone: (303) 352-4502

GUNNISON

Hylanders Inn
412 E. Tanichi Ave., P.O. Box 71
Gunnison, CO 81230
Phone: (303) 641-0700

Pet Restrictions: None
Exercise Area for Pets: Yes
Rates: $45 and up

VETERINARIANS

Town and Country Animal Hosp.
1525 Highway 135 81230
Phone: (303) 641-2215

IDAHO SPRINGS

H&H Motor Lodge
2445 Colorado Blvd., P.O. Box 1359
Idaho Springs, CO 80452
Phone: (303) 567-2838

Pet Restrictions: None
Exercise Area for Pets: Nearby
Rates: $38 to $55

Peoriana Motel
2901 Colorado Blvd., P.O. Box 483
Idaho Springs, CO 80452
Phone: (303) 567-2021

Pet Restrictions: None
Exercise Area for Pets: Yes
Rates: $29 to $38

JULESBURG
BW Platte Valley Inn
P.O. Box 67
Julesburg, CO 80737
Phone: (303) 474-3336

Pet Restrictions: Only in smoking
    rooms
Pet left unattended in room: Yes
Exercise Area for Pets: Yes

LAKEWOOD
Rodeway Inn Foothills
11595 W. 6th Ave.
Lakewood, CO 80215
Phone: (303) 238-7751

Pet Restrictions: $8/pet/day
Exercise Area for Pets: Yes
Rates: $52 to $60

VETERINARIANS
Animal Emergency Service Inc.
9797 W. Colfax Ave. 80215
Phone: (303) 232-6227

The Glens Animal & Bird Hosp.
8775 Wests Colfax 80215
Phone: (303) 238-6464

LAMAR
Cows Palace Inn-BW
1301 N. Main St.
Lamar, CO 81052
Phone: (719) 336-7753

Pet Restrictions: Small pets
Pet left unattended in room: Yes
Exercise Area for Pets: Yes

Economy Inn
1201 N. Main St.
Lamar, CO 81052
Phone: (719) 336-7471

Pet Restrictions: None
Pet left unattended in room: Yes
Exercise Area for Pets: Yes
Rates: $19 to $34

LAS ANIMAS
Best Western Bents Fort Inn
P.O. Box 108
Las Animas, CO 81054
Phone: (719) 456-0011

Pet Restrictions: None
Exercise Area for Pets: Yes
Rates: $37 to $58

LEADVILLE
Silver King Motor Inn
2020 N. Poplar
Leadville CO 80461
Phone: (719) 486-2610

Pet Restrictions: $10 deposit
Exercise Area for Pets: Yes, on leash
Rates: $40 to $72

VETERINARIANS
Linemeyer, Dennis R.
Box 566 80461
Phone: (719) 486-1487

LONGMONT
Budget Host of Longmont
3815 Hwy 119
Longmont, CO 80501
Phone: (303) 776-8700

Pet Restrictions: $5/dog/day
Exercise Area for Pets: Yes
Rates: $32.50 to $56.50

VETERINARIANS
Animal Hospital
1250 Main St. 80501
Phone: (303) 776-3454

Owen, Donald L.
1191 Florida Ave. 80501
Phone: (303) 776-0234

MESA
Wagon Wheel Motel
1090 Hwy 65
Mesa, CO 81643
Phone: (303) 268-5224

Pet Restrictions: None
Pet left unattended in room: Yes
Exercise Area for Pets: Yes
Rates: $40; $5/add. person/children
    under 18 free

NORTHGLENN
Days Inn-N
36 E. 120th Ave.
Northglenn, CO 80233
Phone: (303) 457-0688

Pet Restrictions: $6/pet/day
Pet left unattended in room: Yes, in
    carrier
Exercise Area for Pets: Yes
Rates: $37 to $52

COLORADO — HOTELS (continued)

PUEBLO

BW Town House Motor Hotel
8th St. & Santa Fe Ave.
Pueblo, CO 81003
Phone: (719) 543-6530
Pet Restrictions: None
Rates: $40 to $70

Pueblo Inn
800 Hwy 50 W
Pueblo, CO 81008
Phone: (719) 543-6820
Pet Restrictions: None
Exercise Area for Pets: Yes
Rates: $32 to $48

VETERINARIANS
Pets and Friends Animal Hosp.
3625 Baltimore Ave. 81008
Phone: (719) 542-2022

Pueblo Small Animal Clinic
1400 Highway 50 East 81001
Phone: (719) 545-4350

REDSTONE
Cleveholm Manor
0058 Redstone Blvd.
Redstone, CO 81623
Phone: (303) 963-3463
Pet Restrictions: 100 lbs. or less,
    $100 refund.; 100 lbs. or more
    $200 refund. deposits
Pet left unattended in room: Yes
Exercise Area for Pets: Yes
Rates: $78 to $167

SILVER CREEK
The Inn at Silver Creek
P.O. Box 4222
Silver Creek, CO 80446
Phone: (303) 887-2131
Pet Restrictions: $12/pet/day
Exercise Area for Pets: Yes
Rates: $37 to $218

STEAMBOAT SPRINGS
Holiday Inn of Steamboat
3190 S. Lincoln, P.O. Box 771319
Steamboat Springs, CO 80477
Phone: (303) 879-2250
Pet Restrictions: None
Exercise Area for Pets: Yes
Rates: $65 to $225

VETERINARIANS
Rule, John R.
P.O. Box 774184 80477
Phone: (303) 879-3486

Smith, Earl D.
Box 770026 80477
Phone: (303) 879-1041

STERLING
Colonial Motel
915 S. Division
Sterling, CO 80751
Phone: (303) 522-3382
Pet Restrictions: None
Exercise Area for Pets: Yes
Rates: $24 to $32

Days Inn
12881 Hwy 61
Sterling, CO 80751
Phone: (303) 522-6660
Pet Restrictions: None
Exercise Area for Pets: Yes
Rates: $29 to $44

SOUTH FORK
Wolf Creek Ski Lodge
P.O. Box 283 US 610
South Fork, CO 81154
Phone: (719) 873-5547
Pet Restrictions: None
Pet left unattended in room: Yes
Exercise Area for Pets: Nearby
Rates: $40 to $65

THORNTON
Raddison Graystone Castle
83 E. 120th Ave.
Thornton, CO 80233
Phone: (303) 451-1002
Pet Restrictions: $100 deposit
Exercise Area for Pets: Yes
Rates: $75 to $185

TRINIDAD
Budget Host Derrick Motel
Rt. 1, Box 427B
Trinidad, CO 81082
Phone: (719) 846-3307
Pet Restrictions: $2/pet/day
Exercise Area for Pets: Yes
Rates: $36.95 to $69.95

COLORADO — HOTELS (continued)

WALSENBURG
BW Rambler
P.O. Box 48
Walsenburg, CO 81089
Phone: (719) 738-1121

Pet Restrictions: $10/pet/day
    refund. deposit; 7 rooms
Exercise Area for Pets: Yes
Rates: $55 to $80

WHEATRIDGE
Best Western Country Villa Inn-Foothills
4700 Kipling St.
Wheatridge, CO 80033
Phone: (303) 423-4000

Pet Restrictions: $25 deposit; under
    20 lbs.
Exercise Area for Pets: Yes
Rates: $46 to $56

VETERINARIANS
Wheatridge Small Animal Hosp.
7630 West 39th Ave. 80033
Phone: (303) 424-3325

Gosik, Gary E.
4635 Quail St. 80033

CONNECTICUT — HOTELS

DANBURY

Holiday Inn
80 Newtown Rd.
Danbury, CT 06810
Phone: (203) 792-4000

Pet Restrictions: Owner responsible
for damages
Pet left unattended in room: Yes
Exercise Area for Pets: Yes
Rates: $49 to $84

VETERINARIANS

Brenner, Cary
39 New St. 06810
Phone: (203) 748-8106

DARIEN

Comfort Inn-Darien
50 Ledge Rd.
Darien, CT 06820
Phone: (203) 655-8211

Pet Restrictions: Yes, dogs and
cats, 1st floor
Exercise Area for Pets: Yes
Rates: $54 to $66

Howard Johnson Lodge
150 Ledge Rd.
Darien, CT 06820
Phone: (203) 655-3933

Pet Restrictions: $10 fee
Pet left unattended in room: Yes
Exercise Area for Pets: Yes
Rates: $49 to $85

VETERINARIANS

Ryan, William W.
1297 Post Road 06820
Phone: (203) 655-1449

EAST LYME

Howard Johnson Lodge
265 Flanders Road
East Lyme, CT 06333
Phone: (203) 739-6921

Pet Restrictions: One per room
Exercise Area for Pets: Yes
Rates: $70 to $130

VETERINARIANS

Chester, Janice L.
37 Upper Walnut Hill 06333
Phone: (203) 669-5721

ENFIELD

Red Roof Inn
5 Hazard Ave.
Enfield, CT 06082
Phone: (203) 741-2571

Pet Restrictions: None, notify desk
Pet left unattended in room: Yes
Exercise Area for Pets: Yes
Rates: $24.99 to $59.99

FARMINGTON

Centennial Inn Suites
5 Spring Lane
Farmington, CT 06032
Phone: (203) 677-4647
Fax: (203) 676-0685

Pet Restrictions: None
Pet left unattended in room: Yes
Exercise Area for Pets: Yes
Elizabeth Park
Rates: $85 to $210

VETERINARIANS

Farmington Animal Hospital
204 Farmington Ave. 06032
Phone: (203) 677-4400

Farmington Valley Animal Clinic
1073 Farmington Ave. 06032
Phone: (203) 677-4638

GROTON

Trails Corner Motor Inn
580 Poquannock Rd.
Groton, CT 06340
Phone: (203) 445-0220

Pet Restrictions: $10 fee
Pet left unattended in room: Yes
Rates: Call for rates

VETERINARIANS

Companion Animal Hospital
801 Poquonnock Rd. 06340
Phone: (203) 449-9800

HARTFORD

Holiday Inn
363 Roberts St.
E. Hartford, CT 06108
Phone: (203) 528-9611

Pet Restrictions: None
Exercise Area for Pets: Yes
Rates: $79 to $97

CONNECTICUT — HOTELS (continued)

Holiday Inn-Downtown
50 Morgan St.
Hartford, CT 06120
Phone: (203) 549-2400

Pet Restrictions: None
Exercise Area for Pets: Nearby
Rates: $86 to $175

VETERINARIANS
Bowling, Joyce
47 Willard St. Apt. E 06105
Phone: (203) 377-0235

Chace, Paul A.
40 Allen Place Apt. 1 06106
Phone: (203) 633-8394

LAKEVILLE
Iron Masters Motor Inn
229 Name St., Box 690
Lakeville, CT 06039
Phone: (203) 435-9844

Pet Restrictions: None
Exercise Area for Pets: Yes
Rates: $65 to $120

MERIDEN
Hampton Inn
10 Bee St.
Meriden, CT 06450
Phone: (203) 235-5154

Pet Restrictions: Only 1 per guest
Rates: $48 to $58

VETERINARIANS
Dedrick, Robert S.
785 Paddock Ave. 06450
Phone: (203) 235-1622

St. Clair, Joseph
607 E. Main St. 06450
Phone: (203) 235-1131

MILFORD
Hampton Inn
129 Plains Rd.
Milford, CT 06460
Phone: (203) 874-4400

Pet Restrictions: None
Pet left unattended in room: Yes, no
   housekeeping
Rates: $52 to $58

Red Roof Inn
10 Rowe Ave.
Milford, CT 06460
Phone: (203) 877-6060

Pet Restrictions: None
Pet left unattended in room: No policy
Exercise Area for Pets: Yes
Rates: $42 to $57

VETERINARIANS
Milford Veterinary Hospital
17 Seeman's Lane 06460
Phone: (203) 877-3221

O'Neil, John W.
143 Cherry St. 06460
Phone: (203) 878-7471

Suhie, Richard J.
632 New Haven Ave. 06460
Phone: (203) 878-4646

NEW HAVEN
Holiday Inn
201 Washington Ave.
New Haven, CT 06473
Phone: (203) 239-4225

Pet Restrictions: None
Pet left unattended in room: Yes
Exercise Area for Pets: Yes
Rates: $68 to $73

VETERINARIANS
Aldrich, Robert A.
1297 Whalley Ave. 06515
Phone: (203) 387-6648

Meyer, Patricia A.
146 Springside Ave. #B4 06515
Phone: (203) 799-2364

Parker, Brent B.
196 Norton St. 06511
Phone: (203) 865-0879

NEW LONDON
Red Roof Inn
707 Colman St.
New London, CT 06320
Phone: (203) 444-0001

Pet Restrictions: Notify desk
Pet left unattended in room: Yes
Exercise Area for Pets: Yes
Rates: $31.99 to $67.99

CONNECTICUT — HOTELS (continued)

New London Veterinary Hospital
470 Broad St. 06320
Phone: (203) 442-0611

NORWALK
Holiday Inn-Norwalk
789 Connecticut Ave.
Norwalk, CT 06854
Phone: (203) 853-3477

Pet Restrictions: 2nd floor, $100
deposit
Pet left unattended in room: Yes,
use do not disturb sign
Rates: $61 to $65

Broad River Animal Hospital
89 New Canaan Ave. 06850
Phone: (203) 846-3495

Norwalk Animal Hospital
330 Main St. 06851
Phone: (203) 847-7757

Bellinger, Deborah
726 Connecticut Ave. 06854
Phone: (203) 838-8421

NORWICH
Ramada Norwich
10 Laura Blvd.
Norwich, CT 06360
Phone: (203) 889-5201

Pet Restrictions: None, if well
behaved
Pet left unattended in room: Yes
Exercise Area for Pets: Yes
Rates: $75 to $90

SOUTHINGTON
Howard Johnson Lodge
30 Laning Street
Southington, CT 06489
Phone: (203) 628-0921

Pet Restrictions: Yes, no large dogs
Pet left unattended in room: Yes
Exercise Area for Pets: Yes
Rates: $26.99 to $69

VERNON
Howard Johnson Lodge
451 Hartford Turnpike
Vernon, CT 06066
Phone: (203) 875-0781

Pet Restrictions: $3 fee
Pet left unattended in room: Yes
Exercise Area for Pets: Yes
Rates: Call for rates

WATERBURY
Best Western Red Bull Inn
at top of Schrafft's Dr.
Waterbury, CT 06705
Phone: (203) 597-8000

Pet Restrictions: Must be well
trained, notify desk
Pet left unattended in room: Yes
Exercise Area for Pets: Yes
Rates: $55 to $100

Mattatuck Animal Hospital
1095 Chase Parkway 06708
Phone: (203) 754-2105

WINDSOR
The Residence Inn Hartford - North
100 Dunfey Lane
Windsor, CT 06095
Phone: (203) 688-7474

Pet Restrictions: $50 non-refundable
fee
Pet left unattended in room: Yes
Exercise Area for Pets: Yes
Rates: $109 to $145

DELAWARE — HOTELS

DOVER

Sheraton Inn-Dover
157011 DuPont Highway
Dover, DE 19901
Phone: (302) 678-8500

Pet Restrictions: $10/night, if quiet
   can be unattended
Pet left unattended in room: Yes
Exercise Area for Pets: Yes
Rates: $69 to $80

VETERINARIANS

Howie, Allan G.
1151 S. Governors Ave. 19901
Phone: (302) 674-1515

Jeter, Thomas A.
Rd. #4 Box 156 19901
Phone: (302) 734-3240

NEWARK

Comfort Inn
1120 S. College Ave.
Newark, DE 19713
Phone: (302) 368-8715,
   800-441-7564

Pet Restrictions: None
Pet left unattended in room: Yes
Rates: $44 to $49

Howard Johnson Motor Lodge
1119 South College Ave.
Newark, DE 19713
Phone: (302) 368-8521

Pet Restrictions: Yes, not in suite
   rooms
Exercise Area for Pets: Yes
Rates: $45 to $65

Red Roof Inn
415 Stanton Christiana
Newark, DE 19713
Phone: (302) 292-2870,
   (800) 843-7663

Pet Restrictions: None
Pet left unattended in room: Yes
Exercise Area for Pets: Yes

VETERINARIANS

Newark Animal Hospital
245 E. Cleveland Ave. 19711
Phone: (302) 737-8100

Tammi, Lea ME
1501 Kirkwood Highway 19711
(302) 737-1098

NEW CASTLE

Econo Lodge
232 S. DuPont Highway
New Castle, DE 19720
Phone: (302) 322-4500

Pet Restrictions: Small pets
Pet left unattended in room: Yes
Exercise Area for Pets: Nearby
Rates: $28 to $40

REHOBOTH

Bellbuoy Motel
21 Van Dyke Ave. (Dewey Beach)
Rehoboth Beach, DE 19979
Phone: (302) 227-6000

Pet Restrictions: Off season only,
   $5/pet
Exercise Area for Pets: Nearby
Rates: Vary

WILMINGTON

Best Western Brandywine
1807 Concord Pike
Wilmington, DE 19803
Phone: (302) 656-9436

Pet Restrictions: Small, notify
   management
Pet left unattended in room: Yes
Exercise Area for Pets: Nearby
Rates $54.95 to $79.95

VETERINARIANS

Belvedere Animal Hospital
1211 Newport Gap Pike 19804
Phone: (302) 998-8851

Gaska, Donna J.
201 Portland Ave. 19804
Phone: (301) 398-1331

Stover, Robert M.
806 Silverside 19809
Phone: (302) 792-2777

DIST. OF COLUMBIA — HOTELS

Carlyle Suites
1731 New Hampshire Ave., NW
Washington, DC 20009
Phone: (202) 234-3200

Pet Restrictions: None, must be
    present for housekeeping
Pet left unattended in room: Yes
Rates: $59 to $119

Days Inn
2700 NY Ave. NE
Washington, DC 20002
Phone: (202) 832-5800

Pet Restrictions: Only small pets
Pet left unattended in room: Yes
Rates: $52 to $62

Four Seasons
2800 Pennsylvania Ave. NW
Washington, DC 20007
Phone: (202) 342-0444

Pet Restrictions: None
Pet left unattended in room: Yes,
    well behaved, quiet
Exercise Area for Pets: Nearby
Rates: Vary

Georgetown Dutch Inn
1075 Thomas Jefferson St. NW
Washington, DC 20037
Phone: (202) 337-0900

Pet Restrictions: None, deposit
    refundable
Pet left unattended in room: Yes, on
    leash for housekeeping
Rates: $105 to $250

Guest Quarters - NH Ave.
801 New Hampshire Ave. NW
Washington, DC 20037
Phone: (202) 758-2000

Pet Restrictions: $13/night
Pet left unattended in room: Yes, if
    well trained
Exercise Area for Pets: Nearby
Rates: Vary

Guest Quarters - Penn. Ave.
2500 Penn. Ave. NW
Washington, DC 20037
Phone: (202) 333-8060

Pet Restrictions: $13/night, if well
    trained
Pet left unattended in room: Yes
Exercise Area for Pets: Nearby
Rates: Vary

Hilton & Towers
1919 Connecticut Ave. NW
Washington, DC 20009
Phone: (202) 483-3000

Pet Restrictions: House pet, well
    behaved, sign agreement
Pet left unattended in room: Yes
Exercise Area for Pets: Yes
Rates: Vary

Holiday Inn-Thomas Circle
1155 14th St NW
Washington, DC 20005
Phone: (202) 737-1200

Pet Restrictions: Small, no
    housekeeping
Pet left unattended in room: Yes
Exercise Area for Pets: Nearby
Rates: $59 to $108 availability

Howard Johnson Congress Inn
600 NY Ave NE
Washington, DC 20002
Phone: (202) 546-9200

Pet Restrictions: Small
Rates: $45 to $49

Loews L'Enfant Plaza
480 L'Enfant Plaza SW
Washington, DC 20024
Phone: (202) 484-1000

Pet Restrictions: Well behaved, 20
    lbs. or less, no housekeeping
Pet left unattended in room: Yes
Exercise Area for Pets: Nearby
Rates: $99 to $225

The Madison
15th & M St. NW
Washington, DC 20005
Phone: (202) 862-1600

Pet Restrictions: Only small pets,
    must sign agreement
Exercise Area for Pets: Nearby
Rates: Vary

Park Hyatt
24th & M St. NW
Washington, DC 20037
Phone: (202) 789-1234

Pet Restrictions: None
Exercise Area for Pets: Nearby
Rates: $159 to $1,975

Quality Inn - Capitol Hill
415 New Jersey Ave. NW
Washington, DC 20001
Phone: (202) 638-1616
Pet Restrictions: Deposit required
Pet left unattended in room: Yes
Exercise Area for Pets: Nearby
Rates: Call to check

Savoy Suites Hotel
2505 Wisconsin Ave. NW
Washington, DC 20007
Phone: (202) 337-9700
Pet Restrictions: Small,
    housebroken
Pet left unattended in room: Yes
    except during housekeeping
Rates: $69 to $129

Sheraton Washington
2660 Woodley Rd.
Washington, DC 20008
Phone: (202) 328-2000
Pet Restrictions: Only small animals
Pet left unattended in room: Yes if
    obedient, inform housekeeping
Exercise Area for Pets: Yes
Rates: $79 to $231

Watergate
2650 Virginia Ave., NW
Washington, DC 20037
Phone: (202) 965-2300
Pet Restrictions: Small dogs and
    cats, no vicious animals
Pet left unattended in room: Yes
Exercise Area for Pets: Nearby
Rates: $155 to $1,450

Westin Hotel
24th & M St. NW
Washington, DC 20037
Phone: (202) 429-2400
Pet Restrictions: $50 deposit, small
    animals only
Rates: $185 to $550

VETERINARIANS
Friendship Hospital for Animals
4105 Brandywine St. NW
Phone: (202) 363-7300

MacArthur Animal Hospital
4832 MacArthur Blvd.
Phone: (202) 337-0120

Smith, Melba M.
1519 38th Street SE
Phone: (202) 443-3430

FLORIDA — HOTELS

ALTAMONTE SPRINGS

La Quinta Inn
150 S. Westmonte Dr.
Altamonte Springs, FL 32714
Phone: (407) 788-1411

Pet Restrictions: Small pets, in cage
Pet left unattended in room: Yes, no
   housekeeping
Exercise Area for Pets: Yes
Rates: $61 to $81

Sundance Inn
205 W. Hwy 436
Altamonte Springs, FL 32714
Phone: (407) 862-8200

Pet Restrictions: $10
Pet left unattended in room: Yes
Exercise Area for Pets: Yes
Rates: $38 to $42

BOCA RATON

Radisson Suite Hotel Boca Raton
7920 Glades Rd.
Boca Raton, FL 33434
Phone: (407) 483-3600
Fax: (407) 852-9976

Pet Restrictions: $100 non-
   refundable deposit due upon
   check-in. Animal must be
   leashed at all times.
Pet left unattended in room: No
Exercise Area for Pets: Nearby
Rates: $79 to $189 (seasonal)

**Residence Inn by Marriott-
Boca Raton**
525 N.W. 77th St.
Boca Raton, FL 33487
Phone: (407) 994-3222

Pet Restrictions: $75 fee, $5/day
Pet left unattended in room: Yes
Exercise Area for Pets: Yes
Rates: $89 to $109

VETERINARIANS

Boca Teeca Veterinary Hosp.
170 NW 51st St. 33431
(407) 994-0720

Boca West Animal Clinic
8150 Glades Rd. 33434
(407) 482-1460

Cole Animal Clinic
901 N. Federal Highway 33432
(407) 391-7444

BRADENTON

Knights Inn
668 7th St. Circle E.
Bradenton, FL 34208
Phone: (813) 745-1876

Pet Restrictions: $10/day
Exercise Area for Pets: Yes
Rates: $25 to $30

VETERINARIANS

Bayshore Animal Hosp.
1511 Florida Blvd. 34207
(813) 756-5544

Manatee Veterinary Clinic
3607 Manatee Ave. West 34205
(813) 746-7902

Williams, Donald
2212 53rd Avenue East 34203
(813) 753-2995

CALLAHAN

Friendship Inn
US 23 & 301 P.O. Box 628
Callahan, FL 32011
Phone: (904) 879-3451

Pet Restrictions: None
Pet left unattended in room: Yes
Exercise Area for Pets: Yes
Rates: $36

CAPE CORAL

Quality Inn
1538 Cape Coral Pkwy
Cape Coral, FL 33904
Phone: (813) 542-2121

Pet Restrictions: $5
Exercise Area for Pets: Yes
Rates: $50 to $80

VETERINARIANS

Viscaya-Prado Veterinary Hosp.
920 Country Club Blvd. 33990
(813) 514-6171

CEDAR KEY

Beach Front Motel
P.O. Box 38
Cedar Key, FL 32625
Phone: (904) 543-5113

Pet Restrictions: None
Pet left unattended in room: Yes,
   notify mgmt.
Exercise Area for Pets: Yes
Rates: $41 to $47

COCOA

Best Western Cocoa Inn
4225 W. King St.
Cocoa, FL 32926
Phone: (407) 632-1065

Pet Restrictions: $4/day, small pets,
  notify desk
Pet left unattended in room: Yes, no
  housekeeping
Exercise Area for Pets: Yes
Rates: $39 to $49

Days Inn
5600 Hwy 524
Cocoa, FL 32936
Phone: (407) 636-6500

Pet Restrictions: $5 fee
Pet left unattended in room: Yes, if
  quiet
Rates: Vary

VETERINARIANS
Eden, John S.
329 N. Cocoa Blvd 32922
(407) 632-0445

CORAL GABLES

Howard Johnson Lodge
1430 South Dixie Highway
Coral Gables, FL 33146
Phone: (305) 665-7501

Pet Restrictions: Small
Pet left unattended in room: Yes, no
  housekeeping
Exercise Area for Pets: Yes
Rates: $72 to $76

VETERINARIANS
Richter-Spagnola Animal Hosp.
4569 Ponce De Leon Blvd. 33146
(305) 667-5821

CRESTVIEW

Holiday Inn
P.O. Box 1355
Crestview, FL 32536
Phone: (904) 682-6111

Pet Restrictions: Small pets
Pet left unattended in room: Yes
Exercise Area for Pets: Yes
Rates: $55

VETERINARIANS
Fountain, John E.
402 W. US Hwy 90 32536
(904) 682-2706

CROSS CITY

Carriage Inn
P.O. Box 1360
Cross City, FL 32628
Phone: (904) 498-3910

Pet Restrictions: Small pets
Exercise Area for Pets: Yes
Rates: $32.90 to $38.90

CRYSTAL RIVER

Best Western Plantation Golf Resort
P.O. Box 1116 on King's Bay
Crystal River, FL 32629
Phone: (904) 795-4211

Pet Restrictions: $5, if small
Pet left unattended in room: Yes
Exercise Area for Pets: Yes
Rates: $75 to $259

Econo Lodge
614 NW Hwy 19 & 98
Crystal River, FL 32629
Phone: (904) 795-3171

Pet Restrictions: $3/night
Pet left unattended in room: Yes
Exercise Area for Pets: Yes
Rates: $48 to $55

DAVENPORT

Days Inn/South of Magic Kingdom
2425 Frontage Rd.
Davenport, FL 33837
Phone: (813) 424-2596,
  (800) 424-1880

Pet Restrictions: $5/pet/night
Pet left unattended in room: Yes but
  no cleaning unless present
Exercise Area for Pets: Yes
Rates: $49 to $77

DAYTONA BEACH

Days Inn Interstate
2900 International Speedway
Daytona Beach, FL 32015
Phone: (904) 255-0541

Pet Restrictions: $4
Exercise Area for Pets: Yes
Rates: $42

Holiday Inn-Speedway
1798 International Speedway
Daytona Beach, FL 32014
Phone: (904) 255-2422

Pet Restrictions: Under 15 lbs.
Pet left unattended in room: Yes
Exercise Area for Pets: Yes
Rates: $55 to $65

International Motor Inn
313 S. Atlantic Ave.
Daytona Beach, FL 32018
Phone: (904) 255-7491

Pet Restrictions: Small pet, $25
Pet left unattended in room: Yes
Exercise Area for Pets: Yes
Rates: $29 to $89

La Quinta
2725 International Speedway
Daytona Beach, FL 32014
Phone: (904) 255-7412

Pet Restrictions: Small pets
Exercise Area for Pets: Yes
Rates: $54 to $60

Sea Oats Beach Motel
2539 S. Atlantic Ave.
Daytona Beach Shores, FL 32018
Phone: (904) 767-5684

Pet Restrictions: None
Pet left unattended in room: Yes, no
    housekeeping
Exercise Area for Pets: Yes
Rates: $39 to $78

Paradise Inn
333 S. Atlantic Ave.
Daytona Beach, FL 32018
Phone: (904) 255-8827

Pet Restrictions: Under 25 lbs., $15,
    notify desk
Pet left unattended in room: Yes
Exercise Area for Pets: Nearby
Rates: $89 to $99

VETERINARIANS
Langford, Gary
932 Mason Ave. 32017

DE FUNIAK SPRINGS
Best Western Crossroads Inn
P.O. Box 852
De Funiak Springs, FL 32433
Phone: (904) 892-5111

Pet Restrictions: None
Pet left unattended in room: Yes
Exercise Area for Pets: Yes
Rates: $44

DE LAND
Quality Inn
2801 E. N.Y. Ave.
De Land, FL 32720
Phone: (904) 736-3440

Pet Restrictions: $5/day/pet
Pet left unattended in room: Yes
Exercise Area for Pets: Yes
Rates: $34 to $49

DESTIN
Admiral Benbow Inn
713 Hwy 98E
Destin, FL 32541
Phone: (904) 837-5455

Pet Restrictions: $10/day
Pet left unattended in room: Yes
Exercise Area for Pets: Yes
Rates: $45 to $69

VETERINARIANS
Airport Veterinary Clinic
900 Airport Rd. 32541
(904) 837-3227

EASTPOINT
Sportsman's Lodge Motel & Marina
P.O. Box 606
Eastpoint, FL 32328
Phone: (904) 670-8423

Pet Restrictions: None
Pet left unattended in room: Yes
Exercise Area for Pets: Yes
Rates: $32 to $52

ENGLEWOOD

BW Veranda Inn-Englewood
2073 S. McCall Rd.
Englewood, FL 34224
Phone: (813) 475-6533

Pet Restrictions: $10, under 40 lbs.
Pet left unattended in room: Yes
Exercise Area for Pets: Yes
Rates: $45 to $75

VETERINARIANS

Lemon Bay Animal Hospital
1780 S. McCall Rd. 33533
(813) 474-7711

Botelson, Roger A.
340 N. Indiana Ave. 33533
(813) 474-1295

FLAGLER BEACH

Topaz Motel
1224 S. Oceanshore Blvd.
Flagler Beach, FL 32036
Phone: (904) 439-3301

Pet Restrictions: $25 deposit
Pet left unattended in room: Yes if
    quiet
Exercise Area for Pets: Yes
Rates: $45 to $60

VETERINARIANS

Sprott, Joseph R.
P.O. Box 450 32036
(305) 922-1080

FORT LAUDERDALE

The Trevers Apt. Motel
552 N. Birch Rd. at Terramar St.
Ft. Lauderdale, FL
Phone: (305) 564-9601

Pet Restrictions: $25, if well trained
Pet left unattended in room: Yes
Exercise Area for Pets: Nearby
Rates: $35 to $145

VETERINARIANS

Bixier Animal Hospital
1220 NE 26th St. 33305
(305) 565-1896

Imperial Point Animal Hospital
1570 E. Commercial Blvd. 33334
(305) 771-0156

West Broward Animal Hospital
2875 W. Broward Blvd. 33312
(305) 583-9110

FORT MYERS

Day Inn South/Airport
11435 Cleveland Ave.
Fort Myers, FL 33907
Phone: (813) 936-1311

Pet Restrictions: $5/day
Pet left unattended in room: Yes
Exercise Area for Pets: Yes
Rates: $42 to $48

Econo Lodge
13301 N. Cleveland
Ft. Myers, FL 33903
Phone: (813) 995-0571

Pet Restrictions: Small pets
Exercise Area for Pets: Yes
Rates: $37 to $39

Golf View Motel
3523 Cleveland Ave.
Fort Myers, FL 33901
Phone: (813) 936-1858

Pet Restrictions: $3 fee/day/pet
Pet left unattended in room: Yes
Exercise Area for Pets: Yes
Rates: $35 to $75

Radisson Inn Hotel
20091 Summerlin Rd. SW
Fort Myers, FL 33908
Phone: (813) 466-1200

Pet Restrictions: $50
Pet left unattended in room: Yes
Exercise Area for Pets: Yes
Rates: $79 to $89

VETERINARIANS

Coral Veterinary Clinic
9540 Cypress Lake Dr. 33919
(813) 481-4746

Piper's Riverdale Animal Clinic
14381 Palm Beach Blvd. SE 33905
(813) 693-7387

Small Animal Hospital
3307 Railroad St. 33916
(813) 332-1194

FORT WALTON

Days Inn
135 Miracle Strip Pkwy
Fort Walton, FL 32548
Phone: (904) 244-6184

Pet Restrictions: $3
Exercise Area for Pets: Yes
Rates: $55 to $60

Howard Johnson Lodge
314 Miracle Strip Pkwy
Fort Walton Beach, FL 32548
Phone: (904) 243-6162

Pet Restrictions: Dogs & cats
Exercise Area for Pets: Yes
Rates: $45 to $112

Marina Motel
1345 US 98E Okaloosa Is.
Fort Walton Beach, FL 32548
Phone: (904) 244-1129

Pet Restrictions: Small pets,
$3/night
Pet left unattended in room: Yes
Exercise Area for Pets: Yes
Rates: $29.95 to $85

VETERINARIANS

Friendship Veterinary Clinic
623 A North Beal Pkwy 32548
(904) 862-9813

McClellan, James M.
18 Racetrack Road NE 32548
(904) 862-1005

Stroup, D. Bruce
530 N. Elgin Pkwy 32548
(904) 862-4215

FULTONDALE
Days Inn - Birmingham
616 Decatur Hwy, P.O. Box 476
Fultondale, FL 35068
Phone: (205) 849-0111

Pet Restrictions: $5
Pet left unattended in room: Yes, no
housekeeping
Exercise Area for Pets: Yes
Rates: $45 to $75

GAINESVILLE
Apartment Inn
4401 SW 13th St.
Gainesville, FL 32608
Phone: (904) 371-3811

Pet Restrictions: $5/day,
responsible for damage
Pet left unattended in room: Yes
Exercise Area for Pets: Yes
Rates: $165 week

Days Inn
2820 NW 13th St.
Gainesville, FL 32609
Phone: (904) 376-1211

Pet Restrictions: Small pets
Pet left unattended in room: Yes
Exercise Area for Pets: Yes
Rates: $39 to $44

Howard Johnson Lodge I-75
7400 NW 8th Ave.
Gainesville, FL 32605
Phone: (904) 332-3200

Pet Restrictions: $5 deposit, notify
front desk
Pet left unattended in room: Yes
Exercise Area for Pets: Yes
Rates: Vary

Knights Inn
4021 SW 40th Blvd.
Gainesville, FL 32608
Phone: (904) 373-0392

Pet Restrictions: None
Exercise Area for Pets: Yes
Rates: $29.50 to $43.50

Rush Lake Motel
1410 SW 16th Ave.
Gainesville, FL 32608
Phone: (904) 373-5000

Pet Restrictions: $5, if well behaved
Pet left unattended in room: Yes, no
housekeeping
Exercise Area for Pets: Yes
Rates: $28 to $40

VETERINARIANS

Mill Hopper Veterinary Hosp.
2251-G NW 41st St. 32606
(904) 862-9813

Suburban Animal Hospital
3831 Newberry Rd. 32607
(904) 377-3361

University of Florida
Veterinary Med. Teaching Hosp.
(904) 392-4746

HOMESTEAD

Howard Johnson Lodge
1020 N. Homestead Blvd. (US 1)
Homestead, FL 33030
Phone: (305) 248-2121

Pet Restrictions: Small pets
Exercise Area for Pets: Yes
Rates: $48 to $54

HOMOSASSA SPRINGS

Riverside Inn Downtown
476 S. Suncoast
Homosassa Springs, FL 32647
Phone: (904) 628-4311

Pet Restrictions: $10
Pet left unattended in room: Yes,
    must be present for housekeeping
Exercise Area for Pets: Yes
Rates: $49 to $69

VETERINARIANS

Nayfield, K.C.
1831 S. Suncoast Blvd. 32646
(904) 795-7110

INVERNESS

Central Motel
721 US Hwy 41S
Inverness, FL 32650
Phone: (904) 726-4515

Pet Restrictions: $5, well behaved
Pet left unattended in room: Yes
Exercise Area for Pets: Yes
Rates: $37.91 to $53.46

VETERINARIANS

Dumas Veterinary Hosp.
2225 Hwy 44W 32650
(904) 726-2460

Aultman, Stuart H.
1130 Sterling St. 32650
(904) 726-2830

ISLAMORADA

Sands of Islamorada
Milemarker 80
80051 Overseas Hwy.
Islamorada, FL 33036
Phone: (305) 664-2791

Pet Restrictions: None
Exercise Area for Pets: Yes
Rates: $75 to $125

JACKSONVILLE

Admiral Inn
10550 Balmoral Circle W
Jacksonville, FL 32218
Phone: (904) 757-8338

Pet Restrictions: $10
Pet left unattended in room: Yes, no
    housekeeping
Exercise Area for Pets: Yes
Rates: $28.50 plus

Best Inn of America
8220 Dix Ellis Trail
Jacksonville, FL 32256
Phone: (904) 739-3323

Pet Restrictions: Small pets
Exercise Area for Pets: Yes
Rates: $35.88 to $40.88

Days Inn/Days Lodge
5649 Cagle Rd.
Jacksonville, FL 32216
Phone: (904) 733-3890

Pet Restrictions: $5/night
Exercise Area for Pets: Yes
Rates: $28 to $35

Economy Inns of America
4300 Salisbury Rd.
Jacksonville, FL 32216
Phone: (904) 281-0198

Pet Restrictions: Under 25 lbs.
Exercise Area for Pets: Yes
Rates: $35.90 to $39.90

Economy Inns of America
5959 Youngerman Cir. E
Jacksonville, FL 32244
Phone: (904) 777-0160

Pet Restrictions: Small pets
Exercise Area for Pets: Yes
Rates: $26.90 to $33.90

Holiday Inn East & Conference Center
5865 Arlington Expwy
Jacksonville, FL 32211
Phone: (904) 724-3410

Pet Restrictions: $10 deposit
Pet left unattended in room: Yes
Exercise Area for Pets: Yes
Rates: $49 to $76

FLORIDA — HOTELS (continued)

La Quinta-Baymeadows
8255 Dix Ellis Trail
Jacksonville, FL 32256
Phone: (904) 731-9940
Pet Restrictions: None
Exercise Area for Pets: Yes
Rates: $44 to $56

La Quinta Motor Inn-North
812 Dunn Ave.
Jacksonville, FL 32218
Phone: (904) 751-6960
Pet Restrictions: Under 30 lbs.
Exercise Area for Pets: Yes
Rates: $47 to $54

Holiday Inn East & Conference Center
5865 Arlington Expwy
Jacksonville, FL 32211
Phone: (904) 724-3410
Pet Restrictions: $10 fee
Pet left unattended in room: Yes
Exercise Area for Pets: Yes
Rates: $49 to $76

Ramada Inn-Mandarin
3130 Hartley Rd.
Jacksonville, FL 32217
Phone: (904) 268-8080
Pet Restrictions: Under 25 lbs, if quiet
Pet left unattended in room: Yes
Exercise Area for Pets: Yes
Rates: $46 to $56

Ramada Inn West
510 S. Lane Ave.
Jacksonville, FL 32205
Phone: (904) 786-0500
Pet Restrictions: $10
Pet left unattended in room: Yes
Exercise Area for Pets: Yes
Rates: $29.95 to $65

VETERINARIANS
Briarcliff Animal Clinic
3901 Southside Blvd. 32216
(904) 641-5522

San Jose Beauclerc Animal Clinic
9319 San Jose Blvd. 32257
(904) 733-5022

Snyder Animal Hospital
6003 Phillips Hwy 32216
(904) 733-4080

KEY WEST
Hampton Inn
2801 N. Roosevelt Blvd.
Key West, FL 33040
Phone: (305) 294-2917
Pet Restrictions: $15
Exercise Area for Pets: Yes
Rates: $100 to $115

Ramada Key's End
3420 N. Roosevelt Blvd.
Key West, FL 33040
Phone: (305) 294-5541
Pet Restrictions: $10/night, $25 deposit
Exercise Area for Pets: Yes
Rates: $59 to $119 subject to change

KISSIMMEE
Best Western Eastgate
5565 W. Irlo Bronson Memorial Hwy
Kissimmee, FL 34746
Phone: (407) 396-0707, (800) 223-5361
Pet Restrictions: $5/pet/night
Pet left unattended in room: Yes, must be present for housekeeping
Exercise Area for Pets: Yes
Rates: $48 to $71

Days Inn West
7980 W. Irlo Bronson Memorial Hwy
Kissimmee, FL 34746
Phone: (407) 396-1000, (800) 432-9926, (800) 327-9173
Pet Restrictions: $6/day
Pet left unattended in room: Yes
Exercise Area for Pets: Yes
Rates: $35 to $85

Holiday Inn-Main Gate East
US Hwy I-92 East
Kissimmee, FL 34746
Phone: (407) 396-4488, (800) 366-5437
Pet Restrictions: Under 25 lbs.
Exercise Area for Pets: Yes
Rates: $85 to $126

Howard Johnson Lodge/Kissimmee
2323 Hwy I-92 Ext.
Kissimmee, FL 34744
Phone: (407) 846-4900, (800) 446-4656
Pet Restrictions: Small pets; $5/pet/day
Pet left unattended in room: Yes
Exercise Area for Pets: Yes
Rates: $35 and up

FLORIDA — HOTELS (continued)

Knights Inn Orlando/Main Gate East
2880 Poinciana Blvd
Kissimmee, FL 34746
Phone: (407) 396-8186,
   (800) 843-5644

Pet Restrictions: None
Pet left unattended in room: Yes
Exercise Area for Pets: Yes
Rates: $40 to $49

Red Roof Inn
4970 Kyngs Heath Rd.
Kissimmee, FL 32741
Phone: (407) 396-6065

Pet Restrictions: Under 10 lbs.
Pet left unattended in room: Yes, no
   housekeeping
Exercise Area for Pets: Yes
Rates: $26 to $65

VETERINARIANS
Kissimmee Animal Clinic
403 East Vine St. 32743
(305) 846-3912

Osceola Animal Clinic
1513 North Main St.
(305) 846-7800

LAKE BUENA VISTA
Comfort Inn
8442 Palm Pkwy
Lake Buena Vista, FL 32836
Phone: (407) 239-7300,
   (800) 999-7300

Pet Restrictions: None
Pet left unattended in room: Yes,
   must be present for cleaning
Exercise Area for Pets: Nearby
Rates: $39 to $69

Days Inn Lake Buena Vista Village
12490 Apopka-Vineland Rd.
Lake Buena Vista, FL 32836
Phone: (407) 239-4646,
   (800) 521-3297

Pet Restrictions: Small pets,
   $10/pet/day
Exercise Area for Pets: Nearby
Rates: $39 to $115

LAKE CITY
Econo Lodge
P.O. Box 430, Jct. I75 & US90
Lake City, FL 32055
Phone: (904) 752-7891

Pet Restrictions: $3/room
Exercise Area for Pets: Yes
Rates: $41.44

Howard Johnson Lodge
Route 13, P.O. Box 1082
Lake City, FL 32055
Phone: (904) 752-6262

Pet Restrictions: None
Exercise Area for Pets: Yes
Rates: $39 to $59.95

Quality Inn Lake City
Rt. 13, Box 1075
Lake City, FL 32055
Phone: (904) 752-7550,
   (800) 221-2222

Pet Restrictions: None
Pet left unattended in room: Yes
Exercise Area for Pets: Yes
Rates: $42 to $55

LAKELAND
Crossroads Motor Lodge
3223 Hwy 98 N
Lakeland, FL 33805
Phone: (813) 688-6031

Pet Restrictions: $4/day/pet
Pet left unattended in room: Yes,
   notify desk
Exercise Area for Pets: Yes
Rates: $26 to $30

VETERINARIANS
Animal Medical Clinic
4006 S. Florida Ave. 33813
(813) 646-1476

Lakeland Veterinary Hospital
3003 Highway 98S. 33803
(813) 665-1811

Santa Fe Animal Hospital
3107 US 92 East 33801
(813) 665-5033

FLORIDA — HOTELS (continued)

LAKE WORTH

Montinique Motor Lodge
801 S. Dixie Hwy
Lake Worth, FL 33460
Phone: (407) 585-2502

Pet Restrictions: $7/day; small pets
Pet left unattended in room: Yes
Exercise Area for Pets: Yes
Rates: $28 to $75

VETERINARIANS

Lake Worth Animal Hospital
1110 Second Ave. N. 33480
(305) 582-3364

Hirsch, Cary
3336 Jog Rd. 334167
(305) 968-7888

LEESBURG

Budgett Motel
1225 N. 14th St.
Leesburg, FL 34748
Phone: (904) 787-3534,
    (800) 688-1091

Pet Restrictions: Under 20 lbs.,
    dogs only
Pet left unattended in room: Yes
Exercise Area for Pets: Yes
Rates: $32 to $42

VETERINARIANS

Kiehl, Anita Rene
(904) 787-6733

LONGBOAT KEY

Riviera Beach Motel
5451 Gulf of Mexico Dr.
Longboat Key, FL 34228
Phone: (813) 383-2552

Pet Restrictions: Small dogs
Pet left unattended in room: Yes
Exercise Area for Pets: Yes
Rates: $60 to $95

MARIANNA

Holiday Inn
Hwy 90E, P.O. Box 979
Marianna, FL 32446
Phone: (904) 526-3251

Pet Restrictions: $15/pet/night,
    small pets
Exercise Area for Pets: Yes
Rates: $43 to $52

MIAMI

Hilton Airport & Marina
5101 Blue Lagoon Dr.
Miami, FL 33126
Phone: (305) 262-1000,
    (800) HILTONS

Pet Restrictions: Under 20 lbs., call
    first
Pet left unattended in room: Yes
Exercise Area for Pets: Yes
Rates: $140 to $210

Howard Johnson Motor Lodge-Airport
7330 NW 36th St.
Miami, FL 33166
Phone: (305) 592-5440,
    (800) 654-2000

Pet Restrictions: None
Pet left unattended in room: Yes
Exercise Area for Pets: Yes
Rates: $58 to $100

Quality Inn-South
14501 S. Dixie Hwy
Miami, FL 33176
Phone: (305) 251-2000,
    (800) 221-2222

Pet Restrictions: None
Rates: $59 to $82

Radisson Mart Plaza
711 NW 72nd Ave
Miami, FL 33126
Phone: (305) 261-3800,
    (800) 333-3333

Pet Restrictions: $25
Pet left unattended in room: Yes
Exercise Area for Pets: Nearby
Rates: $140 to $165

Wellesley Inn at Kendall
11750 Mills Dr.
Miami, FL 33183
Phone: (305) 270-0359,
    (800) 444-8880

Pet Restrictions: $10/pet/night
Exercise Area for Pets: Yes
Rates: $120

Wellesley Inn at Miami Lakes
7925 NW 154th St.
Miami, FL 33016
Phone: (305) 821-8274,
    (800) 444-8888

Pet Restrictions: Under 10 lbs.,
    $10/pet/night
Pet left unattended in room: Yes
Exercise Area for Pets: Yes
Rates: $49 to $64

Knowles Animal Hospital
2101 Northwest 25th Ave 33142
(305) 633-2402

Bird Road Animal Hospital
7480 Bird Road 33155
(305) 264-4242

South Kendall Animal Clinic
9501 Southwest 160th St. 33157
(305) 238-2030

MIAMI SPRINGS
Hampton Inn-Airport
5125 NW 36th St.
Miami Springs, FL 33166
Phone: (305) 887-2153,
   (800) 426-7866
Pet Restrictions: None
Exercise Area for Pets: Yes
Rates: $69 to $72

NAPLES
The Spinnaker
6600 Dudley Dr.
Naples, FL 33999
Phone: (813) 434-0444
Pet Restrictions: None
Pet left unattended in room: Yes
Exercise Area for Pets: Yes
Rates: $36 to $75

VETERINARIANS

Saint Francis Animal Clinic
5380 Trail Blvd. N. 33963
(813) 597-3108

OCALA
Davis Bros. Motor Lodge
3924 W. Silver Springs Blvd.
Ocala, FL 34475
Phone: (904) 629-8794,
   (800) 841-9480
Pet Restrictions: $5/pet, 24 rooms
   only
Pet left unattended in room: Yes
Exercise Area for Pets: Yes
Rates: $20 to $42

Days Inn
4040 W. Silver Springs Blvd.
Ocala, FL 34482
Phone: (904) 629-8850,
   (800) 325-2525
Pet Restrictions: $5/pet
Exercise Area for Pets: Yes
Rates: $35 to $60

Hampton Inn
3434 SW College Rd.
Ocala, FL 34474
Phone: (904) 854-3200,
   (800) 854-3205
Pet Restrictions: $5/pet/day
Pet left unattended in room: Yes
Exercise Area for Pets: Yes
Rates: $49 to $54

Howard Johnson Lodge
3811 NW Blitchton Rd.
Ocala, FL 34482
Phone: (904) 629-7041
Pet Restrictions: None
Pet left unattended in room: Yes
Exercise Area for Pets: Yes
Rates: $45 to $55

Howard Johnson Park Square Inn
3712 SW 38th Ave.
Ocala, FL 34474
Phone: (904) 237-8000,
   (800) 821-8272
Pet Restrictions: None
Pet left unattended in room: Yes
Exercise Area for Pets: Yes
Rates: $50 to $55

Quality Inn I-75
3767 NW Blitchton Rd.
Ocala, FL 34474
Phone: (904) 732-2300
Pet Restrictions: $6/pet/night
Pet left unattended in room: Yes
Exercise Area for Pets: Yes
Rates: $30 and up

Radisson Inn
3620 W. Silver Springs Blvd.
Ocala, FL 34474
Phone: (904) 629-0091,
   (800) 333-3333
Pet Restrictions: None
Exercise Area for Pets: Yes
Rates: $35 to $

Scottish Inn
3520 W. Silver Springs Blvd.
Ocala, FL 34470
Phone: (904) 629-7961,
   (800) 251-1962
Pet Restrictions: $3/pet/day
Pet left unattended in room: Yes
Exercise Area for Pets: Yes
Rates: $21 and up

FLORIDA — HOTELS (continued)

VETERINARIANS
Southeast Animal Clinic
4485 SE 53rd Ave. 32671
(904) 624-0300

Edwards, George M.
(904) 867-5553

ORANGE PARK
Econo Lodge
141 Park Ave.
Orange Park, FL 32073
Phone: (904) 264-5107,
(800) 55E-CONO
Pet Restrictions: $3
Pet left unattended in room: Yes
Exercise Area for Pets: Yes
Rates: $38

Holiday Inn-Orange Park
150 Park Ave.
Orange Park, FL 32073
Phone: (904) 264-9513
Pet Restrictions: None
Pet left unattended in room: Yes
Exercise Area for Pets: Yes
Rates: $45 to $61

VETERINARIANS
Guill, Carl A.
Kingsley Ave. 32073
(904) 264-2419

McKee, Douglas C.
1244 Park Ave. 32073
(904) 264-6561

Smith, Daniel J.
2020 Wells Road #20-G 32073
(904) 771-6968

ORLANDO
Days Inn
901 N. Orlando Ave.
Orlando, FL 32789
Phone: (407) 644-8000,
(800) 325-2525
Pet Restrictions: $35, pets not
recommended
Pet left unattended in room: Yes
Rates: $29.95 to $79

Days Inn-International Drive
7200 International Drive
Orlando, FL 32819
Phone: (407) 351-1200
Pet Restrictions: $4/pet/day
Pet left unattended in room: Yes,
caged
Exercise Area for Pets: Yes
Rates: $39 to $74

Days Inn Orlando Airport
2323 McRoy Rd.
Orlando, FL 32809
Phone: (407) 859-6100,
(800) 325-2525
Pet Restrictions: $4/day/pet
Pet left unattended in room: Yes,
must be present for cleaning
Exercise Area for Pets: Yes
Rates: $35 to $58

Economy Inn of America
8222 Jamaican Court
Orlando, FL 32819
Phone: (407) 345-1172,
(800) 826-0778
Pet Restrictions: Under 20 lbs.
Exercise Area for Pets: Yes
Rates: $39 to $59

Gateway Inn
7050 Kirkman Rd.
Orlando, FL 32819
Phone: (407) 351-2000,
(800) 327-3808
Pet Restrictions: Under 20 lbs.
Pet left unattended in room: Yes
Exercise Area for Pets: Yes
Rates: $50 to $78

Holiday Inn-Midtown
929 W. Colonial Dr.
Orlando, FL 32804
Phone: (407) 843-1360,
(800) HOLIDAY
Pet Restrictions: $10/pet/day
Exercise Area for Pets: Yes
Rates: $59 to $81

Howard Johnson Lodge
8820 South Orange Blossom Trail
Orlando, FL 32809
Phone: (407) 851-8200,
(800) 654-2000
Pet Restrictions: Over 25 lbs. call to
confirm
Pet left unattended in room: Yes,
must be present for cleaning
Exercise Area for Pets: Yes
Rates: $40 to $80

Howard Johnson Lodge
2014 W. Colonial Dr.
Orlando, FL 32804
Phone: (407) 841-8600,
    (800) 645-6386
Pet Restrictions: $5/night/pet, under
    25 lbs.
Pet left unattended in room: Yes
Exercise Area for Pets: Yes
Rates: $38 to $54

La Quinta Airport
7931 Daetwyler Dr.
Orlando, FL 32812
Phone: (407) 857-9215,
    (800) 531-5900
Pet Restrictions: Small pets
Pet left unattended in room: Yes
Exercise Area for Pets: Yes
Rates: $59 to $79

Motel 6
5909 American Way
Orlando, FL 38219
Phone: (407) 351-6500
Pet Restrictions: None
Pet left unattended in room: Yes
Exercise Area for Pets: Yes
Rates: $31 to $36

Quality Inn International
7600 International Dr.
Orlando, FL 32819
Phone: (407) 351-1600,
    (800) 825-7600
Pet Restrictions: None
Exercise Area for Pets: Yes
Rates: $29 to $53

Quality Inn-Plaza
9000 International Dr.
Orlando, FL 32819
Phone: (407) 345-8585,
    (800) 999-8585
Pet Restrictions: $5.50
Pet left unattended in room: Yes,
    must be present for cleaning
Exercise Area for Pets: Yes
Rates: $29 to $59

Radisson Plaza
60 S. Ivanhoe Blvd.
Orlando, FL 32804
Phone: (407) 425-4455,
    (800) 333-3333
Pet Restrictions: $25
Pet left unattended in room: Yes
Exercise Area for Pets: Yes
Rates: $59 to $119

Red Roof Inn
9922 Haiwaiian Court
Orlando, FL 32819
Phone: (407) 352-1507
Pet Restrictions: None
Pet left unattended in room: Yes
Exercise Area for Pets: Yes
Rates: $29 to $54

VETERINARIANS

Powers Drive Animal Hospital
2608 North Powers Dr. 32818
(407) 299-4850

Trail Animal Clinic
7306 S. Orange Blossom Trail 32809
(407) 855-1350

Fairvilla Animal Hospital
4020 John Young Parkway 32804
(407) 295-4482

ORMOND BEACH

Days Inn-Ormond Beach/ Oceanfront N.
839 S. Atlantic Ave.
Ormond Beach, FL 32176
Phone: (904) 677-6600,
    (800) 224-5052
Pet Restrictions: Under 20 lbs.,
    dogs only, max. 2 dogs,
    $6/dog/day
Exercise Area for Pets: Yes
Rates: $37 to $150

Driftwood Beach Motel
657 S. Atlantic Ave.
Ormond Beach, FL 32176
Phone: (904) 677-1331
Pet Restrictions: Small pets
Pet left unattended in room: Yes,
    short time
Exercise Area for Pets: Nearby
Rates: $28 to $130

Holiday Inn-I95N
1614 N US1
Ormond Beach, FL 32174
Phone: (904) 672-1060,
    (800) HOLIDAY
Pet Restrictions: None
Exercise Area for Pets: Yes
Rates: $29 to $47

FLORIDA — HOTELS (continued)

Howard Johnson Motor Lodge-Daytona
1633 N. US1, I-95
Ormond Beach, FL 32174
Phone: (904) 677-7310,
    (800) 446-4656
Pet Restrictions: $25 refund.
    deposit, small pets only
Pet left unattended in room: Yes,
    limited time
Exercise Area for Pets: Yes
Rates: $30 to $140

Jamaican Beach Motel
505 S. Atlantic Ave.
Ormond Beach, FL 32176
Phone: (904) 677-3353,
    (800) 336-3353
Pet Restrictions: $3/day/pet
Pet left unattended in room: Yes
Exercise Area for Pets: Yes
Rates: $25 to $70

Shadow Lake Animal Hospital
125North Nova Rd. 32074
(904) 673-0333

Tomoka Pines Veterinary Hosp.
750 S. Nova Rd. 32074
(904) 672-3137

Townsend, James F.
226 Vining Court 32074
(904) 677-0507

PALATKA

Holiday Inn
201 N. First St.
Palatka, FL 32177
Phone: (904) 328-3481
Pet Restrictions: None
Pet left unattended in room: Yes
Exercise Area for Pets: Yes
Rates: $55 to $65

Maltby, Joe H.
Rt. 5, Box 8 32074
(904) 328-4613

PANAMA CITY

Surf High Inn on the Gulf
10611 Front Beach Rd.
Panama City Beach, FL 32407
Phone: (904) 234-2129
Pet Restrictions: $5/pet/day, $20
    refund. deposit
Pet left unattended in room: Yes
Exercise Area for Pets: Yes
Rates: $55 to $89

Pet Health Center Cedar Grove
2620 E. 15th St. 32405
(904) 763-1779

Collier, Stephen E.
739 S. Tyndall Pkwy 32404
(904) 763-8384

Ernst, Gary E.
2640 Jenks Ave. 32405
(904) 769-0305

PENSACOLA

Comfort Inn
6919 Pensacola Ave.
Pensacola, FL 32505
Phone: (904) 478-4499
Pet Restrictions: Small, no snakes
Exercise Area for Pets: Yes
Rates: $29 to $54

Days Inn North
7051 Pensacola Blvd.
Pensacola, FL 32505
Phone: (904) 476-9090
Pet Restrictions: $5/day/pet
Pet left unattended in room: Yes
Exercise Area for Pets: Yes
Rates: $38 to $55

Knights Inn
1953 Northcross Lane
Pensacola, FL 32514
Phone: (904) 477-2554,
    (800) 843-5644
Pet Restrictions: Under 50 lbs.,
    must bring pooper scooper
Exercise Area for Pets: Yes
Rates: $33.95 to $39.95

La Quinta Motor Inn
7750 N. David Hwy
Pensacola, FL 32514
Phone: (904) 474-0411,
    (800) 531-5900

Pet Restrictions: None
Pet left unattended in room: Yes
Exercise Area for Pets: Yes
Rates: $53 to $79

Pensacola Grand Hotel
200 E. Gregory St.
Pensacola, FL 32501
Phone: (904) 433-3336,
    (800) 348-3336

Pet Restrictions: $50
Exercise Area for Pets: Yes
Rates: $49 to $204

Ramada Inn North
6550 Pensacola
Pensacola, FL 32505
Phone: (904) 477-0711

Pet Restrictions: $10
Exercise Area for Pets: Yes
Rates: $53 to $59

Red Roof Inn
7340 Plantation Rd.
Pensacola, FL 32504
Phone: (904) 476-7960

Pet Restrictions: None
Pet left unattended in room: Yes
Exercise Area for Pets: Yes
Rates: $40 to $45

VETERINARIANS

Animal Health Clinic
1224 Old Corry Rd.
(904) 456-6618

Brentwood Animal Hospital
5101 North Palafox
(904) 434-2646

Olive Road Animal Clinic
2605 Olive Rd.
(904) 477-2901

PERRY
Days Inn
2277 S. Byron Buttler Blvd.
Perry, FL 32347
Phone: (904) 584-5311,
    (800) 325-2525

Pet Restrictions: $5
Pet left unattended in room: Yes
Exercise Area for Pets: Yes
Rates: $30 to $53

PINELLAS PARK
Days Inn
9359 US 19N
Pinellas Park, FL 34666
Phone: (813) 577-3838,
    (800) 325-2525

Pet Restrictions: $6/pet/day
Pet left unattended in room: Yes,
    must be present for cleaning
Exercise Area for Pets: Yes
Rates: $35 to $60

La Quinta
7500 US 19N
Pinellas Park, FL 34665
Phone: (813) 545-5611,
    (800) 531-5900

Pet Restrictions: Small pets
Exercise Area for Pets: Yes
Rates: $50 to $77

VETERINARIANS

Park Animal Hosp. Inc.
8065 66th St. N. 33565
(813) 543-9828

Pinellas Animal Hospital and Bird Clinic
8490 49th St. 33565
(813) 546-0005

POMPANO BEACH
Sea Castle Resort Inn
730 N. Ocean Blvd.
Pompano Beach, FL 33062
Phone: (305) 941-2570
Fax: (305) 941-2570

Pet Restrictions: Yes. 1 poolview
    hotel room; 2 poolview eff.
Pet left unattended in room: No
Exercise Area for Pets: Yes
Rates: $39 to $119

PORT RICHEY
Days Inn - Port Richey
11736 US 19
Port Richey, FL 34668
Phone: (813) 863-1502
Fax: (813) 863-1502

Pet Restrictions: $4 per night charge
Pet left unattended in room: No policy
Exercise Area for Pets: Yes
Other: Green Key Beach; Howard Park
Rates: $35 to $85

FLORIDA — HOTELS (continued)

Bayonet Point Animal Clinic
11823 Oak Trailway
(813) 863-2435

Holiday Animal Clinic
4830 State Rd. 54
(813) 847-2150

PUNTA GORDA

Best Western Inn
26560 N. Jones Loop
Punta Gorda, FL 33950
Phone: (813) 637-7200,
    (800) 528-1234
Pet Restrictions: Depends on
    individual and animal
Exercise Area for Pets: Yes
Rates: $31.50 to $45

Holiday Inn
300 Retta Esplanade
Punta Gorda, FL 33950
Phone: (813) 639-1165,
    (800) HOLIDAY
Pet Restrictions: $12/pet/day
Pet left unattended in room: Yes
Exercise Area for Pets: Yes
Rates: $46 to $73

Howard Johnson Lodge
33 Tamiami Trail
Punta Gorda, FL 33950
Phone: (813) 639-2167
Pet Restrictions: None
Pet left unattended in room: Yes,
    must be present for cleaning
Exercise Area for Pets: Nearby
Rates: $40 to $95

Punta Gorda Animal Hospital
25120 Marion Ave. 33950
(813) 639-8717

SANFORD

Days Inn Sanford
4650 W. Rt. 46
Sanford, FL 32771
Phone: (407) 323-6500
Pet Restrictions: $5/day/pet
Exercise Area for Pets: Yes
Rates: $35.99 to $41

Bellhorn, Ted L.
2515 W. 25th St. 32771
(407) 322-8465

SARASOTA

Days Inn-Sarasota Airport
4900 N. Tamiami Trail
Sarasota, FL 34234
Phone: (813) 355-9721,
    (800) 325-2525
Pet Restrictions: $5/day/pet
Pet left unattended in room: Yes,
    must be present for cleaning
Exercise Area for Pets: Yes
Rates: $45 to $75

Holiday Inn Airport (Mariner)
7150 N. Tamiami Trail
Sarasota, FL 34243
Phone: (813) 355-2781,
    (800) HOLIDAY
Pet Restrictions: None
Exercise Area for Pets: Nearby
Rates: $55 to $110

Ramada Inn Airport
8440 N. Tamiami Trail
Sarasota, FL 34243
Phone: (813) 355-7771,
    (800) 228-2828
Pet Restrictions: None
Pet left unattended in room: Yes
Exercise Area for Pets: Nearby
Rates: $45 to $75

Animal Medical Clinic of Gulf Gate, Inc.
2316 Stickney Point Rd.
(813) 922-0756

Bay Road Animal Hospital
1712 Bay Road 33579
(813) 366-2275

Sarasota Animal Hospital
4535 Bee Ridge Rd. 33583
(813) 371-5951

SILVER SPRINGS

Sun Plaza Motel
5461 State Rd. 40 East
Silver Springs, FL 34489-0216
Phone: (904) 236-2343

Pet Restrictions: $4/pet/day
Pet left unattended in room: Yes
Exercise Area for Pets: Yes
Rates: $22.95 to $37.95

ST. AUGUSTINE

Best Western Ocean City
3955 A1A South
St. Augustine, FL 32084
Phone: (904) 471-8010,
    (800) 528-1234

Pet Restrictions: Small pets only
Pet left unattended in room: Yes
Exercise Area for Pets: Yes
Rates: $44 to $99

Comfort Inn Historic Downtown
1111 Ponce de Leon Blvd.
St. Augustine, FL 32084
Phone: (904) 824-5554,
    (800) 221-2222

Pet Restrictions: $5/pet/night, 3
    pets per room
Pet left unattended in room: Yes,
    notify desk
Exercise Area for Pets: Yes
Rates: $29 to $159

Days Inn Downtown
2800 Ponce de Leon Blvd.
St. Augustine, FL 32084
Phone: (904) 829-6581,
    (800) 331-9995

Pet Restrictions: $10/night
Pet left unattended in room: Yes
Exercise Area for Pets: Yes
Rates: $34 to $80

Days Inn Interstate
2560 State Rd. 16
St. Augustine, FL 32092
Phone: (904) 824-4341,
    (800) 325-2525

Pet Restrictions: Yes
Pet left unattended in room: Yes
Exercise Area for Pets: Yes
Rates: $30 to $50

Econo Lodge
2535 State Rd. 16
St. Augustine, FL 32092
Phone: (904) 829-5643,
    (800) 424-4777

Pet Restrictions: Yes
Exercise Area for Pets: Nearby
Rates: $34 to $79

Howard Johnson Lodge
2550 State Rd. 16
St. Augustine, FL 32084
Phone: (904) 829-5686,
    (800) 446-4656

Pet Restrictions: $6/night, dogs
    must be 10 lbs. or under, no cats
Pet left unattended in room: Yes
Rates: $29.95 to $36, higher for
    holidays

Lion Motel
420 Anastasia Blvd.
St. Augustine, FL 32084
Phone: (904) 824-2831

Pet Restrictions: $5/night
Pet left unattended in room: Yes, no
    room service
Exercise Area for Pets: Yes
Rates: $20 to $85

Red Carpet Inn
6 Castillo Dr.
St. Augustine, FL 32084
Phone: (904) 824-4457,
    (800) 251-1962

Pet Restrictions: $6/pet
Exercise Area for Pets: Nearby
Rates: $28 to $85

VETERINARIANS

Beckett, Tachel Sian
1079 Winter Hawk Dr. 32086
(904) 471-3044

ST. PETERSBURG

Valley Forge Motel
6825 Central Ave.
St. Petersburg, FL 33710
Phone: (813) 345-0136

Pet Restrictions: $3/pets under 20
    lbs., $5/over 20 lbs.
Pet left unattended in room: Yes
    except at night
Exercise Area for Pets: Yes
Rates: $30 to $85

FLORIDA — HOTELS (continued)

VETERINARIANS

Bayshore Animal Hosp. of FL
3845 Tyrone Blvd. 33709
(813) 381-3900

Animal Medical Hospital
2540 30th Ave. N. 33713
(813) 896-7127

Tyrone Veterinary Hospital
3451 Tyrone Blvd. 33710
(813) 381-8911

STARKE

Days Inn
1101 North Temple Ave.
Starke, FL 32091
Phone: (904) 964-7600,
        (800) 325-2525
Pet Restrictions: $3, 1 pet per room
Pet left unattended in room: Yes
Exercise Area for Pets: Yes
Rates: $47 to $52

TALLAHASEE

Days Inn North
288 N. Monroe St.
Tallahasee, FL 32301
Phone: (904) 385-0136,
        (800) 325-2525
Pet Restrictions: $5/pet, only in
    certain rooms
Pet left unattended in room: Yes, no
    maid service
Rates: $38 to $47

Collegiate Village Inn
2121 W. Tennessee St.
Tallahassee, FL 32304
Phone: (904) 576-6121
Pet Restrictions: No pets except in
    emergencies
Pet left unattended in room: Yes
Exercise Area for Pets: Yes
Rates: $40, higher for special events

Days Inn
722 Apalachee Pkwy
Tallahassee, FL 32301
Phone: (904) 224-2181,
        (800) 325-2525
Pet Restrictions: $10/night
Exercise Area for Pets: Nearby
Rates: $38 to $53

Knights Inn
2728 Graves Rd.
Tallahasee, FL 32303
Phone: (904) 562-4700,
        (800) 843-5644
Pet Restrictions: Small pet, $50
    refund. deposit
Pet left unattended in room: Yes but
    no cleaning
Exercise Area for Pets: Yes
Rates: $27 to $57

La Quinta Motor Inn
Tallahasee S.
2905 N. Monroe St.
Tallahasee, FL 32303
Phone: (904) 385-7172,
        (800) 531-5900
Pet Restrictions: None
Pet left unattended in room: Yes
Exercise Area for Pets: Yes
Rates: $46 to $52

Motel 6
2738 N. Monroe St.
Tallahassee, FL 32303
Phone: (904) 386-7878,
        (505) 891-6161 (central res.)
Pet Restrictions: 1 small pet/room
Exercise Area for Pets: Yes
Rates: $28.33 to $41.44

Red Roof Inn
2930 North Monroe
Tallahassee, FL 32303
Phone: (904) 385-7884,
        (800) 843-7663
Pet Restrictions: Owner responsible
    for damages, fleas included
Pet left unattended in room: Yes,
    behaved
Exercise Area for Pets: Yes
Rates: $36.99 to $39.99

Tallahasee Travelodge
691 W. Tennessee St.
Tallahasee, FL 32304
Phone: (904) 224-8161,
        (800) 578-7878
Pet Restrictions: None
Pet left unattended in room: Yes
Exercise Area for Pets: Nearby
Rates: $25 to $32

Northwood Animal Hospital
1881 North Blvd. 32303
(904) 385-8181

Mountain, Timothy R.
3552 Gallagher Dr. 32308
(904) 878-8288

Houff-Novey, Patricia
Capitol City Veterinary Hosp.
1826 NE Capitol Circle Rd. 32308
(904) 877-1149

TAMPA

Days Inn Fletcher Ave.
701 E. Fletcher Ave.
Tampa, FL 33612
Phone: (813) 977-1550,
    (800) 325-2525
Pet Restrictions: $5 fee, small pets
    only
Pet left unattended in room: Yes,
    notify desk
Exercise Area for Pets: Nearby
Rates: $35 to $65

Econo Lodge Busch Gardens
9202 N. 30th St.
Tampa, FL 33612
Phone: (813) 935-7855,
    (800) 578-7878
Pet Restrictions: Small pets; $10
    deposit, can't stay more than
    few days
Pet left unattended in room: Yes
Exercise Area for Pets: Yes
Rates: $36 to $48

Embassy Suites
555 N. Westshore Blvd.
Tampa, FL 33609
Phone: (813) 875-1555,
    (800) EMBASSY
Pet Restrictions: $10/night, only
    cats and small dogs
Pet left unattended in room: Yes
Rates: $119 to $139

Holiday Inn-Busch Gardens
2701 E. Fowler Ave.
Tampa, FL 33612
Phone: (813) 971-4710,
    (800) 99-BUSCH
Pet Restrictions: Small pets
Pet left unattended in room: Yes
Exercise Area for Pets: Yes
Rates: $49 to $99

Holiday Inn State Fair
2708 N. 50th St.
Tampa, FL 33619
Phone: (813) 621-2081,
    (800) 237-1510
Pet Restrictions: $25
Pet left unattended in room: Yes, if
    quiet
Exercise Area for Pets: Yes
Rates: $55 and up

Ramada Inn-Univ.-US E
400 E. Bears Ave.
Tampa, FL 33613
Phone: (813) 961-1000,
    (800) 228-2828
Pet Restrictions: Small pets,
    $5/night
Pet left unattended in room: Yes
Exercise Area for Pets: Yes
Rates: $49 to $64

Red Roof Inn
10121 Horace Ave.
Tampa, FL 33619
Phone: (813) 681-8484
Pet Restrictions: 1 pet/must be in
    kennel
Exercise Area for Pets: Yes
Rates: $25 to $45

Red Roof Inn
2307 E. Busch Blvd.
Tampa, FL 33612
Phone: (813) 932-0073
Pet Restrictions: Under 25 lbs.
Pet left unattended in room: Yes, no
    maid service
Exercise Area for Pets: Yes
Rates: $29 to $46

Red Roof Inn
5001 N. US 301
Tampa, FL 33610
Phone: (813) 623-5245
Pet Restrictions: Under 25 lbs., $10
Pet left unattended in room: Yes
Exercise Area for Pets: Yes
Rates: $26 to $41

Murphy Animal Hospital
6845 N. Dale Mabry 33614
(813) 879-6090

Veterinary Medical Clinic, Inc.
4241 Henderson Blvd. 33629
(813) 872-7198

North Bay Animal Hospital
9801 W. Hillsborough Ave. 33615
(813) 885-4477

TARPON SPRINGS
Days Inn/Days Lodge
40050 US Hwy 19 N
Tarpon Springs, FL 34689
Phone: (813) 934-0859,
   (800) 325-2525
Pet Restrictions: $5
Pet left unattended in room: Yes
Exercise Area for Pets: Nearby
Rates: $27 to $50

TAVARES
Howard Johnson Inn
101 W. Burleigh Blvd.
Tavares, FL 32778
Phone: (904) 343-4666,
   (800) 446-4656
Pet Restrictions: Only dogs, $5, no
   attack dogs
Pet left unattended in room: Yes, no
   maid service
Exercise Area for Pets: Yes
Rates: $42 to $47

Inn on the Green
700 E. Burleigh Blvd.
Tavares, FL 32778
Phone: (904) 343-6373,
   (800) 938-4653
Pet Restrictions: Under 10 lbs.
Exercise Area for Pets: Yes
Rates: $39 to $65

TITUSVILLE
Best Western Space Shuttle Inn
3455 Cheney Hwy
Titusville, FL 32780
Phone: (407) 269-9100,
   (800) 523-7654
Pet Restrictions: Small pets
Pet left unattended in room: Yes, if
   caged
Exercise Area for Pets: Nearby
Rates: $46.50 to $75

Quality Inn
3755 Cheney Hwy
Titusville, FL 32780
Phone: (407) 269-4480,
   (800) 221-2222
Pet Restrictions: Small pets, $10
Pet left unattended in room: Yes
Exercise Area for Pets: Yes
Rates: $55 to $90

VETERINARIANS
Dunn Animal Hospital
1202 South Hospital Ave. 32780
(407) 269-0677

TREASURE ISLAND
Lorelei Resort
10273 Gulf Blvd.
Treasure Island, FL 33706
Phone: (813) 360-4351,
   (800) 35-GO-DOG
Pet Restrictions: None
Pet left unattended in room: Yes
Exercise Area for Pets: Yes
Rates: $50 to $65

VENICE
Days Inn
1710 S. Tamiami Trail South
Venice, FL 34293
Phone: (813) 493-4558,
   (800) 241-2323
Pet Restrictions: $15
Pet left unattended in room: Yes
Exercise Area for Pets: Yes
Rates: $46 to $55

VETERINARIANS
Greenwald, Robert J.
2000 S. Tamiami Trail 33595
(813) 493-3300

Jacaranda Animal Hospital
725 Shamrock Blvd. 34293
(813) 497-1676

WEEKIWACHEE
Holiday Inn
6172 Commercial Way
Weekiwachee, FL 34606
Phone: (904) 596-2007,
(800) U-JOIN US
Pet Restrictions: None, have kennels
Pet left unattended in room: Yes
Exercise Area for Pets: Nearby
Rates: $45 to $102

WEST PALM BEACH
Days Inn
2300 W. 45th St.
West Palm Beach, FL 33407
Phone: (407) 689-0450,
   (800) 325-2525

Pet Restrictions: $10, medium size
   or less
Exercise Area for Pets: Yes
Rates: $43 to $69

VETERINARIANS
**Belvedere Academy Animal
Hospital**
429 Belvedere Rd. 33405
(407) 833-0891

Broadway Animal Hospital
4501 Broadway 33407
(407) 844-9777

Golfview Animal Clinic
658 North Military Trail 33415
(407) 689-6750

WINTER HAVEN
Budget Host Driftwood Hotel
970 Cypress Gardens Blvd.
Phone: (813) 294-4229,
   (800) 283-4678

Pet Restrictions: Small pets, $4
Exercise Area for Pets: Yes
Rates: $28 to $66

**Holiday Inn Winter Haven-
Cypress Gardens**
1150 3rd St. SW
Winter Haven, FL 33880
Phone: (813) 294-4451,
   (800) 465-4329

Pet Restrictions: Small pets
Pet left unattended in room: Yes
Exercise Area for Pets: Yes
Rates: $48 to $68

Howard Johnson Lodge
1300 3rd St. SW
Winter Haven, FL 33880
Phone: (813) 294-7321,
   (800) 654-2000

Pet Restrictions: Small Pets
Exercise Area for Pets: Yes
Rates: $48 to $85

VETERINARIANS
Maxwell IV, John N.
3400 Dundee Rd. 33884
(813) 324-3340

GEORGIA — HOTELS

ACWORTH

Econo Lodge
P.O. Box 600
Acworth, GA 30101
Phone: (404) 386-0700

Pet Restrictions: 6 rooms
Exercise Area for Pets: Nearby
Rates: $39.95 to $45.95

ADEL

Days Inn - I-75
I-75 exit 10, 1200 W. Fourth St.
Adel, GA 31620
Phone: (912) 896-4574

Pet Restrictions: None
Pet left unattended in room: Yes, if
    housebroken
Exercise Area for Pets: Nearby
Rates: $28 to $37

Econo Lodge - I-75
1102 West Fourth St.
Adel, GA 31620
Phone: (912) 896-4523

Pet Restrictions: None
Pet left unattended in room: Yes, if
    housebroken
Exercise Area for Pets: Nearby
Rates: $28 to $37

Howard Johnson Inn - King
1103 W. 4th St.
Adel, GA 31620
Phone: (912) 896-2244

Pet Restrictions: None
Pet left unattended in room: Yes, if
    housebroken
Exercise Area for Pets: Nearby
Rates: $28 to $37

ALBANY

Days Inn
422 W. Oglethorpe, P.O. Box 1984
Albany, GA 31701
Phone: (912) 888-2632

Pet Restrictions: None
Exercise Area for Pets: Nearby
Rates: $35 to $44

Heritage House
732 W. Oglethorpe
Albany, GA 31701
Phone: (912) 888-1910

Pet Restrictions: None
Pet left unattended in room: Yes
Exercise Area for Pets: Yes, must
    be on leash
Rates: $42 to $48

Knights Inn
1201 Schley Ave.
Albany, GA 31707
Phone; (912) 888-9600

Pet Restrictions: Under 25 lbs.
Pet left unattended in room: Yes,
    but no maid service
Exercise Area for Pets: Nearby
Rates: $34.95 to $54.95

VETERINARIANS

Bush Animal Clinic
2419 Dawson Rd. 31707
Phone: (912) 439-7073

**Drs. Joiner Lingle Dockery and
Williams Veterinarians**
140 North Magnolia St. 31707
Phone: (912) 435-1431

Hart, Henry A.
410 North Westover Blvd. 31707
Phone: (912) 883-1618

ATHENS

Days Inn
2741 Atlanta Hwy
Athens, GA 30606
Phone: (706) 546-9750

Pet Restrictions: $5 fee
Exercise Area for Pets: Yes
Rates: $31.50 to $43

Howard Johnson Lodge
2465 West Broad St.
Athens, GA 30606
Phone: (706) 548-1111

Pet Restrictions: $100 deposit; must
    sign release form
Exercise Area for Pets: Yes
Rates: $35 to $90

VETERINARIANS

Athens Veterinary Clinic
2575 Atlanta Hgwy 30606
Phone: (706) 543-5547

Maxwell Veterinary Hospital
4120 Lexington Rd. 30605
Pone: (706) 353-1623

ATLANTA

Atlanta Marriott Northwest
200 Interstate North Pkwy
Atlanta, GA 30339
Phone: (404) 952-7900

Pet Restrictions: Under 13 lbs.
Pet left unattended in room: Yes,
    sign waiver, various fees
Exercise Area for Pets: Nearby
Rates: $65 to $123

Executive Villas Hotel
5735 Rosewell Rd. NE
Atlanta, GA 30342
Phone: (404) 252-2868

Pet Restrictions: $100
    non-refundable
Pet left unattended in room: Yes
Exercise Area for Pets: Yes
Rates: $50 to $123

Guest Quarters Suite Hotel
6120 Peachtree-Dunwoody Rd.
Atlanta, GA 30328
Phone: (404) 668-0808

Pet Restrictions: Call first
Exercise Area for Pets: Yes

Hawthorne Suites Hotel
1500 Parkwood Circle
Atlanta, GA 30339
Phone: (404) 952-9595

Pet Restrictions: $5/pet/nite
Pet left unattended in room: Yes, if
    contained
Exercise Area for Pets: Yes
Rates: $55 to $105

Hilton Towers
255 Courtland St. at Harris St.
Atlanta, GA 30043
Phone: (404) 659-2000

Pet Restrictions: Less than 40 lbs;
    must sign waiver
Pet left unattended in room: Yes, if
    quiet
Exercise Area for Pets: Nearby
Rates: $79 to $250

Holiday Inn - I75
1810 Howell Mill Rd. NW
Atlanta, GA 30325
Phone: (404) 351-3831

Pet Restrictions: Yes

La Quinta Motor Inn NE
6187 Dawson Blvd.
Atlanta, GA 30093
Phone: (404) 448-8686

Pet Restrictions: None
Pet left unattended in room: Yes
Rates: $43 to $55

Marriott Gwinnett Place
1775 Pleasant Hill Rd. at Crestwood
Atlanta, GA 30136
Phone: (404) 923-1775

Pet Restrictions: Under 15 lbs.
Pet left unattended in room: Yes
Exercise Area for Pets: Nearby
Rates: $89 to $140

Ramada Inn
1569 Phoenix Blvd.
Atlanta, GA 30349
Phone: (404) 996-4321

Pet Restrictions: Yes
Pet left unattended in room: Yes
Rates: $64 to $74

Ramada Inn
285 at Chamblee-Dunwoody Rd.
Atlanta, GA 30338
Phone: (404) 394-5000

Pet Restrictions: Under 20 lbs.
Pet left unattended in room: Yes
Exercise Area for Pets: Yes
Rates: $59 to $69

Ramada Inn - Near Six Flags
4225 Tilton Industrial Blvd.
Atlanta, GE 30336
Phone: (404) 691-4100

Pet Restrictions: Call first

Red Roof Inn
1960 N. Druid Hill Rd.
Atlanta, GA 30329
Phone: (404) 321-1653

Pet Restrictions: Under 20 lbs.
Rates: $36 to $45

Red Roof Inn - 6 Flags
4265 Shirley Dr. SW
Atlanta, GA 30336
Phone: (404) 696-4391

Pet Restrictions: None
Pet left unattended in room: Yes
Exercise Area for Pets: Yes
Rates: $45.99 to $55.99

Residence Inn by Marriott
Perimeter East, 1901 Savoy Dr.
Atlanta, GA 30341
Phone: (404) 455-4446
Pet Restrictions: $35 non-refundable
    for cleaning
Pet left unattended in room: Yes
Exercise Area for Pets: Yes
Rates: $83 to $103

Sheraton Century Center
2000 Century Blvd. NE
Atlanta, GA 30345
Phone: (404) 325-0000
Pet Restrictions: No puppies
Exercise Area for Pets: Yes
Rates: $90 to $115

Summit Inn
3900 Fulton Industrial Blvd.
Atlanta, GA 30336
Phone: (404) 691-2444
Pet Restrictions: $5/day
Exercise Area for Pets: Yes
Rates: $44 to $49

University Inn
1767 N. Decatur Rd.
Atlanta, GA 30304
Phone: (404) 634-7327
Pet Restrictions: Pet counts as
    person
Pet left unattended in room: Yes
Exercise Area for Pets: Nearby
Rates: $58 to $89

Vantage Hotel
2180 Northlake Pkwy
Atlanta, GA 30084
Phone: (404) 939-8120
Pet Restrictions: $15 cleanup fee;
    10 rooms in back
Pet left unattended in room: Yes
Exercise Area for Pets: Yes
Rates: $49 to $69

VETERINARIANS

Briarcliff Animal Clinic
1850 Johnson Rd. NE 30306
Phone: (404) 874-6393

Vernon Woods Animal Hosp.
270 Vernon Woods Drive NE 30328
Phone: (404) 252-1641

Pets Are People Too
1510 Piedmont Ave. 30324
Phone: (404) 448-8910

AUGUSTA

Hampton Inn
3030 Wash. Rd.
Augusta, GA 30907
Phone: (706) 737-1122
Pet Restrictions: Under 20 lbs.
Pet left unattended in room: Yes,
    w/sign
Exercise Area for Pets: Nearby
Rates: $38 to $49

Holiday Inn I-20
1075 Stevens Creek Rd.
Augusta, GA 30907
Phone: (706) 738-8811
Pet Restrictions: $6/night
Pet left unattended in room: Yes
Exercise Area for Pets: Yes
Rates: $49 to $59

Howard Johnson
1238 Gorden Hwy
Augusta, GA
Phone: (706) 724-9613
Pet Restrictions: $5/day
Pet left unattended in room: Yes
Exercise Area for Pets: Yes
Rates: $27 to $32

Shoneys Inn
3023 Wash. Rd.
Augusta, GA 30907
Phone: (706) 736-2595
Pet Restrictions: Small pets under
    20 lbs.
Pet left unattended in room: Yes
Exercise Area for Pets: Nearby
Rates: $33 to $35

Villager Lodge
210 Boy Scout Rd.
Augusta, GA 30909
Phone: (706) 737-3166
Pet Restrictions: $25 fee
Exercise Area for Pets: Nearby
Rates: $29.95 to $39.95

VETERINARIANS

Aidmore Animal Clinic
1701 North Leg Court 30909
Phone: (706) 733-7181

Highland Animal Hospital
2124 Highland Ave. 30904
Phone: (706) 736-1443

Gayle, Richard
1946 Walton Way
Phone: (706) 733-2288

AUSTELL
Knights Inn-Atlanta West
1595 Blair Bridge Rd.
Austell, GA 30001
Phone: (404) 944-0824

Pet Restrictions: 1 pet/room
Pet left unattended in room: Yes; no maid service
Exercise Area for Pets: Nearby
Rates: $44.95 to $59.95

BREMEN
Shilo Inn Bremer/Carrollton
1077 Alabama Ave.
Bremen, GA 30110
Phone: (404) 537-3833,
(800) 222-2244

Pet Restrictions: $6/pet/day; 3 ground floor rooms only
Exercise Area for Pets: Yes
Rates: $40 to $45

BRUNSWICK
Best Western Brunswick Inn
US 25 & 341, Exit 7B
Brunswick, GA 31520
Phone: (912) 264-0144

Pet Restrictions: None
Exercise Area for Pets: Yes
Rates: $33 to $56

Comfort Inn
490 New Jesup Hwy
Brunswick, GA 31520
Phone: (912) 264-6540

Pet Restrictions: None
Exercise Area for Pets: Yes
Rates: $39 to $59

Days Inn
2307 Gloucester St.
Brunswick, GA 31520
Phone: (912) 265-8830

Pet Restrictions: $4 fee
Pet left unattended in room: Yes, damage will be charged
Rates: $35 to $50

Days Inn
409 Jesup Hwy.
Brunswick, GA 31520
Phone: (912) 264-4330

Pet Restrictions: None
Pet left unattended in room: Yes
Exercise Area for Pets: Nearby
Rates: $34 to $55

Holiday Inn - I95
US 341 at I95
Brunswick, GA 31520
Phone: (912) 264-4033

Pet Restrictions: None
Rates: $59 to $71

Knights Inn
US Hwy 341
Brunswick, GA 31520
Phone: (912) 267-6500

Pet Restrictions: Smoking rooms
Pet left unattended in room: Yes
Exercise Area for Pets: Yes
Rates: $32 to $36.95

VETERINARIANS
Weeks, Billy N.
Route 2, Box 3 31520
Phone: (912) 265-8668

BYRON
Master Economy Inn
Rt. 3, Box 1540
Byron, GA 31008
Phone: (912) 956-5300

Pet Restrictions: $6/pet/night
Exercise Area for Pets: Nearby
Rates: $24.95 to $40.95

Passport Inn
Rt. 1, Box 200
Byron, GA 31008
Phone: (912) 956-5200

Pet Restrictions: None
Exercise Area for Pets: Nearby
Rates: $19.88 to $34.88

Red Carpet Inn
Rt. 3, Box 114X
Byron, GA 31008
Phone: (912) 956-3800

Pet Restrictions: None
Pet left unattended in room: Yes
Exercise Area for Pets: Nearby
Rates: $22.88 to $26.88

CALHOUN
American Inn
1442 Hwy 41N
Calhoun, GA 30701
Phone: (706) 629-1137

Pet Restrictions: $1/pet/night
Exercise Area for Pets: Yes
Rates: $27.95 to $35

GEORGIA — HOTELS (continued)

Best Western of Calhoun
Rt. 3, US 41N
Calhoun, GA 30701
Phone: (706) 629-4521

Pet Restrictions: $4/pet; under 20 lbs.
Exercise Area for Pets: Yes
Rates: $34 to $44

Days Inn
on SR 53
Calhoun, GA 30701
Phone: (706) 629-8271

Pet Restrictions: $4/night
Pet left unattended in room: Yes
Exercise Area for Pets: Yes
Rates: $32 and up

Holiday Inn
P.O. Box 252
Calhoun, GA 30701
Phone: (706) 629-9191

Pet Restrictions: None
Pet left unattended in room: Yes
Exercise Area for Pets: Nearby
Rates: $36 to $60

Red Carpet Inn-Calhoun
915 Hwy 53E
Calhoun, GA 30701
Phone: (706) 629-9501

Pet Restrictions: $3; no fleas
Exercise Area for Pets: Yes
Rates: $31.95 to $45.95

CARTERSVILLE

Budget Host Inn
P.O. Box 1088
Cartersville, GA 30120
Phone: (404) 386-0350

Pet Restrictions: None
Pet left unattended in room: Yes, must be tame
Exercise Area for Pets: Yes
Rates: $19.95 to $60

Economy Inn
P.O. Box 848
Cartersville, GA 30120
Phone: (404) 382-1122

Pet Restrictions: None
Pet left unattended in room: Yes, for short time
Exercise Area for Pets: Yes
Rates: $28 to $38

Red Carpet Inn-Cartersville
35 Carson Loop NW
Cartersville, GA 30120
Phone: (404) 382-8000

Pet Restrictions: None
Pet left unattended in room: Yes, must be tame
Exercise Area for Pets: Yes
Rates: $19.95 to $65

COLLEGE PARK
Holiday Inn-Airport South
5010 Old Natl. Hwy.
College Park, GA 30349
Phone: (404) 761-4000

Pet Restrictions: Call first
Pet left unattended in room: Yes
Exercise Area for Pets: Nearby

Red Roof Inn
2471 Old National Pkwy
College Park, GA 30349
Phone: (404) 761-9701

Pet Restrictions: Under 15 lbs.
Pet left unattended in room: Yes
Exercise Area for Pets: Yes
Rates: $27 to $46

COLUMBUS
Budgetel
2919 Warm Springs Rd.
Columbus, GA 31909
Phone: (706) 323-4344

Pet Restrictions: Under 20 lbs.
Pet left unattended in room: Yes, if quiet
Exercise Area for Pets: Yes
Rates: $37.95 to $52.95

VETERINARIANS
Animal General Hospital
3576 Macon Rd. 31907
Phone: (706) 568-4848

Northside Animal Hospital
5360 Beallwood Connector 31904
Phone: (706) 324-0333

COMMERCE

Bulldog Inns
Rt. 6, Box 270
Commerce, GA 30529
Phone: (706) 335-5147

Pet Restrictions: None
Pet left unattended in room: Yes
Exercise Area for Pets: Yes
Rates: $24.99 to $47.72

CONYERS

Villager Lodge
1297 Dogwood Ave.
Conyers, GA 30207
Phone: (404) 483-1332

Pet Restrictions: $50 fee, for weekly
  rental
Exercise Area for Pets: Nearby
Rates: $29.95 to $41.95

VETERINARIANS

Honey Creek Veterinary Hosp.
1026 Honey Creek Rd. 30208
Phone: (404) 483-7225

Sharp Joseph V.
P.O. Box 566 30207
Phone: (404) 483-1551

DALTON

Days Inn
1518 W. Walnut Ave.
Dalton, GA 30720
Phone: (706) 278-0850

Pet Restrictions: $4/night
Exercise Area for Pets: Yes
Rates: $32 to $68

Welcome Inn
P.O. Box 1794
Dalton, GA 30720
Phone: (706) 277-9323

Pet Restrictions: Call first
Exercise Area for Pets: Nearby

VETERINARIANS

Burger Animal Hospital
1022 South Hamilton St. 30720
Phone: (706) 278-1113

DILLARD

Dillard House
Dillard House Rd., P.O. Box 10
Dillard, GA 30537
Phone: (706) 746-5348

Pet Restrictions: $5 fee
Pet left unattended in room: Yes,
  notify maids
Exercise Area for Pets: Yes
Rates: $45 to $150

DORDELE

Holiday Inn
P.O. Box 916
Dordele, GA 31015
Phone: (912) 273-4117

Pet Restrictions: Small pets only
Rates: $48 to $50

DUBLIN

Holiday Inn
US 441 at Jct. I 16, P.O. Box 768
Dublin, GA 31021
Phone: (912) 272-7862

Pet Restrictions: None
Exercise Area for Pets: Yes
Rates: $40 to $49

EAST POINT

Holiday Inn Airport North
1380 Virginia Ave.
East Point, GA 30344
Phone: (404) 762-8411

Pet Restrictions: None
Pet left unattended in room: Yes
Exercise Area for Pets: Yes
Rates: $49 to $69

FOLHSTON

Red Carpet Inn Tahiti
1201 S. 2nd St.
Folhston, GA 31537
Phone: (912) 496-2514

Pet Restrictions: None
Pet left unattended in room: Yes,
  put up sign
Exercise Area for Pets: Yes
Rates: $30 to $40

FORSYTH

Davis Bros./Days Inn
N. Lee St.
Forsyth, GA 31029
Phone: (912) 994-2900

Pet Restrictions: None
Pet left unattended in room: Yes
Exercise Area for Pets: Yes
Rates: $43

Hampton Inn
Tift College Dr. & Juliette Rd.
P.O. Box 600
Forsyth, GA
Phone: (912) 994-9697

Pet Restrictions: None
Pet left unattended in room: Yes
Exercise Area for Pets: Yes
Rates: $38 to $48

Holiday Inn
P.O. Box 600
Forsyth, GA 31029
Phone: (912) 994-5691

Pet Restrictions: None
Pet left unattended in room: Yes
Exercise Area for Pets: Yes
Rates: $45 plus $5/person

Red Carpet Inn
Rt. 1, Box 45
Forsyth, GA 31029
Phone: (912) 994-5603

Pet Restrictions: Small pets
Pet left unattended in room: Yes
Exercise Area for Pets: Yes
Rates: $25 to $32

GAINESVILLE

Holiday Inn
726 Broad St. SW
Gainesville, GA 30501
Phone: (404) 536-4451

Pet Restrictions: None
Pet left unattended in room: Yes
Exercise Area for Pets: Yes
Rates: $54 to $58

Masters Inn
On 129, P.O. Box CC
Gainesville, GA 30503
Phone: (404) 532-7531

Pet Restrictions: $2 extra
Pet left unattended in room: Yes
Exercise Area for Pets: Yes
Rates: $33 to $38

VETERINARIANS

Dellinger, Wilbur A.
3014 Atlanta Hwy 30501
Phone: (404) 532-4449

Quillian, Edward
4517 Stephens Road 30501
Phone: (404) 532-2849

GLENNVILLE

Cheerie O Motel
P.O. Box 393
Glennville, GA 30427
Phone: (912) 654-2176

Pet Restrictions: Small pets
Exercise Area for Pets: Yes
Rates: $28 to $38.50

HELEN

The Helendorf Inn
Main St., P.O. Box 305
Helen, GA 30545
Phone: (706) 878-2271

Pet Restrictions: Special pet rooms;
     need reservation; $5/pet/night
Pet left unattended in room: Yes
Exercise Area for Pets: Yes
Rates: $59 to $74

JEKYLL ISLAND

Holiday Inn
200 Beachview Dr. S.
Jekyll Island, GA 31520
Phone: (912) 994-5691

Pet Restrictions: None
Pet left unattended in room: Yes
Exercise Area for Pets: Yes
Rates: $45 to $63

Quality Inn Bucaneer
85 Beachview Dr. S.
Jekyll Island, GA 31520
Phone: (912) 635-2261

Pet Restrictions: Up to 20 lbs
Pet left unattended in room: Yes,
     must be in room with pet for
     maid service
Exercise Area for Pets: Yes
Rates: $99 to $169

Seafarer Motel
700 Beachview Dr. N.
Jekyll Island, GA 31520
Phone: (912) 635-2202

Pet Restrictions: $6/day
Exercise Area for Pets: Yes
Rates: $58 to $78

JONESBORO
Holiday Inn-South
6288 Old Dixie Hwy
Jonesboro, GA 30236
Phone: (404) 968-4300

Pet Restrictions: None
Pet left unattended in room: Yes,
    must inform desk
Exercise Area for Pets: Yes
Rates: $40 to $99

VETERINARIANS
Jonesboro Animal Hospital
7944 North Main St. 30236
(404) 478-5521

KENNESAW
Comfort Inn
775 Geo. Busbee Pkwy
Kennesaw, GA 30144
Phone: (404) 424-7666

Pet Restrictions: $5/pet
Pet left unattended in room: Yes
Exercise Area for Pets: Yes
Rates: $55

Red Roof Inn
520 Roberts Ct., NW
Kennesaw, GA 30144
Phone: (404) 429-0323

Pet Restrictions: Small pets only
Pet left unattended in room: Yes
Exercise Area for Pets: Yes
Rates: $28.99 and up

KINGSLAND
Days Inn Kingsland
1050 E. Kings Rd.
Kingsland, GA 31548
Phone: (912) 729-5454

Pet Restrictions: $5/night
Exercise Area for Pets: Yes
Rates: vary

LA GRANGE
Days Inn LaGrange/Callaway Gardens
2606 Whitesville Rd.
La Grange, GA 30240
Phone: (706) 882-8881

Pet Restrictions: $4/night
Exercise Area for Pets: Yes
Rates: $35 to $42

LAKE PARK
Best Western Outpost Inn
Clyattville Exit 2 on I 75
Lake Park, GA 31636
Phone: (912) 559-5181

Pet Restrictions: None
Pet left unattended in room: Yes
Exercise Area for Pets: Yes
Rates: $35 to $40

Shoney's Inn
I 75 & Hwy 376
Lake Park, GA 31636
Phone: (912) 559-5660

Pet Restrictions: Under 30 lbs.,
    smoking rooms only
Pet left unattended in room: Yes, if
    pet is quiet
Exercise Area for Pets: Yes
Rates: $32.95 to $39.95

LAWRENCEVILLE
Days Inn
731 W. Pike St.
Lawrenceville, GA 30245
Phone: (404) 995-7782

Pet Restrictions: None
Pet left unattended in room: Yes,
    must be caged
Exercise Area for Pets: Yes
Rates: $35 to $44

VETERINARIANS
Austin, Gari-Anne Jerry
1577 Scholar Drive 30245
Phone: (404) 963-6903

Pleasant Point Animal Hospital
1455 Pleasant Hill Rd. #201 30245
Phone: (404) 923-5223

LITHONIA
La Quinta Motor Inn East
2859 Panola Rd.
Lithonia, GA 30058
Phone: (404) 981-6411

Pet Restrictions: None
Pet left unattended in room: Yes,
    w/Do not disturb sign
Exercise Area for Pets: Yes
Rates: $49 to $67

VETERINARIANS
Centerville Animal Hospital
3331 Highway 124 30058
Phone: (404) 979-6015

GEORGIA — HOTELS (continued)

Browen, Debbie
4749 Riveredge Cove 30058
Phone: (404) 469-1369

LOCUST GROVE
Super 8
Locust Grove Hwy, P.O. Box 613
Locust Grove, GA 30248
Phone: (404) 957-2936

Pet Restrictions: None
Pet left unattended in room: Yes
Exercise Area for Pets: Yes
Rates: $29 to $36

MACON
Howard Johnson Lodge
2566 Riverside Dr.
Macon, GA 31204
Phone: (912) 746-7671

Pet Restrictions: None
Exercise Area for Pets: Yes
Rates: $25 to $48

The Macon Hilton
108 1st St.
Macon, GA 31202
Phone: (912) 746-1461

Pet Restrictions: None
Rates: $59 to $79

Master's Economy Inn
4295 Pio Nono Ave.
Macon, GA 31206
Phone: (912) 788-8910

Pet Restrictions: $5/day
Pet left unattended in room: Yes,
    but no maid service
Exercise Area for Pets: Yes
Rates: $23.95 to $27.95

Passport Inn
I-475 at US 80
Macon, GA 31206
Phone: (912) 474-2665

Pet Restrictions: Call first
Exercise Area for Pets: Yes
Rates: $21.88 to $40

Quality Inn North
2720 Riverside Dr., P.O. Box 9006
Macon, GA 31298
Phone: (912) 743-1482

Pet Restrictions: None
Pet left unattended in room: Yes, if
    quiet
Exercise Area for Pets: Yes
Rates: $34.88 to $54

Friendship Animal Hospital
1211 Gray Highway 31211
Phone: (912) 745-3941

Northside Animal Hospital
3801 Northside Dive 31210
Phone: (912) 477-6828

Riverside Animal Hospital
2121 Riverside Dr. 31204
Phone: (912) 746-4838

MADISON
Ramada Inn
P.O. Box 602
Madison, GA 30650
Phone: (706) 342-2121

Pet Restrictions: None
Exercise Area for Pets: Yes
Rates: $39 to $46

MARIETTA
Best Inns of America
1255 Franklin Rd.
Marietta, GA 30067
Phone: (404) 955-0004

Pet Restrictions: Under 20 lbs.
Exercise Area for Pets: Yes
Rates: $36.88 to $50.88

Friendship Inn (Exec. Inn)
SR 155
Marietta, GA 30253
Phone: (404) 957-5261

Pet Restrictions: None
Pet left unattended in room: Yes
xercise Area for Pets: Yes
Rates: $27 to $33

Master's Economy Inn
P.O. Box 761
Marietta, GA 30253
Phone: (404) 957-5818

Pet Restrictions: $5/day
Pet left unattended in room: Yes,
    guest responsible for damage
Exercise Area for Pets: Yes
Rates: $23.95 to $65

Terrell Mill Animal Hospital
3258 Powers Ferry Rd. 30067
Phone: (404) 952-9300

The Veterinary Clinic
533 Roswell St. 30062
Phone: (404) 428-3381

Powell, Cynthia
420 North Fairground St. 30060
Phone: (404) 424-9910

McDONOUGH
Welcome Inn
SR 155 at I 75
McDonough, GA 30253
Phone: (404) 957-5858

Pet Restrictions: None
Exercise Area for Pets: Yes
Rates: $32.95 to $38.95

MORROW
Red Roof Inn
1348 Southlake Plaza Dr.
Morrow, GA 30260
Phone: (404) 968-1483

Pet Restrictions: Small pets only
Pet left unattended in room: Yes
Exercise Area for Pets: Yes
Rates: $28 to $44

VETERINARIANS

Lake Harbin Animal Hospital
2056 Lake Harbin Rd.
(404) 961-5036

NEWNAN
Days Inn
P.O. Box 548
Newnan, GA 30263
Phone: (404) 253-8550

Pet Restrictions: Under 20 lbs.
Pet left unattended in room: Yes, if quiet
Exercise Area for Pets: Yes
Rates: $34 to $44

VETERINARIANS

Reeves, R. Scott
Phone: (404) 253-8013

NORCROSS
Red Roof Inn
5171 Indian Trail Industrial Pkwy.
Norcross, GA 30071
Phone: (404) 448-8944

Pet Restrictions: Under 20 lbs.
Pet left unattended in room: Yes
Exercise Area for Pets: Yes
Rates: $26 to $75

The Villager Lodge
5122 Indian Trail
Norcross, GA 30071
Phone: (404) 446-5490

Pet Restrictions: $100 security deposit/wk ($50 non-refundable)
Pet left unattended in room: Yes
Exercise Area for Pets: Yes
Rates: $28 to $40

VETERINARIANS

Cedar Village Animal Clinic
5265 Jimmy Carter Blvd. 30093
Phone: (404) 448-9778

Peachtree Corners Animal Clin.
4020 Holcomb Bridge Rd.
Phone: (404) 448-0700

PERRY
Crossroads Motel
317 Carroll Blvd.
Perry, GA 31069
Phone: (912) 987-3030

Pet Restrictions: None
Pet left unattended in room: Yes, if caged
Exercise Area for Pets: Yes
Rates: $25 to $30

Days Inn of Perry
800 Valley Dr.
Perry, GA 31069
Phone: (912) 987-2142

Pet Restrictions: Smoking rooms only
Pet left unattended in room: Yes
Exercise Area for Pets: Yes
Rates: $44

Holiday Inn
200 Valley Rd., P.O. Box 615
Perry, GA 31069
Phone: (912) 987-3313

Pet Restrictions: None
Exercise Area for Pets: Yes
Rates: $39 to $44

VETERINARIANS

Smith Animal Hospital
US 341 North 31069
Phone: (912) 987-1514

PIKESVILLE

Holiday Inn-Pikesville
1721 Reisterstown Rd.
Pikesville, GA 21208
Phone: (410) 486-5600

Pet Restrictions: Small pets
Exercise Area for Pets: Yes
Rates: $72 and up

PINE MT.

White Columns Motel
P.O. Box 531
Pine Mt., GA 31822
Phone: (706) 663-2312

Pet Restrictions: Waiver form
Pet left unattended in room: Yes
Exercise Area for Pets: Yes
Rates: $33 to $45

POOLER

Knights Inn-Savannah West
500 E. Hwy 80
Pooler, GA 31322
Phone: (912) 748-4124

Pet Restrictions: None
Exercise Area for Pets: Nearby
Rates: $31.95 and up

RICHMOND HILL

Days Inn
P.O. Box 519
Richmond Hill, GA 31324
Phone: (912) 756-3371

Pet Restrictions: $4/night
Exercise Area for Pets: Nearby
Rates: $42

Econo Lodge
P.O. Box 47
Richmond Hill, GA 31324
Phone: (912) 756-3312

Pet Restrictions: $25 deposit
Exercise Area for Pets: Yes
Rates: $28.95

SAVANNAH

Best Western Central
45 Eisenhower Dr.
Savannah, GA 31406
Phone: (912) 355-1000

Pet Restrictions: $10 fee
Pet left unattended in room: Yes
Exercise Area for Pets: Yes
Rates: $40 to $50

Best Western Savannah
1 Gateway Blvd.
Savannah, GA 31419
Phone: (912) 925-2420

Pet Restrictions: None
Pet left unattended in room: Yes
Exercise Area for Pets: Nearby
Rates: $44 to $50

Days Inn Abercorn
11750 Abercorn St.
Savannah, GA 31419
Phone: (912) 927-7720

Pet Restrictions: $10 fee
Pet left unattended in room: Yes
Exercise Area for Pets: Yes
Rates: $47 and up

Gateway Inn
11516 Abercorn St.
Savannah, GA 31419
Phone: (912) 927-6274

Pet Restrictions: Small pet;
    $5/pet/day
Pet left unattended in room: Yes
Exercise Area for Pets: Nearby
Rates: $34.50 to $40.50

The Haslam House
417 E. Charlton St.
Savannah, GA 31401
Phone: (912) 233-6380

Pet Restrictions: Dogs only, house-
    trained; $10 fee
Exercise Area for Pets: Nearby
Rates: $65 to $95

Howard Johnson Lodge
Rt. 4, Box 441C
Savannah, GA 31419
Phone: (912) 925-3680

Pet Restrictions: None
Exercise Area for Pets: Yes
Rates: $38 to $52

La Quinta Motor Inn
6805 Abercorn St.
Savannah, GA 31405
Phone: (912) 355-3004

Pet Restrictions: Under 25 lbs
Pet left unattended in room: Yes
Exercise Area for Pets: Yes
Rates: $42 to $61

Quality Inn Gateway
7 Gateway Blvd. W.
Savannah, GA 31419
Phone: (912) 925-2280

Pet Restrictions: None
Pet left unattended in room: Yes
Exercise Area for Pets: Yes
Rates: $44

Quality Inn Heart of Savannah
300 W. Bay St.
Savannah, GA 31401
Phone: (912) 236-6321

Pet Restrictions: None
Pet left unattended in room: Yes
Exercise Area for Pets: Nearby
Rates: $59 to $68

VETERINARIANS
Case Veterinary Hospital
111 Eisenhower Drive 31406
Phone: (912) 352-3081

Island Veterinary Clinic
416 Johnny Mercer Blvd. 31410
Phone: (912) 897-1121

Grant, Kenneth J.
2357 Ogeechee Rd. 31401
Phone: (912) 233-2614

SMYRNA
Red Roof Inn-North
2200 Corporate Plaza
Smyrna, GA 30080
Phone: (404) 952-6966

Pet Restrictions: None
Pet left unattended in room: Yes
Exercise Area for Pets: Yes
Rates: $28.99 to $43.99

VETERINARIANS
Crowe, Susan M.
991-A Main Street 30080
Phone: (404) 436-2431

Levinson, Roxanne K.
2451 North Matthews St. SE 30080
Phone: (404) 436-5134

SPARKS
Red Carpet Inn
on Barneyville Rd. at Jct. I 75
Sparks, GA 31647
Phone: (912) 549-8243

Pet Restrictions: None
Pet left unattended in room: Yes
Exercise Area for Pets: Yes
Rates: $25 and up

STATESBORO
Bryant's Master Hosts Inn
461 S. Main St., P.O. Box 249
Statesboro, GA 30458
Phone: (912) 764-5666

Pet Restrictions: None
Pet left unattended in room: Yes
Exercise Area for Pets: Yes
Rates: $29 to $35

SUWANEE
Days Inn
I 85 & Hwy 317
Suwanee, GA 30174
Phone: (404) 945-8372

Pet Restrictions: $5/pet/day
Pet left unattended in room: Yes
Exercise Area for Pets: Yes
Rates: $35 to $40

Holiday Inn
on SR 317 at Jct. I 85 exit 44
Suwanee, GA 30174
Phone: (404) 945-4921

Pet Restrictions: Small pets only
Exercise Area for Pets: Yes
Rates: $55

THOMASVILLE
Holiday Inn of Thomasville
US 19 S
Thomasville, GA 31792
Phone: (912) 226-7111

Pet Restrictions: Small pet only
Pet left unattended in room: Yes
Exercise Area for Pets: Yes
Rates: $44 to $46.50

TIFTON
Carson Motel
309 W. 7th St.
Tifton, GA 31794
Phone: (912) 382-3111

Pet Restrictions: None
Pet left unattended in room: Yes
Exercise Area for Pets: Yes
Rates: $17 to $30

Masters Economy Inn
P.O. Box 1310
Tifton, GA 31793
Phone: (912) 382-8100

Pet Restrictions: None
Exercise Area for Pets: Yes
Rates: $22 to $27

Red Carpet Inn
1025 W. 2nd St.
Tifton, GA 31794
Phone: (912) 382-0280

Pet Restrictions: None
Pet left unattended in room: Yes
Exercise Area for Pets: Yes
Rates: $25 and up

TOWNSEND
Best Western Village Inn
On SR 99957 at I 95 exit
Townsend, GA 31331
Phone: (912) 832-4444

Pet Restrictions: None
Pet left unattended in room: Yes
Exercise Area for Pets: Yes
Rates: $32.50

Days Inn
On SR 99 at Jct. I 95 exit 11
Townsend, GA 31331
Phone: (912) 832-4411

Pet Restrictions: $5/pet/day
Exercise Area for Pets: Yes
Rates: $32.95

TUCKER
Knights Inn-Atlanta East
2942 Laurenceville Hwy
Tucker, GA 30084
Phone: (404) 934-5060

Pet Restrictions: One night only
Rates: $30.95 to $38.95

Red Roof Inn-Tucker
2810 Lawrenceville Hwy
Tucker, GA 30084
Phone: (404) 496-1311

Pet Restrictions: $15 lbs. or under
Exercise Area for Pets: Yes
Rates: $26.99 to $40.99

VETERINARIANS
Dekalb Animal Hospital
4070 Lawrenceville 30084
Phone: (404) 938-3900

Pets Are People Too
2015B Montreal Rd. 30084
Phone: (404) 493-1001

UNADILLA
Davis Bros. Quality Inn North
1209 St. Augustine Rd.
Unadilla, GA 310601
Phone: (912) 244-8510

Pet Restrictions: None
Pet left unattended in room: Yes
Exercise Area for Pets: Yes
Rates: $48.95

El Carlo Hotel
2525 N. Ashley St.
Unadilla, GA 31602
Phone: (912) 242-7676

Pet Restrictions: $10 fee
Pet left unattended in room: Yes
Exercise Area for Pets: Nearby
Rates: $20 to $26

Holiday Inn
1309 St. Augustine Rd.,
P.O. Box 1047
Unadilla, GA 31603
Phone: (912) 242-3881

Pet Restrictions: None
Pet left unattended in room: Yes
Exercise Area for Pets: Yes
Rates: $45 to $46

Jolly Inn Motel
I 75 and US 94
Unadilla, GA 31601
Phone: (912) 244-9500

Pet Restrictions: None
Pet left unattended in room: Yes
Exercise Area for Pets: Yes
Rates: $24 to $36

Quality Inn South
1902 W. Hill Ave.
Unadilla, GA 31601
Phone: (912) 244-4520

Pet Restrictions: None
Pet left unattended in room: Yes
Exercise Area for Pets: Yes
Rates: $36.95

Ramada Inn
P.O. Box 931
Unadilla, GA 31603
Phone: (912) 242-1225

Pet Restrictions: None
Exercise Area for Pets: Yes
Rates: $34

GEORGIA — HOTELS (continued)

Scottish Inn
US 41, P.O. Box 759
Unadilla, GA 31091
Phone: (912) 627-3228

Pet Restrictions: $3/pet/day
Exercise Area for Pets: Yes
Rates: $19.88 to $23.88

Shoney's Inn Valdosta
1828 W. Hill Ave.
Unadilla, GA 31610
Phone: (912) 244-7711

Pet Restrictions: None
Exercise Area for Pets: Yes
Rates: $36 to $42

Travel Lodge
1330 St. Augustine Rd.
Unadilla, GA 31601
Phone: (912) 242-3464

Pet Restrictions: None
Exercise Area for Pets: Yes
Rates: $34 to $41

VALDOSTA
Howard Johnson Inn - I 75
I 75 exit 6, N. Valdosta Rd.
Valdosta, GA 31620
Phone: (912) 244-4460

Pet Restrictions: None
Pet left unattended in room: Yes, if
    housebroken
Exercise Area for Pets: Nearby
Rates: $28 to $37

VIENNA
Holiday Inn
Jct. I 75 and SR 215
Vienna, GA 31092
Phone: (912) 268-2221

Pet Restrictions: $2-$3/pet/day
Exercise Area for Pets: Yes
Rates: $26.95 to $34.95

WARNER ROBINS
Holiday Inn of Warner Robins
2024 Watson Blvd.
Warner Robins, GA 31093
Phone: (912) 923-8871

Pet Restrictions: None
Pet left unattended in room: Yes
Exercise Area for Pets: Yes
Rates: $49 to $55

VETERINARIANS
Houston Veterinary Clinic
109 Avalon Circle 31093
Phone: (912) 929-0361

WAYCROSS
Days Inn
2016 Memorial Dr.
Waycross, GA 31501
Phone: (912) 285-4700

Pet Restrictions: None
Rates: $30 and up

HAWAII

No listings due to 120 day quarrantine on all arriving pets

IDAHO — HOTELS

BELLEVUE
High Country Motel
S. Main, P.O. Box 246
Bellevue, Idaho 83313
Phone: (208) 788-2050

Pet Restrictions: House trained
Pet left unattended in room: Yes
Exercise Area for Pets: Yes
Rates: $40 to $60

BLACKFOOT
Riverside Inn
1229 Park Way Dr.
Blackfoot, Idaho 83221
Phone: (208) 785-5000

Pet Restrictions: $5/pet/night,
    responsible for damages
Pet left unattended in room: Yes
Exercise Area for Pets: Yes
Rates: $38 to $44

VETERINARIANS
Animal Health Clinic
Route 3/Box 297 83221
Phone: (208) 785-5580

BLISS
Amber Inn
HC 60, Box 1330
Bliss, Idaho
Phone: (208) 352-4441

Pet Restrictions: Small, house
    trained
Exercise Area for Pets: Yes
Rates: $26 to $40

BOISE
Flying J Motel Inn
8002 Overland Rd.
Boise, ID 83705
Phone: (208) 322-4404

Pet Restrictions: Smoking rooms, if
    well behaved, notify maid
Pet left unattended in room: Yes
Exercise Area for Pets: Yes
Rates: $37 to $41

Holiday Inn
3300 Vista Ave.
Boise, ID 83705
Phone: (208) 344-8365

Pet Restrictions: Outer building, dog
    or cat
Exercise Area for Pets: Nearby
Rates: $69 to $79

Nendels
2155 N. Garden
Boise, ID 83704
Phone: (208) 344-4030

Pet Restrictions: Small pets
Exercise Area for Pets: Yes
Rates: $31 to $41

Ouyhee Plaza Hotel
1109 Main St.
Boise ID 83702
Phone: (208) 343-4611

Pet Restrictions: Small pets
Exercise Area for Pets: Yes
Rates: $51 to $83

Quality Inn
2717 Vista Ave.
Boise, ID 83705
Phone: (208) 343-7505

Pet Restrictions: $5 for large
    animals, notify maid
Pet left unattended in room: Yes
Exercise Area for Pets: Yes
Rates: $45 to $56

Residence Inn by Marriott
1401 Lusk, P.O. Box 6156
Boise, ID 83705
Phone: (208) 344-1200

Pet Restrictions: Responsible for
    damages, $5/pet/night
Pet left unattended in room: Yes
Exercise Area for Pets: Yes
Rates: $103 to $135

Shilo Inn Boise Airport
4111 Broadway Ave.
Boise, ID 83702
Phone: (208) 343-7662

Pet Restrictions: None, $6/day/pet
Exercise Area for Pets: Yes
Rates: $59 to $68

Shilo Inn Riverside
3031 Main
Boise, ID 83702
Phone: (208) 344-3521

Pet Restrictions: $6 fee, 1st floor
    only
Exercise Area for Pets: Yes
Rates: $68

Statehouse Inn
981 Grove St. at 10th St.
Boise ID 83702
Phone: (208) 342-4622
Pet Restrictions: Housebroken
Rates: $53.50 to $65.50

Univ. Inn
2360 Univ. Dr. at Capitol Blvd.
Boise, ID 83706
Phone: (208) 345-7170
Pet Restrictions: Well behaved only
Exercise Area for Pets: Nearby
Rates: $39.50 to $57

VETERINARIANS
Les Bois Veterinary Hospital
1890 West State Street 8702
Phone: (208) 343-2539

Mountain View Animal Clinic
3435 North Cole Rd. 83704
Phone: (208) 375-0251

Hunt, Stephen L.
5402 Franklin Rd. 83705
Phone: (208) 345-6771

BURLEY
Best Western Burley Inn
800 N. Overland Ave.
Burley, ID 83318
Phone: (208) 678-3501
Pet Restrictions: Small pets
Pet left unattended in room: Yes
Exercise Area for Pets: Yes
Rates: $44 to $72

Greenwell Motel
904 E. Main St.
Burley, ID 83318
Phone: (208) 678-5576
Pet Restrictions: None
Exercise Area for Pets: Yes
Rates: $28 to $36

CASCADE
Mt. View Motel
P.O. Box 1053
Cascade, ID 83611
Phone: (208) 382-4238
Pet Restrictions: Small-Medium
   size, $20 deposit
Exercise Area for Pets: Yes
Rates: $29 to $49

COEUR D'ALENE
Comfort Inn
280 W. Appleway
Coeur d'Alene, ID 83814
Phone: (208) 765-5500
Pet Restrictions: Smoking room
Exercise Area for Pets: Yes
Rates: $49 to $69

Days Inn Coeur d'Alene
2200 NW Blvd.
Coeur d'Alene, ID 83814
Phone: (208) 667-8668
Pet Restrictions: Small pets
Exercise Area for Pets: Yes
Rates: $47 to $52

El Rancho Motel
1915 E. Sherman Ave.
Coeur d'Alene, ID 83814
Phone: (208) 664-8794
Pet Restrictions: $3 fee
Exercise Area for Pets: Yes
Rates: $29.95 to $56.95

Holiday Inn
W 414 Appleway
Coeur d'Alene 83814
Phone: (208) 765-3200
Pet Restrictions: Small pets
Pet left unattended in room: Yes
Exercise Area for Pets: Yes
Rates: $67.50 to $89.50

Pines Resort Motel
1422 NW Blvd.
Coeur d'Alene, ID 83814
Phone: (208) 664-8244
Pet Restrictions: Smoking rooms
   only
Exercise Area for Pets: Yes
Rates: $42 to $85

Shilo Inn Coeur D'Alene
702 W. Appleway
Coeur d'Alene, ID 83814
Phone: (208) 664-2300,
   (800) 222-2244
Pet Restrictions: $6/day/pet
Exercise Area for Pets: Yes
Rates: $90 to $100

VETERINARIANS
Lancaster, Howard F.
655 Best Ave. 83814
Phone: (208) 667-1961

EDEN
Amber Inn
Rt. 1
Eden, ID 83325
Phone: (208) 825-5200
Pet Restrictions: No cats, fee for
  large dogs
Exercise Area for Pets: Yes
Rates: $23.95 to $34

GRANGEVILLE
Monty's Motel
700 W. Main
Grangeville, ID 83530
Phone: (208) 983-2500
Pet Restrictions: None
Exercise Area for Pets: Yes
Rates: $30 to $46

IDAHO FALLS
Best Western Driftwood Motel
575 River Pkwy
Idaho Falls, ID 83402
Phone: (208) 523-2242
Pet Restrictions: $3/pet
Pet left unattended in room: Yes
Exercise Area for Pets: Yes
Rates: $40 to $55

Shilo Inn Idaho Falls
780 Lindsay Blvd.
Idaho Falls, ID 83402
Phone: (208) 523-0088
Pet Restrictions: $6 fee/night, 1st
  floor
Exercise Area for Pets: Yes
Rates: $85 to $105

Super 8 Motel
705 N. Lindsay Blvd.
Idaho Falls, ID 83401
Phone: (208) 522-8880
Pet Restrictions: Under 20 lbs., $20
  deposit
Exercise Area for Pets: Yes
Rates: $34.88 to $44.88

VETERINARIANS
Eastside Veterinary Hospital
285 South Woodruff Ave. 83401
Phone: (208) 529-2217

Setter, Stephen M.
1414 South 35th West 83402
Phone: (517) 885-1455

KELLOGG
Silverhorn Motor Inn
699 W. Cameron Ave.
Kellogg, ID 83837
Phone: (208) 783-1151,
  800-437-6437
Pet Restrictions: None, if quiet,
  notify maid
Pet left unattended in room: Yes
Exercise Area for Pets: Yes
Rates: $47 to $70

KETCHUM
Best Western Christiania Lodge
P.O. Box 2196
Ketchum, ID 83340
Phone: (208) 726-3351
Pet Restrictions: $2/night
Rates: $54 to $84

VETERINARIANS
Acker, Randall L.
Phone: (208) 726-5128

LEWISTON
Tapadera Motor Inn
1325 Main St.
Lewiston, ID 83501
Phone: (208) 746-3311
Pet Restrictions: No snakes
Exercise Area for Pets: Yes
Rates: $37 to $65

MACKAY
Wagon Wheel Motel
809 W. Custer
Mackay, ID 83251
Phone: (208) 588-3331
Pet Restrictions: $20 deposit
Pet left unattended in room: Yes
Exercise Area for Pets: Yes
Rates: $26 to $56

McCALL
Woodsman
P.O. Box 884
McCall, ID 83638
Phone: (208) 634-7671
Pet Restrictions: None
Exercise Area for Pets: Yes
Rates: $28 to $55

MOUNTAIN HOME

Best Western Foothills Motor Inn
1080 Hwy 20
Mountain Home, ID 83647
Phone: (208) 587-8477
Pet Restrictions: $50 deposit
Exercise Area for Pets: Yes
Rates: $45 to $100

Hilander Motel & Steak House
615 S. 3rd West
Mountain Home, ID 83647
Phone: (208) 587-3311
Pet Restrictions: Housebroken, notify maids
Pet left unattended in room: Yes
Exercise Area for Pets: Yes
Rates: $26 to $34

Towne Center Motel
410 N. Second E
Mountain Home, ID 83647
Phone: (208) 587-3373
Pet Restrictions: $20 deposit.
Exercise Area for Pets: Yes
Rates: $21 to $34

NAMPA

Desert Inn Motel
115 9th Ave. S.
Nampa, ID 83651
Phone: (208) 467-1161
Pet Restrictions: $3 fee
Exercise Area for Pets: Yes
Rates: $34 to $42.80

Five Crowns Inn
908 3rd St. S
Nampa, ID 83651
Phone: (208) 466-3594
Pet Restrictions: $5 fee
Pet left unattended in room: Yes
Rates: $32.10 to $38.52

Shilo Inn-Nampa
617 Nampa Blvd.
Nampa, ID 83651
Phone: (208) 466-8993
Pet Restrictions: $6 fee, if well behaved
Pet left unattended in room: Yes
Exercise Area for Pets: Yes
Rates: $49 to $55

Shilo Inn Nampa Suites
1401 Shilo Dr.
Nampa, ID 83687
Phone: (208) 465-3250, (800) 222-2244
Pet Restrictions: $6/day/pet
Exercise Area for Pets: Yes
Rates: $65 to $79

VETERINARIANS
Kalbfleisch, Ken
1803 12th Avenue Rd. 83651
Phone: (208) 467-1148

POST FALLS

Best Western Templin's Resort Hotel
414 E. First Ave.
Post Falls, ID 83854
Phone: (208) 773-1611
Pet Restrictions: None
Exercise Area for Pets: Yes
Rates: $81 to $99

PRIEST LAKE

Hills Resort
HCR 5 Box 162A
Priest Lake, ID 83856
Phone: (208) 443-2551
Pet Restrictions: None
Pet left unattended in room: Yes
Exercise Area for Pets: Yes
Rates: $62 to $158

ROXBURY

Best Western Cotton Tree Inn
450 W. 4th St. S.
Roxbury, ID 83440
Phone: (208) 356-4646
Pet Restrictions: Well trained
Exercise Area for Pets: Yes
Rates: $48 to $58

SANDPOINT

Bottle Bay Marina Resort
1360 Bottle Bay Rd.
Sandpoint, ID 83864
Phone: (208) 263-5916
Pet Restrictions: $5/day, leashed
Pet left unattended in room: Yes
Exercise Area for Pets: Yes
Rates: $85 plus $7.50/person

Quality Inn Sandpoint
P.O. Box 187
Sandpoint, ID 83864
Phone: (208) 263-2111

Pet Restrictions: $100 deposit
Pet left unattended in room: Yes
Exercise Area for Pets: Yes
Rates: $38 to $64

STANLEY
Mt. Village Lodge
P.O. Box 150
Stanley, ID 83278
Phone: (208) 774-3661

Pet Restrictions: $5 deposit
Pet left unattended in room: Yes
Exercise Area for Pets: Yes
Rates: $54.88 to $77.28

Redfish Lake Lodge
P.O. Box 9
Stanley, ID 83278
Phone: (208) 774-3536

Pet Restrictions: $4/day
Exercise Area for Pets: Yes
Rates: $67 to $112

SUN VALLEY
Heidelburg Inn
P.O. Box 304
Sun Valley, ID 83353
Phone: (208) 726-5361

Pet Restrictions: Small pets, notify
     housekeeping
Pet left unattended in room: Yes
Exercise Area for Pets: Yes
Rates: $55 to $70

TWIN FALLS
Econo Lodge
320 Main Ave. S.
Twin Falls, ID 83301
Phone: (208) 733-8770

Pet Restrictions: Small pets
Exercise Area for Pets: Yes
Rates: $31 to $39

ILLINOIS — HOTELS

ALSIP
Holiday Inn-Alsip
5000 W. 127th St. at Cicero Ave.
Alsip, IL 60658
Phone: (708) 371-7300
Pet Restrictions: Ground floor back
Rates: $76/1 person, $85/2,
$159/suite

VETERINARIANS
**Lauderdale, Byron N.
Alsip Animal Hospital**
11843 South Pulaski 60658
Phone: (708) 385-6930

ALTAMONT
Aloha Inn
Rt. 2, Box 296
Altamont, IL 62411
Phone: (618) 483-6300
Pet Restrictions: None
Pet left unattended in room: Yes
Exercise Area for Pets: Yes
Rates: $24.95 to $39.95

**Best Western Stuckey's
Carriage Inn**
P.O. Box 303
Altamont, IL 62411
Phone: (618) 483-6101
Pet Restrictions: $5, 2 per room
Pet left unattended in room: Yes,
short period of time
Exercise Area for Pets: Yes
Rates: $25.90 to $46

VETERINARIANS
Wood, Nancy E.
Phone: (314) 443-1170

ALTON
Holiday Inn Alton Pkwy
3800 Homer Adams Pkwy
Alton, IL 62002
Phone: (618) 462-1220
Pet Restrictions: Small pets only
Pet left unattended in room: Yes
Exercise Area for Pets: Yes
Rates: $61 to $75

ARLINGTON HEIGHTS
Red Roof Inn
22 W. Algonquin Rd.
Arlington Heights, IL 60005
Phone: (708) 228-6650
Pet Restrictions: Small pets
Exercise Area for Pets: Yes
Rates: $34.99 to $54.99

VETERINARIANS
**Care Animal Hospital of
Arlington Heights**
1201 E. Palatine Rd.
(312) 394-0455

Civello, Lori A.
2280 W. Nichols Apt. A
(312) 253-1898

BARRINGTON
Barrington Motor Lodge
405 W. Northwest Hwy
Barrington, IL 60010
Phone: (708) 381-2640
Pet Restrictions: Standard room
only
Pet left unattended in room: Yes,
notify desk
Exercise Area for Pets: Nearby
Rates: $54.06

VETERINARIANS
Noyes Animal Hospital
NW Hghwy and Kelsey Rd. 60010
Phone: (708) 381-1920

Veterinary Vision
129 Park Ave. 60010
Phone: (708) 426-8218

BLOOMINGTON
Best Inn of America
1905 W. Market St.
Bloomington, IL 61701
Phone: (309) 827-5333
Pet Restrictions: Small pets only
Pet left unattended in room: Yes
Exercise Area for Pets: Yes
Rates: $31.88 to $38.88

Coachman Inn
408 E. Wash.
Bloomington, IL 61701
Phone: (309) 827-6186
Pet Restrictions: None
Pet left unattended in room: Yes
Exercise Area for Pets: Nearby
Rates: $24 to $28

Days Inn-Airport
1803 E. Empire St.
Bloomington, IL 61701
Phone: (309) 663-1361
Pet Restrictions: $5
Exercise Area for Pets: Yes
Rates: $42 to $47

Ramada Inn
1219 Holiday Lane
Bloomington, IL 61704
Phone: (309) 662-5311

Pet Restrictions: None
Exercise Area for Pets: Yes
Rates: $40 to $77

Ramada Inn
41 Brock Dr.
Bloomington, IL 61701
Phone: (309) 829-7602

Pet Restrictions: $5
Exercise Area for Pets: Nearby
Rates: $35 to $48

VETERINARIANS
Blank-Bottorf, Ruth
1405 Morrissey Dr. 61701
Phone: (309) 662-3241

Brabb, Thea L.
RR #2 61701
Phone: (309) 827-0457

Brunton, Warren R.
510 Guido Dircle 61701
Phone: (309) 662-8535

BRADLEY
Howard Johnson's Ramada
800 N. Kinzie Ave.
Bradley, IL 60915
Phone: (815) 939-3501

Pet Restrictions: None
Exercise Area for Pets: Yes
Rates: $54 to $69

VETERINARIANS
Spurgeon, James J.
Route 50 North
130 South Kinzie 60915
Phone: (815) 932-5011

CARBONDALE
Best Inns of America
1345 E. Main St.
Carbondale, IL 62901
Phone: (618) 529-4801

Pet Restrictions: None
Pet left unattended in room: Yes
Exercise Area for Pets: Yes
Rates: $35.88 to $49.88

Nights Inn
3000 W. Main St.
Carbondale, IL 62901
Phone: (618) 529-2424
Pet Restrictions: None
Exercise Area for Pets: Yes
Rates: $30 to $150

Knight's Court
800 E. Main St.
Carbondale, IL 62901
Phone: (618) 529-1100
Pet Restrictions: None
Exercise Area for Pets: Yes
Rates: $40 to $55

VETERINARIANS
Striegel, Leon F.
RR #7 Striegel Rd. 62901
Phone: (618) 457-4133

CARLINVILLE
Carlinville Motel
Rt. 3, P.O. Box 7
Carlinville, IL 62626
Phone: (217) 854-3201
Pet Restrictions: No barking
Pet left unattended in room: Yes,
    must be present for cleaning
Exercise Area for Pets: Yes
Rates: $28.25 to $49.95

Holiday Inn-Carlinville
P.O. Box 456
Carlinville, IL 62626
Phone: (217) 324-2100
Pet Restrictions: $10
Pet left unattended in room: Yes
Exercise Area for Pets: Nearby
Rates: $44 to $57

CHAMPAIGN
The Chancellor Hotel & Convention Center
1501 S. Neil St.
Champaign, IL 61820
Phone: (217) 352-7891
Pet Restrictions: Caged and quiet
Pet left unattended in room: Yes
Exercise Area for Pets: Nearby
Rates: $59 to $64

Econo Lodge
914 W. Bloomington Rd.
Champaign, IL 61821
Phone: (217) 356-6000
Pet Restrictions: $20 deposit
Exercise Area for Pets: Yes
Rates: $30 to $40

Holiday Inn
1505 N. Neil St.
Champaign, IL 61820
Phone: (217) 359-1601

Pet Restrictions: None
Rates: $50 to $80

La Quinta Motor Inn
1900 Center Dr.
Champaign, IL 61820
Phone: (217) 356-4000

Pet Restrictions: 20 lbs.
Pet left unattended in room: Yes, kennel
Exercise Area for Pets: Nearby
Rates: $47 to $54, $7 extra per person

Red Roof Inn
212 W. Anthony Dr.
Champaign, IL 61820
Phone: (217) 352-0101

Pet Restrictions: None
Pet left unattended in room: Yes
Exercise Area for Pets: Yes
Rates: $29.99 to $50.99

VETERINARIANS
Meadows Animal Hospital
Route 3 61821
Phone: (217) 352-1446

CHICAGO
Essex Inn
800 S. Michigan Ave.
Chicago, IL 60605
Phone: (312) 939-2800

Pet Restrictions: Must use service elevator with pet, sign waiver
Pet left unattended in room: Yes
Exercise Area for Pets: Nearby
Rates: $69.95 to $106

Holiday Inn Mart Plaza
350 N. Orleans
Chicago, IL 60654
Phone: (312) 836-5000

Pet Restrictions: None
Pet left unattended in room: Yes
Exercise Area for Pets: Nearby
Rates: $100 to $180

Marriott
540 N. Michigan Ave.
Chicago, IL 60611
Phone: (312) 836-0100

Pet Restrictions: Under 20 lbs., no barking
Pet left unattended in room: Yes
Exercise Area for Pets: Nearby
Rates: $179 to $209, $99/night weekends

Palmer House & Towers
17 E. Monroe St.
Chicago, IL 60603
Phone: (312) 726-7500

Pet Restrictions: None
Pet left unattended in room: Yes
Exercise Area for Pets: Yes
Rates: $89 to $139

Ritz Carlton
160 E. Pearson St.
Chicago, IL 60611
Phone: (312) 266-1000

Pet Restrictions: None
Pet left unattended in room: No, have grooming kennel during business hours
Rates: $250 to $330

Sheraton Plaza
160 E. Huron St.
Chicago, IL 60611
Phone: (312) 787-2900

Pet Restrictions: None
Rates: $99 to $219

VETERINARIANS
Blum Animal Hospital
3219 North Clark St. 60657
Phone: (312) 327-4446

Bone Animal Hospital
3631 Elston Ave. 60618
Phone: (312) 267-1111

North Center Animal Hospital
1808 West Addison St. 60613
Phone: (312) 327-5050

COLLINSVILLE
Howard Johnson Lodge
301 N. Bluff (Hwy 157)
Collinsville, IL 62234
Phone: (618) 345-1530

Pet Restrictions: None
Pet left unattended in room: Yes
Exercise Area for Pets: Yes
Rates: $35 to $55

Super 8 Motel
2 Gateway Dr.
Collinsville, IL 62234
Phone: (618) 345-8008

Pet Restrictions: Housebroken
Exercise Area for Pets: Yes
Rates: $35 to $40

Pear Tree Inn
552 Ramada Blvd.
Collinsville, IL 62234
Phone: (618) 345-9500

Pet Restrictions: None
Pet left unattended in room: Yes
Exercise Area for Pets: Yes
Rates: $37.95 to $54.95

VETERINARIANS
Douglas Small Animal Hospital
110 North Orient 62234
Phone: (618) 344-4657

Hall, David S.
Route 3, Box 150 62234
Phone: (618) 344-7949

CRYSTAL LAKE
Holiday Inn-Crystal Lake
3 Oaks Rd. & SR 31
Crystal Lake, IL 60014
Phone: (815) 477-7000

Pet Restrictions: Under 18 lbs.
Pet left unattended in room: Yes, if
    in cage
Exercise Area for Pets: Yes
Rates: $59 to $85

VETERINARIANS
Animal Med. Center
41 South Virginia St. 60014
Phone: (815) 455-0770

Krone, James V.
(815) 459-3380

DANVILLE
Redwood Inn
Lynch Rd.
Danville, IL 61832
Phone: (217) 443-3690

Pet Restrictions: None
Exercise Area for Pets: Yes
Rates: $29.95 to $200

Holiday Inn Conf. Resort
US B6W & Wyckles Rd.
Danville, IL 62522
Phone: (217) 422-8800

Pet Restrictions: None
Pet left unattended in room: Yes
Exercise Area for Pets: Yes
Rates: $69 to $79

Ramada Inn
Jct. I 74 Lynch Rd.
Danville, IL 61832
Phone: (217) 446-2400

Pet Restrictions: None
Pet left unattended in room: Yes,
    notify desk
Exercise Area for Pets: Yes
Rates: $42 to $60

VETERINARIANS
East Lake Hospital for Animals
3180 North Vermillion St. 61832
Phone: (217) 446-3010

Hillcrest Hosp. for Small Anim.
3007 East Main 61832
Phone: (217) 442-3088

Vermillion Hillcrest Anim. Hosp.
2722 North Vermillion St. 61832
Phone: (217) 443-0333

DES PLAINES
Comfort Inn - O'Hare
2175 E. Tonky Ave.
Des Plaines, IL 60018
Phone: (708) 635-1300

Pet Restrictions: None
Pet left unattended in room: Yes if
    quiet
Exercise Area for Pets: Yes
Rates: $52.50 to $77

VETERINARIANS
Drazner, Frederick H. Acvim
265 River Road 60016
Phone: (708) 299-0135

Webster, Richards
635 Oakton 60018
Phone: (708) 824-6144

DOWNERS GROVE
Red Roof Inn
1113 Butterfield Rd.
Downers Grove, IL 60515
Phone: (708) 963-4205

Pet Restrictions: Small domestic
    pets
Pet left unattended in room: Yes, no
    housekeeping
Exercise Area for Pets: Yes
Rates: $32 to $57

VETERINARIANS
Arboretum View Animal Hosp.
2551 Warrenville Rd.
(312) 963-0424

Jobe, Jerry
941 63rd St.
(312) 852-1855

EDWARDSVILLE
Knights Inn
P.O. Box 309
Edwardsville, IL
Phone: (618) 656-3000

Pet Restrictions: None
Pet left unattended in room: Yes
Exercise Area for Pets: Yes
Rates: $23 to $56

VETERINARIANS
Helms, Joseph B.
Route 4, Box 4 62025
Phone: (618) 656-4186

EFFINGHAM
Best Inns of America
1209 N. Keller Dr.
Effingham, IL 62401
Phone: (217) 347-5141

Pet Restrictions: Small pets
Pet left unattended in room: Yes, if
    quiet
Exercise Area for Pets: Yes
Rates: $34.88 to $48.88

Best Western
P.O. Box 663
Effingham, IL 62401
Phone: (217) 342-4121

Pet Restrictions: Smoking rooms
    only, small pets
Exercise Area for Pets: Yes
Rates: $35.95 to $56.95

Econo Lodge
SR 32 & 33 at Jct. I 57 & I 70 exit 160
Effingham, IL 62401
Phone: (217) 347-7131

Pet Restrictions: None
Exercise Area for Pets: Yes
Rates: $20 to $48

VETERINARIANS
Slingerland, Marshall V.
202 West Mount Vernon St. 62401
Phone: (618) 483-5225

ELGIN
Howard Johnson Lodge
1585 Dundee Ave.
Elgin, IL 60120
Phone: (708) 695-2100

Pet Restrictions: None
Pet left unattended in room: Yes, if
    in cage
Exercise Area for Pets: Yes
Rates: $54 to $66

VETERINARIANS
Tri-City Animal Hospital
790 Summit 60120
Phone: (708) 741-6770

ELK GROVE VILL.
Holiday Inn of Elk Grove
1000 Busse Rd.
Elk Grove Village, IL 60007
Phone: (708) 437-6010

Pet Restrictions: None
Pet left unattended in room: Yes
Exercise Area for Pets: Yes
Rates: $51 to $78

La Quinta Motor Inn
Elk Grove Village
1900 Oakton St.
Elk Grove Village, IL 60007
Phone: (708) 439-6767

Pet Restrictions: Under 20 lbs.
Exercise Area for Pets: Yes
Rates: $50 to $69

VETERINARIANS
Oakton Animal Clinic
851 Oakton 60007
Phone: (708) 439-8090

FAIRVIEW HEIGHTS

Drury Inn
12 Ludwig Dr.
Fairview Hts., IL 62208
Phone: (618) 398-8530
Pet Restrictions: Must be in cage for
    cleaning
Exercise Area for Pets: Yes
Rates: $50 to $70

Motel 6
1487 N. Henderson St.
Fairview Hts., IL 61401
Phone: (309) 344-2401
Pet Restrictions: Small pets only
Exercise Area for Pets: Yes
Rates: $25.95 and up

VETERINARIANS

Stanley, Susan
701 Lincoln Highway 62208
Phone: (618) 632-6374

FREEPORT

Countryside Motel
1535 W. Galena Ave.
Freeport, IL 61032
Phone: (815) 232-6148
Pet Restrictions: Housebroken
Exercise Area for Pets: Yes
Rates: $25 to $50

Holiday Inn
1¼ mile East on US 20
Freeport, IL 61032
Phone: (815) 235-3121
Pet Restrictions: None
Exercise Area for Pets: Yes
Rates: $48 to $61

GALESBURG

Jumer's Continental Inn
E. Main St.
Galesburg, IL 61401
Phone: (309) 343-7151
Pet Restrictions: $25 refund. deposit
Pet left unattended in room: Yes
Exercise Area for Pets: Yes
Rates: $63 to $80

Ramada Inn
29 Public Sq.
Galesburg, IL 61401
Phone: (309) 343-9161
Pet Restrictions: None
Exercise Area for Pets: Nearby
Rates: $45 to $55

GENESEO

Royal Motel
RR4
Geneseo, IL 61254
Phone: (309) 944-3192
Pet Restrictions: None
Exercise Area for Pets: Yes
Rates: $21 to $27

GLENVIEW

Radisson Suite Hotel Glenview
1400 N. Milwaukee Ave.
Glenview, IL 60025
Phone: (708) 803-9800
Pet Restrictions: Yes

VETERINARIANS

Glen Oak Dog and Cat Hospital
330 Waukegan Rd. 60025
Phone: (708) 729-5200

Glenview Animal Hospital
2400 Waukegan Rd. 60025
Phone: (708) 724-4812

GRAYVILLE

Best Western Windsor Oaks Inn
2200 S. Court St.
Grayville, IL 62844
Phone: (618) 375-7930
Pet Restrictions: $50 refund.
    deposit, $5/night
Pet left unattended in room: Yes
Exercise Area for Pets: Nearby
Rates: $55 to $65

GREENVILLE

Best Western Country View Inn
RR 4, Box 221
Greenville, IL 62246
Phone: (618) 664-3030
Pet Restrictions: $2/night/pet
Pet left unattended in room: Yes
    with approval
Exercise Area for Pets: Yes
Rates: $32 to $49

Budget Host Bel Air
Rt. 4 Box 183
Greenville, IL 62246
Phone: (618) 664-1950
Pet Restrictions: $5/night
Exercise Area for Pets: Yes
Rates: $34 to $43

HOFFMAN ESTATES
Red Roof Inn
2500 Massell Rd.
Hoffman Estates, IL 60195
Phone: (708) 885-7877
Pet Restrictions: None
Exercise Area for Pets: Yes
Rates: $33 to $55

VETERINARIANS

Harper Animal Hospital
1460 W. Algonquin Rd.
(312) 358-6767

Hoffman Estates Animal Clinic
1056 W. Golf Rd.
(312) 310-8668

HILLSBORO
Countryside Inn
P.O. Box 386
Hillsboro, IL 62049
Phone: (217) 532-6176
Pet Restrictions: Call first

HOMEWOOD
Best Western-Homewood
17400 S. Halsted St.
Homewood, IL 60430
Phone: (708) 957-1600
Pet Restrictions: None
Exercise Area for Pets: Nearby
Rates: $53 to $88

VETERINARIANS

Flossmor Animal Hospital Ltd.
19581 Governors Highway 60430
Phone: (708) 798-9030

Mack, William J.
1636 Idlewild Lane 60430
Phone: (708) 375-2433

JACKSONVILLE
Holiday Inn
1717 W. Morton Ave.
Jacksonville, IL 62650
Phone: (217) 245-9571
Pet Restrictions: Small pets only
Pet left unattended in room: Yes
Exercise Area for Pets: Yes
Rates: $48 to $107

Star Lite Motel
1910 W. Morton Ave.
Jacksonville, IL 62650
Phone: (217) 245-7184
Pet Restrictions: None
Pet left unattended in room: Yes but
   notify desk
Exercise Area for Pets: Yes
Rates: $29 and up

JOLIET
Fireside Resort
4200 W. Jeff.
Joliet, IL 60435
Phone: (815) 725-0111
Pet Restrictions: $25 refund. deposit
Exercise Area for Pets: Yes
Rates: $34.95 to $54.95

Red Roof Inn
2500 Massell Rd.
Joliet, IL 60436
Phone: (815) 741-2304
Pet Restrictions: None
Pet left unattended in room: Yes, no
   housekeeping
Exercise Area for Pets: Yes
Rates: $33.99 to $49

VETERINARIANS

**Abou-Youssef, Mamdouh H.
Essington Road Animal Hospital**
1943 Essington Rd. 60435
Phone: (815) 439-2323

Frederickson, Jay
1807 Plainfield Rd. 60435
Phone: (815) 729-1155

KANKAKEE
Days Inn
1975 E. Court St.
Kankakee, IL 60901
Phone: (815) 939-7171
Pet Restrictions: $50 refund.
   deposit, $6/pet/night
Exercise Area for Pets: Nearby
Rates: $26 to $65

VETERINARIANS

Murry, Frank A.
Phone: (815) 933-8831

LANSING

Red Roof Inn
2450 East 173rd St.
Lansing, IL 60438
Phone: (708) 895-9570

Pet Restrictions: None
Pet left unattended in room: Yes
Exercise Area for Pets: Yes
Rates: $34 to $53

VETERINARIANS

Ridge Animal Hospital
3667 Ridge Road
(312) 474-3100

LITCHFIELD

Best Western Gardens
I 55 Exit 52 at Jct. US 66 & 16
Litchfield, IL 62056
Phone: (217) 324-2181

Pet Restrictions: $5/dog/day, under 15 lbs.
Exercise Area for Pets: Yes
Rates: $35 to $50

MACOMB

Holiday Inn
1400 N. Lafayette
Macomb, IL 61455
Phone: (309) 833-5511

Pet Restrictions: None
Pet left unattended in room: Yes, notify desk
Exercise Area for Pets: Yes
Rates: $47 to $65

VETERINARIANS

Larson, Thomas
230 West Washington 61455
Phone: (309) 833-2365

MALTESON

Hampton Inn
5200 W. Lincoln Hwy
Malteson, IL 60443
Phone: (708) 481-3900

Pet Restrictions: None
Pet left unattended in room: Yes, well behaved
Exercise Area for Pets: Nearby
Rates: $54 to $67

MARION

Holiday Inn
P.O. Box 609
Marion, IL 62959
Phone: (618) 997-2326

Pet Restrictions: None
Pet left unattended in room: Yes if quiet
Exercise Area for Pets: Yes
Rates: $42 to $68

Motel 6
P.O. Box 1646
Marion, IL 26959
Phone: (618) 993-2631

Pet Restrictions: None
Exercise Area for Pets: Yes
Rates: $28.03 to $40.99

MOLINE

Exel Inn of Moline
2501 52nd Ave.
Moline, IL 61265
Phone: (309) 797-5580

Pet Restrictions: None
Exercise Area for Pets: Yes
Rates: $30.99 to $46.99

Holiday Inn-Airport Conv. Ctr.
6902 27th St.
Moline, IL 61265
Phone: (309) 762-8811

Pet Restrictions: 329 rooms in separate building
Exercise Area for Pets: Yes
Rates: $48 to $90

Ramada Inn
Airport Road
Moline, IL 61265
Phone: (309) 797-1211

Pet Restrictions: $10 deposit
Exercise Area for Pets: Yes
Rates: $48.75 to $52.75

VETERINARIANS

River Bend Animal Clinic Pc
1500 48th St. 61265
Phone: (309) 764-2471

Greiner, Thomas Paul
3113 41st Street 61265
Phone: (309) 762-9474

Wood, James D.
3113 41st Street 61265
Phone: (309) 762-9474

MORRIS

Holiday Inn
NW of I 80 exit 112 on SR 47
Morris, IL 60450
Phone: (815) 942-6600
Pet Restrictions: Smooking rooms
    only
Pet left unattended in room: Yes, if
    quiet
Exercise Area for Pets: Yes
Rates: $40.50 to $66

VETERINARIANS

Pine Bluff Animal Hospital
7995 East Pine Bluff Rd. 60450
Phone: (815) 942-5365

MT. VERNON

Drury Inn
I 64 & Rt. 15
Mt. Vernon, IL 62864
Phone: (618) 244-4550
Pet Restrictions: None
Exercise Area for Pets: Yes
Rates: $35 to $55

Ramada Hotel
222 Potomac Blvd., P.O. Box 2148
Mt. Vernon, IL 62864
Phone: (618) 244-7100
Pet Restrictions: $10/night
Exercise Area for Pets: Yes
Rates: $44 to $70

MURPHYSBORO

Motel Murphysboro
100 N 2nd St.
Murphysboro, IL 62966
Phone: (618) 687-2345
Pet Restrictions: Housebroken pets
    only
Exercise Area for Pets: Yes
Rates: $30.50 to $40

NAPERVILLE

Exel Inn of Naperville
1585 N. Naperville Rd., Wheaton Rd.
Phone: (708) 357-0022
Pet Restrictions: Contained
Exercise Area for Pets: Yes
Rates: $36.99 to $46.99

Hampton Inn
1087 Diehl Rd.
Naperville, IL 60544
Phone: (708) 505-1400
Pet Restrictions: Call first

Red Roof Inn
1698 W. Diehl Rd.
Naperville, IL 60563
Phone: (708) 369-2500
Pet Restrictions: None
Pet left unattended in room: Yes, no
    housekeeping
Exercise Area for Pets: Yes
Rates: $36 to $54

VETERINARIANS

Dupage River Animal Hosp.
315 South Main St. 60540
Phone: (708) 355-6692

Kilburn, Richard F.
2200 South Washington St. 60565
Phone: (708) 983-5551

NASHVILLE

Nauvoo Village Inn
P.O. Box 191
Nashville, IL 6354
Phone: (217) 453-6634
Pet Restrictions: None
Exercise Area for Pets: Yes
Rates: $24.50 to $56.75

US Inn
I 64 Exit 50
Nashville, IL 62263
Phone: (618) 478-5341
Pet Restrictions: $5 deposit
Pet left unattended in room: Yes
Exercise Area for Pets: Yes
Rates: $27 to $70

NORTHBROOK

Ramada Inn-Northbrook
2875 Milwaukee Ave.
Northbrook, IL 60062
Phone: (708) 298-2525
Pet Restrictions: None
Exercise Area for Pets: Nearby
Rates: $48 to $55

Sheraton North Shore Inn
933 Shokie Blvd.
Northbrook, IL 60062
Phone: (708) 498-6500
Pet Restrictions: Yes

Red Roof Inn
340 Waukegan Rd.
Northbrook, IL 60062
Phone: (708) 205-1755
Pet Restrictions: None
Pet left unattended in room: Yes
Exercise Area for Pets: Yes
Rates: $35 to $55

VETERINARIANS

Countryside Animal Clinic
4091 Dundee Rd. 60062
Phone: (708) 498-5567

Glencoe Animal Hospital Ltd.
1820 Frontage Rd. 60062
Phone: (708) 835-1302

OAK BROOK TERR.

Comfort Suites
17 W. 445 Roosevelt Rd.
Oak Brook Terrace, IL 60181
Phone: (708) 916-1000
Pet Restrictions: Yes

OAK BROOK

Marriott Oak Brook Hotel
1401 W. 22nd St.
Oak Brook, IL 60521
Phone: (708) 573-8555
Pet Restrictions: Small pets only
Pet left unattended in room: Yes, if
   in cage
Exercise Area for Pets: Yes
Rates: $59 to $135

Stouffer Oak Brook Hotel
2100 Spring Rd.
Oak Brook, IL 60521
Phone: (708) 573-2800
Pet Restrictions: Yes

PEKIN

Pekin Inn
2801 E. Court St.
Pekin, IL 61554
Phone: (309) 347-5533
Pet Restrictions: If paying cash $50
   deposit, credit cards,
   responsible for damages
Pet left unattended in room: Yes
Exercise Area for Pets: Yes
Rates: $42 to $55

VETERINARIANS

Pekin Animal Hospital
221 Margaret 61554
Phone: (309) 347-6674

PEORIA

Holiday Inn-Brandywine
4400 N. Brandywine Dr.
Peoria, IL 61614
Phone: (309) 686-8000
Pet Restrictions: $100 refund.
   deposit
Pet left unattended in room: Yes
Exercise Area for Pets: Yes
Rates: $65 and up

Jumer's Castle Lodge
117 N. Western Ave.
Peoria, IL 61604
Phone: (309) 673-8040
Pet Restrictions: Extra charge
   depends on pet
Pet left unattended in room: Yes
Rates: $65 to $150

Red Roof Inn
4031 N. War Memorial Dr.
Peoria, IL 61614
Phone: (309) 685-3911
Pet Restrictions: Small & house
   trained
Rates: $59.99 to $40.99

VETERINARIANS

Whitney Veterinary Hospital
4707 North Sheridan Rd. 61614
Phone: (309) 685-4707

Earp, Norman L.
6115 North Sheridan 61614
Phone: (309) 691-3181

Mills, Jeffrey L.
1217 West Margaret 61604
Phone: (309) 682-6665

PERU

Days Inn
P.O. Box 626
Peru, IL 61354
Phone: (815) 224-1060
Pet Restrictions: Must be leashed at
   all times
Pet left unattended in room: Yes
Exercise Area for Pets: Yes
Rates: $44 to $29.95

PINCKNEYVILLE
Fountain Motel
112 S. Main St.
Pinckneyville IL 62274
Phone: (618) 357-2128

Pet Restrictions: None
Exercise Area for Pets: Yes
Rates: $32 to $34

PRINCETON
Lincoln Inn
P.O. Box 382
Princeton, IL 61356
Phone: (815) 875-3371

Pet Restrictions: None
Exercise Area for Pets: Yes
Rates: $32 to $44

PROSPECT HTS.
Forest Lodge
1246 S. River Rd.
Prospect Hts., IL 60070
Phone: (708) 537-2000

Pet Restrictions: Smaller pets
Pet left unattended in room: Yes
Exercise Area for Pets: Yes
Rates: $29 to $150

QUINCY
Quincy Travelodge
200 S. 3rd St.
Quincy, IL 62301
Phone: (217) 222-5620

Pet Restrictions: None
Exercise Area for Pets: Nearby
Rates: $39 to $44

Klingele Veterinary Clinic
4507 Broadway 62301
Phone: (217) 223-0187

ROCKFORD
Alpine Inn
4404 E. State St.
Rockford, IL 61108
Phone: (815) 399-1890

Pet Restrictions: None
Exercise Area for Pets: Yes
Rates: $31 to $60

Best Western Colonial Inn Motor Lodge
4850 E. State St.
Rockford, IL 61108
Phone: (815) 398-5050

Pet Restrictions: Small pets
Pet left unattended in room: Yes
Exercise Area for Pets: Yes
Rates: $54 to $87

Exel Inn
220 S. Lyford Rd.
Rockford, IL 61108
Phone: (815) 332-4915

Pet Restrictions: None
Exercise Area for Pets: Nearby
Rates: $32.99 to $49.99

Ramada Inn
7550 E. State St.
Rockford, IL 61125
Phone: (815) 398-2200

Pet Restrictions: Small pets only
Pet left unattended in room: Yes
Rates: $61 to $54

Red Roof Inn
7434 E. State St.
Rockford, IL 61108
Phone: (815) 398-9750

Pet Restrictions: None
Pet left unattended in room: Yes
Exercise Area for Pets: Yes
Rates: $33.99 to $57.99

Stephenson Vet. Hosp. Ltd
1211 11th St. 61104
Phone: (815) 963-9685

Helland, David R.
4502 Charles St. 61108
Phone: (815) 399-4808

Thompson, Cary D.
1715 Appaloosa Circle 61107
Phone: (815) 398-4410

ROLLING MEADOWS
Comfort Inn
2801 Algonquin Rd.
Rolling Meadows, IL 60008
Phone: (708) 259-5900

Pet Restrictions: None
Pet left unattended in room: Yes, conditional
Exercise Area for Pets: Nearby
Rates: $70 to $90

ILLINOIS — HOTELS (continued)

VETERINARIANS
McGraw, Jerry
2350 Hicks Rd. 60008
Phone: (312) 577-9044

SALEM
Continental Motel
1600 E. Main, P.O. Box 370
Salem, IL 62881
Phone: (618) 548-3090
Pet Restrictions: House trained
Pet left unattended in room: Yes
Exercise Area for Pets: Yes
Rates: $18.99 to $22.99

Motel Lakewood
1500 E. Main St.
Salem, IL 62881
Phone: (618) 548-2785
Pet Restrictions: None
Exercise Area for Pets: Yes
Rates: $18.90 to $28.90

SCHAUMBERG
Drury Inn
600 N. Martingate Rd.
Schaumberg, IL 60173
Phone: (708) 517-7737
Pet Restrictions: None
Exercise Area for Pets: Yes
Rates: $71 to $60

Schaumberg Marriott Hotel
50 N. Martingate Rd.
Schaumberg, IL 60173
Phone: (708) 240-0100
Pet Restrictions: No large dogs, only
 in certain rooms
Exercise Area for Pets: Yes
Rates: $135 and up

VETERINARIANS
Fink, Debra L.
508 Tebay Place 60194
Phone: (708) 310-8668

SKOKIE
Howard Johnson Hotel
9333 Shokie Boulevard
Skokie, IL 60077
Phone: (708) 679-4200
Pet Restrictions: None
Exercise Area for Pets: Yes
Rates: $81 to $106

VETERINARIANS
North Shore Veterinary Clinic
5225 Golf Road 60077
Phone: (708) 966-3080

Riser Animal Hospital
5335 Touhy Ave. 60077
Phone: (708) 673-2520

Siwek, Share
5138 West Morse Ave. 60077
Phone: (708) 498-7985

SOUTH HOLLAND
Budgetel Inn
17225 S. Halsted
South Holland, IL 60473
Phone: (708) 596-8700
Pet Restrictions: None
Exercise Area for Pets: Yes
Rates: $39.95 to $55.95

Red Roof Inn
17301 S. Halsted Rd.
South Holland, IL 60473
Phone: (708) 331-1621,
 (800) 843-7663
Pet Restrictions: None
Pet left unattended in room: Yes
Exercise Area for Pets: Yes
Rates: $34.99 to $48.99

VETERINARIANS
Dodson, Robert C.
41 West 168th Street 60473
Phone: (708) 333-2444

SPRINGFIELD
Best Inns of America
500 N. First St.
Springfield, IL 62504
Phone: (217) 522-1100
Pet Restrictions: None
Pet left unattended in room: Yes
Rates: $37.69 to $55.88

Best Western Sky Harbor Inn
1701 N. Walnut St.
Springfield, IL 62702
Phone: (217) 753-3446
Pet Restrictions: None
Pet left unattended in room: Yes
Exercise Area for Pets: Yes
Rates: $53 to $58

ILLINOIS — HOTELS (continued)

Days Inn
3000 Stevenson Dr.
Springfield, IL 62703
Phone: (217) 529-0171
Pet Restrictions: Smoking rooms
    only
Pet left unattended in room: Yes
Exercise Area for Pets: Yes
Rates: $38 to $45

Drury Inn
3190 S. Dirksen Pkwy
Springfield, IL 62703
Phone: (217) 529-9100
Pet Restrictions: None
Pet left unattended in room: Yes
Exercise Area for Pets: Yes
Rates: $67 to $75

Holiday Inn-East Conf. Center
Howard Johnson Lodge
3100 S. Dirksen Pkwy
Springfield, IL 62703
Phone: (217) 529-7171
Pet Restrictions: Small-medium size
Exercise Area for Pets: Yes
Rates: $48 to $150

Mansion View Motel
529 S. 4th St.
Springfield, IL 62701
Phone: (217) 544-7411,
    (800) 252-1083 (in IL)
Pet Restrictions: None
Pet left unattended in room: Yes
Exercise Area for Pets: Nearby
Rates: $38 to $50

Red Roof Inn
3200 Singer Ave.
Springfield, IL 62703
Phone: (217) 753-4302
Pet Restrictions: Reservation required
Pet left unattended in room: Yes
Exercise Area for Pets: Yes
Rates: $29.99 to $70

Capitol-Illini Vet. Svcs. Ltd.
1711 Wabash Ave. 62704
Phone: (217) 546-1541

Coble Animal Hospital
2828 South MacArthur Blvd. 62704
Phone: (217) 789-4200

TAYLORVILLE

29 West Motel
709 Springfield Rd.
Taylorville, IL 62568
Phone: (217) 824-2216
Pet Restrictions: $2/night
Pet left unattended in room: Yes
Exercise Area for Pets: Yes
Rates: $27 to $40

Etheridge, R. Keith
1604 West Spressor 62568
Phone: (217) 824-5512

URBANA

Best Western
P.O. Box 605
Urbana, IL 61801-0605
Phone: (217) 367-8331
Pet Restrictions: Not in suites
Pet left unattended in room: Yes
Exercise Area for Pets: Yes
Rates: $49 to $100

Jumer's Castle Lodge
Lincoln Sq. at Race & Green St.
Urbana, IL 61801
Phone: (217) 384-8800
Pet Restrictions: Small pets, $25
    refund. deposit
Exercise Area for Pets: Nearby
Rates: $77 to $145

University of Illinois
Veterinary Med. Teaching Hosp.
1008 West Hazelwood Dr. 61801
Phone: (217) 333-5300

Beaumont, RE
1304 North Cunningham 61801
Phone: (217) 356-6481

Healey, Joanne C.
1711 East Florida Ave.
Phone: (217) 352-2559

VANDALIA

Marke Inn
US 51 just N of Jct. I 70, exit 63
Vandalia, IL 62471
Phone: (618) 283-4400
Pet Restrictions: None
Pet left unattended in room: Yes
Exercise Area for Pets: Yes
Rates: $35 to $39

Vandalia Travelodge
1500 N 6th St.
Vandalia, IL 62471
Phone: (618) 283-2363

Pet Restrictions: None
Pet left unattended in room: Yes
Exercise Area for Pets: Yes
Rates: $32 to $45

WANKEGEN

Best Inns of America
31 N Green Bay Rd.
Wankegen, IL 60085
Phone: (312) 336-9000

Pet Restrictions: Small pets under
50 lbs. (exceptions)
Exercise Area for Pets: Yes
Rates: $41.88 to $65.88

INDIANA — HOTELS

ANDERSON

Best Inns
5706 Scatterfield Rd.
Anderson, IN 46013
Phone: (317) 644-2000,
(800) BEST-INN
Pet Restrictions: Small pets
Pet left unattended in room: Yes,
well behaved
Exercise Area for Pets: Yes
Rates: $36.88 to $50.88

Best Western Sterling House
5901 Scatterfield Rd.
Anderson, IN 76013
Phone: (317) 649-0451,
(800) 528-1234
Pet Restrictions: $25 deposit
Exercise Area for Pets: Yes

Lees Inn
2114 E. 59th St.
Anderson, Indiana 46013
Phone: (317) 649-2500,
(800) 733-5337
Pet Restrictions: Sign waiver
Pet left unattended in room: Yes
Exercise Area for Pets: Nearby
Rates: $58 to $72

Mark Motor Inn
2400 St. Rd. 9
Anderson, IN 46013
Phone: (317) 642-9966
Pet Restrictions: $10
Exercise Area for Pets: Yes
Rates: $31 to $45

VETERINARIANS

Lee, G. Timothy
3405 State Road 9 North 46012
Phone: (317) 649-5218

BEDFORD

Mark III Motel
1709 M St.
Bedford, IN 47421
Phone: (812) 275-5935
Pet Restrictions: None
Pet left unattended in room: Yes
Exercise Area for Pets: Yes
Rates: $32

VETERINARIANS

Bedford Veterinary Med Ctr.
515 Oolitic Road 47421
Phone: (812) 275-7501

BLOOMINGTON

Motel 6
1800 N. Walnut
Bloomington, IN 47401
Phone: (812) 332-0820
Pet Restrictions: Certain rooms
Exercise Area for Pets: Nearby
Rates: $27.99 and up

VETERINARIANS

Hull, Karen Lee
1700 W. That Rd 47401
Phone: (812) 334-1400

Koeppen, Harry E.
P.O. Box 1480
115 North Smith Road 47402
Phone: (812) 339-6115

Webb, Edward M.
115 North Smith Rd. 47402
Phone: (812) 339-6115

CLARKSVILLE

Lakeview Hotel & Resort
505 Marriott Dr.
Clarksville, IN 47130
Phone: (812) 283-4411,
(800) 544-7075, (800) 824-7740
(in Indiana)
Pet Restrictions: $10 deposit
Exercise Area for Pets: Yes
Rates: $54 and up

CLOVERDALE

Holiday Inn
Jct. I 70 & US 231, exit 41
Cloverdale, IN 46120
Phone: (317) 795-3500,
(800) HOLIDAY
Pet Restrictions: None
Pet left unattended in room: Yes, no
maid service, notify desk
Exercise Area for Pets: Yes
Rates: $46 to $65

COLUMBIA CITY

Lees Inn
235 Frontage Rd.
Columbia City, IN 46725
Phone: (219) 244-5300,
(800) 733-5337
Pet Restrictions: Sign waiver
Exercise Area for Pets: Yes
Rates: $49 to $97

COLUMBUS
Days Inn of Columbus
3445 Jonathan Moore Pike
Columbus, IN 47201
Phone: (812) 376-9951
Pet Restrictions: None
Pet left unattended in room: Yes
Exercise Area for Pets: Yes
Rates: $47 to $62.95

Holiday Inn
Jct. SR 46 & I 65, exit 65
Columbus, IN 47201
Phone: (812) 372-1541,
    (800) HOLIDAY
Pet Restrictions: None
Pet left unattended in room: Yes
Exercise Area for Pets: Yes
Rates: $80 to $90

Knights Inn
101 Carrie La.
Columbus, IN 47201
Phone: (812) 378-3100,
    (800) 843-5644
Pet Restrictions: Very small
Pet left unattended in room: Yes
Exercise Area for Pets: Yes
Rates: $34 to $45

VETERINARIANS
Bohm, Paul J.
8700 North US 31 47201
Phone: (812) 526-2697

CRAWFORDSVILLE
Holiday Inn
2500 N. Lafayette Rd.
Crawfordsville, IN 47933
Phone: (317) 362-8700,
    (800) HOLIDAY
Pet Restrictions: None
Pet left unattended in room: Yes
Exercise Area for Pets: Yes
Rates: $50 to $60

ELKHART
Knights Inn
52188 SR 19
Elkhart, IN 46514
Phone: (219) 264-4262
Pet Restrictions: $50 deposit
Exercise Area for Pets: Yes
Rates: $43.95 to $54.95

Red Roof Inn
2902 Lassopolis St.
Elkhart, IN 46515
Phone: (219) 262-3691
Pet Restrictions: None
Pet left unattended in room: Yes
Exercise Area for Pets: Yes
Rates: $35 to $49

VETERINARIANS
Animal Aid Clinic South
24345 Mishawaka Rd.,
County Rd. 30 46517
Phone: (219) 875-5102

Animal Care Clinic
26245 County Rd. 6 East 46514
Phone: (219) 264-9521

Conrad Animal Hospital
3992 East Jackson Blvd 46516
Phone: (219) 293-4555

EVANSVILLE
Howard Johnson
2508 Business 41N
Evansville IN 47711
Phone: (812) 425-1092
Pet Restrictions: None
Pet left unattended in room: Yes
Exercise Area for Pets: Yes
Rates: $33 to $43.95

Regal 8 Inn
4201 US 41N
Evansville, IN 47711
Phone: (812) 424-6431
Pet Restrictions: 1 small pet
Pet left unattended in room: Yes
Exercise Area for Pets: Yes
Rates: $33.12

VETERINARIANS
Greenbrier Animal Hospital
4307 North Green River Rd. 47715
Phone: (812) 479-0867

North Park Veterinary Clinic
2613 North First Ave. 47710
Phone: (812) 426-1435

Hodoval, Leland F.
4705 Bellemeade Ave. 47715
Phone: (812) 477-8866

FORT WAYNE
Days Inn
3527 W. Coliseum Blvd.
Fort Wayne, IN 46808
Phone: (219) 482-4511
Pet Restrictions: None
Pet left unattended in room: Yes
Exercise Area for Pets: Yes
Rates: $27 to $39

Red Roof Inn
2920 Goshen Rd.
Fort Wayne, IN 46808
Phone: (219) 484-8641

Pet Restrictions: None
Pet left unattended in room: Yes
Exercise Area for Pets: Yes
Rates: $35.99 to $44

VETERINARIANS
Southtown Veterinary Hospital
7130 South Calhoun St. 46807
Phone: (219) 745-4967

St. Joe Center Vet. Hosp., Inc.
5812 Maplecrest Rd. 46835
Phone: (219) 485-7372

Waynedale Animal Clinic
6221 Bluffton Rd. 46809
Phone: (219) 747-4196

FRANKLIN
Days Inn
2180 E. King St.
Franklin, IN 46131
Phone: (317) 736-8000

Pet Restrictions: $6 fee; sign waiver
Pet left unattended in room: Yes
Exercise Area for Pets: Yes
Rates: $47 to $55

GOSHEN
Holiday Inn
US 33 Lincolnway E.
Goshen, IN 46526
Phone: (219) 533-9551,
(800) HOLIDAY

Pet Restrictions: None
Pet left unattended in room: Yes
Exercise Area for Pets: Yes
Rates: $66

VETERINARIANS
Maplecrest Animal Hospital
1214 North Main St. 46526
Phone: (219) 543-2441

Kaeser, Terrance J.
2806 South Main St. 46526
Phone: (219) 533-0535

GREENCASTLE
College Castle Motel
315 Bloomington St.
Greencastle, IN 46135
Phone: (317) 653-4167
Pet Restrictions: None
Pet left unattended in room: Yes
Exercise Area for Pets: Yes
Rates: $22 to $30

GREENFIELD
Lees Inn
2270 N. State St.
Greenfield, IN 46140
Phone: (317) 462-7112
Pet Restrictions: Under 20 lbs.
Pet left unattended in room: Yes
Exercise Area for Pets: Yes
Rates: $49 to $56

GREENSBURG
Lees Inn
RR 1 Box 60A
Greensburg, IN 47240
Phone: (812) 663-9998
Pet Restrictions: Sign waiver
Pet left unattended in room: Yes
Exercise Area for Pets: Yes
Rates: $56 to $88

INDIANAPOLIS
Budgetel Inn
2650 Exec. Dr.
Indianapolis, IN 46241
Phone: (317) 244-8100
Pet Restrictions: None
Pet left unattended in room: Yes, no
housekeeping
Exercise Area for Pets: Yes
Rates: $39.95 to $46.95

Comfort Inn
5040 S. East St.
Indianapolis, IN 46227
Phone: (317) 783-6711
Pet Restrictions: None
Pet left unattended in room: Yes
Exercise Area for Pets: Yes
Rates: $43 to $60

Days Inn East
7314 E. 21st St.
Indianapolis, IN 46219
Phone: (317) 359-5500
Pet Restrictions: None
Pet left unattended in room: Yes
Exercise Area for Pets: Yes
Rates: $41

INDIANA — HOTELS (continued)

Days Inn-South
450 Bixler Rd.
Indianapolis, IN 46227
Phone: (317) 788-0811

Pet Restrictions: $5 fee
Pet left unattended in room: Yes,
   not after 9 pm
Exercise Area for Pets: Yes
Rates: $45 to $50

Drury Inn-Indianapolis
9320 N. Mich. Rd.
Indianapolis, IN 46268
Phone: (317) 876-9777

Pet Restrictions: None
Pet left unattended in room: Yes,
   must be caged
Exercise Area for Pets: Yes
Rates: $48 to $60

Holiday Inn-Airport
2501 S. High School Rd.
Indianapolis, IN 46241
Phone: (317) 244-6861,
   (800) HOLIDAY

Pet Restrictions: Under 25 lbs.
Exercise Area for Pets: Yes
Rates: $69 to $96

Holiday Inn-East
6990 E. 21st St.
Indianapolis, IN 46219
Phone: (317) 359-5341,
   (800) HOLIDAY

Pet Restrictions: None
Pet left unattended in room: Yes
Exercise Area for Pets: Yes
Rates: $49.41 to $71

Howard Johnson Lodge
2602 North High School Road
Indianapolis, IN 46224
Phone: (317) 291-8800

Pet Restrictions: None
Rates: $53 and up

Howard Johnson Lodge
2141 North Post Road
Indianapolis, IN 46219
Phone: (317) 897-2000

Pet Restrictions: Small pets; $20
   deposit; sign a waiver
Pet left unattended in room: Yes
Exercise Area for Pets: Yes
Rates: $49 to $65

Indianapolis Motor Speedway
4400 W. 16th St.
Indianapolis, IN 46224
Phone: (317) 241-2500

Pet Restrictions: None
Pet left unattended in room: Yes
Exercise Area for Pets: Yes
Rates: $49 to $66

Knights Inn-North
9402 Hauer Way
Indianapolis, IN 46240
Phone: (317) 848-2423

Pet Restrictions: Small animals
Pet left unattended in room: Yes
Exercise Area for Pets: Yes
Rates: $36.25 to $53.85

Knights Inn-South
4909 Knights Way
Indianapolis, IN 46217
Phone: (317) 788-0125

Pet Restrictions: $5; on leash; no
   cages
Pet left unattended in room: Yes
Exercise Area for Pets: Yes
Rates: $31 to $41

Knights Inn
7101 E. 21st St.
Indianapolis, IN 46219
Phone: (317) 353-8484

Pet Restrictions: $5/day
Pet left unattended in room: Yes
Exercise Area for Pets: Yes
Rates: $30 to $42

La Quinta Inn Airport
5316 W. Southern Ave.
Indianapolis, IN 46241
Phone: (317) 247-4281

Pet Restrictions: Small pets
Exercise Area for Pets: Yes
Rates: $55 to $62

Marriott Hotel
7202 E. 21st St.
Indianapolis, IN 46219
Phone: (317) 352-1231

Pet Restrictions: Sign waiver
Pet left unattended in room: Yes,
   inform housekeepers
Exercise Area for Pets: Yes
Rates: $59 to $130

INDIANA — HOTELS (continued)

Pickwick Farms
Short-Term Apartments
9300 North Ditch Rd.
Indianapolis, IN 46260
Phone: (800) 869-RENT
Fax: (317) 879-7380
Contact: Eva S. Bogar, Director of Sales

Pet Restrictions: None
Pet left unattended in room: No policy
Exercise Area for Pets: Yes

Red Roof Inn-North
9520 Valpariso Ct.
Indianapolis, IN 46268
Phone: (317) 872-3030

Pet Restrictions: None
Pet left unattended in room: Yes
Exercise Area for Pets: Yes
Rates: $30.99 to $56.99

Red Roof Inn-South
5221 Victory Dr.
Jct. Emerson Ave. & I 465
Indianapolis, IN 46203
Phone: (317) 788-9551

Pet Restrictions: None
Pet left unattended in room: Yes
Exercise Area for Pets: Yes
Rates: $36 to $56

The Residence Inn by Marriott
3553 Founders Rd.
Indianapolis, IN 46268
Phone: (317) 872-0462,
(800) 331-3131

Pet Restrictions: $7/night
Pet left unattended in room: Yes, no
maid service
Exercise Area for Pets: Yes
Rates: $89 to $109

Super 8 Motel
4530 S. Emerson Ave.
Indianapolis, IN 46203
Phone: (317) 788-0955

Pet Restrictions: $15 deposit
Exercise Area for Pets: Yes
Rates: $33.88 to $63.88

Michigan Road Animal Hosp.
7720 North Michigan Rd. 46268
Phone: (317) 291-3932

Shelby Street Animal Clinic
3315 Shelby Street 46227
Phone: (317) 787-5323

The Broad Ripple Animal Clinic
6232 North College 46220
Phone: (317) 257-5334

JASPER
Days Inn Jasper
P.O. Box 762
Jasper, IN 47546
Phone: (812) 482-6000

Pet Restrictions: $5; small pets
Exercise Area for Pets: Yes
Rates: $42 to $55

JEFFERSONVILLE
Ramada Hotel
700 W. Riverside Dr.
Jeffersonville, IN 47130
Phone: (812) 284-6711,
(800) 537-3612

Pet Restrictions: None
Pet left unattended in room: Yes
Exercise Area for Pets: Yes
Rates: $57 to $65

Eastside Animal Hospital
1623 East 10th Street 47130
Phone: (812) 282-3855

Spieth, Emmet W.
360 Eastern Blvd. 47130
Phone: (812) 283-8307

KETCHUM
River St. Inn
100 River St. W
Ketchum, IN 83353
Phone: (208) 726-3611

Pet Restrictions: None
Pet left unattended in room: Yes, if
caged
Exercise Area for Pets: Yes
Rates: $115 to $155

LAFAYETTE/
W. LAFAYETTE
Days Inn of Lafayette
400 Sagamore Pkwy S.
Lafayette, IN 47905
Phone: (317) 447-4131

Pet Restrictions: None
Pet left unattended in room: Yes
Exercise Area for Pets: Yes
Rates: $45 to $62

Holiday Inn
Jct. I 65 & SR 43N
W. Lafayette, IN 47906
Phone: (317) 567-2131,
(800) HOLIDAY

Pet Restrictions: None
Exercise Area for Pets: Yes
Rates: $55 to $70

Howard Johnson Plaza Hotel
4343 SR 26 East
Lafayette, IN 47905
Phone: (317) 447-0575

Pet Restrictions: None
Pet left unattended in room: Yes
Exercise Area for Pets: Yes
Rates: $77 to $84

Red Roof Inn
4201 SR 26 E
Lafayette, IN 47905
Phone: (317) 448-4671

Pet Restrictions: None
Pet left unattended in room: Yes
Exercise Area for Pets: Yes
Rates: $33 to $46

Sheraton Univ. Inn & Conf. Ctr.
P.O. Box 2506
W. Lafayette, IN 47906
Phone: (317) 463-5511

Pet Restrictions: Must be leashed or
    caged; need credit card;
    smoking room only; not allowed
    in restaurant or pool
Pet left unattended in room: Yes
Exercise Area for Pets: Yes
Rates: $65 to $79

VETERINARIANS

Lafayette Veterinary Hospital
3532 E. State Rd. 26 47905
Phone: (315) 447-0521

Paw Prints Animal Hosp. Inc
1501 North Sagamore Pkwy 47905
Phone (317) 447-6996

Whitehair, Jon G.
3615-H Liberty St.
Cambridge Estates 47905
Phone: (317) 356-7148

LEBANON
Holiday Inn
SR 39 at Jct. I 65, Exit 139
P.O. Box 582
Lebanon, IN 46052
Phone: (317) 482-0500,
    (800) HOLIDAY

Pet Restrictions: Small pets
Pet left unattended in room: Yes
Exercise Area for Pets: Yes
Rates: $49 to $83

Lees Inn
1245 W. SR 32
Lebanon, IN 46052
Phone: (317) 482-9611

Pet Restrictions: Sign waiver
Pet left unattended in room: Yes
Exercise Area for Pets: Yes
Rates: $56 to $102

Red Roof Inn
8290 Georgia St.
Lebanon, IN 46410
Phone: (219) 738-2430

Pet Restrictions: None
Pet left unattended in room: Yes
Exercise Area for Pets: Yes
Rates: $35 to $50

MARTINSVILLE
Lees Inn
50 Bill Blvd.
Martinsville, IN 46151
Phone: (317) 342-1842

Pet Restrictions: Sign waiver
Pet left unattended in room: Yes
Exercise Area for Pets: Yes
Rates: $49 and up

MERRILLVILLE
Knights Inn
8250 Louisiana St.
Merrillville, IN 46410
Phone: (219) 736-5100

Pet Restrictions: None
Pet left unattended in room: Yes
Exercise Area for Pets: Yes
Rates: $38.95 and up

La Quinta
8210 Louisiana St.
Merrillville, IN 46410
Phone: (219) 738-2870

Pet Restrictions: Under 60 lbs; 1
    pet/room; no exotic pets
Exercise Area for Pets: Yes
Rates: $45 to $58

Red Roof Inn
8290 Georgia St.
Merrillville, IN 46410
Phone: (219) 738-2430

Pet Restrictions: None
Exercise Area for Pets: Yes
Rates: $35 to $55

VETERINARIANS

McMillan, Kenneth W.
4035 West 77th Place #30 46410
Phone: (309) 828-7722

MICHIGAN CITY

City Manor Motel
5225 Franklin St.
Michigan City, IN 46360
Phone: (219) 872-9149

Pet Restrictions: None
Exercise Area for Pets: Yes
Rates: $29

Red Roof Inn
110 W. Kieffer Rd.
Michigan City, IN 46360
Phone: (219) 874-5251

Pet Restrictions: None
Pet left unattended in room: Yes
Exercise Area for Pets: Yes
Rates: $27 to $45

VETERINARIANS

Animal Clinic Inc.
1943 South Woodland Ave 46360
Phone: (219) 879-0249

Hathaway, William J.
3025 East Michigan Blvd. 46360
Phone: (219) 879-8241

Langheinrich, Werner J.
4401 East US 12 46360
Phone: (219) 872-0661

MISHAWAKA

Mishawaka Inn
2754 Lincolnway East
Mishawaka, IN 46544
Phone: (219) 256-2300

Pet Restrictions: $6/day
Exercise Area for Pets: Yes
Rates: $40 to $45

VETERINARIANS

Magrane Animal Hospital
2324 Grape Rd.
(219) 259-5291

Mishawaka Animal Care Center
129 W. Edison Rd.
(219) 255-4130

MUNCIE

Days Inn
2000 N. Broadway Ave.
Muncie, IN 47303
Phone: (317) 288-9953

Pet Restrictions: $20 deposit
Pet left unattended in room: Yes
Exercise Area for Pets: Yes
Rates: $29 to $60

Holiday Inn
3400 S. Madison, P.O. Box 2605
Muncie, IN 47302
Phone: (317) 288-1911,
    (800) HOLIDAY
Pet Restrictions: None
Pet left unattended in room: Yes
Exercise Area for Pets: Yes
Rates: $47 to $52

Lees Inn
3302 Everbrook La.
Muncie, IN 47304
Phone: (317) 282-7557

Pet Restrictions: None
Pet left unattended in room: Yes
Exercise Area for Pets: Yes
Rates: $51 to $58

VETERINARIANS

Maplewood Animal Hosp. Inc.
1811 North Granville Ave. 47303
Phone: (317) 284-3393

Westview Animal Clinic
3712 West Jackson St. 47304
Phone: (317) 288-1881

NEW CASTLE

LK Motel
RR 2 Box 159
New Castle, IN 47362
Phone: (317) 987-8205

Pet Restrictions: No large dogs
Pet left unattended in room: Yes
Exercise Area for Pets: Yes
Rates: $32 to $54

PERU

LK Motel
675 US 31S
Peru, IN 46970
Phone: (317) 472-3971

Pet Restrictions: None
Pet left unattended in room: Yes
Exercise Area for Pets: Yes
Rates: $39 to $50

PORTAGE

Holiday Inn
6200 Melton Rd.
Portage, IN 46368
Phone: (219) 762-5546

Pet Restrictions: None
Exercise Area for Pets: Yes
Rates: $66 to $72

Lees Inn
2300 Willow Creek
Portage, IN 46368
Phone: (219) 763-7177

Pet Restrictions: Yes
Exercise Area for Pets: Yes
Rates: $56 to $70

PRIEST LAKE

Hills Resort
Rt. 5, Box 162A
Priest Lake, IN 83856
Phone: (208) 443-2551

Pet Restrictions: $5/nite
Pet left unattended in room: Yes
Exercise Area for Pets: Yes
Rates: $62 to $248

REMINGTON

Days Inn of Remington
165 & US 24, exit 201
Remington, IN 47977
Phone: (219) 261-2178

Pet Restrictions: $2 fee
Pet left unattended in room: Yes
Exercise Area for Pets: Yes
Rates: $35 to $40

RICHMOND

Days Inn
540 W. Eaton Pike
Richmond, IN 47374
Phone: (317) 966-7591,
    (800) 325-2525

Pet Restrictions: $5/pet
Pet left unattended in room: Yes
Exercise Area for Pets: Yes
Rates: $35 to $50

Holiday Inn
4700 National Rd. E.
Richmond, IN 47374
Phone: (317) 962-5551

Pet Restrictions: None
Pet left unattended in room: Yes
Exercise Area for Pets: Yes
Rates: $55 to $58

Howard Johnson Lodge
2525 Chester Blvd.
Richmond, IN 47374
Phone: (317) 962-7576

Pet Restrictions: None
Pet left unattended in room: Yes
Exercise Area for Pets: Yes
Rates: $32 to $40

Knights Inn
Hwy 40, 419 Commerce Dr.
Richmond, IN 47374
Phone: (317) 966-6682

Pet Restrictions: $5, Smoking
    rooms only,
Pet left unattended in room: Yes
Exercise Area for Pets: Yes
Rates: $28 to $50

ROSELAND

Best Inns of America
425 US 31 North
Roseland, IN 46634
Phone: (219) 277-7700

Pet Restrictions: None
Pet left unattended in room: Yes, if
    caged
Exercise Area for Pets: Yes
Rates: $41 to $53

SCOTTSBURG

Best Western Scottsburg Inn
P.O. Box 429, I 69, SR56
Scottsburg, IN 47170
Phone: (812) 752-2212,
    (800) 528-1234

Pet Restrictions: Under 20 lbs.
Pet left unattended in room: Yes
Exercise Area for Pets: Yes
Rates: $27 to $60

Campbell's Motel
300 N. Gardner
Scottsburg, IN 47170
Phone: (812) 752-4401

Pet Restrictions: None
Pet left unattended in room: Yes
Exercise Area for Pets: Yes
Rates: $20 to $45

SELLERSBURG
Days Inn
7618 SR 60 W
Sellersburg, IN 47172
Phone: (812) 246-4451,
(800) 325-2525

Pet Restrictions: None
Pet left unattended in room: Yes
Exercise Area for Pets: Yes
Rates: $37.95 and up

SEYMOUR
Days Inn-Seymour
302 Frontage Rd.
Seymour, IN 47274
Phone: (812) 522-3678,
(800) 325-2525

Pet Restrictions: $3/night
Exercise Area for Pets: Yes
Rates: $38 and up

Knights Inn
207 N. Frontage Rd.
Seymour, IN 47274
Phone: (812) 522-3523,
(800) 843-5644

Pet Restrictions: None
Pet left unattended in room: Yes
Exercise Area for Pets: Yes
Rates: $31.95 to $52.95

SOUTH BEND
Days Inn
52757 US 31N
South Bend, IN 46637
Phone: (219) 277-0510,
(800) 325-2525

Pet Restrictions: Under 25 lbs.,
$3/night
Exercise Area for Pets: Yes
Rates: $40 to $65

Econo Lodge
3233 Lincoln Way W.
South Bend, IN 16628
Phone: (219) 232-9019,
(800) 55-ECONO

Pet Restrictions: $15 deposit
Exercise Area for Pets: Yes
Rates: $34.95 and up

Holiday Inn-Univ. Ave.
515 Dixie Way N.
South Bend, IN 46637
Phone: (219) 272-6600,
(800) HOLIDAY

Pet Restrictions: None
Pet left unattended in room: Yes
Exercise Area for Pets: Yes
Rates: $66 and up

Howard Johnson Lodge
52939 US 33 North
South Bend, IN 46637-3293
Phone: (219) 272-1500,
(800) 833-3741

Pet Restrictions: None
Pet left unattended in room: Yes, no
maid service
Exercise Area for Pets: Yes
Rates: $24.95 to $75

Knights Inn-South Bend
236 Dixie Way N.
South Bend, IN 46637
Phone: (219) 277-2960

Pet Restrictions: None
Pet left unattended in room: Yes
Exercise Area for Pets: Yes
Rates: $38.95

VETERINARIANS
Ireland Animal Clinic
222 East Ireland Rd. 46614
Phone: (219) 291-1571

Roseland Animal Hospital Inc.
424 Dixie Way North 46637
Phone: (219) 272-6100

South Bend Animal Clinic
3224 Lincolnway West 46628
Phone: (219) 232-1459

TERRE HAUTE
Days Inn
2800 S. Dixie Bee Rd.
Terre Haute, IN 47802
Phone: (812) 234-4268,
(800) 325-2525

Pet Restrictions: None
Exercise Area for Pets: Yes
Rates: $56 to $60

Holiday Inn
3300 Dixie Bee Rd.
Terre Haute, IN 47802
Phone: (812) 232-6081,
(800) HOLIDAY

Pet Restrictions: None
Exercise Area for Pets: Yes
Rates: $58 to $80

Knights Inn
401 Margaret Ave.
Terre Haute, IN 47802
Phone: (812) 234-9931

Pet Restrictions: None
Pet left unattended in room: Yes
Exercise Area for Pets: Yes
Rates: $40

Regal 8 Inn
S on US 41
Terre Haute, IN 47802
Phone: (812) 238-1586

Pet Restrictions: None
Exercise Area for Pets: Yes
Rates: $34.19

Terre Haute Travelodge
530 S. 3rd St.
Terre Haute, IN 47807
Phone: (812) 232-7075

Pet Restrictions: None
Pet left unattended in room: Yes
Exercise Area for Pets: Yes
Rates: $38 to $55

Woodridge Motel
4545 Wabash Ave.
Terre Haute, IN 47803
Phone: (812) 877-1571

Pet Restrictions: $10 deposit
Pet left unattended in room: Yes
Exercise Area for Pets: Yes
Rates: $26 to $34

VINCENNES
Holiday Inn
600 Wheatland Rd.
Vincennes, IN 47591
Phone: (812) 886-9900,
(800) HOLIDAY

Pet Restrictions: None
Pet left unattended in room: Yes
Exercise Area for Pets: Yes
Rates: $47 to $56

WABASH
Days Inn-Wabash
1950 S. Wabash
Wabash, IN 46992
Phone: (219) 563-7451

Pet Restrictions: $25 deposit
Pet left unattended in room: Yes
Exercise Area for Pets: Yes
Rates: $43 to $51

WARSAW
Comfort Inn
2605 E. Center St.
Warsaw, IN 46580
Phone: (219) 267-7337

Pet Restrictions: $50 deposit
Pet left unattended in room: Yes, no
housekeeping
Exercise Area for Pets: Yes
Rates: $65

Holiday Inn
2519 E. Center
Warsaw, IN 46580
Phone: (219) 269-2323,
(800) HOLIDAY

Pet Restrictions: Small pets
Pet left unattended in room: Yes
Exercise Area for Pets: Yes
Rates: $63

VETERINARIANS
Animal Hospital of Warsaw
2031 North Detroit St. 46580
Phone: (219) 269-4745

Woodward, Dennis R.
2031 North Detroit St. 46580
Phone: (219) 269-4745

IOWA — HOTELS

ALBIA

Indian Hills Inn
Rt. 1
Albia, IA 52531
Phone: (515) 932-7181

Pet Restrictions: $6/day
Exercise Area for Pets: Nearby
Rates: $32 to $40

AMES

Best Western Starlite Village
I 35 and 13th St., P.O. Box 1767
Ames, IA 50010
Phone: (515) 232-9260

Pet Restrictions: None
Pet left unattended in room: Yes
Exercise Area for Pets: Nearby
Rates: $52 to $54

New Frontier Motel
RR3
Ames, IA 50010
Phone: (515) 292-2056

Pet Restrictions: $5 deposit/pet
Exercise Area for Pets: Nearby
Rates: $35.58

**Iowa State University
College of Veterinary Medicine**
Small Animal Teaching Hosp. 50010
Phone: (515) 294-4900

Esteban, Lissette R.
637 Pammel Court 50010
Phone: (515) 296-7885

ARNOLD'S PARK

Fillenmarth New Beach Cott.
1 blk off US 71
Arnold's Park, IA 51331
Phone: (712) 332-5646

Pet Restrictions: None
Pet left unattended in room: Yes
Exercise Area for Pets: Nearby
Rates: $70

AUSTIN

Austin Super 8 Motel
P.O. Box 841
Austin, IA 55912
Phone: (507) 433-1801

Pet Restrictions: $10 deposit
Pet left unattended in room: Yes
Exercise Area for Pets: Nearby
Rates: $40.39 to $44.88

BETTENDORF

Jumer's Castle Lodge
909 Middle Rd.
Bettendorf, IA 52722
Phone: (319) 359-7141

Pet Restrictions: $25 deposit
Pet left unattended in room: Yes
Exercise Area for Pets: Nearby
Rates: $83 to $138

Keppy, Kenneth
619 14th Street 52722
Phone: (319) 391-2555

BURLINGTON

Days Inn
1601 N. Roosevelt
Burlington, IA 52601
Phone: (319) 754-4681,
    (800) 325-2525

Pet Restrictions: $5
Pet left unattended in room: Yes, no
    maid service
Exercise Area for Pets: Yes
Rates: $34 to $45

Allgood Animal Hospital
3106 Johannsen Drive 52601
Phone: (319) 752-5983

CEDAR FALLS

Black Hawk Motor Inn
122 Washington St., P.O. Box 307
Cedar Falls, IA 50613
Phone: (319) 277-1161

Pet Restrictions: Pets allowed in
    motor inn only
Exercise Area for Pets: Nearby
Rates: $28 to $37

Holiday Inn
5826 University Ave.
Cedar Falls, IA 50613
Phone: (319) 277-2230,
    (800) HOLIDAY

Pet Restrictions: None
Pet left unattended in room: Yes
Exercise Area for Pets: Yes
Rates: $39 to $59

Midwest Lodge
4410 University Ave.
Cedar Falls, IA 50613
Phone: (319) 277-1550,
    (800) 728-9819

Pet Restrictions: Small pets
Exercise Area for Pets: Yes
Rates: $43 to $65

VETERINARIANS
Cobb, Julie A.
1606 River Bluff Dr. 50613
Phone: (319) 277-1883

CEDAR RAPIDS
Exel Inn
616 33rd Ave. SW
Cedar Rapids, IA 52904
Phone: (319) 366-2475,
(800) 356-8013

Pet Restrictions: Housebroken
Exercise Area for Pets: Yes
Rates: $24.99 to $43.99

Heartland Inn
3315 S. Date Ct.
Cedar Rapids, IA 52404
Phone: (319) 362-9012,
(800) 334-3277

Pet Restrictions: $10/pet/day, 20
lbs. or less
Pet left unattended in room: Yes,
must be in cage
Exercise Area for Pets: Yes
Rates: $39 to $150

Holiday Inn
2501 Williams Blvd. SW
Cedar Rapids, IA 52404
Phone: (319) 365-9441,
(800) 465-4329

Pet Restrictions: Must stay outside
Hollow Dome
Pet left unattended in room: Yes
Exercise Area for Pets: Yes
Rates: $49 to $63

Red Roof Inn
3325 Southgate Court SW
Cedar Rapids, IA 52404
Phone: (319) 366-7523,
(800) THE-ROOF

Pet Restrictions: None
Pet left unattended in room: Yes,
must be caged for maid service
Exercise Area for Pets: Yes
Rates: $24.99 to $35.99

Sheraton Inn
525 33rd Ave. SW
Cedar Rapids, IA 52404
Phone: (319) 366-8671,
(800) 325-3535

Pet Restrictions: $25 deposit
Pet left unattended in room: Yes
Exercise Area for Pets: Yes
Rates: $59 to $79

Stouffer's 5 Season's Hotel
5 Seasons Center; 350 1st Ave. NE
Cedar Rapids, IA 52401
Phone: (319) 363-8161,
(800) 282-4692

Pet Restrictions: None
Pet left unattended in room: Yes,
must be in cage
Exercise Area for Pets: Nearby
Rates: $79 to $119

VETERINARIANS
Frey Animal Clinic
1823 16th Ave. SW 52404
Phone: (319) 364-7149

Graeff, David E.
801 A Ave. NE 52402
Phone: (319) 366-1594

Winterowd, Darrel D.
22 Wilson Ave. SW 52404
Phone: (319) 366-8951

CHARLES CITY
Lamplighter Motel
Hwy 18 & 218 W
Charles City, Iowa 50616
Phone: (515) 228-6711,
(800) 341-8000

Pet Restrictions: $3/pet/day
Exercise Area for Pets: Yes
Rates: $31 to $39

CLINTON
Best Western Frontier Motor Inn
2300 Lincoln Way
Clinton, IA 52732
Phone: (319) 242-7112,
(800) 728-7112

Pet Restrictions: $3/pet/day
Pet left unattended in room: Yes
Exercise Area for Pets: Nearby
Rates: $39.95 to $137.50

Timber Motel
2225 Lincolnway
Clinton, IA 52732
Phone: (319) 243-6901

Pet Restrictions: $10 deposit
Pet left unattended in room: Yes,
notify desk
Exercise Area for Pets: Yes
Rates: $27.21 to $39.04

COLUMBUS JCT
Columbus Motel
Hwy 92E
Columbus Junction, IA 52738
Phone: (319) 728-8080
Pet Restrictions: $5/pet/day
Pet left unattended in room: Yes, no maid servicce
Exercise Area for Pets: Yes
Rates: $30 to $62

COOK
Vermillion Dam Lodge
P.O. Box 1105 AA
Cook, IA 55723
Phone: (218) 666-5418,
(800) 325-5780
Pet Restrictions: $75/pet/week
Pet left unattended in room: Yes
Exercise Area for Pets: Yes
Rates: $700 to $1040

CORALVILLE
Best Western Westfield Inn
1895 27th Ave.
Coralville, IA 52241
Phone: (319) 354-7770,
(800) 528-1234
Pet Restrictions: None
Pet left unattended in room: Yes
Exercise Area for Pets: Yes
Rates: $43.75 to $69.75

Blue Top Motel
1015 5th St.
Coralville, IA 52241
Phone: (319) 351-0900
Pet Restrictions: In certain rooms, $1/night
Exercise Area for Pets: Yes
Rates: $23.50 to $48.50

CORNING
Chalet Motor Lodge
1530 Ave. 9
Corning, IA 51501
Phone: (712) 328-3041
Pet Restrictions: Pets should stay just for a few days
Pet left unattended in room: Yes
Exercise Area for Pets: Yes
Rates: $20 to $42

Comfort Inn Manawa
3208 57th St.
Corning, IA 51501
Phone: (712) 366-9699,
(800) 221-2222
Pet Restrictions: $25/pet deposit
Exercise Area for Pets: Yes
Rates: $44 to $48.29

Days Inn
3619 9th Ave.
Corning, IA 51501
Phone: (712) 323-2200,
(800) 325-2525
Pet Restrictions: $10/pet deposit
Pet left unattended in room: Yes, must be caged
Rates: $37.80 to $42 plus $5 extra per person

Howard Johnson
3537 W. Broadway
Corning, IA 51501
Phone: (712) 328-3171,
(800) 446-4656
Pet Restrictions: None
Pet left unattended in room: Yes, no maid service
Exercise Area for Pets: Yes
Rates: $44 to $61

Motel 6
3032 S. Expwy
Corning, IA 51501
Phone: (712) 366-2405
Pet Restrictions: None
Pet left unattended in room: Yes
Exercise Area for Pets: Yes
Rates: $29 to $34

DAVENPORT
Best Western Riverview Inn
227 Le Claire St.
Davenport, IA 52801
Phone: (319) 324-1921,
(800) 553-1879
Pet Restrictions: $25 deposit, under 25 lbs.
Pet left unattended in room: Yes
Exercise Area for Pets: Nearby
Rates: $39 to $99

IOWA — HOTELS (continued)

Best Western Steeple Gate Inn
100 W. 76th St.
Davenport, IA 52806
Phone: (319) 386-6900,
(800) 373-6900

Pet Restrictions: $3/day
Pet left unattended in room: Yes
Exercise Area for Pets: Yes
Rates: $62 to $69

Kimberly Cret Veterinary Hosp.
1423 East Kimberly Rd. 52807
Phone: (319) 386-1445

DENISON
Best Western Denison's Inn
Hwy 30 & 59
Denison, IA 51442
Phone: (712) 263-5081,
(800) 428-0684

Pet Restrictions: None
Exercise Area for Pets: Yes
Rates: $30 to $42

Lowe, Marilyn
720 Broadway 51442
Phone: (712) 263-6089

DES MOINES
Best Western Colonial Inn
5020 NE 14th St.
Des Moines, IA 50313
Phone: (515) 265-7511,
(800) 528-1234

Pet Restrictions: None
Exercise Area for Pets: Yes
Rates: $30 to $80

Best Western Starlite Village
929 3rd St.
Des Moines, IA 50309
Phone: (515) 282-5251,
(800) 528-1234

Pet Restrictions: None
Pet left unattended in room: Yes
Exercise Area for Pets: Yes
Rates: $72 to $110

Broadway
5100 Hubbell Ave.
Des Moines, IA 50317
Phone: (515) 262-5659

Pet Restrictions: $5, $15 max. if pet stays longer than 5 days
Exercise Area for Pets: Yes
Rates: $30 to $60

Days Inn Capitol City
3501 E. 14th St.
Des Moines, IA 50316
Phone: (515) 265-2541,
(800) DAYS-INN

Pet Restrictions: None
Pet left unattended in room: Yes
Exercise Area for Pets: Yes
Rates: $35 to $66

Hotel Fort Des Moines
10th & Walnut St.
Des Moines, IA 50309
Phone: (515) 243-1161,
(800) 532-1466

Pet Restrictions: None
Pet left unattended in room: Yes
Exercise Area for Pets: Yes
Rates: $69 to $105

Hickman Motor Lodge
6500 Hickman Rd.
Des Moines, IA 50322
Phone: (515) 276-8591

Pet Restrictions: None
Pet left unattended in room: Yes
Exercise Area for Pets: Yes
Rates: $29 to $50

Marriott
700 Grand
Des Moines, IA 50309
Phone: (515) 245-5500,
(800) 228-9290

Pet Restrictions: Must sign waiver
Pet left unattended in room: Yes, must be in cage
Rates: $49 to $134

Motel 6
4817 Fleur Dr.
Des Moines, IA 50321
Phone: (515) 287-6364

Pet Restrictions: 1 small pet per room, in smoking rooms
Exercise Area for Pets: Yes
Rates: $27.99 to $39.99

Savery
4th & Locust St.
Des Moines, IA 50309
Phone: (515) 244-2151,
(800) 798-2151

Pet Restrictions: $40 deposit ($10 non-refund.)
Pet left unattended in room: Yes
Exercise Area for Pets: Nearby
Rates: $45 to $300, $1500 penthouse

Sheraton Inn Des Moines
11040 Hickman Rd.
Des Moines, IA, 50322
Phone: (515) 278-5575

Pet Restrictions: Dogs and cats only
Exercise Area for Pets: Nearby
Rates: $59 to $78

VETERINARIANS
Animal Med Clinic of Merle Hay
4520 Merle Hay Rdwy Rd.
Phone: (515) 276-4511

Bryan Animal Hospital Pc
3009 Ingersoll 50312
Phone: (515) 274-3555

Denhart, James D.
3709 E. University Ave. 50317
Phone: (515) 262-1882

DUBUQUE
Best Western Midway Motor Lodge
3100 Dodge St.
Dubuque, IA 52001
Phone: (319) 557-8000,
    (800) 33-MIDWAY

Pet Restrictions: Small pets
Exercise Area for Pets: Yes
Rates: $48.50 to $135

Heartland Inn
4025 Dodge St.
Dubuque, IA 52001
Phone: (319) 582-3752,
    (800) 334-3277

Pet Restrictions: $6, in smoking rooms
Pet left unattended in room: Yes, must be caged
Exercise Area for Pets: Yes
Rates: $40 to $52.50

VETERINARIANS
Colonial Terrace Animal Hosp.
2777 University 52001
Phone: (319) 556-2667

Ames, Janel R.
331 Kaufman Ave. 52001
Phone: (319) 557-8013

Vanderloo, Merrill M.
3350 Asbury Rd. 52001
Phone: (319) 556-3013

FORT DODGE
Best Western Starlite Village Motel
P.O. Box 1297
Fort Dodge, IA 50501
Phone: (515) 573-7177,
    (800) 528-1234

Pet Restrictions: None
Pet left unattended in room: Yes, notify desk
Exercise Area for Pets: Yes
Rates: $40 to $58

Holiday Inn
P.O. Box 1336
Fort Dodge, IA 50501
Phone: (515) 955-3621,
    (800) HOLIDAY

Pet Restrictions: None
Pet left unattended in room: Yes, only small pets, no kennls in room
Exercise Area for Pets: Yes
Rates: $47 to $63

VETERINARIANS
East Lawn Animal Hospital
2930 5th Ave. South 50501
Phone: (515) 576-5149

Thomas, Charles Alan
2011 1st Ave. South 50501
Phone: (515) 576-7497

FORT MADISON
Best Western Iowan Motor Lodge
Hwy 61 S, P.O. Box 485
Fort Madison, IA 52627
Phone: (319) 372-7510,
    (800) 423-2693

Pet Restrictions: None
Pet left unattended in room: Yes
Exercise Area for Pets: Yes
Rates: $50 to $54

GLENWOOD
Bluff View Motel
RR1 Pacific Junction
Glenwood, IA 51561
Phone: (712) 622-8191,
    (800) 582-9366

Pet Restrictions: None
Exercise Area for Pets: Yes
Rates: $26 to $38

Western Inn of Glenwood
707 S. Locus
Glenwood, IA 52627
Phone: (712) 527-3175
Pet Restrictions: No cats
Exercise Area for Pets: Yes
Rates: $29 to $35

VETERINARIANS
Overmiller, Timothy V.
8 North Hazel 51534
Phone: (712) 527-9454

KEOKUK
Keokuk Motor Lodge
Hwy 218, E. Main St. Rd.
Keokuk, IA 52632
Phone: (319) 524-3252,
(800) 252-2256
Pet Restrictions: Small pets, in cage
Pet left unattended in room: Yes
Exercise Area for Pets: Yes
Rates: $27 to $44

VETERINARIANS
Klauser, Michael A.
1912 Main St. 52632
Phone: (319) 524-6835

MUSCATINE
Holiday Inn
P.O. Box 56
Muscatine, IA 52761
Phone: (319) 264-5550,
(800) HOLIDAY
Pet Restrictions: Not in poolside
rooms
Pet left unattended in room: Yes, in
cage
Exercise Area for Pets: Yes
Rates: $51 to $66

VETERINARIANS
Muscatine Veterinary Hospital
2200 Park Ave. 52761
Phone: (319) 263-2831

Tillie, John E.
3318 Park Ave. West 52761
Phone: (319) 263-5520

OSCEOLA
Best Western Regal Inn
on US 34, P.O. Box 238
Osceola, IA 50213
Phone: (515) 342-2123,
(800) 252-2289
Pet Restrictions: Small pets
Exercise Area for Pets: Yes
Rates: $33 to $43

Traveler Budget Inn
1210 A Ave. East
Osceola, IA 52577
Phone: (515) 673-8333,
(800) 341-8000
Pet Restrictions: None
Pet left unattended in room: Yes
Exercise Area for Pets: Yes
Rates: $28 to $44

OTTUMWA
Colonial Motor Inn
1534 Allsia Rd.
Ottumwa, IA 52501
Phone: (515) 683-1661
Pet Restrictions: $5
Exercise Area for Pets: Yes
Rates: $23.95 to $42.95

Days Inn of Ottumwa
206 Church St.
Ottumwa, IA 52501
Phone: (515) 682-8131,
(800) 325-2525
Pet Restrictions: None
Pet left unattended in room: Yes,
notify desk
Exercise Area for Pets: Yes
Rates: $48 to $62

Heartland Inn
125 W. Joseph St.
Ottumwa, IA 52501
Phone: (515) 682-8526,
(800) 334-3277
Pet Restrictions: $6/day, must sign
waiver
Pet left unattended in room: Yes, no
maid service
Exercise Area for Pets: Yes
Rates: $37.50 to $45.50

NEW HAMPTON
Ferkin's Motel
P.O. Box 249
New Hmpton, IA 50659
Phone: (515) 394-4145,
(800) 728-4145
Pet Restrictions: None
Pet left unattended in room: Yes, if
caged
Exercise Area for Pets: Yes
Rates: $30 to $38

SIOUX CITY
Holiday Inn
1401 Zenith Dr.
Sioux City, IA 51103
Phone: (712) 277-3211,
   (800) 274-3211
Pet Restrictions: Small house pets
Exercise Area for Pets: Yes
Rates: $39 to $70

River Boat Inn
701 Gordon Dr.
Sioux City, IA 51101
Phone: (712) 277-9400
Pet Restrictions: $50 deposit
Exercise Area for Pets: Yes
Rates: $39 to $43

Palmer House Motel
3440 E. Gordon Dr.
Sioux City, IA 51106
Phone: (712) 276-4221
Pet Restrictions: None
Pet left unattended in room: Yes
Exercise Area for Pets: Yes
Rates: $31 to $45

VETERINARIANS
Elk Creek Animal Clinic
6003 Morningside Ave. 51106
Phone: (712) 276-5368

Roach Veterinary Hospital
1909 Pierce 51104
Phone: (712) 277-2232

STORY CITY
Viking Motor Inn
Just W. of I 35, Exit 124
Story City, IA 50248
Phone: (515) 733-4306,
   (800) 233-4306
Pet Restrictions: None
Exercise Area for Pets: Yes
Rates: $32 to $44

URBANDALE
Comfort Inn
5900 Sutton Dr.
Urbandale, IA 50322
Phone: (515) 270-1037,
   (800) 221-2222
Pet Restrictions: None
Pet left unattended in room: Yes
Exercise Area for Pets: Yes
Rates: $44.95 to $63.95

VETERINARIANS
Northwest Veterinary Hospital
7507 Dennis Drive 50322
Phone: (515) 276-4549

WATERLOO
Heartland Inn
1809 La Porte Rd.
Waterloo, IA 50702
Phone: (319) 235-4461,
   (800) 334-3277
Pet Restrictions: $10, smoking
   rooms
Pet left unattended in room: Yes
Exercise Area for Pets: Yes
Rates: $35 to $135

Ramada Hotel
214 Washington St.
Waterloo, IA 50701
Phone: (319) 235-0321,
   (800) 272-6232
Pet Restrictions: $5/day, sign waiver
Pet left unattended in room: Yes
Exercise Area for Pets: Nearby
Rates: $39.95 to $110

VETERINARIANS
Kleaveland University Avenue Veterinary Hospital
556 Progress Ave. 50701
Phone: (319) 232-6895

WAVERLY
Best Western Red Fox Inn
1900 Heritage Way
Waverly, IA 50677
Phone: (319) 352-5330,
   (800) 397-5330
Pet Restrictions: None
Pet left unattended in room: Yes
Exercise Area for Pets: Yes
Rates: $50 to $135

WEBSTER CITY
New Castle Inn
1700 Superior St.
Webster City, IA 50595
Phone: (515) 832-3631
Pet Restrictions: Pets must be in
   portable cage
Exercise Area for Pets: Yes
Rates: $31 to $47

WILLIAMSBURG

Crest Motel
Rt. 1, Box 181
Williamsburg, IA 52361
Phone: (319) 668-1522

Pet Restrictions: None
Pet left unattended in room: Yes
Exercise Area for Pets: Yes
Rates: $30 to $40

Middle America Inn
Exit 220 P.O. Box 749
Williamsburg, IA 52361
Phone: (319) 668-1817

Pet Restrictions: Pets have to be
    bathroom trained
Exercise Area for Pets: Yes
Rates: $27.95 to $32.95

KANSAS — HOTELS

BAXTER SPRINGS

Baxter Inn
2451 Military Road
Baxter Springs, KS 66713
Phone: (316) 856-2106
Pet Restrictions: Small pets, $25 deposit
Exercise Area for Pets: Yes
Rates: $29.35 to $58.75

BELLEVILLE

Best Western Bel Villa Motel
Jct. U.S. 36 & 81
Belleville, KS 66935
Phone: (913) 527-2231
Pet Restrictions: Small pets
Exercise Area for Pets: Yes
Rates: $32 to $38

COFFEYVILLE

Fountain Plaza Inn
104 W 11th St.
Coffeyville, KS 67337
Phone: (316) 251-2250
Pet Restrictions: Small pets, $2
Exercise Area for Pets: Yes
Rates: $36.95 to $42.95

VETERINARIANS

Alter, Ralph E.
1616 West 1st Street
(316) 251-1040

COLBY

Budget Host Inn
1745 W 4th St.
Colby, KS 67701
Phone: (913) 462-3338
Pet Restrictions: Small, well-behaved
Exercise Area for Pets: Yes
Rates: $28 to $47

Best Western Crown Motel
Rt. 1, Box 12M
Colby, KS 67701
Phone: (913) 462-3943
Pet Restrictions: None
Exercise Area for Pets: Yes
Rates: Call for rates

Ramada Inn
1950 S. Range, PO Box 487
Colby, KS 67701
Phone: (913) 462-3933
Pet Restrictions: None
Exercise Area for Pets: Yes
Rates: Call for rates

CONCORDIA

Best Western Thunderbird Inn
N. US 81 Hwy
Concordia, KS 66901
Phone: (913) 243-4545
Pet Restrictions: Well behaved, notify housekeeping
Pet left unattended in room: Yes
Exercise Area for Pets: Yes
Rates: $36 to $46

DODGE CITY

Dodge House Inn
2408 W. Wyatt Earp Blvd.
Dodge City, KS 67801
Phone: (316) 225-9900
Pet Restrictions: $50 deposit
Exercise Area for Pets: Yes
Rates: $40 to $48

Econo Lodge of Dodge City
1610 W. Wyatt Earp Blvd.
Dodge City, KS 67801
Phone: (316) 225-0231
Pet Restrictions: $4 fee
Pet left unattended in room: Yes
Exercise Area for Pets: Yes
Rates: $36 to $45

VETERINARIANS

Posey, Tate D.
2717 Colleen Ave. 67801
(316) 227-8651

Vincent, Tom D.
2105 Thompson 67801
(316) 227-2751

ELLSWORTH

Best Western Garden Motel
PO Box 44
Ellsworth, KS 67439
Phone: (913) 472-3116
Pet Restrictions: Small pets, if well behaved
Pet left unattended in room: Yes
Exercise Area for Pets: Yes
Rates: $35 to $43

GARDEN CITY

Continental Inn
1408 Jones Ave.
Garden City, KS 67846
Phone: (316) 276-7691, (800) 621-0318
Pet Restrictions: None
Pet left unattended in room: Yes
Exercise Area for Pets: Yes
Rates: $29 to $60

Best Western Wheatlands
1311 E. Fulton
Garden City, KS 67846
Phone: (316) 276-2387

Pet Restrictions: None
Exercise Area for Pets: Yes
Rates: $35 to $53

Budget Host
Jct. US 50 & US 83
Garden City, KS 67846
Phone: (316) 275-0677

Pet Restrictions: None
Pet left unattended in room: Yes
Exercise Area for Pets: Yes
Rates: $29 to $40

National 9 Inn
1502 E. Fulton
Garden City, KS 67735
Phone: (316) 276-2394

Pet Restrictions: Small, housebroken
Pet left unattended in room: Yes
    except during room service
Exercise Area for Pets: Yes
Rates: $30 to $39

Plaza Inn
1911 E. Kansas
Garden City, KS 67846
Phone: (316) 275-7471

Pet Restrictions: Must sign damage
    waiver
Pet left unattended in room: Yes, if
    quiet
Exercise Area for Pets: Yes
Rates: Call for rates

GOODLAND
Best Western Buffalo Inn
2520 Hwy 27
Goodland, KS 67735
Phone: (913) 899-3621

Pet Restrictions: Only in smoking
    rooms
Pet left unattended in room: Yes
Exercise Area for Pets: Yes
Rates: Call for rates

Super 8
2520 Hwy 27
Goodland, KS 67735
Phone: (913) 899-7566

Pet Restrictions: Only in smoking
    rooms
Exercise Area for Pets: Yes
Rates: Call for rates

GREAT BEND
Travelers Budget Inn
4200 W. 10th St.
Great Bend, KS 67530
Phone: (316) 793-5448

Pet Restrictions: Small pets
Exercise Area for Pets: Yes
Rates: $23.95 to $59.95

Schrader, Jerry L.
(316) 792-2551

Turner, Terry N.
1205 Patton Rd. 67530
(316) 793-5457

HAYS
Days Inn
3205 N. Vine St.
Hays, KS 67601
Phone: (913) 628-8261

Pet Restrictions: Notify desk
Pet left unattended in room: Yes
Exercise Area for Pets: Yes
Rates: $38 to $84

HUTCHINSON
Best Western Sun Dome Inn
3205 N. Vine St.
S. Hutchinson, KS 67505
Phone: (316) 663-4444

Pet Restrictions: Small pets
Exercise Area for Pets: Yes
Rates: $47 to $52

Quality Inn
15 W. 4th St.
Hutchinson, KS 67501
Phone: (316) 663-1211

Pet Restrictions: None
Exercise Area for Pets: Yes
Rates: $34.95 to $95

Hutchinson Small Animal Hospital
1201 East 30th St. 67502
(316) 665-8743

Scheuermann, Randie L.
1604 N. Pleasant 67501
(316) 665-5119

Schrater, Gerald D.
2911 Apple Lane 67502
(316) 662-0515

IOLA

Best Western Majestic Inn
1315 N. State, PO Box 233
Iola, Kansas
Phone: (316) 365-5161

Pet Restrictions: Small pets
Pet left unattended in room: Yes, as
　　long as not barking
Exercise Area for Pets: Yes
Rates: $24 to $34

JUNCTION CITY

Dreamland Motel
5203 E. Flint Hills Blvd.
Junction City, KS 66441
Phone: (913) 238-1108

Pet Restrictions: Notify desk
Exercise Area for Pets: Yes
Rates: $24 to $32

Harvest Inn
1001 E. 6th St.
Junction City, KS 66441
Phone: (913) 238-8101

Pet Restrictions: None, if quiet
Pet left unattended in room: Yes
Exercise Area for Pets: Yes
Rates: $23 to $37

KANSAS CITY

Best Western Inn Central
501 Southwest Blvd.
Kansas City, KS 66103
Phone: (913) 677-3060

Pet Restrictions: Notify maids
Pet left unattended in room: Yes
Exercise Area for Pets: Yes
Rates: $54 to $64

Home & Hearth Inn
3930 Rainbow Blvd.
Kansas City, KS 66103
Phone: (913) 236-6880

Pet Restrictions: $25 fee
Pet left unattended in room: Yes
Exercise Area for Pets: Yes
Rates: $42 to $54

VETERINARIANS
Smith, Richard D.
3140 North 99th St. 66109
(913) 299-0010

LAWRENCE

Days Inn Lawrence
2309 Iowa St.
Lawrence, KS 66044
Phone: (913) 843-9100

Pet Restrictions: None, if quiet
Pet left unattended in room: Yes
Exercise Area for Pets: Yes
Rates: $30 to $47

Holiday Inn
200 McDonald Rd.
Lawrence, KS 66044
Phone: (913) 841-7077

Pet Restrictions: None
Exercise Area for Pets: Yes
Rates: $56 to $65

Westminster Inn
2525 W. 6th St.
Lawrence, KS 66044
Phone: (913) 841-8410

Pet Restrictions: Small pets,
　　responsible for damage
Pet left unattended in room: Yes
Exercise Area for Pets: Yes
Rates: $26 to $50

VETERINARIANS
Animal Hospital of Lawrence
701 Michigan 66044
(913) 842-0609

Bradley Veterinary Hospital
935 East 23rd St. 66044
(913) 843-9533

Clinton Parkway Animal Hospital
4340 Clinton Parkway 66046
(913) 841-3131

LANSING
The Lansing Inn
504 N. Main
Lansing, KS 66043
Phone: (913) 727-2777

Pet Restrictions: $25 deposit
Pet left unattended in room: Yes
Exercise Area for Pets: Yes
Rates: $30.65 to $45

KANSAS — HOTELS (continued)

LEAVENWORTH

Ramada Inn Leavenworth
103 South 3rd
Leavenworth, KS 66048
Phone: (913) 651-5500

Pet Restrictions: Notify desk
Pet left unattended in room: Yes
Exercise Area for Pets: Yes
Rates: $37 to $41

Meyer Veterinary Hospital
3525 S. Fourth St.
Trafficway 66048
(913) 682-6000

LENEXA

Holiday Inn - Lenexa Holidome
12601 W. 95th St.
Lenexa, KS 66215
Phone: (913) 888-6670

Pet Restrictions: Under 25 lbs.
Pet left unattended in room: Yes, if
    in cage
Exercise Area for Pets: Yes
Rates: $65 to $85

La Quinta
9461 Lenexa Dr.
Lenexa, KS 66215
Phone: (913) 492-5500

Pet Restrictions: Under 20 lbs.
Exercise Area for Pets: Yes
Rates: $44 to $57

LIBERAL

Liberal Travelodge
5643 E. Pancake Blvd.
Liberal, KS 67901
Phone: (316) 624-6203

Pet Restrictions: None
Pet left unattended in room: Yes if
    well behaved
Exercise Area for Pets: Yes
Rates: $23 to $29

LYONS

Lyons Inn
817 W. Main
Lyons, KS 67554
Phone: (316) 257-5185

Pet Restrictions: None
Exercise Area for Pets: Yes
Rates: $26.95 to $45.95

MANHATTAN

Best Western Continental Inn
100 Bluemont
Manhattan, KS 66502
Phone: (913) 776-4771

Pet Restrictions: Small pets
Pet left unattended in room: Yes, if
    well behaved
Exercise Area for Pets: Yes
Rates: $42 to $56

Days Inn
1501 Tuttle Creek Blvd.
Manhattan, KS 66502
Phone: (913) 539-5391

Pet Restrictions: None
Exercise Area for Pets: Yes
Rates: $38.75 to $60

Ramada
17th and Anderson Sts.
Manhattan, KS 66502
Phone: (913) 539-7531

Pet Restrictions: Small pets, deposit
Pet left unattended in room: Yes
Exercise Area for Pets: Yes
Rates: $59 to $67

The Veterinary Hospital
Kansas State University
Veterinary Medical Center 66506
(913) 532-5606

MERRIAM

Drury Inn - Merriam
9009 Shawnee Mission Pkwy
Merriam, KS 66202
Phone: (913) 236-9200

Pet Restrictions: None
Pet left unattended in room: Yes
Exercise Area for Pets: Yes
Rates: $47 to $67

OAKLEY

First Travel Inn
708 Center Ave.
Oakley, KS 67748
Phone: (913) 672-3226

Pet Restrictions: Smoking rooms
Exercise Area for Pets: Yes
Rates: $24 to $37

OVERLAND PARK

Doubletree
10010 College Blvd.
Overland Park, KS 66212
Phone: (913) 451-6100

Pet Restrictions: Deposit
Pet left unattended in room: Yes if
    well behaved
Exercise Area for Pets: Yes
Rates: $65 to $119

Marriott-Overland Park
10800 Metcalf Ave.
Overland, KS 66212
Phone: (913) 451-8000

Pet Restrictions: Notify
    housekeeping
Pet left unattended in room: Yes
Exercise Area for Pets: Nearby
Rates: $79 to $119

Ramada Inn SW
8787 Reeder
Overland Park, KS 66211
Phone: (913) 888-8440

Pet Restrictions: No large dogs
Pet left unattended in room: Yes, in
    cage
Exercise Area for Pets: Yes
Rates: $49.95 to $59.95

Residence Inn by Marriott
6300 W. 110th St.
Overland Park, KS 66211
Phone: (913) 491-3333

Pet Restrictions: None
Pet left unattended in room: Yes,
    notify housekeeping
Exercise Area for Pets: Yes
Rates: $72 to $104

VETERINARIANS

Metcalf South Animal Hospital
7280 West 105th 66212
(913) 381-9100

Overland Pet Clinic
7001 West 79th St. 66204
(913) 648-3616

PITTSBURG

Sunset Motel
Box 737
Pittsburg, KS 66762
Phone: (316) 231-3950

Pet Restrictions: Small pets
Exercise Area for Pets: Yes
Rates: $22.65 to $25.90

RUSSELL

Winchester Inn
Frontage Rd., Hwy 281S
Russell, KS 67665
Phone: (913) 483-6660

Pet Restrictions: $25 deposit
Pet left unattended in room: Yes
Exercise Area for Pets: Yes
Rates: $26 to $41

SMITH CENTER

Modernaire Motel
117 W. Hwy 36
Smith Center, KS 66967
Phone: (913) 282-6644

Pet Restrictions: Up to medium sized
Exercise Area for Pets: Yes
Rates: $23 to $34

SPIN

Best Western Red Baron
Jct U.S. 50 & U.S. 83
Spin, KS 67846
Phone: (316) 275-4164

Pet Restrictions: None
Pet left unattended in room: Yes
Exercise Area for Pets: Yes
Rates: $31 to $41

TOPEKA

Liberty Inn
3839 S. Topeka Blvd.
Topeka, KS 66609
Phone: (913) 266-4700

Pet Restrictions: None
Pet left unattended in room: Yes, no
    housekeeping
Exercise Area for Pets: Yes
Rates: $36 to $42

Ramada Inn - South
3847 S. Topeka Blvd.
Topeka, KS 66609
Phone: (913) 267-1800

Pet Restrictions: Small in carrier
Exercise Area for Pets: Yes
Rates: $25.50 to $40

VETERINARIANS

Animal Clinic of North Topeka
625 West Highway 24, 66608
(913) 357-5188

West Ridge Animal Hosital
2147 Southwest Wesport Dr. 66614
(913) 272-3333

WICHITA
Comfort Inn
4849 S. Laura
Wichita, KS 67216
Phone: (316) 522-1800

Pet Restrictions: Under 25 lbs.
Exercise Area for Pets: Yes
Rates: $46 to $54

La Quinta Inn
7700 E. Kellogg
Wichita, KS 67207
Phone: (316) 681-2881

Pet Restrictions: Small pets
Exercise Area for Pets: Yes
Rates: $48 to $66

VETERINARIANS
Indian Hills Animal Clinic
3223 West 13th St. 67203
(316) 942-3900

Helten Veterinary Clinic
6630 West Central 67212
(916) 942-1002

Bogue Animal Hospital West PA
429 North Maize 67212
(316) 722-1085

KENTUCKY — HOTELS

ASHLAND

Knights Inn
7216 SR60
Ashland, KY 41101
Phone: (606) 928-9501
Pet Restrictions: One night only
Exercise Area for Pets: Yes
Rates: $38 to $43

VETERINARIANS

Academy Animal Hospital
9123 Midland Trail 41101
Phone: (606) 928-9552

BARDSTOWN

Old Kentucky Home Motel
414 W. Stephen Foster Ave.
Bardstown, KY 40004
Phone: (502) 348-5979
Pet Restrictions: None
Exercise Area for Pets: Yes
Rates: Vary

BOWLING GREEN

Budget Inn of Bowling Green
165 Three Springs Rd.
Bowling Green, KY 42105
Phone: (502) 843-3200
Pet Restrictions: Smoking room
Pet left unattended in room: Yes, if
    quiet
Exercise Area for Pets: Yes
Rates: $36 to $52

Holiday Inn I-65
3240 Scottsville Rd.
Bowling Green, KY 42101
Phone: (502) 781-1500
Pet Restrictions: Small pets only
Pet left unattended in room: Yes
Exercise Area for Pets: Yes
Rates: $58 to $64

VETERINARIANS

Denton, Donald G.
2010 Russellville Rd. 42101
Phone: (502) 782-1644

BEREA

Boone Tavern Inn
Main & Prospect Sts.
Berea, KY 40404
Phone: (606) 986-9358,
    (800) 366-9358
Pet Restrictions: Caged or leashed
Pet left unattended in room: Yes
Exercise Area for Pets: Yes
Rates: $52 to $69

CAVE CITY

Days Inn
P.O. Box 2009
Cave City, KY 42127
Phone: (502) 773-2151
Pet Restrictions: None
Pet left unattended in room: Yes if
    in cage
Exercise Area for Pets: Yes
Rates: $48 to $56

Heritage Inn
P.O. Box 2048
Cave City, KY 42127
Phone: (502) 773-3121
Pet Restrictions: None
Exercise Area for Pets: Yes
Rates: $68

Jolly's Motel
P.O. Box 327, US 31W North
Cave City, KY 42127
Phone: (502) 773-3118
Pet Restrictions: $3 fee
Exercise Area for Pets: Yes
Rates: $20 to $35

CORBIN

Days Inn
I75C US 25W
Corbin, KY 40701
Phone: (606) 528-8150
Pet Restrictions: Small pets, if well
    trained
Pet left unattended in room: Yes
Exercise Area for Pets: Yes
Rates: $32.88 to $36.88

Holiday Inn
2615 Cumberland Falls Hwy
Corbin, KY 40701
Phone: (606) 528-6301
Pet Restrictions: If well behaved
Pet left unattended in room: Yes
Exercise Area for Pets: Yes
Rates: $48 to $62

Knights Inn
RR 11, Box 256
Corbin, KY 40701
Phone: (606) 523-1500
Pet Restrictions: None
Exercise Area for Pets: Yes
Rates: $38.50 to $40

Red Carpet Inn
1891 Cumberland Falls Hwy.
Corbin, KY 40701
Phone: (606) 528-7100

Pet Restrictions: $5 fee, if quiet
Exercise Area for Pets: Yes
Exercise Area for Pets: Yes
Rates: $29.88

COVINGTON
Holiday Inn - Riverfront
600 W. 3rd St.
Covington, KY 41011
Phone: (606) 291-4300

Pet Restrictions: Small pets
Exercise Area for Pets: Yes
Rates: $79 to $89

VETERINARIANS

Crescent Springs Animal Hosp.
2521 Ritchie Rd. 41017
Phone: (606) 331-8083

ELIZABETHTOWN
Howard Johnsons
708 E. Dixie Hwy
Elizabethtown, KY 42701
Phone: (502) 765-2185

Pet Restrictions: None
Pet left unattended in room: Yes
Exercise Area for Pets: Yes
Rates: $29.95 to $52.95

VETERINARIANS

Helmwood Veterinary Clinic
804 North Dixie Ave. 42701
Phone: (502) 737-1818

ERLANGER
Comfort Inn
630 Commonwealth Ave.
Erlanger, KY 41018
Phone: (606) 727-3400

Pet Restrictions: None
Pet left unattended in room: Yes, if
    quiet
Exercise Area for Pets: Yes
Rates: $55

FLORENCE
Envoy Inn - Florence
8075 Stetlen Dr.
Florence, KY 41042
Phone: (606) 371-0277

Pet Restrictions: None, notify
    management
Exercise Area for Pets: Yes
Rates: $31.95 to $45.95

Holiday Inn - Florence
8050 US 42
Florence, KY 41042
Phone: (606) 371-2700

Pet Restrictions: None
Pet left unattended in room: Yes if
    quiet
Exercise Area for Pets: Yes
Rates: $59 to $67

Knights Inn - Cincin. South
8049 Dream St.
Florence, KY 41042
Phone: (606) 371-9711

Pet Restrictions: None
Pet left unattended in room: Yes, no
    housekeeping
Exercise Area for Pets: Yes
Rates: $33.31 to $44.64

FORT MITCHELL
Holiday Inn - South
2100 Dixie Hwy
Fort Mitchell, KY 41011
Phone: (606) 331-1500

Pet Restrictions: Under 20 lbs.
Exercise Area for Pets: Yes
Rates: $72 to $82

FORT WRIGHT
Days Inn - Ft. Wright
1945 Dixie Hwy.
Ft. Wright, KY 41011
Phone: (606) 341-8801

Pet Restrictions: Small pets
Pet left unattended in room: Yes if
    well behaved, no maid service
Exercise Area for Pets: Yes
Rates: $35 to $39

FRANKFORT
Blue Grass Inn
635 Versailles Rd.
Frankfort, KY 40601
Phone: (502) 695-1800

Pet Restrictions: None
Exercise Area for Pets: Yes
Rates: $36 to $50

GEORGETOWN
Days Inn
Delaplain Rd.
Georgetown, KY 40324
Phone: (502) 863-5000

Pet Restrictions: $4 fee
Pet left unattended in room: Yes
Exercise Area for Pets: Yes
Rates: $40

KENTUCKY — HOTELS (continued)

GLASGLOW

Glasglow Inn
US68 @31E
Glasglow, KY 42141
Phone: (502) 651-5191

Pet Restrictions: Small pets
Pet left unattended in room: Yes
Exercise Area for Pets: Yes
Rates: $40 to $45

HARDIN

Early American Motel
Hwy 68, Rt. 1
Hardin, KY 42048
Phone: (502) 474-2241

Pet Restrictions: None
Exercise Area for Pets: Yes
Rates: $26.50 to $47.95

HORSE CAVE

Budget Host Inn
P.O. Box 332
Horse Cave, KY 42749
Phone: (502) 786-2165

Pet Restrictions: None
Exercise Area for Pets: Yes
Rates: $24.95 to $100

LEXINGTON

Days Inn
826 New Circle Rd NE
Lexington, KY 40505
Phone: (606) 252-2262

Pet Restrictions: None
Pet left unattended in room: Yes if
    well behaved
Exercise Area for Pets: Yes
Rates: $48

Econo Lodge
5527 Athen-Boonesboro Rd.
Lexington, KY 40509
Phone: (606) 263-5101

Pet Restrictions: None
Pet left unattended in room: Yes if
    quiet
Exercise Area for Pets: Yes
Rates: $31 to $35

Grenelete Inn
2280 Nicholasville Rd.
Lexington, KY 40503
Phone: (606) 277-1191

Pet Restrictions: None
Pet left unattended in room: Yes if
    well behaved, notify maids
Exercise Area for Pets: Yes
Rates: $36 to $51

Holiday Inn - North
1950 Newtown Pike
Lexington, KY 40511
Phone: (606) 233-0512

Pet Restrictions: None, if quiet
Exercise Area for Pets: Yes
Exercise Area for Pets: Yes
Rates: $84 to $89

La Quinta Motor Inn
1919 Stanton Way
Lexington, KY 40511
Phone: (606) 231-7551

Pet Restrictions: Small pets
Pet left unattended in room: Yes
Exercise Area for Pets: Yes
Rates: $52 to 61

Motel 6
2260 Elkhorn Rd.
Lexington, KY 40505
Phone: (606) 293-1431

Pet Restrictions: Small pets
Exercise Area for Pets: Yes
Rates: $31.95

Red Roof Inn
483 Haggard Lane
Lexington, KY 40505
Phone: (606) 293-2626

Pet Restrictions: Under 35 lbs.
Pet left unattended in room: Yes
Exercise Area for Pets: Yes
Rates: $35 to $50

Travelodge - Lexington
1987 N. Broadway
Lexington, KY 40505
Phone: (606) 299-1202

Pet Restrictions: $7 fee
Exercise Area for Pets: Yes
Rates: $35 to $52

VETERINARIANS

Gainesway Small Animal Clinic
1230 Armstrong Mill Rd. 40502
Phone: (606) 272-9625

Jenson, Deane
1410 Village Dr. 40504
Phone: (606) 252-4917

Ashley, Karen Elizabeth
729 Sunset Dr. 40502
Phone: (606) 252-5640

LIBERTY
The Brown Motel
P.O. Box 66
Liberty, KY 42539
Phone: (606) 787-6224

Pet Restrictions: None
Pet left unattended in room: Yes
Exercise Area for Pets: Yes
Rates: $38 to $50

LONDON
Ramada Inn
1025 W. 192 Bypass
London, KY 40741
Phone: (606) 864-7331

Pet Restrictions: None
Exercise Area for Pets: Yes
Rates: $38.95 to $46.95

LOUISVILLE
Holiday Inn Airport East
1465 Gardiner Lane
Louisville, KY 40213
Phone: (502) 452-6361

Pet Restrictions: Under 10 lbs.
Pet left unattended in room: Yes
Exercise Area for Pets: Yes
Rates: $49 to $70

Holiday Inn - Downtown
120 W. Broadway
Louisville, KY 40202
Phone: (502) 582-2241

Pet Restrictions: None
Exercise Area for Pets: Yes
Rates: $71 to $91

Holiday Inn South - Airport
3317 Fern Valley Rd.
Louisville, KY 40213
Phone: (502) 964-3311

Pet Restrictions: None
Pet left unattended in room: Yes if
    well behaved
Exercise Area for Pets: Yes
Rates: $67 to $75

Holiday Inn - Southeast
3255 Bardstown Rd.
Louisville, KY 40205
Phone: (502) 454-0451

Pet Restrictions: Annex building, if
    in cage
Pet left unattended in room: Yes
Exercise Area for Pets: Yes
Rates: $55 to $70

Holiday Inn - Southwest
4110 Dixie Hwy
Louisville, KY 40216
Phone: (502) 448-2020

Pet Restrictions: On leash at all
    times
Pet left unattended in room: Yes if
    in cage
Exercise Area for Pets: Yes
Rates: $54 to $65

Hurstbourne Hotel
9700 Bluegrass Pkwy
Louisville, KY 40299
Phone: (502) 491-4830

Pet Restrictions: $25 fee
Pet left unattended in room: Yes
Exercise Area for Pets: Yes
Rates: $65+

Red Roof Inn
9330 Blairwood Rd.
Louisville, KY 40222
Phone: (502) 426-7621

Pet Restrictions: If quiet, notify maid
Pet left unattended in room: Yes
Exercise Area for Pets: Yes
Rates: $28.99 to $33.99

Residence Inn by Marriott
120 N. Hurstbourne Lane
Louisville, KY 40222
Phone: (502) 425-1821

Pet Restrictions: $10 night
Pet left unattended in room: Yes
Exercise Area for Pets: Yes
Rates: $109 to $140

The Seelback - A Doubletree Hotel
500 Fourth Ave.
Louisville, KY 40202
Phone: (502) 585-3200

Pet Restrictions: None
Pet left unattended in room: Yes
Exercise Area for Pets: Nearby
Rates: $100 to $450

VETERINARIANS

Auburdale Animal Hospital
7136 Southside Dr. 40214
Phone: (502) 361-2622

Fairleigh Animal Hospital
4156 Westport Rd., Suite 206 40207
Phone: (502) 897-1000

Jefferson Animal Hospital and Emergency Center
4505 Outter Loop 40219
Phone: (502) 966-4104

MADISONVILLE

Days Inn
Pennyrite Pkwy, P.O. Box 34
Madisonville, KY 42341
Phone: (502) 821-8620

Pet Restrictions: None, if well
    behaved
Pet left unattended in room: Yes
Exercise Area for Pets: Yes
Rates: $53 to $57

VETERINARIANS

Pennyrile Animal Clinic
Rd. 4/US 41 North Main St. 42431
Phone: (502) 821-7920

OWENSBORO

Days Inn
3720 New Hartford Rd.
Owensboro, KY 42301
Phone: (502) 684-9621

Pet Restrictions: None if well
    behaved
Pet left unattended in room: Yes
Exercise Area for Pets: Yes
Rates: $40 to $44

Holiday Inn
3136 W. Second St.
Owensboro, KY 42301
Phone: (502) 685-3941

Pet Restrictions: None
Exercise Area for Pets: Yes
Rates: $53 to $75

VETERINARIANS

Towne Square Animal Hospital
4804 Towne Square Court 42301
Phone: (502) 685-1111

PADUCAH

Budget Host Inn
1234 Broadway
Paducah, KY 42001
Phone: (502) 443-8401

Pet Restrictions: Small pets
Exercise Area for Pets: Yes
Rates: $31.95 to $36

Drury Inn
Hinkleville Rd.
Paducah, KY 42001
Phone: (502) 443-3313

Pet Restrictions: None, use do not
    disturb sign
Pet left unattended in room: Yes
Exercise Area for Pets: Yes
Rates: $44 to $52

Thrifty Inn
4930 Hinkleville Rd.
Paducah, KY 42001
Phone: (502) 442-4500

Pet Restrictions: Small pets
Exercise Area for Pets: Yes
Rates: $37.70 to $54.88

VETERINARIANS

Paducah Veterinary Clinic
3205 Central Ave. 42001
Phone: (502) 443-8835

PAINTSVILLE

Heart O'Highlands Motel
US 23 S
Paintsville, KY 41240
Phone: (606) 789-3551

Pet Restrictions: None
Pet left unattended in room: Yes
Exercise Area for Pets: Yes
Rates: $32 to $34

RICHMOND

Holiday Inn
100 Eastern Bypass
Richmond, KY 40475
Phone: (606) 623-9220

Pet Restrictions: Smoking rooms, if
    quiet
Pet left unattended in room: Yes
Exercise Area for Pets: Yes
Rates: $45 to $52

KENTUCKY — HOTELS (continued)

Mars Motel
105 N. Killarney La.
Richmond, KY 40475
Phone: (606) 623-8126

Pet Restrictions: None if
  housebroken
Exercise Area for Pets: Yes
Rates: $23 to $45

Motel 6
US 421 & I 75
Richmond, KY 40475
Phone: (606) 623-0880

Pet Restrictions: Small pets
Exercise Area for Pets: Yes
Rates: $27.95+

Thrifty Dutchman Motel
230 Eastern Bypass
Richmond, KY 40475
Phone: (606) 623-8813

Pet Restrictions: Small, quiet
Pet left unattended in room: Yes
Exercise Area for Pets: Yes
Rates: $28 to $32.95

SHEPHERDSVILLE
Days Inn
SR 44 at Jct. I65
Shepherdsville, KY 40165
Phone: (502) 543-3011

Pet Restrictions: None
Exercise Area for Pets: Yes
Rates: $40

Ramada Limited
Paroquet Springs Dr.
Shepherdsville, KY 40165
Phone: (502) 543-4400

Pet Restrictions: $6 fee
Pet left unattended in room: Yes
Exercise Area for Pets: Yes
Rates: $37 to $44

WALTON
Days Inn
1177 Frontage Rd.
Walton, KY 41094
Phone: (606) 485-4151

Pet Restrictions: None
Pet left unattended in room: Yes
Exercise Area for Pets: Yes
Rates: $40

WILLIAMSBURG
Howard Johnson
10 Skyway Dr.
Williamsburg, KY 41097
Phone: (606) 824-7177

Pet Restrictions: Smoking room
Pet left unattended in room: Yes
Exercise Area for Pets: Yes
Rates: $37 to $40

WINCHESTER
Best Western Country Squire Motel
1307 W. Lexington Rd.
Winchester, KY 40391
Phone: (606) 744-7210

Pet Restrictions: $4 fee
Pet left unattended in room: Yes
Exercise Area for Pets: Yes
Rates: $36 to $50

LOUISIANA — HOTELS

ALEXANDRIA

Days Inn
P.O. Box 7026
Alexandria, LA 71306
Phone: (318) 443-7331

Pet Restrictions: Small animals, but
prefer not
Pet left unattended in room: Yes
Exercise Area for Pets: Yes
Rates: $35 to $40

Rodeway Inn
742 MacArthur Dr.
Alexandria, LA 71301
Phone: (318) 448-1611

Pet Restrictions: $25 deposit, small
pets if well behaved
Pet left unattended in room: Yes
Exercise Area for Pets: Yes
Rates: $36 to $51

Fitzgerald Animal Hospital
5119 Mason Dr. 71301
Phone: (318) 445-6428

McGraw, David D.
4801 Masonic Dr. 71301
Phone: (318) 442-4222

BATON ROUGE

Red Roof Inn
11314 Boardwalk Dr.
Baton Rouge, LA 70816
Phone: (504) 275-6600

Pet Restrictions: Only small animals,
please notify
Pet left unattended in room: Yes
Rates: $34.95

Goodwood Animal Hospital
3778 Goodwood Blvd. 70806
Phone: (504) 927-9940

Highland Road Animal Hospital
7280 Highland Rd. 70808
Phone: (504) 766-3200

**Louisiana State University
Vet. Teaching Hosp. & Clinic**
(504) 346-3333

BOSSIER CITY

Days Inn Bossier
200 John Wesley Blvd.
Bossier City, LA 71112
Phone: (318) 742-9200

Pet Restrictions: $5/day fee
Pet left unattended in room: Yes
Exercise Area for Pets: Yes
Rates: $19.95 to $23.95

Residence Inn
1001 Gould Dr.
Bossier City, LA 71111
Phone: (318) 747-6220

Pet Restrictions: Non-refundable
$25, $5/night, guest's discretion,
notify housekeeping
Pet left unattended in room: Yes
Exercise Area for Pets: Nearby
Rates: $75 to $125

Ritter, Glen A.
701 Westgate Drive 7111
Phone: (318) 742-1521

DE RIDDER

Park Motel
806 North Pine
De Ridder, LA 70634
Phone: (318) 463-8605

Pet Restrictions: Keep quiet and well
behaved, no housekeeping if
guest not present
Pet left unattended in room: Yes
Exercise Area for Pets: Yes
Rates: $30 to $54

Kelty, Cecil D.
Deridder Veterinary Clinic 70634
Phone: (318) 463-6040

LAFAYETTE

Red Roof Inn
1718 N. University Dr.
Lafayette, LA 70507
Phone: (318) 233-3339

Pet Restrictions: Under 15 lbs.
Exercise Area for Pets: Yes
Rates: $38 to $44

LOUISIANA — HOTELS (continued)

VETERINARIANS

Els II, EJ
2206 Moss St.
(318) 233-4681

Rausch, ME
1210 Kaliste Saloom Rd.
(318) 984-3889

LAKE CHARLES

Days Inn
1010 Hwy 171N
Lake Charles, LA 70601
Phone: (318) 433-1711

Pet Restrictions: $4 per day
Pet left unattended in room: Yes
Exercise Area for Pets: Yes
Rates: $34 to $41

VETERINARIANS

University Animal Hospital
623 East McNeese Street 70605
Phone: (318) 478-5188

NEW ORLEANS

Quality Inn
3900 Tulane Ave.
New Orleans, LA 70119
Phone: (504) 486-5541

Pet Restrictions: $10/day
Pet left unattended in room: Yes
Rates: $49 to $200

VETERINARIANS

Aurora Animal Hospital Inc.
2123 General Meyer Ave. 70014
Phone: (504) 362-8060

Crowder Animal Hospital Inc.
5427 Crowder Blvd. 70127
Phone: (504) 241-6633

Elysian Fields Animal Clinic Inc.
4237 Elysian Fields Ave. 70122
Phone: (504) 288-4797

PORT ALLEN

Newcourt Inn
P.O. Box 642
Port Allen, LA 70767
Phone: (504) 381-9134

Pet Restrictions: $5/day
Pet left unattended in room: Yes
Exercise Area for Pets: Yes
Rates: $39.95 to $44.95

RUSTON

Best Western King's Inn
1111 N. Trenton St.
Ruston, LA 71270
Phone: (318) 251-0000

Pet Restrictions: Small pets, $2/day
Exercise Area for Pets: Yes
Rates: $36 to $45

Red Roof Inn
7296 Greenwood Rd.
Shreveport, LA 71119
Phone: (318) 938-5342

Pet Restrictions: None
Pet left unattended in room: Yes,
    must notify
Exercise Area for Pets: Yes
Rates: $27 to $42

VETERINARIANS

University Vet. Hospital
7700 E. Kings Hwy.
(318) 797-5522

Wynn, Winburn, N.
850 Havens Rd.
(318) 424-8313

SHREVEPORT

Red Roof Inn
7296 Greenwood Rd.
Shreveport, LA 71119
Phone: (318) 938-5342

Pet Restrictions: None
Pet left unattended in room: Yes,
    must notify
Exercise Area for Pets: Yes
Rates: $27 to $42

VETERINARIANS

University Vet. Hospital
7700 E. Kings Hwy.
(318) 797-5522

Wynn, Winburn N.
850 Havens Rd.
(318) 424-8313

WEST MONROE

Red Roof Inn
102 I 20 Constitution Drive
West Monroe, LA 71291
Phone: (318) 388-2420

Pet Restrictions: Small pets
Pet left unattended in room: Yes
Rates: $30.99 to $35.99

MAINE — HOTELS

AUGUSTA

Best Western Senator Inn
284 Western Ave.
Augusta, ME
Phone: (207) 622-5804

Pet Restrictions: None
Exercise Area for Pets: Yes
Rates: $68

VETERINARIANS

Pine Tree Veterinary Hosp.
220 Western Ave. 04330
Phone: (207) 622-6181

BANGOR

Airport Hilton Inn
308 Godfrey Blvd.
Bangor, ME 04401
Phone: (207) 947-6721

Pet Restrictions: Under 50 lbs.
Exercise Area for Pets: Nearby
Rates: $115 to $130

Best Western White House
155 Littlefield Ave.
Bangor, ME 04401
Phone: (207) 862-3737

Pet Restrictions: None
Exercise Area for Pets: Yes
Rates: $44 to $49

Comfort Inn
750 Hogan Rd.
Bangor, ME 04401
Phone: (207) 942-7899

Pet Restrictions: $6 fee, if quiet
Pet left unattended in room: Yes
Exercise Area for Pets: Yes
Rates: $42.50 to $65

Days Inn
250 Odlin Rd.
Bangor, ME 04401
Phone: (207) 942-8272

Pet Restrictions: Domestic animal, if quiet
Pet left unattended in room: Yes
Exercise Area for Pets: Yes
Rates: $50 to $70

Howard Johnson
482 Odlin Rd.
Bangor, ME 04401
Phone: (207) 942-6301

Pet Restrictions: $5 fee
Exercise Area for Pets: Yes
Rates: $34.95 to $39.95

Quality Inn-Phoenix
20 Westmarket Sq.
Bangor, ME 04401
Phone: (207) 947-3850

Pet Restrictions: None, if quiet
Pet left unattended in room: Yes
Exercise Area for Pets: Yes
Rates: Call for rates

Ramada Inn
357 Odlin Rd.
Bangor, ME 04401
Phone: (207) 947-6961

Pet Restrictions: Small pets, if quiet
Pet left unattended in room: Yes
Exercise Area for Pets: Yes
Rates: $72 to $109

Red Carpet Inn
480 Main St.
Bangor, ME 04401
Phone: (207) 942-5281

Pet Restrictions: None
Exercise Area for Pets: Yes
Rates: $25 to $36

VETERINARIANS

Penobscot Veterinary Hospital
411 Davis Rd. 04401
Phone: (207) 947-6783

BAR HARBOR

Atlantic Oakes by the Sea
P.O. Box 3
Bar Harbor, ME 04609
Phone: (207) 288-5801

Pet Restrictions: Not during July or August
Exercise Area for Pets: Yes
Rates: $113 to $146

Wonderview Motor Lodge
Box 25
Bar Harbor, ME 04609
Phone: (207) 288-3358

Pet Restrictions: None
Pet left unattended in room: Yes
Exercise Area for Pets: Yes
Rates: Vary with season

BELFAST

Admirals Ocean Inn
RR1 Box 99A
Belfast, ME 04915
Phone: (207) 338-4260

Pet Restrictions: $20 deposit
Pet left unattended in room: Yes
Exercise Area for Pets: Yes
Rates: $50 to $100

Belfast Bay Meadows Inn
90 Northport Ave.
Belfast, ME 04915
Phone: 1-(800)-335-2377,
    1-207-338-5715
Fax: 1-(207)-338-5715

Pet Restrictions: None; 2 large
    rooms and one efficiency
Pet left unattended in room: No
Exercise Area for Pets: Yes
Other: Beach, fields and woods on
    premises
Rates: $75 to $135

Penobscot Meadows Inn
US 1; 2 mi. S from jct. SR 3
Belfast, ME 04915
Phone: (207) 338-5320

Pet Restrictions: Give advance
    notice
Exercise Area for Pets: Yes
Rates: $69 to $99

BETHEL
Bethel Inn & Country Club
P.O. Box 49
Bethel, ME 04217
Phone: (207) 824-2175

Pet Restrictions: None, if well
    behaved
Pet left unattended in room: Yes
Exercise Area for Pets: Yes
Rates: $150 to $220 full breakfast &
    dinner

BREWER
Brewer Motor Inn
359 Wilson St.
Brewer, ME 04412
Phone: (207) 989-4478

Pet Restrictions: None, if quiet
Pet left unattended in room: Yes
Exercise Area for Pets: Yes
Rates: $32 to $49

VETERINARIANS
Feher, Robert C.
Route 1, Box 474
Pierce Rd. 04412
Phone: (207) 989-6531

Volz, David M.
Brewer Veterinary Clinic 04412
Phone: (207) 989-6531

BRUNSWICK
The Atrium Motel - Brunswick
Cooks Corner
Brunswick, ME 04011
Phone: (207) 729-5555

Pet Restrictions: Small pets, if quiet
Pet left unattended in room: Yes
Exercise Area for Pets: Yes
Rates: $74 to $86

Mainline Motel
133 Pleasant St.
Brunswick, ME 04011
Phone: (207) 725-8761

Pet Restrictions: Small pets, if quiet
Pet left unattended in room: Yes
Exercise Area for Pets: Yes
Rates: $59 to $79

VETERINARIANS
Bath-Brunswick Vet. Hosp.
257 Bath Rd., P.O. Box 70 04011
Phone: (207) 729-4165

Pietz, W. Guy
304 Maine St. 04011
Phone: (207) 729-3412

BUCKSPORT
Jed Prouty Motel
P.O. Box 826
Bucksport, ME 04416
Phone: (207) 469-3113

Pet Restrictions: Small pets
Exercise Area for Pets: Yes
Rates: $59 to $89

Spring Fountain Motel
RFD2, Box 710
Bucksport, ME 04416
Phone: (207) 469-3139

Pet Restrictions: $5 fee
Exercise Area for Pets: Yes
Rates: $34.95 to $59.95

CAMDEN
Blue Harbor House
67 Elm St.
Camden, ME 04843
Phone: (207) 236-3196

Pet Restrictions: Dogs and cats only
Pet left unattended in room: Yes
Exercise Area for Pets: Yes
Rates: $95 to $125

MAINE — HOTELS (continued)

The Lodge at Camden Hills
P.O. Box 794
Camden, ME 04843
Phone: (207) 236-8478,
    800-832-7058
Pet Restrictions: None
Exercise Area for Pets: Yes
Rates: $75 to $160

CENTER LOVELL
Westways on Kezar Lake
Rt. 5
Center Lovell, ME 04016
Phone: (207) 928-2663
Pet Restrictions: In 3 cottages
Pet left unattended in room: Yes;
    well mannered
Exercise Area for Pets: Yes
Rates: $90 and up

CAPE NEDDICK
Country View Motel & Greenhouse
1521 Rte. 1
Cape Neddick, ME 03902
Phone: (207) 363-7160
Pet Restrictions: None; 14 units -
    large rooms
Pet left unattended in room: No
Rates: $45 to $84 - summer

CASTINE
The Manor
P.O. Box 276
Castine, ME 04421
Phone: (207) 326-4861
Pet Restrictions: Well behaved only
Rates: $15 to $55

DAMARISCOTTA
County Fair Motel
RFD Box 36
Damariscotta, ME 04543
Phone: (207) 563-3769
Pet Restrictions: None
Exercise Area for Pets: Yes
Rates: $52 to $58

EAST BOOTHBAY
Smugglers Cove Motor Inn
East Boothbay, ME 04544
Phone: (207) 633-2800
Pet Restrictions: Fee and deposit
Exercise Area for Pets: Yes
Rates: $62 to $120

ELLSWORTH
Colonial Motor Lodge
Bar Harbor Rd.
Ellsworth, ME 04605
Phone: (207) 667-5548
Pet Restrictions: None, owner
    responsible
Exercise Area for Pets: Yes
Rates: $40 to $80

Holiday Inn
High St.
Ellsworth, ME 04605
Phone: (207) 667-9341
Pet Restrictions: None
Exercise Area for Pets: Yes
Rates: $89 to $110

Jaspers Motel
200 High St.
Ellsworth, ME 04605
Phone: (207) 667-5318
Pet Restrictions: Domestic animals
Exercise Area for Pets: Yes
Rates: $62 to $66

The White Birches
P.O. Box 743
Ellsworth, ME 04605
Phone: (207) 667-3621
Pet Restrictions: No horses, if well
    behaved
Pet left unattended in room: Yes
Exercise Area for Pets: Yes
Rates: $59 to $74

VETERINARIANS
Small Animal Clinic
275 High St. 04605
Phone: (207) 667-2341

FALMOUTH
The Buoy Motel
374 US 1
Falmouth, ME 04105
Phone: (207) 781-3145
Pet Restrictions: Dogs and cats, at
    management's discretion
Exercise Area for Pets: Yes
Rates: $40 to $65

VETERINARIANS
Falmouth Foreside Vet. Clinic
174 US Route 1 04105
Phone: (207) 781-4028

FARMINGTON
Mount Blue Motel
RFD 4, Box 5060
Farmington, ME 04938
Phone: (207) 778-6004

Pet Restrictions: $7 fee
Exercise Area for Pets: Yes
Rates: $40 to $74

VETERINARIANS
Dingley, Peter Y.
90 High St. 04938
Phone: (207) 778-2061

Rockwood, Kenneth H.
RFD #2 04938
Phone: (207) 778-2840

FREEPORT
Freeport Inn
335 US Route 1
Freeport, ME 04032
Phone: (207) 865-3106

Pet Restrictions: None, if well
    behaved
Pet left unattended in room: Yes
Exercise Area for Pets: Yes
Rates: $89 to $99

Isaac Randall House
Indepedence Drive
Freeport, ME 04032
Phone: (207) 865-9295

Pet Restrictions: None
Exercise Area for Pets: Yes
Rates: $70 to $110

GREENVILLE JCT.
Greenwood Motel
P.O. Box 307
Greenville Junction, ME 04442
Phone: (207) 695-3321

Pet Restrictions: $5/nite/pet
Exercise Area for Pets: Yes
Rates: $50 to $55

Indian Hill Motel
P.O. Box 1181
Greenville, ME 04441
Phone: (207) 695-2623

Pet Restrictions: None, check with
    management, $5 fee, some
    rules apply
Exercise Area for Pets: Yes
Rates: $40 to $45

KENNEBUNKPORT
Captain Jefferds Inn
Box 691 Pearl St.
Kennebunkport, ME 04046
Phone: (207) 967-2311

Pet Restrictions: House trained
Exercise Area for Pets: Yes
Rates: $85 to $125 includes full
    breakfast

The Colony
Kings Rd. and Ocean Ave.
Kennebunkport, ME
Phone: (207) 967-3331

Pet Restrictions: $15 per day
Exercise Area for Pets: Yes
Rates: $165 to $295

VETERINARIANS
Vigue, Frank R.
1470 Ocean Ave. 04046

KITTERY
Kittery Motor Inn
Rt. 1 Bypass
Kittery, ME 03904
Phone: (207) 439-2000

Pet Restrictions: None
Exercise Area for Pets: Yes
Rates: $39 to $69

LUBEC
The Eastland Motel
Box 220
Lubec, ME 04652
Phone: (207) 733-5501

Pet Restrictions: Dogs and cats
Exercise Area for Pets: Yes
Rates: $48 to $56

MACHIAS
The Bluebird Motel
RFD Box 45
Machias, ME 04654
Phone: (207) 255-3332

Pet Restrictions: None
Exercise Area for Pets: Yes
Rates: $50 to $64

Machias Motor Inn
26 E. Main St.
Machias, ME 04654
Phone: (207) 255-4861

Pet Restrictions: $5 fee, if well
    behaved, owner responsible
Pet left unattended in room: Yes
Exercise Area for Pets: Yes
Rates: $56 to $60

MILLINOCKET
The Atrium Inn & Health Club
740 Central St.
Millinocket, ME 04462
Phone: (207) 723-4555

Pet Restrictions: None
Exercise Area for Pets: Yes
Rates: $60 to $90

NEWPORT
Lovely's Motel
P.O. Box 147
Newport, ME 04953
Phone: (207) 368-4311

Pet Restrictions: None
Exercise Area for Pets: Yes
Rates: $59.90 to $79.90

NORTH ANSON
Embden Lake Resorts
RR1, Box 3395
North Anson, ME 04958
Phone: (207) 566-7501

Pet Restrictions: $10 fee
Pet left unattended in room: Yes
Exercise Area for Pets: Yes
Rates: $52 and up

NORWAY
Ledgewood Motel
RFD 2, Box 30
Norway, ME 04268
Phone: (207) 743-6347

Pet Restrictions: None
Exercise Area for Pets: Yes
Rates: $49

VETERINARIANS
Norway Veterinary Hospital
Lower Main St. 04268
Phone: (207) 743-6384

OGUNQUIT
Studio East Motor Inn
P.O. Box 1827
Ogunquit, ME 03907
Phone: (207) 646-7297

Pet Restrictions: Quiet &
    well-behaved
Pet left unattended in room: Yes, on
    trial basis
Exercise Area for Pets: Yes
Rates: $70 to $89

ORONO
University Motor Inn
5 College Ave.
Orono, ME 04473
Phone: (207) 866-4921

Pet Restrictions: None
Exercise Area for Pets: Yes
Rates: $68

SOUTH PORTLAND
Comfort Inn
90 Main Mall Rd.
South Portland, ME 04100
Phone: (207) 775-0409

Pet Restrictions: $5/night
Exercise Area for Pets: Yes
Rates: $77 to $89

PORTLAND
Holiday Inn West
81 Riverside St.
Portland, ME 04103
Phone: (207) 774-5601

Pet Restrictions: Smoking rooms
    only, no housekeeping
Pet left unattended in room: Yes
Exercise Area for Pets: Yes
Rates: $82 to $109

Howard Johnson's Lodge
155 Riverside St.
Portland, ME 04103
Phone: (207) 774-5861

Pet Restrictions: $50 deposit, not
    for long periods of time
Pet left unattended in room: Yes
Exercise Area for Pets: Yes
Rates: $94 to $160

VETERINARIANS
North Deering Vet. Hosp.
456 Auburn St. 04103
Phone: (207) 797-4855

MAINE — HOTELS (continued)

PRESQUE ISLE
Keddy's Inn
P.O. Box 270
Presque Isle, ME 04769
Phone: (207) 764-3321
Pet Restrictions: None
Exercise Area for Pets: Yes
Rates: $28 to $82

Northern Lights Motel
692 Main St.
Presque Isle, ME 04764
Phone: (207) 764-4441
Pet Restrictions: No large dogs
Exercise Area for Pets: Yes
Rates: $24.95 to $42.75

RANGELEY
Country Club Inn
P.O. Box 680
Rangeley, ME 04970
Phone: (207) 864-3831
Pet Restrictions: $10/day, if well behaved
Pet left unattended in room: Yes
Exercise Area for Pets: Yes
Rates: $67 to $76

Rangeley Inn & Motor Lodge
Box 160
Rangeley, ME 04970
Phone: (207) 864-3341
Pet Restrictions: $8 fee/night, certain number of rooms
Exercise Area for Pets: Yes
Rates: $65 to $110

ROCKLAND
Navigator Motor Inn
520 Main St.
Rockland, ME 04841
Phone: (207) 594-2131
Pet Restrictions: None
Pet left unattended in room: Yes
Exercise Area for Pets: Yes
Rates: $65 to $95

Trade Winds Motor Inn
2 Park View Dr.
Rockland, ME 04841
Phone: (207) 596-6661
Pet Restrictions: Housebroken, if quiet
Pet left unattended in room: Yes
Exercise Area for Pets: Yes
Rates: $70 to $125

VETERINARIANS
Davis, Sybil S.
355 Old County Rd. 04841
Phone: (207) 594-5850

Sidwell II, Walter L.
RFD #1, Box 644 04841
Phone: (207) 594-2581

ROCKPORT
Deep Harbor Motel
Rt. 1, Box 616
Rockport, ME 04856
Phone: (207) 236-2205
Pet Restrictions: $50 deposit
Pet left unattended in room: Yes
Exercise Area for Pets: Yes
Rates: $55 per night, $335 week in summer

VETERINARIANS
Steinglass, Victor J.
Route 1 04856
Phone: (207) 236-2311

RUMFORD
Linnell Motel
US 2
Rumford, ME 04276
Phone: (207) 364-4511, 800-446-9038
Pet Restrictions: Dog or cat, notify reservations
Exercise Area for Pets: Yes
Rates: $42 to $58

Madison Motor Inn
P.O. Box 398
Rumford, ME 04276
Phone: (207) 364-7973
Pet Restrictions: No housekeeping
Pet left unattended in room: Yes
Exercise Area for Pets: Yes
Rates: $60 to $85

SACO
Tourist Haven Motel
757 Portland Rd.
Saco, ME 04072
Phone: (207) 284-7251
Pet Restrictions: Out of season only
Exercise Area for Pets: Yes
Rates: $35 to $75

MAINE — HOTELS (continued)

SANFORD
Bar H Motel
SR 109
Sanford, ME 04073
Phone: (207) 324-4662

Pet Restrictions: None
Pet left unattended in room: Yes
Exercise Area for Pets: Yes
Rates: $45 to $65

Down Maine Veterinary Clinic
Route 4 04073
Phone: (207) 324-4683

SEARSPORT
Light's Motel and Restaurant
US 1, RFD Box 349
Searsport, ME 04974
Phone: (207) 548-2405

Pet Restrictions: Well mannered
Pet left unattended in room: Yes
Exercise Area for Pets: Yes
Rates: $30 to $36

SOUTHPORT ISLAND
The Lawnmeer Inn
Rt. 27
Southport Island, ME 04576
Phone: (207) 633-2544

Pet Restrictions: $5 deposit, rooms
    overlook water
Pet left unattended in room: Yes
Exercise Area for Pets: Yes
Rates: $70 to $90

WATERVILLE
The Atrium Motel
332 Main St.
Waterville, ME 04901
Phone: (207) 873-2777

Pet Restrictions: None
Exercise Area for Pets: Yes
Rates: $50 to $75

Holiday Inn
375 Upper Main St.
Waterville, ME 04901
Phone: (207) 873-0111

Pet Restrictions: None
Exercise Area for Pets: Yes
Rates: $84 to $89

Howard Johnson Lodge
356 Main St
Waterville, ME 04901
Phone: (207) 873-3335

Pet Restrictions: Advanced notice
Exercise Area for Pets: Yes
Rates: $45 to $85

WEST PARIS
Mollyockett Motel
P.O. Box 248
West Paris, ME 04289
Phone: (207) 674-2345

Pet Restrictions: None
Pet left unattended in room: Yes
Exercise Area for Pets: Yes
Rates: $55 to $85

YORK
Dockside Guest Quarters
Harris Island Road, Box 205
York, ME
Phone: (207) 363-2868

Pet Restrictions: Yes, only guests
    who had pets previously here,
    owner responsible
Pet left unattended in room: Yes
Exercise Area for Pets: Yes
Rates: $60 to $134

MARYLAND — HOTELS

ABERDEEN

Days Inn
783 West Bel Air Ave.
Aberdeen, MD 21001
Phone: (410) 272-8500,
    (800) 325-2525

Pet Restrictions: None
Pet left unattended in room: Yes,
    short time
Exercise Area for Pets: Yes
Rates: $38 to $42

Econo Lodge
820 West BelAir Ave.
Aberdeen, MD 21001
Phone: (410) 272-5500,
    (800) 424-4777 (central res.)

Pet Restrictions: small domestic pets
Pet left unattended in room: Yes,
    must be quiet
Exercise Area for Pets: Yes
Rates: $35.95 to $45.95

Holiday Inn Chesapeake House
1007 Beardshill Rd.
Aberdeen, MD 21001
Phone: (410) 272-8100

Pet Restrictions: Small domestic pets
Pet left unattended in room: Yes,
    must be quiet
Exercise Area for Pets: Yes
Rates: $78

Howard Johnson
793 W. Belaire Ave.
Aberdeen, MD 21001
Phone: (410) 272-6000,
    (800) GO HO JO (central res.)

Pet Restrictions: Small domestic pets
Exercise Area for Pets: Yes
Rates: $38.80 to $58

VETERINARIANS
Moffa, John V.
728 South Philadelphia Blvd. 21001
(410) 272-0655

ANNAPOLIS

Holiday Inn
210 Holiday Ct.
Annapolis, MD 21401
Phone: (410) 224-3150,
    (800) HOLIDAY (central res.)

Pet Restrictions: Under 30 lbs.
Pet left unattended in room: Yes, no
    housekeeping
Exercise Area for Pets: Yes
Rates: $69 to $125

Howard Johnson Lodge
69 Old Mill Bottom Rd.-North
Annapolis, MD 21401
Phone: (410) 757-1600,
    (800) 446-4656 (central res.)

Pet Restrictions: $25/stay deposit,
    under 50 lbs.
Pet left unattended in room: Yes, no
    housekeeping, must be quiet
Exercise Area for Pets: Yes
Rates: $29.95 to $89

Loews Annapolis Hotel
126 West St.
Annapolis, MD 21401
Phone: (410) 263-7777
Fax: (410) 268-7777

Pet Restrictions: No animals indoors
    above 100 lbs.
Pet left unattended in room: Yes
Exercise Area for Pets: Yes. Sandy
    Point State Park and Beach,
    Quiet Waters Park
Rates: $105 to $165

VETERINARIANS
**Greater Annapolis Veterinary
Hosp.**
1901 Generals Highway 21401
(410) 224-3800

Dougherty, Paul G.
490 Fawns Walk/Annapolis 21401
(410) 948-6707

BALTIMORE
BWI Airport-Mariott
1743 W. Nursery Rd.
Baltimore, MD 21240
Phone: (410) 859-8300,
    (800) 228-9290 (central res.)

Pet Restrictions: Very small pets,
    must sign waiver
Exercise Area for Pets: Yes
Rates: $49 to $135

Comfort Inn Airport
6921 Baltimore/Annapolis Blvd.
Baltimore, MD 21225
Phone: (410) 789-9100,
    (800) 221-2222 (central res.)

Pet Restrictions: Under 50 lbs.,
    dogs and cats
Exercise Area for Pets: Yes
Rates: $49 to $92

Holiday Inn Belmont
1800 Belmont Ave.
Baltimore, MD 21207
Phone: (410) 265-1400,
    (800) HOLIDAY (central res.)
Pet Restrictions: First level only,
    small and medium pets only,
    credit card needed
Pet left unattended in room: Yes, no
    housekeeping
Exercise Area for Pets: Yes
Rates: $59 to $65

Holiday Inn - Inner Harbor
301 W. Lombard St.
Baltimore, MD 21201
Phone: (410) 685-3500,
    (800) HOLIDAY
Pet Restrictions: Small caged pet
Pet left unattended in room: Yes, no
    housekeeping
Exercise Area for Pets: Yes
Rates: $109 to $119

Holiday Inn-Moravia
6510 Frankford Ave.
Baltimore, MD 21206
Phone: (410) 485-7900
Pet Restrictions: None
Pet left unattended in room: Yes
Exercise Area for Pets: Yes
Rates: $69

Howard Johnson Motor Lodge
5701 Baltimore National Pike
Baltimore, MD 21228
Phone: (410) 747-8900,
    (800) 654-2000
Pet Restrictions: Quiet
Pet left unattended in room: Yes,
    quiet
Exercise Area for Pets: Yes
Rates: $37.95 to $60

Marriott Inner Harbor
110 S. Eutaw St.
Baltimore, MD 21201
Phone: (410) 962-0202,
    (800) 228-9290
Pet Restrictions: Small pets only
    (under 15 lbs.), over that $50
    deposit
Pet left unattended in room: Yes,
    quiet
Exercise Area for Pets: Yes
Rates: $79 to $650

Motel 6
1654 Whitehead Ct.
Baltimore, MD 21207
Phone: (410) 265-7660
Pet Restrictions: 1 small pet
Exercise Area for Pets: Yes
Rates: $38 to $45

Ramada Hotel & Conf. Center
1701 Belmont Ave.
Baltimore, MD 21244
Phone: (410) 265-1100,
    (800) 272-6232 (central res.)
Pet Restrictions: $10/day/pet
Pet left unattended in room: Yes,
    quiet
Exercise Area for Pets: Yes
Rates: $54 to $75

Sheraton Inner Harbor
300 S. Charles St.
Baltimore, MD 21201
Phone: (410) 962-8300,
    (800) 325-3535 (central res.)
Pet Restrictions: Not too big
Pet left unattended in room: Yes,
    quiet
Exercise Area for Pets: Yes
Rates: $135 to $170

Sheraton International Hotel at BWI
7032 Elm Rd.
BWI Airport, Baltimore, MD 21240
Phone: (410) 859-3300,
    (800) 638-5858
Pet Restrictions: Small pets only
Pet left unattended in room: Yes
Exercise Area for Pets: Yes
Rates: $117 to $127

Tremont Baltimore
8 E. Pleasant St.
Baltimore, MD 21202
Phone: (410) 576-1200
Pet Restrictions: $3 per night
Pet left unattended in room: Yes
Rates: $89 to $109

VETERINARIANS

Falls Road Animal Hospital
6314 Falls Rd. 21209
(410) 825-9100

Pulaski Veterinary Clinic
9707 Pulaski Highway 21220
(410) 686-6310

Westview Animal Hospital
5800 Johnnycake Rd. 21207
(410) 744-4800

BETHESDA

Residence Inn by Marriott
7335 Wisconsin Ave.
Bethesda, MD 20814
Phone: (301) 718-0200

Pet Restrictions: Pet floor, $100 flat
fee plus $5 per night
Pet left unattended in room: Yes
Exercise Area for Pets: Nearby
Rates: $89 to $199

VETERINARIANS

Benson Jr., Albert
4981 Cordell Ave. 20814
(301) 652-8819

Currey, Gordon R.
5439 Butler Rd. 20816
(301) 654-3000

CAMBRIDGE

Econo Lodge
P.O. Box 1170
Cambridge, MD 21613
Phone: (410) 221-0800

Pet Restrictions: Small 10-14 lbs.,
$5 fee
Exercise Area for Pets: Yes
Rates: $50.50 to $54

CAPITOL HEIGHTS

Days Inn Washington Capitol Center
55 Hampton Place Blvd.
Capitol Heights, MD 20743
Phone: (301) 336-8900

Pet Restrictions: $5 fee
Pet left unattended in room: Yes,
notify housekeeping
Exercise Area for Pets: Yes
Rates: $39 to $65

CATONSVILLE

Econolodge
5801 Baltimore Nat'l Pike
Catonsville, MD 21228
Phone: (410) 744-5000,
(800) 237-2218

Pet Restrictions: None
Exercise Area for Pets: Yes
Rates: $35.05 to $45.95

VETERINARIANS

College Park Animal Hospital
6003 Burnt Oak Rd.
(301) 788-1612

CHEVY CHASE

Holiday Inn Chevy Chase
5520 Wisconsin Ave.
Chevy Chase, MD 20815
Phone: (301) 656-1500

Pet Restrictions: Small pets
Pet left unattended in room: Yes, no
housekeeping
Exercise Area for Pets: Yes
Rates: $75 to $135, $125-$149 for
suites

VETERINARIANS

Chevy Chase Veterinary Clinic
8815 Connecticut Ave. 20815
(301) 656-6655

COLUMBIA

The Columbia Inn
10207 Wincopin Circle
Columbia, MD 21044
Phone: (410) 730-3900

Pet Restrictions: Only in the Inn,
$75 deposit
Pet left unattended in room: Yes
Exercise Area for Pets: Yes
Rates: $69 to $125

VETERINARIANS

Columbia Animal Hospital
10788 Hickory Ridge Rd. 21044
(301) 730-2122

Haupt, Barbara
6310 Leafy Screen 21045
(301) 381-0284

EASTON

Easton Days Inn
P.O. Box 968
Easton, MD 21601
Phone: (410) 822-4600

Pet Restrictions: Yes
Pet left unattended in room: Yes,
use do not disturb sign
Exercise Area for Pets: Yes
Rates: $40 to $60

Econo Lodge
U.S. 50
Easton, MD 21601
Phone: (410) 822-6330

Pet Restrictions: Small pets
Pet left unattended in room: Yes, if
   caged
Exercise Area for Pets: Yes
Rates: $46.06 to $54

Holiday Inn
999 W. Patrick St.
Easton, MD 21701
Phone: (301) 662-5141

Pet Restrictions: None
Pet left unattended in room: Yes
Exercise Area for Pets: Yes
Rates: $59 to $79

Knights Inn
6005 Urban Pike
Easton, MD 21701
Phone: (301) 698-0555

Pet Restrictions: $10 deposit
Exercise Area for Pets: Yes
Rates: $37 to $61

VETERINARIANS

Community Animal Hospital
Route 2, Box 172
(410) 822-4475

Schriver, Michael D.
507 Decatur Pl.
(410) 822-2965

FREDERICK
Best Western Red Horse Motor Inn
998 W. Patrick St.
Frederick, MD 21701
Phone: (301) 662-0281

Pet Restrictions: None
Pet left unattended in room: Yes, if
   quiet
Exercise Area for Pets: Yes
Rates: $34 to $54

Holiday Inn
5400 Sheraton Drive
Frederick, MD 21701
Phone: (301) 694-7500

Pet Restrictions: None
Exercise Area for Pets: Yes
Rates: $72 to $91

VETERINARIANS

McClellan Veterinary Clinic
142A W. Patrick St.
(301) 663-6531

Opossum Pike Veterinary Clinic
1550 O'Possumtown Pike
(301) 662-2322

West Frederick Veterinary Hospital
1519 W. Patrick Street, A-1
(301) 695-6133

FROSTBURG
Comfort Inn
Rt. 36
Frostburg, MD 21532
Phone: (301) 689-2050

Pet Restrictions: $10 fee
Pet left unattended in room: Yes
Exercise Area for Pets: Yes
Rates: $45 to $125

GAITHERSBURG
Red Roof Inn
497 Quince Orchard Rd.
Gaithersburg, MD 20878
Phone: (301) 977-3311

Pet Restrictions: None
Pet left unattended in room: Yes,
   notify desk
Exercise Area for Pets: Yes
Rates: $40 to $60

VETERINARIANS

Seneca Valley Vet. Hospital
14023 Darnestown Rd.
(301) 926-1400

Walnut Hill Animal Hosp.
615 S. Frederick Ave.
(301) 977-8680

GLEN BURNIE
Holiday Inn Glen Burnie #2
6323 Ritchie Highway
Glen Burnie, MD 21061
Phone: (410) 636-4300

Pet Restrictions: None if behaves well
Pet left unattended in room: Yes, if
   quiet
Rates: $55 to $69

MARYLAND — HOTELS (continued)

Holiday Inn Glen Burnie #1S
6600 Ritchie Highway
Glen Burnie, MD 21061
Phone: (410) 761-8300

Pet Restrictions: None
Pet left unattended in room: Yes
Exercise Area for Pets: Yes
Rates: $55 to $69

VETERINARIANS
Glen Burnie Animal Hospital
408 Crain Highway North
(410) 766-1500

GRANTSVILLE
Holiday Inn
Rt. 48, P.O. Box 216
Grantsville, MD 21532
Phone: (301) 895-5993

Pet Restrictions: None
Exercise Area for Pets: Yes
Rates: $39 to $89

HAGERSTOWN
Holiday Inn
900 Dual Highway
Hagerstown, MD 21740
Phone: (301) 739-9050

Pet Restrictions: None
Pet left unattended in room: Yes
Exercise Area for Pets: Yes
Rates: $49 to $52

Travel Lodge
101 Massey Blvd.
Hagerstown, MD 21740
Phone: (301) 582-4445

Pet Restrictions: None
Exercise Area for Pets: Yes
Rates: $40 to $65

Best Western
Rt. 6, P.O. P.O. Box 195
Hagerstown, MD 21740
Phone: (301) 791-3560

Pet Restrictions: Small pets,
$2.50/pet/day
Pet left unattended in room: Yes,
not for the whole day
Exercise Area for Pets: Yes
Rates: $35 to $43

Ramada Inn Convention Center
901 Dual Highway
Hagerstown, MD 21740
Phone: (301) 733-5100

Pet Restrictions: Special pet rooms
Pet left unattended in room: Yes if
quiet
Exercise Area for Pets: Yes
Rates: $44 to $69

Sheraton Inn
1910 Dual Highway
Hagerstown, MD 21740
Phone: (301) 790-3010

Pet Restrictions: Well behaved pets
only
Pet left unattended in room: Yes
Exercise Area for Pets: Yes
Rates: $58 to $72

State Line Motel
Rt. 6, Box 195C
Hagerstown, MD 21740
Phone: (301) 733-8262

Pet Restrictions: $2.50/day
Rates: $24 to $37

Wellsley Inn
1101 Dual Highway
Hagerstown, MD 21740
Phone: (301) 733-2700

Pet Restrictions: None
Pet left unattended in room: Yes, if
housebroken/quiet
Exercise Area for Pets: Yes
Rates: $39.99 to $69.99

VETERINARIANS
Park Circle Animal Hospital
362 Virginia Ave.
(301) 791-2180

HANCOCK
Hampton Inn Hunt Valley
11200 York Rd.
Hancock, MD 21030
Phone: (410) 527-1500

Pet Restrictions: None
Pet left unattended in room: Yes, no
maid service
Exercise Area for Pets: Yes
Rates: $49 to $59

HUNT VALLEY

Marriott Hunt Valley Inn
Shawan Rd.
Hunt Valley, MD 21031
Phone: (301) 785-7000

Pet Restrictions: None
Pet left unattended in room: Yes,
    must be caged
Exercise Area for Pets: Yes
Rates: $69 to $97

Residence Inn by Marriott
10710 Bever Dorm Rd.
Hunt Vally, MD 21030
Phone: (301) 584-7370

Pet Restrictions: $50 one time, $5
    per day
Pet left unattended in room: Yes
Exercise Area for Pets: Yes
Rates: $74 to $139

VETERINARIANS

Frank, Allan
11206 York Rd.
(301) 666-0800

INNER HARBOR

Sheraton Inner Harbor Hotel
300 S. Charles St.
Inner Habor, MD 21201
Phone: (410) 962-8300

Pet Restrictions: None
Pet left unattended in room: Yes, but
    no housekeeping, notify maids
Exercise Area for Pets: Yes
Rates: $135 to $1300

JESSUP

Red Roof Inn - Columbia/Jessup
8000 Washington Blvd.
Jessup, MD 20794
Phone: (410) 796-0380

Pet Restrictions: None
Rates: $40.99 to $54.99

LANHAM

Holiday Inn
5910 Princess Garden Pkwy.
Lanham, MD 20706
Phone: (301) 459-1000

Pet Restrictions: Small pets
Pet left unattended in room: Yes
Exercise Area for Pets: Yes
Rates: $72 to $132

Red Roof Inn
9050 Lanham Severn Rd.
Lanham, MD 20706
Phone: (301) 731-8830

Pet Restrictions: None
Exercise Area for Pets: Yes
Rates: $30 to $68

LAUREL

Howard Johnson Lodge
#1 Second St.
Laurel, MD 20707
Phone: (301) 725-8800

Pet Restrictions: Small pets only
Exercise Area for Pets: Yes
Rates: $39 to $80

Knights Inn
3380 Fort Meade Rd.
Laurel, MD 20707
Phone: (301) 498-5553

Pet Restrictions: None
Pet left unattended in room: Yes, for
    short period, no housekeeping
Exercise Area for Pets: Yes
Rates: $33.95 to $55.95

Red Roof Inn
Laurel 12525 Laurel Boivie Rd.
Laurel, MD 20708
Phone: (301) 498-8811

Pet Restrictions: Under 16 lbs.
Pet left unattended in room: Yes,
    notify desk
Exercise Area for Pets: Yes
Rates: $24.99 to $37.99

VETERINARIANS

Brenner Animal Hospital
10100 Washington Blvd.
U.S. Route One South
(301) 725-5400

North Laurel Animal Hospital
Whiskey Bottom Center
9105 All Saints Rd.
(301) 953-7387

Rhody, Jeffrey
14709 Baltimore Ave. #11
(301) 498-8387

MARYLAND — HOTELS (continued)

LINTHICUM

Holiday Inn BWi Airport
890 Elkridge Landing Rd.
Linthicum, MD 21090
Phone: (410) 859-8400,
    (800) HOLIDAY (central res.)
Pet Restrictions: None
Pet left unattended in room: Yes, no
    housekeeping
Exercise Area for Pets: Yes
Rates: $99

LINTHIUM HEIGHTS

Red Roof Inn
827 Elkridge Landing Rd.
Linthium Heights, MD 21090
Phone: (301) 850-7600
Pet Restrictions: None
Pet left unattended in room: Yes
Exercise Area for Pets: Yes
Rates: $31.99 to $47.99

NEW CARROLLTON

Sheraton Hotel
8500 Annapolis Rd.
New Carrollton, MD 20782
Phone: (301) 459-6700
Pet Restrictions: Special pet rooms
Exercise Area for Pets: Yes
Rates: $69 to $92

Trinh, Thu-suong (Sue)
8513 Carrollton Parkway
(301) 258-0333

OCEAN CITY

Days Inn Bayside
4201 Coastal Hwy.
Ocean City, MD 21842
Phone: (410) 289-6488
Fax: (410) 289-1617
Pet Restrictions: No poisonous
    snakes. Pets contained to
    second floor rooms
Pet left unattended in room: Yes
Exercise Area for Pets: Yes
Other Areas: One block to beach -
    seasonal restriction (Memorial to
    Labor Day)
Rates: $29.95 to $229.95

Sheraton Ocean City Resort & Conference Center
10100 Ocean Highway
Ocean City, MD 21842
Phone: (410) 524-3535
Pet Restrictions: $14/pet/day
Pet left unattended in room: Yes
Exercise Area for Pets: Yes
Rates: $55 to $180

OXON HILL

Red Roof Inn - Oxon Hill
6170 Oxon Hill Rd.
Oxon Hill, MD 20745
Phone: (301) 567-8030
Pet Restrictions: None except notify
    if large dog is coming
Pet left unattended in room: Yes,
    but no maid service
Exercise Area for Pets: Yes
Rates: $29.99 to $58.99

POCOMOKE

Days Inn
Rt. 2, Box 216 A1
Pocomoke, MD 21851
Phone: (410) 957-3000
Pet Restrictions: None
Exercise Area for Pets: Yes
Rates: $35 to $76

Quality Inn of Pocomoke
P.O. Box 480
Pocomoke City, MD 21851
Phone: (410) 957-1300
Pet Restrictions: None
Exercise Area for Pets: Yes
Rates: $54 to $61

ROCKVILLE

Days Inn
16001 Shady Grove Rd.
Rockville, MD 20850
Phone: (301) 948-4300
Pet Restrictions: Small pets only
Pet left unattended in room: Yes,
    inform housekeeping
Exercise Area for Pets: Yes
Rates: $39 to $80

Sheraton Potomac
#3 Research Ct.
Rockville, MD 20850
Phone: (301) 840-0200
Pet Restrictions: $100 deposit
Pet left unattended in room: Yes
Exercise Area for Pets: Yes
Rates: $42 to $68

Metropolitan Animal Clinic
12213 Nebel St.
(310) 770-5225

Montgomery Animal Hospital
12200 Rockville Pike
(301) 881-6447

SALISBURY

Atlantic Budget Inn
P.O. Box 370
Salisbury, MD 21875
Phone: (410) 896-3434

Pet Restrictions: $25 deposit, $10 fee
Rates: $39 to $49

Days Inn
U.S. 13N, RD 6, P.O. Box 978
Salisbury, MD 21801
Phone: (410) 749-6200

Pet Restrictions: $5 fee
Pet left unattended in room: Yes, if
   caged or small
Exercise Area for Pets: Yes
Rates: $30 to $69

VETERINARIANS

Salisbury Animal Hospital
925 Boundary St.
(410) 749-4393

**Johnson-McKee Animal
Hospital**
RR3 Box 228/Mt. Harmon Church
(410) 749-9422

SALOMONS

**Holiday Inn Hotel & Conference
Center & Marina**
P.O. Box 1099
Salomons, MD 20688
Phone: (410) 326-6311

Pet Restrictions: 1 pet floor
Pet left unattended in room: Yes
Exercise Area for Pets: Yes
Rates: $67 to $73

ST. MICHAELS

**St. Michaels Motor Inn &
Conference Center**
P.O. Box 437
St. Michaels, MD 21663
Phone: (410) 745-3333

Pet Restrictions: Small pets
Exercise Area for Pets: Yes
Rates: $63 to $80

TIMONIUM

Holiday Inn Hotel
2004 Graen Spring Dr.
Timonium, MD 21093
Phone: (410) 252-7373

Pet Restrictions: None
Pet left unattended in room: Yes
Exercise Area for Pets: Yes
Rates: $69 to $89

Red Roof Inn
111 West Timonium Rd.
Timonium, MD 21093
Phone: (410) 666-0380

Pet Restrictions: None
Pet left unattended in room: Yes
Exercise Area for Pets: Yes
Rates: $35 to $60

VETERINARIANS

Spikloser, Ronald
2135 York Rd.
(410) 252-8820

TOWNSON

Quality Inn
1015 York Rd.
Townson, MD 21204
Phone: (410) 825-9190

Pet Restrictions: None
Pet left unattended in room: Yes
Exercise Area for Pets: Yes
Rates: $52 to $58

Holiday Inn Cromwell Bridge
1100 Cromwell Bridge Rd.
Townson, MD 21204
Phone: (410) 823-4410,
   (800) HOLIDAY (central res.)

Pet Restrictions: Small, quiet
Pet left unattended in room: Yes,
   quiet
Exercise Area for Pets: Yes
Rates: $69 to $84

Ramada Inn
8712 Lochraven Blvd.
Townson, MD 21286
Phone: (410) 823-8750,
   (800) 2 RAMADA (central res.)

Pet Restrictions: Housebroken
Pet left unattended in room: Yes, no
   housekeeping
Exercise Area for Pets: Yes
Rates: $49 to $69

Townson EconoLodge/Days Inn
8801 Lock Raven Blvd.
Townson, MD 21204
Phone: (410) 882-0900

Pet Restrictions: Under 50 lbs., $25 deposit
Pet left unattended in room: Yes, if quiet
Exercise Area for Pets: Yes
Rates: $42 to $56

UPPER MARLBORO
Upper Marlboro Bragg Motel
7001 SW Crain Highway
Upper Marlboro, MD 20772
Phone: (301) 627-1880

Pet Restrictions: None
Pet left unattended in room: Yes, must be caged
Exercise Area for Pets: Yes
Rates: $36 to $55

VETERINARIANS
Anderson, Scott K.
15222 Marlboro Pike
(301) 627-4664

Jackson, Robert K.
11204 Lenox Dr.
(301) 295-0566

WALDORF
Econo Lodge of Waldorf
4 Business Park Dr.
Waldorf, MD 20772
Phone: (301) 645-0022

Pet Restrictions: $15 fee
Pet left unattended in room: Yes, no housekeeping
Exercise Area for Pets: Yes
Rates: $33 to $46

Holiday Inn
1st St. Patricks Dr.
Waldorf, MD 20601-4507
Phone: (301) 645-8200

Pet Restrictions: $50 deposit
Pet left unattended in room: Yes, notify desk
Exercise Area for Pets: Yes
Rates: $48 to $110

Knights Inn
Highway 301, P.O. Box 99
Waldorf, MD 20772
Phone: (301) 932-5090

Pet Restrictions: $10 fee
Exercise Area for Pets: Yes
Rates: $41 to $50

VETERINARIANS
Neuman, Neal B.
Three Doolittle Dr.
(301) 645-2550

WILLIAMSPORT
Wolf's End Farm
14940 Falling Waters Rd.
Williamsport, MD 21795
Phone: (301) 223-6888

Pet Restrictions: None
Pet left unattended in room: Yes
Exercise Area for Pets: Yes
Activities: Gettysburg
Rates: $60 to $100

MASSACHUSETTS — HOTELS

ANDOVER

Boston Marriott Andover
123 Old River Rd.
Andover, MA 01810
Phone: (508) 975-3600

Pet Restrictions: None
Pet left unattended in room: Yes
Exercise Area for Pets: Yes
Rates: $85 to $130

VETERINARIANS
Andover Animal Hospital Inc.
233 Lowell Street 01810
Phone: (508) 475-3600

John K. Prentiss
366 Salem Street 01810
(508) 682-9905

AUBURN

Budgetel Inn
444 Southbridge St.
Auburn, MA 01501
Phone: (508) 832-7000

Pet Restrictions: 2 rooms for pets
Exercise Area for Pets: Yes
Rates: $50 to $60

BOSTON

Copley Plaza
138 St. James Ave.
Boston, MA 02116
Phone: (617) 267-5300

Pet Restrictions: None
Exercise Area for Pets: Yes
Rates: $215 to $235

Four Seasons
200 Boylston St.
Boston, MA
Phone: (617) 338-4400

Pet Restrictions: None, will do
anything for pet as they would a
human
Pet left unattended in room: Yes
Exercise Area for Pets: Nearby
Rates: $260 to $420

Hilton — Back Bay
40 Dalton St.
Boston, MA 02115
Phone: (617) 236-1100

Pet Restrictions: None
Pet left unattended in room: Yes
Exercise Area for Pets: Nearby
Rates: $145 to $215

Hilton — Logan Airport
75 Service Rd.
Boston, MA 02128
Phone: (617) 569-9300

Pet Restrictions: Pet agreement
Rates: $180 to $220

Howard Johnson Hotel
575 Commonwealth Ave.
Boston, MA 02215
Phone: (617) 267-3100

Pet Restrictions: Small pets
Exercise Area for Pets: Yes
Rates: $80 to $165

Meridien
250 Franklin St.
Boston, MA 02110
Phone: (617) 451-1900

Pet Restrictions: Small dogs
Exercise Area for Pets: Yes
Rates: $125 to $255

Ritz Carlton
Arlington and Newbury Streets
Boston, MA 02117
Phone: (617) 536-5700

Pet Restrictions: None
Exercise Area for Pets: Nearby
Rates: $195 to $380

Sheraton Boston Hotel & Towers
39 Dalton St.
Boston, MA 02199
Phone: (617) 236-2000

Pet Restrictions: None
Exercise Area for Pets: Nearby
Rates: $155 to $475

The Westin Hotel, Copley Place
10 Huntington Ave.
Boston, MA 02116
Phone: (800) 228-3000

Pet Restrictions: Small pets
Pet left unattended in room: Yes
Exercise Area for Pets: Yes
Rates: $109 to $245

VETERINARIANS:
Angell Memorial Animal Hospital
350 South Huntington Avenue 02130
(617) 522-7282

South Bay Veterinary Group
587 Tremont Street 02118
(617) 266-6619

BURLINGTON

Boston Marriott-Burlington
Rt. 128 & 3A
Burlington, MA 01803
Phone: (617) 229-6565
Pet Restrictions: 40 rooms, 1st floor
    only
Exercise Area for Pets: Nearby
Rates: $79 to $139

Howard Johnson Lodge
98 Middlesex Turnpike
Burlington, MA 01803
Phone: (617) 272-6550
Pet Restrictions: 1 pet per room
Pet left unattended in room: Yes but
    no housekeeping unless pet is
    supervised
Exercise Area for Pets: Nearby
Rates: $82 to $86

CAMBRIDGE

The Charles Hotels
1 Bennett St.
Cambridge, MA 02138
Phone: (617) 864-1200
Pet Restrictions: Small only, sign
    contract
Exercise Area for Pets: Nearby
Rates: $139 to $259

Howard Johnson Hotel
777 Memorial Drive
Cambridge, MA 02139
Phone: (617) 492-7777
Pet Restrictions: None
Exercise Area for Pets: Yes
Rates: $110 to $165

VETERINARIANS

Grant J. Mayne
Fresh Pond Animal Hospital
769 Concord Ave. 02138
(617) 492-0808

CENTERVILLE

**Centerville Corners Motor
Lodge**
So. Main St. & Craigville Beach Rd.
P.O. Box 507
Centerville, MA 02632
Phone: (508) 775-7223
Pet Restrictions: $5/pet/day
Exercise Area for Pets: Yes
Rates: $53 to $91

CHELMSFORD

Howard Johnson Hotel
187 Chelmsford St.
Chelmsford, MA 01824
Phone: (508) 256-7511
Pet Restrictions: Ground floor only,
    27 rooms
Pet left unattended in room: Yes
Exercise Area for Pets: Yes
Rates: $52 to $62

CHICOPEE

**Best Western-Chicopee Motor
Lodge**
463 Memorial Dr.
Chicopee, MA 01020
Phone: (413) 592-6171
Pet Restrictions: Small pets only
Pet left unattended in room: Yes
Exercise Area for Pets: Yes
Rates: $49 and up

DANVERS

Motel 6
US Rt 1, 65 Newbury St.
Danvers, MA 01923-1072
Phone: (508) 774-8045
Pet Restrictions: 1 pet per room
Exercise Area for Pets: Yes
Rates: $37.99 to $43.99

VETERINARIANS

George D. Myers
367 Maple St. 01923
(508) 774-0045

EASTHAM

Town Crier Motel
P.O. Box 457
Eastham, MA 02642
Phone: (508) 255-4000
Pet Restrictions: $10 per night,
    housekeeping will not clean
    room if pet is unattended
Exercise Area for Pets: Yes
Rates: $49 to $75

FALMOUTH

Marina Hotel
555 Main St.
Falmouth, MA 02540
Phone: (800) 233-2939
Pet Restrictions: None
Pet left unattended in room: No
Exercise Area for Pets: Yes
Rates: $49 to $99

Quality Inn - Falmouth
291 Jones Rd.
Falmouth, MA 02540
Phone: (508) 540-2000
Fax: (508) 548-2712

Pet Restrictions: None
Pet left unattended in room: No
Exercise Area for Pets: Yes
Rates: $45 to $119

Shore Haven Inn
321 Shore St.
Falmouth, MA 02540
Phone: (800) 828-3255

Pet Restrictions: Well behaved
Pet left unattended in room: No
Exercise Area for Pets: Yes
Rates: $59 to $149

FRAMINGHAM

Red Roof Inn
650 Cochituate Rd.
Framingham, MA 01701
Phone: (508) 872-4499

Pet Restrictions: None
Pet left unattended in room: Yes
Exercise Area for Pets: Yes
Rate: $50

VETERINARIANS

Slade Vet. Hospital
334 Concord St.
(508) 875-7086

Herman, Judith K.
757 Southwest St.
(508) 877-0900

HAVERHILL

Best Western
401 Lowell Ave.
Haverhill, MA 01832
Phone: (508) 373-1511

Pet Restrictions: $10 refundable
    deposit
Exercise Area for Pets: Yes
Rates: $49 to $59

VETERINARIANS

Daniel J. Pelletier
89 Plaistow Rd. 01830
(508) 373-3251

HYANNIS

Harbor Village
P.O. Box 625
Hyannis Port, MA 02647
Phone: (508) 775-7581

Pet Restrictions: $25 fee (dogs only)
Pet left unattended in room: Yes
Exercise Area for Pets: Nearby
Rates: $9.75 to $12.25

HYANNIS PORT

Sea Breeze Cottages
397 Sea St. Rear
Hyannis Port, MA 02647
Phone: (508) 775-4269

Pet Restrictions: Well behaved at all
    times
Exercise Area for Pets: Yes
Rates: $750 weekly

VETERINARIANS

Hyannis Animal Hospital
711 Yarmouth Rd 02601
(508) 775-4521

KINGSTON

Howard Johnson Lodge
Rt. 3 or 3A - 149 Main St.
Kingston, MA 02364
Phone: (508) 585-3831

Pet Restrictions: None
Exercise Area for Pets: Yes
Rates: $69 to $114

VETERINARIANS

Kingston Animal Hospital
192 Main St. 02364
(508) 585-6525

NEW BEDFORD

Days Inn — New Bedford
500 Hathaway Rd.
New Bedford, MA 02740
Phone: (508) 997-1231

Pet Restrictions: None
Exercise Area for Pets: Yes
Rates: $54 to $82

VETERINARIANS

Buttonwood Pet Hospital
922 Kempton St. 02740
(508) 996-3159

NEWTON

Days Inn-Newton
399 Grove St.
Newton, MA 02162
Phone: (617) 969-5300,
    (800) 325-2525

Pet Restrictions: $50 refundable
    deposit, housekeeping will not
    clean if pet is unattended
Pet left unattended in room: Yes
Exercise Area for Pets: Yes
Rates: $99 to $109

VETERINARIANS

Sidney M. Mael
160 Charlemont St. 02161
(617) 527-5507

William S. Walker
Rotherwood Animal Clinic
1100 Beacon St. 02161
(617) 244-4367

PROVINCETOWN

Holiday Inn
Shore Dr., P.O. Box 392
Provincetown, MA 02657
Phone: (508) 487-1711

Pet Restrictions: None
Pet left unattended in room: Yes if
    caged
Exercise Area for Pets: Yes
Rates: $80 to $130

VETERINARIANS

Kevin R. Clarke
Provincetown Veterinary Hospital
140 Commercial St. 02657
(508) 487-2191

SALEM

Salem Inn
7 Summer St.
Salem, MA 01970
Phone: (508) 741-0680
Fax: (508) 744-8924

Pet Restrictions: None
Pet left unattended in room: No
    policy
Exercise Area for Pets: Nearby
Rates: $89 to $150

SCITUATE

Clipper Ship Motor Lodge
7 Beaver Dam Rd.
Scituate, MA 02066
Phone: (617) 545-5550

Pet Restrictions: None
Exercise Area for Pets: Yes
Rates: $69 to $135

SOUTHBOROUGH

Red Roof Inn
367 Turnpike Rd.
Southborough, MA 01772
Phone: (508) 481-3904

Pet Restrictions: Under 50 lbs.
Pet left unattended in room: Yes
Exercise Area for Pets: Yes
Rates: $36 to $65

SPRINGFIELD

Howard Johnson Plaza Hotel
1150 Riverdale St.
Springfield, MA 01089
Phone: (413) 739-7261

Pet Restrictions: None
Pet left unattended in room: Yes
Exercise Area for Pets: Yes
Rates: $44 to $65

VETERINARIANS

Boston Road Animal Hospital
1235 Boston Road 01119
(413) 783-1203

Community Animal Clinic
839 Chicopee St.,
Chicopee, MA 01020
(413) 536-3113

WESTBOROUGH

Westborough Marriott Hotel
5400 Computer Dr.
Westborough, MA 01581
Phone: (508) 366-5511

Pet Restrictions: Small dogs only
Exercise Area for Pets: Yes
Rates: $79 to $128

WEST SPRINGFIELD

Ramada Hotel
1080 Riverdale St.
W. Springfield, MA 01089
Phone (413) 781-8750

Pet Restrictions: 1st floor, outside
    ent.
Pet left unattended in room: Yes
Exercise Area for Pets: Yes
Rates: $54 to $84

Red Roof Inn
1254 Riverdale St.
West Springfield, MA 01089
Phone: (413) 731-1010

Pet Restrictions: None
Pet left unattended in room: Yes
Exercise Area for Pets: Yes
Rates: $35 to $55

VETERINARIANS
West Springfield Animal Hospital
288 Westfield St. 01089
(413) 781-5275

WILLIAMSTOWN
The Williamstown Inn
On The Green @ Williams College
Williamstown, MA 01267
Phone: (413) 458-9371

Pet Restrictions: $5 p.p. p.d.
Pet left unattended in room: Yes
Exercise Area for Pets: Yes
Rates: $80 to $150

WOBURN
Ramada Hotel-Woburn
15 Middlescx Canal Pk Rd.
Woburn, MA 01801
Phone: (617) 935-8760

Pet Restrictions: Under 15 lbs.
Exercise Area for Pets: Yes
Rates: $69 to $89-$150

VETERINARIANS
Paul V. Marino
Woburn Animal Hospital
373 Russell St. 01801
(617) 933-0170

Anne G. Schless
Woburn Animal Hospital
373 Russell St. 01801
(617) 933-0170

MICHIGAN — HOTELS

ALLEN PARK

Allen Park Motor Lodge
14887 South Field Rd.
Allen Park, MI 48101
Phone: (313) 386-6900

Pet Restrictions: $25 per stay
Exercise Area for Pets: Yes
Rates: $34 to $56

ALPENA

Fletcher Motel
1001 Hwy 23N
Alpena, MI 49707
Phone: (517) 354-4191

Pet Restrictions: None
Pet left unattended in room: Yes
Exercise Area for Pets: Yes
Rates: $42 to $100

Parker House Motel
11505 Hwy 23N
Alpena, MI 49707
Phone: (517) 595-6484

Pet Restrictions: $5 per night
Pet left unattended in room: Yes
Exercise Area for Pets: Yes
Rates: $40 to $55

ANN ARBOR

Red Roof Inn
3621 Plymouth Rd.
Ann Arbor, MI 48105
Phone: (313) 996-5800

Pet Restrictions: None
Pet left unattended in room: Yes,
   if caged
Exercise Area for Pets: Yes
Rates: $41 and up

Residence Inn by Marriott
800 Visitors Way
Ann Arbor, MI 48108
Phone: (313) 996-5666

Pet Restrictions: 10 days or less
   $50, 11-29 = $100, 30+$150
Pet left unattended in room: Yes
Exercise Area for Pets: Yes
Rates: $55 to $150

VETERINARIANS

Ann Arbor Animal Hosp.
2150 West Liberty
Phone: (313) 662-4474

Westarbor Animal Hosp.
6011 Jackson Rd.
Phone: (313) 769-5391

Visiting Vet
2862 Kimberly St.
Phone: (313) 996-9474

BARAGA

Lake Shore Motel
On Keweenan Bay, Rt. 1, Box 233
Baraga, MI
Phone: (906) 353-6256

Pet Restrictions: $3 small dog, $5
   for larger dogs
Rates: $24 to $44

BARK RIVER

Parcells' Bayside Resort
316 N. 35
Bark River, MI 49807
Phone: (906) 789-9555

Pet Restrictions: None
Exercise Area for Pets: Yes
Rates: $42 to $38

BATTLE CREEK

Comfort Inn
165 Capital Ave. SW
Battle Creek, MI 49015
Phone: (616) 965-3976

Pet Restrictions: No large pets,
   small pets in carrier
Exercise Area for Pets: Nearby
Rates: $37.95 to $61.95

Howard Johnson Lodge
2590 Capital Ave. SW
Battle Creek, MI 49015
Phone: (616) 965-3201,
   (800) 1 GO-HOJO

Pet Restrictions: None
Pet left unattended in room: Yes
Exercise Area for Pets: Yes
Rates: $41 to $70

Knights Inn
2595 Capital Ave. SW
Battle Creek, MI 49015
Phone: (616) 964-2600

Pet Restrictions: Small pet
Pet left unattended in room: Yes
Exercise Area for Pets: Yes
Rates: $34.95 to $51.95

Michigan Motel
30475 Capital Ave. NE
Battle Creek, MI 49017
Phone: (616) 963-1566

Pet Restrictions: $1.50/night/pet
Exercise Area for Pets: Yes
Rates: $30 to $39.95

VETERINARIANS
Rost, David R.
2150 Columbia Ave. West
Phone: (616) 979-1115

Turner, Sally A.
3070 W. Michigan Ave.
Phone: (616) 962-9955

BAY CITY
Holiday Inn
501 Saginaw St.
Bay City, MI 48708
Phone: (517) 892-3501

Pet Restrictions: None
Pet left unattended in room: Yes
Exercise Area for Pets: Yes
Rates: $57 to $140

VETERINARIANS
Murray, Alex P.
1699 Midland Rd.
Phone: (517) 684-2625

BELLEVILLE
Red Roof Inn Metro Airport
45501 I 94 N Expwy
Belleville, MI 48111
Phone: (313) 697-2244

Pet Restrictions: None
Pet left unattended in room: Yes
Exercise Area for Pets: Yes
Rates: $29.99 to $59

VETERINARIANS
Belleville Animal Hospital
437 Sumpter Rd.
Phone: (313) 697-9142

BENTON HARBOR
Days Inn
2699 Michigan Route 139
Benton Harbor, MI 49022
Phone: (616) 925-7025

Pet Restrictions: $5/night/pet
Pet left unattended in room: Yes
Exercise Area for Pets: Yes
Rates: $41 to $63

Motel 6
2063 Pipestone Rd.
Benton Harbor, MI 49022
Phone: (616) 925-5100

Pet Restrictions: 1 small pet
(registered)
Exercise Area for Pets: Yes
Rates: $27.51 to $40.23

Red Roof Inn
1630 Mall Dr.
Benton Harbor, MI 49022
Phone: (313) 697-2244

Pet Restrictions: None
Pet left unattended in room: Yes, no
housekeeping
Exercise Area for Pets: Yes
Rates: $39 to $46

VETERINARIANS
Freier Animal Hospital
1298 Colfax Avenue
Phone: (616) 925-8835

BEULAH
Sunny Woods Retreat
14065 Honor Hwy
Beulah, MI 49617
Phone: (616) 325-3952

Pet Restrictions: Kept on leash
Pet left unattended in room: Yes
Exercise Area for Pets: Yes
Rates: $34.90 to $55

BLOOMFIELD HILLS
Holiday Inn
1801 S. Telegraph Rd.
Bloomfield Hills, MI 48013
Phone: (313) 334-2444

Pet Restrictions: Small pets
Pet left unattended in room: Yes
Exercise Area for Pets: Yes
Rates: $49 to $99

VETERINARIANS
Ross, Burton A.
880 W. Long Lake Rd.
Phone: (313) 642-2050

CADILLAC
South Shore Motel & Resort
1246 Sunnyside Dr.
Cadillac, MI 49601
Phone: (616) 775-7641

Pet Restrictions: None
Pet left unattended in room: Yes
Exercise Area for Pets: Yes
Rates: $45 to $60

CHARLEVOIX

The Lodge Motel
US 31 N
Charlevoix, MI
Phone: (616) 547-6565

Pet Restrictions: None
Exercise Area for Pets: Yes
Rates: $36 to $95

VETERINARIANS

Charlesvoix Veterinary Hospital
05560 US 31
Phone: (616) 547-9841

Vickers, James E.
06300 Boyne City Rd.
Phone: (616) 582-9024

CHEBOYGAN

Cheboygan Motor Lodge
1355 Mackinaw Ave.
Cheboygan, MI 49721
Phone: (616) 627-3129

Pet Restrictions: $4 or $5
Exercise Area for Pets: Yes
Rates: Varies

COLDWATER

Little King Motel
847 E. Chicago Rd.
Coldwater, MI 49036
Phone: (517) 278-6660

Pet Restrictions: None
Exercise Area for Pets: Yes
Rates: $35.70 to $48.30

COPPER HARBOR

Bella Vista Motel
P.O. Box 26
Copper Harbor, MI 49918
Phone: (906) 289-4213

Pet Restrictions: None
Exercise Area for Pets: Yes
Rates: $38 to $50

Norland Motel
beyond entrance to Fort Williams
    State Park
Copper Harbor, MI 49918
Phone: (906) 289-4815

Pet Restrictions: $4/night
Exercise Area for Pets: Yes
Rates: $28 to $49

DEARBORN

Holiday Inn
22900 Michigan Ave.
Dearborn, MI 48124
Phone: (313) 278-4800

Pet Restrictions: None
Pet left unattended in room: Yes
Exercise Area for Pets: Yes
Rates: $85 to $61

Red Roof Inn
24130 Michigan Ave.
Dearborn, MI 48124
Phone: (313) 278-9732

Pet Restrictions: Small pets only
Pet left unattended in room: Yes
Exercise Area for Pets: Yes
Rates: $37 to $45

VETERINARIANS

Burns Animal Hospital
24604 Michigan Ave.
Phone: (313) 561-5920

Barnes, Richard D.
14437 Michigan Ave.
Phone: (313) 581-8525

DETROIT

Comfort Inn
11401 Hall Rd.
Detroit, MI 48087
Phone: (313) 739-7111

Pet Restrictions: Small pets only
Pet left unattended in room: Yes
Exercise Area for Pets: Yes
Rates: $37.79 to $78.99

Hampton Inn
32652 Stephenson Hwy
Detroit, MI 48071
Phone: (313) 585-8881

Pet Restrictions: Smaller pets
Pet left unattended in room: Yes
Exercise Area for Pets: Yes
Rates: $48 to $59

Knights Inn
21880 West Rd.
Detroit, MI 48183
Phone: (313) 676-8550

Pet Restrictions: None
Exercise Area for Pets: Yes
Rates: $28 to $79

Marriott-Airport Metropolitan
Detroit, MI 48242
Phone: (313) 941-9400

Pet Restrictions: None
Pet left unattended in room: Yes
Exercise Area for Pets: Yes
Rates: $114 to $128

Red Roof Inn
21230 Eureka Rd.
Detroit, MI 48180
Phone: (313) 374-1150

Pet Restrictions: None
Pet left unattended in room: Yes
Exercise Area for Pets: Yes
Rates: $25.99 to $55

Red Roof Inn
24130 Michigan Ave.
Detroit, MI 48124
Phone: (313) 278-9732

Pet Restrictions: 1 pet per room,
    smoking rooms only
Pet left unattended in room: Yes
Exercise Area for Pets: Yes
Rates: $35.99 to $54.99

Residence In by Marriott - Southfield
26700 Central Pk Blvd.
Detroit, MI 48076
Phone: (313) 352-8900

Pet Restrictions: $200 deposit,
    $5/day
Pet left unattended in room: Yes
Exercise Area for Pets: Yes
Rates: $59 up

VETERINARIANS

Northeast Veterinary Hospital
14003 E. Seven Mile Rd.
Phone: (313) 839-4042

Westcott Hospital
24429 Grand River
Phone: (313) 255-2400

Yates, Kathleen AK
14520 Plymouth Rd.
Phone: (313) 837-0115

ESCANABA

Ramada Inn
2603 N. Lincoln Rd.
Escanaba, MI 49829
Phone: (906) 789-1200

Pet Restrictions: $35 ref. deposit
Pet left unattended in room: Yes
Exercise Area for Pets: Yes
Rates: $55 to $74

FARMINGTON HILLS

Knights Inn
37527 Grand River Rd.
Farmington Hills, MI 48042
Phone: (313) 477-3200

Pet Restrictions: None
Pet left unattended in room: Yes
Exercise Area for Pets: Yes
Rates: $28.95 to $55.95

Red Roof Inn
24300 Sinacola Ct.
Farmington Hills, MI 48335
Phone: (313) 478-8640

Pet Restrictions: None
Pet left unattended in room: Yes
Exercise Area for Pets: Nearby
Rates: $27 to $44

VETERINARIANS

Westcott Hospital - Farmington Hills
32732 Northwestern Hwy
Phone: (313) 855-3095

Kulinski, Laura E.
29953 Mirlon Dr.
Phone: (313) 661-0845

FLINT

Best Western Flint
64380 W. Pierson Rd.
Flint, MI 48504
Phone: (313) 733-7570

Pet Restrictions: None
Pet left unattended in room: Small
    pets
Exercise Area for Pets: Yes
Rates: $29.95 to $43.95

Days Inn - Flint
2207 W. Bristol Rd.
Flint, MI 48507
Phone: (313) 239-4681

Pet Restrictions: $5 fee
Pet left unattended in room: Yes
Exercise Area for Pets: Yes
Rates: $25 to $54

Econo Lodge
932 South Center Rd.
Flint, MI 48503
Phone: (313) 744-0200

Pet Restrictions: None
Exercise Area for Pets: Yes
Rates: $29.95 to $47.95

Red Roof Inn
G3219 Miller Rd.
Flint, MI 48507
Phone: (313) 733-1660

Pet Restrictions: None
Pet left unattended in room: Yes
Exercise Area for Pets: Yes
Rates: $53.99 to $31.99

VETERINARIANS

Eascor Animal Hospital
2845 East Court St.
Phone: (313) 239-9457

Babich, Peter J.
G3252 Miller Rd.
Phone: (313) 732-0000

GAYLORD

Downtown Motel
208 S. Otsego Ave.
Galyord, MI 49735
Phone: (517) 732-5010

Pet Restrictions: None
Exercise Area for Pets: Nearby
Rates: $28 to $48

Holiday Inn
833 W. Main St., P.O. Box 116
Gaylord, MI 49735
Phone: (517) 732-2431

Pet Restrictions: None
Exercise Area for Pets: Yes
Rates: $59 to $88

VETERINARIANS

Gaylord Veterinary Hospital
1893 US 27 North
Phone: (517) 732-4545

GRAND MARAIS

Alverson's Motel
P.O. Box 188, opp. Grand Marais
    Harbor
Grand Marais, MI 49839
Phone: (906) 494-2681

Pet Restrictions: None
Exercise Area for Pets: Nearby
Rates: $28 to $38

GRAND RAPIDS

Econo Lodge
250 285th St. SW
Grand Rapids, MI 49508
Phone: (616) 452-2131

Pet Restrictions: $25 refund. deposit
Pet left unattended in room: Yes
Exercise Area for Pets: Yes
Rates: $33.95 to $43.95

Exel Inn
4855 28th St. ES
Grand Rapids, MI 49508
Phone: (616) 957-3000

Pet Restrictions: None
Exercise Area for Pets: Yes
Rates: $32.99 to $45.99

Holiday Inn Crown Plaza
5700 28th St. SE
Grand Rapids, MI 49506
Phone: (616) 957-1770

Pet Restrictions: Smaller pets & in a
    cage, sign waiver
Exercise Area for Pets: Yes
Rates: $89 to $109

Holiday Inn East
3333 28th St. SE
Grand Rapids, MI 49508
Phone (616) 949-9222

Pet Restrictions: None
Exercise Area for Pets: Yes
Rates: $60 to $88

Holiday Inn North
270 Ann St. NW
Grand Rapids, MI 49504
Phone: (616) 363-9001

Pet Restrictions: Small pets
Exercise Area for Pets: Nearby
Rates: $60 to $85

Howard Johnson
35 28th St. SW
Grand Rapids, MI 49508
Phone: (616) 452-5141

Pet Restrictions: None
Exercise Area for Pets: Yes
Rates: $29.95 to $50

Red Roof Inn
5131 East 28th St.
Grand Rapids, MI 49512
Phone: (616) 942-0800

Pet Restrictions: None
Pet left unattended in room: Yes
Exercise Area for Pets: Yes
Rates: $35 to $50

Animal Clinic
133 28th St. Southeast
Phone: (616) 241-3651

Cascade Hospital for Animals
6730 Cascade Rd.
Phone: (616) 949-0960

Kelley's Animal Clinic
4011 Remembrance Rd. NW
Phone: (616) 453-7422

HARBOR SPRINGS

Harbor Springs Motor Inn
145 Zoll St.
Harbor Springs, MI 49740
Phone: (616) 526-5431

Pet Restrictions: $5/night
Pet left unattended in room: Yes
Exercise Area for Pets: Yes
Rates: $72 to $130

VETERINARIANS

McDonald, Michael
8769 M-119
Phone: (616) 347-4552

Zehnder, David
8769 M-119
Phone: (616) 347-4552

HARPER WOODS

Parkcrest
20000 Harper Ave.
Harper Woods, MI 48225
Phone: (313) 884-8800

Pet Restrictions: None
Pet left unattended in room: Yes
Exercise Area for Pets: Yes
Rates: $55 to $80

VETERINARIANS

Harper Woods Veterinary Hosp.
20102 Harper Ave.
Phone: (313) 881-8061

HAZEL PARK

Quality Inn - Hazel Park
1 W 9 Mill Rd.
Hazel Park, MI 48030
Phone: (313) 399-5800

Pet Restrictions: None
Pet left unattended in room: Yes
Exercise Area for Pets: Yes
Rates: $49 to $89

HOUGHTON LAKE

Hillside Motel
3419 W. Houghton Lake Dr.
Houghton Lake, MI 48629
Phone: (517) 366-5711

Pet Restrictions: None
Exercise Area for Pets: Yes
Rates: $34 to $44

Holiday On The Lake
100 Clearview Rd.
Houghton Lake, MI 48629
Phone: (517) 422-5195

Pet Restrictions: $5/stay/pet
Exercise Area for Pets: Yes
Rates: $38 to $60

HOWELL

Howell Park Inn
125 Holiday Lane
Howell, MI 48843
Phone: (517) 546-6800

Pet Restrictions: No snakes
Pet left unattended in room: Yes
Exercise Area for Pets: Yes
Rates: $42 to $53

Knights Inn
124 Holiday Lane
Howell, MI 48843
Phone: (517) 548-3510

Pet Restrictions: $5/night
Pet left unattended in room: Yes
Exercise Area for Pets: Yes
Rates: $31.50 to $40

VETERINARIANS

Countryside Veterinary Clinic
2745 East Grand River
Phone: (517) 546-5714

INDIAN RIVER

Caravan Motel & Cottages
4904 S. Straits Hwy
Indian River, MI 49749
Phone: (616) 238-7481

Pet Restrictions: No exotic animals
Exercise Area for Pets: Yes
Rates: $36 to $75

Star Gate Motel
4646 S. Straits Hwy
Indian River, MI 49749
Phone: (616) 238-7371

Pet Restrictions: Leashed
Exercise Area for Pets: Yes
Rates: $36 to $48

VETERINARIANS
Indian River Veterinary Clinic
5338 S. Straits Hwy
Phone: (616) 238-7022

JACKSON
Holiday Inn
2000 Holiday Inn Dr.
Jackson, MI 49202
Phone: (517) 783-2681

Pet Restrictions: None
Pet left unattended in room: Yes
Exercise Area for Pets: Nearby
Rates: $105 to $120

Motel 6
830 Royal Dr.
Jackson, MI 49202
Phone: (517) 789-7186

Pet Restrictions: None
Exercise Area for Pets: Yes
Rates: $27.99 to $39.99

VETERINARIANS
Gorczyca, Patrick J.
1606 W. Ganson St.
Phone: (517) 784-5928

North, Catherine
1606 W. Ganson St.
Phone: (517) 784-8457

KALAMAZOO
Days Inn
1912 East Kilgore Rd.
Kalamazoo, MI 49002
Phone: (616) 382-2303

Pet Restrictions: Caged pets
Exercise Area for Pets: Yes
Rates: $39.95 to $44.95

Holiday Inn-Expressway
3522 Sprinkle Rd.
Kalamazoo, MI 49002
Phone: (616) 381-7070

Pet Restrictions: Sign waiver
Exercise Area for Pets: Yes
Rates: $70 to $59

Red Roof Inn - East
3701 E. Cork St.
Kalamazoo, MI 49001
Phone: (616) 382-6350

Pet Restrictions: None
Pet left unattended in room: Yes
Exercise Area for Pets: Yes
Rates: $33.99 to $48.99

Red Roof Inn - West
5425 W. Michigan Ave.
Kalamazoo, MI 49009
Phone: (616) 375-7400

Pet Restrictions: None
Pet left unattended in room: Yes
Exercise Area for Pets: Yes
Rates: $29 to $47

Roadway Inn
619 S. Nicolet St.
Kalamazoo, MI 49701
Phone: (616) 436-5332

Pet Restrictions: None
Exercise Area for Pets: Yes
Rates: $33.50 to $38.50

VETERINARIANS
Portage Animal Hospital
8037 Portage Rd.
Phone: (616) 327-3459

LAKE CITY
Northcrest Motel
P.O. Box M, 1 mi. S on SR 55 & 66
Lake City, MI 49651
Phone: (616) 839-2075

Pet Restrictions: None
Pet left unattended in room: Yes
Exercise Area for Pets: Yes
Rates: $38 to $49

LANSING
Days Inn
6501 S. Penn. Ave.
Lansing, MI 48911
Phone: (517) 393-1650

Pet Restrictions: None
Exercise Area for Pets: Yes
Rates: $44 to $49

Knights Inn South
1100 Ramada Dr.
Lansing, MI 48910
Phone: (517) 394-7200

Pet Restrictions: None
Exercise Area for Pets: Yes
Rates: $34.50 to $50

Motel 6
7326 W. Saginaw Hwy.
Lansing, MI 48917
Phone: (517) 321-1444

Pet Restrictions: 1 small pet
Exercise Area for Pets: Yes
Rates: $27.99 up

Red Roof Inn - East
3615 Dunckle Rd.
Lansing, MI 48910
Phone: (517) 332-2575

Pet Restrictions: None
Pet left unattended in room: Yes
Exercise Area for Pets: Yes
Rates: $34.99 to $50.99

Red Roof Inn - West
7412 W. Saginaw Hwy
Lansing, MI 48917
Phone: (517) 321-7246

Pet Restrictions: None
Pet left unattended in room: Yes
Exercise Area for Pets: Yes
Rates: $34.99 to $51.99

Regal 8 Inn
6501 S. Cedar St.
Lansing, MI 48910
Phone: (517) 393-2030

Pet Restrictions: None
Pet left unattended in room: Yes
Exercise Area for Pets: Yes
Rates: $24.95 to $36.95

Residence Inn by Marriott
1600 E. Grand River
Lansing, MI 48823
Phone: (517) 332-7711

Pet Restrictions: $60 non-refund.
  deposit, $6/day
Pet left unattended in room: Yes
Exercise Area for Pets: Yes
Rates: $99 to $129

Sheraton Inn - Lansing
925 S. Creyts Rd.
Lansing, MI 48917
Phone: (517) 323-7100

Pet Restrictions: 1st floor only
Exercise Area for Pets: Yes
Rates: $96 to $106

VETERINARIANS

Waverly Animal Hospital
233 South Waverly Rd.
Phone: (517) 323-4156

Atma, Mark S.
4124 Woodbridge
Phone: (517) 393-1777

LIVONIA

Holiday Inn - Livonia West
17123 Laurel Park Dr. N
Livonia, MI 48152
Phone: (313) 464-1300

Pet Restrictions: Small pets
Pet left unattended in room: Yes
Exercise Area for Pets: Yes
Rates: $76 to $84

VETERINARIANS

Allen Animal Hospital
19066 Farmington Rd.
Phone: (313) 476-0570

Bloom Animal Hospital
31205 Five Mil Rd.
Phone: (313) 425-2270

McClure, Glenn R.
29212 Five Mile Rd.
Phone: (313) 427-6360

LUDINGTON

Nova Motel
472 US 31 S
Ludington, MI 49431
Phone: (616) 843-3454

Pet Restrictions: $5/pet, under 40
  lbs.
Exercise Area for Pets: Yes
Rates: $28 to $69

MACHINAW CITY

American Motel
Nicolet St. & SR 108, P.O. Box 928
Machinaw City, MI 49701
Phone: (616) 436-5231

Pet Restrictions: None
Exercise Area for Pets: Yes
Rates: $20 to $55

Econo Lodge
412 Nicolet St., P.O. Box 354
Machinaw City, MI 49701
Phone: (616) 436-5026

Pet Restrictions: None
Exercise Area for Pets: Yes
Rates: $28 to $128

Lamplighter Motel
303 Janet St.
Machinaw, MI 49701
Phone: (616) 436-5350

Pet Restrictions: None
Pet left unattended in room: Yes
Exercise Area for Pets: Nearby
Rates: $24.50 to $42.50

MADISON HTS
Knights Inn
32703 Stephenson Hwy
Madison Hts., MI 48671
Phone: (313) 583-7700

Pet Restrictions: None
Pet left unattended in room: Yes
Exercise Area for Pets: Yes
Rates: $33.95 to $46.95

Knights Inn - North Central II
26091 Dequindre Rd.
Madison Hts., MI 48071
Phone: (313) 545-9930

Pet Restrictions: None
Pet left unattended in room: Yes
Exercise Area for Pets: Yes
Rates: $28.95 to $30.95

Red Roof Inn
32511 Concord
Madison Heights, MI 48071
Phone: (313) 583-4700

Pet Restrictions: None
Pet left unattended in room: Yes
Exercise Area for Pets: Yes
Rates: $27 to $46

Residence Inn by Marriott - Troy Southeast
32650 Stephenson Hwy
Madison Hts., MI 48071
Phone: (313) 583-4322

Pet Restrictions: $75 non-ref. fee, $6/night
Pet left unattended in room: Yes
Exercise Area for Pets: Yes
Rates: $104 to $139

VETERINARIANS
Madison Veterinary Hospital
240 East 12 Mile Rd.
Phone: (313) 399-5225

MANISTIQUE
City Motel
1030 W. Lake Shore Dr.
Manistique, MI 49854
Phone: (906) 341-5212

Pet Restrictions: $2/night/pet
Exercise Area for Pets: Yes
Rates: $26 to $36

Holiday Motel
opp. Schoolcraft County Airport, Rt. 1, Box 1514
Manistique, MI 49854
Phone: (906) 341-2710

Pet Restrictions: $5/night
Exercise Area for Pets: Yes
Rates: $29 to $50

Howard Johnson Lodge
726 East Lake Shore Dr. US-2
Manistique, MI 49854
Phone: (906) 341-6981

Pet Restrictions: $5/day/pet
Exercise Area for Pets: Yes
Rates: $33 to $65

Ramada Inn
P.O. Box 485
Manistique, MI 49854
Phone: (906) 341-6911

Pet Restrictions: None
Pet left unattended in room: Yes
Exercise Area for Pets: Yes
Rates: $35 to $75

MARQUETTE
Holiday Inn
1951 US 41 W
Marquette, MI 49855
Phone: (906) 225-1351

Pet Restrictions: None
Exercise Area for Pets: Yes
Rates: $45 to $75

Ramada Inn
412 W. Washington
Marquette, MI 49855
Phone: (906) 228-6000

Pet Restrictions: None
Pet left unattended in room: Yes
Exercise Area for Pets: Yes
Rates: $65 to $85

VETERINARIANS
Engstrom, David V.
2270 US 41 South
Phone: (906) 249-1456

Ryan, Randy O.
2270 US 41 South
Phone: (906) 249-1456

MIDLAND

Holiday Inn
1500 W. Wacherly
Midland, MI 48640
Phone: (517) 631-4220

Pet Restrictions: Outside rooms
    usually
Pet left unattended in room: Yes
Exercise Area for Pets: Yes
Rates: $41 to $79

VETERINARIANS

Midland Animal Clinic
1500 E. Patrick Rd.
Phone: (517) 631-0220

Robbins, Laura J.
1926 N. Saginaw Rd.
Phone: (517) 631-9740

MILAN

Star Motel
335 Lewis Ave.
Milan, MI 48160
Phone: (313) 439-2448

Pet Restrictions: $10
Pet left unattended in room: Yes
Exerclse Area for Pets: Yes
Rates: $34 to $39

VETERINARIANS

Milan Veterinary Clinic
140 West Main St.
Phone: (313) 439-1112

MONROE

Hometown Inn
1885 Welcome Way
Monroe, MI 48161
Phone: (313) 289-1080

Pet Restrictions: None
Pet left unattended in room: Yes
Exercise Area for Pets: Yes
Rates: $25.95 to $34.95

Knights Inn
1250 N. Dixie Hwy
Monroe, MI 48161
Phone: (313) 243-0597,
    (800) 843-5644

Pet Restrictions: None
Pet left unattended in room: Yes
Exercise Area for Pets: Yes
Rates: $31.75 to $34.93

MT. PLEASANT

Mt. Pleasant Inn
5665 E. Pickard Ave.
Mt. Pleasant, MI 48858
Phone: (517) 772-2905

Pet Restrictions: None
Pet left unattended in room: Yes
Exercise Area for Pets: Yes
Rates: $58 to $85

MUNISING

Sunset Motel
P.O. Box 291
Munising, MI 49862
Phone: (906) 387-4574

Pet Restrictions: $3/night
Exercise Area for Pets: Yes
Rates: $39 to $54

MUSKEGON

Econo Lodge
3450 Hoyt St.
Muskegon, MI 49444
Phone: (616) 733-2601,
    (800) 424-4777

Pet Restrictions: None
Pet left unattended in room: Yes
Exercise Area for Pets: Yes
Rates: $44.95 up

VETERINARIANS

Martin, Charles R.
1703 W. Sherman Blvd.
Phone: (616) 755-2205

NEWBERRY

Best Western Village Inn
S. Newbury Ave.
Newberry, MI 49868
Phone: (906) 293-5114

Pet Restrictions: None
Exercise Area for Pets: Yes
Rates: $34 to $62

Green Acres Motel
Rt. 1, Box 736
Newberry, MI 49868
Phone: (906) 293-5932,
    (800) 800-5398

Pet Restrictions: None
Pet left unattended in room: Yes
Exercise Area for Pets: Yes
Rates: $38 to $48

MICHIGAN — HOTELS (continued)

NEW BUFFALO

Grand Beach Motel
19189 US 12W
New Buffalo, MI 49117
Phone: (616) 469-1555

Pet Restrictions: None
Pet left unattended in room: Yes
Exercise Area for Pets: Yes
Rates: $50 to $45

NILES

Holiday Inn
930 S. 11th St.
Niles, MI 49120
Phone: (616) 684-3000,
    (800) HOLIDAY

Pet Restrictions: None
Exercise Area for Pets: Yes
Rates: $52 up

VETERINARIANS

County Line Animal Clinic
2164 Oak St.
Phone: (616) 683-6511

Schleiffarth, Robert A.
1040 Tomahawk Lane
Phone: (616) 684-0082

NOVI

Novi Hilton
2111 Haggerty Rd.
Novi, MI 48050
Phone: (313) 349-4000

Pet Restrictions: None
Pet left unattended in room: Waiver,
    25 lb. and under
Exercise Area for Pets: Yes
Rates: $69 to $134

OSCODO

Northern Traveler Motel
5493 US 23 N
Oscodo, MI 48750
Phone: (517) 739-9261

Pet Restrictions: $5/night
Exercise Area for Pets: Yes
Rates: $34 to $58

PLYMOUTH

Motel 6
41216 Ford Rd.
Plymouth, MI 48187
Phone: (313) 981-5000

Pet Restrictions: None
Exercise Area for Pets: Yes
Rates: $26.95 up

Red Roof Inn
39700 Ann Arbor Rd.
Plymouth, MI 48170
Phone: (313) 459-3300

Pet Restrictions: None
Pet left unattended in room: Yes
Exercise Area for Pets: Yes
Rates: $27 to $45

VETERINARIANS

Parkway Veterinary Clinic
41395 Wilcox Rd.
Phone: (313) 453-2577

Leininger, Steven
725 Wing St.
Phone: (313) 453-0485

Roose, Kevin C.
8909 S. Main
Phone: (313) 459-1400

PORT AUSTIN

The Castaway Beach Resort
1404 Port Austin Rd.
Port Austin, MI 48467
Phone: (517) 738-5101

Pet Restrictions: Only in cottages
Pet left unattended in room: Yes
Exercise Area for Pets: Yes
Rates: $60 up

PORT HURON

Economy Lodge of Port Huron
1720 Hancock St.
Port Huron, MI 48060
Phone: (313) 984-2661

Pet Restrictions: $5/night
Exercise Area for Pets: Yes
Rates: $51.50 up

Knights Inn
2160 Water St.
Port Huron, MI 48060
Phone: (313) 982-1022

Pet Restrictions: None
Pet left unattended in room: Yes
Exercise Area for Pets: Yes
Rates: $46.95 to $72.95

VETERINARIANS

North River Animal Hospital
2909 N. River Rd.
Phone: (313) 985-6117

Veterinary Associates
3801 Lapeer Rd.
Phone: (313) 985-6144

DeMerritt, DE
4740 W. Water St.
Phone: (313) 985-5624

RAPID RIVER
The Right Bower Motel
9912 US 2
Rapid River, MI 49878
Phone: (906) 474-6078

Pet Restrictions: None
Pet left unattended in room: Yes
Exercise Area for Pets: Yes
Rates: $23 to $36

ROCHESTER HILLS
Red Roof Inn
2580 Crooks Rd.
Rochester Hills, MI 48309
Phone: (313) 853-6400

Pet Restrictions: None
Pet left unattended in room: Yes
Exercise Area for Pets: Yes
Rates: $29 to $49

VETERINARIANS
Rochester Vet. Hospital
2155 Crooks Rd.
(313) 852-3650

Spring Hill Vetny. Hospital
2905 Walton Blvd.
(313) 375-1440

ROMULUS
Holiday Inn Metro Airport/ Holidome
31200 Detroit Industrial Expwy
Romulus, MI 48174
Phone: (313) 728-2800,
(800) 221-2222

Pet Restrictions: None
Pet left unattended in room: Yes
Exercise Area for Pets: Yes
Rates: $79 to $49

VETERINARIANS
Willowood Acres Vet. Clinic
29490 Sibley Rd.
Phone: (313) 753-4424

ROSEVILLE
Red Roof Inn
31800 Little Mack Rd.
Roseville, MI 48066
Phone: (313) 296-0310,
(800) THE ROOF

Pet Restrictions: None
Pet left unattended in room: Yes
Exercise Area for Pets: Yes
Rates: $48.99 to $42.99

SAGINAW
Best Western Saginaw
3325 Davenport Ave.
Saginaw, MI 48602
Phone: (517) 793-2080,
(800) 654-3309

Pet Restrictions: Smaller Pets
Exercise Area for Pets: Yes
Rates: $52 to $39

Knights Inn
2225 Tittabawasee Rd.
Saginaw, MI 48604
Phone: (517) 791-1411,
(800) 843-5644

Pet Restrictions: Smaller pets
Pet left unattended in room: Yes
Exercise Area for Pets: Yes
Rates: $34.95 to $48.95

Red Roof Inn
966 S. Outer Dr.
Saginaw, MI 48601
Phone: (517) 754-8414,
(800) 843-7663

Pet Restrictions: None
Pet left unattended in room: Yes
Exercise Area for Pets: Yes
Rates: $29.99 to $52.99

VETERINARIANS
Cole Veterinary Hospital
2615 Schust Rd.
Phone: (517) 790-2230

Riverside Animal Clinic
1855 Midland Rd.
Phone: (517) 799-6490

Millerick, MT
305 N. Center Rd.
Phone: (517) 793-2490

SAULT STE. MARIE

Admirals Inn
2701 I 75 business spur
Sault Ste. Marie, MI 49783
Phone: (906) 632-1130

Pet Restrictions: None
Exercise Area for Pets: Yes
Rates: $40 to $33

Seaway Motel
1800 Ashman St.
Sault Ste. Marie, MI 49783
Phone: (906) 632-8201,
(800) 782-0466

Pet Restrictions: None
Exercise Area for Pets: Yes
Rates: $52 to $42

SMYRNA

Double R. Ranch Resort
4424 Whites Bridge Rd.
Smyrna, MI 48887
Phone: (616) 794-0520

Pet Restrictions: None
Exercise Area for Pets: Yes
Rates: $34.65 to $50

SOUTH HAVEN

Friendship Inn
09817 140-M Hwy
South Haven, MI 49090
Phone: (616) 637-5141,
(800) 955-1831

Pet Restrictions: Under 40 lbs.,
leashed
Pet left unattended in room: Yes
Exercise Area for Pets: Yes
Rates: $55 to $90

ST. IGNACE

Bay View Motel (Wishing Well)
1133 N. State St.
St. Ignace, MI 49781
Phone: (906) 643-9444

Pet Restrictions: $5/night
Exercise Area for Pets: Yes
Rates: $44 to $52

Howard Johnson Lodge
913 Blvd. Drive
St. Ignace, MI 49781
Phone: (906) 643-9700,
(800) 1-GO-HOJO

Pet Restrictions: $6/pet
Pet left unattended in room: Yes
Exercise Area for Pets: Yes
Rates: $42 to $68

STURGIS

Holiday Inn
1300 S. Centerville Rd.
Sturgis, MI 49091
Phone: (616) 651-7881

Pet Restrictions: Smaller pets
Pet left unattended in room: Yes
Exercise Area for Pets: Yes
Rates: $46 to $59

TAWAS CITY

Tawas Motel
1124 US 23 S, P.O. Box 248
Tawas City, MI 28763
Phone: (517) 362-3822

Pet Restrictions: $5 refund. deposit
Exercise Area for Pets: Yes
Rates: $55 to $85

TAYLOR

Red Roof Inn
21230 Eureka Rd.
Taylor, MI 48180
Phone: (313) 374-1150,
(800) 843-7663

Pet Restrictions: Yes
Pet left unattended in room: Yes
Exercise Area for Pets: Yes
Rates: $42 to $52

VETERINARIANS

Rossoni Animal Hospital
23737 Van Born Rd.
(313) 291-6400

THREE RIVERS

Three Rivers Inn
1200 W. Broadway, PO Box 349
Three Rivers, MI 49093
Phone: (616) 273-9521,
(800) 553-4626

Pet Restrictions: W/authorization
number, $5.20/night
Exercise Area for Pets: Yes
Rates: $75 to $52

TRAVERSE CITY

Fox House Motor Lodge
704 Munson Ave.
Traverse City, MI 49684
Phone: (616) 947-4450

Pet Restrictions: None
Exercise Area for Pets: Yes
Rates: $89 to $99

Main St. Inn
618 E. Front St.
Traverse City, MI 49684
Phone: (616) 929-0410,
  (800) 255-7180
Pet Restrictions: None
Pet left unattended in room: Yes
Exercise Area for Pets: Yes
Rates: $49.95 to $69.95

VETERINARIANS

Cherry Bend Animal Hospital
10351 Cherry Bend Rd.
Phone: (616) 922-0500

Clarke-Everett Dog/Cat Hosp.
1525 Cass St.
Phone: (616) 947-3900

Grand Traverse Vet. Hosp.
3805 Town Hall Rd. N
Phone: (616) 946-3770

TROY
Holiday Inn
2537 Rochester Ct.
Troy, MI 48083
Phone: (313) 689-7500
Pet Restrictions: None
Pet left unattended in room: Yes
Exercise Area for Pets: Yes
Rates: $49 to $85

Red Roof Inn
2350 Rochester Rd.
Troy, MI 48083
Phone: (313) 689-4391
Pet Restrictions: None
Pet left unattended in room: Yes -
  no maid service
Exercise Area for Pets: Yes
Rates: $30 to $45

Residence Inn by Marriott - Troy Ctr.
26000 Livernois Rd.
Troy, MI 48043
Phone: (313) 689-6856,
  (800) 331-3131
Pet Restrictions: $75 nonrefundable
  deposit, $6/night
Pet left unattended in room: Yes
Exercise Area for Pets: Yes
Rates: $119 to $159

WARREN
Budgetel Inn
30900 N. Van Dyke
Warren, MI 48093
Phone: (313) 574-0550,
  (800) 428-3438
Pet Restrictions: None
Pet left unattended in room: Yes
Exercise Area for Pets: Yes
Rates: $31.95 to $45.95

Motel 6
8300 Chicago Rd.
Warren, MI 48093
Phone: (313) 826-9300
Pet Restrictions: Small pets
Exercise Area for Pets: Yes
Rates: $26.95 to $40.85

Red Roof Inn
26300 Dequindre Rd.
Warren, MI 48091
Phone: (313) 573-4300
Pet Restrictions: None
Pet left unattended in room: Yes
Exercise Area for Pets: Yes
Rates: $30 to $47

VETERINARIANS

Abbey East Animal Hospital
30824 Dequindre Rd.
Phone: (313) 751-7611

MINNESOTA — HOTELS

AITKIN

Ripple River Motel
P.O. Box 346
Aitkin, MN 56431
Phone: (218) 927-3734,
 (800) 258-3734

Pet Restrictions: Yes
Exercise Area for Pets: Nearby
Rates: $19.95 to $51.65

ALBERT LEA

Days Inn
2306 E. Main St.
Albert Lea, MN 56007
Phone: (507) 373-6471,
 (800) 325-2525

Pet Restrictions: None
Exercise Area for Pets: Yes
Rates: $46 to $75

AUSTIN

Albert Lea Super 8 Lodge
2019 E. Main St.
Austin, MN 56007
Phone: (507) 377-0591,
 (800) 800-8000

Pet Restrictions: $10 deposit
Pet left unattended in room: Yes,
 owner responsible for damages
Exercise Area for Pets: Nearby
Rates: $34.88 and up

Bel Aire Motor Inn
just SW of jct. SR 13 & SR 69
Austin, MN 56007
Phone: (507) 373-3983

Pet Restrictions: None
Pet left unattended in room: Yes
Exercise Area for Pets: Yes
Rates: $20 to $60

BABBITT

Timber Bay Lodge & Houseboats
P.O. Box 248
Babbitt, MN 55706
Phone: (218) 827-3682,
 (800) 846-6821

Pet Restrictions: $5/pet/day,
 $25/pet/week if staying weekly
Exercise Area for Pets: Yes
Rates: $80 to $250

BEMIDJI

Ruttgers Birchmont Lodge
530 Birchmont Beach Rd. NE
Bemidji, MN 56601
Phone: (218) 751-1630,
 (800) 726-3866

Pet Restrictions: Only in cabins,
 $4/pet/night
Pet left unattended in room: Yes
Exercise Area for Pets: Yes
Rates: $138 to $225

BLOOMINGTON

Bloomington Marriott
220 E. 79th St.
Bloomington, MN 55424
Phone: (612) 854-7441,
 (800) 228-9292

Pet Restrictions: None
Pet left unattended in room: Yes
Exercise Area for Pets: Yes
Rates: $79 to $102

Crown Sterling Suites Airport
7901 34th Ave.
Bloomington, MN 55420
Phone: (612) 854-1000,
 (800) 433-4600

Pet Restrictions: Small pets under
 30 lbs.
Pet left unattended in room: Yes
Exercise Area for Pets: Yes
Rates: $129 to $149

Excel Inn
2701 E. 78th St.
Bloomington, MN 55425
Phone: (612) 854-7200,
 (800) 356-8012

Pet Restrictions: Small pets
Exercise Area for Pets: Yes
Rates: $43.99 to $125

Thunderbird Hotel & Conv. Ctr.
2201 E. 78th St.
Bloomington, MN 55425-1228
Phone: (612) 854-3411,
 (800) 328-1931

Pet Restrictions: None
Pet left unattended in room: Yes
Exercise Area for Pets: Yes
Rates: $68 to $91

VETERINARIANS
Bloomington Veterinary Hosp.
8830 Lyndale Ave. South
Phone: (612) 884-3228

South Hyland Pet Hospital
5400 West Old Shakopee
Phone: (612) 884-1868

Schulz, Vicki A.
8716 Utah Ave. South
Phone: (612) 942-7304

BRAINERD

Holiday Inn
P.O. Box 608
Brainerd, MN 56401
Phone: (218) 829-1441,
    (800) HOLIDAY
Pet Restrictions: Yes
Exercise Area for Pets: Yes
Rates: $43 to $74

River View Motel
324 NW Wash. St., P.O. Box 588
Brainerd, MN 56401
Phone: (218) 829-8771
Pet Restrictions: None
Pet left unattended in room: Yes,
    should be house trained
Rates: $26 to $54

BROOKLYN CENTER

Park Inn
1501 Freeway Blvd.
Brooklyn Center, MN 55430
Phone: (612) 566-4140,
    (800) 437-7275
Pet Restrictions: Small pets
Exercise Area for Pets: Yes
Rates: $44 to $85

BURNSVILLE

Red Roof Inn
12920 Aldrich Ave.
Burnsville, MN 55337
Phone: (612) 890-1420
Pet Restrictions: Under 25 lbs.
Pet left unattended in room: Yes, no
    maid service
Exercise Area for Pets: Yes
Rates: $30 to $48

VETERINARIANS

Crossroads Animal Hospital
14321 Nicollet Court, Suite 900
(612) 435-2655

CHANHASSEN

Chanhassen Inn Motel
531 W. 79th St.
Chanhassen, MN 55317
Phone: (612) 934-7373,
    (800) 242-6466
Pet Restrictions: No cats, $20
    deposit
Exercise Area for Pets: Yes
Rates: $38 to $49

CLEARWATER

Budget Inn
P.O. Box 266
Clearwater, MN 55320
Phone: (612) 558-2221,
    (800) 950-7751
Pet Restrictions: $2
Exercise Area for Pets: Yes
Rates: $30.90 to $40.90

CRANE LAKE

Handberg's Campbell's Cabins
Canadian side of Lac La Croix
Crane Lake, MN 55725
Phone: (807) 485-2441
Pet Restrictions: None
Pet left unattended in room: Yes
Exercise Area for Pets: Yes
Rates: $45 per person

CROOKSTON

Northland Inn
P.O. Box 117
Crookston, MN 56716
Phone: (218) 281-5210
Pet Restrictions: $3/day/pet
Pet left unattended in room: Yes
Exercise Area for Pets: Nearby
Rates: $50 to $56

DEER RIVER

Bahr's Motel
109 Division St., P.O. Box 614
Deer River, MN 56636
Phone: (218) 246-8271
Pet Restrictions: None
Pet left unattended in room: Yes
Exercise Area for Pets: Yes
Rates: $25 to $39

DETROIT LAKES

Budget Host
895 Hwy 10E
Detroit Lakes, MN 56501
Phone: (218) 847-4454,
 (800) 888-2124

Pet Restrictions: None
Exercise Area for Pets: Yes
Rates: $47.95 to $57.95 plus tax

VETERINARIANS

McCormack, James K.
P.O. Box 1382
Phone: (218) 547-5674

DULUTH

Best Western Downtown Motel
131 W 2nd St.
Duluth, MN 55802
Phone: (218) 727-6851,
 (800) 528-1234

Pet Restrictions: In kennel if left alone
Pet left unattended in room: Yes
Exercise Area for Pets: Yes
Rates: $59 to $69

Best West. Edgewater E. Motel
2330 London Rd.
Duluth, MN 55812
Phone: (218) 728-3601,
 (800) 777-7925

Pet Restrictions: Only in original
 bldg., not in atrium
Exercise Area for Pets: Nearby
Rates: $79 to $99

Best West. Edgewater W. Motel
2211 London Rd.
Duluth, MN 55812
Phone: (218) 728-5141,
 (800) 777-7925

Pet Restrictions: Only in original
 bldg., not in atrium
Exercise Area for Pets: Nearby
Rates: $63 to $130

Duluth Motel
4415 Grand Ave.
Duluth, MN 55807
Phone: (218) 628-1008

Pet Restrictions: Small pet, in cage
 only
Exercise Area for Pets: Nearby
Rates: $25 to $40

VETERINARIANS

North Shore Veterinary Hosp.
6001 E. Superior St.
Phone: (218) 525-1937

Dougherty, Thomas
Central Entrance & 14th St.
Phone: (218) 722-3963

Ferrin, David
2548 London Rd.
Phone: (218) 728-3616

EAGAN

Residence Inn by Marriott
3040 Eagandale Pl.
Eagan, MN 55121
Phone: (612) 688-0363

Pet Restrictions: $150-$5/day, 20
 lb. limit
Exercise Area for Pets: Nearby
Rates: $117 to $147

EDEN PRAIRIE

Residence Inn by Marriott
7780 Flying Cloud Dr.
Eden Prairie, MN 55344
Phone: (612) 829-0033,
 (800) 331-3131

Pet Restrictions: $50 or $8/day
Pet left unattended in room: Yes
Exercise Area for Pets: Yes
Rates: $99 to $149

VETERINARIANS

Harris, Steven M.
8300 Flying Cloud Dr.
Phone: (612) 941-8676

Vogt, Judi C.
8743 Bentwood Dr.
Phone: (612) 944-1597

EVELETH

Holiday Inn - Eveleth Virginia
Hat Trick Ave., P.O. Box 708
Eveleth, MN 55734
Phone: (218) 744-2703,
 (800) 465-4329

Pet Restrictions: None
Exercise Area for Pets: Nearby
Rates: $53.50 to $79.50

FAIRMONT

Super 8 Motel-Fairmont
P.O. Box 902
Fairmont, MN 56031
Phone: (507) 238-9444,
    (800) 800-8000

Pet Restrictions: None
Pet left unattended in room: Yes
Exercise Area for Pets: Yes
Rates: $39.88 to $47.88 plus tax
    and $5 per add'l person

FERGUS FALLS

Holiday Inn
I94 & SR 210, P.O. Box 103
Fergus Falls, MN 56537
Phone: (218) 739-2211

Pet Restrictions: None
Pet left unattended in room: Yes
Exercise Area for Pets: Nearby
Rates: $60 to $68

FOREST LAKE

Americinn Motel
1291 W. Broadway
Forest Lake, MN 55025
Phone: (612) 464-1930,
    (800) 634-3444

Pet Restrictions: $6/dog/night, only
    dogs
Pet left unattended in room: Yes
Exercise Area for Pets: Nearby
Rates: $51.90 to $55.90 2 people,
    $6 per add'l person

VETERINARIANS

Leblond Jr., John
5475 Upper 183rd Street
Phone: (612) 460-8985

FRIDLEY

Best Western Skywood Inn
5203 Central Ave. NE
Fridley, MN 55421
Phone: (612) 571-9440

Pet Restrictions: $100 deposit
Exercise Area for Pets: Nearby,
    scooper needed
Rates: $55

GRAND MARAIS

Gunflint Lodge
on Gunflint Trail, P.O. Box 100 GTA
Grand Marais, MN 55604
Phone: (218) 388-2294,
    (800) 328-3325

Pet Restrictions: On leash,
    $5/night/pet
Pet left unattended in room: Yes
Rates: $89 to $149

Gunflint Motel
P.O. Box 1028 Gunflint Trail
Grand Marais, MN 55604
Phone: (218) 387-1454

Pet Restrictions: May require
    deposit, reserve in advance
Pet left unattended in room: Yes
Exercise Area for Pets: Yes
Rates: $40 to $52

Nor Wester Lodge
P.O. Box 60 AAA
Grand Marais, MN 55604
Phone: (218) 388-2252,
    (800) 992-4386

Pet Restrictions: $40/wk or $6/day
    in cabin, on leash please
Exercise Area for Pets: Yes
Rates: $72 to $150

Tom Teboda Motel
1800 W. Hwy 61, P.O. Box 112
Grand Marais, MN 55604
Phone: (218) 387-1585,
    (800) 622-2622

Pet Restrictions: None
Exercise Area for Pets: Yes
Rates: $45 to $62

GRAND RAPIDS

Days Inn Motel
5 blocks E. on Hwy 2 & 129E
Grand Rapids, MN 55744
Phone: (218) 326-3457

Pet Restrictions: Smoking rooms only
Exercise Area for Pets: Nearby
Rates: $55

Sawmill Inn
2301 S. Pokegama
Grand Rapids, MN 55744
Phone: (218) 326-8501,
    (800) 235-6455

Pet Restrictions: None
Exercise Area for Pets: Yes
Rates: $60 to $62 (2 people)

HIBBING
Days Inn Motel
1520 Hwy 37E, P.O. Box 862
Hibbing, MN 55746
Phone: (218) 263-8306,
  (800) 325-2525
Pet Restrictions: None
Exercise Area for Pets: Yes
Rates: $36 to $43

VETERINARIANS
Toivola, Brian E.
Star Route 2, Box 11
Phone: (218) 262-1051

INT'L FALLS
Days Inn
P.O. Drawer O
International Falls, MN 56679
Phone: (218) 283-9441,
  (800) 325-2525
Pet Restrictions: Small pets
Exercise Area for Pets: Yes
Rates: $49 to $51 (2 people)

Island View Lodge
Rt. 8
International Falls, MN 56649
Phone: (218) 286-3511,
  (800) 777-7856
Pet Restrictions: Only in cabins
Exercise Area for Pets: Yes
Rates: $60 to $195

MANKATO
Budgetel Inn
111 W. Lind Ct.
Mankato, MN 56001
Phone: (507) 345-8800
Pet Restrictions: Smoking rooms
  only
Exercise Area for Pets: Yes
Rates: $33.95 to $43.95

VETERINARIANS
Fischer, George
1606 S. Riverfront Dr.
Phone: (507) 388-7783

N. MANKATO
Best Western Garden Inn
1111 Range St.
N. Mankato, MN 56001
Phone: (507) 625-9333,
  (800) 528-1234
Pet Restrictions: Small
Exercise Area for Pets: Yes
Rates: $45 to $60

VETERINARIANS
Berndt, Julie S.
1540 Meyer Lane
Phone: (507) 345-5900

MARSHALL
Crown Sterling Suites
425 S 7th St.
Marshall, MN 55415
Phone: (612) 333-3111,
  (800) 433-4600
Pet Restrictions: $50 deposit or
  credit card imprint
Exercise Area for Pets: Nearby
Rates: $99 to $225

Holiday Inn Metrodome
1500 Wash. Ave.
Marshall, MN 55434
Phone: (612) 333-4646,
  (800) HIT-DOME
Pet Restrictions: None
Pet left unattended in room: Yes if
  in kennel or no service
Exercise Area for Pets: Nearby
Rates: $83.50 for 2

Park Inn International
1313 Nicolet Mall
Marshall, MN 55403
Phone: (612) 332-0371,
  (800) 437-7275
Pet Restrictions: Small dogs & cats
Exercise Area for Pets: Nearby
Rates: $79 to $89

VETERINARIANS
Somers, Dennis R.
Highway 59 North
Phone: (507) 537-1537

MINNEAPOLIS
Aqua City Motel
5739 Lyndale Ave. S
Minneapolis, MN 55419
Phone: (612) 861-6061
Pet Restrictions: $2/night
Pet left unattended in room: Yes, no
  service
Exercise Area for Pets: Nearby
Rates: $41.95 for 2

Best Western Golden Valley Hse
4820 Olson Mem. Hwy
Minneapolis, MN 55422
Phone: (612) 588-0511
Pet Restrictions: $50 deposit, small
  pets only
Exercise Area for Pets: Nearby
Rates: $39 to $65

Budgetel
7815 Nicollet Ave. S.
Minneapolis, MN 55420
Phone: (612) 881-7311,
 (800) 428-3438
Pet Restrictions: None
Pet left unattended in room: Yes
Exercise Area for Pets: Yes
Rates: $42 to $49

Budgetel Inn Brooklynn Ctr.
6415 James Circle
Minneapolis, MN 55430
Phone: (612) 561-8400,
 (800) 428-3438
Pet Restrictions: 2 pet rooms
Exercise Area for Pets: Yes, please
 clean up
Rates: $35.95 to $52.95

Crown Sterling Suites
425 S. 7th St.
Minneapolis, MN 55415
Phone: (612) 333-3111
Pet Restrictions: $50 deposit or
 credit card imprint
Exercise Area for Pets: Nearby
Rates: $59 to $67

Exel Inn
2701 E. 78th St.
Minneapolis, MN 55425
Phone: (612) 854-7200,
 (800) 356-8013
Pet Restrictions: Small pets
Rates: $50.99 to $52.99 for 2

Normandy Hotel
405 S. 8th St.
Minneapolis, MN 55404
Phone: (612) 370-1400,
 (800) 372-3131
Pet Restrictions: Small dogs, no
 cats
Exercise Area for Pets: Nearby
Rates: $59.50 to $66

Radisson Hotel Metrodome
615 Wash. Ave. SE
Minneapolis, MN 55414
Phone: (612) 379-8888,
 (800) 822-6757
Pet Restrictions: No cougars
Exercise Area for Pets: Nearby
Rates: $92 to $102

VETERINARIANS
Brooklyn Pet Hospital
4902 France Avenue North
Phone: (612) 537-3669

Kenwood Pet Clinic
2107 Penn Ave. South
Phone: (612) 377-5551

Teachout, Debra
2528 Taylor St. NE
Phone: (612) 487-3255

NEW ULM
Colonial Inn Motel
1315 N. Broadway
New Ulm, MN 56073
Phone: (507) 354-3128
Pet Restrictions: None
Exercise Area for Pets: Nearby
Rates: $24 to $40

Crossroads Motel
1118 Main St., P.O. Box 546
New Ulm, MN 55065
Phone: (612) 674-7074,
 (800) 422-0160
Pet Restrictions: $25 deposit or
 credit card imprint
Exercise Area for Pets: Nearby
Rates: $36.50 to $39.50

VETERINARIANS
Hurley, Sharon
512 N7
Phone: (507) 354-5310

OLIVIA
Sheep Shedde Inn
US 91 & 212 W
Olivia, MN 56277
Phone: (612) 523-5000
Pet Restrictions: Kennel if possible
Exercise Area for Pets: Yes
Rates: $34.08 to $41.54

PROCTOR
Spirit Mountain Lodge
9315 Westgate Blvd.
Proctor, MN 55810
Phone: (218) 628-3691,
 (800) 777-8530
Pet Restrictions: None
Exercise Area for Pets: Nearby
Rates: $51 to $59 for 2

PLYMOUTH
Red Roof Inn
2600 Annapolis
Plymouth, MN 55441
Phone: (612) 553-1751

Pet Restrictions: None
Pet left unattended in room: Yes
Exercise Area for Pets: Yes
Rates: $33 to $55

VETERINARIANS
Fleming, Pierce
3401 County Rd.
(612) 544-4141

ROCHESTER
Blondell's Crown Sq. Motel & Mall
1406 2nd St. SW
Rochester, MN 55902
Phone: (507) 282-9444,
    (800) 441-5209

Pet Restrictions: None
Pet left unattended in room: Yes
Exercise Area for Pets: Nearby
Rates: $41 to $91

Comfort Inn
111 SE 28th St.
Rochester, MN 55901
Phone: (507) 286-1001,
    (800) 221-2222

Pet Restrictions: Smoking room
Exercise Area for Pets: Nearby
Rates: $55 for 2

Days Inn-South
106 21st St. SE
Rochester, MN 55901
Phone: (507) 282-1756,
    (800) 325-2525

Pet Restrictions: $25 deposit
Pet left unattended in room: Yes
Exercise Area for Pets: Nearby
Rates: $44 for 2

Days Inn West
435 16th Ave NW
Rochester, MNB 55901
Phone: (507) 288-9090,
    (800) 325-2525

Pet Restrictions: Smaller
Exercise Area for Pets: Yes
Rates: $43 to $75

Holiday Inn Downtown
220 S. Broadway
Rochester, MN 55904
Phone: (507) 288-3231,
    (800) 465-4329

Pet Restrictions: None
Rates: $69 to $84 for 2

Radisson Hotel Centerplace
150 S. Broadway
Rochester, MN 55904
Phone: (507) 281-8000,
    (800) 333-3333

Pet Restrictions: None
Pet left unattended in room: Yes,
    must be caged for service
Exercise Area for Pets: Nearby
Rates: $115 for 2

Royalty Suites
1620 1st Ave. SE
Rochester, MN 55904
Phone: (507) 282-8091,
    (800) 544-2717

Pet Restrictions: $5/night
Pet left unattended in room: Yes,
    must be caged for service
Rates: $69 to $74

VETERINARIANS
Cascade Animal Hospital
602 Seventh St. NW
Phone: (507) 282-8611

ROGERS
Americinn of Rogers
Box 13
Rogers, MN 55347
Phone: (612) 428-4346,
    (800) 634-3444

Pet Restrictions: $15 deposit, 2 pet rooms
Exercise Area for Pets: Yes
Rates: $42.90 plus $5 each extra

Super 8 Motel
21130 134th Ave.
Rogers, MN 55374
Phone: (612) 428-4000,
    (800) 800-8000

Pet Restrictions: $3/night
Exercise Area for Pets: Nearby
Rates: $39 to $47

ST. CLOUD

Budgetel Inn
70 37th Ave. S
St. Cloud, MN 56301
Phone: (612) 253-4444,
  (800) 428-3438

Pet Restrictions: In smoking rooms
Pet left unattended in room: Yes
Exercise Area for Pets: Nearby
Rates: $35 to $45

Holiday Inn
75 S. 37th Ave.
St. Cloud, MN 56301
Phone: (612) 253-9000,
  (800) HOLIDAY

Pet Restrictions: Not in public areas,
  must have kennel
Pet left unattended in room: Yes
Exercise Area for Pets: Nearby
Rates: $60 to $90

Kleis Motel
30 25th Ave. S
St. Cloud, MN 56301
Phone: (612) 251-7450

Pet Restrictions: $5
Pet left unattended in room: Yes
Exercise Area for Pets: Yes
Rates: $24 to $31

ST. PAUL

Best Western Kelly Inn-St. Paul
161 St. Anthony
St. Paul, MN 55119
Phone: (612) 227-8711,
  (800) 528-1234

Pet Restrictions: $50 cash deposit
Pet left unattended in room: Yes
Exercise Area for Pets: Yes
Rates: $59 to $67

Best Western Maplewood Inn
1780 E County Rd.
St. Paul, MN 55109
Phone: (612) 770-2811,
  (800) 528-1234

Pet Restrictions: Small pets, leash in
  lobby
Pet left unattended in room: Yes
Exercise Area for Pets: Nearby
Rates: $60 to $85

Embassy Suites Hotel
175 E. 10th St.
St. Paul, MN 55101
Pone: (612) 224-5400,
  (800) 433-4600

Pet Restrictions: None
Pet left unattended in room: Yes
Exercise Area for Pets: Nearby
Rates: $56 to $112 for 2

Golden Steer Motel Hotel
1010 S. Concord
St. Paul, MN 55075
Phone: (612) 455-8541,
  (800) 346-3552

Pet Restrictions: None
Pet left unattended in room: Yes
Exercise Area for Pets: Yes
Rates: $31.90

Holiday Inn East
2201 Burns Ave.
St. Paul, MN 55119
Phone: (612) 731-2220,
  (800) HOLIDAY

Pet Restrictions: None
Pet left unattended in room: Yes
Exercise Area for Pets: Yes
Rates: $71 to $80

Radisson
11 E Kellogg Blvd.
St. Paul, MN 55101
Phone: (612) 292-1900,
  (800) 333-3333

Pet Restrictions: Cage when alone
Pet left unattended in room: Yes if
  in cage
Exercise Area for Pets: Nearby
Rates: $55 to $110

Sheraton Midway, St. Paul
400 North Hamilton Ave.
St. Paul, MN 55104
Phone: (612) 642-1234,
  (800) 325-3535

Pet Restrictions: None
Pet left unattended in room: Yes
Exercise Area for Pets: Nearby
Rates: $80 to $90

VETERINARIANS

Minnesota Veterinary Hospital
3434 Hodgson Rd.
Phone: (612) 484-3331

MINNESOTA — HOTELS (continued)

Kleckner, Sharon
1322 Goodrich Ave.
Phone: (612) 698-2714

SHOREVIEW
Holiday Inn Shoreview
1000 Gramsie Rd.
Shoreview, MN 55126
Phone: (612) 482-0402

Pet Restrictions: None
Exercise Area for Pets: Yes
Rates: $59 to $89

SPRING VALLEY
66 Motel
½ Mi. on US 16 & 63
Spring Valley, MN 55975
Phone: (507) 346-9993

Pet Restrictions: None
Exercise Area for Pets: Yes
Rates: $22.37 to $25.56

STEWARTVILLE
American Inn Motel
1700 NW 2nd Ave.
Stewartville, MN 55976
Phone: (507) 533-4747,
    (800) 634-3444

Pet Restrictions: $20 deposit &
    $5/night
Exercise Area for Pets: Nearby
Rates: $46.86 to $51.12 for 2

TOFTE
Bluefin Bay
On US 61, P.O. Box 2125
Tofte, MN 55615
Phone: (218) 663-7296,
    (800) 258-3346

Pet Restrictions: None
Pet left unattended in room: Yes
Exercise Area for Pets: Yes
Rates: $69 to $165

TWO HARBORS
Superior Shores Lodge
10 Superior Shores Dr.
Two Harbors, MN 55616
Phone: (218) 834-5671,
    (800) 242-1988

Pet Restrictions: None
Pet left unattended in room: Yes
Exercise Area for Pets: Yes
Rates: $59 to $159

Lake Country Veterinary Clinic
W Star Route, Box 66
Phone: (218) 834-4234

VIRGINIA
Ski View Motel
903 N. 17th St.
Virginia, MN 55792
Phone: (218) 741-8918

Pet Restrictions: None
Exercise Area for Pets: Nearby
Rates: $32 to $38 for 2

WALKER
Moore's Lodge
P.O. Box 786
Walker, MN 56484
Phone: (218) 547-1542

Pet Restrictions: $10day/$50wk
    deposit (never refund more than
    half)
Exercise Area for Pets: Yes
Rates: $337 to $800 per week

WARROAD
The Patch Motel
P.O. Box N
Warroad, MN 56763
Phone: (218) 386-2723

Pet Restrictions: None
Pet left unattended in room: Yes
Exercise Area for Pets: Yes
Rates: $31 to $44

MISSISSIPPI — HOTELS

BILOXI

Breakers Inn
2506 Beach Blvd
Biloxi, MS 39531
Phone: (601) 388-6320

Pet Restrictions: Under 200 lbs.,
  deposit
Pet left unattended in room: Yes
Exercise Area for Pets: Yes
Activities: Beach (pets on leash)
Rates: $93.50 to $137.50

Juls Beach Hotel Resort
2428 Beach Blvd
Biloxi, MS 39531
Phone: (601) 385-5555

Pet Restrictions: $25 deposit, lower
  floor
Exercise Area for Pets: Yes
Rates: $55 to $80

COLUMBUS

Holiday Inn
Hwy 45N
Columbus, MS 39701
Phone: (601) 328-5202

Pet Restrictions: Small, quiet
Pet left unattended in room: Yes
Rates: $39 to $75

VETERINARIANS
Bounds, Louis A.
P.O. Box 2163
Phone: (601) 328-8395

Wilcox, Samuel
2601 Highway 45 North
Phone: (601) 327-9414

HATTIESBURG

Quality Inn
6528 Hwy 49N
Hattiesburg, MS 39401
Phone: (601) 544-4530

Pet Restrictions: Small, house
  broken, dogs and cats
Pet left unattended in room: Yes
Rates: $36.95 to $43.95

HOLLY SPRINGS

Heritage Inn
P.O. Box 476
Holly Springs, MS 38635
Phone: (601) 252-1120

Pet Restrictions: None
Pet left unattended in room: Yes
Exercise Area for Pets: Yes
Attractions: Parks

JACKSON

Days Inn East
716 Hwy 80E, P.O. Box 5707
Jackson, MS 39208
Phone: (601) 939-8200

Pet Restrictions: $6/day, cats, dogs
Pet left unattended in room: Yes
Exercise Area for Pets: Yes
Rates: $29.95 to $38.95

Holiday Inn North
5075 I55 North
Jackson, MS
Phone: (601) 366-9411

Pet Restrictions: Small
Exercise Area for Pets: Yes
Rates: $48 to $53

Passport Inn
5035 I 55N
Jackson, MS 39236
Phone: (601) 982-1011

Pet Restrictions: None
Pet left unattended in room: Yes
Exercise Area for Pets: Yes
Rates: $40 plus $4 per person

VETERINARIANS
Ward, Hugh
1471 Canton Mart Rd.
Phone: (601) 956-5030

McCOMB

Holiday Inn
1900 Delaware Ave.
McComb, MS 39648
Phone: (601) 684-6211

Pet Restrictions: Small, house broken
Pet left unattended in room: Yes
Exercise Area for Pets: Yes
Rates: $42 to $50

MERIDIAN
Holiday Inn Northeast
610 Hwy 11 and 80
Meridian, MS 39301
Phone: (601) 485-5101

Pet Restrictions: If quiet
Pet left unattended in room: Yes
Exercise Area for Pets: Yes
Rates: $43 to $56

RIDGELAND
Red Roof Inn North
810 Adcock St.
Ridgeland, MS 39157
Phone: (601) 956-7707

Pet Restrictions: Dogs under 20
    lbs., no cats, owner present for
    housekeeping
Pet left unattended in room: Yes
Exercise Area for Pets: Yes
Rates: $34.99 to $44.99

SENATOBIA
Howard Johnson Lodge
501 E. Main St.
Senatobia, MS 38668
Phone: (601) 562-5241

Pet Restrictions: Dog or cat, $10
    deposit
Pet left unattended in room: Yes
Rates: $40.13 to $50.83

VICKSBURG
Anchuca
1010 First St. E
Vicksburg, MS 39180
Phone: (601) 636-4931

Pet Restrictions: Small animals
Pet left unattended in room: Yes
Exercise Area for Pets: Yes
Rates: $75 to $145

VETERINARIANS
Brunton, Adam
P.O. Box 444
Phone: (601) 636-8112

MISSOURI — HOTELS

ABERDEEN

Red Roof Inn
988 Beards Hill
Aberdeen, MO 21001
Phone: (410) 273-7800,
   (800) 843-7663
Pet Restrictions: 20 lbs.
Pet left unattended in room: Yes
Exercise Area for Pets: Yes
Rates: $43 to $60

ARNOLD

White Wing Resort
HCR1, P.O. Box 840
Arnold, MO 65616
Phone: (417) 338-2318
Pet Restrictions: Small dogs only
Exercise Area for Pets: Nearby
Rates: $42 to $53

VETERINARIANS

Kohne, Keirn J.
2009 Key West #K
(314) 296-7060

Wilson, Donald G.
1105 Jeffco Blvd.
(314) 296-7066

BRIDGETON

Air Way Motel
4125 N. Lindbergh Blvd.
Bridgeton, MO 63044
Phone: (314) 291-3414
Pet Restrictions: $50 deposit
Pet left unattended in room: Yes
Exercise Area for Pets: Nearby
Rates: $28.95 to $42.95

Holiday Inn-Airport North
4545 N. Lindburgh Blvd.
Bridgeton, MO 63044
Phone: (314) 731-2100
Pet Restrictions: None
Pet left unattended in room: Yes
Exercise Area for Pets: Nearby
   (leash required)
Rates: $73 to $83

Knights Inn-Bridgeton
12433 St. Charles Rock Rd.
Bridgeton, MO 63044
Phone: (314) 291-8545
Pet Restrictions: $25 refund. dep.
Pet left unattended in room: Yes
Exercise Area for Pets: Nearby
Rates: $37.95 to $38.95

Red Roof Inn
3470 Hollenberg Dr.
Bridgeton, MO 63044
Phone: (314) 291-3350
Pet Restrictions: Small pet only
Pet left unattended in room: Yes
Exercise Area for Pets: Nearby
Rates: $49.99 to $55.99

BROOKFIELD

Country Inn
800 S. Main St.
Brookfield, MO 64628
Phone: (816) 258-7262
Pet Restrictions: Small pet only
Exercise Area for Pets: Nearby
Rates: $31 to $36.11

VETERINARIANS

Vahle, John L.
150 Ridgecrest Dr.
(816) 258-3308

CAMERON

Best Western Rambler Motel
P.O. Box 431
Cameron, MO 64429
Phone: (816) 632-6571
Pet Restrictions: Small pets only
Exercise Area for Pets: Nearby
Rates: $38.42 to $44.82

CAPE GIRARDEAU

Drury Inn
P.O. Box 910, Rt 1C at I55
Cape Girardeau, MO 63701
Phone: (314) 334-7151
Pet Restrictions: None
Pet left unattended in room: Yes
Exercise Area for Pets: Yes
Rates: $63 to $68

VETERINARIANS

Skyview Animal Clinic
855 South Kings Highway
(314) 334-6300

Sprigg, Cynthia
605 North Kings Highway
(314) 447-3565

CARTHAGE
Econo Lodge
1441 W. Central
Carthage, MO 64836
Phone: (417) 358-3900

Pet Restrictions: Smoking room
    only; $15 refund. deposit
Exercise Area for Pets: Nearby
Rates: $40.95 to $45.95

CHESTERFIELD
Residence Inn by Marriott
15431 Conway Rd.
Chesterfield, MO 63017
Phone: (314) 537-1444

Pet Restrictions: $25 non-refundable
    deposit; $10/day
Pet left unattended in room: Yes
Exercise Area for Pets: Nearby
Rates: $69 to $109

VETERINARIANS

Petropolis
16830 Chesterfield Airport Rd.
(314) 537-2322

Long, Grace
14355 Stablestone Court
(314) 469-6415

Thornberry, Kenneth
16361 Westboro Circle Dr.
(314) 394-7501

CHILLICOTHE
Grand River Inn
P.O. Box 868
Chillicothe, MO 64601
Phone: (816) 646-6590

Pet Restrictions: Yes
Exercise Area for Pets: Nearby
Rates: $56 to $63

CLAYTON
Holiday Inn-Clayton Plaza
7730 Bonhomme Ave.
Clayton, MO 63105
Phone: (314) 863-0400

Pet Restrictions: None
Pet left unattended in room: Yes
Exercise Area for Pets: Nearby
Rates: $64 to $78

Radisson Hotel Clayton
7750 Carondelet Ave.
Clayton, MO 63105
Phone: (314) 726-5400

Pet Restrictions: Under 15 lbs.
Exercise Area for Pets: Nearby
Rates: $89

COLUMBIA
Budget Host Inn
900 Vandiver
Columbia, MO 65202
Phone: (314) 449-1065

Pet Restrictions: Domestic pets
    only; 20 rooms
Pet left unattended in room: Yes
Exercise Area for Pets: Yes
Activities: Finger Lakes State Park,
    Cosmopolitan Park
Rates: $20.95 to $49.95

Budgetel Inn-Columbia
2500 I 70 Dr. SW
Columbia, MO 65203
Phone: (314) 445-1899

Pet Restrictions: None
Pet left unattended in room: Yes
Exercise Area for Pets: Nearby
Rates: $43.95 to $45.95

Days Inn Univ. Cntr
1900 I 70 Dr. SW
Columbia, MO 65203
Phone: (314) 445-8511

Pet Restrictions: Small pet only
Pet left unattended in room: Yes
Exercise Area for Pets: Nearby
Rates: $54 to $56

Econolodge
900 I-70 Dr. SW
Columbia, MO 65203
Phone: (314) 442-1191

Pet Restrictions: $4/day/pet
Exercise Area for Pets: Nearby
Rates: $40 to $45

Holiday Inn East
1612 N. Providence Rd.
Columbia, MO 65202
Phone: (314) 449-2491

Pet Restrictions: Certain rooms only
Pet left unattended in room: Yes
Exercise Area for Pets: Nearby
Rates: $66 to $68

Holiday Inn Exec. Cntr.
2200 I 70 Dr. SW
Columbia, MO 65203
Phone: (314) 445-8531

Pet Restrictions: Small dogs only
Pet left unattended in room: Yes
Exercise Area for Pets: Nearby
Rates: $69 to $79

Red Roof Inn
201 East Texas Ave.
Columbia, MO 65202
Phone: (314) 442-0145

Pet Restrictions: None
Pet left unattended in room: Yes, if
   caged
Exercise Area for Pets: Yes
Rates: $40 to $58

VETERINARIANS

University of Missouri
Teaching Hospital
(314) 882-4648

Buttonwood Animal Hospital
3505 Buttonwood Dr.
(314) 449-7387

Rose, Thomas D.
4380 Santa Barbara
(314) 449-3791

DONIPHAN
Econolodge Motel
State Route 142 & 21
Doniphan, MO 63935
Phone: (314) 996-2101

Pet Restrictions: None
Exercise Area for Pets: Nearby
Rates: $32.93 to $36.12

DRURY
Holiday Inn at Cape Girardeau
P.O. Box 1570
Drury, MO 63701
Phone: (314) 334-4491

Pet Restrictions: Small pets only
Pet left unattended in room: Yes
Exercise Area for Pets: Nearby
Rates: $74 to $80

Thrifty Inn
William St.
Drury, MO 63701
Phone: (314) 334-3000

Pet Restrictions: Small pets only
Exercise Area for Pets: Nearby
Rates: $40.88 to $46.88

EUREKA
Best Rest Motel
1725 W. Fifth St.
Eureka, MO 63027
Phone: (314) 938-5348

Pet Restrictions: Small pet only; $20
   refund. deposit
Pet left unattended in room: Yes
Exercise Area for Pets: Nearby
Rates: $54.95 to $64.95

Days Inn
1400 W. Liberty St., P.O. Box 161
Eureka, MO 63640
Phone: (314) 756-8951

Pet Restrictions: $4/day/pet; 3
   rooms only
Pet left unattended in room: Yes
Exercise Area for Pets: Nearby
Rates: $41.95

Days Inn at 6 Flags
15 Hilltop Village Cntr.
Eureka, MO 63025
Phone: (314) 587-7000

Pet Restrictions: $5/day
Exercise Area for Pets: Nearby
Rates: $69 to $79

Oak Grove Inn
1733 W. 5th St.
Eureka, MO 63025
Phone: (314) 938-4368

Pet Restrictions: $10 deposit
Pet left unattended in room: Yes
Exercise Area for Pets: Nearby
Rates: $47.95 to $51.95

Ramada Inn at 6 Flags
P.O. Box 999
Eureka, MO 63025
Phone: (314) 938-6661

Pet Restrictions: Small pets only
Pet left unattended in room: Yes
Exercise Area for Pets: Nearby
Rates: $54 to $98

VETERINARIANS

Jones, Michael A.
17245 Thunder Valley
(314) 227-4041

FARMINGTON

Best Western Tradition Inn
1627 W. Columbia, P.O. Box 856
Farmington, MO 63640
Phone: (314) 756-8031

Pet Restrictions: Small pets only
Pet left unattended in room: Yes
Exercise Area for Pets: Nearby
Rates: $48.95

VETERINARIANS

Protheroe, Margo M.
Route 3, P.O. Box 3816
(314) 756-3301

FENTON

Drury Inn-St. Louis Southwest
1088 S. Drury Dr.
Fenton, MO 63026
Phone: (314) 343-7822

Pet Restrictions: None
Exercise Area for Pets: Yes
Rates: $45

Motel 6 Southwest
1860 Intertech Dr.
Fenton, MO 63026
Phone: (314) 349-1800

Pet Restrictions: None
Exercise Area for Pets: Nearby
Rates: $40.61

Thrifty Inn
1100 South Highway Dr.
Fenton, MO 63026
Phone: (314) 343-8820

Pet Restrictions: Small pets only
Exercise Area for Pets: Nearby
Rates: $54.88 to $59.88

FESTUS

Drury Inn-Festus
1001 Veterans Blvd.
Festus, MO 63028
Phone: (314) 933-2400

Pet Restrictions: Small pet only
Exercise Area for Pets: Nearby
Rates: $52 to $57

FLORISSANT

Red Roof Inn
307 Dunn Rd.
Florissant, MO 63031
Phone: (314) 831-7900

Pet Restrictions: None
Pet left unattended in room: Yes
Exercise Area for Pets: Nearby
Rates: $40.89 to $47.99

VETERINARIANS

Florissant Animal Hospital
605 N. Lindbergh
(314) 921-0500

Ferm, Diane
2156 Flordawn Dr. #5
(501) 273-9573

Jones, Walter N.
2685 North Highway
(314) 837-4617

FULTON

Budget Host Westwoods Motel
422 Gaylord Dr.
Fulton, MO 65251
Phone: (314) 642-5991

Pet Restrictions: None
Exercise Area for Pets: Nearby
Rates: $36 to $75

VETERINARIANS

Barnett, Robert E.
Highway 54 South
(214) 642-3724

HANNIBAL

Hannibal Travel Lodge
502 Mark Twain Ave.
Hannibal, MO 63401
Phone: (314) 221-4100

Pet Restrictions: Smoking rooms only
Exercise Area for Pets: Nearby
Rates: $48 to $64

Holiday Inn
4141 Market St.
Hannibal, MO 63401
Phone: (314) 221-6610

Pet Restrictions: None
Exercise Area for Pets: Nearby
Rates: $70 to $73

MISSOURI — HOTELS (continued)

HIGGINSVILLE

Super 8 Motel
P.O. Box 306
Higginsville, MO 64037
Phone: (816) 584-7781

Pet Restrictions: $10 refund. deposit
Exercise Area for Pets: Nearby
Rates: $37.88

INDEPENDENCE

Howard Johnson Lodge
4200 South Noland Rd.
Independence, MO 64055
Phone: (816) 373-8856

Pet Restrictions: $25 refund. deposit
Pet left unattended in room: Yes
Exercise Area for Pets: Nearby
Rates: $50 to $65

Red Roof Inn
13712 E. 42nd Terrace
Independence, MO 64055
Phone: (816) 373-2800

Pet Restrictions: None
Pet left unattended in room: Yes
Exercise Area for Pets: Nearby
Rates: $40.99 to $50.99

VETERINARIANS

Schondelmeyer Animal Hosp.
1102 East 23rd St.
(816) 833-1300

Falk, Mel H.
300 South Noland
(816) 254-4282

JACKSON

Howard Johnson Lodge
2655 I-55 South
Jackson, MO 39204
Phone: (601) 372-1006

Pet Restrictions: Small pets only
Exercise Area for Pets: Yes
Rates: $33.19 to $36.88

JEFFERSON CITY

Capitol Plaza Hotel
415 W. McCarty
Jefferson City, MO 65101
Phone: (314) 635-1234

Pet Restrictions: None
Exercise Area for Pets: Nearby
Rates: $58.50 to $73

Days Inn Downtown
422 Monroe St.
Jefferson City, MO 65101
Phone: (314) 636-5101

Pet Restrictions: $10 for big dogs;
    no charge for small pets
Exercise Area for Pets: Yes
Rates: $49 to $54

VETERINARIANS

Howard, James P.
610 Dix Rd.
(314) 636-4626

Russell, Sherri W.
2402 East McCarty
(314) 635-0435

JOPLIN

Days Inn
3500 Range Line Rd.
Joplin, MO 64801
Phone: (417) 623-0100

Pet Restrictions: Small pets only
    (major credit card deposit)
Exercise Area for Pets: Nearby
Rates: $40 to $45

Holiday Inn Hotel & Conv. Cntr
3615 Range Line Rd.
Joplin, MO 64801
Phone: (417) 782-1000

Pet Restrictions: None
Exercise Area for Pets: Nearby
Rates: $70

VETERINARIANS

Dahlstrom, Carol K.
115 E. 34th St.
(417) 623-2032

KANSAS CITY

Americana on Convention Sq.
1301 Wyandotte St.
Kansas City, MO 64105
Phone: (816) 221-8800

Pet Restrictions: $20 fee
Pet left unattended in room: Yes
Exercise Area for Pets: Nearby
Rates: $59.95 to $67

Best Western Airport Inn
P.O. Box 819
Kansas City, MO 64079
Phone: (816) 464-2300

Pet Restrictions: $25 deposit
Pet left unattended in room: Yes
Exercise Area for Pets: Yes
Rates: $48.95 to $49.95

Budgetel Inn
2214 Taney
Kansas City, MO 64116
Phone: (816) 221-1200

Pet Restrictions: None
Exercise Area for Pets: Nearby
Rates: $41.95 to $46.95

Econo Lodge KCI Airport
11300 NW Prairie View Rd.
Kansas City, MO 64153
Phone: (816) 464-5082

Pet Restrictions: $10 refund.
  deposit; small pets only
Exercise Area for Pets: Nearby
Rates: $39.95 to $49.95

Econo Lodge - Southeast
8500 Blue Pkwy Hwy 350
Kansas City, MO 64133
Phone: (816) 353-3000

Pet Restrictions: $5/day
Pet left unattended in room: Yes
Exercise Area for Pets: Nearby
Rates: $28 to $39.95

Howard Johnson Lodge
1600 NE Parvin Rd.
Kansas City, MO 64116
Phone: (816) 453-5210

Pet Restrictions: $15 refund. deposit
Exercise Area for Pets: Nearby
Rates: $37 to $49.95

Kansas City Airport Marriott
775 Brasilia Ave.
Kansas City, MO 64153
Phone: (816) 464-2200

Pet Restrictions: Responsible for
  damages
Pet left unattended in room: Yes
Exercise Area for Pets: Nearby
Rates: $109 to $129

Marriott Downtown Hotel
200 W. 12th St.
Kansas City, MO 64105
Phone: (816) 421-6800

Pet Restrictions: $25 fee
Pet left unattended in room: Yes
Exercise Area for Pets: Nearby
Rates: $79 to $150

Motel 6
6400 E. 87th St.
Kansas City, MO 64138
Phone: (816) 333-4468

Pet Restrictions: None
Pet left unattended in room: Yes
Exercise Area for Pets: Nearby
Rates: $38.02

Park Place
1601 N. Universal Ave.
Kansas City, MO 64120
Phone: (816) 483-9900

Pet Restrictions: $25 refund. deposit;
  small pets only
Exercise Area for Pets: Yes
Rates: $79 to $89

Ramada Inn SE
6101 E. 87th St.
Kansas City, MO 64138
Phone: (816) 765-4331

Pet Restrictions: $25 fee
Exercise Area for Pets: Yes
Rates: $54.90 to $61

Red Roof Inn-North
3636 NE Randolph Rd.
Kansas City, MO 64161
Phone: (816) 452-8585

Pet Restrictions: None
Pet left unattended in room: Yes
Exercise Area for Pets: Nearby
Rates: $41.99 to $46.99

Residence Inn by Marriott
9900 NW Prairie View Rd.
Kansas City, MO 64190
Phone: (816) 891-9009,
  (800) 331-3131

Pet Restrictions: $5/day; $50 - single;
  $100 - penthouse cleaning
  deposit depending on your room
Pet left unattended in room: Yes, or
  in kennel
Exercise Area for Pets: Yes
Rates: $85 to $115

Residence Inn by Marriott at Union Hill
2975 Main St.
Kansas City, MO 64108
Phone: (816) 561-3000,
(800) 331-3131
Pet Restrictions: $50 charge
Exercise Area for Pets: Yes
Rates: $75 and up

Sheraton KCI Hotel & Conf. Cntr.
7301 New Tiffany Springs Rd.
Kansas City, MO 64153
Phone: (816) 741-9500;
(800) 234-9501
Pet Restrictions: Under 15 lbs; on
1st floor only; in cage
Exercise Area for Pets: Yes, on leash
Rates: $32 to $74

Westin Crown Center
1 Pershing Rd.
Kansas City, MO 64108
Phone: (816) 474-4400,
(800) 228-3000
Pet Restrictions: Small pets only,
$20/night
Exercise Area for Pets: Yes
Rates: $85 to $144

N. KANSAS CITY
Budgetel Inn
2214 Faney
N. Kansas City, MO 64116
Phone: (816) 221-1200,
(800) 428-3438
Pet Restrictions: None
Exercise Area for Pets: Yes
Rates: $34.95 to $51.95

VETERINARIANS

Kansas City CAT Clinic
8251 Wornall Rd.
(816) 361-4888

Donnelly, Amanda L.
5612 NW 87th Terrace #245
(816) 741-2247

Kovac, Lawrence P.
4207 N. Colorado Dr.
(816) 454-1772

KIMBERLING CITY
Kimberling Heights Resort Motel
Rt. 3, P.O. Box 980
Kimberling City, MO 65686
Phone: (417) 779-4158
Pet Restrictions: None
Exercise Area for Pets: Yes
Rates: $44 and up

VETERINARIANS

Kimberling Pet Clinic
15 Greenview Dr., P.O. Box 605
(417) 739-4090

KIRKSVILLE
Best Western Shamrock Inn
P.O. Box 1005
Kirksville, MO 63501
Phone: (816) 665-8352,
(800) 528-1234
Pet Restrictions: Small dogs only
Exercise Area for Pets: Yes
Rates: $34 to $48

Travelers Hotel
301 W. Washington
Kirksville, MO 63501
Phone: (816) 665-5191
Pet Restrictions: None
Pet left unattended in room: Yes
Exercise Area for Pets: Nearby
Rates: $27.95 to $55

LAKE OZARK
Howard Johnson Lodge
P.O. Box 8, Hwy 54 & Business 54
Lake Ozark, MO 65049
Phone: (314) 365-5353,
(800) 654-2000
Pet Restrictions: Small pets only
Exercise Area for Pets: Yes
Rates: $67 to $81

LEBANON
Brentwood Motel
1320 S. Highway 5
Lebanon, MO 65536
Phone: (417) 532-6131
Pet Restrictions: $50 deposit on
large animals
Pet left unattended in room: Yes,
short periods of time
Exercise Area for Pets: Yes
Rates: $29.95 to $32.95

LEES SUMMIT

Best Western Summit Inn
625 Murray Rd.
Lees Summit, MO 64063
Phone: (816) 525-1400,
    (800) 666-3638

Pet Restrictions: $25 refund. deposit
Exercise Area for Pets: Yes
Rates: $44 to $60

VETERINARIANS

Cedar Creek Veterinary Hosp.
400 South 291 Hwy.
(816) 524-9536

MARYLAND HTS

Drury Inn-Westport
12220 Dorsett Rd.
Maryland Hts., MO 63043
Phone: (314) 576-9966,
    (800) 325-8300

Pet Restrictions: Under 20 lbs.;
    dogs or cats only
Exercise Area for Pets: Yes
Rates: $56 to $71

MOBERLY

Noll Motel
P.O. Box 146
Moberly, MO 65265
Phone: (816) 263-5000

Pet Restrictions: None
Pet left unattended in room: Yes
Exercise Area for Pets: Yes
Rates: $26 to $30

NEOSHO

Neosho Inn
2 mi. NW on US 71 at
Jct. US 60
Neosho, MO 64850
Phone: (417) 451-6500,
    (800) 777-1362

Pet Restrictions: None
Pet left unattended in room: Yes, if
    quiet
Exercise Area for Pets: Yes
Rates: $42 to $60

OSAGE BEACH

Holiday Inn-South I55
4234 Butter Hill Rd.
Osage Beach, MO 63129
Phone: (314) 894-0700,
    (800) HOLIDAY

Pet Restrictions: None
Exercise Area for Pets: Yes
Rates: $65 to $76

**Howard Johnson
Hampton Hotel**
5915 Wilson Ave.
Osage Beach, MO 63110
Phone: (314) 645-0700,
    (800) I-GO-HOJO

Pet Restrictions: None
Exercise Area for Pets: Yes
Rates: $45 to $85

Motel 6
6500 S. Lindburgh Blvd.
Osage Beach, MO 63123
Phone: (314) 892-3664

Pet Restrictions: Caged
Exercise Area for Pets: Yes,
    attended
Rates: $33.84 and up

Red Roof Inn-Hampton
5823 Wilson Ave.
Osage Beach, MO 63110
Phone: (314) 645-0101,
    (800) 843-7663

Pet Restrictions: Small pets only
Pet left unattended in room: Yes
Exercise Area for Pets: Yes
Rates: $44.99 to $79.99

Red Roof Inn-Westport
11837 Lackland Rd.
Osage Beach, MO 63146
Phone: (314) 991-4900,
    (800) 843-7663

Pet Restrictions: None
Pet left unattended in room: Yes
Exercise Area for Pets: Yes
Rates: $27.99 to $50.99

MISSOURI — HOTELS (continued)

OVERLAND PARK

Doubletree Hotel
10100 College Blvd.
Overland Park, MO 66210
Phone: (913) 451-6100,
(800) 222-TREE
Pet Restrictions: Under 15 lbs., $50
deposit; room checked ½ hr
before checkout
Pet left unattended in room: Yes, no
maid service
Exercise Area for Pets: Yes
Rates: $109 to $139

PERRYVILLE

Budget Host Park-ET
Rt. 2, P.O. Box 8
Perryville, MO 63775
Phone: (314) 547-4516,
(800) BUD-HOST
Pet Restrictions: None
Pet left unattended in room: Yes
Exercise Area for Pets: Yes
Rates: $24 to $42

ROLLA

Econo Lodge
1417 Martin Springs Dr.
Rolla, MO 65401
Phone: (314) 341-3130,
(800) 424-4777
Pet Restrictions: None
Rates: $36.95 and up

Howard Johnson Lodge
I44 and Business at 127 HJ Drive
Rolla, MO 65401
Phone: (314) 364-7111,
(800) 654-2000
Pet Restrictions: None
Pet left unattended in room: Yes, if
quiet
Exercise Area for Pets: Yes
Rates: $38 to $60

Interstate Bestway Inn
1631 Martin Spring Dr.
Rolla, MO 65401
Phone: (314) 341-2158
Pet Restrictions: None
Exercise Area for Pets: Yes
Rates: $21.95 to $30

SEDALIOR

Knights Court
3501 W. Broadway
Sedalior, MO 65301
Phone: (816) 826-8400
Pet Restrictions: $6/day/pet
Pet left unattended in room: Yes
Exercise Area for Pets: Nearby
Rates: $39 to $45

SIKESTON

Ramada Inn
P.O. Box 869
Sikeston, MO 63801
Phone: (314) 471-4700,
(800) 358-5347
Pet Restrictions: Outside rooms only
Pet left unattended in room: Yes,
owner responsible
Exercise Area for Pets: Yes
Rates: $48 to $50

ST. ANN

Drury Inn-St. Louis Airport
10800 Pear Tree Lane
St. Ann, MO 63074
Phone: (314) 423-7700,
(800) 325-8300
Pet Restrictions: None
Exercise Area for Pets: Nearby
Rates: $61 to $73

ST. CHARLES

Comfort Inn St. Louis/St. Charles
2750 Plaza Way
St. Charles, MO 63303
Phone: (314) 949-8700
Fax:　(314) 946-8996
Pet Restrictions: $50 Pet deposit
required. Pet must be kept on a
leash when in public areas. Pets
are restricted from breakfast room.
Pet left unattended in room: Must
be in carrier
Exercise Area for Pets: Yes
Other Areas: Dog museum
Rates: $43 to $120

Monarch Budget Motel
3717 I-70
St. Charles, MO 63303
Phone: (314) 724-3717
Pet Restrictions: $5
Exercise Area for Pets: Yes
Rates: $22.60 to $32.80

Red Roof Inn
2010 Zumbehl Rd.
St. Charles, MO
Phone: (314) 947-7770
Pet Restrictions: Carrier required
Pet left unattended in room: Yes
Exercise Area for Pets: Yes
Rates: $30 to $54

VETERINARIANS

Harvester Animal Clinic
10L San Miguel Dr.
(314) 447-3565

Kress, Mel Arthur
229 Riverbluff Dr. #E-111
(314) 946-7643

Polley, Don
#46 Daniel Boone Village
(314) 928-6441

ST. JOSEPH

Ramada Inn
4016 Frederick Ave.
St. Joseph, MO 64506
Phone: (816) 233-6192,
(800) 2-RAMADA
Pet Restrictions: None
Exercise Area for Pets: Yes
Rates: $52 to $85

ST. LOUIS

Comfort Inn Southwest
3730 S. Lindbergh Blvd.
St. Louis, MO 63127
Phone: (314) 842-1200,
(800) 221-2222
Pet Restrictions: None
Pet left unattended in room: Yes, in cage
Exercise Area for Pets: Yes, attended
Rates: $46 to $59

Daniele Hilton
216 N. Meramec Ave.
St. Louis, MO 63105
Phone: (314) 721-0101,
(800) 325-8302
Pet Restrictions: Under 20 lbs.; $25 deposit
Pet left unattended in room: Yes
Exercise Area for Pets: Nearby
Rates: $70 to $99

Days Inn Airport
4545 Woodson Rd., P.O. Box 10365
St. Louise, MO
Phone: (314) 423-6770,
(800) 325-2525
Pet Restrictions: None
Pet left unattended in room: Yes, well behaved
Exercise Area for Pets: Yes
Rates: $44.95 to $56.95

Days Inn at the Arch
333 Washington Ave.
St. Louis, MO 63102
Phone: (314) 621-7900,
(800) 325-2525
Pet Restrictions: None
Exercise Area for Pets: Yes
Rates: $69 to $99

Days Inn
2560 South Outer Rd.
St. Louis, MO 63367
Phone: (314) 625-1711,
(800) 325-2525
Pet Restrictions: $2/night
Pet left unattended in room: Yes, not at night
Exercise Area for Pets: Yes
Rates: $39 to $90

Drury Inn Union Station
201 S. 20th St.
St. Louis, MO 63103
Phone: (314) 231-3900,
(800) 325-8300
Pet Restrictions: None
Exercise Area for Pets: Nearby
Rates: $79 to $149

Embassy Suites
901 N. 1st St.
St. Louis, MO 63102
Phone: (314) 241-4200
Pet Restrictions: Small dogs only
Pet left unattended in room: Yes
Exercise Area for Pets: Nearby
Rates: $125 to $140

Holiday Inn
9th St. at Convention Plaza
St. Louis, MO 63101
Phone: (314) 421-4000,
(800) 289-8338
Pet Restrictions: Under 25 lbs.
Pet left unattended in room: Yes, on leash
Exercise Area for Pets: Yes
Rates: $79 and up

MISSOURI — HOTELS (continued)

Howard Johnson
1200 S. Kirkwood Rd.
St. Louis, MO 63122
Phone: (314) 821-3950,
(800) 435-4656
Pet Restrictions: $5/night
Pet left unattended in room: Yes
Exercise Area for Pets: Yes
Rates: $55 to $75

Howard Johnson Hotel
5915 Wilson Ave.
St. Louis, MO 63110
Phone: (314) 645-0700,
(800) I-GO-HOJO
Pet Restrictions: None
Exercise Area for Pets: Yes
Rates: $45 to $85

Marriott Airport
I70 at Lambert Airport
St. Louis, MO 63134
Phone: (314) 423-9700,
(800) 228-9290
Pet Restrictions: $25 fee; drive up
rooms
Exercise Area for Pets: Yes
Rates: $74 to $124

Oakgrove Inn
6602 S. Lindbergh Blvd.
St. Louis, MO
Phone: (314) 894-9449,
(800) 435-7144
Pet Restrictions: None
Pet left unattended in room: Yes, no
maid service
Rates: $29 to $56

Ramada Inn-Westport
12031 Lackland Rd.
St. Louis, MO 63146
Phone: (314) 878-1400,
(800) 272-6232
Pet Restrictions: None
Pet left unattended in room: Yes
Exercise Area for Pets: Yes
Rates: $49 to $62

Red Roof Inn
11837 Lackland Rd.
St. Louis, MO 63146
Phone: (314) 991-4900
Pet Restrictions: Under 25 lbs.
Pet left unattended in room: Yes
Exercise Area for Pets: Yes
Rates: $29 to $65

Red Roof Inn
5823 Wilson Ave.
St. Louis, MO 63110
Phone: (314) 645-0101
Pet Restrictions: None
Pet left unattended in room: Yes
Exercise Area for Pets: Yes
Rates: $50 to $80

Regal Riverfront
200 S. 4th St.
St. Louis, MO
Phone: (314) 241-9500,
(800) 325-7353
Pet Restrictions: Under 50 lbs.; $50
refund. deposit
Pet left unattended in room: Yes
Exercise Area for Pets: Yes
Rates: $65 to $1,000

Sheraton-West Port Inn
191 West Port Plaza
St. Louis, MO 63146
Phone: (314) 878-1500,
(800) 822-3535
Pet Restrictions: 1st floor only;
notify desk
Pet left unattended in room: Yes,
quiet; notify desk, no maid service
Exercise Area for Pets: Yes
Rates: $64 to $120

VETERINARIANS

County Animal Hospital
14020 Manchester Rd.
(314) 256-7387

Lemay Animal Hospital
211 Lemay Ferry Rd.
(314) 631-4020

Webster Groves Animal Hospital
7979 Big Bend Blvd.
(314) 968-4310

SPRINGFIELD
Bass Country Inn
2610 North Glenstone
Springfield, MO 65803
Phone: (417) 866-6671,
(800) 587-BASS
Pet Restrictions: Small pets only
Pet left unattended in room: Yes,
quiet
Exercise Area for Pets: Yes
Rates: $44 to $56

MISSOURI — HOTELS (continued)

Days Inn-Springfield I44
2700 N. Glenstone Ave.
Springfield, MO 65803
Phone: (417) 865-5511,
(800) 325-2525

Pet Restrictions: None
Pet left unattended in room: Yes
Exercise Area for Pets: Yes
Rates: $40 to $55

Markham Inn
2820 N. Glenstone Ave.
Springfield, MO 65803
Phone: (417) 866-3581,
(800) 658-0476

Pet Restrictions: $12 deposit, $6 fee
Pet left unattended in room: Yes;
notify desk
Exercise Area for Pets: Yes
Rates: $39.50 to $64.50

Residence Inn by Marriott
1550 E. Raynell Pl.
Springfield, MO 65804
Phone: (417) 883-7300,
(800) 331-3131

Pet Restrictions: $100 deposit, $75
is refundable
Exercise Area for Pets: Yes
Rates: $74 to $134

Skyline Motel
2120 N. Glenstone Ave.
Springfield, MO 65803
Phone: (417) 866-4356

Pet Restrictions: $5/night
Exercise Area for Pets: Yes
Rates: $28 to $52

VETERINARIANS

Great Avenue Pet Hospital
1037 S. Grant Ave.
(417) 869-1581

SULLIVAN
Sullivan Super 8 Motel
601 N. Service, Rd., P.O. Box 69
Sullivan, MO 63080
Phone: (314) 468-8076,
(800) 800-8000

Pet Restrictions: None
Pet left unattended in room: Yes,
quiet
Exercise Area for Pets: Yes
Rates: $37.05 to $62.55

TROY
Oak Grove Inn
P.O. Box 241
Troy, MO 63379
Phone: (314) 528-6124

Pet Restrictions: None
Pet left unattended in room: Yes,
owner responsible for damage,
quiet
Exercise Area for Pets: Yes, on leash
Rates: $30.55

VILLA RIDGE
Best Western Diamond Inn Motel
RR 2, P.O. Box 416
Villa Ridge, MO 63809
Phone: (314) 742-3501

Pet Restrictions: None
Pet left unattended in room: Yes, if
in cage
Exercise Area for Pets: Yes
Rates: $49 to $79

WARRENSBURG
Super 8 Motel
440 Russell Ave.
Warrensburg, MO 64093
Phone: (816) 429-2183,
(800) 800-8000

Pet Restrictions: $10 deposit
Pet left unattended in room: Yes
Exercise Area for Pets: Yes
Rates: $30.88 and up

WENTZVILLE
Budget Host Inn
1500 Continental Dr., P.O. Box 412
Wentzville, MO 63385
Phone: (314) 327-5212,
(800) 283-4678

Pet Restrictions: None
Pet left unattended in room: Yes
Exercise Area for Pets: Yes
Rates: $19.95 and up

Heritage Motel
404 N. Hwy 61 Business Rt.
Wentzville, MO 63385
Phone: (314) 327-6263

Pet Restrictions: None
Exercise Area for Pets: Yes
Rates: $22 to $26.50

Super 8
4 Pontera Dr.
Wentzville, MO 63385
Phone: (314) 327-5300,
    (800) 800-8000

Pet Restrictions: $50 deposit
    w/permission
Pet left unattended in room: Yes
Exercise Area for Pets: Yes
Rates: $31.88 to $42.88

WEST PLAINS

Way-Station Motel
North Hwy. 63, P.O. Box 278
West Plains, MO 65775
Phone: (417) 256-4135
Fax: (417) 256-1106

Pet Restrictions: None
Pet left unattended in room: No
Exercise Area for Pets: Nearby
Rates: $30 to $48

MONTANA — HOTELS

BILLINGS

The Billings Inn
880 N. 29th St.
Billings, MT 59101
Phone: (406) 252-6800

Pet Restrictions: None, $5/night
Exercise Area for Pets: Yes
Rates: $33.50 to $49.50, $5 extra person

Cherry Tree Inn
823 N. Broadway
Billings, MT 59101
Phone: (406) 252-5603

Pet Restrictions: None
Exercise Area for Pets: Yes
Rates: $30 and up

Juniper Motel
1315 N. 27th St.
Billings, MT 59101
Phone: (406) 245-4128

Pet Restrictions: None
Pet left unattended in room: Yes if well behaved
Exercise Area for Pets: Nearby
Rates: $32 to $40

Kelly Inn
5425 Midland Rd.
Billings, MT 59101
Phone: (406) 252-2700

Pet Restrictions: None
Exercise Area for Pets: Yes
Rates: $33 to $45

VETERINARIANS
Moore Lane Veterinary Hosp.
50 Moore Lane
Phone: (406) 252-4159

Herren, Roy
533 South 24th St. West
Phone: (406) 656-6320

Kuehn, Diana E.
1239 Landscape Dr.
Phone: (406) 245-6703

BOZEMAN

The Bozeman Inn
1235 N. 7th Ave.
Bozeman, MT 59715
Phone: (406) 587-3176

Pet Restrictions: None, $5/day/pet
Pet left unattended in room: Yes
Exercise Area for Pets: Yes
Rates: $35 to $58

Holiday Inn
5 Baxter Lane
Bozeman, MT 59715
Phone: (406) 587-4561

Pet Restrictions: Yes, dogs and cats
Pet left unattended in room: Yes, if quiet
Exercise Area for Pets: Yes
Rates: $53 to $65

Royal 7 Motel
310 N. 7th Ave.
Bozeman, MT 59715
Phone: (406) 587-3103

Pet Restrictions: Yes, smoking rooms
Exercise Area for Pets: Yes
Rates: $26 to $53.95

VETERINARIANS
All West Vet Hospital
81770 Gallatin Rd.
Phone: (406) 586-4919

Lougren, Gregs
2605 West Main
Phone: (406) 587-4458

COLUMBUS

Super 8 of Columbus
P.O. Box 88
Columbus, MT 59019
Phone: (406) 322-4101

Pet Restrictions: None, $4/day/pet
Pet left unattended in room: Yes
Exercise Area for Pets: Yes
Rates: $31.39 plus $3/person

GARDENER

Best Western by Mammoth Hot Springs
US 89
Gardener, MT 59030
Phone: (406) 848-7311, 800-828-9080

Pet Restrictions: No large animals, smoking rooms
Pet left unattended in room: Yes
Exercise Area for Pets: Nearby
Rates: $71 to $102

MONTANA — HOTELS (continued)

Yellowstone Village Motel
P.O. Box 297
Gardner, MT 59030
Phone: (406) 848-7417,
    800-228-8158
Pet Restrictions: Smoking room,
    $5/night
Exercise Area for Pets: Yes
Rates: $33.75 to $150

GLENDINE
El Centro Motel
112 S. Kendrick Ave.
Glendine, MT 59330
Phone: (406) 365-5211
Pet Restrictions: None
Exercise Area for Pets: Yes
Rates: $23.98 to $38.58

GREAT FALLS
Best Western Heritage Inn
1700 Fox Farm Rd.
Great Falls, MT 59404
Phone: (406) 761-1900
Pet Restrictions: None
Exercise Area for Pets: Yes
Rates: $60 to $66

Townhouse Inn
1411 10th Ave. S
Great Falls, MT 59405
Phone: (406) 761-4600
Pet Restrictions: None
Rates: $47 to $74

VETERINARIANS
Animal Medical Clinic
5100 Ninth Ave. South
Phone: (406) 761-8183

Davis, Elmer G.
316 Central Avenue West
Phone: (406) 761-7055

HARDIN
Lariat Motel
709 N. Center Ave.
Hardin, MT 59034
Phone: (406) 665-2683
Pet Restrictions: $4/day/pet
Pet left unattended in room: Yes
Exercise Area for Pets: Yes
Rates: $30 to $54

HARLOWTON
Corral Motel
P.O. Box 721
Harlowton, MT 59036
Phone: (406) 632-4331
Pet Restrictions: None
Exercise Area for Pets: Yes
Rates: $24 to $45

Super 8 Motel
166 19th Ave. W
Harlowton, MT 59501
Phone: (406) 265-1411
Pet Restrictions: None, smoking
    rooms
Exercise Area for Pets: Yes
Rates: $32.20 to $44.72

HELENA
Days Inn
2001 Prospect Ave.
Helena, MT 59601
Phone: (406) 442-3280
Pet Restrictions: None, smoking
    rooms
Exercise Area for Pets: Nearby
Rates: $40 to $58

Lamplighter Motel
1006 Madison
Helena, MT 59601
Phone: (406) 442-9200
Pet Restrictions: None, $4/day/pet
Exercise Area for Pets: Yes
Rates: $25 to $55

Shilo Inn Helena
2020 Prospect Ave.
Helena, MT 59601
Phone: (406) 442-0320,
    (800) 222-2244
Pet Restrictions: $6 p.p. p.d.
Pet left unattended in room: Yes
Exercise Area for Pets: Yes
Rates: $49 to $73

KALISPELL
Best Western Outlaw Inn
1701 Hwy 93 S
Kalispell, MT 59901
Phone: (406) 755-6100
Pet Restrictions: None, $3/day
Exercise Area for Pets: Nearby
Rates: $52 to $61

Cavanaugh's at Kalispell
20 N. Main St.
Kalispell, MT 59901
Phone: (406) 752-6660
Pet Restrictions: Only dogs & cats
Exercise Area for Pets: Yes
Rates: $55 to $140

LIBBY
Caboose Motel
P.O. Box 792
Libby, MT 59923
Phone: (406) 293-6201
Pet Restrictions: Smoking rooms,
    $20 deposit, no housekeeping
Pet left unattended in room: Yes
Exercise Area for Pets: Yes
Rates: $31.50 to $39.90

Super 8
448 Hwy 2 West
Libby, MT 59923
Phone: (406) 293-2771
Pet Restrictions: None, $5/pet/day
Exercise Area for Pets: Yes
Rates: $36.37 to $48.89

LINCOLN
Leeper's Motel
PO Box 611
Lincoln, MT 59639
Phone: (406) 362-4333
Pet Restrictions: None, not allowed
    on furniture
Exercise Area for Pets: Yes
Rates: $28.50 to $41.75

MILES CITY
Best Western War Bonnet Inn
1015 S. Haynes Ave.
Miles City, MT 59301
Phone: (406) 232-4560
Pet Restrictions: None
Exercise Area for Pets: Yes
Rates: $30 to $45

Buckboard Inn
1006 S. Haynes Ave.
Miles City, MT 59301
Phone: (406) 232-3550
Pet Restrictions: None
Exercise Area for Pets: Yes
Rates: $29.20 to $43.80

Budget Host Custer's Inn
1209 S. Haynes Ave.
Miles City, MT 59301
Phone: (406) 232-5170
Pet Restrictions: Small pets, $20
    deposit
Pet left unattended in room: Yes
Exercise Area for Pets: Yes
Rates: $28 to $48

MISSOULA
Reserve St. Inn
4825 N. Reserve St.
Missoula, MT 59802
Phone: (406) 721-0990
Pet Restrictions: None
Exercise Area for Pets: Yes
Rates: $38 to $74

Village Red Lion Inn
100 Madison
Missoula, MT 59802
Phone: (406) 728-3100
Pet Restrictions: None
Pet left unattended in room: Yes
Exercise Area for Pets: Yes
Rates: $62 to $82

VETERINARIANS
Ancare Veterinary Clinic
1440 Russell Avenue
Phone: (406) 728-0408

Animal Clinic
920 SW Higgins
Phone: (406) 728-6900

Big Sky Veterinary Clinic
2411 Dearborn Avenue
Phone: (406) 721-3069

PRAY
Chico Hot Springs Lodge
PO Box 127
Pray, MT 59645
Phone: (406) 333-4933
Pet Restrictions: $2 fee
Exercise Area for Pets: Yes
Rates: $36 to $275

RED LODGE

Chateau Rouge
HCR 49, Box 3410
Red Lodge, MT 59068
Phone: (406) 446-1601

Pet Restrictions: None, inform
    management
Pet left unattended in room: Yes
Exercise Area for Pets: Yes
Rates: $57.35 to $156.42

ST. REGIS

St. Regis Super 8
PO Drawer 2
St. Regis, MT 59866
Phone: (406) 649-2422

Pet Restrictions: None, $20 deposit
Exercise Area for Pets: Yes
Rates: $29.92 to $50.97

THREE FORKS

Broken Spur Motel
PO Box 1009
Three Forks, MT 59752
Phone: (406) 285-3237

Pet Restrictions: $4/day
Exercise Area for Pets: Yes
Rates: $28 to $50

Sacajawea Inn
5 North Main
Three Forks, MT 59752
Phone: (800) 821-7326,
    406-285-6515

Pet Restrictions: Yes, 1st floor only,
    well-behaved, domestic, call in
    advance
Pet left unattended in room: Yes, in
    carrier
Exercise Area for Pets: Yes
Activities: National forests
Rates: $49 to $99

W. YELLOWSTONE

Best Western Desert Inn
133 Canyon, PO Box 340
West Yellowstone, MT 59758
Phone: (406) 646-7376

Pet Restrictions: None
Exercise Area for Pets: Nearby
Rates: $36 to $68

Cross Winds Inn
201 Firehole, PO Box 340
West Yellowstone, MT 59758
Phone: (406) 646-9557

Pet Restrictions: None
Exercise Area for Pets: Yes
Rates: $40 to $80

NEBRASKA — HOTELS

AINSWORTH
Remington Arms Hotel
1000 E. 4th
Ainsworth, NB 69210
Phone: (402) 387-2220
Pet Restrictions: $2/night
Rates: $23.50 to $34, add'l per
    extra per person

ALLIANCE
West Way Motel
1207 W Hwy 2 & 385, PO Box O
Alliance, NB 69301
Phone: (308) 762-4040
Pet Restrictions: None
Exercise Area for Pets: Yes
Rates: $34 to $74.75

AURORA
Ken's Motel Best Western
1515 11th St.
Aurora, NB 68818
Phone: (402) 694-3141
Pet Restrictions: Small, well
    behaved
Exercise Area for Pets: Yes
Rates: $26 to $38

BEATRICE
Beatrice Inn
3500 US 77 N
Beatrice, NB 68310
Phone: (402) 223-4074
Pet Restrictions: Small pets, outside
    pens available for hunting dogs
Exercise Area for Pets: Yes
Rates: $32.75 to $38.75

BEAVER CITY
Furnas County Inn
Hwy 89 & 10th St.
Beaver City, NB 68926
Phone: (308) 268-7705
Pet Restrictions: Small pets, pens
    available for hunting dogs
Pet left unattended in room: Yes
Rates: $25 to $36

BELLEVUE
American Family Inn
1110 Fort Crook Rd. S
Bellevue, NB 68005
Phone: (402) 291-0804
Pet Restrictions: $5 charge, in
    special rooms only
Pet left unattended in room: Yes, in
    carrier for maid service
Exercise Area for Pets: Yes
Rates: $38 to $53

VETERINARIANS
Bellevue Animal Hospital
10410 South 25th St.
Phone: (402) 291-1255

BRIDGEPORT
Bell Motel
US Hwy 385, PO Box 854
Bridgeport, NB 69336
Phone: (308) 262-0557
Pet Restrictions: Extra charge
    depending on number & size
Exercise Area for Pets: Yes
Rates: $29.50 to $48.50

CENTRAL CITY
Crawford Motel
E. Hwy 30
Central City, NB 68826
Phone: (308) 946-3051
Pet Restrictions: None
Exercise Area for Pets: Yes
Rates: $17 to $24

CRETE
Villa Madrid Motel
Hwy 33W
Crete, NB 68333
Phone: (402) 826-4341
Pet Restrictions: Small trained pets
Exercise Area for Pets: Yes
Rates: $31 to $39

GRAND ISLAND
Holiday Inn - Interstate 80
Grand Is. - Hastings, exit 312
P.O. Box 1501
Grand Island, NB 68802
Phone: (308) 384-7770
Pet Restrictions: None, responsible
    for damage
Exercise Area for Pets: Nearby
Rates: $42 to $69

NEBRASKA — HOTELS (continued)

Holiday Inn - Midtown
2503 S. Locust St.
Grand Island, NB 68801
Phone: (308) 384-1330
Pet Restrictions: None, kennels on
  grounds
Exercise Area for Pets: Yes
Rates: $54 to $61

Lazy V Motel
2703 E. Hwy 30
Grand Island, NB 68801
Phone: (308) 384-0700
Pet Restrictions: Small, fee
  depending on pet
Exercise Area for Pets: Yes
Rates: $17 to $36

Riverside Inn
3333 Ramada Rd.
Grand Island, NB 68801
Phone: (308) 384-5150,
  (800) 422-3485
Pet Restrictions: Must be house
  trained, responsible for damages
Pet left unattended in room: Yes if
  caged
Exercise Area for Pets: Nearby
Rates: $48 to $98

HASTINGS
Midlands Lodge
910 W. J St.
Hastings, NB 68901
Phone: (402) 463-2428
Pet Restrictions: Small, well
  behaved
Exercise Area for Pets: Nearby
Rates: $24.50 to $50

VETERINARIANS
Guthrie, Carl A.
2424 Bateman
Phone: (402) 463-9805

KEARNEY
Holiday Inn
301 S 2nd Ave., PO Box 1118
Kearney, NB 68847
Phone: (308) 237-3141
Pet Restrictions: Must be
  housebroken
Rates: $43.40 to $70

Western Inn South
510 Third Ave.
Kearney, NB 68847
Phone: (308) 234-1876
Pet Restrictions: Small
Exercise Area for Pets: Yes
Rates: $30 to $70

KIMBALL
1st Interstate Inn
Jct. I-80, US 71 exit 20
Rt. 1, Box 136
Kimball, NB 69145
Phone: (308) 235-4601
Pet Restrictions: Cats in carrier
  w/litter
Exercise Area for Pets: Nearby
Rates: $24.26 to $51.95

LINCOLN
Airport Lodge
2410 NW 12th
Lincoln, NB 68521
Phone: (402) 474-1311
Pet Restrictions: None, designated
  rooms
Exercise Area for Pets: Yes
Rates: $23.95 to $25.95

Ramada Hotel & Conference Center
141 N. 9th St.
Lincoln, NB 68508
Phone: (402) 475-4011
Pet Restrictions: Small
Rates: $49 to $109

Residence Inn
200 S. 68th St.
Lincoln, NB 68510
Phone: (402) 483-4900
Pet Restrictions: $50 cleaning fee
Pet left unattended in room: Yes, in
  carrier for maid service
Exercise Area for Pets: Yes
Rates: $94 to $114

Stop-n Sleep Motel
1140 Calvert St.
Lincoln, NB 68502
Phone: (402) 423-7111
Pet Restrictions: Small pets under
  20 lbs., $4/day
Exercise Area for Pets: Nearby
Rates: $31.95 to $51.95

VETERINARIANS

Pitts, Terry W.
2225 Highway 2
Phone: (402) 423-4120

Starr-Chichester, Roberta
7110 South 70th St.
Phone: (402) 426-3043

Stine, Lisa C.
5620 Abbey Court #69
Phone: (402) 895-6900

McCOOK

Best Western Chief Motel
612 West B St., P.O. Box 650
McCook, NB 69001
Phone: (308) 345-3700

Pet Restrictions: None
Exercise Area for Pets: Yes
Rates: $46 to $68

MINDEN

Harold Warp Pioneer Village Motel
Rt. 1, Box 1
Minden, NB 68959
Phone: (308) 832-2750

Pet Restrictions: None
Exercise Area for Pets: Nearby
Rates: $30.44 to $45.20

NORTH PLATTE

1st Interstate Inn
P.O. Box 1201
North Platte, NB 69101
Phone: (308) 532-6980

Pet Restrictions: None
Exercise Area for Pets: Yes
Rates: $29.95 to $36.95

Rambler Motel
1420 Rodeo Rd.
North Platte, NB 69101
Phone: (308) 532-9290

Pet Restrictions: None
Exercise Area for Pets: Yes
Rates: $20 to $26

The Stockman Inn
1402 S. Jeffers St., PO Box 2003
North Platte, NB 69103
Phone: (308) 534-3630

Pet Restrictions: None
Exercise Area for Pets: Yes
Rates: $30.72 to $40.95

OMAHA

Best Western Central
3650 South 72nd St.
Omaha, NB 68124
Phone: (402) 397-3700

Pet Restrictions: Small, in caddy
Pet left unattended in room: Yes if
    well behaved & quiet
Exercise Area for Pets: Yes
Rates: $48 to $71

Budgetel Inn
10760 M St.
Omaha, NB 68127
Phone: (402) 592-5200

Pet Restrictions: No more than 2
    per room
Exercise Area for Pets: Yes
Rates: $34.95 to $41.95

Clarion Carlisle
10909 M St.
Omaha, NB 68137
Phone: (402) 331-8220

Pet Restrictions: Small, quiet pets
Exercise Area for Pets: Yes
Rates: $45 to $175

Embassy Suites
7270 Cedar St.
Omaha, NB 68124
Phone: (402) 397-5141,
    (800) 362-2779 (central res.)

Pet Restrictions: $25/stay, refundable
    if no damage
Pet left unattended in room: Yes
Exercise Area for Pets: Nearby
Rates: $99 to $119

Hampton Inn S.W.
10728 L St.
Omaha, NB 68127
Phone: (402) 593-2380

Pet Restrictions: None
Exercise Area for Pets: Yes
Rates: $43 to $57

La Quinta
3330 N 104th Ave.
Omaha, NB 68134
Phone: (402) 493-1900

Pet Restrictions: None
Exercise Area for Pets: Yes
Rates: $43 to $50

Marriott Hotel
10220 Regency Circle
Omaha, NB 68114
Phone: (402) 399-9000

Pet Restrictions: None
Exercise Area for Pets: Yes
Rates: $65 to $140

Ramada Inn Airport
2002 E. Locus
Omaha, NB 68110
Phone: (402) 342-5100

Pet Restrictions: In caddy, quiet, on first floor
Exercise Area for Pets: Yes
Rates: $44 to $63

Ramada Central Hotel
7007 Grover St.
Omaha, NB 68106
Phone: (402) 397-7030

Pet Restrictions: None
Exercise Area for Pets: Yes
Rates: $59 to $91

Residence Inn by Marriott
6990 Dodge St.
Omaha, NB 68132
Phone: (402) 553-8898

Pet Restrictions: None
Pet left unattended in room: kennels available
Exercise Area for Pets: Yes
Rates: $69 to $130

Sheraton Inn Omaha
4888 S. 118th St.
Omaha, NB 68137
Phone: (402) 895-1000

Pet Restrictions: Under 20 lbs.
Pet left unattended in room: Yes if quiet
Exercise Area for Pets: Nearby
Rates: $49.95 to $97

VETERINARIANS

Animal Medical Center
2323 South 64th Avenue
Phone: (402) 558-1522

Harvey Oaks Animal Hospital
2706 South 148th Ave. Circle
Phone: (402) 334-0200

Curry, Carol, J.
12229 Bel Drive
Phone: (402) 330-3096

O'NEILL
Elms Motel
O'Neill, NB 68763
Phone: (402) 336-3800

Pet Restrictions: $2/pet, must be well behaved
Exercise Area for Pets: Yes
Rates: $25 to $40

PAPILLON
Ben Franklin Motel
I 80 & 144th St.
Papillon, NB 68138
Phone: (402) 895-2200

Pet Restrictions: $5, specific rooms
Exercise Area for Pets: Yes
Rates: $22.63 to $81

SCOTTS BLUFF
Capri Motel
2424 Ave. I
Scotts Bluff, NB 69361
Phone: (308) 635-2057,
(800) 642-2774 (res.)

Pet Restrictions: $3, small only
Exercise Area for Pets: Yes
Rates: $28 to $48

NEVADA — HOTELS

BATTLE MOUNTAIN

Best Western Big Chief Motel
434 W. Front St.
Battle Mt., NV 89820
Phone: (702) 635-2416

Pet Restrictions: $10 cash deposit
Pet left unattended in room: Yes,
    quiet
Exercise Area for Pets: Yes
Rates: $35 to $53.42

BEATTY

Burro Inn
3rd St. at Hwy 95, P.O. Box 7
Beatty, NV 89003
Phone: (702) 553-2225

Pet Restrictions: $4 fee
Pet left unattended in room: Yes,
    must be quiet
Exercise Area for Pets: Yes
Rates: $31.80 to $47.70

ELY

Fireside Inn
HC 33 Box 33400
Ely, NV 89301
Phone: (702) 289-3765

Pet Restrictions: $4 fee
Exercise Area for Pets: Yes
Rates: $33 to $57

ELKO

Holiday Inn
3015 Idaho St.
Elko, NV 89801
Phone: (702) 738-8425

Pet Restrictions: None
Rates: $53 to $79

Red Lion Inn and Casino
2065 Idaho St.
Elko, NV 89801
Phone: (702) 738-2111

Pet Restrictions: Small
Pet left unattended in room: Yes,
    must be quiet and contained
Exercise Area for Pets: Nearby
Rates: $59 to $250

Shilo Inn - Elko
2401 Mountain City Hwy
Elko, NV 89801
Phone: (702) 738-5522,
    (800) 222-2244

Pet Restrictions: $6/pet/day
Exercise Area for Pets: Yes
Rates: $55 to $75

VETERINARIANS

Bergin, Richard J.
700 South 5th St.
(702) 738-5010

LAS VEGAS

Best Western Nellis Motor Inn
5330 E. Craig Rd.
Las Vegas, NV 89115
Phone: (702) 643-6111

Pet Restrictions: $5/pet/night; $50
    deposit
Exercise Area for Pets: Yes
Rates: $36 to $95

Best Western Park View Inn
905 Las Vegas Blvd. N.
Las Vegas, NV 89101
Phone: (702) 385-1213

Pet Restrictions: Small; $6/pet/night
Pet left unattended in room: Yes, if
    quiet & well behaved
Exercise Area for Pets: Nearby
Rates: $38 to $92

Boardwalk Hotel
3750 Las Vegas Blvd. S.
Las Vegas, NV 89109
Phone: (702) 735-1167

Pet Restrictions: Limited number of
    rooms; $50 deposit; $10/pet/night
Pet left unattended in room: Yes,
    must be quiet, and maid can
    clean room
Exercise Area for Pets: Yes
Rates: $35 to $100

E-Z 8 Motel - Las Vegas
5201 S. Industrial Ave.
Las Vegas, NV 89118
Phone: (702) 739-9513

Pet Restrictions: Dogs must be on
    leash while walking on premises
    Pet deposit for large dogs
Pet left unattended in room: No
Exercise Area for Pets: Nearby
Rates: $21.88 to $36.88

Ferguson's Motel
1028 E. Freemont St.
Las Vegas, NV 89101
Phone: (702) 382-3500

Pet Restrictions: $25 refundable
    deposit
Exercise Area for Pets: Nearby
Rates: $27 to $65

La Quinta Inn
3782 Las Vegas Blvd. S.
Las Vegas, NV 89109
Phone: (702) 739-7457

Pet Restrictions: 1 small & quiet pet
Pet left unattended in room: Yes,
    must be quiet
Exercise Area for Pets: Nearby
Rates: $45 to $78

Marianna Inn
1322 E. Femont St.
Las Vegas, NV 89101
Phone: (702) 385-1150

Pet Restrictions: $10 fee
Pet left unattended in room: Yes,
    but room won't get cleaned
Exercise Area for Pets: Yes
Rates: $38 to $100

Meadows Inn
525 E. Bonanza Rd.
Las Vegas, NV 89101
Phone: (702) 366-0456

Pet Restrictions: $50 refundable
    deposit
Exercise Area for Pets: Nearby
Rates: $22.50 to $80

Motel Monaco
3073 Las Vegas Blvd. S.
Las Vegas, NV 89109
Phone: (702) 735-9222

Pet Restrictions: 1 small house pet
    only
Exercise Area for Pets: Nearby
Rates: $24 to $46

Rodeway Inn
3786 Las Vegas Blvd.
Las Vegas, NV 89109
Phone: (702) 736-1434,
    (800) 350-1132

Pet Restrictions: $10/day/pet
Pet left unattended in room: Yes if
    well behaved
Exercise Area for Pets: Yes
Rates: $49 to $69

VETERINARIANS

Animal Kindness
Vetny Hospital
4909 E. Bonanza Rd.
(702) 453-2990

Animal Medical Hospital
1914 E. Sahara
(702) 457-8043

Gentle Doctor Animal Hospital
1725 S. Rainbow Blvd.
(702) 363-7300

LAUGHLIN
Best Western Riverside Resort
P.O. Box 500
Laughlin, NV 89029
Phone: (702) 298-2535

Pet Restrictions: Less than 30 lbs.;
    $8/pet/night
Exercise Area for Pets: Yes
Rates: $19 to $91

MESQUITE
Peppermill Resort Hotel/Casino
P.O. Box 360
Mesquite, NV 89024
Phone: (702) 346-5233,
    (800) 621-0187

Pet Restrictions: Dogs, cats only;
    housetrained; Deposit
    $25/pet/stay
Pet left unattended in room: Yes
Exercise Area for Pets: Yes
Rates: $39 to $70

OVERTON
Echo Bay Resort
Lake Meade
Overton, NV 89040
Phone: (702) 394-4000

Pet Restrictions: $25/pet deposit;
    maximum 2 pets; $5/pet/day
Exercise Area for Pets: Nearby
Rates: $45 to $84

RENO
Days Inn
701 E. 7th St.
Reno, NV 89512
Phone: (702) 786-4070

Pet Restrictions: $6/pet/day
Pet left unattended in room: Yes,
    must be quiet; out of room
    during cleaning
Exercise Area for Pets: Yes
Rates: $36 to $53

Donner Inn Motel
720 W. 4th St.
Reno, NV 89503
Phone: (702) 323-1851

Pet Restrictions: $5/pet/day
Exercise Area for Pets: Nearby
Rates: $25 to $50

NEVADA — HOTELS (continued)

Harrah's Hotel
Center & 2nd St., P.O. Box 10
Reno, NV 89520
Phone: (702) 786-3232

Pet Restrictions: Pet in free kennel,
  not in room; $15 deposit for
  kennel key
Exercise Area for Pets: Nearby
Rates: $69 to $375

Holiday Inn Convention Cntr
5051 S. Virginia St.
Reno, NV 89502
Phone: (702) 825-2940

Pet Restrictions: Special rooms for
  small domestic pets
Pet left unattended in room: Yes, no
  housekeeping if pet alone
Exercise Area for Pets: Yes
Rates: $39 to $65

Holiday Inn Downtown
1000 E. 6th St.
Reno, NV 89512
Phone: (702) 786-5151

Pet Restrictions: Small
Exercise Area for Pets: Yes
Rates: $45 to $119

Vagabond Inn
3131 S. Virginia St.
Renov, NV 89502
Phone: (702) 825-7134

Pet Restrictions: $5/night
Pet left unattended in room: Yes
Rates: $36 to $54

VETERINARIANS

Animal Medical Center of Reno
855 E. Peckham Lane
(702) 827-3033

Truckee Meadows Vetny Hospital
465 W. Moana Lane
(702) 825-0400

Green, Cathleen A.
1660 Marla Dr.
(702) 356-7729

TONOPAH
Sundowner Motel
700 Hwy 95
Tonopah, NV 89049
Phone: (702) 482-6224

Pet Restrictions: None
Rates: $26.20 to $39.05

WELLS
Best Western Sage Motel
P.O. Box 343
Wells, NV 89835
Phone: (702) 752-3353

Pet Restrictions: $10/pet/night
Exercise Area for Pets: Nearby
Rates: $50 to $80

NEW HAMPSHIRE — HOTELS

BARTLETT

The Villager Motel
P.O. Box 427
Bartlett, NH 03812
Phone: (603) 374-2742

Pet Restrictions: prior approval only,
always on leash
Exercise Area for Pets: Yes
Rates: $39 to $95

BERLIN

Traveler Motel
25 Pleasant St.
Berlin, NH 03570
Phone: (603) 752-2500

Pet Restrictions: Only on occasion
Exercise Area for Pets: Yes
Rates: $29 to $68

CENTER CONWAY

Saco River Motor Lodge
Rt. 302, P.O. Box 9A
Center Conway, NH 03813
Phone: (603) 447-3720

Pet Restrictions: sometimes
additional fee
Exercise Area for Pets: Yes
Rates: $39 to $139

CONCORD

Brick Tower Motor Inn
414 S. Main St.
Concord, NH 03301
Phone: (603) 224-9565

Pet Restrictions: None
Exercise Area for Pets: Yes
Rates: $35 to $75

Econo Lodge
Gulf St.
Concord, NH 03301
Phone: (603) 224-4011

Pet Restrictions: small pets
Rates: $40 to $48

Ramada Inn
172 N. Main St.
Concord, NH 03301
Phone: (603) 224-9534,
(800) 228-2828

Pet Restrictions: None
Pet left unattended in room: Yes,
quiet
Exercise Area for Pets: Nearby
Rates: $59.95 to $119

VETERINARIANS

Russell Animal Hospital
286 Pleasant St.
(603) 224-2361

Berliner, David H.
37 Iron Works Rd.
(603) 224-9549

Mara, Kevin Joseph
1307 Alton Woods Dr.
(603) 228-2077

DOVER

Friendship Inn
181 Silver St.
Dover, NH 03820
Phone: (603) 742-4100

Pet Restrictions: Domestic only
Exercise Area for Pets: Yes
Rates: $48 to $75

VETERINARIANS

Central Park Veterinary Hosp.
53 Somersworth Rd.
(603) 742-1203

Dover Veterinary Hospital
Durham Rd.
(603) 742-6438

EXETER

Exeter Inn
90 Front St, P.O. Box 508
Exeter, NH 03833-0508
Phone: (603) 772-5901,
(800) 782-8444

Pet Restrictions: Quiet, well trained
Exercise Area for Pets: Yes
Rates: $57.50 to $165

FRANCISTOWN

The Inn at Crotched Mtn.
Mountain Road
Francistown, NH 03043
Phone: (603) 588-6840

Pet Restrictions: $5/pet/night
Exercise Area for Pets: Yes
Rates: $60 to $140

GORHAM

Gorham Motor Inn
324 Main St.
Gorham, NH 03581
Phone: (603) 466-3381

Pet Restrictions: None
Exercise Area for Pets: Yes
Rates: $38 to $60

Northern Peaks Motel
289 Main St.
Gorham, NH 03581
Phone: (603) 466-3374

Pet Restrictions: No cats
Exercise Area for Pets: Yes
Rates: $29 to $88

Tourist Village Motel
130 Main St.
Gorham, NH 03581
Phone: (603) 466-3312

Pet Restrictions: None
Exercise Area for Pets: Yes
Rates: $47 to $64

Town & Country Motor Inn
P.O. Box 220
Gorham, NH 03581
Phone: (603) 466-3315,
    (800) 325-4386

Pet Restrictions: None
Exercise Area for Pets: Yes
Rates: $48 to $82

HAMPTON

Hampton Motor Inn
815 Lafayette Rd.
Hampton, NH 03842
Phone: (603) 926-6771,
    (800) 423-4561

Pet Restrictions: Not in non-
    smoking room, not in pool area
Pet left unattended in room: Yes,
    quiet only
Exercise Area for Pets: Yes
Rates: $69 to $79

HANOVER

Hanover Inn
P.O. Box 151
Hanover, NH 03755
Phone: (603) 643-4300,
    (800) 443-7024

Pet Restrictions: $15/night
Exercise Area for Pets: Yes
Rates: $164 to $224

VETERINARIANS

Smith, Alcott L.
P.O. Box 997
(603) 643-3313

HILLSBORO

1830 House Motel
626 W. Main St.
Hillsboro, NH 03244
Phone: (603) 478-3135

Pet Restrictions: Quiet, small,
    $5/night
Pet left unattended in room: Yes, if
    quiet
Exercise Area for Pets: Yes
Rates: $45 and up

HOLDERNESS

Olde Colonial Eagle on Squam
P.O. Box R
Holderness, NH 03245
Phone: (603) 968-3233

Pet Restrictions: Small dogs only
Exercise Area for Pets: Yes
Rates: $38 to $75

INTERVALE

Riverside Inn
P.O. Box 42
Intervale, NH 03845
Phone: (603) 356-9060

Pet Restrictions: Notify in advance,
    well behaved, $5/night
Pet left unattended in room: Yes
Exercise Area for Pets: Yes
Rates: $44 to $85

Swiss Chalets Motel
Rt. 16A
Intervale, NH 03845
Phone: (603) 356-2232,
    (800) 831-2727

Pet Restrictions: $10/pet/night
Exercise Area for Pets: Yes
Rates: $35 to $135

JAFFREY

Woodbound Inn
Woodbound Road
Jaffrey, NH 03452
Phone: (603) 532-8341,
    (800) 668-7770

Pet Restrictions: In cabins only
Pet left unattended in room: Yes
Exercise Area for Pets: Yes
Rates: $75 to $260

NEW HAMPSHIRE — HOTELS (continued)

KEENE
Ramada Inn
401 Winchester St.
Keene, NH 03431
Phone: (603) 357-3038,
   (800) 2-RAMADA

Pet Restrictions: Domestic only
Pet left unattended in room: Yes, if
   quiet
Exercise Area for Pets: Yes
Rates: $55 to $85

VETERINARIANS
Cheshire Animal Hospital
505 Winchester St.
(603) 352-8585

Righter, Richard S.
686 Court St.
(603) 357-2455

LANCASTER
Pinetree Motel
RFD2, P.O. Box 281
Lancaster, NH 03584
Phone: (603) 636-2479

Pet Restrictions: None
Exercise Area for Pets: Yes
Rates: $25 to $35

LITTLETON
Continental 93 Motor Inn
I-93 exit 42 at US 302
Littleton, NH 03561
Phone: (603) 444-5366,
   (800) 544-9366

Pet Restrictions: designated rooms;
   $5/night
Pet left unattended in room: Yes, if
   caged
Exercise Area for Pets: Yes
Rates: $39 and up

Eastgate Motor Inn
Cottage St.
Littleton, NH 03561
Phone: (603) 444-3971

Pet Restrictions: Owner responsible
   for damage
Exercise Area for Pets: Yes
Rates: $39.50 and up

Maple Leaf Motel & Annex
297 W. Main St.
Littleton, NH 03561
Phone: (603) 444-5105

Pet Restrictions: $5/pet/night
Exercise Area for Pets: Yes
Rates: $34 to $57

VETERINARIANS
Littleton Veterinary Clinic
268 W. Main St.
(603) 444-0132

MANCHESTER
Center of NH - Holiday Inn
700 Elm St.
Manchester, NH 03101
Phone: (603) 625-1000,
   (800) HOLIDAY

Pet Restrictions: None
Exercise Area for Pets: Yes
Rates: $76 to $86

Days Hotel Manchester
55 John E. Devine Dr.
Manchester, NH 03103
Phone: (603) 668-6110,
   (800) 325-2525

Pet Restrictions: None
Exercise Area for Pets: Yes
Rates: $62.95 to $91

Howard Johnson Hotel
298 Queen City Ave.
Manchester, NH 03102
Phone: (603) 668-2600,
   (800) 446-4656

Pet Restrictions: Smoking rooms
Exercise Area for Pets: Yes
Rates: $49.90 to $99.90

Travelodge
21 Front St.
Manchester, NH 03102
Phone: (603) 669-2660

Pet Restrictions: Quiet pets only,
   smoking rooms
Pet left unattended in room: Yes,
   quiet
Exercise Area for Pets: Yes
Rates: $39 to $45

VETERINARIANS
Davidson, Steve D.
805 Northbrook Dr.
(603) 641-1228

Lewis, Matthew F.
1 Roosevelt St.
(603) 668-0369

Lockridge, Thomas J.
1153 Hanover St.
(603) 624-4378

MERRIMACK
Residence Inn by Marriott
246 Daniel Webster Hwy.
Merrimack, NH 03054
Phone: (603) 424-8100,
(800) 331-3131
Pet Restrictions: $100 refundable
deposit; $10 or $25 wk fee
Exercise Area for Pets: Yes
Rates: $99 to $120 (suites)

VETERINARIANS
Clough, Eric
235 Daniel Webster Hwy.
(603) 424-9922

MOULTONBORO
Olde Orchard Inn
RR1, Box 256
Moultonboro, NH 03254
Phone: (800) 598-5845
Pet Restrictions: Portable kennel or
stall in barn
Pet left unattended in room: No
Rates: $70 to $80

NASHUA
Holiday Inn
9 Northeastern Blvd.
Nashua, NH 03060
Phone: (603) 888-1200,
(800) 465-4329
Pet Restrictions: Sign damage slip;
no deposit if on credit card
Exercise Area for Pets: Yes
Rates: $45 to $69

Red Roof Inn
77 Spitbrook Rd.
Nashua, NH 03063
Phone: (603) 888-1893,
(800) 843-7663
Pet Restrictions: None
Pet left unattended in room: Yes,
take out for housekeeeping
Rates: $29.99 to $39.99

Sheraton-Tara Hotel
Spitbrook Rd.
Nashua, NH 03062
Phone: (603) 888-9970,
(800) 325-3535
Pet Restrictions: None
Exercise Area for Pets: Yes
Rates: $85 to $125

VETERINARIANS
The Animal Clinic of Nashua
155 Main Dunstable Rd.
(603) 880-3034

Huston Jr., Roland E.
325 South DW Highway
(603) 888-2751

Nashoba Valley Veterinary Hosp
15 Royal Crest Dr. #8
(617) 692-2302

NORTH CONWAY
The 1785 Inn
P.O. Box 1785
North Conway, NH 03860
Phone: (603) 356-9025,
(800) 421-1785
Pet Restrictions: Individual
discretion
Pet left unattended in room: Yes, if
well behaved
Exercise Area for Pets: Yes
Rates: $69 to $129

VETERINARIANS
Hussey, Eugene R.
Westside River Road
(603) 356-5538

OSSIPEE
Pine Cove Motel
at Jct. Rte 16 & 28 Ossipee
Ossipee, NH 03864
Phone: (603) 539-4491
Pet Restrictions: None
Exercise Area for Pets: Yes
Rates: $39 to $79

VETERINARIANS
The Kindness Animal Hospital
Route 171
(603) 539-2272

PITTSBURG
The Glen
77 The Glen Rd.
Pittsburg, NH 03592
Phone: (603) 538-6500,
(800) 445-4536
Pet Restrictions: Not in main lodge;
designated rooms
Exercise Area for Pets: Yes, if
supervised
Rates: $60 to $72

PLYMOUTH

Days Inn-White Mtns.
RR-1, P.O. Box 355
Plymouth, NH 03264
Phone: (603) 536-3520,
(800) 370-8666
Pet Restrictions: $5/pet/day
Pet left unattended in room: Yes,
no housekeeping
Exercise Area for Pets: Yes
Rates: $64 to $85

Knoll Motel
US Rte 3
Plymouth, NH 03264
Phone: (603) 536-1245
Pet Restrictions: In cottages only;
in summer
Exercise Area for Pets: Yes
Rates: $36 to $47

PORTSMOUTH

The Port Motor Inn
Rte 1 Bypass, South
Portsmouth, NH 03801
Phone: (603) 436-4378,
(800) 282-PORT
Pet Restrictions: None
Pet left unattended in room: Yes,
quiet
Exercise Area for Pets: Yes
Rates: $39.95 to $48.95

ROCHESTER

Anchorage Motor Inn
P.O. Box 7325
Rochester, NH 03867
Phone: (603) 332-3350
Pet Restrictions: None
Exercise Area for Pets: Yes
Rates: $35.95 to $65.95

VETERINARIANS
Moon, Thomas A.
3 Rochester Neck Rd.
(603) 332-5893

SALEM

Red Roof Inn
15 Red Roof Lane
Salem, NH 03079
Phone: (603) 898-6422,
(800) 843-7663
Pet Restrictions: None
Exercise Area for Pets: Yes
Rates: $29.99 to $41.99

Salem Hotel
Keewaydin Dr.
Salem, NH 03079
Phone: (603) 893-5511
Pet Restrictions: Small dogs only
Exercise Area for Pets: Yes
Rates: $35 to $40

VETERINARIANS
Salem Animal Hospital
193 South Broadway
(603) 893-3565

SHELBURNE

Philbrook Farm Inn
North Rd.
Shelburne, NH 03581
Phone: (603) 466-3831
Pet Restrictions: In cottages
Exercise Area for Pets: Yes
Rates: $122/night w/meals to
$475/wk no meals

SUNAPEE

Dexter's Inn
P.O. Box 703A, Winn Hill Rd.
Sunapee, NH 03782
Phone: (603) 763-5571,
(800) 232-5571
Pet Restrictions: In annex only;
$10/day
Exercise Area for Pets: Yes
Rates: $130 to $187.50 (both
include breakfast & dinner)

TWIN MOUNTAIN

Charlmont Motor Inn
On US Rte 3
Twin Mountain, NH 03595
Phone: (603) 846-5549,
(800) 286-5549 in N.H.
Pet Restrictions: $10/day
Exercise Area for Pets: Yes
Rates: $49 to $100

WOLFEBORO

Museum Lodges
HC 69, P.O. Box 680
Wolfeboro, NH 03894
Phone: (603) 569-1551
Pet Restrictions: Off-season only
Exercise Area for Pets: Yes
Rates: $80 to $130

WOODSVILLE

All Seasons Motel
36 Smith St.
Woodsville, NH 03785
Phone: (603) 747-2157,
(800) 660-0644 in N.H.
Pet Restrictions: None
Exercise Area for Pets: Yes
Rates: $34 to $50

NEW JERSEY — HOTELS

CLARK

Howard Johnson Lodge
70 Central Ave., P.O. Box 792
Clark, NJ 07066
Phone: (908) 381-6500,
(800) 654-2000

Pet Restrictions: None
Pet left unattended in room: Yes but
room won't be cleaned
Rates: $49 to $75

CLIFTON

Howard Johnson Hotel
680 Route 3 West
Clifton, NJ 07014
Phone: (201) 471-3800,
(800) 654-2000

Pet Restrictions: Small, domestic
Pet left unattended in room: Yes,
but no cleaning
Exercise Area for Pets: Yes
Rates: $49 to $85

VETERINARIANS

Antelmans Animal Hospital
1071 Paulson Ave.
(201) 478-0097

Foster Animal Hospital
1347 Broad St.
(201) 777-0064

EATONTOWN

Crystal Motor Lodge
170-174 Hwy. 35
Eatontown, NJ 07724
Phone: (908) 542-4900,
(800) 562-5290

Pet Restrictions: None
Pet left unattended in room: Yes,
but no cleaning
Exercise Area for Pets: Yes
Rates: $42 to $46

EDISON

Red Roof Inn
860 New Durham Rd.
Edison, NJ 08817
Phone: (908) 248-9300,
(800) 843-7663

Pet Restrictions: Yes
Pet left unattended in room: Yes
Exercise Area for Pets: Nearby
Rates: $43 to $53

Wellesley Inn Edison
831 Route 1, South
Edison, NJ 08817
Phone: (908) 287-0171
Fax: (908) 287-8364
Contact: John Gallagher

Pet Restrictions: None
Pet left unattended in room: Yes
Exercise Area for Pets: Yes
Rates: $55.99 to $79.99

VETERINARIANS

Raritan Hospital for Animals
1850 Lincoln Hwy
(908) 985-0278

FAIRFIELD

Sheraton Hotel
690 US 46E
Fairfield, NJ 07006
Phone: (201) 227-9200,
(800) 325-3535

Pet Restrictions: $25 deposit, small
domestic pets
Exercise Area for Pets: Yes
Rates: $130 to $350

HAZLET

Wellesley Inn
3215 SR-35
Hazlet, NJ 07730
Phone: (908) 888-2800

Pet Restrictions: Quiet, $3/day
Pet left unattended in room: Yes,
but quiet
Exercise Area for Pets: Yes
Rates: $39.99 to $75.99

KENILWORTH

Holiday Inn
S. 31st St at Garden State Pkwy
Kenilworth, NJ 07033
Phone: (908) 241-4100,
(800) HOLIDAY

Pet Restrictions: None
Pet left unattended in room: Yes,
but no cleaning
Exercise Area for Pets: Yes
Rates: $64 to $78

LAWRENCEVILLE

Howard Johnson Lodge
2995 Brunswick Pike, Rte. 1
Lawrenceville, NJ 08648
Phone: (609) 896-1100,
(800) 654-2000

Pet Restrictions: $10/day
Pet left unattended in room: Yes, no
cleaning
Rates: $63.50 to $90

Red Roof Inn-Princeton
3203 Brunswick Pike
Lawrenceville, NJ 08648
Phone: (609) 896-3388,
    (800) 843-7663

Pet Restrictions: None
Pet left unattended in room: Yes, no
    cleaning
Exercise Area for Pets: Yes
Rates: $35.99 to $47.99

LYNDHURST
Novatel Meadowlands
1 Polito Ave.
Lyndhurst, NJ 07071
Phone: (201) 896-1137
Fax: (201) 507-0419

Pet Restrictions: None
Pet left unattended in room: No
    policy
Exercise Area for Pets: Nearby
Other Areas: Bergen County Park,
    Lavalette Beach
Rates: $59 to $114

MAHWAH
Ramada Inn
180 Rt. 17
Mahwah, NJ 07430
Phone: (201) 529-5880,
    (800) 2-RAMADA

Pet Restrictions: None
Pet left unattended in room: Yes
Exercise Area for Pets: Yes
Rates: $59 to $74.50

Sheraton Hotel & Towers Corporate Hdqrts.
On SR-17N
Mahwah, NJ 07430
Phone: (201) 529-1660,
    (800) 325-3535

Pet Restrictions: $5/day
Exercise Area for Pets: Yes
Rates: $79 to $750

MILLVILLE
Millville Motor Inn
Rte 47 Delsea Dr.
Millville, NJ 08332
Phone: (609) 327-3300,
    (800) 428-4373

Pet Restrictions: $5/day/pet, small
    domestic pets
Pet left unattended in room: Yes,
    but quiet
Rates: $54 to $100

VETERINARIANS
Animal Hospital of Millville
2206 N. Delsea Dr.
(609) 825-3434

MONMOUTH JUNCTION
Red Roof Inn
603 Fellowship Rd.
Monmouth Junction, NJ 08852
Phone: (908) 821-8800

Pet Restrictions: None
Pet left unattended in room: Yes
Exercise Area for Pets: Yes
Rates: $40 to $55

MT. ARLINGTON
Sheraton
15 Howard Blvd.
Mt. Arlington, NJ 07856
Phone: (201) 770-2000,
    (800) 325-3535

Pet Restrictions: With manager's
    approval
Exercise Area for Pets: Yes
Rates: $85.50 to $150

MT. HOLLY
Howard Johnson Lodge
P.O. Box 73
Mt. Holly, NJ 08060
Phone: (609) 267-6550,
    (800) 654-2000

Pet Restrictions: Not allowed in
    exec. section
Pet left unattended in room: No,
    prefer animal crated in room
Exercise Area for Pets: Yes
Rates: $62 to $70

VETERINARIANS
BuLaga, Leslie L.
13 Ridgley St.
(609) 267-1609

Cady, Errol J.
Marne Highway
(609) 267-1609

Campbell, Helen E.
1100 Monmouth Rd.
(609) 888-3400

MT. LAUREL

Red Roof Inn
603 Fellowship Rd.
Mt. Laurel, NJ 08054
Phone: (609) 234-5589,
    (800) 843-7663
Pet Restrictions: None
Pet left unattended in room: Yes, in
    cage
Exercise Area for Pets: Yes
Rates: $32.99 to $52.99

VETERINARIANS

Lipman, Janet L.
114 Banwell Lane
(609) 267-0296

NEWARK

Ramada Hotel
Rt. 1 & 9 South
Newark, NJ 07114
Phone: (201) 824-4000,
    (800) 2-RAMADA
Pet Restrictions: Pet deposit, must
    be caged
Pet left unattended in room: Yes,
    must be caged
Exercise Area for Pets: Yes
Rates: $70 to $150

NORTH PLAINFIELD

Howard Johnson Lodge
US 22 W at West End Ave.
North Plainfield, NJ 07060
Phone: (908) 753-6500
Pet Restrictions: Notify in advance,
    only in certain rooms
Pet left unattended in room: Yes if
    quiet
Exercise Area for Pets: Yes
Rates: $50 to $75

PARAMUS

Howard Johnson Lodge
393 Route 17
Paramus, NJ 07652
Phone: (201) 265-4200,
    (800) 446-4656
Pet Restrictions: Clean
Exercise Area for Pets: Yes
Rates: $48 to $65

PARSIPPANY

Red Roof Inn
855 US 46
Parsippany, NJ 07054
Phone: (201) 334-3737,
    (800) 843-7663
Pet Restrictions: Yes
Exercise Area for Pets: Yes
Rates: $31 to $59.99

PHILLIPSBURG

Howard Johnson Lodge
US 22 & I-78
Phillipsburg, NJ 08865
Phone: (908) 454-6461
Pet Restrictions: Small pets only
Pet left unattended in room: Yes, if
    well behaved
Exercise Area for Pets: Yes
Rates: $57 to $84.80

VETERINARIANS

Epple, William B.
2200 Beluidire Rd.
(201) 454-5600

PRINCETON

**Princeton Residence Inns by
Marriott**
4225 Rt. 1
Princeton, NJ 08540
Phone: (908) 329-9600,
    (800) 331-3131
Pet Restrictions: $10/day plus pay
    for damages
Exercise Area for Pets: Yes
Rates: $99 to $200

VETERINARIANS

Garruba, Christopher N.
3975 Old Princeton Pike
(609) 924-2293

RAMSEY

Howard Johnson Lodge
1255 Rt. 17
S. Ramsey, NJ 07446
Phone: (201) 327-4550,
    (800) I-GO-HOJO
Pet Restrictions: None
Pet left unattended in room: Yes,
    but must be removed from
    room during cleaning
Rates: $45 to $55

VETERINARIANS

Lynch Veterinary Hospital
Grove St.
(201) 327-1877

Krazinski, Gerard L.
3 Meadowbrook Rd.
(201) 825-4545

RUNNEMEDE
Holiday Inn-Runnemede
109 9th Ave.
Runnemede, NJ 08078
Phone: (609) 939-4200,
  (800) HOLIDAY
Pet Restrictions: Deposit, $10/day,
  dogs and cats only
Exercise Area for Pets: Yes
Rates: $52 to $62

SADDLE BROOK
Holiday Inn & Conference Ctr.
50 Kenney Place
Saddlebrook, NJ 07662
Phone: (201) 843-0600,
  (800) HOLIDAY
Pet Restrictions: Not too big,
  deposit required, while in lobby
  must be caged or leashed
Pet left unattended in room: Yes if
  caged
Exercise Area for Pets: Yes
Rates: $65 to $99

Howard Johnson Plaza-Hotel
129 Pehle Ave.
Saddle Brook, NJ 07662
Phone: (201) 845-7800
Pet Restrictions: Small pets only
Pet left unattended in room: Yes
Rates: $59 to $99

SECAUCUS
Red Roof Inn
15 Meadowlands Pkwy
Secaucus, NJ 07094
Phone: (201) 319-1000
Pet Restrictions: None
Pet left unattended in room: Yes
Exercise Area for Pets: Yes
Rates: $50 to $75

Secaucus Animal Hospital
1250 Paterson Plank
(201) 867-4795

SOMERSET
Ramada Inn
Weston Canal Rd. & Rt. 287
Somerset, NJ 08873
Phone: (908) 560-9880,
  (800) 2-RAMADA
Pet Restrictions: Dogs & cats only
Pet left unattended in room: Yes if
  caged
Exercise Area for Pets: Yes
Rates: $49.95 to $125

Bacon, James D.
1760 Easton Ave.
(201) 469-5133

SOUTH PLAINFIELD
Comfort Inn
Stelton Rd. & I-287
South Plainfield, NJ 07080
Phone: (908) 561-4488,
  (800) 221-2222
Pet Restrictions: Cats & dogs only
Pet left unattended in room: Yes
Rates: $45 to $70

South Plainfield Animal Hosp.
2201 Park Avenue
(201) 755-2428

Quin, Kenneth L.
226 Oakmoor Avenue
(201) 754-2049

WAYNE
Howard Johnson Lodge
1850 Route 23
Wayne, NJ 07470
Phone: (201) 696-8050
Pet Restrictions: Clean up after
Exercise Area for Pets: Yes
Rates: $55.50 to $72

North Jersey Animal Hospital
197 Hamburg Tpke
(201) 595-8600

Perez, Maritza M.
Salisburry Rd. #16-B
(201) 595-8600

Wayne Animal Hospital
2411 Hamberg Tpke
(201) 839-3737

WHIPPANY
Howard Johnson Lodge
1255 Rt. 10
Whippany, NJ 07981
Phone: (201) 539-8350
Pet Restrictions: Notify housekeeping
Pet left unattended in room: Yes but
  maid will not service room
Exercise Area for Pets: Yes
Rates: $49 to $62.50

NEW MEXICO — HOTELS

ALBUQUERQUE

Albuquerque Super 8 Mid-Town
2500 University Blvd. NE
Albuquerque, NM 87107
Phone: (505) 888-4884,
    (800) 800-8000 (central res.)
Pet Restrictions: $5/pet/night
Pet left unattended in room: Yes, for
    short time only
Exercise Area for Pets: Yes
Rates: $35.88 to $56.88

Amberley Suite Hotel
7620 Pan American Frwy, NE
Albuquerque, NM 87109
Phone: (505) 823-1300,
    (800) 333-9806
Pet Restrictions: $2/pet/night
Pet left unattended in room: Yes
Exercise Area for Pets: Yes
Rates: $69 to $94

Best Western American Motor Inn
12999 Central Ave. NE
Albuquerque, NM 87123
Phone: (505) 298-7426,
    (800) 366-5252
Pet Restrictions: No larger dogs
Rates: $41 to $65

Best Western Winrock Inn
18 Winrock Center NE
Albuquerque, NM 87110
Phone: (505) 883-5252,
    (800) 866-5252
Pet Restrictions: $35/pet/stay deposit
    Exercise Area for Pets: Nearby
Rates: $62 to $105

Comfort Inn Albuquerque Airport
2300 Yale SE
Albuquerque, NM 87106
Phone: (505) 243-2244
Pet Restrictions: Must be leashed
    outside; quiet; not allowed in
    non smoking rooms
Pet left unattended in room: Yes, no
    room service
Exercise Area for Pets: Nearby
Rates: $44.10 to $69

Comfort Inn Mid-Town
2015 Menaul NE
Albuquerque, NM 87107
Phone: (505) 881-3210,
    (800) 221-2222
Pet Restrictions: $25/pet/stay
    refund. deposit
Pet left unattended in room: Yes, if
    well behaved
Exercise Area for Pets: Yes
Rates: $43 to $53

Days Inn
13317 Central Ave. NE
Albuquerque, NM 87123
Phone: (505) 294-3297,
    (800) 325-2525
Pet Restrictions: $5/pet/stay
Pet left unattended in room: Yes
Exercise Area for Pets: Nearby
Rates: $42 to $52

De Anza
4301 Central Ave, NE
Albuquerque, NM 87108
Phone: (505) 255-1654
Pet Restrictions: Well behaved
Pet left unattended in room: Yes,
    but no room service
Exercise Area for Pets: Nearby
Rates: $19.95 to $37

Hampton Inn
5105 Ellison St. NE
Albuquerque, NM 87109
Phone: (505) 344-1555,
    (800) 426-7866
Pet Restrictions: No very large dogs
Pet left unattended in room: Yes, for
    short time
Exercise Area for Pets: Nearby
Rates: $43 to $52.50

Holiday Inn-Midtown
2020 Menaul Blvd. NE
Albuquerque, NM 87107
Phone: (505) 884-2511,
    (800) 545-0599
Pet Restrictions: None
Exercise Area for Pets: Yes
Rates: $67.20 to $94

Holiday Inn Pyramid
5151 San Francisco Rd. NE
Albuquerque, NM 87109
Phone: (505) 821-3333
Pet Restrictions: Responsible for
   damages or clean up
Pet left unattended in room: Yes, for
   short time
Exercise Area for Pets: Yes
Rates: $98 to $132

La Quinta
2424 San Mateo Blvd. NE
Albuquerque, NM 87110
Phone: (505) 884-3591,
   (800) 531-5900
Pet Restrictions: Under 20 lbs.
Exercise Area for Pets: Nearby
Rates: $47 to $70

La Quinta Motor Inn at the Airport
2116 Yale Blvd. SE
Albuquerque, NM 87106
Phone: (505) 243-5500,
   (800) 531-5900
Pet Restrictions: Small to medium
   size. No large dogs.
Exercise Area for Pets: Yes
Rates: $51 to $66

La Quinta San Antonio
5241 San Antonio Dr. NE
Albuquerque, NM 87109
Phone: (505) 821-9000,
   (800) 531-5900
Pet Restrictions: Under 20 lbs. only;
   must be leashed at all times
Exercise Area for Pets: Yes
Rates: $48 to $68

Radison Inn
1901 University SE
Albuquerque, NM 87106
Phone: (505) 247-0512,
   (800) 333-3333
Pet Restrictions: Small only; must
   notify in advance; Rooms in
   Building B only
Pet left unattended in room: Yes
Exercise Area for Pets: Nearby
Rates: $84 to $95

Ramada Hotel Classic
6815 Menaul, NE
Albuquerque, NM 87110
Phone: (505) 881-0000,
   (800) 252-7772
Pet Restrictions: Well trained
Pet left unattended in room: Yes,
   but no cleaning
Exercise Area for Pets: Nearby
Rates: $87 to $97

Rio Grande Inn
1015 Rio Grande Blvd. NW
Albuquerque, NM 87104
Phone: (505) 843-9500,
   (800) 959-4726
Pet Restrictions: None
Exercise Area for Pets: Yes
Rates: $34.95 and up

Riteway Inn
5201 Central Ave., NE
Albuquerque, NM 87108
Phone: (505) 265-8413,
   (800) 888-8413
Pet Restrictions: None
Pet left unattended in room: Yes, no
   maid service
Rates: $34 to $38

Royal Motor Hotel of Albuquerque
4119 Central Ave., NE
Albuquerque, NM 87108
Phone: (505) 265-3585,
   (800) 843-8572
Pet Restrictions: 12 rooms w/private
   outside areas; $20/pet/stay
   deposit
Pet left unattended in room: Yes,
   but no room service
Exercise Area for Pets: Nearby
Rates: $24.90 to $49.90

Motel 6
5701 Lliff Rd.
Albuquerque, NY 87105
Phone: (505) 831-8888
Pet Restrictions: None
Exercise Area for Pets: Yes
Rates: $28.76 to $42.05

VETERINARIANS

Animal Medical Clinic
2632 Pennsylvania NW
(505) 897-2363

Manzano Animal Clinic
1041 Juan Tabo NE
(505) 298-5543

Veterinary Care Clinic
3601 Eubank NE
(505) 292-5353

ALTO
High Country Lodge
P.O. Box 137
Alto, NM 88312
Phone: (505) 336-4321,
    (800) 845-7265

Pet Restrictions: None
Pet left unattended in room: Yes, if
    quiet
Exercise Area for Pets: Yes
Rates: $59 to $89

La Junta Guest Ranch
P.O. Box 139
Alto, NM 88312
Phone: (505) 336-4361,
    (800) 443-8423

Pet Restrictions: None
Exercise Area for Pets: Yes
Rates: $70 to $200

CARLSBAD
Park Inn International
3706 Nat'l Park Hwy
Carlsbad, NM 88220
Phone: (505) 887-2861,
    (800) 321-2861

Pet Restrictions: Small; must notify
    desk; not allowed in public areas
Exercise Area for Pets: Yes
Rates: $35 to $50

DEMING
Grand Motor Inn
1721 E. Spruce St.
Deming, NM 88030
Phone: (505) 546-2632

Pet Restrictions: None
Exercise Area for Pets: Yes
Rates: $32 to $65

ELEPHANT BUTTE
Elephant Butte Resort Inn
P.O. Box E
Elephant Butte, NM 87935
Phone: (505) 744-5431

Pet Restrictions: 4 rooms; $10/stay
Exercise Area for Pets: Yes
Rates: $40 to $59

GALLUP
Gallup Travelodge
1709 W. Hwy. 66
Gallup, NM 87301
Phone: (505) 863-9301,
    (800) 255-3050

Pet Restrictions: None
Pet left unattended in room: Yes
Exercise Area for Pets: Yes
Rates: $35/bed; $45/2 beds

Red Rock Animal Hospital
816 S. Boardman
(505) 722-4283

GRANTS
Econolodge
1509 E. Santa Fe Ave.
Grants, NM 87020
Phone: (505) 287-4426

Pet Restrictions: None
Pet left unattended in room: Yes
Exercise Area for Pets: Nearby
Rates: $27.95 to $54.95

HOBBS
The Innkeepers
309 N. Marland Blvd.
Hobbs, NM 88240
Phone: (505) 397-7171,
    (800) 628-4074

Pet Restrictions: Small pets; must
    be leashed outdoors; $20/stay
    refund. deposit
Pet left unattended in room: Yes, if
    nice
Exercise Area for Pets: Yes
Rates: $35.95 to $59.95

Great Plains Vetny Clinic
2720 Lovington Highway
(505) 392-5513

LAS CRUCES
Desert Lodge Motel
1900 W. Picacho St.
Las Cruces, NM 88005
Phone: (505) 524-1925

Pet Restrictions: Clean; $5/day
    deposit
Exercise Area for Pets: Nearby
Rates: $20 to $39

Lundeen Inn of the Arts
618 S. Alameda
Las Cruces, NM 88005
Phone: (505) 526-3327

Pet Restrictions: Small, if you have
    cage; larger dogs limited to one
    room; $10/night deposit
Exercise Area for Pets: Yes
Rates: $57 to $895

VETERINARIANS
Alta Vist Animal Clinic
725 South Solano
(505) 524-7176

Paisano Mobile Animal Clinic
2608 Westwind Rd.
(505) 523-5654

Schumacher, William J.
701 S. Valley Dr.
(505) 524-2894

LAS VEGAS
Plaza Hotel
230 on the Old Town Plaza
Las Vegas, NM 87701
Phone: (505) 425-3591,
    (800) 328-1882

Pet Restrictions: $25/stay refund.
    deposit
Pet left unattended in room: Yes
Exercise Area for Pets: Nearby
Rates: $55 to $90

VETERINARIANS
Nelson, Ben Scott
Box 74 Mora Route
(505) 425-3538

MESILLA
Meson de Mesilla
1803 Avenida de Mesilla
Mesilla, NM 88046
Phone: (505) 525-9212,
    (800) 732-6025

Pet Restrictions: Small-medium
    only; $10-$25/stay refund.
    deposit (depends on size)
Exercise Area for Pets: Yes
Rates: $45 to $82

PORTALES
Dunes Motel
P.O. Box 127
Portales, NM 88130
Phone: (505) 356-6668

Pet Restrictions: None
Pet left unattended in room: Yes
Exercise Area for Pets: Yes
Rates: $23 to $40

RATON
Capri Motel
304 Canyon Dr.
Raton, NM 87740
Phone: (505) 445-3641

Pet Restrictions: $10 refund. deposit
Exercise Area for Pets: Yes
Rates: $29 to $55

Melody Lane Motel
136 Canyon Dr.
Raton, NM 87740
Phone: (505) 445-3655,
    (800) 421-5210

Pet Restrictions: $5/night deposit
Exercise Area for Pets: Yes
Rates: $40 to $45 (1 extra person)

RED RIVER
Golden Eagle Lodge
P.O. Box 869
Red River, NM 87558
Phone: (505) 754-2227,
    (800) 621-4046

Pet Restrictions: Leashed/Seasonal
Exercise Area for Pets: Yes
Rates: $36 to $146

Terrace Towers Lodge
P.O. Box 149
Red River, NM 87558
Phone: (505) 754-2962,
    (800) 695-6343

Pet Restrictions: Pets in lodge
    building; notify in advance;
    $1/day, $5 max. deposit
Pet left unattended in room: Yes
Exercise Area for Pets: Nearby
Rates: $33.95 to $90

ROSWELL

Budget Inn
2300 W 2nd St.
Roswell, NM 88201
Phone: (505) 623-3811,
(800) 752-4667

Pet Restrictions: No cats; quiet; must clean after pet; not allowed near pool; $2/day deposit; $20 undeclared pet charge
Exercise Area for Pets: Yes
Rates: $22.10 to $39.10

VETERINARIANS

Country Club Animal Hospital
301 W. Country Club Rd.
(505) 623-9191

Humphreys, James Louis
502 E. College
(505) 624-2424

RUIDOSO

Swiss Chalet Inn
1451 Mechem Dr.
Ruidoso, NM 88345
Phone: (505) 258-3333,
(800) 47SWISS

Pet Restrictions: Small pets only
Exercise Area for Pets: Yes
Rates: $77

VETERINARIANS

Ruidoso Animal Clinic
160 Sudderth
(505) 257-4027

SANTA FE

Alexander's Inn
529 E. Palace Ave.
Santa Fe, NM 87501
Phone: (505) 986-1431

Pet Restrictions: None
Pet left unattended in room: Yes
Exercise Area for Pets: Yes
Other: Mountains
Rates: $65 to $150

Holiday Inn
4048 Cerrillos Rd.
Santa Fe, NM 87505
Phone: (505) 473-4646

Pet Restrictions: 1st floor
Pet left unattended in room: Yes
Exercise Area for Pets: Nearby
Rates: $65 to $250

Hotel La Fonda De Taos
P.O. Box 1447
Santa Fe, NM 87571
Phone: (505) 758-2211,
(800) 833-2211

Pet Restrictions: None
Pet left unattended in room: Yes, depends on pet behavior
Exercise Area for Pets: Nearby
Rates: $65 to $85

Inn on the Alameda
303 E. Alameda
Santa Fe, NM 87501
Phone: (505) 984-2121,
(800) 289-2122

Pet Restrictions: $50; designated rooms w/patios
Pet left unattended in room: Yes
Exercise Area for Pets: Yes
Rates: $155 to $330

La Quinta
4298 Cerrillos Rd.
Santa Fe, NM 87505
Phone: (505) 471-1142,
(800) 531-5900 (central res.)

Pet Restrictions: Small, 20 lbs or under
Exercise Area for Pets: Nearby
Rates: $53 to $74

Motel 6
3007 Cerrillos Rd.
Santa Fe, NM 87501
Phone: (505) 473-1380

Pet Restrictions: Small pets only
Exercise Area for Pets: Nearby
Rates: $32 to $45

Quality Inn
3011 Cerrillos Rd.
Santa Fe, NM 87501
Phone: (505) 471-1211,
(800) 228-5151 (central res.)

Pet Restrictions: None
Pet left unattended in room: Yes
Exercise Area for Pets: Yes
Rates: $50 to $70

Ramada Inn
2907 Cerrillos Rd.
Santa Fe, NM 87501
Phone: (505) 471-3000,
(800) 2 Ramada

Pet Restrictions: $5/pet/night deposit
Pet left unattended in room: Yes
Exercise Area for Pets: Nearby
Rates: $35 to $88

VETERINARIANS

Acoma Animal Hospital
1605 Llano St.
(505) 983-8631

Sangre De Cristo Animal Hosp.
6820 Cerrillos Rd.
(505) 471-6594

Lauer, Jean L.
1089 Mansion Ridge Dr.
(505) 982-4469

SILVER CITY

Bear Mt. Guest Ranch
P.O. Box 1163
Silver City, NM 88062
Phone: (505) 538-2538

Pet Restrictions: Must be leashed
when outside
Pet left unattended in room: Yes, no
longer than a meal
Exercise Area for Pets: Yes
Rates: $90 to $105

TAOS

El Rincon Bed and Breakfast Inn
114 E. Kit Carson St.
Taos, NM 87571
Phone: (505) 758-4874

Pet Restrictions: Stay off furniture
Pet left unattended in room: Yes
Exercise Area for Pets: Yes
Rates: $49 to $99

La Posada de Taos
309 Juanita Lane, P.O. Box 1118
Taos, NM 87571
Phone: (505) 758-8164

Pet Restrictions: 3 rooms; must be
leashed on street
Exercise Area for Pets: Yes
Rates: $68 to $100

Quality Inn
1043 S. Santa Fe Rd., P.O. Box 2319
Taos, NM 87571
Phone: (505) 758-2200,
(800) 845-0648

Pet Restrictions: $25/stay
refundable deposit
Exercise Area for Pets: Yes
Rates: $55 to $80

Sagebush Inn
P.O. Box 2319, S. Santa Fe Rd.
Taos, NM 87571
Phone: (505) 758-2254,
(800) 428-3626

Pet Restrictions: $25/stay refund.
deposit
Pet left unattended in room: Yes, if
quiet
Exercise Area for Pets: Yes
Rates: $60 to $140

VETERINARIANS

Schupbach, Theodore A.
P.O. Box 2678
(505) 758-7310

TUCUMCARI

Best Western Aruba Motel
1700 E. Tucumcari Blvd.
Tucumcari, NM 88401
Phone: (505) 461-3335,
(800) 528-1234 (central res.)

Pet Restrictions: None
Pet left unattended in room: Yes, if
quiet
Exercise Area for Pets: Yes
Rates: $36 to $46

Best Western Discovery Motor Inn
200 E. Estrella
Tucumcari, NM 88401
Phone: (505) 461-4884

Pet Restrictions: Small pets only
Exercise Area for Pets: Yes
Rates: $46

VAUGHN

Bel Air Motel
P.O. Box 68
Vaughn, NM 88353
Phone: (505) 584-2241

Pet Restrictions: Smaller pets
Pet left unattended in room: Yes, if
quiet & well-behaved
Exercise Area for Pets: Yes
Rates: $28 to $55

NEW YORK — HOTELS

ALBANY

Albany Ramada Inn
1228 Western Ave.
Albany, NY 12203
Phone: (518) 489-2981,
  (800)-2-Ramada (central res.)

Pet Restrictions: Quiet, well
  behaved, damages will be charged
Pet left unattended in room: Yes if
  quiet
Exercise Area for Pets: Yes
Rates: $49 to $88

Albany Quality Inn Motel
1-3 Watervliet Ave.
Albany, NY 12206
Phone: (518) 438-8431,
  (800) 221-2222 (central res.)

Pet Restrictions: None
Pet left unatted in room: Yes,
  notify desk or leave note on door
Exercise Area for Pets: Yes
Rates: $63 to $92

Howard Johnson Lodge
416 Southern Blvd.
Albany, NY 12209
Phone: (518) 462-6555,
  (800) 562-7253

Pet Restrictions: None
Pet left unattended in room: Yes, let
  desk know, no cleaning
Exercise Area for Pets: Yes
Rates: $50 to $80

Red Roof Inn
188 Wolf Rd.
Albany, NY 12205
Phone: (518) 459-1971,
  (800) 843-7665

Pet Restrictions: Yes
Pet left unattended in rooms: Yes
Exercise Area for Pets: Yes
Rates: $43 to $53

VETERINARIANS
Albany County Vetny Hospital
1506 Western Avenue
Phone: (518) 456-6333

Central Veterinary Hospital
388 Central Avenue
Phone: (518) 434-2115

Colonie Animal Hospital
1946 Central Avenue
Phone: (518) 456-1613

AMHERST

Lord Amherst
5000 Main St.
Amherst, NY 14226
Phone: (716) 839-2200,
  (800) 544-2200

Pet Restrictions: None
Exercise Area for Pets: Yes
Rates: $59 to $99

Motel 6
4400 Maple Rd.
Amherst, NY 14226
Phone: (716) 834-2231

Pet Restrictions: Quiet at night,
  must be caged for room service
Exercise Area for Pets: Yes
Rates: $48 plus $6/person

Red Roof Inn - Amherst
42 Flint Rd.
Amherst, NY 14226
Phone: (716) 689-7474,
  (800) 843-7663 (central res.)

Pet Restrictions: Up to 10 lbs.
Pet left unattended in room: Yes
Exercise Area for Pets: Yes
Rates: $38.99 to $70

VETERINARIANS
Greater Buffalo Vetny Svcs.
4949 Main St.
Phone: (716) 839-4044

AVOCA

Goodrich Center Motel
Rte. 415
Avoca, NY 14809
Phone: (607) 566-2216

Pet Restrictions: None
Exercise Area for Pets: Yes
Rates: $38 to $60, $4/extra person

BATAVIA

Sheraton Inn Batavia
8250 Park Rd.
Batavia, NY 14020
Phone: (716) 344-2100

Pet Restrictions: Must sign pet
  waiver, deposit $25/night
  (refundable), room will not be
  serviced if dog is alone
Exercise Area for Pets: Yes
Rates: $60 to $110

Treadway Inn Batavia
8204 Park Rd.
Batavia, NY 14020
Phone: (716) 343-1000,
    (800) 228-2842
Pet Restrictions: None
Exercise Area for Pets: Yes
Rates: $48 to $80

VETERINARIANS
Batavia Animal Hospital
3699 W. Main Rd.
Phone: (716) 343-4046

BINGHAMTON
Howard Johnson's Inn
700 Front St.
Binghamton, NY 13905
Phone: (607) 724-1341,
    (800) 446-4646 (central res.)
Pet Restrictions: Not in non-
    smoking room
Pet left unattended in room: Yes
Exercise Area for Pets: Yes
Rates: $39.95 to $95.95

VETERINARIANS
Chenango Valley Animal Hosp.
1443 Front St.
Phone: (607) 724-3033

BUFFALO
Holiday Inn Downtown
620 Delaware Ave.
Buffalo, NY 14202
Phone: (716) 886-2121
    (800) 465-1329
Pet Restrictions: None
Pet left unattended in room: Yes, if
    caged
Exercise Area for Pets: Yes
Rates: $72 to $93

Wellesley Inn Buffalo Airport
4630 Genesee St.
Buffalo, NY 14225
Phone: (716) 631-8966,
    (800) 444-8888
Pet Restrictions: $5 charge
Exercise Area for Pets: Yes
Rates: $57 to $75

VETERINARIANS
Blue Cross Small Animal Clinic
3921 Main St.
Phone: (716) 832-2800

Ellicott Small Animal Hospital
455 Ellicott St.
Phone: (716) 852-8276

Town and Country Animal Clinic
3095 Genesee St.
Phone: (716) 896-2424

CAMBRIDGE
Town House Motor Inn
RR2, Box 140 or 56 North Park St.
Cambridge, NY 12816
Phone: (518) 677-5524
Pet Restrictions: None, deposit
    $25/stay
Pet left unattended in room: Yes,
    short time only
Exercise Area for Pets: Yes
Rates: $45

CANANDAIGUA
Econo Lodge Muar Lake
170 Eastern Blvd.
Canandaigua, NY 14424
Phone: (716) 394-9000,
    (800) 424-4777
Pet Restrictions: Proof of rabies
    vaccine, must sign pet waiver
Exercise Area for Pets: Yes
Rates: $37.75 to $65.95

VETERINARIANS
Ferraglio, Susan
4410 Lakeshore Dr.
Phone: (716) 394-3340

CANTON
Best Western Univ. Inn
Rt. 11
Canton, NY 13617
Phone: (315) 386-8522,
    (800) 528-1234 (central res.)
Pet Restrictions: Well behaved
Pet left unattended in room: Yes,
    notify desk
Exercise Area for Pets: Yes
Rates: $55 to $90

CASTLETON-ON-HUDSON

Bel-Air Motel
RD 2
Castleton-On-Hudson, NY 12033
Phone: (518) 732-7744

Pet Restrictions: 1 room only, $4/day
Pet left unattended in room: Yes, if caged
Exercise Area for Pets: Yes
Rates: $39.95 to $55

CAZENOVIA

Lincklaen House
79 Albany St., Box 36
Cazenovia, NY 13035
Phone: (315) 655-3461

Pet Restrictions: None, leash law
Pet left unattended in room: Yes but no service
Exercise Area for Pets: Nearby
Rates: $70 to $130

CHEEKTOWAGA

Holiday Inn Gateway
601 Dingens St.
Cheektowaga, NY 14206
Phone: (716) 896-2900,
    (800) 465-1329 (central res.)

Pet Restrictions: Small & well trained, quiet, deposit $10/stay
Exercise Area for Pets: Yes, clean up after pet
Rates: $76 to $87

VETERINARIANS

Keem, Michael D.
957 Dick Rd.
Phone: (716) 634-8736

COBLESKILL

Best Western Inn of Cobleskill
P.O. Box 189
Cobleskill, NY 12043
Phone: (518) 234-4321

Pet Restrictions: None
Exercise Area for Pets: Yes
Rates: $56 to $89

COMMACK

Howard Johnson Bed & Breakfast
450 Moreland Rd.
Commack, NY 11725
Phone: (516) 864-8820,
    (800) 446-4646 (central res.)

Pet Restrictions: Quiet
Pet left unattended in room: Yes but no housekeeping
Exercise Area for Pets: Nearby
Rates: $65 to $85

CORFU

Darien Lakes Econo Lodge
8493 Rt. 77
Corfu, NY 14036
Phone: (716) 599-4681,
    (800) 424-4777 (central res.)

Pet Restrictions: Must be caged all the time
Pet left unattended in room: Yes if quiet
Exercise Area for Pets: Yes
Rates: $42.95 to $75

DELHI

Buena Vista Motel
1 mile south on SR 28
Delhi, NY 13753
Phone: (607) 746-2135

Pet Restrictions: Dogs only
Exercise Area for Pets: Yes
Rates: $40 to $57

DUNKIRK

South Shore Motor Lodge
5040 W. Lake Rd.
Dunkirk, NY 14048
Phone: (716) 366-2822

Pet Restrictions: Dogs only, cottages only, clean up after
Exercise Area for Pets: Yes

EAST HAMPTON

Dutch Motel
488 Montauk Hwy
East Hampton, NY 11937
Phone: (516) 324-4550

Pet Restrictions: 5 rooms only, deposit $7/night
Exercise Area for Pets: Nearby
Rates: $55 to $145

ELMIRA

Coachman Motor Lodge
908 Pennsylvania Ave.
Elmira, NY 14904
Phone: (607) 733-5526

Pet Restrictions: Small pets
Exercise Area for Pets: Yes
Rates: $53 to $63

Holiday Inn - Downtown
1 Holiday Plaza
Elmira, NY 14901
Phone: (607) 734-4211

Pet Restrictions: None
Pet left unattended in room: Yes
Exercise Area for Pets: Yes
Rates: $60 to $90

VETERINARIANS

Broadway Animal Hospital
855 Broadway
Phone: (607) 734-1272

Yealy, Jeanne E.
511½ W. Hudson St.
Phone: (607) 733-3916

ELMSFORD

Ramada Inn
540 Sawmill River Rd.
Elmsford, NY 10523
Phone: (914) 592-3300

Pet Restrictions: None
Exercise Area for Pets: Yes
Rates: $69.50 to $124.50

FALCONER

Motel 6
1980 E. Main St.
Falconer, NY 14733
Phone: (716) 665-3670

Pet Restrictions: Small pets, 1 per
   room, no snakes
Exercise Area for Pets: Yes
Rates: $31.99 to $37.99

FLEISCHMANNS

River Run
Main Street
Fleischmanns, NY 12430
Phone: (914) 254-4884

Pet Restrictions: Dogs only, if quiet
Pet left unattended in room: Yes
Exercise Area for Pets: Yes
Rates: $45 to $85

FREDONIA

Days Inn
10455 Bennett Rd.
Fredonia, NY 14063
Phone: (716) 673-1351

Pet Restrictions: None, must pay for
   damages
Pet left unattended in room: Yes
Exercise Area for Pets: Yes
Rates: $39.95 to $60

FULTONVILLE

The Poplar's Inn
Riverside Dr.
Fultonville, NY 12072
Phone: (518) 853-4511

Pet Restrictions: None
Pet left unattended in room: Yes
Exercise Area for Pets: Yes
Rates: $43.20 to $60

VETERINARIANS

Van Wagenen, Victor F.
RD 1, Box 5F
Phone: (518) 853-3835

GLEN FALLS

Queensbury Motel
88 Ridge St.
Glen Falls, NY 12801
Phone: (518) 792-1121,
   (800) 554-4526

Pet Restrictions: Small pets, well
   behaved, responsible for damages
Exercise Area for Pets: Nearby
Rates: $62 to $124

Ramada Inn Glen Falls
I87 & Aviation Rd.
Glen Falls, NY 12801
Phone: (518) 793-7701,
   (800) 272-6232 (central res.)

Pet Restrictions: None
Exercise Area for Pets: Yes
Rates: $69 to $128

VETERINARIANS

Glens Falls Animal Hospital
66 Glenwood Avenue
Phone: (518) 792-6575

Edwards, Allen
RR #1 Box 110
Phone: (518) 793-6663

Evans, Patricia A.
108 Main St.
Phone: (518) 793-0994

NEW YORK — HOTELS (continued)

GRAND ISLAND

Chateau Motor Lodge
1810 Grand Island Blvd.
Grand Island, NY 14072
Phone: (716) 773-2868

Pet Restrictions: Small pets, must
be housebroken, responsible for
damages, pet deposit
Exercise Area for Pets: Yes
Rates: $39 to $69

Holiday Inn on Grand Island
100 Whitehaven Rd.
Grand Island, NY 14072
Phone: (716) 773-1111,
(800) 465-4329 (central res.)

Pet Restrictions: Small pets, 1st
floor only, credit card imprint in
case of damage, more than 3
complaints you will be asked to
leave
Pet left unattended in room: Yes
Exercise Area for Pets: Yes
Rates: $70 to $120

Grand Isl. Small Animal Hosp.
2323 Whitehaven Rd.
Phone: (716) 773-7645

Loree, Ruth L.
2057 Bush Rd.
Phone: (716) 773-3131

HAMBURG
Red Roof Inn
5370 Camp Rd.
Hamburg, NY 14075
Phone: (716) 648-7222

Pet Restrictions: None
Pet left unattended in room: Yes, no
housekeeping
Exercise Area for Pets: Yes
Rates: $45 to $61

Swart, Donald A.
5576 Camp Rd.
(716) 649-6865

HENRIETTA
Red Roof Inn
4820 W. Henrietta Rd.
Henrietta, NY 14467
Phone: (716) 359-1100,
(800) 843-7663 (central res.)

Pet Restrictions: Special rooms for
pets, notify front desk
Pet left unattended in room: Yes but
room will not be serviced
Exercise Area for Pets: Yes
Rates: $34 to $70

Henrietta Animal Hospital
3156 E. Henrietta Rd.
Phone: (716) 334-3800

HERKIMER
Herkimer Motel
100 Marginal Rd.
Herkimer, NY 13350
Phone: (315) 866-0490

Pet Restrictions: None
Exercise Area for Pets: Yes
Rates: $38 to $82

HICKSVILLE
Econo Lodge
429 Duffy Ave.
Hicksville, NY 11801
Phone: (516) 433-3900

Pet Restrictions: Dogs & cats only
Pet left unattended in room: Yes,
room will not be serviced unless
pet is caged
Exercise Area for Pets: Yes
Rates: $60 to $80

Mid-Island Animal Hospital
264 Old Country Rd.
Phone: (516) 681-5477

HORSEHEADS
Holiday Inn
602 Corning Rd.
Horseheads, NY 14845
Phone: (607) 739-3681

Pet Restrictions: Small pets
Exercise Area for Pets: Yes
Rates: $60 to $90

Howard Johnson Lodge
Rt. 17 & 14
Horseheads, NY 14845
Phone: (607) 739-5636

Pet Restrictions: None
Exercise Area for Pets: Yes
Rates: $42 to $64

ITHACA
Howard Johnson Lodge
2700 North Triphammer Rd.
Ithaca, NY 14850
Phone: (607) 257-1212

Pet Restrictions: Small pets only
Pet left unattended in room: Yes
Exercise Area for Pets: Yes
Rates: $45 to $80

Ithaca Ramada Inn & Executive Towers
222 S. Cayuga St.
Ithaca, NY 14850
Phone: (607) 272-1000,
    (800) 753-8485

Pet Restrictions: Main building only,
    deposit $10/stay
Pet left unattended in room: Yes,
    must be caged
Exercise Area for Pets: Yes
Rates: $60 to $90

VETERINARIANS
Colonial Veterinary Hospital
2369 N. Triphammer
Phone: (607) 257-3650

Cornell Univ. Veterinary Med.
(607) 253-3030

Slater, Margaret R.
203 Snyder Hill Rd.
Phone: (607) 253-3572

JAMAICA
Travelodge
Van Wyck Expwy (JFK Bldg. 144)
Jamaica, NY 11430
Phone: (718) 995-9000

Pet Restrictions: $30/stay deposit
Exercise Area for Pets: Nearby
Rates: $119 to $129

VETERINARIANS
Animal Hospital of Queens Blvd.
139-54 Queens Blvd.
Phone: (718) 291-0200

JAMESTOWN
Comfort Inn
2800 N. Main St. Extension
Jamestown, NY 14701
Phone: (716) 664-5920,
    (800) 453-7155

Pet Restrictions: Must sign release
    form in case of damages
Exercise Area for Pets: Yes
Rates: $52.95 to $59.95

VETERINARIANS
Jamestown Veterinary Hosp.
236 Fluvanna Ave.
Phone: (716) 664-4204

Pet Animal Hospital
9 Glidden Avenue West
Phone: (716) 483-1762

JOHNSON CITY
Red Roof Inn
590 Fairview St.
Johnson City, NY 13790
Phone: (607) 729-8940

Pet Restrictions: None
Pet left unattended in room: Yes,
    notify front desk
Exercise Area for Pets: Yes
Rates: $40 to $61

KINGSTON
Holiday Inn Kingston
503 Wash. Ave.
Kingston, NY 12401
Phone: (914) 338-0400

Pet Restrictions: None
Exercise Area for Pets: Yes
Rates: $59 to $129

Howard Johnson Lodge
129 Rte. 28
Kingston, NY 12401
Phone: (914) 338-4200

Pet Restrictions: No snakes
Pet left unattended in room: Yes, if
    caged
Exercise Area for Pets: Yes
Rates: $47 to $68

VETERINARIANS

Hoppenstedt Animal Hospital
RD #4 Rosendale Rd.
Phone: (914) 331-1050

Ulster Animal Hospital
Route 32, Flatbush Rd.
Phone: (914) 336-8700

Rugg, Arnold
456 Albany Ave.
Phone: (914) 331-0240

LAKE GEORGE

Econo-Lodge Lake George Motel
431 Canada St.
Lake George, NY 12845
Phone: (518) 668-2689,
    (800) 477-3529

Pet Restrictions: Well trained, 5
    rooms only, 1st floor type B
    room, deposit $3-$5/day
    according to size
Pet left unattended in room: Yes
Exercise Area for Pets: Nearby
Rates: $77 to $98

LAKE PLACID

**Best Western
Golden Arrow Hotel**
150 Main St.
Lake Placid, NY 12946
Phone: (518) 523-3353
Fax: (518) 523-3353, Ext. 614

Pet Restrictions: One time Pet Fee
    $10-$25 rooms with 2 double
    beds/first floor, north wing, on
    lake
Pet left unattended in room: No
Exercise Area for Pets: Yes
Rates: $70 to $138

Howard Johnson Resort Lodge
90 Saranac Ave.
Lake Placid, NY 12946
Phone: (518) 523-9555,
    (800) 858-4656

Pet Restrictions: None
Exercise Area for Pets: Yes
Rates: $45 to $150

LANCASTER

Red Roof Inn
146 Maple Dr.
Lancaster, NY 14026
Phone: (716) 633-1100

Pet Restrictions: 1 small house pet
Pet left unattended in room: Yes,
    notify
Exercise Area for Pets: Yes
Rates: $40 to $60

VETERINARIANS

Burgwardt, Meldina R.
5600 Broadway
(716) 681-5676

LATHAM

Comfort Inn Airport
866 Albany Shaker Rd.
Latham, NY 12110
Phone: (518) 783-1216,
    (800) 274-9429

Pet Restrictions: None
Exercise Area for Pets: Yes
Rates: $49 to $70

Howard Johnson Lodge
611 Troy Schenectady Rd.
Latham, NY 12946
Phone: (518) 785-5891

Pet Restrictions: Responsible for
    damages
Pet left unattended in room: Yes but
    no room service
Exercise Area for Pets: Nearby
Rates: $33.50 to $78

VETERINARIANS

Capitaland Animal Hospital
890 Troy-Schenectady
Phone: (518) 785-5531

Shaker Veterinary Hospital
223 Maxwell Rd.
Phone: (518) 458-9669

LIBERTY

Holiday Inn Express
Rtes. 17 & 52
Liberty, NY 12754
Phone: (914) 292-7171

Pet Restrictions: Dogs and cats
    only. Allowed in hallway rooms
    only.
Pet left unattended in room: Yes if
    quiet
Exercise Area for Pets: Yes
Rates: $50 to $80

LITTLE FALLS

Best West. Little Falls Motor Inn
20 Albany St.
Little Falls, NY 13365
Phone: (315) 823-4954

Pet Restrictions: Deposit $10/stay
Pet left unattended in room: Yes
Exercise Area for Pets: Yes
Rates: $48 to $60

LIVERPOOL

Arborgate Inn
430 Electronics Pkwy
Liverpool, NY 13088
Phone: (315) 453-6330

Pet Restrictions: Leash law, $5/day
Pet left unattended in room: Yes but
no room service unless caged
Exercise Area for Pets: Yes
Rates: $35.95 to $53.95

Econo Lodge Syracuse-Liverpool
401 7th North St.
Liverpool, NY 13088
Phone: (315) 451-6000

Pet Restrictions: $3/night, smoking
room, 1 pet per room
Exercise Area for Pets: Nearby
Rates: $40 to $45

VETERINARIANS

Liverpool Animal Health Center
8203 Oswego Rd.
Phone: (315) 622-2882

Liverpool Veterinary Hospital
7906 Oswego Rd.
Phone: (315) 652-6216

Liverpool Village Animal Hosp.
206 Salina St.
Phone: (315) 451-5455

MASSENA

Econo Lodge Meadow View Motel
Rt 37
Massena, NY 13662
Phone: (315) 764-0246

Pet Restrictions: 6 rooms only, cats
& dogs only
Exercise Area for Pets: Yes
Rates: $50 to $63

McGRAW

Econo Lodge of Cortland
3775 US Rt 11
McGraw, NY 13101
Phone: (607) 753-7594

Pet Restrictions: Small pets
Exercise Area for Pets: Yes
Rates: $39 to $55

MIDDLETOWN

Middletown Motel
501 Rt. 211 E
Middletown, NY 10940
Phone: (914) 342-2535

Pet Restrictions: Smoking rooms only
Pet left unattended in room: Yes if
quiet, no room service
Exercise Area for Pets: Yes
Rates: $49.95 to $99.95

Super 8 Lodge
563 Rt. 211 E
Middletown, NY 10940
Phone: (914) 692-5828

Pet Restrictions: Deposit $25/stay
refundable
Pet left unattended in room: Yes
Exercise Area for Pets: Yes
Rates: $55.88 and up

VETERINARIANS

Animal Clinic Lloyds
Route 211
Phone: (914) 343-1323

Middletown Veterinary Hosp.
189 Wawayanda Ave.
Phone: (914) 343-7012

Orange Community Pet Hospital
7 Beakes Rd.
Phone: (914) 343-4364

MONTAUK

Sepp's Surf-Sound Cottages
Ditch Plains Rd.
Montauk, NY 11954
Phone: (516) 668-2215

Pet Restrictions: None
Exercise Area for Pets: Yes
Rates: $80 and up

MT. KISCO

Holiday Inn
1 Holiday Dr.
Mt. Kisco, NY 10549
Phone: (914) 241-2600

Pet Restrictions: None
Exercise Area for Pets: Yes, no
   room service
Rates: $96 and up

VETERINARIANS

Haddad, Joseph E.
474 Lexington Avenue
Phone: (914) 241-3337

NEW YORK

Box Tree
250 E. 49th St.
New York, NY 10017
Phone: (212) 758-8320

Pet Restrictions: None
Pet left unattended in room: Yes
Exercise Area for Pets: Nearby
Rates: $160 to $260

Carlyle
Madison Ave. at E. 76th St.
New York, NY 10021
Phone: (212) 744-1600
   (800) 227-5737

Pet Restrictions: $10/day
Pet left unattended in room: Yes
Exercise Area for Pets: Nearby
Rates: $250 to $375

Inn on 57th Street
440 W. 57th St.
New York, NY 10019
Phone: (212) 581-8100

Pet Restrictions: $10/night
Exercise Area for Pets: Nearby
Rates: $89.99 to $159

Essex House
160 Central Park S.
New York, NY 10019
Phone: (212) 247-0300
   (800) 645-5687

Pet Restrictions: $100/stay ($75
   refundable)
Exercise Area for Pets: Nearby
Rates: $195 to $245

Four Seasons, The Pierre
5th Ave. at 61st
New York, NY 10019
Phone: (212) 838-8000,
   (800) 743-7734

Pet Restrictions: Leashed in
   hallways
Pet left unattended in room: Yes
Exercise Area for Pets: Nearby
Rates: $280 to $1600

The Lowell
28 E 63rd St.
New York, NY 10021
Phone: (212) 838-1400,
   (800) 221-4444

Pet Restrictions: Sign pet waiver,
   small-medium size pets only
Pet left unattended in room: Yes
Exercise Area for Pets: Nearby
Rates: $290 to $1500

Marriott Marquis
1535 Broadway
New York, NY 10036
Phone: (212) 398-1900,
   (800) 228-9290 (central res.)

Pet Restrictions: Leave credit card
   imprint
Pet left unattended in room: Yes, for
   service pet must be caged or
   owner present
Exercise Area for Pets: Nearby
Rates: $159 to $350

Mayflower Hotel
15 Central Park W.
New York, NY 10023
Phone: (212) 265-0600,
   (800) 223-4164

Pet Restrictions: None
Pet left unattended in room: Yes
Exercise Area for Pets: Nearby
Rates: $145 to $165

New York Hilton & Towers at Rockefeller Center
1335 Ave. of the Americas
New York City, NY 10019
Phone: (212) 586-7000

Pet Restrictions: Sign release for
   damages
Pet left unattended in room: Yes
Exercise Area for Pets: Nearby
Rates: $159 to $279

Novotel N.Y.
226 W. 52nd St.
New York, NY 10019
Phone: (212) 315-0100,
(800) 221-3185
Pet Restrictions: Notify in advance
Pet left unattended in room: Yes
Exercise Area for Pets: Nearby
Rates: $109 to $169

The Plaza
Fifth Ave. at Central Park South
New York, NY 10019
Phone: (212) 759-3000,
(800) 759-3000
Pet Restrictions: Small pets only
Exercise Area for Pets: Nearby
Rates: $175 to $1400

The Plaza Athenee
37 E. 64th St.
New York, NY 10021
Phone: (212) 734-9100
Pet Restrictions: Very small dogs &
cats only
Pet left unattended in room: Yes,
only in cage
Exercise Area for Pets: Nearby
Rates: $275 to $390

Sheraton Park Ave.
45 Park Ave.
New York, NY 10016
Phone: (212) 685-7676,
(800) 537-0075
Pet Restrictions: Very small pets only
Pet left unattended in room: Yes if
caged
Exercise Area for Pets: Nearby
Rates: $135 to $270

VETERINARIANS

Animal Medical Center
510 East 62nd Street
Phone: (212) 838-8100

Bergh Memorial Animal Hosp. of the ASPCA
441 East 92nd St.
Phone: (212) 876-7700

Westside Veterinary Clinic
220 West 83rd St.
Phone: (212) 580-1800

NEWBURGH

Howard Johnson Lodge
95 Rte. 17K
Newburgh, NY 12550
Phone: (914) 564-4000
Pet Restrictions: None
Pet left unattended in room: Yes, if
quiet
Exercise Area for Pets: Yes
Rates: $60 to $85

VETERINARIANS

Flannery Animal Hospital
1006 Union Ave.
Phone: (914) 564-6760

Ackerman, David B.
384 N. Plank Rd.
Phone: (914) 564-2660

NIAGARA FALLS

Holiday Inn on Buffalo Ave.
114 Buffalo Ave.
Niagara Falls, NY 14303
Phone: (716) 285-2521
Pet Restrictions: Small pets,
chaperoned at all times
Exercise Area for Pets: Nearby
Rates: $59 to $125

Howard Johnson Motor Lodge-East
6505 Niagara Falls Blvd.
Niagara Falls, NY 14304
Phone: (716) 283-8791
Pet Restrictions: None
Pet left unattended in room: Yes,
well-behaved
Exercise Area for Pets: Yes
Rates: $39 to $96

Pelican Motel
6817 Niagara Falls Blvd.
Niagara Falls, NY 14304
Phone: (716) 283-2278
Pet Restrictions: House-trained
Pet left unattended in room: Yes
Exercise Area for Pets: Yes
Rates: $29 to $99

Ramada Inn
401 Buffalo Ave.
Niagara Falls, NY 14303
Phone: (716) 285-2541
Pet Restrictions: 1st floor rooms
only, must sign pet waiver
Exercise Area for Pets: Yes
Rates: $49 to $129

VETERINARIANS

Ford Veterinary Hospital
527 Hyde Park Blvd.
Phone: (716) 285-5734

Leveson, Lawrence
151 Buffalo Ave. #1204
Phone: (716) 282-6682

NORWICH

Howard Johnson Hotel
75 N. Broad St.
Norwich, NY 13815
Phone: (607) 334-2200
Pet Restrictions: Leashed in public
    areas of building
Pet left unattended in room: Yes
Exercise Area for Pets: Nearby
Rates: $50 to $100

OSWEGO

Sunrise Motel
Rt 17C West, Box 249
Oswego, NY 13827
Phone: (607) 687-5666
Pet Restrictions: $2 fee/day, not too
    big
Pet left unattended in room: Yes
Exercise Area for Pets: Yes
Rates: $32.65 to $49

PAINTED POST

Stiles Motel
9239 Victory Hwy
Painted Post, NY 14870
Phone: (607) 962-5221,
    (800) 331-3920
Pet Restrictions: Leash law, deposit
    $3/day/pet
Exercise Area for Pets: Yes
Rates: $22 to $42

PLATTSBURGH

Howard Johnson Lodge
Rt. 3
Plattsburgh, NY 12901
Phone: (518) 561-7750,
    (800) 243-4656
Pet Restrictions: Well-behaved
Pet left unattended in room: Yes
Exercise Area for Pets: Yes
Rates: $52 to $83

ROCHESTER

Comfort Inn
395 Buell Rd.
Rochester, NY 14624
Phone: (716) 436-4400
    (800) 221-2222
Pet Restrictions: None
Exercise Area for Pets: Yes
Rates: $39 to $59.95

Comfort Inn - West
1501 W. Ridge Rd.
Rochester, NY 14615
Phone: (800) 221-2222 (central res.)
Pet Restrictions: Must sign a pet
    waiver
Pet left unattended in room: Yes
Exercise Area for Pets: Yes
Rates: $59.95 to $74.95

Econo Lodge
940 Jefferson Rd.
Rochester, NY 14623
Phone: (716) 427-2700
Pet Restrictions: Small pets only
Exercise Area for Pets: Yes
Rates: $35 to $49.95

Hampton Inn
717 E. Hampton Rd.
Rochester, NY 14623
Phone: (716) 272-7800,
    (800) 426-7896
Pet Restrictions: Must sign waiver
Exercise Area for Pets: Yes
Rates: $60 to $77

Holiday Inn - Airport
911 Brooks Ave.
Rochester, NY 14624
Phone: (716) 328-6000
Pet Restrictions: Small pets
Exercise Area for Pets: Yes
Rates: $90 to $116

Holiday Inn - Genesee Plaza
120 Main St. E.
Rochester, NY 14604
Phone: (716) 546-6400
Pet Restrictions: None
Pet left unattended in room: Yes
Exercise Area for Pets: Yes
Rates: $96 to $106

Howard Johnson Airport Hotel
1100 Brooks Ave.
Rochester, NY 14624
Phone: (716) 235-6030
Pet Restrictions: Small, house
trained
Pet left unattended in room: Yes
Exercise Area for Pets: Yes
Rates: $65 to $79

Marketplace Inn
800 Jefferson Rd.
Rochester, NY 14623
Phone: (716) 475-9190,
(800) 888-8102
Pet Restrictions: Medium size, sign
liability agreement to clean up or
pay for damage
Pet left unattended in room: Yes if
caged
Exercise Area for Pets: Yes
Rates: $59 to $75

Marriott Airport
1890 W. Ridge Rd.
Rochester, NY 14615
Phone: (716) 225-6880
Pet Restrictions: 1st floor rooms,
responsible for damages
Exercise Area for Pets: Yes
Rates: $85 to $99

Residence Inn by Marriott
1300 Jeff. Rd.
Rochester, NY 14623
Phone: (716) 272-8850
Pet Restrictions: Leashed in public
areas of hotel, deposit $8/day
Pet left unattended in room: Yes
Exercise Area for Pets: Yes
Rates: $108 to $114

Wellesley Inn
797 E. Henrietta Rd.
Rochester, NY 14623
Phone: (716) 427-0130,
(800) 444-8888
Pet Restrictions: $3/day, small and
medium only
Rates: $41 to $75

Wellesley Inn - Greece
1635 W. Ridge Rd.
Rochester, NY 14615
Phone: (716) 621-2060,
(800) 444-8888
Pet Restrictions: $5/day
Pet left unattended in room: Yes but
no service
Exercise Area for Pets: Yes
Rates: $43.95 to $85

VETERINARIANS

Animal Hospital of Pittsford
41 E. Squire Dr. #4
Phone: (716) 271-7700

East Ridge Animal Hospital
1825 Ridge Rd. East
Phone: (716) 467-2120

Wiseman, Linda
617 Paul Rd.
Phone: (716) 889-3662

ROCK HILL
Howard Johnson Motor Lodge
P.O. Box 469
Rock Hill, NY 12775
Phone: (914) 796-3000
Pet Restrictions: $50 dep. refund.
Exercise Area for Pets: Yes if quiet
and well-behaved
Exercise Area for Pets: Yes
Rates: $65 to $89

ROME
Adirondack 13 Pines Motel
7353 River Rd.
Rome, NY 13440
Phone: (315) 337-4930
Pet Restrictions: None
Exercise Area for Pets: Yes
Rates: $30 to $45

Family Inns of America
145 E. Whitesboro St.
Rome, NY 13440
Phone: (315) 337-9400
(800) 348-3377
Pet Restrictions: None
Pet left unattended in room: Yes but
no service
Exercise Area for Pets: Yes
Rates: $39.77

SARATOGA SPRINGS
Holiday Inn
Broadway at Circular St.
Saratoga Springs, NY 12866
Phone: (518) 584-4550
Pet Restrictions: Well-behaved
Pet left unattended in room: Yes
Exercise Area for Pets: Nearby
Rates: $49 to $189

VETERINARIANS

Saratoga Veterinary Hospital
Phone: (518) 587-3832

Manning, James L.
86 Congress St.
Phone: (518) 583-0609

SAVGERTIES
Howard Johnson Lodge
1001 Rte. 32
Savgerties, NY 12477
Phone: (914) 246-9511
    (800) 654-2000

Pet Restrictions: None
Pet left unattended in room: Yes
Exercise Area for Pets: Yes
Rates: $57 to $80

VETERINARIANS
Rothstein, Howard
163 Ulster Avenue
Phone: (914) 246-6150

SOUTH BUFFALO
Howard Johnson Inn
5245 Camp Rd.
South Buffalo, NY 14075
Phone: (716) 648-2000

Pet Restrictions: None
Exercise Area for Pets: Yes, must
    be leashed
Rates: $38 to $65

SPRING GLEN
Gold Mountain Chalet Resort
Tice Road, Box 456
Spring Glen, NY 12483
Phone: (800) 295-5200

Pet Restrictions: Up to 100 lbs. on
    leash. We provide pooper
    scoopers. Not allowed in
    restaurant or by pools
Pet left unattended in room: Yes
Exercise Area for Pets: Yes
Other: Minnawaska State Park; Ice
    Cave National Monument
Rates: $218 to $359

STAMFORD
Red Carpet Motor Inn
Jct. SR 10 & 23
Stamford, NY 12167
Phone: (607) 652-7394,
    (800) 932-1090

Pet Restrictions: None
Pet left unattended in room: Yes,
    brief period of time only
Exercise Area for Pets: Yes
Rates: $48 to $68

SUFFERN
Wellesley Inn
17 N. Airmont Rd.
Suffern, NY 10901
Phone: (914) 368-1900,
    (800) 444-8888 (central res.)

Pet Restrictions: $3/day, no snakes
Pet left unattended in room: Yes
Exercise Area for Pets: Yes
Rates: $55 to $80

VETERINARIANS
French, James M.
8 Chestnut St.
Phone: (914) 357-0317

SYRACUSE
Days Inn - Syracuse East
6609 Thompson Rd. at Carrier Circle
Syracuse, NY 13206
Phone: (315) 437-5998,
    (800) 325-2525

Pet Restrictions: $3 fee/day,
    smoking rooms only
Exercise Area for Pets: Yes
Rates: $40 to $60

Holiday Inn
6701 Buckley Rd.
N. Syracuse, NY 13212
Phone: (315) 457-4000

Pet Restrictions: None
Pet left unattended in room: Yes,
    notify desk
Exercise Area for Pets: Nearby
Rates: $69 to $89

Howard Johnson Lodge
Thompson Rd. & Carrier Circle
Syracuse, NY 13206
Phone: (315) 437-2711

Pet Restrictions: Well-behaved,
    small pets
Pet left unattended in room: Yes
Exercise Area for Pets: Yes
Rates: $52 to $85

Red Roof Inn
6614 N. Thompson Rd.
Syracuse, NY 13206
Phone: (315) 437-3309,
    (800) 843-7663 (central res.)

Pet Restrictions: None
Exercise Area for Pets: Yes
Rates: $48.99 to $64.99

VETERINARIANS

Boulevard Animal Hospital
2406 Erie Blvd. East
Phone: (315) 446-7740

Fairmount Animal Hospital
3705 W. Genesee St.
Phone: (315) 468-3446

Stack Veterinary Hospital
5092 Velasko Rd.
Phone: (315) 478-3161

UNIONDALE

Long Island Marriott
101 James Doolittle Blvd.
Uniondale, NY 11553
Phone: (516) 794-3800
Pet Restrictions: Leashed out of
    room & on property
Pet left unattended in room: Yes
Exercise Area for Pets: Nearby
Rates: $99 to $135

VETERINARIANS

Hempstead Animal Hospital
1138 Hempstead Turnpike
Phone: (516) 481-1332

UTICA

Howard Johnson Lodge
302 North Genesee St.
Utica, NY 13502
Phone: (315) 724-4141
Pet Restrictions: None
Exercise Area for Pets: Yes
Rates: $35 to $85

Red Roof Inn
20 Weaver St.
Utica, NY 13502
Phone: (315) 724-7128
Pet Restrictions: Small pets only
Pet left unattended in room: Yes
Exercise Area for Pets: Yes
Rates: $50 to $65

VETERINARIANS

De Bliss Animal Hospital
5674 Horatio St. Arterial
Phone: (315) 724-0182

VALATIE

Blue Spruce Motel
Rt 9
Valatie, NY 12184
Phone: (518) 758-9711
Pet Restrictions: Cats & dogs only
Exercise Area for Pets: Yes
Rates: $42 to $60

VESTAL

Holiday Inn S.U.N.Y.
4105 Vestal Pkwy.
Vestal, NY 13850
Phone: (607) 729-6371,
    (800) 465-4329 (central res.)
Pet Restrictions: Notify in advance,
    $10/day
Exercise Area for Pets: Yes
Rates: $49.95 to $100

Residence Inn by Marriott
4610 Vestal Pkwy. E
Vestal, NY 13850
Phone: (607) 770-8500,
    (800) 331-3131 (central res.)
Pet Restrictions: $250 refundable
    deposit, fee $10/day
Pet left unattended in room: Yes, no
    room service unless caged
Exercise Area for Pets: Yes
Rates: $99 and up

VETERINARIANS

The Vestal Veterinary Hospital
2316 Vestal Parkway
Phone: (607) 754-3933

Valley Animal Hospital
205 Front St.
Phone: (607) 754-7164

WATKINS GLEN

Glen Motor Inn
3380 Rt 14
Watkins Glen, NY 14891
Phone: (607) 535-2706
Pet Restrictions: Well-behaved
Pet left unattended in room: Yes but
    no room service
Exercise Area for Pets: Yes
Rates: $73 to $90

WAVERLY

O'Brien's Inn; America's Most Scenic
Waverly Hill
Waverly, NY 14892
Phone: (607) 565-2817

Pet Restrictions: $10/refundable deposit
Pet left unattended in room: Yes
Exercise Area for Pets: Yes
Rates: $43 to $58

WEEDSPORT

Best Western Weedsport Inn
2709 Erie Dr.
Weedsport, NY 13166
Phone: (315) 834-6623

Pet Restrictions: $2/day/pet, no large animals
Pet left unattended in room: Yes, if well-behaved
Exercise Area for Pets: Yes
Rates: $37 to $76

VETERINARIANS
Weedsport Animal Hospital
2602 West Brutus
Phone: (315) 834-6432

WEST NYACK

Nyack Motor Lodge
Rt. 303
West Nyack, NY 10994
Phone: (914) 358-4100

Pet Restrictions: Deposit $25/stay
Pet left unattended in room: Yes but no room service unless caged
Exercise Area for Pets: Yes
Rates: $44.59 to $68.75

WILLIAMSVILLE

Residence Inn by Marriott, Buffalo
100 Maple Rd.
Williamsville, NY 14221
Phone: (716) 632-6622,
      (800) 331-3131

Pet Restrictions: Limited to certain buildings, $3/day/pet
Pet left unattended in room: Yes but no room service unless caged
Exercise Area for Pets: Yes, must be leashed
Rates: $80 to $200

Wellesley Inn Buffalo Airport
4630 Genesee St.
Williamsville, NY 14225
Phone: (716) 631-8966,
      (800) 444-8888 (central res.)

Pet Restrictions: $5/night
Pet left unattended in room: Yes only if caged
Exercise Area for Pets: Yes
Rates: $44 to $65

VETERINARIANS
Afton Animal Hospital
6543 Main St.
Phone: (714) 634-0344

Georgetown Small Animal Clinic
5155 Sheridan Dr.
Phone: (716) 633-7123

Harris Hill Animal Hospital
8470 Main St.
Phone: (716) 634-1000

WILMINGTON

Grand View Motel
1 mi. E. on SR 86
Wilmington, NY 12997
Phone: (518) 946-2209

Pet Restrictions: No younger than 2, 1 pet per room
Exercise Area for Pets: Yes
Rates: $49 to $59

Hungry Trout Motor Inn
2 mi. SW on SR 86
Wilmington, NY 12997
Phone: (518) 946-2217,
      (800) 766-9137

Pet Restrictions: Small-medium dogs only
Pet left unattended in room: Yes
Exercise Area for Pets: Yes
Rates: $79

Winkleman Resort Motel
Center on SR 86
Wilmington, NY 12997
Phone: (518) 946-7761

Pet Restrictions: None
Pet left unattended in room: Yes, house trained
Exercise Area for Pets: Yes
Rates: $48 and up

NORTH CAROLINA

ABERDEEN

Best Western Pinehurst Motor Inn
1500 Sand Hills Blvd.
Aberdeen, NC 28315
Phone: (919) 944-2367,
(800) 528-1234
Pet Restrictions: Small dogs only, no cats
Pet left unattended in room: Yes, no housekeeping
Exercise Area for Pets: Yes
Rates: $36.95 to $69.95

Motel 6
1408 N. Sand Hills Blvd.
Aberdeen, NC 28315
Phone: (919) 944-5633
Pet Restrictions: Well behaved
Exercise Area for Pets: Yes
Rates: $27.99 add'l by person

ASHEVILLE

Econo Lodge Biltmore
190 Tunnel Rd.
Asheville, NC 28805
Phone: (704) 254-9521,
(800) 424-4777
Pet Restrictions: None
Exercise Area for Pets: No, unless in carrier & quiet
Exercise Area for Pets: Yes
Rates: $30 to $65

Days Inn Downtown
120 Patton Ave.
Asheville, NC 28801
Phone: (704) 254-9661
Pet Restrictions: $10/night, prior notice
Pet left unattended in room: Yes
Rates: $25 to $75

Red Roof Inn
16 Crowell Rd.
Asheville, NC 28806
Phone: (704) 667-9803,
(800) 843-7663
Pet Restrictions: Under 25 lbs., on leash or in carrier
Pet left unattended in room: Yes but no housekeeping unless caged
Exercise Area for Pets: Yes
Rates: $28.99 to $54.99

VETERINARIANS

Animal Hosp. of N. Asheville
1 Beaverdam Rd.
(704) 253-3393

Animal Hospital East
1275 Tunnel Rd.
(704) 298-6585

Mountain Valley Vet. Hospital
348 New Leicester Hwy
(704) 254-2122

ATLANTIC BEACH

Atlantis Lodge
Salter Path Rd., Pine Knolls Shore
Atlantic Beach, NC 28512
Phone: (919) 726-5168,
(800) 682-7057
Pet Restrictions: 2 rooms $2/pet/room with minimum of $5 only in efficiency apt.
Pet left unattended in room: Yes, no housekeeping
Exercise Area for Pets: Yes, leash law
Rates: $51 to $109

BANNER ELK

Holiday Inn Banner Elk
P.O. Box 1478
Banner Elk, NC 28604
Phone: (704) 898-4571,
(800) HOLIDAY (central res.)
Pet Restrictions: Not in rooms, kennels avail.
Exercise Area for Pets: Yes
Rates: $49 to $95

BRATTLEBORO

Days Inn Rocky Mount
Rt 1, Box 155
Brattleboro, NC 27809
Phone: (919) 446-0621,
(800) 325-2505 (central res.)
Pet Restrictions: $3/night/pet
Exercise Area for Pets: Yes
Rates: $35 to $40 plus

CHARLOTTE

Bradley Motel
4200 S. Interstate 85
Charlotte, NC 28214
Phone: (704) 392-3206
Pet Restrictions: Small only
Exercise Area for Pets: Yes
Rates: $27 to $32

Holiday Inn Center City
230 N. College St.
Charlotte, NC 28202
Phone: (800) 327-3318

Pet Restrictions: None
Pet left unattended in room: Yes, quiet
Exercise Area for Pets: Nearby
Rates: $75 to $93

Homewood Suites
4920 S. Tryon St.
Charlotte, NC 28217
Phone: (704) 525-2600,
    (800) CALL HOM

Pet Restrictions: $7/night
Exercise Area for Pets: Yes
Rates: $59 to $79

Hyatt Charlotte
5501 Carnegie Blvd
Charlotte, NC 28211
Phone: (800) 233-1234

Pet Restrictions: Special rooms, under 25 lbs.
Exercise Area for Pets: Nearby
Rates: $59 to $125

La Quinta Motor Inn
3100 S. I-85 Service Rd.
Charlotte, NC 28208
Phone: (704) 393-5306,
    (800) 531-5900

Pet Restrictions: Small & caged
Exercise Area for Pets: Yes
Rates: $40 to $60

La Quinta South
7900 Nations Ford Rd.
Charlotte, NC 28217
Phone: (704) 522-7110,
    (800) 531-5900

Pet Restrictions: Under 25 lbs.
Pet left unattended in room: Yes, no housekeeping
Exercise Area for Pets: Yes
Rates: $42 to $49

Red Roof Inn-Airport
3300 I-85 S.
Charlotte, NC 28208
Phone: (704) 392-2316,
    (800) 843-7663

Pet Restrictions: None
Exercise Area for Pets: Yes
Rates: $25.99 to $43.99

Red Roof Inn
5116 I-85 N.
Charlotte, NC 28206
Phone: (704) 596-8222,
    (800) 843-7663

Pet Restrictions: None
Exercise Area for Pets: Yes
Rates: $24.99 to $55.99

Red Roof Inn Coliseum
131 Greenwood Dr.
Charlotte, NC 28217
Phone: (704) 529-1020,
    (800) 843-7663

Pet Restrictions: Small, trained, caged, common house pet
Exercise Area for Pets: Yes
Rates: $27.99 to $40.99

Residence
5800 W. Park Dr.
Charlotte, NC 28217
Phone: (704) 527-8110,
    (800) 331-3131

Pet Restrictions: $50 non-refundable, $10/day
Exercise Area for Pets: Yes
Rates: $79 to $110

Sheraton Airport Plaza Hotel
3315 S. I-85
Charlotte, NC 28208
Phone: (704) 392-1200,
    (800) 325-3535 (central res.)

Pet Restrictions: None
Pet left unattended in room: Yes
Exercise Area for Pets: Yes
Rates: $79 to $104

Villager Lodge
7901 Nations Ford Rd.
Charlotte, NC 28217
Phone: (704) 522-0364,
    (800) 328-7829

Pet Restrictions: Nightly only $5/night/pet
Exercise Area for Pets: Yes
Rates: $23.95 to $36.95

Wyndhan Garden Hotel
4200 Wilmount Rd.
Charlotte, NC 28208
Phone: (704) 357-9100,
    (800) 822-4200 (central res.)

Pet Restrictions: $15/stay plus $50 refundable deposit
Pet left unattended in room: Yes
Exercise Area for Pets: Yes
Rates: $89 to $109

Yorkshire Inn
9900 York Rd.
Charlotte, NC 28273
Phone: (704) 588-3949
Pet Restrictions: Under 25 lbs., $10 deposit
Exercise Area for Pets: Yes
Rates: $31.95 to $70

VETERINARIANS
Animal Medical Hospital
3832 Monroe Rd.
(704) 334-4684

Clear Creek Animal Hospital
6916 Harrisburg Rd.
(704) 537-8405

Sharon Lakes Animal Hosp.
7619 Sharon Lakes Rd.
(704) 552-0647

DUNN
Econo Lodge
Exit 72 I-95 & Pope Rd.
Dunn, NC 28334
Phone: (919) 892-6181,
(800) 424-4777
Pet Restrictions: $5/night
Pet left unattended in room: Yes
Exercise Area for Pets: Yes
Rates: $26.95 to $49.95

Ramada Inn
1011 E. Cumberland
Dunn, NC 28334
Phone: (919) 892-8101,
(800) 2-RAMADA (central res.)
Pet Restrictions: Small domestic pets
Pet left unattended in room: Yes, must be in carrier
Exercise Area for Pets: Yes
Rates: $52 to $69

DURHAM
Best Western
I-85 & 70 W, Rt 2, Box 560
Durham, NC 27705
Phone: (919) 383-2508,
(800) 528-1234 (central res.)
Pet Restrictions: None
Pet left unattended in room: Yes, no housekeeping
Exercise Area for Pets: Yes
Rates: $38 to $58

Carolina Duke Motor Inn
2517 Guess Rd.
Durham, NC 27705
Phone: (919) 286-0771,
(800) 438-1158
Pet Restrictions: No cats, $5/night/small dog only
Exercise Area for Pets: Yes
Rates: $26.98 to $38.98

Hampton Inn
1816 Hillandale Rd.
Durham, NC 27701
Phone: (919) 471-6100,
(800) 876-6338
Pet Restrictions: $6/night/pet
Pet left unattended in room: Yes, no housekeeping
Exercise Area for Pets: Yes
Rates: $48.50 to $50.50

Holiday Inn Raleigh-Durham Airport
Page Rd. exit 282, I-40
Durham, NC 27709
Phone: (919) 941-6000,
(800) HOLIDAY (central res.)
Pet Restrictions: Only in suites
Exercise Area for Pets: Yes
Rates: $125

Red Roof Inn
5623 Chapel Hill Blvd.
Durham, NC 27707
Phone: (919) 489-9421,
(800) 843-7663
Pet Restrictions: None
Pet left unattended in room: Yes, no housekeeping
Exercise Area for Pets: Yes
Rates: $32.99 to $46.99

Red Roof Inn
2000 I-85 Service Rd.
Durham, NC 27705
Phone: (919) 471-9882,
(800) 843-7663 (central res.)
Pet Restrictions: Up to 45 lbs.
Exercise Area for Pets: Yes
Rates: $29.99 to $45.99

Red Roof Inn RTP
4405 Hwy 55E
Durham, NC 27713
Phone: (919) 361-1950,
(800) THE ROOF (central res.)
Pet Restrictions: Small domestic pets, special rooms
Exercise Area for Pets: Yes
Rates: $25.85 to $48.83

Sheraton Inn University Ctr.
2800 Middleton Ave.
Durham, NC 27705
Phone: (919) 383-8575,
   (800) 633-5379 (8-5pm)
Pet Restrictions: Small domestic
   pets only
Exercise Area for Pets: Yes
Rates: $85 to $150

VETERINARIANS

Academy Vet. Hosp. of Durham
247 Village Shopping Center
(919) 688-6628

Cornwallis Rd. Animal Hosp.
200 W. Cornwallis Rd.
(919) 489-9194

Triangle Vet. Hosp.
3301 Chapel Hill Rd.
(919) 489-2391

FAYETTEVILLE
Comfort Inn
1922 Skibo Rd.
Fayetteville, NC 28314
Phone: (919) 867-1777,
   (800) 537-2268
Pet Restrictions: Small caged dogs
Exercise Area for Pets: Yes
Rates: $48 to $56

Comfort Inn
1957 Cedar Creek Rd.
Fayetteville, NC 28301
Phone: (919) 323-8333
Pet Restrictions: None
Pet left unattended in room: Yes, no
   housekeeping
Exercise Area for Pets: Yes
Rates: $35 to $45.95

VETERINARIANS

Cumberland Animal Hospital
1775 Pamalee Dr.
(919) 822-3337

Northgate Animal Hosp.
2921 Ramsey St.
(919) 822-3141

FORT MILL
Best Western Motor Lodge
3482 Hwy 21
Fort Mill, SC 29715
Phone: (803) 548-8000
Pet Restrictions: None
Pet left unattended in room: Yes, no
   housekeeping
Exercise Area for Pets: Yes
Rates: $38.25 to $49.95

GASTONIA
Days Inn Gastonia-Charlotte
1700 North Chester
Gastonia, NC 28052
Phone: (704) 864-9981,
   (800) 325-2525 (central res.)
Pet Restrictions: $5/night/pet
Exercise Area for Pets: Yes
Rates: $35 to $45

Knights Inn
1721 Broadcast St.
Gastonia, NC 28052
Phone: (704) 868-4900,
   (800) 843-5644
Pet Restrictions: Well trained,
   special rooms
Exercise Area for Pets: Yes
Rates: $31.95 to $38.95

VETERINARIANS

Dickson Animal Clinic
1654 Wilkinson Blvd.
(704) 866-8741

Gaston Vet. Hospital
2022 Wilkinson Blvd.
(704) 864-5739

GREENSBORO
Airport Marriott Hotel
1 Marriott Dr.
Greensboro, NC 27409
Phone: (919) 852-6450,
   (800) 228-9290
Pet Restrictions: Small domestic
   pets, caged
Pet left unattended in room: Yes, in
   cage
Rates: $99 to $116

Hampton Inn
20004 Veasley St.
Greensboro, NC 27407
Phone: (800) 426-7866

Pet Restrictions: Under 25 lbs.,
domestic pets
Pet left unattended in room: Yes,
with notification
Exercise Area for Pets: Yes
Rates: $41 to $54

Ramada Inn-Airport
7067 Albert Pick Rd.
Greensboro, NC 27409
Phone: (919) 668-3900,
(800) 2-RAMADA

Pet Restrictions: Under 25 lbs.,
domestic pet
Pet left unattended in room: Yes,
must be caged
Exercise Area for Pets: Yes
Rates: $56 to $68

Red Roof Inn
615 S. Regional Rd.
Greensboro, NC 27409
Phone: (919) 271-2636,
(800) 843-7663 (central res.)

Pet Restrictions: None
Pet left unattended in room: Yes,
must be caged
Exercise Area for Pets: Yes
Rates: $31 to $41

VETERINARIANS

Animal Medical Centre
4113 Spring Garden St.
(919) 855-5821

Cobb Animal Clinic
3224 Battleground Ave.
(919) 288-2827

GREENVILLE

Arborgate Inn
3435 S. Memorial Dr.
Greenville, NC 27834
Phone: (919) 355-5699,
(800) 843-5644

Pet Restrictions: Small domestic
pets, special rooms
Exercise Area for Pets: Yes
Rates: $26.95 to $32.95

VETERINARIANS

Bateman, Joseph
200 Memorial Dr.
(919) 752-3148

Thompson, A.G.
1523 East 14th St.
(919) 752-1890

HENDERSONVILLE

Comfort Inn
206 Mitchelle Dr.
Hendersonville, NC 28792
Phone: (704) 693-8800,
(800) 221-2222 (central res.)

Pet Restrictions: Special rooms
Exercise Area for Pets: Yes
Rates: $49.95 to $59.95

VETERINARIANS

Parsons, Brenda J.
704 Kanuga Rd.
(704) 692-0941

HICKORY

Holiday Inn
1385 Lenoir Rhyne Blvd.
Hickory, NC 28602
Phone: (704) 323-1000,
(800) HOLIDAY (central res.)

Pet Restrictions: $25/night/pet,
small domestic animal
Exercise Area for Pets: Yes
Rates: $66 to $77

Howard Johnson Lodge
483 Hwy 70 SW
Hickory, NC 28601
Phone: (704) 323-1600,
(800) 654-2000 (central res.)

Pet Restrictions: Special rooms
Exercise Area for Pets: Yes
Rates: $39 to $45

Red Roof Inn
1184 Lenoir Rhyne Blvd.
Hickory, NC 28602
Phone: (704) 323-1500,
(800) 843-7663 (central res.)

Pet Restrictions: Small, domestic
pets
Pet left unattended in room: Yes, no
housekeeping
Exercise Area for Pets: Yes
Rates: $27.99 to $42.99

HIGH POINT

Holiday Inn
236 S. Main St.
High Point, NC 27261
Phone: (919) 886-7011,
(800) 465-4329 (central res.)

Pet Restrictions: None
Pet left unattended in room: Yes
Exercise Area for Pets: Yes
Rates: $50 to $63

VETERINARIANS

Sink, E. Max
2513 S. Main St.
(919) 885-8129

JACKSONVILLE

Onslow Inn
201 Marene Blvd.
Jacksonville, NC 28540
Phone: (919) 347-3151,
(800) 763-3151

Pet Restrictions: Small domestic pets
Pet left unattended in room: Yes
Exercise Area for Pets: Yes
Rates: $37 to $42

VETERINARIANS

Jacksonville Vet. Hospital
131 Wilmington Hwy
(919) 347-3186

Onslow Animal Hospital
10 Doris Ave. E.
(919) 347-1219

JONESVILLE

Country Inn
Rt 1, Box 266
Jonesville, NC 28642
Phone: (919) 835-2261

Pet Restrictions: Small domestic
pets, dogs under 10 lbs.
Exercise Area for Pets: Yes
Rates: $22 to $65

KILL DEVIL HILL

Comfort Inn
401 N. Virginia Dare Trail
Kill Devil Hill, NC 27948
Phone: (919) 480-2600,
(800) 854-5286

Pet Restrictions: $50 deposit,
$5/night/pet, special rooms
Exercise Area for Pets: Yes
Rates: $35 to $150

MARION

Econo Lodge
Rt 5, Box 68A
Marion, NC 28752
Phone: (704) 659-7940,
(800) 424-4777 (central res.)

Pet Restrictions: Small pets
Pet left unattended in room: Yes, no
barking
Exercise Area for Pets: Yes
Rates: $33.70 to $47.70

MORGANTON

Holiday Inn
2400 S. Sterling St.
Morganton, NC 28655
Phone: (704) 437-0171

Pet Restrictions: None
Pet left unattended in room: Yes
Exercise Area for Pets: Yes
Rates: $47 to $49

VETERINARIANS

Wellborn, Sanford
119 Evans St.
(704) 437-4524

MORRISVILLE

Budgetel Inn
1001 Aerial Ctr. Pkwy.
Morrisville, NC 27560
Phone: (919) 481-3600,
(800) 428-3438 (central res.)

Pet Restrictions: Special rooms
Exercise Area for Pets: Yes
Rates: $37.95 to $38.95

MURPHY

Comfort Inn
114 Hwy 64 W.
Murphy, NC 28906
Phone: (704) 837-8030,
(800) 221-2222 (central res.)

Pet Restrictions: $30 room deposit
Exercise Area for Pets: Yes
Rates: $40 to $75

NAGS HEAD

Care Free Cottages
6721 S. Virginia Dare Trail
Nags Head, NC 27959
Phone: (919) 441-5340 or (704)
249-1114 (evenings)

Pet Restrictions: $25 per dog
Pet left unattended in room: Yes
Exercise Area for Pets: Yes
Rates: $150 to $1,550 per week

RALEIGH

Hampton Inn-North Raleigh
1001 Wake Towne Dr.
Raleigh, NC 27609
Phone: (919) 828-1813,
(800) HAMPTON (central res.)
Pet Restrictions: Small domestic
pets, special rooms
Pet left unattended in room: Yes, no
housekeeping
Exercise Area for Pets: Yes
Rates: $49 to $59

The Plantation Inn Resort
6401 North Blvd.
Raleigh, NC 27604
Phone: (919) 876-1411,
(800) 992-9662 (out of state)
Pet Restrictions: $10/pet/visit,
special rooms
Pet left unattended in room: Yes, no
damage
Exercise Area for Pets: Yes
Rates: $36.95 to $65

Red Roof Inn
3520 Maitland Dr.
Raleigh, NC 27610
Phone: (919) 231-0200,
(800) 843-7663 (central res.)
Pet Restrictions: Must be caged,
under 50 lbs.
Pet left unattended in room: Yes, no
housekeeping
Exercise Area for Pets: Yes
Rates: $27.99 to $36.99

Residence Inn by Marriott
1000 Navaho Dr.
Raleigh, NC 27609
Phone: (919) 878-6100,
(800) 331-3131 (central res.)
Pet Restrictions: $100/stay, $5/day
Pet left unattended in room: Yes
Exercise Area for Pets: Yes
Rates: $95 to $125

Velvet Cloak Inn
1505 Hillsborough St.
Raleigh, NC 27605
Phone: (919) 828-0333,
(800) 334-4372 (outside NC)
Pet Restrictions: Small domestic
pets under 30 lbs.
Pet left unattended in room: Yes,
prior notice
Exercise Area for Pets: Yes
Rates: $69 to $99

VETERINARIANS

Animal Hospital-North Raleigh
8819 Six Forks Rd.
(919) 847-1972

Capital Animal Hospital
6841 Glenwood Ave.
(919) 787-3341

Six Forks Animal Hosp.
7130 Six Forks Rd.
(919) 847-5854

ROANOKE RAPIDS

Comfort Inn
1911 Weldon Rd.
Roanoke Rapids, NC 27870
Phone: (919) 537-5252,
(800) 221-2222 (central res.)
Pet Restrictions: Small domestic pets
Pet left unattended in room: Yes, no
noise
Exercise Area for Pets: Yes
Rates: $37.95 to $45.95

Holiday Inn
100 Holiday Dr.
Roanoke Rapids, NC 27870
Phone: (919) 537-1031,
(800) 465-4329
Pet Restrictions: Under 20 lbs.
Exercise Area for Pets: Yes
Rates: $52 to $56

VETERINARIANS

Rick, Benjamin R.
824 Weldon Rd.
(919) 535-3117

ROCKY MOUNT

Comfort Inn
200 Gateway Blvd.
Rocky Mount, NC 27804
Phone: (919) 937-7765,
(800) 221-2222 (central res.)
Pet Restrictions: $10/night/pet
Exercise Area for Pets: Yes
Rates: $51 to $64

VETERINARIANS

Hicks, Robert F.
283 N. Main St.
(919) 442-1771

Turner, Ben S.
1902 Sunset Ave.
(919) 442-3636

ROWLAND

Days Inn
Rte 2, Box 187
Rowland, NC 28383
Phone: (919) 422-3366,
    (800) 325-2525 (central res.)
Pet Restrictions: Must not bother
    other customers
Pet left unattended in room: Yes
Exercise Area for Pets: Yes
Rates: $32 to $60

ROXBORO

Innkeeper Motel
906 Durham Rd.
Roxboro, NC 27573
Phone: (919) 599-3800,
    (800) 822-9899 (central res.)
Pet Restrictions: Must sign
    statement of responsibility
Exercise Area for Pets: Yes
Rates: $59.95

VETERINARIANS

Berryhill, Claudia K.
430 S. Morgan Dr.
(919) 599-0611

SALISBURY

Days Inn
1810 Lutheran Sinod Dr.
Salisbury, NC 28144
Phone: (704) 633-4211,
    (800) 325-2525 (central res.)
Pet Restrictions: $5/night/pet
Pet left unattended in room: Must
    be quiet
Exercise Area for Pets: Yes
Rates: $36 to $50

VETERINARIANS

James, Ted L.
3002 S. Main St.
(704) 636-1100

Stehle, Janice E.
126 Mitchell Ave.
(704) 637-0227

SANFORD

Palomino Motel
PO Box 777
Sanford, NC 27330
Phone: (919) 776-7531
Pet Restrictions: Must be
    responsible
Exercise Area for Pets: Yes
Rates: $34

SKYLAND

**Glenn & Edna's Vacation
    Cottage**
P.O. Box 98 - Skyland
Skyland, NC 28776
Phone: (704) 684-9938
Pet Restrictions: Cottage - 4 rooms;
    Redmond Boarding Kennel on
    premises
Exercise Area for Pets: Yes
Other: Biltmore House, Chimney
    Rock Lake, Blue Ridge Mountain
    & Great Smoky Mtns.,
    Gatlinburg, Cherokee, Dollywood
Rates: $55 to $60

STATESVILLE

Howard Johnsons
1215 Garner Bagnal Blvd.
Statesville, NC 28677
Phone: (704) 878-9691,
    (800) 160-HOJO (central res.)
Pet Restrictions: Small domestic pets
Exercise Area for Pets: Yes
Rates: $48 to $69

Red Roof Inn
1508 E. Broad St.
Statesville, NC 28677
Phone: (704) 878-2051,
    (800) 843-7663 (central res.)
Pet Restrictions: Small domestic
    pets, special rooms
Pet left unattended in room: Yes,
    well behaved
Exercise Area for Pets: Yes
Rates: $25.99 to $49.99

VETERINARIANS

Parks, David J.
Rte. 12, Box 355A
(704) 872-3625

WADE

Days Inn
Rte. I, Box 216 BB
Wade, NC 28395
Phone: (919) 323-1255, (800) DAYS
    INN (central res.)
Pet Restrictions: Large dogs in
    kennel, special rooms
Exercise Area for Pets: Yes
Rates: $37 to $42

WELDON

Econo Lodge
1615 Roanoke Rapids Rd.
Weldon, NC 27890
Phone: (919) 536-2131,
    (800) 424-4777 (central res.)

Pet Restrictions: None
Exercise Area for Pets: Yes
Rates: $30.47 to $42.46

WILLIAMSTON

Holiday Inn
Intersection Hwy. 17 & 64
Williamston, NC 27892
Phone: (919) 792-3184,
    (800) HOLIDAY (central res.)

Pet Restrictions: Small, domestic
    pets, quiet
Exercise Area for Pets: Yes
Rates: $43 to $58.40

WILSON

Quality Inn South
Hwy 301 South
Wilson, NC 27893
Phone: (919) 243-5165

Pet Restrictions: Small domestic
    pets, well trained
Pet left unattended in room: Must
    be quiet
Exercise Area for Pets: Yes
Rates: $44 to $60

VETERINARIANS

Brentwood Vet. Center
103 N. Ward Blvd.
(919) 243-6252

WINSTON-SALEM

Residence Inn by Marriot
7835 Northpoint
Winston-Salem, NC 27106
Phone: (919) 759-0777

Pet Restrictions: $75, be
    responsible
Pet left unattended in room: Yes
Exercise Area for Pets: Yes
Rates: $86 to $106

VETERINARIANS

Ard-Vista Animal Hospital
527 S. Stratford Rd.
(919) 765-3070

Old Town Veterinary Hospital
3744 Reynolds Rd.
(919) 924-4176

NORTH DAKOTA — HOTELS

BEACH

Buckwood Inn
HC2 Box 109A
Beach, ND 58621
Phone: (701) 872-4794
Pet Restrictions: Smoking rooms only
Exercise Area for Pets: Yes
Rates: $28.35 to $32.55

Select Inn
1505 Interchange Ave.
Beach, ND 58501
Phone: (701) 223-8060
Pet Restrictions: Smoking rooms only
Exercise Area for Pets: Yes
Rates: $25.90 to $39.90

VETERINARIANS

Bismarck Animal Clinic
1414 E. Calgary Ave.
Phone: (701) 222-8255

BISMARK

Select Inn
1505 Interchange Ave.
Bismark, ND 58501
Phone: (701) 223-8060,
(800) 641-1000
Pet Restrictions: Smoking rooms only
Exercise Area for Pets: Yes
Rates: $24.46 to $43.49

VETERINARIANS

Buchholz, Gerald R.
(701) 222-8255

BOWMAN

Super 8 Motel
P.O. Box 675
Bowman, ND 58623
Phone: (701) 523-5613
Pet Restrictions: None
Exercise Area for Pets: Yes
Rates: $31.20 to $54.95

DEVILS LAKE

Trails West Motel
Highway 2 West
Devils Lake, ND 58301
Phone: (701) 662-5011,
(800) 453-5011
Pet Restrictions: $10/pet refund. deposit
Exercise Area for Pets: Yes
Rates: $24.95 to $37.95

DICKINSON

Comfort Inn
493 Elk Dr.
Dickinson, ND 58601
Phone: (701) 264-7300,
(800) 221-2222 (central res.)
Pet Restrictions: Not allowed in pool area
Exercise Area for Pets: Yes
Rates: $24.50 to $42.50

Hospitality Inn & Conv. Ctr.
P.O. Box 1778
Dickinson, ND 58301
Phone: (701) 227-1853
Pet Restrictions: No pit bulls
Pet left unattended in room: Yes, if quiet
Exercise Area for Pets: Yes
Rates: $48 to $80

Select Inn
642 12th St. W.
Dickinson, ND 58601
Phone: (701) 227-1891,
(800) 437-6445
Pet Restrictions: 4 rooms only
Pet left unattended in room: Yes, notify desk
Exercise Area for Pets: Yes
Rates: $19.85 to $48.85

Super 8 Motel
637 12th St. West
Dickinson, ND 58601
Phone: (701) 227-1215
Pet Restrictions: Smoking room
Exercise Area for Pets: Nearby
Rates: $28.94 to $45.97

FARGO

Select Inn
1025 38th St. South
Fargo, ND 58103
Phone: (701) 282-6300,
(800) 641-1000 (central res.)
Pet Restrictions: None
Exercise Area for Pets: Yes
Rates: $27.90 to $41.90

Town House Inn
301 3rd Ave. N.
Fargo, ND 58102
Phone: (701) 232-8851,
(800) 437-4682
Pet Restrictions: None
Pet left unattended in room: Yes
Exercise Area for Pets: Yes
Rates: $49 to $69

VETERINARIANS

Animal Health Clinic
1441 S. University Dr.
Phone: (701) 237-9310

Valley Veterinary Hospital
3210 Main Avenue
Phone: (701) 232-3391

GRAND FORKS

Motel 6
1211 47th St. North
Grand Forks, ND 58201
Phone: (701) 775-0511
Pet Restrictions: None
Exercise Area for Pets: Yes
Rates: $26.95 to $31.91

HETTINGER

Mirror Lake Lodge
East Hwy 12
Hettinger, ND 58639
Phone: (701) 567-4571
Pet Restrictions: Deposit, large pets
     must be caged in room
Exercise Area for Pets: Yes
Rates: $29.43 plus $5/person

MINOT

Holiday Inn
2315 N. Broadway
Minot, ND 58702
Phone: (701) 852-4161
Pet Restrictions: Smoking rooms
     only
Exercise Area for Pets: Yes
Rates: $54 to $59

VETERINARIANS

Minot Vet Clinic North
2029 N. Broadway
Phone: (701) 852-2770

Pinkerton Animal Hospital
2105 N. Broadway
Phone: (701) 852-3055

RUGBY

Econo Lodge
Hwy 2 East
Rugby, ND 58368
Phone: (701) 776-5776,
     (800) 367-8429
Pet Restrictions: None
Exercise Area for Pets: Yes
Rates: $36 to $56

WILLISTON

Travel Host Motel
3801 2nd Ave. (West)
Williston, ND 58801
Phone: (701) 774-0041,
     (800) 322-8029
Pet Restrictions: Smoking rooms
     only, well behaved
Pet left unattended in room: Yes, if
     well behaved
Exercise Area for Pets: Yes
Rates: $24.85 to $34.85

OHIO — HOTELS

AKRON

Cascade Plaza Hotel
S. Cascade Plaza
Akron, OH 44308
Phone: (216) 762-0661

Pet Restrictions: Pet dep. $25
    p/stay refund.
Pet left unattended in room: Yes
Exercise Area for Pets: Nearby
Rates: $66 to $195

Knights Inn
3237 S. Arlington Rd.
Akron, OH 44312
Phone: (216) 644-1204,
    (800) 843-5644

Pet Restrictions: None
Pet left unattended in room: Yes
Exercise Area for Pets: Yes
Rates: $35.15 to $56.94

Red Roof Inn
99 Rothrock Rd.
Akron, OH 44321
Phone: (216) 666-0566

Pet Restrictions: None
Pet left unattended in room: Yes
Exercise Area for Pets: Yes
Rates: $35 to $50

Red Roof Inn
2939 S. Arlington Rd.
Akron, OH 44312
Phone: (216) 644-7748

Pet Restrictions: None
Exercise Area for Pets: Yes
Rates: $30 to $55

Residence Inn by Marriott
120 Montrose W. Ave.
Akron, OH 44321
Phone: (216) 666-4811,
    (800) 331-3131

Pet Restrictions: $50-$100 dep
    p/stay, set a time for cleaning
    with staff, you must be there.
    Has to be caged.
Pet left unattended in room: Yes
Exercise Area for Pets: Yes
Rates: $80 to $132

VETERINARIANS

Bingham, Keith Daniel
490 E Cuyahoga Falls Ave.
(216) 928-6514

Keller, Frederick J.
1635 Copley Rd.
(216) 836-0481

Southerland, Ronald M.
1415 Dietz Ave.
(216) 773-9960

AUSTINTOWN

Budget Luxury Inn
5425 Clarkins Dr.
Austintown, OH 44515
Phone: (216) 793-9808

Pet Restrictions: $5/pet
Pet left unattended in room: Yes
Exercise Area for Pets: Yes
Rates: $29.95 to $47.95

Knights Inn-West
5431 76th Dr.
Austintown, OH 44515
Phone: (216) 793-9305,
    (800) 843-5644

Pet Restrictions: None
Pet left unattended in room: Yes -
    talk to housekeeping
Exercise Area for Pets: Yes
Rates: $40.95

BEACHWOOD

Cleveland Marriott East
3663 Park E. Dr.
Beachwood, OH 44122
Phone: (216) 464-5950

Pet Restrictions: $50 chge. unrefund.
Pet left unattended in room: Yes
Exercise Area for Pets: Nearby
Rates: $74 to $138

BEDFORD HEIGHTS

Ramada - Cleveland S.E.
24801 Rockside Rd.
Bedford Heights, OH 44146
Phone: (216) 439-2500

Pet Restrictions: 2nd floor only
Pet left unattended in room: Yes -
    no housekeeping, coordinate
    with housekeeping for cleaning
Exercise Area for Pets: Yes
Rates: $64 to $95

BOWLING GREEN

Buckeye Budget Motor Inn
1740 E. Wooster St.
Bowling Green, OH 43402
Phone: (419) 352-1520

Pet Restrictions: None
Pet left unattended in room: Yes
Exercise Area for Pets: Yes
Rates: $39.95

Holley Lodge
1630 E. Wooster St.
Bowling Green, OH 43402
Phone: (419) 352-2521

Pet Restrictions: None
Pet left unattended in room: Yes -
   room will not be serviced, clean
   up after pet
Exercise Area for Pets: Yes
Rates: $43 to $60

BROADVIEW HEIGHTS

Days Inn
4501 E. Royalton Rd.
Broadview Hts., OH 44147
Phone: (216) 526-0640

Pet Restrictions: Dogs in control
Pet left unattended in room: Yes -
   but must talk to housekeeping
Exercise Area for Pets: Yes
Rates: $36 to $46

VETERINARIANS

Burge, Robert A.
407 E. Royalton Rd.
(216) 526-2915

BROOKPARK

Budget Inn of America
14043 Brookpark Rd.
Brookpark, OH 44142
Phone: (216) 267-2350

Pet Restrictions: Pet dep., $20
   p/stay refund.
Pet left unattended in room: Yes
Exercise Area for Pets: Yes
Rates: $34.95 to $40.02

CAMBRIDGE

Holiday Inn
2248 Southgate Pkwy
Cambridge, OH 43725
Phone: (614) 432-7313

Pet Restrictions: Small pets
Pet left unattended in room: Yes, if
   well behaved
Exercise Area for Pets: Yes
Rates: $66 to $71

VETERINARIANS

Small, D.S.
2103 E. Wheeling Ave.
(614) 432-5980

CANTON

Motel 6
6880 Sunset Strip Ave. NW
Canton, OH 44720
Phone: (216) 494-7611

Pet Restrictions: Small pets
Exercise Area for Pets: Yes
Rates: $29.91 to $43.23

Red Roof Inn
5353 Inn Circle Ct. NW
N. Canton, OH 44720
Phone: (216) 499-1970

Pet Restrictions: None
Pet left unattended in room: Yes -
   let front desk know
Exercise Area for Pets: Yes
Rates: $34.99 to $47.99

VETERINARIANS

Mellett Animal Hospital
3802 W. Tuscarawas St.
(216) 477-3491

Schneiders Pet Hospital
2610 Fulton Dr. NW
(216) 452-7987

Stark Animal Hospital
3900 Cleveland Ave.
(216) 492-2444

CHILLICOTHE

Holiday Inn
1250 N. Bridge St.
Chillicothe, OH 45601
Phone: (614) 775-7000

Pet Restrictions: Responsible for
   damages, well-behaved
Exercise Area for Pets: Yes
Rates: $50 to $75

Travel Lodge
1135 E. Main St.
Chillicothe, OH 45601
Phone: (614) 775-2500,
(800) 255-3050
Pet Restrictions: None
Exercise Area for Pets: Yes, for 1
hour max.
Exercise Area for Pets: Yes
Rates: $38 to $48

CINCINNATI
Clarion
141 W 6th St.
Cincinnati, OH 45202
Phone: (513) 352-2100,
(800) 876-2100
Pet Restrictions: Dep. $25/stay; up
to 15 lbs.; well-behaved
Pet left unattended in room: Yes -
quiet
Exercise Area for Pets: Nearby,
clean up after pet
Rates: $91 to $425

Days Inn - Cincinnati East
4056 Mt. Carmel-Tabasco Rd.
Cincinnati, OH 45255
Phone: (513) 528-3800
Pet Restrictions: Small pets
Pet left unattended in room: Yes, if
caged
Exercise Area for Pets: Yes
Rates: $35 to $99

Holiday Inn - Cincinnati North
2235 Sharon Rd.
Cincinnati, OH 45241
Phone: (513) 771-0700
Pet Restrictions: Small pets, they
must be leashed in public
Exercise Area for Pets: Yes
Rates: $69 to $175

Holiday Inn Queensgate
800 W 8th St.
Cincinnati, OH 45203
Phone: (513) 241-8660,
(800) 465-4329
Pet Restrictions: Small, quiet
Pet left unattended in room: Yes
Exercise Area for Pets: Nearby
Rates: $69 to $89

Howard Johnson Plaza-Hotel
11440 Chester Rd.
Cincinnati, OH 45245
Phone: (513) 771-3400
Pet Restrictions: Small pets only
Pet left unattended in room: Yes, in
cage
Exercise Area for Pets: Yes
Rates: $35 to $79

Marriott
11320 Chester Rd.
Cincinnati, OH 45246
Phone: (513) 772-1720,
(800) 950-8883
Pet Restrictions: Notify in advance,
lower level rooms only
Pet left unattended in room: Yes
Exercise Area for Pets: Yes
Rates: $69 to $125

Motel 6
3960 Nine Mile Rd
Cincinnati, OH 45255
Phone: (513) 752-2262
Pet Restrictions: Small pets
Exercise Area for Pets: Yes
Rates: $23.99 to $25.99

Ramada Inn & Conf. Ctr.
5901 Pfeiffer Rd.
Cincinnati, OH 45242
Phone: (513) 793-4500,
(800) 272-6232
Pet Restrictions: Small-med. dogs &
cats, 1st floor rooms only
Exercise Area for Pets: Yes
Rates: $67 to $73

Red Roof Inn
5900 Pfeiffer Rd.
Cincinnati, OH 45252
Phone: (513) 793-8811,
(800) 843-7663 (central res.)
Pet Restrictions: Under 30 lbs.
Notify desk when arriving.
Responsible for damages.
Pet left unattended in room: Yes
Exercise Area for Pets: Yes
Rates: $30 to $75

Red Roof Inn
2301 E. Sharon Rd.
Cincinnati, OH 45241
Phone: (513) 771-5552,
　　(800) 843-7663 (central res.)

Pet Restrictions: 20 lbs. or under
Pet left unattended in room: Yes
Exercise Area for Pets: Yes
Rates: $32.99 to $57.99

Red Roof Inn
5300 Kennedy Dr.
Cincinnati, OH 45213
Phone: (513) 531-6589

Pet Restrictions: None
Pet left unattended in room: Yes
Exercise Area for Pets: Yes
Rates: $45 to $60

Red Roof Inn
4035 Mt. Carmel-Tabasco Rd.
Cincinnati, OH 45255
Phone: (513) 528-2741

Pet Restrictions: None
Pet left unattended in room: Yes
Exercise Area for Pets: Yes
Rates: $39 to $50

Red Roof Inn
11345 Chester Rd.
Cincinnati, OH 45246
Phone: (513) 771-5141

Pet Restrictions: None
Pet left unattended in room: Yes
Exercise Area for Pets: Nearby
Rates: $44 to $57

Residence Inn By Marriott
11689 Chester Rd.
Cincinnati, OH 45246
Phone: (513) 771-2525,
　　(800) 331-3131 (central res.)

Pet Restrictions: Dep. $10/day not
　　exceed $100
Pet left unattended in room: Yes but
　　no housekeeping
Exercise Area for Pets: Nearby
Rates: $49 to $129

Rodeway Inn
400 Glensprings Dr.
Cincinnati, OH 45246
Phone: (513) 825-3129

Pet Restrictions: Under 15 lbs.
　　Deposit $25/pet/stay
Pet left unattended in room: Yes,
　　day hours only
Exercise Area for Pets: Yes
Rates: $34.95 to $60

VETERINARIANS

Grady Veterinary Hospital
9211 Winton Rd.
(513) 931-8675

Montgromery Animal Hospital
7700 Montgomery Rd.
(513) 791-7912

Tennessee Avenue Animal Hospital
1381 Tennessee Ave.
(513) 242-2141

CIRCLEVILLE

Hometown Inn
23897 US-23S
Circleville, OH 43113
Phone: (614) 474-6006

Pet Restrictions: Walked in back of
　　property only
Pet left unattended in room: Yes
Exercise Area for Pets: Yes
Rates: $37.75 to $41.95

COLUMBUS

Days Inn
1212 E. Dubln-Granville Rd.
Columbus, OH 43229
Phone: (614) 885-9696

Pet Restrictions: Small pets under
　　20 lbs. Dep. $6/day. Not in pool
　　area.
Pet left unattended in room: Yes,
　　well-behaved
Exercise Area for Pets: Yes
Rates: $32.95 to $45

Holiday Inn
175 E. Town St.
Columbus, OH 43215
Phone: (614) 221-3281

Pet Restrictions: Small pets
Exercise Area for Pets: Yes
Rates: $79 to $89

Holiday Inn-Columbus/ Worthington Avenue
175 Hutchinson Ave.
Columbus, OH 43235
Phone: (614) 885-3334

Pet Restrictions: 25 lbs. or under
　　leashed in public spaces
Exercise Area for Pets: Yes
Rates: $69 to $85

OHIO — HOTELS (continued)

Knights Inn - I-71
1300 E. Dublin-Granville Rd.
Columbus, OH 43229
Phone: (614) 846-7635

Pet Restrictions: None
Exercise Area for Pets: Yes - no
    maid service
Rates: $31.50 to $47.40

Motel 6
5500 Renner Rd.
Columbus, OH 43228
Phone: (614) 870-0993

Pet Restrictions: 15 lbs. or under; 1
    pet per owner
Exercise Area for Pets: Yes
Rates: $25.95 to $37.99

Quality Inn-North
1213 E. Dublin-Granville Rd.
Columbus, OH 43229
Phone: (614) 885-4084,
    (800) 221-2222 (central res.)

Pet Restrictions: 50 lbs. or under.
    Dep. $25 p/stay refund.
Exercise Area for Pets: Yes
Rates: $50 to $60

Radisson Hotel-Columbus North
4900 Sinclair Rd.
Columbus, OH 43229
Phone: (614) 846-0300

Pet Restrictions: None
Pet left unattended in room: Yes -
    notify front desk
Exercise Area for Pets: Yes
Rates: $59 to $118

Ramada Inn West
4601 W. Broad St.
Columbus, OH 43228
Phone: (614) 878-5301

Pet Restrictions: No snakes
Exercise Area for Pets: Yes
Rates: $30 to $60

Red Roof Inn-OSU
441 Ackerman Rd.
Columbus, OH 43202
Phone: (614) 267-9941,
    (800) 843-7663

Pet Restrictions: Dep. Well behaved.
    Notify desk when checking in.
Pet left unattended in room: Yes -
    tell front desk
Exercise Area for Pets: Yes
Rates: $33.99 to $59.99

Red Roof Inn-Worthington
7474 N. High St.
Columbus, OH 43235
Phone: (614) 846-3001

Pet Restrictions: None
Pet left unattended in room: Yes
Exercise Area for Pets: Yes
Rates: $38.99 to $50.99

Red Roof Inn
750 Morse Rd.
Columbus, OH 43229
Phone: (614) 846-8520

Pet Restrictions: None
Pet left unattended in room: Yes
Exercise Area for Pets: Yes
Rates: $30 to $44

Red Roof Inn
5001 Renner Rd.
Columbus, OH 43228
Phone: (614) 878-9245

Pet Restrictions: None
Pet left unattended in room: Yes
Exercise Area for Pets: Yes
Rates: $33 to $55

Residence Inn by Marriott-Columbus East
2084 S. Hamilton Rd.
Columbus, OH 43232
Phone: (614) 864-8844

Pet Restrictions: Sign pet waiver.
    Pet dep. 5 nights or less $50, 6
    or more $ p/d, p/pet (non-refnd.)
Pet left unattended in room: Yes -
    arrange time for housekeeping
Exercise Area for Pets: Nearby
Rates: $119 to $149

Residence Inn by Marriott-Columbus North
6191 W. Zumstein Dr.
Columbus, OH 43229
Phone: (614) 431-1819

Pet Restrictions: Must be leashed
    when not in room. Dep. $ p/day
    p/pet, max. charge will be no
    greater than $150
Pet left unattended in room: Yes -
    arrange time with housekeeping
    for cleaning
Exercise Area for Pets: Yes -
    cleanup
Rates: $45 to $115

VETERINARIANS

Beechwold Veterinary Hospital
4590 Indianola Ave.
(614) 268-8666

Ohio State University Veterinary Hospital
1935 Coffey Rd.
(614) 292-7105

Westgate Medical and Surgical Hospital
3578 W. Broad St.
(614) 279-8415

DAYTON

Holiday Inn South
2455 Dryden Rd.
Dayton, OH 45439
Phone: (513) 294-1471

Pet Restrictions: 40 lbs. or under. Dep. $25 p/stay refundable
Pet left unattended in room: Yes but room will not be serviced
Exercise Area for Pets: Nearby
Rates: $60 to $103

Knights Inn-North
3663 Maxton Rd.
Dayton, OH 45414
Phone: (513) 898-1212, (800) 428-7228

Pet Restrictions: Med.-small pets only
Exercise Area for Pets: Yes
Rates: $31.95 to $42.95

Red Roof Inn
7370 Miller Ln.
Dayton, OH 45414
Phone: (513) 898-1054

Pet Restrictions: None
Pet left unattended in room: Yes
Exercise Area for Pets: Yes
Rates: $34 to $47

Red Roof Inn-North
7570 Miller Lane
Dayton, OH 454144
Phone: (513) 898-1054, (800) 843-7663 (central res.)

Pet Restrictions: None
Pet left unattended in room: Yes
Exercise Area for Pets: Yes
Rates: $38.92 to $42.99

Residence Inn by Marriott-Dayton North
7070 Poe Ave.
Dayton, OH 45414
Phone: (513) 898-7764

Pet Restrictions: 1-6 nites $70/stay; 6-more $100/stay; Penthse. 1-6 ngts. $120/stay; 6-more $150
Pet left unattended in room: Yes, no cleaning unless pet is caged
Exercise Area for Pets: Yes
Rates: $89 to $114

Rodeway Inn North
7575 Poe Rd.
Dayton, OH 45414
Phone: (513) 454-0550

Pet Restrictions: None
Pet left unattended in room: Yes - well behaved
Exercise Area for Pets: Yes
Rates: $37 to $48.95

Travel Lodge
7911 Brandt Pike
Dayton, OH 45424
Phone: (513) 236-9361

Pet Restrictions: Owner responsible for any damage, must pay w/credit card. No housekeeping.
Pet left unattended in room: Yes
Exercise Area for Pets: Yes
Rates: $35 to $58

VETERINARIANS

Apt Veterinary Clinic
2409 Wilmington Pike
(513) 299-5700

Beavercreek Animal Hospital
3609 Dayton Xenia Rd.
(513) 426-1773

Tinney, Leonard M.
8970 N. Dixie Dr.
(513) 890-6341

DUBLIN

Red Roof Inn
5125 Post Rd.
Dublin, OH 43017
Phone: (614) 764-3993

Pet Restrictions: None
Exercise Area for Pets: Yes
Rates: $27 and up

VETERINARIANS
Animal Med. & Emerg. Hosp.
3859 W. Dublin-Granville Rd.
(614) 889-2556

ELYRIA
Knights Inn-Elyria/Lorain
523 Griswold Rd.
Elyria, OH 44035
Phone: (216) 324-3911

Pet Restrictions: 1 pet/room; notify
desk when checking in.
Pet left unattended in room: Yes
Exercise Area for Pets: Yes
Rates: $45.95 to $53.95

VETERINARIANS
Murray Ridge Animal Clinic
7855 N. Murray Ridge Rd.
(216) 323-9568

ENGLEWOOD
Motel 6
1212 S. Main St.
Englewood, OH 45322
Phone: (513) 832-3770

Pet Restrictions: None
Exercise Area for Pets: Yes
Rates: $28.11 to $34.86

VETERINARIANS
McKenzie, Larry D.
539 S. Main St.
(513) 836-9636

FAIRBORN
Red Roof Inn
2580 Colonel Glen Hwy.
Fairborn, OH 45324
Phone: (513) 426-6116

Pet Restrictions: Under 25 lbs.
Pet left unattended in room: Yes
Exercise Area for Pets: Yes
Rates: $36 to $52

VETERINARIANS
Towne & Country Animal Clinic
801 N. Broad St.
(513) 878-4009

FRANKLIN
Knights Inn-Franklin
8500 Claude Thomas Rd.
Franklin, OH 45005
Phone: (513) 746-2841

Pet Restrictions: None
Exercise Area for Pets: Yes - room
will not be cleaned
Exercise Area for Pets: Yes
Rates: $32.95 to $77.70

FREMONT
Travel Lodge
1750 Cedar St.
Fremont, OH 43420
Phone: (419) 334-9517,
(800) 578-7878 (central res.)

Pet Restrictions: Small pets only
Pet left unattended in room: Yes, if
caged
Exercise Area for Pets: Yes
Rates: $39 to $61

FINDLAY
Knights Inn
1901 Broad Ave.
Findlay, OH 45840
Phone: (419) 424-1133

Pet Restrictions: None
Pet left unattended in room: Yes
Exercise Area for Pets: Yes
Rates: $27.85 to $49.95

GIRARD
Days Inn North
1610 Motor Inn Dr.
Girard, OH 44420
Phone: (216) 759-3410

Pet Restrictions:$5/pet/day
Pet left unattended in room: Yes,
quiet
Exercise Area for Pets: Yes
Rates: $41.95 to $47.95

GROVE CITY
Ramada Inn South
1879 Stringtown Rd.
Grove City, OH 43123
Phone: (614) 871-2990

Pet Restrictions: None
Exercise Area for Pets: Yes
Rates: $45 to $57

Red Roof Inn
1900 Stringtown Rd.
Grove City, OH 43123
Phone: (614) 875-8543

Pet Restrictions: None
Pet left unattended in room: Yes
Exercise Area for Pets: Yes
Rates: $30 to $36

VETERINARIANS
Arndt, Martha J.
4350 Grove City Rd.
(614) 875-4321

Griffiths, Joyce Perlman
2288 Quartz
(614) 292-1391

HEATH
Holiday Inn
733 Hebron Rd.
Heath, OH 43056
Phone: (614) 522-1165

Pet Restrictions: Leashed when in
    public
Pet left unattended in room: Yes -
    if quiet
Rates: $58 to $67

HILLIARD
Motel 6
3950 Parkway Lane
Hilliard, OH 43026
Phone: (614) 771-1500

Pet Restrictions: 1 small pet
Rates: $25.99 to $6 per extra person

VETERINARIANS
Kukor, George A.
5125 Cemetary Rd.
(614) 876-5125

Vesper, Richard Z.
4084 Main St.
(614) 876-5641

HOLLAND
Residence Inn by Marriott
6101 Trust Dr.
Holland, OH 43528
Phone: (419) 867-9555

Pet Restrictions: Studio
    $10/pet/nite, max. $100;
    Penthse $15/pet/nite, max. $150.
Pet left unattended in room: Yes, if
    in cage, notify desk
Exercise Area for Pets: Yes
Rates: $99 to $129

INDEPENDENCE
Budgetel Inn
6161 Quarry Lane
Independence, OH 44131
Phone: (216) 447-1133,
    (800) 428-3438

Pet Restrictions: None
Exercise Area for Pets: Yes
Rates: $39.95 to $49.95

Holiday Inn-Independence
6001 Rockside Rd.
Independence, OH 44131
Phone: (216) 524-8050

Pet Restrictions: Not on club floor,
    unless caged.
Pet left unattended in room: Yes, if
    caged
Exercise Area for Pets: Yes
Rates: $69 to $89

Red Roof Inn
6020 Quarry Lane
Independence, OH 44131
Phone: (216) 447-0030

Pet Restrictions: Caged when in
    room and leashed in public
Pet left unattended in room: Yes, for
    short time
Exercise Area for Pets: Yes
Rates: $40.99 to $56.99

KENT
Knights Inn-Akron E.
4423 State Route 43
Kent, OH 44240-6997
Phone: (216) 678-5250

Pet Restrictions: None
Pet left unattended in room: Yes
Exercise Area for Pets: Yes
Rates: $40 to $55

VETERINARIANS
Stow-Kent Animal Hospital
4559 Kent Rd.
(216) 673-0049

Banks, Fred E.
2222 Kent-Revenna Rd.
(216) 678-2770

KINGS ISLAND

Quality Inn Kings Island Conference Center
Jct. Kings Mills Rd. & I-71
Kings Island, OH 45034
Phone: (513) 398-8075,
    (800) 227-7100

Pet Restrictions: None
Pet left unattended in room: Yes - if
    caged
Exercise Area for Pets: Yes
Rates: $32 to $175

LANCASTER

Holiday Inn
1858 N. Memorial Drive
Lancaster, OH 43130
Phone: (614) 653-3040

Pet Restrictions: Owner liable
Pet left unattended in room: Yes - if
    well behaved
Exercise Area for Pets: Yes
Rates: $52 to $85

MARIETTA

Econo Lodge
702 Pike St.
Marietta, OH 45750
Phone: (614) 374-8481

Pet Restrictions: $5/day
Pet left unattended in room: Yes -
    not for long, notify front desk
Exercise Area for Pets: Yes
Rates: $28.95 to $43.95

Knights Inn
506 Pike St.
Marietta, OH 45750
Phone: (614) 373-7373,
    (800) 526-5947

Pet Restrictions: Small pets only
Exercise Area for Pets: Yes
Rates: $34.95 $54.95

Marietta Animal Hospital
416 Front St.
(614) 374-7419

MARION

Travel Lodge
1952 Marion-Mt. Gilead Rd.
Marion, OH 43302
Phone: (614) 389-4671

Pet Restrictions: $5/pet/night
Pet left unattended in room: Yes
    with front desk permission
Exercise Area for Pets: Yes
Rates: $43.95 to $65.95

Kantzer, John W.
P.O. Box 585
(614) 382-6613

MARYSVILLE

Country Hearth Inn
16510 Square Dr.
Marysville, OH 43040
Phone: (513) 644-8821

Pet Restrictions: Small pets only
Pet left unattended in room: Yes -
    no housekeeping
Exercise Area for Pets: Yes
Rates: $47 to $66

MASON

Best Western-Northeast
9847 Escort Dr.
Mason, OH 45040
Phone: (513) 398-3633

Pet Restrictions: None
Exercise Area for Pets: Yes
Rates: $29 to $150

Days Inn Kings Island
9735 Mason Montgomery Rd.
Mason, OH 45040
Phone: (513) 398-3297

Pet Restrictions: Small pets only
Pet left unattended in room: Yes -
    if caged
Exercise Area for Pets: Yes
Rates: $33 to $125

County Animal Hospital
1185 Reading Rd.
(513) 398-8000

Johnson, Richard W.
424 Reading Rd.
(513) 398-3070

MAUMEE

Hampton Inn Toledo South
1409 Reynolds Rd.
Maumee, OH 43537
Phone: (419) 893-1004,
(800) 426-7866
Pet Restrictions: Not in lobby during breakfast
Exercise Area for Pets: Yes
Rates: $46 to $54

Knights Inn-Toledo West
1520 Holland-Sylvania Rd.
Maumee, OH 43537
Phone: (419) 865-1380
Pet Restrictions: None
Exercise Area for Pets: Yes
Rates: $29.95 to $45.95

Red Roof Inn
1570 S. Reynolds Rd.
Maumee, OH 43537
Phone: (419) 893-0292
Pet Restrictions: None
Exercise Area for Pets: Yes
Rates: $29 to $50

MAYFIELD HEIGHTS

Budgetel Inn
1421 Golden Gate Blvd.
Mayfield Hts, OH 44124
Phone: (216) 442-8400,
(800) 428-3438 (central res.)
Pet Restrictions: None
Exercise Area for Pets: Yes
Rates: $38.95 to $52.95

MEDINA

Knights Inn
5200 Montville Dr.
Medina, OH 44256
Phone: (216) 722-4335
Pet Restrictions: None
Exercise Area for Pets: Yes
Rates: $25 to $67

VETERINARIANS

Nova Veterinary Service
4483 Wemouth Rd.
(216) 723-3200

Sternecker, W.T.
730 W Smith Rd.
(216) 722-0041

MENTOR

Arborgate Inn
7677 Reynolds St.
Mentor, OH 44060
Phone: (216) 946-0749,
(800) 843-5644
Pet Restrictions: Guest responsible for damages
Pet left unattended in room: Yes, must be caged or attended
Exercise Area for Pets: Yes
Rates: $34.95 to $50.95

Terrace Inn
9260 Mentor Ave.
Mentor, OH 44060
Phone: (216) 255-3456
Pet Restrictions: None
Exercise Area for Pets: Yes - except dogs
Rates: $35 to $50

VETERINARIANS

Lake Shore Animal Hospital
7761 Lake Shore Blvd.
(216) 257-7285

Sasala, James S.
8790 Munson Rd.
(216) 255-9761

MIAMISBURG

Knights Inn-South
185 Byers Rd.
Miamisburg, OH 45342
Phone: (513) 859-8797
Pet Restrictions: Owner liable. Pay with credit card.
Pet left unattended in room: Yes - if not caged room will not be serviced.
Exercise Area for Pets: Yes
Rates: $32.95 to $45

Motel 6
8101 Springboro Pike
Miamisburg, OH 45342
Phone: (513) 434-8750
Pet Restrictions: 1 small pet
Rates: $28.07 to $41.57

Red Roof Inn-South
222 Byers Rd.
Miamisburg, OH 45342
Phone: (513) 866-0705

Pet Restrictions: Under 25 lbs.
  Responsible for damages
Pet left unattended in room: Yes -
  only if caged
Exercise Area for Pets: Yes
Rates: $28.99 to $50

Residence Inn by Marriott-Dayton South
155 Prestige Rd.
Miamisburg, OH 45342
Phone: (513) 434-7881

Pet Restrictions: $10/nite for 1-10
  nights; $8/nite for 11-30 nights;
  $6/nite for 30 or more nights
Pet left unattended in room: Yes -
  no service unless caged
Exercise Area for Pets: Yes
Rates: $79 to $140

MIDDLEBURY HEIGHTSVILLE
Red Roof Inn
17555 Bagley Rd.
Middlebury Hts., OH 44130
Phone: (216) 243-2441

Pet Restrictions: None
Pet left unattended in room: Yes -
  but not at night
Exercise Area for Pets: Yes
Rates: $36.99 to $52.99

MONTPELIER
Holiday Inn Resort & Conference Center
on State Route 15
Montpelier, OH 43543
Phone: (419) 485-5555

Pet Restrictions: None
Pet left unattended in room: Yes -
  if quiet
Exercise Area for Pets: Yes
Rates: $45 to $200

NAPOLEON
Holiday Inn
2395 N. Scott St., P.O. Box 68
Napoleon, OH 43545
Phone: (419) 592-5010

Pet Restrictions: None
Exercise Area for Pets: Yes
Rates: $44 to $46

NEW PHILADELPHIA
Best Western-Valley Inn
131 Bluebell Dr. SW
New Philadelphia, OH 44663
Phone: (216) 339-7731

Pet Restrictions: $5/stay refund. dep.
Pet left unattended in room: Yes -
  if quiet
Exercise Area for Pets: Yes
Rates: $52 to $59

VETERINARIANS
Town and Country Veterinary Clinic
1396 E. High Ave.
(216) 339-2363

NEWARK
Howard Johnson Lodge
775 Hebron Rd.
Newark, OH 43055
Phone: (614) 522-3191

Pet Restrictions: Front wing rooms
  only
Pet left unattended in room: Yes -
  has to be caged
Exercise Area for Pets: Yes
Rates: $34.95 to $75

VETERINARIANS
Fuller, R.R.
1625 W. Church St.
(614) 344-2606

NILES
Park Inn International
1225 Youngstown-Warren Rd.
Niles, OH 44446
Phone: (216) 652-1761

Pet Restrictions: $25/stay only in
  certain rooms
Pet left unattended in room: Yes
Exercise Area for Pets: Yes
Rates: $49 to $69

NORTH CANTON
Red Roof Inn
5353 Inn Circle Ct.
North Canton, OH
Phone: (216) 499-1970

Pet Restrictions: None
Pet left unattended in room: Yes
Exercise Area for Pets: Yes
Rates: $35 to $47

VETERINARIANS

North Canton Veterinary Clinic
517 N. Main St.
(216) 499-5742

NORTH LIMA

Comfort Inn
10076 Market St.
North Lima, OH 44452
Phone: (216) 549-2187

Pet Restrictions: $5/pet/day
Pet left unattended in room: Yes
Exercise Area for Pets: Yes
Rates: $35 to $110

NORWALK

Econo-Lodge
342 Milan Ave.
Norwalk, OH 44857
Phone: (419) 668-8255,
     (800) 766-6868

Pet Restrictions: $20/stay deposit
Exercise Area for Pets: Yes
Rates: $33 to $88

LK Motel
283 Benedict Ave.
Norwalk, OH 44857
Phone: (419) 668-8255,
     (800) 282-5711

Pet Restrictions: None
Exercise Area for Pets: Yes
Rates: $30 to $119

VETERINARIANS

Maple View Animal Hospital
59 Benedict Ave.
(419) 668-1367

NORWOOD

Quality Hotel
4747 Montgomery Rd.
Norwood, OH 45212
Phone: (513) 351-6000,
     (800) 292-2079 (central res.)

Pet Restrictions: Small, well trained
Pet left unattended in room: Yes -
     if caged
Exercise Area for Pets: Yes
Rates: $64

OXFORD

College View Motel
4000 Oxford-Millville Rd.
Oxford, OH 45056
Phone: (513) 523-6311

Pet Restrictions: Quiet
Exercise Area for Pets: Yes
Rates: $32 to $48

PERRYSBURG

Best Western Executive Inn
27441 Helen Dr.
Perrysburg, OH 43551
Phone: (419) 874-9181

Pet Restrictions: None
Exercise Area for Pets: Yes
Rates: $44.95, + $5 p/person

Holiday Inn - French Quarter
10630 Freemont Pike, P.O. Box 268
Perrysburg, OH 43551
Phone: (419) 874-3111

Pet Restrictions: Outside rooms
     only. Leashed when out of room
Pet left unattended in room: Yes, if
     quiet
Exercise Area for Pets: Yes, leashed
Rates: $88 to $111

Holiday Inn-Perrysburg I-75
10621 Fremont Pike
Perrysburg, OH 43551
Phone: (419) 874-3101

Pet Restrictions: Small pets
Exercise Area for Pets: Yes
Rates: $57 to $66

VETERINARIANS

Perrysburg Animal Care
29098 Hufford Rd.
(419) 874-1836

Igoe, Denise A.
28315 Simmons Rd. #2
(419) 423-7232

Knepper, Donald R.
399 W. Boundary St.
(419) 874-3148

PORT CLINTON

LK Inn
1811 Harbor Rd.
Port Clinton, OH 43452
Phone: (419) 732-2111

Pet Restrictions: None
Exercise Area for Pets: Yes
Rates: $29.95 to $85

VETERINARIANS
Geiger, Robert R.
2360 E. Harbor Rd.
(419) 734-5202

PORTSMOUTH
Holiday Inn
State Highway 23
Portsmouth, OH 45662
Phone: (614) 354-2851
Pet Restrictions: Tell desk, must
check in with credit card
Pet left unattended in room: Yes
Exercise Area for Pets: Yes
Rates: $58 to $62

REYNOLDSBURG
La Quinta Motor Inn
2447 Brice Rd.
Reynoldsburg, OH 43068
Phone: (614) 866-6456
Pet Restrictions: Small-med.
pets only
Pet left unattended in room: Yes -
room will not be serviced
Exercise Area for Pets: Nearby
Rates: $41 to $62

Lenox Inn
13700 Reynoldsburg-Baltimore Rd.
P.O. Box 346
Reynoldsburg, OH 43068
Phone: (614) 861-7800,
(800) 821-0007
Pet Restrictions: $10/stay
Pet left unattended in room: Yes -
room will not be serviced
Exercise Area for Pets: Yes
Rates: $45 to $61

Red Roof Inn-East
2449 Brice Rd.
Reynoldsburg, OH 43068
Phone: (614) 864-3683
Pet Restrictions: Under 20 lbs.;
smoking rooms only
Pet left unattended in room: Yes
Exercise Area for Pets: Yes
Rates: $33.99 to $48.99

RICHFIELD
Holiday Inn Richfield
4742 Brecksville Rd., Rt. 21
Richfield, OH 44286
Phone: (216) 659-6151
Pet Restrictions: None
Pet left unattended in room: Yes
Exercise Area for Pets: Yes
Rates: $56 to $76

SHARONVILLE
Days Inn of Cincinnati
I-275 & Route 42
Sharonville, OH 45241
Phone: (513) 554-1400
Pet Restrictions: None
Pet left unattended in room: Yes
Exercise Area for Pets: Yes
Rates: $36 to $99

Envoy Inn
11620 Chester Rd.
Sharonville, OH 45246
Phone: (513) 771-0370,
(800) 358-2301
Pet Restrictions: Small pets
Pet left unattended in room: Yes -
room will not be serviced
Exercise Area for Pets: Yes
Rates: $27.95 to $44.95

Motel 6
3850 Hauck Rd.
Sharonville, OH 45241
Phone: (513) 563-1123
Pet Restrictions: 1 small pet.
Smoking rooms only
Exercise Area for Pets: Yes
Rates: $23.99 to $47.99

SIDNEY
Holiday Inn
400 Folkerth Ave.
Sidney, OH 45365
Phone: (513) 492-1131
Pet Restrictions: None
Pet left unattended in room: Yes -
notify front desk
Exercise Area for Pets: Yes, clean
up after
Rates: $45 and up

SPRINGDALE
Budgetel Inn
12150 Springfield Pike
Springdale, OH 45246
Phone: (513) 671-2300

Pet Restrictions: 1 small pet/room
Exercise Area for Pets: Yes
Rates: $36.95 to $52.95

Sheraton-Springdale
11911 Sheraton Ave.
Springdale, OH 45246
Phone: (513) 671-6600

Pet Restrictions: Dep. $25/day;
leashed when in public
Pet left unattended in room: Yes
Exercise Area for Pets: Yes
Rates: $74 to $125

VETERINARIANS
Eastview Veterinary Clinic
2754 E. Main St.
(513) 323-3719

Valley Veterinary Hospital
1233 W. First St.
(513) 325-4644

Henry, Charles D.
3681 Middle Urbana Rd.
(513) 390-2283

SPRINGFIELD
Drake Motel
3200 E. Main St.
Springfield, OH 45505
Phone: (513) 325-7334

Pet Restrictions: None
Exercise Area for Pets: Yes
Rates: $38

VETERINARIANS
Eastview Veterinary Clinic
2754 E. Main St.
(513) 323-3719

Valley Veterinary Hospital
1233 W. First St.
(513) 325-4644

ST. CLAIRSVILLE
Days Inn
52601 Holiday Dr.
St. Clairsville, OH 43950
Phone: (614) 695-0100,
(800) 551-0186

Pet Restrictions: None
Pet left unattended in room: Yes
Exercise Area for Pets: Yes
Rates: $47

Fischer Motel
P.O. Box 63
St. Clairsville, OH 43950
Phone: (614) 782-1715

Pet Restrictions: Cats & dogs only
housetrained
Exercise Area for Pets: Yes
Rates: $28.80 to $35.20

Red Roof Inn
68301 Red Roof Lane
St. Clairsville, OH 68301
Phone: (614) 695-4057

Pet Restrictions: None
Pet left unattended in room: Yes
Exercise Area for Pets: Yes
Rates: $37 to $50

STEUBENVILLE
Holiday Inn
University Blvd.
Steubenville, OH 43952
Phone: (614) 282-0901

Pet Restrictions: None
Pet left unattended in room: Yes -
if well-behaved
Exercise Area for Pets: Yes
Rates: $45 to $53

VETERINARIANS
Argos Veterinary Hospital
4357 Sunset Blvd.
(614) 264-3321

STOW
Stow Inn
4601 Darrow Rd.
Stow, OH 44224
Phone: (216) 688-3508

Pet Restrictions: None
Pet left unattended in room: Yes
Exercise Area for Pets: Yes, not in
court area
Rates: $36 to $62

Graham Road Animal Hospital
713 Graham Rd.
(216) 928-2625

STRONGSVILLE
Holiday Inn-Strongsville
15471 Royalton Rd.
Strongsville, OH 44136
Phone: (216) 238-8800

Pet Restrictions: Dep. $25 p/stay;
    small pets only
Exercise Area for Pets: Yes
Rates: $65 to $80

Red Roof Inn
15385 Royalton Rd.
Strongsville, OH 44136
Phone: (216) 238-0170

Pet Restrictions: None
Pet left unattended in room: Yes
Exercise Area for Pets: Yes
Rates: $36 to $52

VETERINARIANS
Bloze, Dalia M.
8260 Oxford Dr.
(216) 243-0141

Price, Loretta
16541 Pearl Rd.
(216) 238-4940

Sorm, Emilie A.
12514 Pearl Rd.
(216) 238-7797

TOLEDO
Red Roof Inn
3530 Executive Pkwy.
Toledo, OH 43606
Phone: (419) 536-0118

Pet Restrictions: None
Pet left unattended in room: Yes
Exercise Area for Pets: Yes
Rates: $25 to $54

VETERINARIANS
Bowers Animal Hospital
5104 Lewis Ave.
(419) 476-9105

Graber's Animal Hospital
3311 Laskey Rd.
(419) 475-3456

Sieben, Susan K.
4569 Forestview Dr.
(419) 536-4035

WADSWORTH
Knights Inn-Akron W.
810 High St.
Wadsworth, OH 44281
Phone: (216) 336-6671,
    (800) 843-5644

Pet Restrictions: Leash law in town.
    Notify when making reservation.
    Owner liable.
Pet left unattended in room: Yes,
    notify front desk
Exercise Area for Pets: Yes, clean
    up after
Rates: $32.95 to $47.95

WASHINGTON COURTHOUSE
Knights Inn
1820 Columbus Ave.
Washington Courthouse, OH 43160
Phone: (614) 335-9133

Pet Restrictions: Quiet
Pet left unattended in room: Yes, if
    small
Exercise Area for Pets: Yes
Rates: $32.95 to $40.95

VETERINARIANS
Junk, Gary D.
1973 US-62 NE
(614) 335-6161

WESTERVILLE
Knights Inn-Westerville
32 Heatherdown Dr.
Westerville, OH 43081
Phone: (614) 890-0426

Pet Restrictions: Quiet
Pet left unattended in room: Yes - if
    caged. No housekeeping unless
    owner is present
Exercise Area for Pets: Yes
Rates: $29.95 to $89

VETERINARIANS
Cryan, John H.
298 NW Street
(614) 882-4184

Stoughton, John E.
6147 Westerville Rd.
(614) 882-2332

WILMINGTON
LK Motel
264 W. Curry Rd.
Wilmington, OH 45177
Phone: (513) 382-6605,
　　(800) 282-5711
Pet Restrictions: None
Pet left unattended in room: Yes -
　caged if you want housekeeping
Exercise Area for Pets: Yes
Rates: $39 to $59

VETERINARIANS
Peterson, Stanley E.
960 W. Locust St.
(513) 382-0994

WILLOUGHBY
Red Roof Inn-Willoughby
4166 State Route 306
Willoughby, OH 44094
Phone: (216) 946-9872,
　　(800) 843-7663 (central res.)
Pet Restrictions: Small pets, notify
　when making reservations
Pet left unattended in room: Yes,
　quiet
Exercise Area for Pets: Yes
Rates: $41.99 to $57.99

VETERINARIANS
Pet Hospital of Willoughby
4131 Kirtland Rd.
(216) 942-8181

WOOSTER
L-K Motel
969 Timken Rd.
Wooster, OH 44691
Phone: (216) 264-9222,
　　(800) 282-5711 (central res.)
Pet Restrictions: Quiet
Pet left unattended in room: Yes
Exercise Area for Pets: Yes
Rates: $32 to $50

WORTHINGTON
Red Roof Inn
7474 High St.
Worthington, OH 43235
Phone: (614) 846-3001
Pet Restrictions: None
Pet left unattended in room: Yes
Exercise Area for Pets: Yes
Rates: $32 to $60

VETERINARIANS
Animal Hosp. of Worthington
5756 N. High St.
(614) 885-0333

Linworth Animal Hospital
2133 W. Granville Rd.
(614) 885-5170

YOUNGSTOWN
Best Western Meander Inn
870 N. Camfield-Niles Rd.
Youngstown, OH 44515
Phone: (216) 544-2378
Pet Restrictions: Dep. $6/night;
　smoking rooms only
Pet left unattended in room: Yes -
　short time only
Exercise Area for Pets: Yes
Rates: $48 to $95

Days Inn
8392 Market St.
Youngstown, OH 44512
Phone: (216) 758-2371
Pet Restrictions: $4/pet/day;
　weekdays only
Exercise Area for Pets: Yes
Rates: $38 to $185

VETERINARIANS
Austintown Veterinary Clinic
229 S. Canfield Niles
(216) 793-4621

Belmont Veterinary Clinic
2900 Belmont
(216) 759-9207

Craver Animal Hospital
234 5th Ave.
(216) 744-8607

ZANESVILLE
Holiday Inn
4645 E. Pike
Zanesville, OH 43701
Phone: (614) 453-0771
Pet Restrictions: Certain rooms only
Pet left unattended in room: Yes,
　quiet
Exercise Area for Pets: Yes
Rates: $63 to $72

VETERINARIANS
Brandywine Hospital for Pets
1384 Brandywine Blvd.
(614) 453-0539

Rostek, Deborah A.
2010 N. Hazel Avenue
(614) 454-6295

OKLAHOMA — HOTELS

ARDMORE

Holiday Inn
2705 Holiday Dr.
Ardmore, OK 73401
Phone: (405) 223-7130

Pet Restrictions: Housebroken
Exercise Area for Pets: Yes
Rates: $44 to $64

Lake Murray Resort
P.O. Box 1329
Ardmore, OK 73402
Phone: (405) 223-6600,
    (800) 654-8240

Pet Restrictions: Cabins only, must
    be leashed in public
Pet left unattended in room: Yes
Exercise Area for Pets: Yes
Rates: $43 to $195

Ramada Inn
Hwy 199
Ardmore, OK 73401
Phone: (405) 226-1250

Pet Restrictions: Small pets only
Pet left unattended in room: Yes
Exercise Area for Pets: Yes
Rates: $42 to $52

VETERINARIANS

Nightengale, Louis W.
P.O. Box 1814, 73401
(405) 223-0472

BROKEN ARROW

Holiday Inn South
2600 N. Aspen
Broken Arrow, OK 74012
Phone: (918) 258-7085

Pet Restrictions: 10 lbs. and under
Exercise Area for Pets: Nearby
Rates: $48 to $59

VETERINARIANS

Nail, Nicholas A.
550 West Florence St., 74011
(918) 455-7107

CATOOSA

Travelers Inn
19250 Timbercrest Circle
Catoosa, OK 74015
Phone: (918) 266-7000

Pet Restrictions: No cats, small pets
Exercise Area for Pets: Nearby
Rates: $19.76 to $35.95

CLINTON

Budget Inn
1413 Neptune Dr.
Clinton, OK 73601
Phone: (405) 323-9333

Exercise Area for Pets: Yes
Rates: $19.34 to $37.61

Park Inn International
2140 Gary Blvd.
Clinton, OK 73601
Phone: (405) 323-2010

Pet Restrictions: Domestic pets only
Pet left unattended in room: Yes
Exercise Area for Pets: Yes
Rates: $28 to $38

Travel Inn
1116 US 66
Clinton, OK 73601
Phone: (405) 323-1888

Pet Restrictions: Small, well behaved
Exercise Area for Pets: Yes
Rates: $25 and up

DEL CITY

La Quinta Motor Inn Del City
5501 Tinker Diagonal
Del City, OK 73115-4613
Phone: (405) 672-0067

Pet Restrictions: 15 lbs. and under
Exercise Area for Pets: Nearby
Rates: $47 to $69

DUNCAN

Travelodge
2535 Hwy 81 N.
Duncan, OK 73533
Phone: (405) 252-0810

Pet Restrictions: House trained
Pet left unattended in room: Yes
Exercise Area for Pets: Yes
Rates: $33 to $51

DURANT

Durant Inn
2121 W. Main St.
Durant, OK 74701
Phone: (405) 924-5432

Pet Restrictions: Housebroken, quiet
Pet left unattended in room: Yes, if
    quiet
Exercise Area for Pets: Yes
Rates: $24.77 to $43.95

ELK CITY

Best Western Elk City Inn
2015 W 3rd St.
Elk City, OK 73644
Phone: (405) 225-2331

Pet Restrictions: 2 per room
    maximum, prefer small pets
Exercise Area for Pets: Yes
Rates: $35 to $42

Flamingo Inn & Restaurant
2000 W 3rd St.
Elk City, OK 73644
Phone: (405) 225-1811,
    (800) 466-1811
Pet Restrictions: Small pets
Exercise Area for Pets: Yes
Rates: $26 to $36

Holiday Inn-Elk City
101 Meadow Ridge
Elk City, OK 73648
Phone: (405) 225-6637
Pet Restrictions: None
Pet left unattended in room: Yes
Exercise Area for Pets: Yes
Rates: $43 to $87

ERICK

Econo Lodge
I-40 & Hwy 30
Erick, OK 73645
Phone: (405) 526-3315,
    (800) 424-4777
Pet Restrictions: None
Exercise Area for Pets: Yes
Rates: $27.95 to $30.45

GUTHRIE

Harrison House
124 W. Harrison
Guthrie, OK 73044
Phone: (405) 282-1000,
    (800) 375-1001
Pet Restrictions: Very well-behaved,
    notify in advance
Exercise Area for Pets: Nearby
Rates: $57 to $102

GUYMON

Best Western Townsman Motel
E. Hwy. 54
Guymon, OK 73942
Phone: (405) 338-6556,
    (800) 245-0335
Pet Restrictions: Small pets,
    deposit, only through AAA
Exercise Area for Pets: Yes
Rates: $35 to $52

VETERINARIANS
Town and Country Veterinary Clinic
Highway 54 East 73942
(405) 338-5448

KINGSTON

Lake Texoma Resort
P.O. Box 248
Kingston, OK 73439
Phone: (405) 564-2311,
    (800) 654-8240

Pet Restrictions: Cabins only, not in
    lodge, must be leashed when
    outside
Pet left unattended in room: Yes
Exercise Area for Pets: Yes
Rates: $62 to $96

LAWTON

Howard Johnson Hotel
1125 E. Gore Blvd.
Lawton, OK 73501
Phone: (405) 353-0200

Pet Restrictions: $15, dog cannot be
    chained alone, deposit required
Pet left unattended in room: Yes,
    use do not disturb sign
Exercise Area for Pets: Yes
Rates: $44 to $140

Park Inn International Executive-Lawton
3110 Cashe Rd.
Lawton, OK 73505
Phone: (405) 353-3104

Pet Restrictions: Small pets; $5
Pet left unattended in room: Yes
Exercise Area for Pets: Yes
Rates: $37 to $50

Ramada Inn
601 N. 2nd St.
Lawton, OK 73507
Phone: (405) 355-7155,
    (800) 749-7155

Exercise Area for Pets: Yes
Rates: $42 to $50

VETERINARIANS
Great Plains Veterinary Hospital
6731 Cache Road 73505
(405) 563-5755

Midtown Animal Hospital
1101 Park Ave. 73501
(405) 353-3438

LONE WOLF
Quartz Mountain Resort
Rt. 1
Lone Wolf, OK 73655
Phone: (405) 563-2424,
   (800) 654-8240

Pet Restrictions: Small pets, in
   cabins only, leashed when
   outside, not allowed in lodge
Pet left unattended in room: Yes
Exercise Area for Pets: Yes
Rates: $57 to $88

McALASTER
Days Inn
1217 S. George Nigh Expwy
McAlaster, OK 74501
Phone: (918) 426-5050

Pet Restrictions: None
Pet left unattended in room: Yes, if
   quiet
Exercise Area for Pets: Yes
Rates: $32.56 to $47

MIDWEST CITY
Coachman Inn-Midwest
5653 Tinker Diagonal
Midwest City, OK 73110
Phone: (405) 733-1339,
   (800) THE INNS

Pet Restrictions: $25 deposit,
   checkout between 9-11:30 so
   housekeeping can inspect
Pet left unattended in room: Yes, no
   maid service, if quiet
Exercise Area for Pets: Yes
Rates: $35.95 to $50.95

Motel 6
5801 Tinker Diagonal
Midwest City, OK 73110
Phone: (405) 737-8851

Pet Restrictions: 1 small pet per
   room
Exercise Area for Pets: Yes
Rates: $22.95 and up

VETERINARIANS
Midwest Veterinary Hospital
720 South Air Depot 73110
(405) 732-4505

Easton, Marlys
1824 Suth Midwest Blvd 73110
(405) 737-4444

MUSKOGEE
Best Western Trade Winds Inn
534 S. 32nd St.
Muskogee, OK 74401
Phone: (918) 683-2951

Pet Restrictions: Back must
   measure less than 9″ unless
   with kennel club, no room
   cleaning
Exercise Area for Pets: Nearby
Rates: $41 to $49

Ramada Inn
800 S. 32nd St.
Muskogee, OK 74401
Phone: (918) 682-4341,
   (800) 722-9467

Pet Restrictions: Small, owner liable
   for damages
Pet left unattended in room: Yes
Exercise Area for Pets: Yes
Rates: $45 to $50/person

NORMAN
Residence Inn by Marriott
2681 Jefferson St.
Norman, OK 73069
Phone: (405) 366-0900

Pet Restrictions: $75 deposit, quiet
Pet left unattended in room: Yes if
   quiet, well behaved
Exercise Area for Pets: Nearby
Rates: $79 to $99

Sheraton Norman
1000 N. Interstate Dr.
Norman, OK 73072
Phone: (405) 364-2882,
   (800) 325-3535 (central res.)

Pet Restrictions: Small, owner liable
   for damage
Exercise Area for Pets: Yes
Rates: $60 to $125

VETERINARIANS
Fritzler, Beverly A.
14915 E. Imhoff Rd. 73071
(405) 321-3361

Harrington, Nancy Y.
501 Willow Branch Rd. 73072
(405) 364-6413

Hartung, Therese C.
111 North Mercedes 73069
(405) 364-1100

OKLAHOMA CITY

Best Western Saddleback Inn
4300 SW 3rd St.
Oklahoma City, OK 73108
Phone: (405) 947-7000,
    (800) 228-3903
Pet Restrictions: $25 deposit
Pet left unattended in room: Yes,
    notify desk
Exercise Area for Pets: Yes
Rates: $53 to $75

Century-Center Hotel
1 N. Broadway
Oklahoma City, OK 73102
Phone: (405) 235-2780,
    (800) 285-2780
Pet Restrictions: Under 10 lbs.
Pet left unattended in room: Yes, if
    quiet
Exercise Area for Pets: Nearby
Rates: $109 to $500

Days Inn Meridian
4712 W I-40
Oklahoma City, OK 73128
Phone: (405) 947-8721
Pet Restrictions: $5/stay, deposit
Pet left unattended in room: Yes,
    well behaved
Exercise Area for Pets: Yes
Rates: $31.95 and up

Days Inn-Northwest
2801 NW 39th St.
Oklahoma City, OK 73112
Phone: (405) 946-0741,
    (800) 992-3297
Pet Restrictions: Smoking rooms
    only, $15 deposit
Pet left unattended in room: Yes, if
    quiet
Exercise Area for Pets: Nearby
Rates: $38 to $60

Holiday Inn-Northwest
3535 NW 39th Expy
Oklahoma City, OK 73112
Phone: (405) 947-2351
Pet Restrictions: No cats
Pet left unattended in room: Yes, if
    caged
Exercise Area for Pets: Nearby
Rates: $49 to $58

Holiday Inn-West
801 S. Meridian Ave.
Oklahoma City, OK 73108
Phone: (405) 942-8511
Pet Restrictions: Not allowed in
    main building
Pet left unattended in room: Yes,
    must be caged
Exercise Area for Pets: Yes
Rates: $55 to $76

Howard Johnson Lodge
400 S. Meridian
Oklahoma City, OK 73108
Phone: (405) 943-9841
Pet Restrictions: Nothing over 10
    lbs.
Pet left unattended in room: Yes, if
    caged
Exercise Area for Pets: Yes
Rates: $34 to $46

Lincoln Plaza Hotel & Conference Center
4445 Lincoln Blvd.
Oklahoma City, OK 73105
Phone: (405) 528-2741,
    (800) 741-2741
Pet Restrictions: Under 15 lbs., $20
    deposit
Pet left unattended in room: Yes
Exercise Area for Pets: Yes
Rates: $65 to $175

Marriott
3233 NW Expwy
Oklahoma City, OK 73112
Phone: (405) 842-6633
Pet Restrictions: Must sign waiver
Pet left unattended in room: Yes,
    notify desk
Exercise Area for Pets: Nearby
Rates: $119 and up

Motel 6
12121 NE Expwy
Oklahoma City, OK 73131
Phone: (405) 478-4030
Pet Restrictions: 1 small pet per
    room, smoking rooms only,
    notify desk
Exercise Area for Pets: Yes
Rates: $25.10 to $31.66

OKLAHOMA — HOTELS (continued)

Motel 6
4200 W. I-40
Oklahoma City, OK 73108
Phone: (405) 947-6550
Pet Restrictions: 1 small pet
Exercise Area for Pets: Yes
Rates: $27.95 to $33.95

Radisson Inn
401 S. Meridian
Oklahoma City, OK 73108
Phone: (405) 947-7681
Pet Restrictions: Under 25 lbs.
Exercise Area for Pets: Yes
Rates: $57.67 to $79.89

Ramada Inn South
6800 S I-35
Oklahoma City, OK 73149
Phone: (405) 631-3321
Pet Restrictions: Pay with credit
  card, no large dogs
Exercise Area for Pets: Yes
Rates: $45 to $49

Red Carpet Inn
8217 I-35
Oklahoma City, OK 73149
Phone: (405) 632-0807
Pet Restrictions: Small pets, $25
  deposit
Pet left unattended in room: Yes,
  notify desk
Exercise Area for Pets: Yes
Rates: $21.95 to $39.95

Residence Inn by Marriott
4361 W. Reno Ave.
Oklahoma City, OK 73107
Phone: (405) 942-4500
Pet Restrictions: No snakes, $25
  plus $6/day/pet, $10/day/2 pets,
  no more than 2 pets per room
Pet left unattended in room: Yes
Exercise Area for Pets: Yes
Rates: $90 to $110

Rodeway Inn
4601 SW 3rd St.
Oklahoma City, OK 73128
Phone: (405) 947-2400,
  (800) 292-7929
Pet Restrictions: Quiet, well behaved
Pet left unattended in room: Yes but
  no room service
Exercise Area for Pets: Yes
Rates: $34 to $38

Southgate Inn
5245 S. I-35
Oklahoma City, OK 73129
Phone: (405) 672-5561
Pet Restrictions: None

Trade Winds Central Motor Inn-Best Western
1800 E. Reno
Oklahoma City, OK 73117
Phone: (405) 235-4531
Pet Restrictions: Prefer them to be
  caged
Pet left unattended in room: Yes, no
  cleaning unless caged
Rates: $41 to $49

VETERINARIANS

Crestwood Animal Hospital
9100 North MacArthur 73132
(405) 721-9276

Grant Square Animal Hospital
2124 SW 44th St. 73119
(405) 685-0131

Quail Creek Veterinary Clinic
2915 NW 122nd St. 73120
(405) 755-0746

PAULS VALLEY
Amish Inn Motel
Rt. 3, P.O. Box 298
Pauls Valley, OK 73075
Phone: (405) 238-7545
Pet Restrictions: None
Pet left unattended in room: Yes
Exercise Area for Pets: Yes
Rates: $26

PERRY
Best Western Cherokee Strip Motel
Hwy 6477 & I-65
Perry, OK 73077
Phone: (405) 238-7545
Pet Restrictions: None
Pet left unattended in room: Yes, if
  caged
Exercise Area for Pets: Yes
Rates: $35 to $54

SALLISAW

Green Country Motel
2403 E. Cherokee, Hwy 64 & I-40
Sallisaw, OK 74955
Phone: (918) 775-7981
Pet Restrictions: None
Pet left unattended in room: Yes
Exercise Area for Pets: Yes
Rates: $21 to $23.76

Holiday Inn Express
1300 E. Cherokee
Sallisaw, OK 74955
Phone: (918) 775-7791
Pet Restrictions: None
Pet left unattended in room: Yes,
notify desk
Exercise Area for Pets: Yes
Rates: $36 to $42

VETERINARIANS
Talley, Mike
P.O. Box 642, 74955
(918) 775-6182

SHAWNEE

Best Western Cinderella Motor Hotel
623 Kickapoo Spur
Shawnee, OK 74801
Phone: (405) 273-7010
Pet Restrictions: No hoofed animals
Pet left unattended in room: Yes
Exercise Area for Pets: Yes
Rates: $41 to $61

Holiday Habor Motel
12510 Valley View Rd.
Shawnee, OK 74801
Phone: (405) 275-1005
Pet Restrictions: No large dogs,
$5/pet/day
Pet left unattended in room: Yes
Exercise Area for Pets: Yes
Rates: $22 to $26

VETERINARIANS
Barker, Robert R.
Route 8, Lake Rd., 74801
(405) 273-5617

STILLWATER

Executive Inn
5010 W. 6th St.
Stillwater, OK 74074
Phone: (405) 743-2570
Pet Restrictions: None
Pet left unattended in room: Yes
Exercise Area for Pets: Yes
Rates: $28 to $52

VETERINARIANS
Baker Animal Clinic
2003 N. Boomer Rd. 74074
(405) 372-4525

Boren Veterinary Medical Teaching Hospital
Oklahoma State University
(405) 624-6731

STROUD

Best Western Stroud Motor Lodge
1200 N. 8th St.
Stroud, OK 74079
Phone: (918) 968-9515
Pet Restrictions: Small animals
Exercise Area for Pets: Yes
Rates: $38 to $40

TULSA

Best Western Trade Winds Central Inn
3141 E. Skelly Dr.
Tulsa, OK 74105
Phone: (918) 749-5561
Pet Restrictions: None
Pet left unattended in room: Yes,
inform housekeeping
Exercise Area for Pets: Yes
Rates: $56 to $87

Best Western Trade Winds East
3337 E. Skelly Dr.
Tulsa OK 74135
Phone: (918) 743-7931
Pet Restrictions: Small pets
Exercise Area for Pets: Yes
Rates: $42 to $56

Days Inn Tulsa
8201 E. Skelly Dr.
Tulsa, OK 74129
Phone: (918) 665-6800
Pet Restrictions: $25 deposit, under
25 lbs.
Pet left unattended in room: Yes
Exercise Area for Pets: Yes
Rates: $38 then $4/person, under
18 free

Doubletree Hotel at Warren Place
610 S. Yale
Tulsa, OK 74136
Phone: (918) 495-1000
Pet Restrictions: $100 deposit, under 100 lbs.
Pet left unattended in room: Yes, if caged
Exercise Area for Pets: Yes
Rates: $64 to $148

Hawthorne Suites Hotel
3509 S 79th East Ave.
Tulsa, OK 74145
Phone: (918) 663-3900, (800) 527-1133
Pet Restrictions: Not too large, $150 deposit ($25 non-refund.)
Pet left unattended in room: Yes
Exercise Area for Pets: Yes
Rates: $76 to $110

Holiday Inn-East Airport
1010 N. Garnett Rd.
Tulsa, OK 74116
Phone: (918) 437-7660
Pet Restrictions: Owner liable for damages
Pet left unattended in room: Yes, no cleaning
Exercise Area for Pets: Yes
Rates: $66

Holiday Inn-Tulsa Cental Holidome
8181 E. Skelly Dr.
Tulsa, OK 74129
Phone: (918) 663-4541
Pet Restrictions: Small pets only
Pet left unattended in room: Yes, well behaved
Exercise Area for Pets: Yes
Rates: $49 to $70

La Quinta Motor Inn
10829 E. 41st St. South
Tulsa, OK 74146
Phone: (918) 665-0220, (800) 531-5900
Pet Restrictions: 1 pet/room, under 25 lbs, register at desk
Pet left unattended in room: Yes, notify desk
Exercise Area for Pets: Yes
Rates: $44 to $60

La Quinta Motor Inn
35 N. Sheridan Rd.
Tulsa, OK 74115
Phone: (918) 836-3931, (800) 531-5900
Pet Restrictions: Under 20 lbs.
Pet left unattended in room: Yes, no housekeeping
Exercise Area for Pets: Yes
Rates: $47 to $55

Marriott
10918 E. 41st St.
Tulsa, OK 74146
Phone: (918) 627-5000
Pet Restrictions: Notify in advance
Pet left unattended in room: Yes, short time only
Exercise Area for Pets: Yes

Quality Inn
222 North Garnet Rd.
Tulsa, OK 74116
Phone: (918) 438-0780, (800) 221-2222
Pet Restrictions: $5/pet/night
Exercise Area for Pets: Yes
Rates: $42 to $48

VETERINARIANS

Capron Veterinary Hospital
6705 E 51st 74145
(918) 627-5188

Veterinary Associates
6925 S 69 East Ave. 74133
(918) 492-4200

Woodland Animal Hospital
4720 East 51st St. 74135
(918) 496-2111

WAGONER
Western Hills Guest Ranch
P.O. Box 509
Wagoner, OK 74477
Phone: (918) 772-2545
Pet Restrictions: Only in cabins, owner liable for damages
Pet left unattended in room: Yes
Exercise Area for Pets: Yes
Rates: $45 to $98

WATONGA
Roman Nose Resort
Rt. 1
Watonga, OK 73772
Phone: (405) 623-7281,
(800) 654-8240

Pet Restrictions: Not in lodge,
housed in kennel, allowed in
cabins, leash law
Exercise Area for Pets: Yes
Rates: $50 to $73

WEATHERFORD
Best Western Mark Motel
525 E. Main
Weatherford, OK 73096
Phone: (405) 772-3325

Pet Restrictions: Owner liable for
damages
Pet left unattended in room: Yes, if
caged
Exercise Area for Pets: Yes
Rates: $36 to $49

VETERINARIANS
Cox, Thomas K.
Route 4, P.O. Box 19, 73096
(405) 774-2915

OREGON — HOTELS

ASHLAND

Best Western Bard's Inn Motel
132 N. Main St.
Ashland, OR 97520
Phone: (503) 482-0049

Pet Restrictions: 1 building only;
    $10/pet/night deposit; leash &
    scoop law
Pet left unattended in room: Yes, no
    housekeeping
Exercise Area for Pets: Nearby
Rates: $48 to $125

Knights Inn Motel
2359 Hwy 66
Ashland, OR 97520
Phone: (503) 482-5111

Pet Restrictions: $6/day/pet; must
    have credit card
Exercise Area for Pets: Yes
Rates: $33 to $52

Windmill's Ashland Hills Inn
2525 Ashland St.
Ashland, OR 97520
Phone: (503) 482-8310,
    (800) 547-4747 (central res.)

Pet Restrictions: In smoking rooms
Pet left unattended in room: Yes
Exercise Area for Pets: Yes
Rates: $45 to $225

Vandijk, Leo J.
1525 Highway 99 North
Phone: (503) 482-2786

BEND

Best Western Entrada Lodge
19221 Century Dr.
Bend, OR 97702
Phone: (503) 382-4080

Pet Restrictions: Must have credit
    card; $5/pet/night
Pet left unattended in room: No, will
    be picked up by shelter
Exercise Area for Pets: Yes
Rates: $55 to $85

Best Western Woodstone Inn
721 NE 3rd
Bend, OR 97701
Phone: (503) 382-1515

Pet Restrictions: $5/pet/night; stay
    off pool area
Exercise Area for Pets: Yes
Rates: $45 to $75

Hampton Inn
15 NE Butler Rd.
Bend, OR 97701
Phone: (503) 388-4114,
    (800) 426-7866

Exercise Area for Pets: Yes
Rates: $44 to $63

The Riverhouse Motor Inn
3075 N Hwy 97
Bend, OR 97701
Phone: (503) 389-3111,
    (800) 547-3928

Pet Restrictions: Must be leashed at
    all times (leash law in town)
Pet left unattended in room: Yes, if
    caged
Exercise Area for Pets: Yes
Rates: $55 to $150

Westward Ho Motel
904 SE 3rd St.
Bend, OR 97702
Phone: (503) 382-2111,
    (800) 999-8143

Pet Restrictions: $2/pet/night
Exercise Area for Pets: Yes
Rates: $28 to $115

Central Oregon Animal Hospital
366 Northeast Underwood
Phone: (503) 382-7067

Loomis, Susan C.
1474 NW Hill St.
Phone: (503) 382-2481

McKim, Frank W.
2124 NE Division St.
Phone: (503) 382-0741

BOARDMAN

Nugget Inn
105 South Front St.
Boardman, OR 97818
Phone: (503) 481-2375,
    (800) 336-4485

Pet Restrictions: $5/pet/stay
Exercise Area for Pets: Nearby
Rates: $32 to $69

BURNS

Ponderosa Best Western
577 W. Monroe
Burns, OR 97720
Phone: (503) 573-2047
Pet Restrictions: No intimidating
   large dogs
Exercise Area for Pets: Yes

Royal Inn
999 Oregon Ave.
Burns, OR 97720
Phone: (503) 573-5295
Pet Restrictions: Stay off furniture,
   housebroken, $10/day deposit
Exercise Area for Pets: Yes
Rates: $39 to $74

CAMP SHERMAN

House on the Metolius
P.O. Box 601, Forest Svc. Rd. 1420
Camp Sherman, OR 97730
Phone: (503) 595-6620 summer
Pet Restrictions: None
Exercise Area for Pets: Yes
Rates: $100 to $150

CANNON BEACH

Best Western Surfsand Resort
P.O. Box 219
Cannon Beach, OR 97110
Phone: (503) 436-2274,
   (800) 547-6100
Pet Restrictions: $5/pet/day
Exercise Area for Pets: Yes
Rates: $64 to $209

COOS BAY

Best Western Holiday Motel
411 N. Bayshore Dr.
Coos Bay, OR 97420
Phone: (503) 269-5111,
   (800) 228-8655
Pet Restrictions: Under 20 lbs., 1
   pet/room; $3/day
Exercise Area for Pets: Yes
Rates: $50 to $64

VETERINARIANS
Morgan Veterinary Hospital
230 Market St.
Phone: (503) 269-5846

CORVALLIS

Shanico Inn
1113 NW 9th Ave.
Corvallis, OR 97330
Phone: (503) 754-7474,
   (800) 432-1233
Pet Restrictions: Ground floor
   rooms only; $5/day
Exercise Area for Pets: Yes
Rates: $38 to $60

VETERINARIANS
Corvallis Veterinary Hospital
1543 Northwest 9th St.
Phone: (503) 752-5595

Pioneer Veterinary Clinic
5610 SW Philomath Blvd.
Phone: (503) 753-4681

Williamette Veterinary Clinic
650 Southwest 3rd St.
Phone: (503) 753-2223

COTTAGE GROVE

BW Village Green Motor Hotel
725 Row River Rd.
Cottage Grove, OR 97424
Phone: (503) 942-2491,
   (800) 343-7666
Pet Restrictions: Smoking rooms
   only. Leashed while in public
   areas of hotel
Pet left unattended in room: Yes, no
   housecleaning
Exercise Area for Pets: Yes
Rates: $69 to $82

VETERINARIANS
Forest Valley Veterinary Clinic
2555 Mosby Creek Rd.
Phone: (503) 942-9132

EUGENE

Best West. New Oregon Motel
1655 Franklin Blvd.
Eugene, OR 97440
Phone: (503) 683-3669
Pet Restrictions: Leashed while on
   hotel property; Refund. deposit
   $25/stay
Exercise Area for Pets: Nearby
Rates: $66 to $70.50

Eugene Hilton
66 E. 6th & Oak St.
Eugene, OR 97401
Phone: (503) 342-2000,
   (800) 937-6660

Pet Restrictions: $25/stay
Pet left unattended in room: Yes
Exercise Area for Pets: Nearby
Rates: $112 to $132

VETERINARIANS
Animal Health Associates
2835 S. Willamette
Phone: (503) 345-1544

Eugene Animal Hospital
1432 Orchard St.
Phone: (503) 342-1178

The Veterinary Med. Center
621 River Avenue
Phone: (503) 689-9191

FLORENCE
Park Motel
85034 Hwy 101
Florence, OR 97439
Phone: (503) 997-2634,
   (800) 392-0441

Pet Restrictions: $4/pet/night; on leash
Exercise Area for Pets: Yes
Rates: $29 to $73

GLENEDEN BEACH
Salishan Lodge
7760 Hwy 101
Gleneden Beach, OR 97388
Phone: (503) 764-2371,
   (800) 452-2300

Pet Restrictions: $10/night/pet deposit
Exercise Area for Pets: Yes
Rates: $104 to $207

GOLD BEACH
Jot's Resort
94360 Webberburn Loop Rd.
Gold Beach, OR 97444
Phone: (503) 247-6676,
   (800) 367-5687

Pet Restrictions: Rooms with 2 queen beds only; $5/day
Exercise Area for Pets: Yes
Rates: $50 to $165

River Bridge Inn
1010 Jerry's Flat Rd.
Gold Beach, OR 97444
Phone: (503) 247-4533,
   (800) 759-4533

Pet Restrictions: None
Pet left unattended in room: Yes
Exercise Area for Pets: Nearby
Rates: $32 to $69

Tu Tu Ton Lodge
96550 North Bank Rogue
Gold Beach, OR 97444
Phone: (503) 247-6664

Pet Restrictions: No pets in July, Aug.
Pet left unattended in room: Yes
Exercise Area for Pets: Yes
Rates: $100 to $189

Western Village Motel
975 S. Ellensburg
Gold Beach, OR 97444
Phone: (503) 247-6611

Pet Restrictions: Small to medium pets; $5/stay
Exercise Area for Pets: Nearby
Rates: $27 to $58

GRANTS PASS
Riverside Inn
971 SE 6th St.
Grants Pass, OR 97526
Phone: (503) 476-6873,
   (800) 334-4567

Pet Restrictions: $15 charge, $5 each add'l pet
Exercise Area for Pets: Yes
Rates: $55 to $225

SHILO INN GRANTS PASS
1880 NW 6th St.
Grants Pass, OR 97526
Phone: (503) 479-8391,
   (800) 222-2244

Pet Restrictions: $6/pet
Exercise Area for Pets: Yes
Rates: $48 to $58

VETERINARIANS
Grant's Pass Veterinary Clinic
535 SW Lincoln Rd.
Phone: (503) 476-7769

Redwood Veterinary Hospital
1326A Dowell Rd.
Phone: (503) 476-2271

HUNTINGTON

Farewell Bend Motor Inn
I 84 exit 353 or Rt 2 Box 17
Huntington, OR 97907
Phone: (503) 869-2211
Pet Restrictions: None
Pet left unattended in room: Yes; for
    a short while
Exercise Area for Pets: Yes
Rates: $34 to $46

JOHN DAY

Best Western Inn
315 W. Main
John Day, OR 97845
Phone: (503) 575-1700
Pet Restrictions: Smoking rooms
    only; small - medium pets;
    $2.50/pet
Pet left unattended in room: Yes, for
    short time
Exercise Area for Pets: Yes
Rates: $48.50 to $54.50

Dreamers Lodge
144 N. Canyon Blvd.
John Day, OR 97845
Phone: (503) 575-0526,
    (800) 654-2849
Pet Restrictions: None
Exercise Area for Pets: Yes
Rates: $34 to $46

John Day Sunset Inn
390 W. Main
John Day, OR 97845
Phone: (503) 575-1462
Pet Restrictions: Not allowed in
    pool; $2/pet/night
Exercise Area for Pets: Yes
Rates: $40 to $42

LAKE OSWEGO

Best Western Sherwood Inn
15700 SW Upper Boones Ferry Rd.
Lake Oswego, OR 97035
Phone: (503) 620-2980
Pet Restrictions: Under 40 lbs.
    Leashed on hotel property;
    $5/pet/day
Exercise Area for Pets: Yes
Rates: $56

The Residence Inn/Portland S.
15200 SW Bangy Rd.
Lake Oswego, OR 97035
Phone: (503) 684-2603
Pet Restrictions: $10/night (1-6
    nights) $100 & $15 (7 or more
    nights) fee
Pet left unattended in room: Yes
Exercise Area for Pets: Yes
Rates: $108 to $142

VETERINARIANS

Groves Animal Clinic
433 3rd St.
Phone: (503) 635-3573

Lake Grove Vet. Clinic
17131 Southwest Boones Ferry
Phone: (503) 636-5681

LINCOLN CITY

Coho Inn
1635 NW Harbor Ave.
Lincoln City, OR 97367
Phone: (503) 994-3684,
    (800) 848-7006 (WA & OR only)
Pet Restrictions: Small-med pets;
    $6/stay
Exercise Area for Pets: Nearby
Rates: $62 to $78

Shilo Inn Lincoln City
1501 NW 40th St.
Lincoln City, OR 97367
Phone: (503) 994-3655,
    (800) 222-2244
Pet Restrictions: $6/pet/night; 1st
    floor (40 rooms)
Exercise Area for Pets: Yes
Rates: $48 to $94

MADRAS

Leisure Inn
12 SW 4th St.
Madras, OR 97741
Phone: (503) 475-6141
Pet Restrictions: Smoking rooms
    only; $4/stay
Exercise Area for Pets: Yes
Rates: $27 to $53

OREGON — HOTELS (continued)

Sonny's Motel
1539 SW Hwy 97
Madras, OR 97741
Phone: (503) 475-7217,
   (800) 624-6137
Pet Restrictions: $5/stay
Exercise Area for Pets: Yes
Rates: $32 to $65

MEDFORD
Horizon Motor Inn
1150 E. Barnett Rd.
Medford, OR 97504
Phone: (503) 779-5085,
   (800) 452-2255
Pet Restrictions: $10/stay
Exercise Area for Pets: Nearby
Rates: $50 to $150

Shilo Inn Medford
2111 Biddle Rd.
Medford, OR 97504
Phone: (503) 770-5151,
   (800) 222-2244
Pet Restrictions: $6/pet/day
Exercise Area for Pets: Yes
Rates: $49 to $80

Windmill Inn of Medford
1950 Biddle Rd.
Medford, OR 97504
Phone: (503) 779-0050
Pet Restrictions: None
Pet left unattended in room: Yes
Exercise Area for Pets: Yes
Rates: $48 to $69

NEWBERG
Shilo Inn - Newberg
501 Sitka Ave.
Newberg, OR 97132
Phone: (503) 537-0303,
   (800) 222-2244
Pet Restrictions: $6/pet/day
Pet left unattended in room: Yes,
   quiet
Exercise Area for Pets: Nearby
Rates: $62 to $68

VETERINARIANS
Holveck, Robert K.
18220 N.E. Chehalem Dr.
(503) 538-8334

NEWPORT
Shilo Inn - Newport
536 SW Elizabeth
Newport, OR 97365
Phone: (503) 265-7701,
   (800) 222-2244
Pet Restrictions: $6/pet/day
Exercise Area for Pets: Nearby

VETERINARIANS
Animal Medical Care of Newport
159 NE Tenth St.
(503) 265-6671

Grove Veterinary Clinic
448 East Olive St.
(503) 265-2381

NORTH BEND
Pony Village Motor Lodge
at Pony Village Shopping Center
North Bend, OR 97459
Phone: (503) 756-3191
Pet Restrictions: 12 rooms only;
   $3/pet/day
Exercise Area for Pets: Yes
Rates: $46 to $65

VETERINARIANS
Harbor Lights Animal Hospital
1710 Virginia Avenue
Phone: (503) 756-5156

OREGON CITY
Val-U-Inn Motel
1900 Clackamette Dr.
Oregon City, OR 97045
Phone: (503) 655-7141,
   (800) 443-7777
Pet Restrictions: $5/pet/day
Exercise Area for Pets: Nearby
Rates: $66 to $120

PENDLETON
Econo Lodge
201 SW Court
Pendleton, OR 97801
Phone: (503) 276-5252
Pet Restrictions: $5/day
Exercise Area for Pets: Yes
Rates: $28 to $50

Tapadera Motor Inn
105 SE Court Ave.
Pendleton, OR 97801
Phone: (503) 276-3231,
   (800) 722-8277
Pet Restrictions: None
Exercise Area for Pets: Nearby
Rates: $19.50 to $51.50

PORTLAND

Holiday Inn - Airport
8439 NE Columbia Blvd.
Portland, OR 97220
Phone: (503) 256-5000
Pet Restrictions: $50 refund. deposit
Pet left unattended in room: Yes,
   quiet
Exercise Area for Pets: Yes
Rates: $83 to $225

Imperial Hotel
400 SW Broadway
Portland, Or 97205
Phone: (503) 228-7221,
   (800) 452-2323
Pet Restrictions: Small pets;
   $10/stay
Exercise Area for Pets: Nearby
Rates: $70 to $85

Lloyd Center Shilo
1506 NE 2nd Ave.
Portland, OR 97232
Phone: (503) 231-7665
Pet Restrictions: $6/day
Exercise Area for Pets: Yes
Rates: $51 to $59

Mallory Motor Hotel
729 SW 15th
Portland, OR 97205
Phone: (503) 223-6311,
   (800) 228-8657
Pet Restrictions: $10/stay
Pet left unattended in room: Yes, if
   well behaved
Exercise Area for Pets: Nearby
Rates: $45 to $75

Portland Marriott
1401 SW Front Ave.
Portland, OR 97201
Phone: (503) 226-7600
Pet Restrictions: Sign waiver; owner
   responsible for damages
Exercise Area for Pets: Nearby
Rates: $125 to $450

Quality Inn
8247 NE Sandy Blvd
Portland, OR 97220
Phone: (503) 256-4111,
   (800) 221-2222
Pet Restrictions: $10/stay
Pet left unattended in room: Yes
Exercise Area for Pets: Yes
Rates: $50 to $85

Red Lion Inn Columbia River
1401 N. Hayden Island Dr.
Portland, OR 97217
Phone: (503) 283-2111,
   (800) 547-8010 (central res.)
Pet Restrictions: Under 20 lbs.;
   $15/stay
Exercise Area for Pets: Yes
Rates: $99 to $114

Red Lion - Downtown
310 W. Lincoln St.
Portland, OR 97217
Phone: (503) 221-0450
Pet Restrictions: Under 35 lbs.
Pet left unattended in room: Yes,
   notify desk
Exercise Area for Pets: Yes
Rates: $108 to $118

Red Lion Motor Inn - Jantzen Beach
909 N. Hayden Island Dr.
Portland, OR 97217
Phone: (503) 283-4466,
   (800) 547-8010
Pet Restrictions: 1st floor only;
   under 35 lbs.
Pet left unattended in room: Yes,
   notify housekeeping
Exercise Area for Pets: Yes
Rates: $105 to $140

Red Lion Inn - Lloyd Ctr
1000 NE Multnomah St.
Portland, OR 97232
Phone: (503) 281-6111
Pet Restrictions: Notify in advance
Exercise Area for Pets: Nearby
Rates: $77 to $160

The Riverplace Hotel
1510 SW Harbor Way
Portland, OR 97201
Phone: (503) 228-3233,
   (800) 426-0670 (central res.)
Pet Restrictions: Leash law in town;
   sign waiver
Exercise Area for Pets: Yes
Rates: $145 to $500

Shilo Inn Portland Airport
3828 NE 82nd Ave.
Portland, OR 97220
Phone: (503) 256-2550,
    (800) 222-2244
Pet Restrictions: $8/pet/day
Exercise Area for Pets: Nearby
Rates: $45 to $75

Shilo Inn Lloyd Center
1506 NE 2nd Ave.
Portland, OR 97232
Phone: (503) 231-7665,
    (800) 222-2244
Pet Restrictions: $6/day
Exercise Area for Pets: Nearby
Rates: $61 to $69

Travelodge-Portland-Troutdale
23705 NE Sandy Blvd.
Portland, OR 97060
Phone: (503) 666-6623
Pet Restrictions: No big dogs;
    $6/day
Exercise Area for Pets: Yes
Rates: $38 to $60

VETERINARIANS

Fremont Veterinary Clinic
5055 NE Fremont St.
Phone: (503) 282-0991

North Portland Animal Clinic
2009 N. Killingsworth
Phone: (503) 285-0462

REEDSPORT
Western Hills Motel
1821 Winchester Ave.
Reedsport, OR 97467
Phone: (503) 271-2149
Pet Restrictions: $5/pet/day
Exercise Area for Pets: Nearby
Rates: $36 to $105

ROCKAWAY
Tradewinds Motel
523 N. Pacific St.
Rockaway Beach, OR 97136
Phone: (503) 355-2112
Pet Restrictions: $10/stay; cats
    declawed; 1 pet/family
Exercise Area for Pets: Yes
Rates: $51.40 to $219.15

ROSEBURG
Windmill Inn
1450 Mulholland Dr.
Roseburg, OR 97470
Phone: (503) 673-0901,
    (800) 547-4747 (central res.)
Pet Restrictions: Downstairs,
    smoking rooms only
Pet left unattended in room: Yes
Exercise Area for Pets: Yes
Rates: $52 to $74

VETERINARIANS

Parkway Animal Hospital
2655 Northwest Broad St.
Phone: (503) 672-1621

Bailey, Robert B.
1356 NW Troost St.
Phone: (503) 673-4403

SALEM
Quality Inn Hotel & Conv. Ctr.
3301 Market St. NE
Salem, OR 97301
Phone: (503) 370-7888,
    (800) 248-6273
Pet Restrictions: $10/stay
Pet left unattended in room: Yes,
    quiet
Exercise Area for Pets: Yes
Rates: $42 to $150

City Center Motel
510 Liberty SE
Salem, OR 97301
Phone: (503) 364-0121,
    (800) 289-0121
Pet Restrictions: $3/day
Pet left unattended in room: Yes, if
    quiet
Exercise Area for Pets: Nearby
Rates: $40 to $48

VETERINARIANS

Animal Clinic
3230 Triangle Dr. SE
Phone: (503) 581-1438

Keizer Veterinary Clinic
4815 River Road North
Phone: (503) 393-3633

OREGON — HOTELS (continued)

SISTERS
Lake Creek Lodge
Star Route
Sisters, OR 97759
Phone: (503) 595-6331
Pet Restrictions: $3/day; off season only
Exercise Area for Pets: Yes
Rates: $55 to $140

SPRINGFIELD
Red Lion Inn/Eugene-Sprgfld
3280 Gateway Rd.
Springfield, OR 97477
Phone: (503) 726-8181,
(800) 547-8010
Pet Restrictions: Smoking rooms only
Pet left unattended in room: Yes
Exercise Area for Pets: Nearby
Rates: $59 to $92

Shilo Inn Eugene/Springfield
3350 Gateway
Springfield, Or 97477
Phone: (503) 747-0332,
(800) 222-2244
Pet Restrictions: $6/pet/day
Pet left unattended in room: Yes
Exercise Area for Pets: Nearby
Rates: $49 to $64

VETERINARIANS
McKenzie Animal Clinic
5303 Main St.
Phone: (503) 747-3859

SURTHERLIN
Ponderosa Inn
1470 Central
Surtherlin, OR 97479
Phone: (503) 459-2236
Pet Restrictions: $5/stay
Exercise Area for Pets: Yes
Rates: $36.75 to $55.65

THE DALLES
Shilo Inn
3223 Bret Clodfelter Way
The Dalles, OR 97058
Phone: (503) 298-5502
Pet Restrictions: Ground floor rooms only; $6/pet/day
Exercise Area for Pets: Yes
Rates: $48 to $165

Tillicum Motor Inn
2114 W. Sixth St.
The Dalles, OR 97058
Phone: (503) 298-5161,
(800) 848-9378
Pet Restrictions: Quiet; $2/pet/day
Pet left unattended in room: Yes, no cleaning
Exercise Area for Pets: Yes
Rates: $38 to $75

VETERINARIANS
Skov, Milton
404 West Third
Phone: (503) 296-9191

TIGARD
Shilo Inn Hotel
7300 SW Hazel Fern Rd.
Tigard, OR 97223
Phone: (503) 620-3460
Pet Restrictions: $6/day; no snakes
Exercise Area for Pets: Nearby
Rates: $55 to $175

Shilo Inn Tigard/Wash. Sq.
10830 SW Greenburg Rd.
Tigard, OR 97223
Phone: (503) 620-4320,
(800) 222-2244
Pet Restrictions: $6/pet/day
Exercise Area for Pets: Yes
Rates: $49 to $78

VETERINARIANS
Canterbury Animal Hosp.
14350 SW Pacific Hwy
(503) 620-1300

Greenway Pet Clinic
12196 SW Scholls Ferry Rd.
(503) 639-8295

TILLSMOOK
Shilo Inn Tillsmook
2515 N. Main St.
Tillsmook, OR 97141
Phone: (503) 842-7971,
(800) 222-2244
Pet Restrictions: $6/pet/day
Exercise Area for Pets: Yes
Rates: $73 and up

OREGON — HOTELS (continued)

TOLOVANA

Tolovana Inn
3400 S. Hemlock
Tolovana Pk, OR 97145
Phone: (503) 436-2211,
   (800) 333-8890
Pet Restrictions: $4/pet/night; Can't
   leave them locked in car in
   parking lot
Exercise Area for Pets: Yes
Rates: $61 to $225

TROUTDALE

Burns West Hotel
790 NW Frontage Rd.
Troutdale, OR 97060
Phone: (503) 667-6212
Pet Restrictions: $3/pet/day
Exercise Area for Pets: Yes
Rates: $32 to $43

TUALATIN

Sweet Briar Inn
7125 SW Nyberg Rd.
Tualatin, OR 97062
Phone: (503) 692-5800,
   (800) 551-9167
Pet Restrictions: $25/stay refund.
   deposit
Pet left unattended in room: Yes
Exercise Area for Pets: Yes
Rates: $68 to $73

VETERINARIANS

Evergreen Veterinary Clinic
8970 SW Tualatin Sherwood Rd.
Phone: (503) 692-4840

Bertelsen, Lynn E.
8575 Southwest Tualatin
Phone: (503) 692-3340

UMATILLA

The Heather Inn
705 Willamette Ave.
Umatilla, OR 97882
Phone: (503) 922-4871,
   (800) 447-7529
Pet Restrictions: $10/stay; leashed
   when in hotel public areas
Exercise Area for Pets: Nearby
Rates: $52 to $57, $7/person

WARM SPRINGS

Kahneeta Vacation Resort
P.O. Box K
Warm Springs, OR 97761
Phone: (503) 553-1112,
   (800) 831-0100
Pet Restrictions: $8/pet/day;
   leashed when out of cabin.
   Cabins in village area only. Not
   allowed in patio area
Pet left unattended in room: Yes
Exercise Area for Pets: Yes
Rates: $49.95 to $99.95

WARRENTON

Shilo Inn Warrenton
1609 E. Harbour Dr.
Warrenton, OR 97146
Phone: (503) 861-2181,
   (800) 222-2244
Pet Restrictions: $6/pet/day
Exercise Area for Pets: Yes
Rates: $85

WILSONVILLE

Best Western Willamette Inn
30800 SW Pkwy Ave
Wilsonville, OR 97070
Phone: (503) 682-7275
Pet Restrictions: Under 25 lbs.; 4
   rooms only; notify in advance
Exercise Area for Pets: Yes
Rates: $53.50 to $95.15

Holiday Inn - Portland South
25425 SW Boones Ferry Rd.
Wilsonville, OR 97070
Phone: (503) 682-2211
Pet Restrictions: $5/stay
Exercise Area for Pets: Nearby
Rates: $56 to $95

Hotel Orleans
8815 SW Sun Place
Wilsonville, Or 97070
Phone: (503) 682-3184,
   (800) 626-1900
Exercise Area for Pets: Yes
Rates: $33 to $68

Snooze Inn
30245 Parkway Ave.
Wilsonville, OR 97070
Phone: (503) 682-2333
Pet Restrictions: $10/pet/day; leash
   law in town
Exercise Area for Pets: Yes
Rates: $39.50 to $46.90

Super 8
25438 SW Parkway Ave.
Wilsonville, OR 97070
Phone: (503) 682-2088
Pet Restrictions: $25/stay
Exercise Area for Pets: Nearby
Rates: $41.88 to $53.88

VETERINARIANS
Calkins, Raymond L.
9275 Barber
Phone: (503) 682-3737

WOODBURN
Comfort Inn Woodburn
120 Arney Rd. NE
Woodburn, OR 97071
Phone: (503) 982-1727
Pet Restrictions: Smoking rooms
    only
Exercise Area for Pets: Yes
Rates: $49 to $95

WOOD VILLAGE
Shilo Inn Wood Village/Gresham
2252 NE 238th Dr.
Wood Village, OR 97060
Phone: (503) 667-1414,
    (800) 222-2244
Pet Restrictions: $6/pet/day
Exercise Area for Pets: Yes
Rates: $30 to $45

YACHATS
Adobe Resort Motel
1555 Highway 101 N
Yachats, OR 97498
Phone: (503) 982-1727,
    (800) 522-3623
Pet Restrictions: $5/day/pet
Pet left unattended in room: Yes, if
    good
Exercise Area for Pets: Yes
Rates: $55 to $140

The Fireside Motel
1881 Highway 101 N
Yachats, OR 97498
Phone: (503) 547-3636,
    (800) 336-3573 (US only)
Pet Restrictions: $4/pet/night; No
    exotic pets. Leash law; keep off
    furniture
Exercise Area for Pets: Yes
Rates: $40 to $72

Shamrock Lodgettes
PO Box 346
Yachats, OR 97498
Phone: (503) 547-3312,
    (800) 845-5028
Pet Restrictions: $2/pet/day; cabins
    only
Pet left unattended in room: Yes
Exercise Area for Pets: Yes
Rates: $65 to $103 and up

PENNSYLVANIA — HOTELS

ALLENTOWN

Days Inn of Lehigh Valley
1715 Plaza Lane
Allentown, PA 18104
Phone: (215) 435-7880

Pet Restrictions: $3 fee
Pet left unattended in room: Yes
Exercise Area for Pets: Yes
Rates: $48 to $50

Red Roof Inn
1846 Catasauqua Rd.
Allentown, PA 18103
Phone: (215) 264-5404,
    (800) 874-9000 (central res.)

Pet Restrictions: Well-behaved
Exercise Area for Pets: Nearby
Rates: $48.99 to $58.99

VETERINARIANS

Myers, Carla
Road #1, Box 28
Phone: (215) 252-8276

Rush, James H.
2102 Walbert Ave.
Phone: (215) 820-9224

BEDFORD

Best Western Hoss's Inn
RD 2, Box 33B
Bedford, PA 15522
Phone: (814) 623-9006,
    (800) 752-8592

Pet Restrictions: Dep. $50 p/stay
Exercise Area for Pets: Yes
Rates: $54 to $58

Quality Inn Bedford
Route 20 North
Bedford, PA 15522
Phone: (814) 623-5188

Pet Restrictions: None
Pet left unattended in room: Yes,
    quiet
Exercise Area for Pets: Yes
Rates: $54 to $60

BENSALEM

Comfort Inn
3660 Street Rd.
Bensalem, PA 19020
Phone: (215) 245-0100,
    (800) 458-6886

Pet Restrictions: Under 40 lbs.
Pet left unattended in room: Yes
Exercise Area for Pets: Yes
Rates: $49 to $96

VETERINARIANS

Bridgewater Veterinary Hosp.
1740 Byberry Rd.
Phone: (215) 638-9275

BERWYN

Residence Inn by Marriott
600 W. Swedesford Rd.
Berwyn, PA 19312
Phone: (215) 640-9494,
    (800) 331-3131 (central res.)

Pet Restrictions: $100 non ref. dep.,
    $6 p/day
Pet left unattended in room: Yes
Exercise Area for Pets: Yes
Rates: $79 to $130

VETERINARIANS

Berwyn Veterinary Center
1058 Lancaster Ave. Box 123
Phone: (215) 640-9188

BLOOMSBURG

The Inn at Turkey Hill
991 Central Rd.
Bloomsburg, PA 17815
Phone: (717) 387-1500

Pet Restrictions: $15/stay
Pet left unattended in room: Yes
Exercise Area for Pets: Yes
Rates: $84 to $150

VETERINARIANS

Laudermilch, John A.
108 Shawnee Rd.
Phone: (717) 784-6440

BROOKVILLE

Econo Lodge
235 Allegheny Blvd.
Brookville, PA 15825
Phone: (814) 849-8381

Pet Restrictions: $5/day; Small pets
Exercise Area for Pets: Yes
Rates: $29 to $48

BURNHAM

Holiday Inn of lewiston
Rt. 322
Burnham, PA 17009
Phone: (717) 248-4961

Pet Restrictions: None
Pet left unattended in room: Yes,
    quiet
Exercise Area for Pets: Yes
Rates: $39 to $56

CARLISLE

Budget Host
125 Harrisburg Pike
Carlisle, PA 17013
Phone: (717) 243-8585

Pet Restrictions: Smoking rooms only
Pet left unattended in room: Yes
Exercise Area for Pets: Yes
Rates: $33 to $45.50

Embers Inn
1700 Harrisburg Pike
Carlisle, PA 17013
Phone: (717) 249-7622,
    (800) 692-7315

Pet Restrictions: None
Exercise Area for Pets: Yes
Rates: $53 to $58

Holiday Inn
1450 Harrisburg Pike
Carlisle, PA 17013
Phone: (717) 245-2400

Pet Restrictions: None
Pet left unattended in room: Yes -
    notify housekeeping
Exercise Area for Pets: Yes
Rates: $62 to $65

Howard Johnson Motor Lodge
1255 Harrisburg Pike
Carlisle, PA 17013
Phone: (717) 243-6000

Pet Restrictions: No snakes
Pet left unattended in room: Yes,
    quiet
Exercise Area for Pets: Yes
Rates: $55

Knights Inn
1153 Harrisburg Pike
Carlisle, PA 17013
Phone: (717) 249-7622

Pet Restrictions: None
Pet left unattended in room: Yes
Exercise Area for Pets: Yes
Rates: $45 to $90

VETERINARIANS

Barnett, Curt M.
25 Shady Lane
Phone: (717) 243-2717

CHAMBERSBURG

Scottish Inn
1620 Lincoln Way E
Chambersburg, PA 17201
Phone: (717) 264-4108,
    (800) 251-1962 (res. only)

Pet Restrictions: Small pets
Pet left unattended in room: Yes
Exercise Area for Pets: Yes
Rates: $32 to $39

Travelodge
565 Lincoln Way East
Chambersburg, PA 17201
Phone: (800) 255-3050

Pet Restrictions: None
Pet left unattended in room: No
Exercise Area for Pets: Yes
Rates: $44 to $60

VETERINARIANS

Chambersburg Animal Hospital
1340 Lincolnway East
Phone: (717) 264-4712

CLARION

Holiday Inn
Rt. 68 & I80
Clarion, PA 16214
Phone: (814) 226-8850

Pet Restrictions: Quiet, well
    behaved. Leashed in public
    areas & hotel
Exercise Area for Pets: Yes
Rates: $65 to $77

Knights Inn
SR 68 at Jct. I80
Clarion, PA 16214
Phone: (814) 226-4550,
    (800) 843-5644 (central res.)

Pet Restrictions: None
Pet left unattended in room: Yes
Exercise Area for Pets: Yes
Rates: $35.95 to $48.95

CLARKS SUMMIT

Days Inn Scranton N.
811 Northern Blvd.
Clarks Summit, PA 18411
Phone: (717) 586-9100

Pet Restrictions: $3/day/pet
Exercise Area for Pets: Yes
Rates: $44.99 to $56.99

Summit Inn
649 Northern Blvd.
Clarks Summit, PA 18411
Phone: (717) 586-1211

Pet Restrictions: $2/pet/day
Exercise Area for Pets: Yes
Rates: $56.99

CLEARFIELD
Days Inn of Clearfield
RD 2, PO Box 245B
Clearfield, PA 16830-9794
Phone: (814) 765-5381,
    (800) 325-2525 (central res.)

Pet Restrictions: None
Pet left unattended in room: Yes - if
    well-behaved
Exercise Area for Pets: Yes
Rates: $52 to $56

VETERINARIANS
Wootton, Laurence A.
P.O. Box 380
Phone: (814) 765-6541

CORAOPOLIS
Hampton Inn - Airport
1420 Beers School Rd.
Coraopolis, PA 15108
Phone: (412) 264-0020,
    (800) 426-7866 (central res.)

Pet Restrictions: None
Pet left unattended in room: Yes
Exercise Area for Pets: Yes
Rates: $55 to $65

Holiday Inn - Airport
1406 Beers School Rd.
Coraopolis, PA 15108
Phone: (412) 262-3600,
    (800) 333-4835

Pet Restrictions: Caged when in
    room
Pet left unattended in room: Yes
Exercise Area for Pets: Yes

La Quinta Motor Inn - Airport
1433 Beers School Rd.
Coraopolis, PA 15108
Phone: (412) 269-0400

Pet Restrictions: 1st floor rooms;
    smoking rooms only
Pet left unattended in room: Yes -
    notify front desk
Exercise Area for Pets: Yes
Rates: $53 to $69

Ramada Inn - Airport
1412 Beers School Rd.
Coraopolis, PA 15108
Phone: (412) 264-8950

Pet Restrictions: Deposit; call for
    further information

Red Roof Inn
1454 Beers School Rd.
Coraopolis, PA 15108
Phone: (412) 264-5678,
    (800) 843-7663 (central res.)

Pet Restrictions: Notify at check in
Pet left unattended in room: Yes
Exercise Area for Pets: Yes
Rates: $37.99 to $60.99

DANVER
Holiday Inn - Lancaster County
Rt. 272 & Exit 21 PA Turnpike
Danver, PA 17517
Phone: (215) 267-7541,
    (800) 437-5711

Pet Restrictions: None
Exercise Area for Pets: Yes
Rates: $70 to $105

DANVILLE
Countryside Inn
Exit 33 I80 and Rt 54
Danville, PA 17821
Phone: (717) 275-4640

Pet Restrictions: 1st floor rooms
    only
Pet left unattended in room: Yes,
    well-behaved
Exercise Area for Pets: Yes
Rates: $33.50 to $39.50

Days Inn
Exit 33 & I-80
Danville, PA 17821
Phone: (717) 275-5510,
    (800) 325-2525

Pet Restrictions: $5/day
Exercise Area for Pets: Yes
Rates: $60 to $70

Howard Johnson Lodge
15 Valley West Rd.
Danville, PA 17821
Phone: (717) 275-5100

Pet Restrictions: Smoking rooms
    only. Leashed when outside.
Pet left unattended in room: Yes
Exercise Area for Pets: Yes
Rates: $29.95 to $65

Red Roof Inn
Box 88
Danville, PA 17821
Phone: (717) 275-7600

Pet Restrictions: None
Pet left unattended in room: Yes
Exercise Area for Pets: Yes
Rates: $35 to $58

Leighow Veterinary Hospital
RD #4, Box 14, Route 11
Phone: (717) 275-0202

DUBOIS
Holiday Inn
US 219 & I-80
Dubois, PA 15801
Phone: (814) 371-5100

Pet Restrictions: None
Pet left unattended in room: Yes
Exercise Area for Pets: Yes - parking
    lot only
Rates: $49.50 to $61

Animal Hospital of Dubois
Road 3, Box 147
Phone: (814) 375-9206

DUNMORE
Days Inn
1226 O'Neil Hwy
Dunmore, PA 18512
Phone: (717) 348-6101

Pet Restrictions: None
Exercise Area for Pets: Yes
Rates: $53.99 to $68.99

EASTON
Days Inn
25th St. Shopping Ctr.
Easton, PA 18042
Phone: (215) 253-0546,
    (800) 325-2525 (central res.)

Pet Restrictions: $5/day
Exercise Area for Pets: Yes - must
    be leashed
Rates: $55.99 to $65.99

EPHRATA
Smithton Inn
900 W. Main St.
Ephrata, PA 17522
Phone: (717) 733-6094

Pet Restrictions: Dogs only, well-
    behaved, not on furniture
Exercise Area for Pets: Nearby
Rates: $65 to $170

ERIE
Holiday Inn Downtown
18 W 18th St.
Erie, PA 16501
Phone: (814) 456-2961,
    (800) 832-9101

Pet Restrictions: No big pets
Pet left unattended in room: Yes
Exercise Area for Pets: Yes
Rates: $64 to $80

Holiday Inn - South
8040 Perry Hwy
Erie, PA 16509
Phone: (814) 864-4911

Pet Restrictions: None
Pet left unattended in room: Yes -
    if caged
Exercise Area for Pets: Yes
Rates: $65 to $85

Howard Johnson Motor Lodge
7575 Peach St.
Erie, PA 16509
Phone: (814) 864-4811

Pet Restrictions: None
Exercise Area for Pets: Yes
Rates: $49 to $92

Knights Inn
7455 Schultz Rd.
Erie, PA 16509
Phone: (814) 868-0879,
    (800) 843-5644

Pet Restrictions: None
Pet left unattended in room: Yes -
    room will not be cleaned
Exercise Area for Pets: Yes
Rates: $45.95 and up

Ramada Inn
6101 Wattsburg Rd.
Erie, PA 16509
Phone: (814) 825-3100

Pet Restrictions: Dep.; 1st floor
    rooms only $5/day
Pet left unattended in room: Yes
Exercise Area for Pets: Yes
Rates: $46 to $50

Red Roof Inn
7865 Perry Hwy
Erie, PA 16509
Phone: (814) 868-5246

Pet Restrictions: None
Pet left unattended in room: Yes -
   no cleaning service
Exercise Area for Pets: Yes
Rates: $29 to $59

VETERINARIANS

Erie Animal Hospital
3024 West 26th Street
Phone: (814) 838-7638

Kester, Richard A.
5065 Buffalo rd.
Phone: (814) 899-0694

Sorenson, DN
3853 Peach St.
Phone: (814) 864-3019

ESSINGTON
Holiday Inn Airport
45 Industrial Hwy
Essington, PA 19029
Phone: (215) 521-2400,
   (800) 685-6110

Pet Restrictions: Owner liable for
   damages
Pet left unattended in room: Yes
Exercise Area for Pets: Yes
Rates: $103 to $119

Red Roof Inn Airport
49 Industrial Hwy
Essington, PA 19029
Phone: (215) 521-5090

Pet Restrictions: Small pets
Pet left unattended in room: Yes
Exercise Area for Pets: Yes
Rates: $43.99 to $57.99

FAYETTEVILLE
Rite Spot Motel
5651 Lincoln Way E
Fayetteville, PA 17222
Phone: (717) 352-2144

Pet Restrictions: $1/day, small pets
Pet left unattended in room: Yes,
   short time only
Exercise Area for Pets: Yes
Rates: $34 and up

GETTYSBURG
Howard Johnson Lodge
301 Steinwehr Ave.
Gettysburg, PA 17325
Phone: (717) 334-1188

Pet Restrictions: Owner liable for
   any damages
Exercise Area for Pets: Nearby

Quality Inn Gettysburg Motor Lodge
380 Steinwehr Ave.
Gettysburg, PA 17325
Phone: (717) 334-1103

Pet Restrictions: Small,
   well-behaved
Pet left unattended in room: Yes,
   quiet
Exercise Area for Pets: Nearby
Rates: $46 to $89

GREENTREE
Hampton Inn-Greentree
555 Trumbull Dr.
Greentree, PA 15205
Phone: (412) 922-0100

Pet Restrictions: Notify when
   checking in
Pet left unattended in room: Yes -
   if caged
Exercise Area for Pets: Yes
Rates: $65 to $69

HARRISBURG
Red Roof Inn
400 Corporate Circle
Harrisburg, PA 17110
Phone: (717) 657-1445

Pet Restrictions: None
Pet left unattended in room: Yes
Exercise Area for Pets: Yes
Rates: $38 to $46

Red Roof Inn
950 Eisenhower Blvd.
Harrisburg, PA 17111
Phone: (717) 939-1331

Pet Restrictions: None
Pet left unattended in room: Yes
Exercise Area for Pets: Yes
Rates: $40 to $51.99

Super 8 Motel
4125 N. Front St.
Harrisburg, PA 17110
Phone: (717) 233-5891

Pet Restrictions: Dep. quiet at night
Pet left unattended in room: Yes,
    not at night
Exercise Area for Pets: Yes
Rates: $50.88

VETERINARIANS

Capitol Area Animal Clinic
6 North Progress Avenue
Phone: (717) 652-0713

Guise, Mark B.
5399 Jonestown Rd.
Phone: (717) 545-5803

HARMARVILLE
Holiday Inn - North
2801 Freeport Rd.
Harmarville, PA 15238
Phone: (412) 828-9300

Pet Restrictions: None
Exercise Area for Pets: Yes
Rates: $78 to $82

HAZLETON
Mt. Laurel Motel
Rt. 309 S. 1039 S. Church St.
Hazleton, PA 18201-7626
Phone: (717) 455-6391

Pet Restrictions: No puppies
Exercise Area for Pets: Nearby
Rates: $38 to $55

HERMITAGE
Royal Motel
301 S. Hermitage Rd.
Hermitage, PA 16148
Phone: (412) 347-5546,
    (800) 831-8348

Pet Restrictions: Cats must be
    caged or have litter box
Pet left unattended in room: Yes,
    quiet
Exercise Area for Pets: Yes
Rates: $32 and up

KING OF PRUSSIA
Holiday Inn of King of Prussia
260 Goddard Blvd.
King of Prussia, PA 19406
Phone: (215) 265-7500

Pet Restrictions: $10/stay
Pet left unattended in room: Yes -
    caged
Exercise Area for Pets: Yes
Rates: $99 to $119

VETERINARIANS

Church, John R.
560 West De Kalb St.
Phone: (215) 265-4313

KULPSVILLE
Holiday Inn
1750 Sumney Town Pike
Kulpsville, PA 19443
Phone: (215) 368-3800

Pet Restrictions: Sign a pet waiver.
    They have a kennel
Pet left unattended in room: Yes
Exercise Area for Pets: Yes
Rates: $71 to $86

LANGHORNE
Red Roof Inn
3100 Cabot Blvd. West
Langhorne, PA 19047
Phone: (215) 750-6200,
    (800) 843-7663

Pet Restrictions: Yes
Pet left unattended in room: Yes
Exercise Area for Pets: Yes
Rates: $40 to $50

VETERINARIANS

Flowers Mill Vet. Hospital
10 S. Flowers Mill Rd.
(215) 752-1010

LEVITTOWN
Levittown - Econo-Lodge
6201 Bristol Pike
Levittown, PA 19057
Phone: (215) 946-1100

Pet Restrictions: 1st floor rooms;
    not allowed in public area in
    hotel. Leashed when out of room
    & on hotel property.
Pet left unattended in room: Yes, if
    caged
Exercise Area for Pets: Yes
Rates: $39.95

VETERINARIANS

Jeffers, Shirley A.
55 Tallpine Lane
Phone: (215) 547-2704

LUMBERVILLE

Black Bass Hotel
Route 32, River Rd.
Lumberville, PA 18933
Phone: (215) 297-5770
Fax: (215) 297-0262

Pet Restrictions: None
Exercise Area for Pets: Yes
Rates: $55 to $175

MANSFIELD

Mansfield Inn
26 S Main St.
Mansfield, PA 16933
Phone: (717) 662-2136

Pet Restrictions: Pets not allowed in
    court area
Pet left unattended in room: Yes
Exercise Area for Pets: Yes, in back
Rates: $49 to $65

West's Deluxe Motel
Rt 15 South
Mansfield, PA 16933
Phone: (717) 659-5141,
    (800) 995-9378

Pet Restrictions: None
Exercise Area for Pets: Yes
Rates: $30 to $40

MARS

Hampton Inn - Cranberry
210 Executive Dr.
Mars, PA 16046
Phone: (412) 776-1000,
    (800) 426-7866 (central res.)

Pet Restrictions: Notify desk; owner
    liable for damages
Pet left unattended in room: Yes -
    if caged
Exercise Area for Pets: Nearby
Rates: $50 to $69

Red Roof Inn
20009 Route 19 & Mauguierite Rd.
Mars, PA
Phone: (412) 776-5670

Pet Restrictions: Small pets
Pet left unattended in room: Yes
Exercise Area for Pets: Yes
Rates: $51 to $60

MEADVILLE

Days Inn
240 Conneaut Lake Rd.
Meadville, PA 16335
Phone: (814) 337-4264,
    (800) 325-2525 (central res.)

Pet Restrictions: Pet waiver; $5/day
Pet left unattended in room: Yes
Exercise Area for Pets: Nearby
Rates: $70

VETERINARIANS

**Langdon and Leveto Vet. Hosp.
    & Emergency Ctr.**
316 Conneault Lake Rd.
Phone: (814) 337-3271

MERCER

Howard Johnson Lodge
835 Perry Hwy.
Mercer, PA 16137
Phone: (412) 748-3030,
    (800) 542-7674

Pet Restrictions: None
Pet left unattended in room: Yes
Exercise Area for Pets: Yes
Rates: $64 to $67

MILFORD

Tourist Village Motel
P.O. Box 487
Milford, PA 18337
Phone: (717) 491-4414

Pet Restrictions: Housebroken
Exercise Area for Pets: Yes

MILL HALL

Comfort Inn
RR 3, Box 600
Mill Hall, PA 17751
Phone: (717) 726-4901,
    (800) 228-5150

Pet Restrictions: No snakes
Pet left unattended in room: Yes
Exercise Area for Pets: Yes
Rates: $39 to $49

MONROEVILLE

Red Roof Inn
2729 Mosside Blvd.
Monroeville, PA 15146
Phone: (412) 856-4738

Pet Restrictions: None
Pet left unattended in room: Yes
Exercise Area for Pets: Yes
Rates: $41.99 to $60.99

VETERINARIANS

Lynch, Robert K.
232 Center Rd.
Phone: (412) 372-1100

MYERSTOWN

Motel of Frystown
90 Fort Motel Dr.
Myerstown, PA 17067
Phone: (717) 933-4613

Pet Restrictions: Notify front desk
Pet left unattended in room: Yes -
    if quiet
Exercise Area for Pets: Yes
Rates: $30 and up

VETERINARIANS

Myerstown Animal Hospital
410 South Broad St.
Phone: (717) 866-7515

NEW CUMBERLAND

Keystone Motor Inn
353 Motor Inn
New Cumberland, PA 17070
Phone: (717) 774-1310,

Pet Restrictions: None
Pet left unattended in room: Yes, if
    clean and quiet
Exercise Area for Pets: Yes
Rates: $41 to $70

VETERINARIANS

West Shore Veterinary Hosp.
719 Limekiln Rd.
Phone: (717) 774-0685

NEW HOPE

Holiday Inn
Route 202
New Hope, PA 18938
Phone: (215) 862-5221

Pet Restrictions: 1 pet p/room. Sign
    a waiver
Pet left unattended in room: Yes -
    if quiet
Exercise Area for Pets: Yes
Rates: $85 to $105

NEW STANTON

Howard Johnson Motor Lodge
112 W. Byers Ave.
New Stanton, PA 15672
Phone: (412) 925-3511

Pet Restrictions: Well-behaved
Pet left unattended in room: Yes, no
    cleaning
Exercise Area for Pets:
Rates: $38 and up

OAKDALE

Comfort Inn - Parkway W
7011 Old Steubenville Pike
Oakdale, PA 15071
Phone: (412) 787-2600,
    (800) 221-2222 (central res.)

Pet Restrictions: 10 rooms only.
    Notify in advance. $8/day
Exercise Area for Pets: Yes
Rates: $49.50 to $55

OIL CITY

Holiday Inn
1 Seneca St.
Oil City, PA 16301
Phone: (814) 677-1221

Pet Restrictions: None
Exercise Area for Pets: Yes
Rates: $62 to $79

PHILADELPHIA

Barclay
237 S. 18th St.
Philadelphia, PA 19103
Phone: (215) 545-0300,
    (800) 421-6662

Pet Restrictions: $50/stay deposit;
    small pets; must be leashed
    when in public areas of hotel.
Pet left unattended in room: Yes -
    no service
Exercise Area for Pets: Nearby
Rates: $135 to $185

Ramada Suites Convention Ctr.
1010 Race St.
Philadephia, PA 19106
Phone: (215) 922-1730,
    (800) 628-8932

Pet Restrictions: $100 deposit; sign
    a pet release. Must be leashed.
Exercise Area for Pets: Nearby
Rates: $55 to $109

PENNSYLVANIA — HOTELS (continued)

Warwick Hotel
1701 Locust St.
Philadelphia, PA 19103
Phone: (215) 735-6000,
      (800) 523-4210 (res. only)
Pet Restrictions: $25/stay; under 15 lbs.
Pet left unattended in room: Yes - no cleaning
Exercise Area for Pets: Nearby
Rates: $95 to $165

VETERINARIANS

Cat Hospital of Philadelphia
226 South 20th St.
Phone: (215) 567-6446

Mount Airy Animal Hospital
114 East Mount Airy Avenue
Phone: (215) 248-1886

Veterinary Hosp. Univ. of Penn.
3850 Spruce St.
Phone: (215) 898-4161

PHILIPSBURG
Harbor Inn
Jct. Rts. 322 & 53
Philipsburg, PA 16866
Phone: (814) 342-0250
Pet Restrictions: Call for more information

PITTSBURGH
Econo-Lodge
4800 Steubenville Pike
Pittsburgh, PA 15205
Phone: (412) 922-6900
Pet Restrictions: Notify when checking in
Pet left unattended in room: Yes - no cleaning
Exercise Area for Pets: Yes
Rates: $38 to $42.68

Hilton Airport Inn
1 Hilton Dr.
Pittsburgh, PA 15231
Phone: (412) 262-3800
Pet Restrictions: Small animals, sign waiver
Exercise Area for Pets: Yes
Rates: $70 to $125

Holiday Inn - Parkway East
915 Brinton Rd.
Pittsburgh, PA 15221
Phone: (412) 247-2700
Pet Restrictions: None
Pet left unattended in room: Yes
Exercise Area for Pets: Yes
Rates: $78 to $84

Holiday Inn Green Tree - Central
401 Holiday Dr.
Pittsburgh, VA 15220
Phone: (412) 922-8100
Pet Restrictions: Small, notify front desk
Pet left unattended in room: Yes
Exercise Area for Pets: Yes
Rates: $59 to $114

Holiday Inn - McKnight Rd.
4859 McKnight Rd.
Pittsburgh, PA 15237
Phone: (412) 366-5200,
      (800) 465-4329
Pet left unattended in room: Yes - no cleaning
Exercise Area for Pets: Yes
Rates: $77 to $89

Howard Johnson Univ Ctr Hotel
3401 Blvd. of the Allies
Pittsburgh, PA 15213
Phone: (412) 683-6100,
      (800) 245-4444
Pet Restrictions: Small, sign pet waiver
Exercise Area for Pets: Yes
Rates: $62 to $72

Marriott Greentree
101 Marriott Dr.
Pittsburgh, PA 15205
Phone: (412) 922-8400
Pet Restrictions: Small
Pet left unattended in room: Yes
Exercise Area for Pets: Yes
Rates: $65 to $117

New Allegheny Motor Inn
1464 Beers School Rd.
Pittsburgh, PA 15108
Phone: (412) 264-7790
Pet Restrictions: None
Pet left unattended in room: Yes
Exercise Area for Pets: Nearby
Rates: $31.95 and up

Red Roof Inn
6404 Steubenville Pike
Pittsburgh, PA 15205
Phone: (412) 787-7870,
(800) TheRoof
Pet Restrictions: Small pets only
Pet left unattended in room: Yes
Exercise Area for Pets: Yes -
scooper needed
Rates: $49.95 to $60.99

Red Roof Inn
1464 Steubenville Pike
Pittsburgh, PA 15205
Phone: (412) 787-7870
Pet Restrictions: Under 20 lbs.
Pet left unattended in room: Yes
Exercise Area for Pets: Yes
Rates: $40.99 to $48.99

Residence Inn by Marriott Greentree
700 Mansfield Ave.
Pittsburgh, PA 15205
Phone: (412) 279-6300
Pet Restrictions: $50/stay deposit +
$6/day
Pet left unattended in room: Yes
Exercise Area for Pets: Yes
Rates: $114 to $144

Sheraton South Hills
164 Ft. Couch Rd.
Pittsburgh, PA 15241
Phone: (412) 343-4600
Pet Restrictions: Well-trained
Pet left unattended in room: Yes -
no cleaning
Rates: $67 to $105

Castle Shannon Vetny Hosp.
3610 Library Rd.
Phone: (412) 885-2500

North Boros Vetny Hosp.
2255 Babcock Blvd.
Phone: (412) 821-5600

Northview Animal Hospital
223 Siebert Rd.
Phone: (412) 364-5353

PITTSTON

Howard Johnson Motor Lodge
347 Rt. 315
Pittston, PA 18640
Phone: (717) 654-3301
Pet Restrictions: None
Pet left unattended in room: Yes -
well-behaved
Exercise Area for Pets: Yes
Rates: $42 to $65

Knight Inn
310 St. Rt. 315
Pittston, PA 18640
Phone: (717) 654-6020,
(800) 843-5644
Pet Restrictions: Quiet
Pet left unattended in room: Yes -
well-behaved
Exercise Area for Pets: Yes
Rates: $32.95 to $45.95

POTTSTOWN

Modern Motel
1417 S. Hanover on Rt. 100
Pottstown, PA 19464
Phone: (215) 323-6650
Pet Restrictions: Not on furniture.
No snakes
Pet left unattended in room: Yes
Exercise Area for Pets: Yes
Rates: $35 to $55

Peterman Rd. Animal Hospital
RD #1, Box 226A
Phone: (215) 323-9454

Stephan, Steve C.
200 Eschuylk Rd.
Phone: (215) 326-6330

PUNXSUTAWNEY

Pantall Hotel
135 E. Mahoney St.
Punxsutawney, PA 15767
Phone: (814) 938-6600,
(800) 872-6825
Pet Restrictions: None
Pet left unattended in room: Yes
Exercise Area for Pets: Nearby
Rates: $47 to $93

QUAKERTOWN

Econo Lodge
1905 Rt. 663
Quakertown, PA 18104
Phone: (215) 538-3000

Pet Restrictions: Owner liable for
damages; deposit depends,
negotiate
Pet left unattended in room: Yes
Exercise Area for Pets: Yes
Rates: $36 to $65

VETERINARIANS

Pleasant Valley Animal Hosp.
Pleasant Valley Star Route
Phone: (215) 346-7854

Quakertown Vetny Clinic
2250 Old Bethlehem Pike
Phone: (215) 536-6245

Brake, Karen Caccese
RD 2, Box 106
Phone: (215) 322-6776

READING

Dutch Colony Inn
4635 Perkiomen Ave.
Reading, PA 19606
Phone: (215) 779-2345,
(800) 828-2830

Pet Restrictions: $4/day
Pet left unattended in room: Yes
Exercise Area for Pets: Yes
Rates: $60 and up

Holiday Inn
2545 N. 5th St. Hwy
Reading, PA 19605
Phone: (215) 929-4741

Pet Restrictions: None
Pet left unattended in room: Yes -
if quiet
Exercise Area for Pets: Yes
Rates: $49 to $129

Wellesley Inn Reading
910 Woodland Ave.
Reading, PA 19610
Phone: (610) 374-1500
Fax: (610) 374-2554
Contact: Paul Maddry

Pet Restrictions: None
Pet left unattended in room: Yes
Exercise Area for Pets: Yes
Rates: $43.99 to $79.99

VETERINARIANS

Detwiler Veterinary Clinic
22 Kenhorst Blvd.
Phone: (215) 777-6546

Willow Creek Animal Hospital
RD #2 Box 2037
Phone: (717) 866-7512

SELINSGROVE

Comfort Inn
Rt. 11 & 15
Selinsgrove, PA 17870
Phone: (717) 374-8880,
(800) 627-7366

Pet Restrictions: $25/stay deposit
Pet left unattended in room: Yes
Exercise Area for Pets: Yes
Rates: $48 to $53

VETERINARIANS

Jacobson, Louis H.
Star Route
Phone: (717) 374-8441

SHIPPENSBURG

Best Western Univ. Lodge
720 Walnut Bottom Rd.
Shippensburg, PA
Phone: (717) 532-7311

Pet Restrictions: None
Exercise Area for Pets: Yes
Rates: $28 to $80

Budget Host Shippensburg Inn
10 Hershey Rd.
Shippensburg, PA
Phone: (717) 530-1234,
(800) BUD-HOST

Pet Restrictions: None
Pet left unattended in room: Yes
Exercise Area for Pets: Nearby
Rates: $38.80 to $68.48

VETERINARIANS

Burnt Mill Veternary Center
118 Timber Lane
Phone: (717) 423-6536

SHOMOKIN DAM

Days Inn
Rt. 11 & 15
Shomokin Dam, PA 17876
Phone: (717) 743-1111

Pet Restrictions: Well-behaved
Pet left unattended in room: Yes
Exercise Area for Pets: Yes
Rates: $39 to $47

SOMERSET

Knights Inn
Turnpike Entrance, Exit 10
Somerset, PA 15501
Phone: (814) 445-8933,
   (800) 843-5644

Pet Restrictions: None
Pet left unattended in room: Yes -
   if caged
Exercise Area for Pets: Yes
Rates: $37.95 to $64.95

VETERINARIANS
Laurel Highlands Animal Hosp.
Road 2, Box 241
Phone: (814) 445-8575

STRASBURG

Historic Strasburg Inn
Rt. 896, 2½ Mi. S of US 30
Strasburg, PA 17579
Phone: (717) 687-7691,
   (800) 872-0201

Pet Restrictions: $25/stay deposit
Pet left unattended in room: Yes
Exercise Area for Pets: Yes
Rates: $38.50 to $75

TANNERSVILLE

Howard Johnson Inn
I-80 & Rt. 215
Tannersville, PA 18372
Phone: (717) 629-4100,
   (800) 441-2193

Pet Restrictions: None
Pet left unattended in room: Yes
Exercise Area for Pets: Yes
Rates: $42.95 to $99.95

TOWANDA

Towanda Motel & Restaurant Inc.
383 York Ave.
Towanda, PA 18848
Phone: (717) 265-2178

Pet Restrictions: Well-trained
Pet left unattended in room: Yes -
   notify front desk
Exercise Area for Pets: Yes
Rates: $37 to $55

TREVOSE

Red Roof Inn
3100 Lincoln Hwy. US 1
Trevose, PA 19047
Phone: (800) 843-7663

Pet Restrictions: Yes
Pet left unattended in room: Yes
Exercise Area for Pets: Yes
Rates: $32 to $52

ULYSSES

Pine Log Motel
US Rt. 66, RR 1, Box 15
Ulysses, PA 16948
Phone: (814) 435-6400

Pet Restrictions: None
Exercise Area for Pets: Yes
Rates: $32 to $38

WARREN

Holiday Inn
210 Ludlow St.
Warren, PA 16365
Phone: (814) 726-3000,
   (800) 446-6814

Pet Restrictions: Under 35 lbs. Sign
   pet release
Pet left unattended in room: Yes -
   no barking
Exercise Area for Pets: Yes
Rates: $51 to $64

VETERINARIANS
Warren Veterinary Hospital
2848 Pennsylvania Avenue West
Phone: (814) 723-7123

WASHINGTON

Knights Inn
125 Knights Inn Dr.
Washington, PA 15301
Phone: (412) 223-8040,
   (800) 843-5644 (central res.)

Pet Restrictions: Dogs leashed when
   in public
Pet left unattended in room: Yes -
   taken care of
Exercise Area for Pets: Yes
Rates: $43.95 and up

PENNSYLVANIA — HOTELS (continued)

Red Roof Inn
1399 W. Chestnut St.
Washington, PA 15301
Phone: (412) 228-5750

Pet Restrictions: None
Pet left unattended in room: Yes
Exercise Area for Pets: Yes
Rates: $36.99 to $48.99

Gardner, Katherine H.
1200 Washington Rd.
Phone: (412) 228-2040

Roe, Muriel O.
1099 Redstone Rd.
Phone: (412) 225-1109

WELLSBORO
Canyon Motel
18 East Ave.
Wellsboro, PA 16901
Phone: (717) 724-1681,
    (800) 255-2718

Pet Restrictions: Smoking rooms
    only
Exercise Area for Pets: Yes
Rates: $45 to $48

WHITE HAVEN
Pocono Mountain Lodge
Rt. 940
White Haven, PA 18661
Phone: (717) 443-8461,
    (800) 443-4049

Pet Restrictions: No snakes
Exercise Area for Pets: Yes
Rates: $50 to $68

WILKES-BARRE
Holiday Inn
800 Kidder St.
Wilkes-Barre, PA 18703
Phone: (717) 824-8901

Pet Restrictions: Quiet
Pet left unattended in room: Yes quiet
Exercise Area for Pets: Yes
Rates: $59 to $79

Red Roof Inn
1035 Hwy 315
Wilkes-Barre, PA 18702
Phone: (717) 829-6422,
    (800) 843-7663 (central res.)

Pet Restrictions: Owner liable for
    damages; under 50 lbs.
Pet left unattended in room: Yes -
    no cleaning
Exercise Area for Pets: Yes
Rates: $35.99 to $50.99

WILLIAMSPORT
Days Inn of Williamsport
1840 E. 3rd St.
Williamsport, PA 17701
Phone: (717) 326-1981

Pet Restrictions: 11 rooms; notify
    when making reservations
Pet left unattended in room: Yes
Exercise Area for Pets: Yes
Rates: $39 to $55

Beck, Lester L.
1900 Northway Rd.
Phone: (717) 326-1709

WIND GAP
Travel Inn
499 E. Morrestown Rd.
Wind Gap, PA 18091
Phone: (215) 863-4146

Pet Restrictions: No cats; $5/day
Exercise Area for Pets: Yes
Rates: $42 to $65 subject to change

WYOMISSING
Econo Lodge - Reading
635 Spring St.
Wyomissing, PA 19610
Phone: (215) 378-5105

Pet Restrictions: Small pets; $4/day
Pet left unattended in room: Yes
Exercise Area for Pets: Yes
Rates: $43.99 to $53.99

Wellesley Inn
910 Woodland Ave.
Wyomissing, PA 19610
Phone: (215) 374-1500

Pet Restrictions: $3/day; inform
    when making reservations,
    smoking rooms only
Exercise Area for Pets: Yes
Rates: $40 to $65

YORK

Bridgeton Hotel & Conference Center
222 Arsenal Rd.
York, PA 17402
Phone: (717) 843-9971

Pet Restrictions: None
Pet left unattended in room: Yes
Exercise Area for Pets: Yes
Rates: $54 to $68

Holiday Inn
2600 E. Market St.
York, PA 17402
Phone: (717) 755-1966

Pet Restrictions: Smoking rooms only
Pet left unattended in room: Yes - no cleaning
Exercise Area for Pets: Yes
Rates: $49 to $79

Ramada Inn
1650 Toronita St.
York, PA 17402
Phone: (717) 846-4940

Pet Restrictions: Smoking rooms only
Exercise Area for Pets: Yes
Rates: $65 and up

Red Roof Inn
323 Arsenal Rd.
York, PA 17402
Phone: (717) 843-8181

Pet Restrictions: None
Pet left unattended in room: Yes - if caged
Exercise Area for Pets: Yes
Rates: $34.99 to $55.99

VETERINARIANS

Hill Street Veterinary Hospital
555 Hill St.
Phone: (717) 843-6060

Leader Heights Animal Hospital
199 Leaders Heights Rd.
Phone: (717) 741-4618

Yorkshire Animal Hospital
3434 East Market St.
Phone: (717) 755-4935

RHODE ISLAND

MIDDLETOWN

Newport Comfort Inn & Conference Center
936 W. Main Rd.
Middletown, RI 02840
Phone: (401) 846-7600, (800) 556-6464

Pet Restrictions: Under 100 lbs., leash law in town, bring just one pet, $5/day
Pet left unattended in room: Yes, if caged
Exercise Area for Pets: Yes
Rates: $55 to $109

Howard Johnson Hotel
351 W. Main Rd.
Middletown, RI 02840
Phone: (401) 849-2000

Pet Restrictions: Certain rooms, notify while making reservations
Exercise Area for Pets: Yes
Rates: $69 to $129

VETERINARIANS

Newport Animal Hospital
170 East Main Rd.
(401) 849-3400

PROVIDENCE

Holiday Inn-Downtown
21 Atwells Ave.
Providence, RI 02903
Phone: (401) 831-3900

Pet Restrictions: Under 60 lbs.
Pet left unattended in room: Yes
Exercise Area for Pets: Nearby
Rates: $85 to $95

VETERINARIANS

Hoffman Animal Hospital
1338 Broad Street
(401) 941-7345

Northern RI Animal Hospital
38 Windmill St.
(401) 762-2400

The Cat Clinic
205 Gano St.
(401) 421-5836

WAKEFIELD

Larchwood Inn
521 Main St.
Wakefield, RI 02879
Phone: (401) 783-5454

Pet Restrictions: $5 day
Pet left unattended in room: Yes
Exercise Area for Pets: Yes
Rates: $60 to $75

SOUTH CAROLINA — HOTELS

AIKEN

Holiday Inn
Highway 19N
Aiken, SC 29801
Phone: (803) 648-4272
Pet Restrictions: $50 dep. small pet
    only
Exercise Area for Pets: Nearby
Rates: $45 to $68

VETERINARIANS

Vet Services
1310 Whiskey Rd.
(803) 648-5489

Bagshaw, Clarence
1511 Alpine Dr.
(803) 733-7458

ANDERSON

Howard Johnson Lodge
4420 Clemson Blvd.
Anderson, SC 29621
Phone: (803) 226-3457
Pet Restrictions: $6 day, small pet
    only
Pet left unattended in room: Yes
Exercise Area for Pets: Nearby
Rates: $38 to $58

Quality Inn
3569 Clemson Rd.
Anderson, SC 29621
Phone: (803) 226-1000
Pet Restrictions: Small pet only
Exercise Area for Pets: Nearby
Rates: $53 to $75

CAYCE

Knights Inn
1987 Airport Blvd.
Cayce, SC 29033
Phone: (803) 794-0222,
    (800) 235-8339
Pet Restrictions: $25 dep.
Pet left unattended in room: Yes
Exercise Area for Pets: Yes
Rates: $36.95

Tremont Motor Inn
111 Knox Abbott Dr.
Cayce, SC 29033
Phone: (803) 796-6240
Pet Restrictions: House trained,
    owner responsible for damages
Pet left unattended in room: Yes
Exercise Area for Pets: Yes
Rates: $32 to $35

CHARLESTON

Comfort Inn-Airport
5055 N. Arco Lane
Charleston, SC 29418
Phone: (803) 554-6485
Pet Restrictions: Under 25 lbs,
    $10/day
Pet left unattended in room: Yes, no
    cleaning
Rates: $45 to $55

Holiday Inn Charleston-Mt. Pleasant
250 Hwy 17 Bypass
Charleston, SC 29464
Phone: (803) 884-6000
Pet Restrictions: None
Pet left unattended in room: Yes,
    notify desk
Exercise Area for Pets: Yes
Rates: $69 to $143

Holiday Inn-Riverview
301 Savannah Hwy
Charleston, SC 29407
Phone: (803) 556-7100
Pet left unattended in room: Yes,
    dealt with on a case to case basis
Exercise Area for Pets: Yes
Rates: $49 to $115

Howard Johnson-Downtown Riverview
250 Spring St.
Charleston, SC 29403
Phone: (803) 722-4000,
    (800) 654-2000
Pet Restrictions: Dogs under 10
    lbs., cats must have cage & litter
    box, 1st floor rooms only
Exercise Area for Pets: Yes
Rates: $49 to $89

La Quinta
2499 La Quinta Lane
Charleston, SC 29420
Phone: (803) 797-8181
Pet Restrictions: No large dogs,
    $20/stay
Pet left unattended in room: Yes, do
    not disturb sign on door
Exercise Area for Pets: Yes
Rates: $44 to $60

Super 8 Motel
2311 Ashley-Phosphate Rd.
Charleston, SC 29418
Phone: (803) 572-2228

Pet Restrictions: Under 20 lbs.
Exercise Area for Pets: Yes
Rates: $34.88 to $58.88

NORTH CHARLESTON

Days Inn
2998 W. Montague Ave.
N. Charleston, SC 29418
Phone: (803) 747-4101
　　　　(800) 325-2525 (central res.)
Pet Restrictions: $4/day/pet
Pet left unattended in room: Yes, no
　　cleaning
Exercise Area for Pets: Yes
Rates: $42 to $55

Hampton Inn-Airport
4701 Saul White Blvd.
N. Charleston, SC 29418
Phone: (803) 554-7154

Pet Restrictions: None
Pet left unattended in room: Yes, no
　　cleaning
Exercise Area for Pets: Yes
Rates: $46 to $63

Holiday Inn-Airport
6099 Fain St.
N. Charleston, SC 29418
Phone: (803) 744-1621

Pet Restrictions: House trained
Pet left unattended in room: Yes,
　　notify desk
Exercise Area for Pets: Yes
Rates: $45 to $85

Red Roof Inn
7480 Northwoods Blvd.
N. Charleston, SC 29418
Phone: (803) 572-9100

Pet left unattended in room: Yes,
　　notify desk
Exercise Area for Pets: Yes
Rates: $45.99 to $49.99

Residence Inn by Marriott
7645 Northwoods Blvd.
N. Charleston, SC 29418
Phone: (803) 572-5757

Pet Restrictions: $50-$75/stay
　　(non-refundable)
Pet left unattended in room: Yes, no
　　cleaning
Exercise Area for Pets: Yes
Rates: $90 to $120

VETERINARIANS

Bradford Veterinary Clinic
2517 Ashley River Rd.
(803) 763-4128

Charles Towne Veterinary Clinic
850 Savannah Hwy.
(803) 571-4291

Smith, Cynthia P.
17 Pinckney St.
(803) 723-1443

COLUMBIA

Days Inn
7128 Parklane Rd.
Columbia, SC 29223
Phone: (803) 736-0000

Pet Restrictions: Under 30 lbs.,
　　$25/stay deposit
Exercise Area for Pets: Yes
Rates: $33 to $37

Econo-Lodge
494 Piney Grove Rd.
Columbia, SC 29210
Phone: (803) 731-4060,
　　(800) 424-4777 (central res.)
Pet Restrictions: Small pets, deposit
　　depends
Pet left unattended in room: Yes
Exercise Area for Pets: Yes
Rates: $28.95 to $33.95

Holiday Inn-Northeast
7510 Two Notch Rd.
Columbia, SC 29223
Phone: (803) 736-3000

Pet Restrictions: Small
Pet left unattended in room: Yes
Exercise Area for Pets: Yes
Rates: $65 to $75

Knights Inn Columbia-Northwest
1803 Bush River Rd.
Columbia, SC 29210
Phone: (803) 772-0022

Pet left unattended in room: Yes, no
　　cleaning
Exercise Area for Pets: Yes
Rates: $23.95 to $38.95

Red Roof Inn
7580 Two Notch Rd.
Columbia, SC 29223
Phone: (803) 736-0850
Pet Restrictions: None
Pet left unattended in room: Yes
Exercise Area for Pets: Yes
Rates: $39 to $43

Red Roof Inn-West
10 Berryhill Rd.
Columbia, SC 29210
Phone: (803) 798-9220
Pet Restrictions: None
Pet left unattended in room: Yes
Exercise Area for Pets: Yes
Rates: $32.99 to $42.99

WEST COLUMBIA
Hampton Inn-Columbia West
1094 Chris Dr.
West Columbia, SC 29169
Phone: (803) 791-8940,
(800) 426-7866
Pet Restrictions: Under 15 lbs.
Exercise Area for Pets: Yes
Rates: $42 to $49 plus $6/person

VETERINARIANS
Columbia Hospital for Animals
1502 Highway 31 North
(615) 388-7756

Saint Andrews Animal Hospital
1330 Omarest Dr.
(803) 772-8411

Spring Valley Animal Hospital
8913 Two Notch Rd.
(803) 788-8481

DILLON
Days Inn
Rt. 1, P.O. Box 70
Dillon, SC 29536
Phone: (803) 774-6041
Pet Restrictions: $5/day/pet, owner
liable for damages
Pet left unattended in room: Yes
Exercise Area for Pets: Yes
Rates: $39 to $69

Holiday Inn Express
I-95 and Hwy 9
Dillon, SC 29536
Phone: (803) 774-5111
Pet Restrictions: Under 20 lbs.
Exercise Area for Pets: Yes
Rates: $33.75 to $85

Travelodge
SR 9 and I-95 exit 193
Dillon, SC 29536
Phone: (803) 774-4161
Pet Restrictions: None
Exercise Area for Pets: Yes
Rates: $25.63 to $41.76

FLORENCE
Knights Inn-Florence North
1834 W. Lucas St.
Florence, SC 29501
Phone: (803) 667-6100
Pet Restrictions: No barnyard
animals
Pet left unattended in room: Yes, for
a short time
Exercise Area for Pets: Yes
Rates: $31 to $49

Quality Inn-I95
T.V. Road
Florence, SC 29503
Phone: (803) 669-1715
Pet Restrictions: None
Pet left unattended in room: Yes, if
quiet
Exercise Area for Pets: Yes
Rates: $41 and up

Ramada Inn
2038 W. Lucas St.
Florence, SC 29501
Phone: (803) 669-4241
(800) 2 RAMADA
Pet Restrictions: Small pets
Pet left unattended in room: Yes
Exercise Area for Pets: Yes
Rates: $54 to $60

Red Roof Inn
2690 David McLeod Blvd.
Florence, SC 29501
Phone: (803) 678-9000,
(800) 843-7663 (central res.)
Pet Restrictions: Under 25 lbs.
Pet left unattended in room: Yes
Exercise Area for Pets: Yes
Rates: $29.99 to $41.99

Shoney's Inn

Jct I-95 & US 52
Florence, SC 29503
Phone: (803) 669-1921,
(800) 222-2222 (central res.)
Pet Restrictions: Not allowed in VIP
section
Pet left unattended in room: Yes, if
quiet
Exercise Area for Pets: Yes
Rates: $44 to $54

Young's Plantation Inn

Ext 157 off I-95
Florence, SC 29502
Phone: (803) 669-4171,
(800) 476-2299
Pet Restrictions: $4/day/pet, small
pets
Pet left unattended in room: Yes, if
quiet
Exercise Area for Pets: Yes

VETERINARIANS

Harris, James M.
2221 2nd Loop Rd.
(803) 667-6720

Hoffmeyer, Thompson P.
111 South Cashua Dr.
(803) 669-5231

Reeves, Richard B.
2222 West Palmetto St.
(803) 669-1420

GAFFNEY

Comfort Inn

143 Corona Dr.
Gaffney, SC 29340
Phone: (803) 489-4200
Pet Restrictions: 3 rooms only,
notify in advance, $5/stay/pet
Exercise Area for Pets: Yes
Rates: $47 and up

Days Inn at Gaffney

136 Peachold Rd.
Gaffney, SC 29341
Phone: (803) 489-7172
Pet Restrictions: Housebroken,
$10/stay
Pet left unattended in room: Yes
Exercise Area for Pets: Yes
Rates: $38.95 to $45.95

GREENVILLE

Phoenix Inn

246 N. Pleasantbury Dr.
Greenville, SC 29601
Phone: (803) 233-4651
(800) 257-3529
Pet Restrictions: None
Pet left unattended in room: Yes,
short time only
Exercise Area for Pets: Yes
Rates: $32 to $60

Red Roof Inn

2801 Laurens Rd.
Greenville, SC 29607
Phone: (803) 297-4458
Pet Restrictions: None
Pet left unattended in room: Yes
Exercise Area for Pets: Yes
Rates: $26.99 to $45.99

VETERINARIANS

East North Veterinary Clinic
550 Old Howell Rd.
(803) 268-6312

Bing Jr., Carroll V.
2902 N. Pleasantburg
(803) 233-4347

Creel, Wayne
594 Haywood Rd.
(803) 288-7472

HARDEEVILLE

Days Inn

Hwy 17 & I-95
Hardeeville, SC 29927
Phone: (803) 784-2221
Pet Restrictions: $2/day/pet
Pet left unattended in room: Yes
Exercise Area for Pets: Yes
Rates: $35 and up

Holiday Inn

P.O. Box 1109
Hardeeville, SC 29927
Phone: (803) 784-2151
Pet Restrictions: None
Pet left unattended in room: Yes, if
quiet
Exercise Area for Pets: Yes
Rates: $48 plus $6/person

Howard Johnson Motor Lodge
P.O. Box 1107
Hardeeville, SC 29927
Phone: (803) 784-2271

Pet Restrictions: $5/day/pet
Pet left unattended in room: Yes,
notify desk
Exercise Area for Pets: Yes
Rates: $29.95 and up

Thunderbird Lodge
P.O. Box 1126
Hardeeville, SC 29927
Phone: (803) 784-2196

Pet Restrictions: Maximum 2-day
stay
Exercise Area for Pets: Yes
Rates: $21.95 to $37.95

HILTON HEAD ISLAND
Comfort Inn
2 Tanglewood Dr.
Hilton Head Island, SC 29928
Phone: (803) 842-6662

Pet Restrictions: $5/day/pet
Pet left unattended in room: Yes, if
caged
Exercise Area for Pets: Yes
Rates: $54.95 to $73.95

Red Roof Inn
5 Regency Pwy.
Hilton Head, SC 29928
Phone: (803) 686-6808

Pet Restrictions: None
Pet left unattended in room: Yes
Exercise Area for Pets: Yes
Rates: $47.99 to $55.99

LATTA
Patrick Henry Motor Lodge
203 N. Richardson St.
Latta, SC 29565
Phone: (803) 752-5861

Pet Restrictions: Reservations
suggested
Pet left unattended in room: Yes
Exercise Area for Pets: Yes
Rates: $20 to $35

LITTLE RIVER
Harbor Inn
P.O. Box 548 on US-17
Little River, SC 29566
Phone: (803) 249-3535
(800) 292-0404

Pet Restrictions: Small pets, $5/stay
Exercise Area for Pets: Yes
Rates: $36 to $62

VETERINARIANS
Brucks, E.W.
Highway 17 North
(803) 249-3421

MANNING
Budget Inn
I-95 & US 301 ext 115
Manning, SC 29102
Phone: (803) 473-2561, call collect
for reservations

Pet Restrictions: Housebroken,
notify at check-in, must be
leashed when out of room
Pet left unattended in room: Yes, if
quiet
Exercise Area for Pets: Yes
Rates: $19 to $26.95

MT. PLEASANT
Comfort Inn-East
310 Hwy. 17 Bypass
Mt. Pleasant, SC 29464
Phone: (803) 884-5853

Pet Restrictions: Leashed at all
times, prefer no large dogs
Pet left unattended in room: Yes, no
cleaning
Exercise Area for Pets: Nearby
Rates: $45 to $67

VETERINARIANS
George Veterinary Clinic
993 Highway 17 Bypass
(803) 884-6171

Thompson, Susan B.
307 Mill St.
(803) 884-7387

MYRTLE BEACH
South Wind Villas
5310 N. Ocean Blvd.
Myrtle Beach, SC 29577
Phone: (803) 449-5211,
(800) 842-1871

Pet Restrictions: Sept. 15-May 15
only, Under 25 lbs., $5-$10/day
Pet left unattended in room: Yes
Exercise Area for Pets: Yes
Rates: $133 to $1030

Super 8 Northgate
3450 Hwy 17 Bypass S.
Myrtle Beach, SC 29577
Phone: (803) 293-6100
(800) 264-1140

Pet Restrictions: None
Exercise Area for Pets: Nearby
Rates: $64.88

VETERINARIANS
Mavris, Zita N.
13 Southgate Rd.
(803) 238-1414

PORT ROYAL
Battery Creek Inn
US Hwy 802, P.O. Box 208
Port Royal, SC 29935
Phone: (803) 521-1441

Pet Restrictions: $50/stay
Pet left unattended in room: Yes,
well-behaved
Exercise Area for Pets: Yes, clean
up after
Rates: $74.90

Days Inn-Beaufort
1809 S. Ribant
Port Royal, SC 29935
Phone: (803) 524-1551

Pet Restrictions: Leash law in town,
$5/stay
Pet left unattended in room: Yes
Exercise Area for Pets: Nearby
Rates: $50 plus $5/person

RIDGELAND
Palms Motel
P.O. Box 547
Ridgeland, SC 29936
Phone: (803) 726-5511

Pet Restrictions: None
Pet left unattended in room: Yes
Exercise Area for Pets: Yes
Rates: $23 to $30

ROCK HILL
Howard Johnson Lodge
2625 Cherry Rd.
Rock Hill, SC 29730
Phone: (803) 329-3121

Pet Restrictions: Under 50 lbs.
Pet left unattended in room: Only
cats if caged
Exercise Area for Pets: Yes
Rates: $52 to $65

VETERINARIANS
Troutman, Roger J.
2241 India Hook Rd.
(803) 366-8188

ST. GEORGE
National 9 Economy Inn
Highway 78
St. George, SC 29477
Phone: (803) 563-4195

Pet Restrictions: $2 per day, small
pets only
Pet left unattended in room: Yes
Exercise Area for Pets: Nearby
Rates: $28 to $30

SANTEE
Days Inn
Hwy S.C. 6 P.O. Box 9
Santee, SC 29142
Phone: (803) 854-2175

Pet Restrictions: $5/day/pet
Pet left unattended in room: Yes,
notify housekeeping
Exercise Area for Pets: Yes
Rates: $45 to $50

Holiday Inn
Jct. Hwys 301 & 6 & 15
Santee, SC 29142
Phone: (803) 854-2121

Pet Restrictions: None
Exercise Area for Pets: Yes
Rates: $39.50 plus $5/person

Quality Inn-Clarks
P.O. Box 26
Santee, SC 29142
Phone: (803) 854-2141
(800) 531-9658

Pet Restrictions: In original building
only
Pet left unattended in room: Yes, do
not disturb sign on door
Exercise Area for Pets: Yes
Rates: $37 plus $5/person

SPARTANBURG

Days Inn
1355 Boiling Springs Rd.
Spartanburg, SC 29303
Phone: (803) 585-2413,
     (800) 325-2525

Pet Restrictions: None
Pet left unattended in room: Yes
Exercise Area for Pets: Yes
Rates: $22.40 to $35

Ramada Inn
1000 Hearon Circle
Spartanburg, SC 29303
Phone: (803) 578-7170

Pet Restrictions: Under 30 lbs.
Pet left unattended in room: Yes, no
    cleaning
Exercise Area for Pets: Yes
Rates: $45 to $54

VETERINARIANS

Harrison, Wendel R.
980 South Pine St.
(803) 585-0231

Hughston, Nancy
121 S. Blackstock Rd.
(803) 574-2430

Nichols, Shari L.
113 Windyrush Rd.
(803) 574-6200

SUMMERTON

Summerton Inn
P.O. Box 640
Summerton, SC 29148
Phone: (803) 485-2635

Pet Restrictions: None
Pet left unattended in room: Yes,
    short time only
Exercise Area for Pets: Yes
Rates: $17.95 to $39

SUMMERVILLE

Holiday Inn-Summerville
I-26 at Jct US-17A exit 199A
Summerville, SC 29483
Phone: (803) 875-3300

Pet Restrictions: Under 20 lbs.,
    housebroken
Exercise Area for Pets: Yes
Rates: $46 to $64

VETERINARIANS

Flynn, Anne
1720 Trolley Rd.
(803) 871-2900

Grant III, John B.
605 Miles Rd.
(803) 871-4560

SUMTER

Ramada Inn
226 N. Wash St.
Sumter, SC 29150
Phone: (803) 775-2323,
    (800) 457-6884

Pet Restrictions: Under 15 lbs.
Pet left unattended in room: Yes, do
    not disturb sign on door
Exercise Area for Pets: Yes
Rates: $39.90 to $75

VETERINARIANS

Animal Medical Clinic
21 Pinewood Rd.
(803) 773-1616

Shaw, John W.
463 N. Guignard
(803) 773-5506

WALTERBORO

Comfort Inn
1109 Snider's Hwy.
Walterboro, SC 29488
Phone: (803) 538-5403

Pet Restrictions: None
Pet left unattended in room: Yes
Exercise Area for Pets: Yes
Rates: $33 to $55

Econo Lodge
1057 Sniders Hwy.
Walterboro, SC 29488
Phone: (803) 538-3830

Pet Restrictions: Well-trained
Pet left unattended in room: Yes, if
    well-behaved
Exercise Area for Pets: Yes
Rates: $31.95 to $38.95

Holiday Inn
1120 Snider's Hwy.
Walterboro, SC 29488
Phone: (803) 538-5473

Pet Restrictions: None
Pet left unattended in room: Yes,
    quiet
Exercise Area for Pets: Yes
Rates: $53 and up

Super 8 Motel
Ext 57 - I95
Walterboro, SC 29488
Phone: (803) 538-5383

Pet Restrictions: No puppies
Exercise Area for Pets: Yes
Rates: $25.99 to $58.88

Town & Country Inn
1139 Snider's Hwy.
Walterboro, SC 29488
Phone: (803) 538-5911

Pet Restrictions: None
Exercise Area for Pets: Yes
Rates: $21.95 to $29.95

WINNSBORO
Fairfield Motel
US-321 Bypass 115 S.
Winnsboro, SC 29180
Phone: (803) 635-4681,
        (800) 292-1509

Pet Restrictions: None
Pet left unattended in room: Yes
Exercise Area for Pets: Yes
Rates: $27.80 to $45.47

YEMASSEE
Days Inn - Point South
Jct. US-17 & I-95, exit 33
Yemassee, SC 29945
Phone: (803) 726-8156

Pet Restrictions: $3/pet/day
Pet left unattended in room: Yes
Exercise Area for Pets: Yes
Rates: $48 to $58

Palmetto Lodge
Jct I-95 & SR 68, exit 38
Yemassee, SC 29945
Phone: (803) 589-2361

Pet Restrictions: Housebroken
Exercise Area for Pets: Yes
Rates: $20.95 to $32.95

SOUTH DAKOTA — HOTELS

ABERDEEN

Best Western Ramkota Inn
1400 8th Ave. NW
Aberdeen, SD 57401
Phone: (605) 229-4040

Pet Restrictions: None
Pet left unattended in room: Yes, if
    quiet
Exercise Area for Pets: Yes
Rates: $46 to $54

VETERINARIANS

Cooper Animal Clinic
6155 East Highway
Phone: (605) 225-3500

Nelson, Robin K.
704 South Melgaard Rd.
Phone: (605) 229-1691

BELLE FOURCHE

Motel Lariat
1033 Elkhorn
Belle Fourche, SD 57717
Phone: (605) 892-2601

Pet Restrictions: Housebroken
Pet left unattended in room: Yes
Exercise Area for Pets: Yes
Rates: $18 to $58

Sunset Motel
HC30, Box 65
Belle Fourch, SD 57717
Phone: (605) 892-2508

Pet Restrictions: Small, deposit
    $3/day, dog only
Exercise Area for Pets: Yes
Rates: $22 to $48

BERESFORD

Crossroads Motel
1409 W. Cedar
Beresford, SD 57004
Phone: (605) 763-2020

Pet Restrictions: $5 per day, small
    pet only
Exercise Area for Pets: Yes
Rates: $27.30 to $31.50

BROOKINGS

Best Western Starlite Inn
2515 E. 6th St.
Brookings, SD 57006
Phone: (605) 692-9421

Pet Restrictions: None
Exercise Area for Pets: Yes
Rates: $43 to $58

VETERINARIANS

McKnight, James H.
420 South 12th St.
Phone: (605) 692-2815

CANOVA

Skoglund Farm
Rte. 1, Box 45
Canova, SD 57321
Phone: (605) 247-3445

Pet Restrictions: None
Pet left unattended in room: No
Exercise Area for Pets: Yes
Rates: Adults $30; Teens $20;
    Children $15. Includes evening
    dinner, overnight and breakfast

CUSTER

Dakota Cowboy Inn
208 W. Mt. Rushmore Rd.
Custer, SD 57730
Phone: (605) 673-4659

Pet Restrictions: Certain rooms,
    deposit $5/day/pet
Exercise Area for Pets: Yes
Rates: $32 to $70

Roost Resort
HCR 83, Box 120
Custer, SD 57730
Phone: (605) 673-2326

Pet left unattended in room: Yes,
    notify desk
Exercise Area for Pets: Yes, clean
    up after pets
Rates: $34 to $58

State Game Lodge
HCR, Box 74
Custer, SD 57730
Phone: (605) 255-4541,
    (800) 658-3530

Pet Restrictions: $5 per day, cabins
    only
Pet left unattended in room: Yes
Exercise Area for Pets: Nearby
Rates: $60 to $70

FAITH

Prairie Vista Hotel
1st St & E. 1st Ave.
Faith, SD 57626
Phone: (605) 967-2343,
    (800) 341-8000 (IMA)

Pet Restrictions: Small pets
Exercise Area for Pets: Yes
Rates: $34.95 to $39.95

SOUTH DAKOTA — HOTELS (continued)

INTERIOR

Badlands Inn
P.O. Box 103
Interior, SD 57626
Phone: (605) 433-5401

Pet Restrictions: Well-behaved
Exercise Area for Pets: Yes
Rates: $27 to $62.40

Cedar Pass Lodge
P.O. Box 5
Interior, SD 57750
Phone: (605) 433-5460
Pet Restrictions: Well-behaved
Exercise Area for Pets: Yes
Rates: $37 to $56

KEYSTONE

4 Presidents Motel
Hwy. 16, P.O. Box 690
Keystone, SD 57751
Phone: (605) 666-4472,
    (800) 528-1234
Pet Restrictions: Small pet only
Exercise Area for Pets: Yes
Rates: $75 to $85

KODOKA

Cuckleburr Motel
P.O. Box 575
Kodoka, SD 57543
Phone: (605) 837-2151,
    (800) 323-7988
Pet Restrictions: None
Pet left unattended in room: Yes,
    if quiet
Exercise Area for Pets: Yes
Rates: $24 to $60

MADISON

Lake Park Motel
P.O. Box 44
Madison, SD 57042
Phone: (605) 256-3524,
    (800) 341-8000
Pet Restrictions: None
Exercise Area for Pets: Nearby
Rates: $31.80 to $34.96

MILBANK

Manor Motel
E. Hwy. 12, Box 26
Milbank, SD 57252
Phone: (605) 432-4527

Pet Restrictions: Small pets only
Exercise Area for Pets: Yes
Rates: $32 to $34

MITCHELL

Coachlight
1000 W. Haven St.
Mitchell, SD 57301
Phone: (605) 996-5686

Pet Restrictions: None
Exercise Area for Pets: Yes
Rates: $28 to $35 plus $3/person

Siesta Motel
1210 W. Hawn St.
Mitchell, SD 57301
Phone: (605) 996-5544,
    (800) 424-0537

Pet Restrictions: No snakes
Exercise Area for Pets: Yes
Rates: $32 to $48 plus $4/person

OACOMA

Oasis Inn
I90 exit 260
Oacoma, SD 57365
Phone: (605) 734-6061,
    (800) 341-8000 (IMA reserv. only)
Pet Restrictions: Owner responsible
    for damages, deposit $5/day for
    large dogs
Exercise Area for Pets: Yes
Rates: $35 to $55

PIERRE

Best Western Ramkota Inn
920 W. Sioux Ave.
Pierre, SD 57501
Phone: (605) 224-6877

Pet Restrictions: None
Exercise Area for Pets: Nearby
Rates: $57 to $150

RAPID CITY

Gold Nugget Motel
Mt. Rushmore Rd.
Rapid City, SD 57701
Phone: (605) 348-2082

Pet Restrictions: Deposit $5/day/pet
Exercise Area for Pets: Yes
Rates: $30 to $67

SOUTH DAKOTA — HOTELS (continued)

Rapid City Hilton Inn
445 Mt. Rushmore Rd.
Rapid City, SD 57701
Phone: (605) 348-8300,
   (800) 456-3750
Pet Restrictions: Knee high only,
   deposit $25/stay
Exercise Area for Pets: Nearby
Rates: $77 to $100

Rockervill Trading Post
HCR 33, P.O. Box 1607
Rapid City, SD 57701
Phone: (605) 341-4880
Pet Restrictions: Deposit $5/pet/day
Exercise Area for Pets: Yes
Rates: $22.95 to $68.95

VETERINARIANS
Canyon Lake Veterinary Clinic
4230 Canyon Lake Dr.
Phone: (605) 348-6510

Meiners Animal Clinic
Route 4, Box 121 Deadwood Ave.
Phone: (605) 343-5089

Twitero, Geroge A.
2909 South Highway 79
Phone: (605) 343-6066

SIOUX FALLS
Best Western Ramkota Inn
2400 N. Louise Ave.
Sioux Falls, SD 57107
Phone: (605) 336-0650
Pet Restrictions: None
Exercise Area for Pets: Yes
Rates: $57 to $160

Excel Inn
1300 W. Russel St.
Sioux Falls, SD 57104
Phone: (605) 331-5800,
   (800) 356-8013
Pet Restrictions: None
Exercise Area for Pets: Yes
Rates: $20.95 to $44.99

Holiday Inn
100 W. 8th St.
Sioux Falls, SD 57102
Phone: (605) 339-2000,
   (800) 843-9821
Pet Restrictions: None
Exercise Area for Pets: Nearby
Rates: $69 to $85

Howard Johnson Hotel
3300 West Russell St.
Sioux Falls, SD 57101
Phone: (605) 336-9000
Pet Restrictions: Well behaved,
   quiet
Exercise Area for Pets: Yes
Rates: $60 to $66

Surburban Motel
3308 E. 10th St.
Sioux Falls, SD 57103
Phone: (605) 336-3668
Pet Restrictions: $3/day/pet
Exercise Area for Pets: Yes
Rates: $24 to $40

VETERINARIANS
Brost, Douglas R.
1102 East 10th St.
Phone: (605) 338-3223

Christensen, Robert
1010 East 41st St.
Phone: (605) 336-1650

SPEARFISH
Queens Motel
305 Main St.
Spearfish, SD 57783
Phone: (800) 658-5564
Pet Restrictions: Small pets only
Exercise Area for Pets: Yes
Rates: $26 to $60

VETERINARIANS
Boke, James W.
710 East Colorado Blvd.
Phone: (605) 642-5771

WATERTOWN
Best Western Ramkota Inn
1901 9th Ave. SW
Watertown, SD 57201
Phone: (605) 886-8011
Pet Restrictions: None
Exercise Area for Pets: Yes
Rates: $45 to $95

Drake Motor Inn
P.O. Box 252
Watertown, SD 57201
Phone: (605) 886-8411
Pet Restrictions: Deposit $25/stay
Exercise Area for Pets: Yes
Rates: $27.95 to $32.95 plus
   $5/person

WINNER

Buffalo Trail Motel

West Hwy 18
Winner, SD 57580
Phone: (605) 842-2212,
   (800) 341-8000 (IMA)

Pet Restrictions: None
Pet left unattended in room: Yes,
   short time only, if caged
Exercise Area for Pets: Yes
Rates: $27 to $70

TENNESSEE — HOTELS

ALCOA

Quality Inn - Airport
2306 Airport Hwy
Alcoa, TN 97701
Phone: (615) 970-3140,
   (800) 221-2222 (central res.)
Pet Restrictions: None
Pet left unattended in room: Yes
Exercise Area for Pets: Yes
Rates: $45 to $65

ANTIOCH

Days Inn Bell Rd.
501 Collins Park Dr.
Antioch, TN 37013
Phone: (615) 731-7800
Pet Restrictions: $5/day
Pet left unattended in room: Yes
Exercise Area for Pets: Yes
Rates: $43.95 to $49.95

ATHENS

Days Inn at Athens
I 75 & US 30
Athens, TN 37303
Phone: (615) 745-5800
Pet Restrictions: None
Pet left unattended in room: Yes
Exercise Area for Pets: Yes
Rates: $32 to $40

Homestead Inn
1827 Holiday
Athens, TN 37303
Phone: (615) 744-9002
Pet Restrictions: $5/day, small pets
   only
Exercise Area for Pets: Nearby
Rates: $32.95 to $39.95

BRISTOL

Econolodge
P.O. Box 1016
Bristol, TN 37621
Phone: (615) 968-9119
Pet Restrictions: Small pets only
Pet left unattended in room: Yes
Exercise Area for Pets: Nearby
Rates: $38 to $44

Holiday Inn I-81
111 Holiday Dr.
Bristol, TN 37620
Phone: (615) 968-1101
Pet Restrictions: None
Pet left unattended in room: Yes,
   well-behaved
Exercise Area for Pets: Yes
Rates: $42 to $58

VETERINARIANS

Animal Medical Clinic
2012 W. State Street
Phone: (615) 764-2428

Hill, Neal G.
2616 Volunteer Pkwy
Phone: (615) 968-7241

CAREYVILLE

Holiday Inn - Cove Lake
Rt. 1, Box 14
Careyville, TN 37714
Phone: (615) 562-8476
Pet Restrictions: Deposit $15, owner
   liable for damages
Pet left unattended in room: Yes if
   quiet
Exercise Area for Pets: Yes
Rates: $43 to $55

CHATTANOOGA

Days Inn Chatanooga Lookout
101 E. 20th St.
Chattanooga, TN 37408
Phone: (615) 267-9761,
   (800) 325-2525 (central res.)
Pet Restrictions: $4/pet/day deposit
Exercise Area for Pets: Yes
Rates: $39 plus $5/person

Days Inn & Convention Center
1400 N. Mack Smith Rd.
Chattanooga, TN 37412
Phone: (615) 894-0440,
   (800) 251-7624
Pet Restrictions: Smoking rooms only
Pet left unattended in room: Yes
Exercise Area for Pets: Yes
Rates: $44 and up

Howard Johnson Hotel
100 West 21st St.
Chattanooga, TN 37408
Phone: (615) 265-3151,
   (800) 828-4656
Pet Restrictions: Small pets,
   $6/pet/day deposit
Rates: $39 to $69

Motel 6
7707 Lee Hwy
Chattanooga, TN 37421
Phone: (615) 892-7707
Pet Restrictions: 1-2 pets per room
Exercise Area for Pets: Yes
Rates: $24.99 to $30.99

TENNESSEE — HOTELS (continued)

Red Roof Inn
7014 Shallowford Rd.
Chattanooga, TN 37421
Phone: (615) 899-0143
Pet Restrictions: None
Exercise Area for Pets: Yes
Rates: $33.99 to $55

VETERINARIANS
Animal Clinic Inc. 23rd Street
2223 East 23rd Street
Phone: (615) 698-2401

Ashland Terrace Animal Hosp.
907 Ashland Terrace
Phone: (615) 877-4576

Northgate Animal Hospital
1600 Hamill Rd. at Hixson Pike
Phone: (615) 875-9033

CLARKSVILLE
Days Inn of Clarksville
1100 Hwy 76 Connector Rd.
Clarksville, TN 37043
Phone: (615) 358-3194
Pet Restrictions: None
Pet left unattended in room: Yes
Exercise Area for Pets: Yes
Rates: $30 to $40

Holiday Inn I24
3095 Guthrie Hwy
Clarksville, TN 37040
Phone: (615) 648-4848
Pet Restrictions: None
Exercise Area for Pets: Nearby
Rates: $46 to $59

Quality Inn
803 N. 2nd St.
Clarksville, TN 37040
Phone: (615) 645-9084,
(800) 228-5151
Pet Restrictions: Leashed on hotel
property-state law
Pet left unattended in room: Yes,
use do not disturb sign
Exercise Area for Pets: Nearby

Skyway Motel
2581 Ft. Campbell Blvd.
Clarkesville, TN 37042
Phone: (615) 431-5225
Pet Restrictions: Small, $25/stay
deposit
Pet left unattended in room: Yes if
caged, no cleaning
Exercise Area for Pets: Yes
Rates: $23 to $35

VETERINARIANS
Hackett, Mark E.
P.O. Box 2128
Phone: (615) 647-1534

CLEVELAND
Cleveland Travel Inn
Ext 25 I-75 at 25th St.
Cleveland, TN 37311
Phone: (615) 472-2185
Pet Restrictions: None
Exercise Area for Pets: Yes
Rates: $26 to $42

Days Inn of Cleveland
2550 Georgetown Rd.
Cleveland, TN 37311
Phone: (615) 476-2112
Pet Restrictions: $5/day/pet
Exercise Area for Pets: Yes
Rates: $35 to $45

Ramada Inn of Cleveland
P.O. Box 3896
Cleveland, TN 37320
Phone: (615) 479-4531
Pet Restrictions: Small,
housebroken
Pet left unattended in room: Yes,
if quiet
Exercise Area for Pets: Yes
Rates: $30 to $53

VETERINARIANS
Keith Street Animal Clinic
1990 Keith Street
Phone: (615) 476-1804

Taylor Animal Hospital
2954 Keith Street NW
Phone: (615) 476-6551

CONCORD
Days Inn - Lovell Rd.
200 Lovell Rd.
Concord, TN 37922
Phone: (615) 966-5801
Pet Restrictions: $5/day/pet, no
large dogs
Exercise Area for Pets: Yes
Rates: $41 to $56

VETERINARIANS
Brown, George W.
10226 Kingston Pike
Phone: (615) 693-0401

COOKEVILLE

Best West. Thunderbird Motel
900 S. Jefferson
Cookeville, TN 38501
Phone: (615) 526-7115
Pet Restrictions: Smoking only
Exercise Area for Pets: Nearby
Rates: $39.95

Holiday Inn - Cookville
920 S. Jefferson Ave.
Cookeville, TN 38501
Phone: (615) 526-7125
Pet Restrictions: No large dogs
Pet left unattended in room: Yes, no
    problems
Exercise Area for Pets: Yes
Rates: $55 to $58

Howard Johnson Motor Lodge
2021 E. Spring St.
Cookeville, TN 38501
Phone: (615) 526-3333
Pet Restrictions: Deposit $5/day/pet
Exercise Area for Pets: Yes
Rates: $40 to $44

Super 8 Inn
1330 Bunker Hill Rd.
Cookeville, TN 38501
Phone: (615) 528-2020
Pet Restrictions: Small pets only,
    $10 deposit
Exercise Area for Pets: Nearby
Exercise Area for Pets: Yes
Rates: $39 to $45

CUMBERLAND GAP

Holiday Inn-Cumberland Gap
Hwy 25 E
Cumberland Gap, TN 37724
Phone: (615) 869-3631
Pet Restrictions: Small pets
Exercise Area for Pets: Yes
Rates: $47 and up

FRANKLIN

Best Western Goose Creek Inn
Paytonsville Rd. - Spring Hill exit 61
Franklin, TN 37064
Phone: (615) 794-7200
Pet Restrictions: No large dogs,
    $8/day/pet deposit
Pet left unattended in room: Yes,
    use do not disturb sign
Exercise Area for Pets: Yes
Rates: $38 to $54

Holiday Inn
1307 Murffeesboro Rd.
Franklin, TN 37065
Phone: (615) 794-7591
Pet Restrictions: Small-med pets
Pet left unattended in room: Yes,
    notify desk
Exercise Area for Pets: Yes
Rates: $49 to $60

GALLATIN

Shoney's Inn
221 W. Main St.
Gallatin, TN 37066
Phone: (615) 452-5433,
    (800) 222-2222 (central res.)
Pet Restrictions: Housebroken
Exercise Area for Pets: Yes, must
    be leashed
Rates: $42 to $48

GATLINBURG

Creekstone Motel
104 Oglewood Lane
Gatlinsburg, TN 37738
Phone: (615) 436-4628,
    (800) 572-7770
Pet Restrictions: None
Exercise Area for Pets: Yes
Rates: $40 to $54

Holiday Inn
520 Airport Rd.
Gatlinburg, TN 37738
Phone: (615) 436-9201,
    (800) 435-9201
Pet Restrictions: None
Exercise Area for Pets: Yes
Rates: $39 to $99

GOODLETSVILLE

Budgetel Inn Nashville N.
120 Cartwright Ct.
Goodletsville, TN 37072
Phone: (615) 851-1891
Pet Restrictions: Under 10 lbs.
Exercise Area for Pets: Yes
Rates: $45.95 to $51.95

Econolodge
320 Long Hollow Pike
Goodlettesville, TN 37072
Phone: (615) 859-4988,
    (800) 424-4777
Pet Restrictions: None
Pet left unattended in room: Yes
Exercise Area for Pets: Yes
Rates: $25.95 to $52.95

Red Roof Inn
110 Northgate Dr.
Goodlettsville, TN 37072
Phone: (615) 859-2537

Pet Restrictions: Small pet only
Exercise Area for Pets: Nearby
Rates: $44.95 to $49.95

JACKSON
Budgetel Inn
2370 N. Highland Ave.
Jackson, TN 38305
Phone: (901) 664-1800

Pet Restrictions: 2 rooms, smoking
    rooms, make reservations
Exercise Area for Pets: Yes
Rates: $29.95 to $36.95

Quality Inn
2262 N. Highland
Jackson, TN 38350
Phone: (901) 668-1066

Pet Restrictions: Small pets only
Exercise Area for Pets: Nearby
Rates: $34.95 to $37.95

VETERINARIANS
Northside Veterinary Clinic
3327 Humboldt Highway
Phone: (901) 668-9350

JELICO
Days Inn
P.O. Box 299, I-75 & US 25
Jelico, TN 37762
Phone: (615) 784-7281

Pet Restrictions: $4/day, small pet
    only
Exercise Area for Pets: Yes
Rates: $33 to $38

JOHNSON CITY
Garden Plaza Hotel
211 Mockingbird Lane
Johnson City, TN 37604
Phone: (615) 929-2000,
    (800) 342-7336

Pet Restrictions: Small pets, quiet
Pet left unattended in room: Yes,
    quiet
Exercise Area for Pets: Yes
Rates: $65 to $110

Holiday Inn
2406 Roan St.
Johnson City, TN 37601
Phone: (615) 282-2161

Pet Restrictions: Well-behaved
Pet left unattended in room: Yes,
    if quiet
Exercise Area for Pets: Yes
Rates: $39 to $75

Red Roof Inn
210 Broyles Dr.
Johnson City, TN 37601
Phone: (615) 282-3040

Pet Restrictions: Small dog 45 lb. or
    under
Pet left unattended in room: Yes
Exercise Area for Pets: Yes
Rates: $31 to $45

VETERINARIANS
Cherokee Hospitals for Animals
708 Cherokee Rd.
Phone: (615) 928-7272

Tri-City Veterinary Med. Ctr.
205 Princeton Rd.
Phone: (615) 282-4113

KINGSPORT
Comfort Inn
100 Indian Center Ct.
Kingsport, TN 37660
Phone: (615) 378-4418

Pet Restrictions: Owner liable for
    damages, deposit $8/pet/day
Pet left unattended in room: Yes
Exercise Area for Pets: Yes
Rates: $48 to $75

Holiday Inn
700 Lynn Garden Dr.
Kingsport, TN 37660
Phone: (615) 247-3133

Pet Restrictions: None
Pet left unattended in room: Yes
Exercise Area for Pets: Yes
Rates: $50 to $56

VETERINARIANS
Colonial Heights Animal Hosp.
P.O. Box 5316
Phone: (615) 239-5116

KINGSTON SPRINGS

Friendship Motel
123 Luyven Hills Rd.
Kingston Springs, TN 37082
Phone: (615) 952-2900
Pet Restrictions: None
Exercise Area for Pets: Nearby
Rates: $38 to $42.95

KNOXVILLE

Econolodge
402 Lovell Rd.
Knoxville, TN 37922
Phone: (615) 675-7200,
    (800) 424-4777 (central res.)
Pet Restrictions: Quiet, small-med
    pets, smoking rooms only
Rates: $32 to $49

Holiday Inn-Knoxville West
1315 Kirby Rd.
Knoxville, TN 37909
Phone: (615) 584-3911,
    (800) 854-8315
Pet Restrictions: None
Exercise Area for Pets: Yes
Rates: $69 to $89

Howard Johnson Motor Lodge
118 Merchants Rd. NW
Knoxville, TN 37912
Phone: (615) 688-3141,
    (800) 446-4656
Pet Restrictions: $50 deposit, quiet
Rates: $45 to $75

Hyatt Regency - Knoxville
500 Hill Ave. SE
Knoxville, TN 37901
Phone: (615) 637-1234,
    (800) 233-1234
Pet Restrictions: Deposit $35, under
    35 lbs.
Pet left unattended in room: Yes
Exercise Area for Pets: Yes
Rates: $135 to $600 (suite)

La Quinta Motor Inn
258 Peters Rd. N.
Knoxville, TN 37923
Phone: (615) 690-9777,
    (800) 531-5900
Pet left unattended in room: Yes
Exercise Area for Pets: Yes
Rates: $55 to $62 plus $6/person

Quality Inn West
7621 Kingston Pike
Knoxville, TN 37919
Phone: (615) 693-8111
Pet Restrictions: Housebroken,
    deposit $5/pet/day
Exercise Area for Pets: Yes
Rates: $66.50 plus $10/person

Red Roof Inn-Knoxville North
5640 Merchants Center Blvd.
Knoxville, TN 37912
Phone: (615) 689-7100,
    (800) 843-7663
Pet Restrictions: Under 20 lbs
Pet left unattended in room: Yes
Exercise Area for Pets: Yes
Rates: $29.99 to $47.99

Red Roof Inn-Knoxville West
106 North Advantage Place
Knoxville, TN 37923
Phone: (615) 691-1664
Pet Restrictions: Small pets
Pet left unattended in room: Yes
Exercise Area for Pets: Yes
Rates: $37.95 to $47.99

West Town Inn
7723 Kingston Pike
Knoxville, TN 37919
Phone: (615) 693-6111
Pet Restrictions: Under 35 lbs, 5
    smoking rooms, no pets over 5
    days
Pet left unattended in room: Yes, no
    cleaning
Exercise Area for Pets: Yes
Rates: $28.80 to $41

VETERINARIANS

Crossroads Animal Clinic
7426 Maynardville Hwy
Phone: (615) 922-7749

Lange Animal Hospital
110 Center Park Drive
Phone: (615) 690-6481

Univ. of Tenn. College Vet Hosp.
(615) 546-9240

KODAK

Best West. Dumplin Valley Inn
3426 Winfield Dunn Pkwy
Kodak, TN 37764
Phone: (615) 933-3467

Pet Restrictions: Small pets only
Exercise Area for Pets: Yes
Rates: $49.95 to $89.95

MADISON

Friendship Motel
625 N. Gallatin Rd.
Madison, TN 37115
Phone: (615) 865-2323

Pet Restrictions: $4/day
Pet left unattended in room: Yes
Exercise Area for Pets: Yes
Rates: $32 to $41

VETERINARIANS

Head, Michael A.
124 Harris St.
Phone: (615) 865-4310

MANCHESTER

Ambassador Inn & Luxury Suites
Ext. 110 I-29
Manchester, TN 37355
Phone: (615) 728-2200,
    (800) 237-9228

Pet Restrictions: Small number of
    rooms only, reserve in advance
Pet left unattended in room: Yes
Exercise Area for Pets: Yes
Rates: $33.90 to $56

MEMPHIS

Brownstone Hotel
300 N. 2nd St.
Memphis, TN 38105
Phone: (901) 525-2511,
    (800) 468-3515 (res. only)

Pet Restrictions: Under 8 lbs.
Exercise Area for Pets: Yes
Rates: $90

Budgetel Inn-Memphis Airport
3005 Millbranch Rd.
Memphis, TN 38114
Phone: (901) 396-5411

Pet Restrictions: Under 10 lbs, 3
    rooms only, make reservations
Pet left unattended in room: Yes
Rates: $37.95 to $44.95

Days Inn - Brooks Rd.
1533 Brooks Rd.
Memphis, TN 38116
Phone: (901) 345-2470

Pet Restrictions: Deposit
    $4/day/room
Pet left unattended in room: Yes
Exercise Area for Pets: Yes
Rates: $35 and up

Days Inn-East
5877 Poplar Ave.
Memphis, TN 38119
Phone: (901) 767-6300,
    (800) 325-2525

Exercise Area for Pets: Yes
Rates: $57 to $60

La Quinta - Medical Center
42 S. Camilla Dr.
Memphis, TN 38104
Phone: (901) 526-1050,
    (800) 531-5900

Pet Restrictions: Small pets
Pet left unattended in room: Yes, no
    cleaning unless caged
Exercise Area for Pets: Yes
Rates: $46 to $60

Memphis Airport Hotel
2240 Democrat Rd.
Memphis, TN 38132
Phone: (901) 332-1130

Pet Restrictions: Under 15 lbs., pet
    deposit varies
Pet left unattended in room: Yes
Exercise Area for Pets: Yes
Rates: $33.50 to $275

Motel 6
1360 Springbrook Rd.
Memphis, TN 38116
Phone: (901) 396-3620

Pet Restrictions: None
Exercise Area for Pets: Nearby
Rates: $31.65 to $45.44

Red Roof Inn
3875 American Way
Memphis, TN 38118
Phone: (901) 363-2335

Pet Restrictions: None
Pet left unattended in room: Yes
Exercise Area for Pets: Yes
Rates: $29.99 to $48.99

Sheraton Inn - Airport
2411 Winchester Rd.
Memphis, TN 38116
Phone: (901) 332-2370
Pet Restrictions: Small,
　　housebroken & quiet
Pet left unattended in room: Yes, if
　　quiet
Exercise Area for Pets: Yes
Rates: $72 to $82

VETERINARIANS
Frayser Raleigh Animal Hosp.
3147 Frayser Raleigh Rd.
Phone: (901) 353-9452

Hickory Ridge Animal Hospital
6466 Winchester
Phone: (901) 362-8321

Stage Road Animal Hosp.
4359 Stage Rd.
Phone: (901) 382-1950

MURFREESBORO
Howard Johnson Lodge
I-24 & US 231 S
Murfressboro, TN 37130
Phone: (615) 896-5522
Pet Restrictions: Sign waiver,
　　$5/pet/night
Exercise Area for Pets: Yes
Rates: $41 to $50

Wayside Inn
2025 S. Church St.
Murfreesboro, TN 37130
Phone: (615) 896-2320
Pet Restrictions: Under 20 lbs.,
　　quiet
Pet left unattended in room: Yes, if
　　caged
Exercise Area for Pets: Yes
Rates: $28 to $69.50

VETERINARIANS
Jackson, George A.
2050 Salem Rd.
Phone: (615) 896-3434

NASHVILLE
Airport Inn at Briley Parkway
1 International Plaza
Nashville, TN 37217
Phone: (615) 361-7666,
　　(800) 851-1962
Pet Restrictions: Small pets
Exercise Area for Pets: Yes
Rates: $50 to $75

Budgetel Inn
531 Donelson Pike
Nashville, TN 37214
Phone: (615) 885-3100,
　　(800) 428-3438
Pet Restrictions: None
Exercise Area for Pets: Yes
Rates: $51.99

Days Inn
1400 Brick Church Pike
Nashville, TN 37207
Phone: (615) 228-5977,
　　(800) 325-2525
Pet Restrictions: Deposit $5/pet/day
Pet left unattended in room: Yes
Exercise Area for Pets: Yes
Rates: $45 plus $5/person

Drury Inn - Airport
837 Briley Pkwy
Nashville, TN 37217
Phone: (615) 361-6999
Pet Restrictions: Small
Pet left unattended in room: Yes, for
　　short time
Exercise Area for Pets: Yes
Rates: $57 to $62

Econo Lodge
2460 Music Valley Dr.
Nashville, TN 37214
Phone: (615) 889-0090,
　　(800) 424-4777
Pet Restrictions: Under 10 lbs.
Pet left unattended in room: Yes, if
　　quiet
Exercise Area for Pets: Yes
Rates: $55.95 plus $5/person

Hampton Inn - Briley Pkwy
2350 Elm Hill Pike
Nashville, TN 37214
Phone: (615) 871-0222
Pet Restrictions: Under 20 lbs., 1
　　pet per room
Pet left unattended in room: Yes,
　　dogs must be caged
Rates: $49 to $63

Hampton Inn - North
2407 Brick Church Pike
Nashville, TN 37207
Phone: (615) 226-3300,
　　(800) 426-7866 (central res.)
Pet Restrictions: Smoking rooms only
Pet left unattended in room: Yes, if
　　quiet
Exercise Area for Pets: Yes
Rates: $55

Holiday Inn Express-Southeast
981 Murfreesboro Rd.
Nashville, TN 37217
Phone: (615) 367-9150

Pet Restrictions: None
Pet left unattended in room: Yes,
short time
Exercise Area for Pets: Yes
Rates: $61

Holiday Inn - Vanderbilt
2613 West End Ave.
Nashville, TN 37203
Phone: (615) 327-4707,
(800) 777-5871

Pet Restrictions: Under 30 lbs.
Pet left unattended in room: Yes
Exercise Area for Pets: Nearby
Rates: $75 to $81

Howard Johnson Inn
323 Harding Place
Nashville, TN 37211
Phone: (615) 834-0570

Pet Restrictions: $10
Pet left unattended in room: Yes,
notify desk
Exercise Area for Pets: Yes
Rates: $29 to $32

La Quinta Inn
4311 Sidco Dr.
Nashville, TN 37204
Phone: (615) 834-6900

Pet Restrictions: Under 35 lbs.,
must be leashed on hotel property
Pet left unattended in room: Yes, no
cleaning
Exercise Area for Pets: Yes, but
leashed on hotel property
Rates: $55

Nashville Marriott-Airport
600 Marriott Dr.
Nashville, TN 37214
Phone: (615) 889-9300

Pet Restrictions: None
Pet left unattended in room: Yes
Exercise Area for Pets: Yes
Rates: $118 to $144

Red Roof Inn
510 Claridge Dr.
Nashville, TN 37214
Phone: (615) 872-0735

Pet Restrictions: None
Pet left unattended in room: Yes
Exercise Area for Pets: Yes
Rates: $35.99 to $47.99

Red Roof Inn-Med. Ctr.
210 S. Pauline
Nashville, TN 38104
Phone: (901) 528-0650

Pet Restrictions: None
Pet left unattended in room: Yes, no
maid service
Exercise Area for Pets: Yes
Rates: $40.99 and up

Red Roof Inn - South
4271 Sidco Dr.
Nashville, TN 37204
Phone: (615) 832-0093

Pet Restrictions: Under 40 lbs.
Pet left unattended in room: Yes
Exercise Area for Pets: Yes
Rates: $29.99 to $55.99

Sheraton - Music City
777 McGavock Pike
Nashville, TN 37214
Phone: (615) 885-2200

Pet Restrictions: Under 15 lbs.
Pet left unattended in room: Yes, if
caged
Exercise Area for Pets: Yes
Rates: $120 to $130

Stouffer Nashville Hotel
611 Commerce St.
Nashville, TN 37203
Phone: (615) 255-8400, call collect
for reservations

Pet Restrictions: Notify desk, under
15 lbs.
Pet left unattended in room: Yes,
use do not disturb sign
Rates: $139 to $219

VETERINARIANS

Airport Animal Clinic
215 Pineway Dr.
Phone: (615) 367-9319

Elm Hill Veterinary Clinic
2733 Elm Hill Pike
Phone: (615) 885-0813

Fitzpatrick Veterinary Clinic
3926 Nolensville Rd.
Phone: (615) 832-6535

NEWPORT

Holiday Inn
I-40 & Hwy 32
Newport, TN 37821
Phone: (615) 623-8622

Pet Restrictions: None
Pet left unattended in room: Yes, if
    quiet
Exercise Area for Pets: Yes
Rates: $38 to $75

Ramsey Motel
P.O. Box 1148, Hwy 2570
Newport, TN 37821
Phone: (615) 625-1521

Pet Restrictions: 1 small pet
Exercise Area for Pets: Yes
Rates: $24 to $45

VETERINARIANS

Appalachian Veterinary Hosp.
1002 West Broadway
Phone: (615) 625-1616

Cedarwood Veterinary Clinic
101 Hedrick Dr.
Phone: (615) 623-4362

OAK RIDGE

Days Inn
206 S. Illinois Ave.
Oak Ridge, TN 37830
Phone: (615) 483-5615

Pet Restrictions: None
Pet left unattended in room: Yes,
    notify desk
Exercise Area for Pets: Yes
Rates: $50 to $52

VETERINARIANS

McArthur Animal Hospital
2190 Oak Ridge Turnpike
Phone: (615) 482-1797

ONEIDA

The Galloway Inn
Hwy 27 South
Oneida, TN 37841
Phone: (615) 569-8835

Pet Restrictions: Owner responsible
    for damages, notify desk
Exercise Area for Pets: Yes
Rates: $22 to $29

PIGEON FORGE

Econo Lodge
2440 Parkway
Pigeon Forge, TN 37863
Phone: (615) 428-1231

Pet Restrictions: Small, $5/day/pet
Pet left unattended in room: Yes
Exercise Area for Pets: Yes
Rates: $69 to $89

SWEETWATER

Comfort Inn
S. Main St., P.O. Box 48
Sweetwater, TN 37874
Phone: (615) 337-6646

Pet Restrictions: None
Pet left unattended in room: Yes
Exercise Area for Pets: Yes
Rates: $36 and up

TEXAS — HOTELS

ABILENE

Best Western Classic Inn
3950 Ridgemont Dr.
Abilene, TX 79606
Phone: (915) 695-1262,
   (800) 346-1574

Pet Restrictions: Small pets
Pet left unattended in room: Yes, if
   caged
Exercise Area for Pets: Yes
Rates: $39.95 to $60

Economy Inn
I20 & Hwy 351 Exit 288
Abilene, TX 79601
Phone: (915) 673-5251

Pet Restrictions: Deposit, $20 for
   large dog
Pet left unattended in room: Yes
Exercise Area for Pets: Yes
Rates: $28.95 to $22.95

VETERINARIANS

Abilene Veterinary Clinic
1365 S. Daville
(915) 675-0372

Elm Creek Veterinary Clinic
5925 South First
(915) 692-1488

ALICE

Kings Inn Motel
815 Hwy. 2815
Alice, TX 78332
Phone: (512) 664-4351

Pet Restrictions: None
Exercise Area for Pets: Yes
Rates: $28 to $32

AMARILLO

Best Western Amarillo Inn
1610 Coulter Dr.
Amarillo TX 79106
Phone: (806) 358-7861

Pet Restrictions: Small pets, deposit
   $6/day/pet
Exercise Area for Pets: Yes
Rates: $55 to $61

Comfort Inn
2100 S. Coulter Rd.
Amarillo, TX 79106
Phone: (806) 358-6141,
   (800) 628-5013

Pet Restrictions: None
Exercise Area for Pets: Yes
Rates: $34 to $68

Comfort Inn
15151-40E
Amarillo, TX 79102
Phone: (806) 376-9993

Pet Restrictions: Certain rooms
Exercise Area for Pets: Yes
Rates: $42 to $59

Hampton Inn
1700 I-40E
Amarillo, TX 79103
Phone: (806) 372-1425,
   (800) 426-7866 (central res.)

Pet Restrictions: Quiet
Exercise Area for Pets: Yes
Rates: $49 to $58

La Quinta Inn
1708 I-40E
Amarillo, TX 79103
Phone: (806) 373-7486

Pet Restrictions: Smoking rooms
   only, under 25 lbs.
Pet left unattended in room: Yes, no
   housekeeping
Exercise Area for Pets: Yes
Rates: $53 to $63

La Quinta Motor Inn Medical Center
2108 South Coulter Dr.
Amarillo, TX 79106
Phone: (806) 352-6311,
   (800) 531-5900

Pet Restrictions: None
Exercise Area for Pets: Yes
Rates: $39 to $53

Travelodge East
3205 I-40E
Amarillo, TX 79104
Phone: (806) 372-8171

Pet Restrictions: Small pets, under
   20 lbs.
Exercise Area for Pets: Yes
Rates: $45 to $50

VETERINARIANS

Acoma Pines Animal & Bird Clinic
4010 West 34th St.
(806) 358-7608

Animal Medical Center
6201 Amarillo Blvd. West
(806) 358-7831

Henley Animal Hospital
5127 Canyon Dr.
(806) 355-5629

ARLINGTON

Days Inn
910 N. Collins St.
Arlington, TX 76011
Phone: (817) 261-8444

Pet Restrictions: Under 15 lbs., pet deposit $5/day/pet
Pet left unattended in room: Yes, if caged
Exercise Area for Pets: Yes
Rates: $55 to $68

Hawthorne Suites Hotel
2401 Brookhollow Plaza Dr.
Arlington, TX 76006
Phone: (817) 640-1188,
       (800) 527-1133

Pet Restrictions: Dogs only, small, deposit $250, $50 kept for cleaning
Pet left unattended in room: Yes
Exercise Area for Pets: Yes
Rates: $120 to $200

Park Inn Ltd.
703 Benge Dr. at 1200 S. Cooper
Arlington, TX 76013
Phone: (817) 860-2323,
       (800) 437-7275

Pet Restrictions: None
Pet left unattended in room: Yes, for short time
Exercise Area for Pets: Yes
Rates: $40.95 to $45

Ramada Inn
700 E. Lamar Blvd.
Arlington, TX 76011
Phone: (817) 265-7711,
       (800) 228-2828

Pet Restrictions: 20 lbs. under
Pet left unattended in room: Yes, if quiet
Exercise Area for Pets: Yes
Rates: $58 to $68

VETERINARIANS

Farrell Animal Hospital
2890 W. Pioneer Pkwy
(817) 265-6276

I-20 Animal Medical Center
4501 Hawkins Cemetery Rd.
(817) 478-9238

Sanford Oaks Animal Clinic
2000 W. Sanford
(817) 460-4441

AUSTIN

Best Western-Seville
4323 I-35S
Austin, TX 78744
Phone: (512) 447-5511

Pet Restrictions: Small pets, deposit $20/per stay, refundable
Pet left unattended in room: Yes
Exercise Area for Pets: Yes
Rates: $38 to $42

Doubletree Hotel
6505 I-35 North
Austin, TX 78752
Phone: (512) 454-3737,
       (800) 222-8733

Pet Restrictions: Under 25 lbs., enter lobby thru garage, deposit $25/stay, refundable
Exercise Area for Pets: Yes
Rates: $115 to $175

Four Seasons Hotel Austin
98 San Jancinto Blvd.
Austin, TX 78701
Phone: (512) 478-4500,
       (800) 332-3442

Pet Restrictions: Notify when making reservations
Pet left unattended in room: Yes
Exercise Area for Pets: Yes
Rates: $152 to $1000

Hawthorne Suites Austin Central
935 La Posada Dr.
Austin, TX 78752
Phone: (512) 459-3335,
       (800) 526-1133 (central res.)

Pet Restrictions: Under 25 lbs., 1 pet per room, notify in advance, $50/stay
Pet left unattended in room: Yes, if caged
Exercise Area for Pets: Yes
Rates: $133

Heart of Texas Motel
5303 US-290 W
Austin, TX 78735
Phone: (512) 892-0644

Pet Restrictions: Smoking rooms only, $1/pet/day
Pet left unattended in room: Yes, leave phone number where you can be reached
Exercise Area for Pets: Yes
Rates: $35 to $48

Holiday Inn Northwest Plaza
8401 Business Park Drive
Austin, TX 78759
Phone: (512) 343-0888

Pet Restrictions: Small pets, 1st
  floor only, deposit varies
Pet left unattended in room: Yes, if
  quiet
Exercise Area for Pets: Yes
Rates: $78 to $88

Holiday Inn - Town Lake
20 I-35 N
Austin, TX 78701
Phone: (512) 472-8211

Pet Restrictions: Smoking floors only
Pet left unattended in room: Yes, if
  quiet
Exercise Area for Pets: Yes
Rates: $74

Red Lion
6121 I-35N
Austin, TX 78752
Phone: (512) 323-5466

Pet Restrictions: Owner responsible
  for damages
Exercise Area for Pets: Yes
Rates: $104 to $124

Royce Hotel
3401 I-35S
Austin, TX 78741
Phone: (512) 448-2444

Pet Restrictions: None
Pet left unattended in room: Yes
Exercise Area for Pets: Yes
Rates: $78 to $104

Stouffer Austin Hotel
9721 Arboretum Blvd.
Austin, TX 78759
Phone: (512) 343-2626

Pet Restrictions: Small pets, must
  be leashed on hotel property,
  sign pet release, leave credit
  card imprint
Pet left unattended in room: Yes
Exercise Area for Pets: Yes
Rates: $142 to $182

VETERINARIANS

Animal Medical Center-Central
7701 Cameron Rd.
(512) 454-3518

North Austin Animal Hospital
5608 Burnet Rd.
(512) 459-7676

West Lake Animal Hospital
3930 Bee Caves Rd.
(512) 327-1703

BAYTOWN

La Quinta-Baytown
4911 I-10E
Baytown, TX 77521
Phone: (713) 421-5566

Pet Restrictions: Notify desk
Pet left unattended in room: Yes,
  notify desk
Exercise Area for Pets: Yes
Rates: $62 to $69

VETERINARIANS

Casey, Gwenn D.
3108 Elvinta
(713) 427-1760

Guinn, Joy Beth
1101 Knowlton
(713) 427-5671

BEAUMONT

Beaumont Hilton Hotel
2355 I-10S
Beaumont, TX 77705
Phone: (409) 842-3600,
  (800) 445-8667

Pet Restrictions: Deposit $50/stay,
  refundable
Pet left unattended in room: Yes
Exercise Area for Pets: Yes
Rates: $99 to $109

Best Western Beaumont Inn
2155 N. 11th St.
Beaumont, TX 77703
Phone: (409) 898-8150

Pet Restrictions: None
Pet left unattended in room: Yes,
  notify desk
Exercise Area for Pets: Yes, leash law
Rates: $42.95 and up

Econolodge
11551 - 10S
Beaumont, TX 77701
Phone: (409) 835-5913

Pet Restrictions: $5/pet/night
Pet left unattended in room: Yes if
  housetrained
Exercise Area for Pets: Yes
Rates: $29.95 to $44.95

Howard Johnson Inn
2690 I-10E
Beaumont, TX 77703
Phone: (409) 892-8111

Pet Restrictions: Under 20 lbs.,
  deposit $5/day/pet
Exercise Area for Pets: Yes
Rates: $21.95 to $34.95

Road Runner
3985 College St.
Beaumont, TX 77707
Phone: (409) 842-4420
Pet Restrictions: Small pets
Pet left unattended in room: Yes, if
    quiet, no housekeeping
Exercise Area for Pets: Yes
Rates: $28.95 to $36.95

VETERINARIANS

Delaware Animal Clinic
4010 Delaware
(409) 892-2821

Jones, Darlene E.
Route 6, P.O. Box 1033
(409) 866-8208

BEDFORD

La Quinta-Bedford
1450 W. Airport Frwy.
Bedford, TX 76022
Phone: (817) 267-5200
Pet Restrictions: Small
Exercise Area for Pets: Yes
Rates: $57 to $64

VETERINARIANS

Bedford Meadows Animal Clinic
2102 Harwood Rd.
(817) 571-4088

BIG BEND NATIONAL PARK

Chisos Mt. Lodge
Basin Rural Station
Big Bend Nat. Park, TX 79834-9999
Phone: (915) 477-2291
Pet Restrictions: Advance
    notification
Pet left unattended in room: Yes -
    no maid service
Exercise Area for Pets: Yes
Rates: $53 to $112.36

BIG SPRING

Ponderosa Motor Inn
2701 S. Gregg St.
Big Spring, TX 79720
Phone: (915) 267-5237
Pet Restrictions: Small, quiet
Exercise Area for Pets: Yes
Rates: $27 plus $3/person

BRADY

Plateau Motel
2023 Southbridge St.
Brady, TX 76825
Phone: (915) 597-2185
Pet Restrictions: Housebroken
Pet left unattended in room: Yes
Exercise Area for Pets: Yes
Rates: $27 to $40

BROWNSVILLE

Holiday Inn-Brownsville
1945 N. Expressway
Brownsville, TX 78521
Phone: (210) 546-4591
Pet Restrictions: Owner responsible
    for damages, under 10 lbs.
Exercise Area for Pets: Yes
Rates: $50 to $59

La Quinta Motor Inn
55 Sam Perl Blvd.
Brownsville, TX 78520
Phone: (512) 546-0381,
    (800) 531-5900
Pet Restrictions: None
Pet left unattended in room: Yes
Exercise Area for Pets: Yes
Rates: $52

CANTON

Best Western Canton Inn
Rt. 2, P.O. Box 6B
Canton, TX 75103
Phone: (903) 567-6591
Pet Restrictions: Deposit
    $10/pet/stay, refundable
Pet left unattended in room: Yes
Exercise Area for Pets: Yes
Rates: $40 to $69

CASTROVILLE

Best Western Inn
1650 Hwy. 90W
Castroville, TX 78009
Phone: (210) 538-2262,
    (800) 446-8528
Pet Restrictions: Deposit $5/day/pet
Pet left unattended in room: Yes,
    notify desk
Exercise Area for Pets: Nearby
Rates: $54 to $59

TEXAS — HOTELS (continued)

CHILDRESS
Childress Classic Inn
1805 Ave. F NW
Childress, TX 79201
Phone: (817) 937-6353,
   (800) 346-1576

Pet Restrictions: Small
Exercise Area for Pets: Yes
Rates: $46.95 to $58.95

CISCO
Oak Motel
300 I-20 E
Cisco, TX 76437
Phone: (817) 442-2100

Pet Restrictions: None
Pet left unattended in room: Yes -
   no maid service
Exercise Area for Pets: Yes
Rates: $22 to $36.30

COLLEGE STATION
Comfort Inn
104 S. Texas Ave.
College Station, TX 77840
Phone: (409) 846-7333

Pet Restrictions: Under 10 lbs.,
   deposit $5/day/pet
Pet left unattended in room: Yes, if
   caged
Exercise Area for Pets: Yes
Rates: $47 to $75

Holiday Inn-College Station
1502 S. Texas Ave.
College Station, TX 77840
Phone: (409) 693-1736
Pet Restrictions: Under 20 lbs.
Pet left unattended in room: Yes
Exercise Area for Pets: Nearby
Rates: $49 to $53

La Quinta Motor Inn
607 Texas Ave. S.
College Station, TX 77840
Phone: (409) 696-7777,
   (800) 531-5900

Pet Restrictions: Under 40 lbs.
Pet left unattended in room: Yes, if
   caged
Exercise Area for Pets: Yes
Rates: $49 to $67

Ramada Inn-Aggieland Hotel
1502 S. Texas Ave.
College Station, TX 77840
Phone: (409) 693-9891

Pet Restrictions: Under 15 lbs.,
   deposit $10/week
Pet left unattended in room: Yes, if
   caged
Exercise Area for Pets: Yes
Rates: $44 to $48

VETERINARIANS
Southwood Valley Animal Hospital
1305 FM 2818
(409) 693-9898

Van Stavern Animal Hospital
3102 Texas Avenue South
(409) 693-8870

CONWAY
S&S Motel
I-40
Conway, TX 79068
Phone: (806) 537-5111

Pet Restrictions: Housebroken
Exercise Area for Pets: Yes
Rates: $20 to $28

CORPUS CHRISTI
Airport Holiday Inn
5549 Leopard St.
Corpus Christi, TX 78408
Phone: (512) 289-5100,
   (800) 465-4329

Pet Restrictions: Notify in advance
Pet left unattended in room: Yes,
   notify desk
Exercise Area for Pets: Yes
Rates: $69

Best Western-Sandy Shores Beach Hotel
3200 Surfside
Corpus Christi, TX 78403
Phone: (512) 883-7456

Pet Restrictions: Small, motel
   section only, deposit $6/day/pet
Exercise Area for Pets: Yes
Rates: $59 to $109

Comfort Inn-Airport
6301 I-37
Corpus Christi, TX 78409
Phone: (512) 289-6925

Pet Restrictions: 2nd and 3rd floors
   only, deposit $5/day/pet
Pet left unattended in room: Yes, no
   large dogs
Exercise Area for Pets: Yes
Rates: $44 to $70

Days Inn
901 Navigation Dr.
Corpus Christi, TX 78408
Phone: (512) 888-8599,
   (800) 233-3297

Pet Restrictions: None, deposit
   $6/day/pet
Pet left unattended in room: Yes, no
   housekeeping
Exercise Area for Pets: Yes
Rates: $56 to $74

Drury Inn
2021 North Padre Island Dr.
Corpus Christi, TX 78408
Phone: (512) 289-8200,
   (800) 325-8300

Pet Restrictions: Housebroken,
   prefer smaller dogs
Pet left unattended in room: Yes, if
   quiet
Exercise Area for Pets: Yes
Rates: $65 to $72

Embassy Suites
4337 S. Padre Island Dr.
Corpus Christi, TX 78411
Phone: (512) 853-7899,
   (800) 678-7533

Pet Restrictions: Fee $10/day/pet
Pet left unattended in room: Yes,
   notify desk
Exercise Area for Pets: Yes
Rates: $84 to $125

Emerald Beach Holiday Inn
1102 Shoreline Dr.
Corpus Christi, TX 78401
Phone: (512) 883-5731,
   (800) 465-4329

Pet Restrictions: None
Pet left unattended in room: Yes
Exercise Area for Pets: Yes
Rates: $83 to $99

La Quinta Motor Inn
6225 S. Padre Island Dr.
Corpus Christi, TX 78412
Phone: (512) 991-5730,
   (800) 531-5900

Pet Restrictions: None
Pet left unattended in room: Yes, if
   quiet
Rates: $55 to $78

Shilo Inn Corpus Christi
5224 IH-37 at Navigation
Corpus Christi, TX 78407
Phone: (512) 883-2951

Pet Restrictions: None
Exercise Area for Pets: Yes
Rates: $29.95 to $35.95

Surfside Condo Apts.
15005 Windward Dr.
Corpus Christi, TX 78418
Phone: (512) 949-8128

Pet Restrictions: $3/day
Pet left unattended in room: Yes
Exercise Area for Pets: Yes
Rates: $85 and up

VETERINARIANS

Nueces Veterinary Hospital
10656 Up River Rd.
(512) 242-3337

Padre Animal Hospital
9501 South Padre Island
(512) 937-2631

Santa Fe Animal Hospital
4100 Santa Fe
(512) 854-5911

CORSICANA
Holiday Inn
2000 S. Hwy. 287
Corsicana, TX 75110
Phone: (903) 874-7413

Pet Restrictions: None
Pet left unattended in room: Yes
Exercise Area for Pets: Yes
Rates: $49 to $56

CROCKETT

Crockett Inn
1600 Loop 304 E.
Crockett, TX 75835
Phone: (409) 544-5611

Pet Restrictions: None
Pet left unattended in room: Yes
Exercise Area for Pets: Yes
Rates: $35 and up

DALLAS

Airport Hilton
611 NW Loop 410
Dallas, TX 78216
Phone: (210) 340-6060,
   (800) 455-8667

Pet Restrictions: 30 lbs. and under,
   $50 refund. deposit
Pet left unattended in room: Yes
Exercise Area for Pets: Yes
Rates: $69 to $139

Bristol Suites
7800 Alpha Rd.
Dallas, TX 75240
Phone: (214) 233-7600.
   (800) 922-9222

Pet Restrictions: Deposit $125
   ($100 refundable)
Pet left unattended in room: Yes
Exercise Area for Pets: Yes
Rates: $104 to $134

Drury Inn North
2421 Walnut Hill
Dallas, TX 75229
Phone: (214) 484-3330

Pet Restrictions: Quiet, taken care
   of, well behaved, small
Pet left unattended in room: Yes
Rates: $45 to $50

Embassy Suites
1313 Central Expwy
Dallas, TX 75243
Phone: (214) 234-3300,
   (800) 362-2779

Pet Restrictions: $25 refund. deposit
Pet left unattended in room: Yes
Exercise Area for Pets: Yes
Rates: $89 to $109

Embassy Suites Dallas Market Center
2727 Stemmons Freeway
Dallas, TX 75207
Phone: (214) 630-5332

Pet Restrictions: $25/night/pet
Pet left unattended in room: Yes
Exercise Area for Pets: Yes
Rates: $79 to $159

Executive Inn
3232 W. Mockingbird Lane
Dallas, TX 75235
Phone: (214) 357-5601

Pet Restrictions: $10
Pet left unattended in room: Yes,
   notify desk
Exercise Area for Pets: Yes
Rates: $36 to $72

Harvey Hotel
7815 LBJ Freeway
Dallas, TX 75240
Phone: (214) 960-7000

Pet Restrictions: $125 deposit ($25
   non-refundable)
Pet left unattended in room: Yes
Exercise Area for Pets: Yes
Rates: $65 to $79

Harvey Hotel-Addison
14315 Midway Rd.
Dallas, TX 75244
Phone: (214) 980-8877

Pet Restrictions: $125 deposit ($25
   non-refund.)
Pet left unattended in room: Yes
Exercise Area for Pets: Yes
Rates: $55 to $109

Hawthorne Suites Hotel-Dallas
7900 Brook River Dr.
Dallas, TX 75240
Phone: (214) 688-1010,
   (800) 527-1133

Pet Restrictions: Under 15 lbs.,
   $150 deposit ($50 non-refund.)
Exercise Area for Pets: Yes
Rates: $59 to $140

Hilton and Towers-Richardson
1981 N. Central Expressway
Dallas, TX 75080
Phone: (214) 644-4000,
   (800) 285-3434

Pet Restrictions: 20 lbs. and under,
   $20 refund. deposit
Pet left unattended in room: No, in
   carrier at all times
Exercise Area for Pets: Yes
Rates: $59 to $109

Holiday Inn-North Park Plaza
10650 N. Central Expressway
Dallas, TX 75231
Phone: (214) 373-6000,
   (800) HOLIDAY
Pet Restrictions: $20
Pet left unattended in room: Yes
Exercise Area for Pets: Yes
Rates: $39 to $80

Holiday Inn-Park Central
8102 LBJ Freeway
Dallas, TX 75251
Phone: (214) 239-7211,
   (800) HOLIDAY
Pet Restrictions: Small pets only
Exercise Area for Pets: Yes
Rates: $49 to $89

Hotel Crescent Court
400 Crescent Court
Dallas, TX 75201
Phone: (214) 871-3200
Pet Restrictions: $50 deposit
Pet left unattended in room: Yes,
   must be caged
Exercise Area for Pets: Yes
Rates: $280 to $340

La Quinta Motor Inn Central
4440 N. Central Expressway
Dallas, TX 75206
Phone: (214) 821-4220,
   (800) 531-5900
Pet Restrictions: 1 small pet per room
Exercise Area for Pets: Yes
Rates: $53 to $75

La Quinta Motor Inn-North Park
10001 N. Central Expressway
Dallas, TX 75231
Phone: (214) 361-8200,
   (800) 531-5900
Pet Restrictions: None
Exercise Area for Pets: Yes
Rates: $51 to $64

Marriott Park Central
7750 LBJ Freeway
Dallas, TX 75251
Phone: (214) 233-4421
Pet Restrictions: 15-20 rooms, 1st
   floor only
Pet left unattended in room: Yes,
   must be present for cleaning
Exercise Area for Pets: Yes
Rates: Up to $99

Motel 6
2660 Forest Lane
Dallas, TX 75234
Phone: (214) 484-9111
Pet Restrictions: None
Pet left unattended in room: Yes
Exercise Area for Pets: Yes
Rates: Up to $38

Motel 6-Addison
4325 Beltline
Dallas, TX 75244
Phone: (214) 386-4577
Pet Restrictions: Housekeeping will
   not clean if pet unattended
Pet left unattended in room: Yes,
   must be present for cleaning
Exercise Area for Pets: Yes
Rates: $31 to $37

Preston House
6104 LBJ Freeway
Dallas, TX 75240
Phone: (214) 458-2626,
   (800) 524-7038
Pet Restrictions: $75
Exercise Area for Pets: Yes
Rates: $45 to $123

Radisson Central
6060 N. Central Expy
Dallas, TX 75206
Phone: (214) 750-6060
Pet Restrictions: Only small pets,
   $50
Pet left unattended in room: Yes
Exercise Area for Pets: Nearby
Rates: $114

Radisson Hotel Stemmons
2330 W. Northwest Hwy
Dallas, TX 72550
Phone: (214) 351-4477,
   (800) 333-3333
Pet Restrictions: $50 deposit
Pet left unattended in room: Yes
Exercise Area for Pets: Nearby
Rates: $99 to $119

Red Roof Inn
8108 Erl Thornton Freeway
Dallas, TX 75228
Phone: (214) 506-8100
Pet Restrictions: None
Pet left unattended in room: Yes -
   no maid
Exercise Area for Pets: Yes
Rates: $26.99 and up

Red Roof Inn-Market Center
1550 Empire Central Dr.
Dallas, TX 75235
Phone: (214) 638-5151,
    (800) 843-7663

Pet Restrictions: None
Pet left unattended in room: Yes,
    must be present for cleaning
Exercise Area for Pets: Yes
Rates: $24 to $50

Red Roof Inn Northwest
10335 Gardner Rd.
Dallas, TX 75220
Phone: (214) 506-8100,
    (800) 843-7663

Pet Restrictions: Small pets
Pet left unattended in room: Yes
Exercise Area for Pets: Yes
Rates: $24 to $45

Residence Inn Marriot-Dallas North
13636 Goldmark Dr.
Dallas, TX 75240
Phone: (214) 669-0478,
    (800) 331-3131

Pet Restrictions: $60, $6/day/pet
Pet left unattended in room: Yes
Exercise Area for Pets: Yes
Rates: $50 to $130

Westin Hotel Dallas
1334 Dallas Parkway
Dallas, TX 75240
Phone: (214) 934-9494,
    (800) 228-3000

Pet Restrictions: Under 10 lbs.
Pet left unattended in room: Yes,
    must be present for cleaning
Exercise Area for Pets: Nearby
Rates: $110 and up

VETERINARIANS
Animal Referral Clinic
2353 Royal Lane
(214) 241-6266

Holt Veterinary Clinic
5619 Yale Blvd.
(214) 361-2834

Park Cities Animal Hospital
4520 Lovers Lane
(214) 368-8573

DELHART
Comfort Inn
HCR 2
Delhart, TX 79022
Phone: (806) 249-8585

Pet Restrictions: None
Exercise Area for Pets: Nearby
Rates: $45 to $55

Sands Motel
301 Liberal St.
Delhart, TX 79022
Phone: (806) 249-4568

Pet Restrictions: None
Pet left unattended in room: Yes, if
    quiet
Exercise Area for Pets: Yes
Rates: $21 to $40

DEL RIO
Best Western Inn of Del Rio
810 Ave. F
Del Rio, TX 78840
Phone: (210) 775-7511,
    (800) 336-3537

Pet Restrictions: $4/pet, 25 lbs. and
    under
Pet left unattended in room: Yes
Exercise Area for Pets: Yes
Rates: $41 and up

DENTON
Exel Inn of Denton
4211 I-35 E. N.
Denton, TX 76201
Phone: (817) 383-1471,
    (800) 356-8013

Pet Restrictions: None
Pet left unattended in room: Yes
Exercise Area for Pets: Yes
Rates: $25.99 to $31.99

VETERINARIANS
Companion Animal Hospital
2010 Denison
(817) 382-8689

University Dr. Veterinary Hospital
1620 W. University Dr.
(817) 387-3116

Westgate Veterinary Hospital
4501 N. Mesa Dr.
(817) 387-9522

TEXAS — HOTELS (continued)

EAGLE PASS
Eagle Pass Inn
2150 N. U.S. Highway 277
Eagle Pass, TX 78852
Phone: (210) 773-9531,
    (800) 272-9786

Pet Restrictions: None
Pet left unattended in room: Yes
Exercise Area for Pets: Yes
Rates: $35 to $55

EASTLAND
Budget Host Inn
I-20 Farm Rd. 570
Eastland, TX 76448
Phone: (817) 629-2655

Pet Restrictions: None
Exercise Area for Pets: Yes
Rates: $31.50 to $37.50

EL PASO
Comfort Inn
900 N. Yarborough St.
El Paso, TX 79915
Phone: (915) 594-9111,
    (800) 221-2222

Pet Restrictions: $25 refund.
    deposit, 2nd or 3rd floor only
Pet left unattended in room: Yes,
    must be present for cleaning
Exercise Area for Pets: Yes
Rates: $41 to $45

El Paso Airport Hilton
2227 Airway Blvd.
El Paso, TX 79925
Phone: (915) 778-4241,
    (800) 742-7248

Pet Restrictions: None
Exercise Area for Pets: Yes
Rates: $65 to $109

El Paso Marriot Hotel
1600 Airway Blvd.
El Paso, TX 79925
Phone: (915) 779-3300,
    (800) 228-9290

Pet Restrictions: None
Pet left unattended in room: Yes
Exercise Area for Pets: Yes
Rates: $69 to $114

Howard Johnson Lodge
8887 Gateway West
El Paso, TX 79925
Phone: (915) 591-9471,
    (800) 446-4656

Pet Restrictions: None
Pet left unattended in room: Yes
Exercise Area for Pets: Yes
Rates: $45 to $57

VETERINARIANS
Crossroads Animal Clinic
5021 Crossroads Dr.
(915) 584-3459

Johnsen Animal Hospital
1851 Lee Tevino Dr.
(915) 592-6200

Zarges Animal Clinic
5820 Doniphan Dr.
(915) 584-9471

FORT DAVIS
Prude Ranch
P.O. Box 1431
Fort Davis, TX 79734
Phone: (915) 426-3347,
    (800) 458-6232

Pet Restrictions: On leash when not
    near you
Exercise Area for Pets: Yes
Rates: $49 to $75

FORT WORTH
Best Western West Branch Inn
7301 W. Freeway
Fort Worth, TX 76116
Phone: (817) 244-7444,
    (800) 528-1234

Pet Restrictions: Small pets
Pet left unattended in room: Yes
Exercise Area for Pets: Yes

Country Suites
8401 I-30 W.
Fort Worth, TX 76116
Phone: (817) 560-0060

Pet Restrictions: $25 ref. deposit
Pet left unattended in room: Yes
Exercise Area for Pets: Yes
Rates: $46 to $52

Green Oaks Inn & Conference Center
6901 W. Freeway
Fort Worth, TX 76116
Phone: (817) 738-7311,
(800) 772-2341

Pet Restrictions: None
Pet left unattended in room: Yes,
must be present for cleaning
Exercise Area for Pets: Yes
Rates: $55 to $78

Holiday Inn-North
2540 Meacham Blvd.
Fort Worth, TX 76106
Phone: (817) 625-9911,
(800) HOLIDAY

Pet Restrictions: 20 lbs. and under
Pet left unattended in room: Yes
Exercise Area for Pets: Yes
Rates: $59 to $75

Holiday Inn-South & Conference Center
100 Alta Mesa East Blvd.
Fort Worth, TX 76134
Phone: (817) 293-3088,
(800) HOLIDAY

Pet Restrictions: None
Pet left unattended in room: Yes
Exercise Area for Pets: Yes
Rates: $75

La Quinta-Northeast
7920 Bedford-Euless Rd.
Fort Worth, TX 76180
Phone: (817) 485-2750,
(800) 531-5900

Pet Restrictions: Small pets
Pet left unattended in room: Yes,
must be present for cleaning
Exercise Area for Pets: Yes
Rates: $43 to $53

La Quinta-West
7888 I-30 West
Fort Worth, TX 76108
Phone: (817) 246-5511,
(800) 531-5900

Pet Restrictions: None
Pet left unattended in room: No
unless caged
Exercise Area for Pets: Yes
Rates: $43 to $79

Plaza-Forth Worth
2000 Beach St.
Fort Worth, TX 76103
Phone: (817) 534-4801

Pet Restrictions: Depends on
availability
Exercise Area for Pets: Yes
Rates: $48 to $89

Ramada Inn
125 NE Loop 20
Fort Worth, TX 76053
Phone: (817) 284-9461

Pet Restrictions: None
Pet left unattended in room: Yes
Exercise Area for Pets: Yes
Rates: $42 to $65

Residence Inn Fort Worth
1701 S. University Dr.
Fort Worth, TX 76107
Phone: (817) 870-1011,
(800) 331-3131

Pet Restrictions: $5 day
Pet left unattended in room: Yes
Exercise Area for Pets: Nearby
Rates: $92 to $102

VETERINARIANS

Eastern Hills Animal Clinic
5600 Meadowbrook Dr.
(817) 451-2260

Ridglea Animal Hospital
6824 Highway 80 West
(817) 738-2186

Wedgwood Animal Hospital
5201 Wonder Dr.
(817) 292-3100

FREDERICKSBURG

Best Western Sunday House
501 East Main
Fredericksburg, TX 78624
Phone: (210) 997-4484

Pet Restrictions: Very small pets
Exercise Area for Pets: Yes
Rates: $64

Dietzel Motel
I-290 W & 87 N
Fredericksburg, TX 78624
Phone: (210) 997-3330

Pet Restrictions: 6 rooms only, $2
day
Pet left unattended in room: Yes
Exercise Area for Pets: Yes
Rates: $35 to $48

Save Inn Motel
514 E. Main St.
Fredericksburg, TX 78624
Phone: (210) 997-6568
Pet Restrictions: Small pets
Exercise Area for Pets: Nearby
Rates: $43.50 to $58.50

GARLAND
La Quinta Motor Inn-Garland
12721 LBJ Freeway
Garland, TX 75041
Phone: (214) 271-7581,
    (800) 531-5900
Pet Restrictions: None
Pet left unattended in room: Yes
Exercise Area for Pets: Nearby
Rates: $51 to $58

VETERINARIANS
Centerville Road Animal Clinic
145 E. Centerville Rd.
(214) 271-4637

Springhill Veterinary Clinic
3214 Big Springs Rd.
(214) 495-5314

King, David F.
747 Valiant Circle
(214) 262-2684

GEORGETOWN
Comfort Inn
1005 Leander Rd.
Georgetown, TX 78628
Phone: (512) 863-7504
Pet Restrictions: None
Pet left unattended in room: Yes
Exercise Area for Pets: Yes
Rates: $39 to $59

VETERINARIANS
Koy Animal Clinic
3501 Williams Dr.
(512) 863-0327

GRAHAM
Gateway Inn Motor Hotel
1401 Highway 16S
Graham, TX 76450
Phone: (817) 549-0222
Pet Restrictions: $5/pet/day, small
    pets only
Pet left unattended in room: Yes
Exercise Area for Pets: Nearby
Rates: $40 to $55

HARLINGEN
Best Western Hotel
6779 W. Expressway 83
Harlingen, TX 78552
Phone: (210) 425-7070,
    (800) 528-1234
Pet Restrictions: None
Pet left unattended in room: Yes
Exercise Area for Pets: Nearby
Rates: $51 to $65

Holiday Inn
1901 W. Tyler
Harlingen, TX 78550
Phone: (210) 425-1810
Pet Restrictions: Yes
Pet left unattended in room: Yes
Exercise Area for Pets: Nearby
Rates: $54 to $77

VETERINARIANS
Moseley Jr., William T.
1649 North 77 Sunshine Strip
(210) 428-4002

HENDERSON
Holiday Inn
1500 Hwy 259 S.
Henderson, TX 75652
Phone: (903) 657-9561
Pet Restrictions: $30
Exercise Area for Pets: Nearby
Rates: $42 to $44

HOUSTON
Days Inn Airport
17607 Eastex Freeway
Houston Vic., TX 77396
Phone: (713) 446-4611,
    (800) 325-2525
Pet Restrictions: $10, small pets only
Exercise Area for Pets: Yes
Rates: $45 to $49

Days Inn East
4039 E. Houston St.
Houston, TX 78220
Phone: (210) 337-6753,
    (800) 325-2525
Pet Restrictions: None
Pet left unattended in room: Yes
Exercise Area for Pets: Yes
Rates: $80 to $90

TEXAS — HOTELS (continued)

Days Inn I-10 W. Gessner
Katy Freeway
Houston, TX 77024
Phone: (713) 468-7801,
(800) 325-2525

Pet Restrictions: None
Pet left unattended in room: Yes
Exercise Area for Pets: Yes
Rates: $53 to $64

Doubletree Hotel
15747 JFK Blvd.
Houston, TX 77032
Phone: (713) 442-8000,
(800) 528-0444

Pet Restrictions: $50 deposit ($25 non-refund.), under 15 lbs.
Exercise Area for Pets: Nearby
Rates: $85 to $103

Doubletree Hotel-Allen Ctr.
400 Dallas St.
Houston, TX 77002
Phone: (713) 759-0202,
(800) 222-TREE

Pet Restrictions: $20 deposit, under 20 lbs.
Pet left unattended in room: Yes
Exercise Area for Pets: Nearby
Rates: $125 to $155

Four Seasons-Houston Center
1300 Lamar St.
Houston, TX 77010
Phone: (713) 650-1300,
(800) 332-3442

Pet Restrictions: $25, 30 lbs. and under
Pet left unattended in room: Yes
Exercise Area for Pets: Nearby
Rates: $200 to $450

Guest Quarters-Galleria W.
5353 W. Heimer Rd.
Houston, TX 77056
Phone: (713) 961-9000,
(800) 424-2900

Pet Restrictions: $10/pet/day
Pet left unattended in room: Yes
Exercise Area for Pets: Yes
Rates: $134 to $154

Holiday Inn Hobby Airport
9100 Gulf Freeway
Houston, TX 77017
Phone: (713) 943-7979,
(800) HOLIDAY

Pet Restrictions: 20 lbs. and under, call first
Rates: $88 to $104

Holiday Inn Houston West
14703 Park Row
Houston, TX 77079
Phone: (713) 558-5580,
(800) HOLIDAY

Pet Restrictions: $15
Pet left unattended in room: Yes
Exercise Area for Pets: Yes
Rates: $59 to $90

Houston Greenport Marriott
255 N. Sam Houston Pkwy
Houston, TX 77060
Phone: (713) 875-4000,
(800) 228-9290

Pet Restrictions: Must sign waiver
Exercise Area for Pets: Yes
Rates: $55 to $115

Lancaster Hotel
701 Texas Ave.
Houston, TX 77002
Phone: (713) 228-9500,
(800) 325-2580

Pet Restrictions: $75, under 20 lbs.
Pet left unattended in room: Yes, owner responsible for damages
Exercise Area for Pets: Nearby
Rates: $95 to $165

La Quinta-Greenway Plaza
4015 Southwest Freeway
Houston, TX 77027
Phone: (713) 623-4750,
(800) 531-5900

Pet Restrictions: None
Exercise Area for Pets: Yes
Rates: $57 to $84

La Quinta Motor Inn-Intercontinental
6 N. Belt E.
Houston, TX 77060
Phone: (713) 447-6888,
(800) 531-5900

Pet Restrictions: Small pets only
Pet left unattended in room: Yes
Exercise Area for Pets: Yes
Rates: $57 to $64

La Quinta Motor Inn-N.W.
11002 Northwest Freeway
Houston, TX 77092
Phone: (713) 688-2581,
(800) 531-5900

Pet Restrictions: 20 lbs. and under
Pet left unattended in room: Yes
Exercise Area for Pets: Yes
Rates: $54 to $85

Marriott Astrodome
2100 S. Braeswood
Houston, TX 77030
Phone: (713) 797-9000,
  (800) 722-1368
Pet Restrictions: 25 lbs. and under,
  $10 deposit, waiver
Pet left unattended in room: Yes
Exercise Area for Pets: Yes
Rates: $99 to $109

Marriott Brookhollow
3000 N. Loop W.
Houston, TX 77092
Phone: (713) 688-0100,
  (800) 688-3000
Pet Restrictions: None
Pet left unattended in room: Yes
Exercise Area for Pets: Yes
Rates: $90 to $119

Marriott Hotel-By the Galleria
1750 W. Loop South
Houston, TX 77027
Phone: (713) 960-0111,
  (800) 228-9290
Pet Restrictions: Sign waiver
Pet left unattended in room: Yes
Exercise Area for Pets: Nearby
Rates: $109 to $129

Marriott-Houston Airport
18700 Kennedy Blvd.
Houston, TX 77032
Phone: (713) 443-2310,
  (800) 228-9290
Pet Restrictions: None
Exercise Area for Pets: Yes
Rates: $115 to $135

Motel 6
10 at TX 6
Houston, TX 77094
Phone: (713) 497-5000
Pet Restrictions: None
Exercise Area for Pets: Yes
Rates: $32.95 to $43.95

Motel 6
5555 W. 34th
Houston, TX 77092
Phone: (713) 682-8588
Pet Restrictions: None
Pet left unattended in room: Yes,
  must be present for cleaning
Exercise Area for Pets: Yes
Rates: $31.95 to $43.95

Omni on the Park
4 River Way
Houston, TX 77056
Phone: (713) 871-8181
Pet Restrictions: 20 lbs. and under
Pet left unattended in room: Yes, in
  carrier
Exercise Area for Pets: Nearby
Rates: $79 to $179

Premier Inn
2929 Southwest Fwy.
Houston, TX 77098
Phone: (713) 528-6161
Fax: (713) 528-2985
Pet Restrictions: Dogs must be on
  leash while walking on premises
  Pet deposit may be required
Pet left unattended in room: No
Exercise Area for Pets: Nearby
Rates: $32.95 to $75.95

Quality Inn Intercontinental-Airport
6115 Will Clayton Parkway
Houston, TX 77205
Phone: (713) 446-9131,
  (800) 221-2222
Pet Restrictions: $15
Exercise Area for Pets: Yes
Rates: $56 to $63

Ramada Hotel-NW
12801 NW Freeway
Houston, TX 77040
Phone: (713) 462-9977,
  (800) 2-RAMADA
Pet Restrictions: Small pets, pool
  side rooms
Pet left unattended in room: Yes
Exercise Area for Pets: Yes
Rates: $78 to $88

The Ramada Inn
157 25 Bamble
Houston, TX 77014
Phone: (713) 893-5666,
  (800) 2-RAMADA
Pet Restrictions: $25
Pet left unattended in room: Yes
Exercise Area for Pets: Yes
Rates: $37 to $65

Residence Inn by Marriott
6910 SW Freeway
Houston, TX 77074
Phone: (713) 785-3415
Pet Restrictions: $25, $5/pet/day,
  under 50 lbs.
Pet left unattended in room: Yes
Exercise Area for Pets: Yes
Rates: $104 to $134

Residence Inn by Marriott-Astrodome
7710 S. Main St.
Houston, TX 77030
Phone: (713) 660-7993,
(800) 331-3131
Pet Restrictions: $25 cleaning fee,
$5/day/pet, 25 lbs. and under
Pet left unattended in room: Yes
Exercise Area for Pets: Yes
Rates: $95 to $125

The Rings Inn
1301 Nasa Rd. 1
Houston, TX 77058
Phone: (713) 488-0220,
(800) 255-7345
Pet Restrictions: None
Exercise Area for Pets: Yes
Rates: $55 to $87

Stouffer Greenway Plaza
6 Greenway Plaza E
Houston, TX 77046
Phone: (713) 629-1200
Pet Restrictions: 25 lbs. and under
Pet left unattended in room: Yes
Exercise Area for Pets: Yes
Rates: $79 to $159

The Westin Galleria
5060 W. Alabama
Houston, TX 77056
Phone: (713) 960-8100,
(800) 228-3000
Pet Restrictions: Small pets
Exercise Area for Pets: Yes
Rates: $135 to $1300

VETERINARIANS
Alief-Bellaire Animal Clinic
12816 Bellaire Blvd.
(713) 498-3977

Beechnut Animal Clinic
8541 Beechnut
(713) 774-9731

Wilcrest Animal Hospital
704 Wilcrest Dr.
(713) 781-3770

IRVING
Drury Inn
4210 W. Airport Freeway
Irving, TX 75062
Phone: (214) 986-1200,
(800) 325-8300
Pet Restrictions: None
Exercise Area for Pets: Yes
Rates: $52 to $67

Four Seasons Resort & Hotel
4150 N. MacArthur Blvd.
Irving, TX 75062
Phone: (214) 717-0700
Pet Restrictions: Small-medium only
Pet left unattended in room: Yes,
notify desk
Exercise Area for Pets: Yes
Rates: $185 to $250

Holiday Inn DFW Airport
4441 Highway 114 at Esters
Irving, TX 75063
Phone: (214) 929-8181,
(800) HOLIDAY
Pet Restrictions: $50 deposit
Exercise Area for Pets: Yes
Rates: $54 to $87

La Quinta DFW-Irving
4105 W. Airport Freeway
Irving, TX 75062
Phone: (214) 252-6546,
(800) 531-5900
Pet Restrictions: None
Pet left unattended in room: Yes,
must be present for cleaning
Exercise Area for Pets: Yes
Rates: $49 to $60

Marriott-DFW Airport
8440 Freeport Parkway
Irving, TX 75063
Phone: (214) 929-8800
Pet Restrictions: 15 lbs. and under
Exercise Area for Pets: Yes

Omni-Mandalay
221 E. Las Colinas Blvd.
Irving, TX 75039
Phone: (214) 556-0800,
(800) THE OMNI
Pet Restrictions: $30
Pet left unattended in room: Yes
Exercise Area for Pets: Yes
Rates: $59 to $125

Red Roof Inn
8150 Esters Blvd.
Irving, TX 75063
Phone: (214) 929-0020,
(800) 843-7663
Pet Restrictions: Yes
Pet left unattended in room: Yes
Exercise Area for Pets: Yes
Rates: $30 to $39

VETERINARIANS

Animal Medical and Surgical Hospital
600 Airport Freeway West
(214) 438-7113

Story Road Animal Hospital
600 North Story Road
(214) 790-3585

Vaeth, Judith E.
1010 West Airport Freeway
(214) 579-0115

JACKSBORO

Jacksboro Inn
704 S. Main Hwy 281
Jacksboro, TX 76458
Phone: (817) 567-3751
Pet Restrictions: Small pets only
Exercise Area for Pets: Yes
Rates: $30 and up

JASPER

Ramada Inn
239 E. Gibson
Jasper, TX 75951
Phone: (409) 384-9021,
(800) 2-RAMADA
Pet Restrictions: None
Pet left unattended in room: Yes
Exercise Area for Pets: Yes
Rates: $36 to $54

KERRVILLE

Holiday Inn
2033 Sidney Baker St.
Kerrville, TX 78028
Phone: (210) 257-4440,
(800) HOLIDAY
Pet Restrictions: None
Pet left unattended in room: Yes but
maid won't enter
Exercise Area for Pets: Yes
Rates: $42 to $230

Inn of the Hills River Resort
1001 Junction Highway
Kerrville, TX 78028
Phone: (210) 895-5000
Pet Restrictions: Small pets
Exercise Area for Pets: Yes
Rates: $75 to $200

Sunday House Motor Inn
2124 Sidney Baker Rd.
Kerrville, TX 78028
Phone: (210) 896-1313,
(800) 677-9477
Pet Restrictions: None
Exercise Area for Pets: Yes
Rates: $64 to $89.95

VETERINARIANS

Brittmoore Animal Hospital
1236 Brittmore Rd.
(210) 468-8253

Memorial/Town & Country Animal Clinic
12661 Memorial Dr.
(210) 464-4686

Southwest Freeway Animal Hospital
10710 West Bellfort
(210) 495-0130

KILGORE

Ramada Inn
3501 Highway 255 N
Kilgore, TX 75662
Phone: (903) 983-3456,
(800) 2-RAMADA
Pet Restrictions: None
Pet left unattended in room: Yes
Exercise Area for Pets: Yes
Rates: $42 to $60

VETERINARIANS

Kilgore Small Animal Veterinary Hospital
1508 North Highway 259
(903) 984-0621

LAREDO

Royce
One S. Main Ave.
Laredo, TX 78040
Phone: (210) 722-2411,
(800) 937-6923
Pet Restrictions: $75 deposit, no
deposit required with credit card
Pet left unattended in room: Yes
Exercise Area for Pets: Nearby
Rates: $59 to $95

TEXAS — HOTELS (continued)

LLANO

Llanno Classic Inn
901 W. Young
Llano, TX 78643
Phone: (915) 247-4101,
    (800) 346-1578

Pet Restrictions: None
Pet left unattended in room: No, if
    pets are loud, no maid service
Exercise Area for Pets: Nearby
Rates: $34.95 to $36.95

LONGVIEW

Econo Lodge
3120 Estes Pkwy
Longview, TX 75602
Phone: (903) 753-4884,
    (800) 424-4777

Pet Restrictions: Small pets only
Pet left unattended in room: Yes
    with sign on door
Exercise Area for Pets: Yes
Rates: $29.95 to $37.95

La Quinta Motor Inn
502 S. Access Rd.
Longview TX 75602
Phone: (903) 757-3663,
    (800) 531-5900

Pet Restrictions: Under 30 lbs.
Pet left unattended in room: Yes
Exercise Area for Pets: Yes
Rates: $44 to $57

Ramada Inn
3304 S. Eastman Rd.
Longview, TX 75602
Phone: (903) 758-0711,
    (800) 2-RAMADA

Pet Restrictions: In cage at all times
Pet left unattended in room: Yes
Exercise Area for Pets: Yes
Rates: $30 to $55

Kimbrough Animal Hospital North
1613 Judson Rd.
(903) 757-5543

Taylor Veterinary Clinic
P.O. Box 5854
(903) 759-7611

Zimicki Jr., M.P.
812 Gilmer Rd.
(903) 759-1292

LUBBOCK

Holiday Inn Civic Center
801 Avenue Q
Lubbock, TX 79401
Phone: (806) 763-1200,
    (800) HOLIDAY

Pet Restrictions: None
Pet left unattended in room: Yes
Exercise Area for Pets: Yes
Rates: $68 to $79

Paragon Hotel
4115 Brownfield Highway
Lubbock, TX 79407
Phone: (806) 792-0065,
    (800) 333-1146

Pet Restrictions: Under 30 lbs.
Pet left unattended in room: Yes in
    cage
Exercise Area for Pets: Nearby
Rates: $49 and up

Residence Inn by Marriott Lubbock
2551 S. Loop 289
Lubbock, TX 79423
Phone: (806) 745-1963,
    (800) 331-3131

Pet Restrictions: $75 cleaning fee,
    $6/pet/day
Pet left unattended in room: Yes
Exercise Area for Pets: Yes
Rates: $82 to $105

Southwest Animal Clinic
4808 50th St.
(806) 792-3291

Key, John C.
5006 50th St.
(806) 792-6226

MARATHON

The Gage Hotel
West Highway 90, P.O. Box 46
Marathon, TX 79842
Phone: (915) 386-4205

Pet Restrictions: House trained
Rates: $40 to $60

MARSHALL

Best Western of Marshall
5565 E. End Blvd. S.
Marshall, TX 75270
Phone: (903) 935-1941,
    (800) 528-1234
Pet Restrictions: None
Pet left unattended in room: Yes,
    must be quiet
Exercise Area for Pets: Nearby
Rates: $42 to $62

Holiday Inn
100 I-20 West
Marshall, TX 75670
Phone: (903) 935-7923,
    (800) HOLIDAY
Pet Restrictions: $25 deposit or
    credit card
Rates: $42 to $54

NEW BOSTON

Red Carpet
906 N. McCoy Blvd.
New Boston, TX 75570
Phone: (903) 628-2546,
    (800) 251-1962
Pet Restrictions: None
Pet left unattended in room: Yes
Exercise Area for Pets: Yes
Rates: $29.95 to $59.95

ODESSA

Odessa Exec. Inn
2505 E. Second St.
Odessa, TX 79761
Phone: (915) 333-1528
Pet Restrictions: None
Exercise Area for Pets: Yes
Rates: $19.99 to $32

ORANGE

Best Western Inn
2630 I-10, P.O. Box 1839
Orange, TX 77630
Phone: (409) 883-6616,
    (800) 528-1234
Pet Restrictions: Small pets only
Pet left unattended in room: Yes
Exercise Area for Pets: Nearby
Rates: $40 to $48

VETERINARIANS

Pachar Veterinary Hospital
3423 West Park
(409) 883-3191

Ludwig, Christine M.
3424 West Park
(409) 883-3191

PLAINVIEW

Holiday Inn
4005 Alton Rd., P.O. Box 1925
Plainview, TX 79072
Phone: (806) 293-4181,
    (800) HOLIDAY
Pet Restrictions: None
Exercise Area for Pets: Yes
Rates: $43 to $63

PLANO

Harvey Hotel-Plano
1600 N. Central Expressway
Plano, TX 75074
Phone: (214) 578-8555
Pet Restrictions: $120 deposit ($20
    non-refund.)
Exercise Area for Pets: Yes
Rates: $78 to $83

La Quinta-Plano
1820 N. Central Expwy
Plano, TX 75074
Phone: (214) 423-1300,
    (800) 531-5900
Pet Restrictions: 35 lbs. and under
Pet left unattended in room: Yes
Exercise Area for Pets: Yes
Rates: $42 to $58

Motel 6
2550 N. Central Expressway
Plano, TX 75074
Phone: (214) 578-1626
Pet Restrictions: One pet only
Exercise Area for Pets: Yes
Rates: $29 to $38

VETERINARIANS

Animal Hospital of Plano
1512 N. Central Expressway
(214) 424-8521

Chalkley, Lorraine W.
1101 N. Murphy Rd.
(214) 424-2677

Reeves, Lee
3207 Independence
(214) 596-3413

QUANAH

Quanah Parker Motel
1415 W. 287
Quanah, TX 79252
Phone: (817) 663-6366,
    (800) 441-7971

Pet Restrictions: None
Pet left unattended in room: Yes
Exercise Area for Pets: Yes
Rates: $26 to $58

RICHARDSON

Hawthorne Suites-Richardson
250 Municipal Dr.
Richardson, TX 75080
Phone: (214) 669-1000,
    (800) 527-1133

Pet Restrictions: $250 deposit ($50
    non-refund.)
Pet left unattended in room: Yes,
    must be present for cleaning
Exercise Area for Pets: Nearby
Rates: $100 to $140

Richardson Hilton Inn
1981 N. Central Expwy
Richardson, TX 75080
Phone: (214) 644-4000,
    (800) 285-3434

Pet Restrictions: Under 20 lbs., in
    carrier, 1st floor
Exercise Area for Pets: Yes
Rates: $59 to $109

VETERINARIANS

Spring Valley Veterinary Clinic
162 East Spring Valley
(214) 231-3411

Frey, Cynthia
1217 Brush Creek Dr.
(214) 235-0549

Taurog, JoAnn W.
1401 E. Arapahoe Rd.
(214) 690-8741

SAN ANGELO

Inn of Concons
2021 N. Bryant Blvd.
San Angelo, TX 76902
Phone: (915) 658-2811,
    (800) 621-6041

Pet Restrictions: None
Pet left unattended in room: Yes
Exercise Area for Pets: Yes
Rates: $30 to $90

La Quinta Motor Inn
2307 Loop 306
San Angelo, TX 76904
Phone: (915) 949-0515,
    (800) 531-5900

Pet Restrictions: None
Exercise Area for Pets: Yes
Rates: $52 to $74

VETERINARIANS

Animal Medical Clinic
3209 Knickerbocker
(915) 944-3557

Miller, Charles F.
4240 Sherwood Way
(915) 949-1976

SAN ANTONIO

Days Inn Northeast
3434 I-35 N.
San Antonio, TX 78219
Phone: (210) 225-4521,
    (800) 325-2525

Pet Restrictions: None
Pet left unattended in room: Yes
Exercise Area for Pets: Yes
Rates: $58 to $98

Drury Inn
143 NE Loop 14
San Antonio, TX 78216
Phone: (210) 366-4300,
    (800) 325-8300

Pet Restrictions: 25 lbs. and under,
    1st floor only
Pet left unattended in room: Yes
Exercise Area for Pets: Yes
Rates: $68 to $78

Embassy Suites
7750 Briaridge
San Antonio, TX 78230
Phone: (210) 340-5421

Pet Restrictions: $25, 20 lbs. and
    under
Exercise Area for Pets: Yes
Rates: $109 to $169

Hilton Palacio Del Rio
200 South Alamo
San Antonio, TX 78205
Phone: (210) 222-1400,
    (800) HILTON

Pet Restrictions: Under 20 lbs.
Pet left unattended in room: Yes,
    caged
Exercise Area for Pets: Nearby
Rates: $99 to $200

Holiday Inn-Airport
77 NE Loop I-410 E
San Antonio, TX 78216
Phone: (210) 349-9900

Pet Restrictions: None
Pet left unattended in room: Yes
Exercise Area for Pets: Yes
Rates: $89 to $114

Holiday Inn-Market Sq.
318 West Durango
San Antonio, TX 78204
Phone: (210) 225-3211,
   (800) HOLIDAY

Pet Restrictions: None
Pet left unattended in room: Yes
Exercise Area for Pets: Yes
Rates: $84 to $109

Holiday Inn-Northeast
3855 Pan Am Highway
San Antonio, TX 78219
Phone: (210) 226-4361,
   (800) HOLIDAY

Pet Restrictions: None
Pet left unattended in room: Yes
Exercise Area for Pets: Yes
Rates: $53 to $75

Holiday Inn Northwest Loop
3233 NW Loop 410
San Antonio, TX 78213
Phone: (210) 377-3900

Pet Restrictions: Yes
Pet left unattended in room: Yes
Exercise Area for Pets: Yes
Rates: $69 to $107

Holiday Inn-Riverwalk
217 N. St. Mary's
San Antonio, TX 78205
Phone: (210) 224-2500,
   (800) HOLIDAY

Pet Restrictions: One only
Pet left unattended in room: Yes
Exercise Area for Pets: Yes
Rates: $115 to $125

Knight's Court
6370 I-35 N.
San Antonio, TX 78218
Phone: (210) 646-6336

Pet Restrictions: $25
Pet left unattended in room: Yes,
   must be present for cleaning
Exercise Area for Pets: Yes
Rates: $45 to $65

La Quinta-Airport East
333 NE Loop I-410
San Antonio, TX 78216
Phone: (210) 828-0781,
   (800) 531-5900

Pet Restrictions: None
Pet left unattended in room: Yes
Exercise Area for Pets: Yes
Rates: $73

La Quinta-Market
900 Dolorosa
San Antonio, TX 78207
Phone: (210) 271-0001,
   (800) 531-5900

Pet Restrictions: None
Pet left unattended in room: Yes, no
   housekeeping
Exercise Area for Pets: Yes
Rates: $79 to $86

La Quinta Motor Inn-South
7202 S. Pan Am Expressway
San Antonio, TX 78224
Phone: (210) 922-2111,
   (800) 531-5900

Pet Restrictions: Under 20 lbs., 1
   pet per room
Pet left unattended in room: No,
   only in carrier
Exercise Area for Pets: Yes
Rates: $58 to $75

Marriott
San Antonio Marriot Riverwalk
889 E. Market
San Santonio, TX 78205
Phone: (210) 224-4555,
   (800) 228-9290

Pet Restrictions: Sign waiver
Pet left unattended in room: Yes
Exercise Area for Pets: Nearby
Rates: $115 to $199

Marriott River Center
101 Bowie St.
San Antonio, TX 78205
Phone: (210) 223-1000

Pet Restrictions: Sign waiver, small
   pets
Exercise Area for Pets: Yes
Rates: $99 to $225

TEXAS — HOTELS (continued)

Marriott Riverwalk
711 E. River Walk
San Antonio, TX 78205
Phone: (210) 224-4555,
    (800) 228-9290

Pet Restrictions: None
Pet left unattended in room: Yes
Exercise Area for Pets: Yes
Rates: $139 to $159

Oak Motor Lodge
150 Humphreys Ave.
San Antonio, TX 78209
Phone: (210) 826-6368

Pet Restrictions: None
Pet left unattended in room: Yes
Exercise Area for Pets: Yes
Rates: $25 to $60

Plaza San Antonio
555 S. Alamo
San Antonio, TX 78205
Phone: (210) 229-1000,
    (800) 421-1172

Pet Restrictions: None
Exercise Area for Pets: Yes
Rates: $160 to $230

Ramada Inn-Airport
1111 NE Loop 410
San Antonio, TX 78209
Phone: (210) 828-9031,
    (800) 228-2828

Pet Restrictions: Medium sized
Pet left unattended in room: Yes
Exercise Area for Pets: Yes
Rates: $85 to $95

Texas Guested Suites
13101 E. Loop 1604N
San Antonio, TX 78233
Phone: (210) 655-9491,
    (800) 537-4238

Pet Restrictions: Small pets, one-
time fee - daily $25 - monthly
$100
Pet left unattended in room: Yes
Exercise Area for Pets: Yes
Rates: $69 to $159

VETERINARIANS

Castle Hills Companion Animal Hospital
2313 Northwest Military #115
(210) 341-3252

Oak Hills Veterinary Hospital
6614 Southpoint
(210) 342-9518

Wiseman Animal Hospital
2210 Loop 410 NW
(210) 344-9741

SHAMROCK
Best Western Irish Inn
301 I-40E
Shamrock, TX 79079
Phone: (806) 256-2106

Pet Restrictions: None
Pet left unattended in room: Yes
Exercise Area for Pets: Yes
Rates: $40 to $51

Budget Inn
711 E. 12th St.
Shamrock, TX 79079
Phone: (806) 256-3257

Pet Restrictions: Only 2 pets
Pet left unattended in room: Yes if
housebroken
Exercise Area for Pets: Nearby
Rates: $16 to $22

The Western Motel
104 E. 12th St.
Shamrock, TX 79079
Phone: (806) 256-3244

Pet Restrictions: None
Exercise Area for Pets: Yes
Rates: $22 to $32

SONORA
Devils River Motel
I-10 & Golf Course Rd. N.
Sonora, TX 76950
Phone: (915) 387-3516

Pet Restrictions: $2/night
Exercise Area for Pets: Yes
Rates: $31 to $37

VETERINARIANS

Fields, John W.
P.O. Box 441
(915) 387-3636

SOUTH PADRE ISLAND

Best Western Raintree Inn
5701 Padre Blvd.
South Padre Island, TX 78597
Phone: (210) 761-4913,
(800) 528-1234

Pet Restrictions: $25 deposit
Pet left unattended in room: Yes
Exercise Area for Pets: Yes
Rates: $54 to $118

Bridgepoint
334 Padre Blvd.
South Padre Island, TX 78597
Phone: (210) 761-7969,
(800) 221-1402

Pet Restrictions: None
Pet left unattended in room: Yes
Exercise Area for Pets: Yes
Rates: $150 to $425

STRATFORD

Ranger Motel
402 Texas Hwy 54
Stratford, TX 79084
Phone: (806) 396-5574

Pet Restrictions: Yes
Exercise Area for Pets: Yes
Rates: $25 to $31

SWEETWATER

Holiday Inn
Int. 20 & Georgia St., P.O. Box 167
Sweetwater, TX 79556
Phone: (915) 236-6887,
(800) HOLIDAY

Pet Restrictions: None
Exercise Area for Pets: Yes
Rates: $46

Ranch House Motel/Restaurant
Int. 20 & Hwy. 70
Sweetwater, TX 79556
Phone: (915) 236-6341

Pet Restrictions: Small pets
Exercise Area for Pets: Yes
Rates: $26 to $46

TEMPLE

Holiday Inn
802 N. General Bruce Dr.
Temple, TX 76504-2334
Phone: (817) 778-4411,
(800) HOLIDAY

Pet Restrictions: Quiet pets
Pet left unattended in room: Yes, no barking
Exercise Area for Pets: Yes
Rates: $45 to $62

Ramada Inn
400 S.W. HK Dodgen Loop 363
Temple, TX 76504
Phone: (817) 773-1515,
(800) 228-2828

Pet Restrictions: Small, housebroken
Pet left unattended in room: Yes
Exercise Area for Pets: Yes
Rates: $41 to $57

VETERINARIANS
Temple Veterinary Hospital
2211 South 57th St.
(817) 773-1411

TERLINGUA

Lajitas on the Rio Grande
P.O. Box 400 Star Route 70
Terlingua, TX 79852
Phone: (915) 424-3471

Pet Restrictions: None
Exercise Area for Pets: Yes
Rates: $52 to $65

TERRELL

Comfort Inn
1705 Highway 34 South
Terrell, TX 75160
Phone: (214) 563-1511,
(800) 221-2222

Pet Restrictions: Smaller than 24", cats must be caged
Pet left unattended in room: Yes but caged
Exercise Area for Pets: Nearby
Rates: $45 to $75

TEXARKANA
Holiday Inn Texarkana
5100 N. State Line Ave.
Texarkana, TX 75502
Phone: (501) 774-3521,
　　(800) HOLIDAY

Pet Restrictions: Outside, must be
　　on leash
Pet left unattended in room: Yes
Exercise Area for Pets: Yes
Rates: $61 to $71

VETERINARIANS
Pfluger, Cynthia N.
4005 Poinsettia
(501) 832-4559

Wisdom, David
2403 Texas Blvd.
(501) 793-1193

TYLER
Best Western Inn of Tyler
2828 NNW Loop 323
Tyler, TX 75702
Phone: (903) 595-2681,
　　(800) 528-1234

Pet Restrictions: $25/day
Pet left unattended in room: Yes
Exercise Area for Pets: Yes
Rates: $35 to $44

Days Inn
3300 Mineola Hwy.
Tyler, TX 75702
Phone: (903) 595-2451

Pet Restrictions: None
Pet left unattended in room: Yes,
　　prefer cage
Exercise Area for Pets: Yes
Rates: $32 to $47

Holiday Inn-Southeast Crossing
3310 Troup Highway
Tyler, TX 75701
Phone: (903) 593-3600,
　　(800) HOLIDAY

Pet Restrictions: None
Pet left unattended in room: Yes, no
　　housekeeping
Exercise Area for Pets: Yes
Rates: $58 to $68

Residence Inn by Marriott
3303 Troup Highway
Tyler, TX 75701
Phone: (903) 595-5188

Pet Restrictions: $50
Pet left unattended in room: Yes
Exercise Area for Pets: Yes
Rates: $86 to $102

Travelodge
2616 NNW Loop 323
Tyler, TX 75702
Phone: (903) 593-8361,
　　(800) 578-7878

Pet Restrictions: $25 deposit
Pet left unattended in room: Yes
Exercise Area for Pets: Yes
Rates: $35 to $61

VETERINARIANS
Starnes Animal Clinic
6622 S. Broadway
(903) 561-3211

Arnold, John P.
118 Shelley Dr.
(903) 561-7373

VAN HORN
Best Western Inn of Van Horn
1705 W. Broadway
Van Horn, TX 79855
Phone: (915) 283-2410,
　　(800) 367-7589

Pet Restrictions: None
Pet left unattended in room: Yes
Exercise Area for Pets: Yes
Rates: $35 to $43

Friendship Inn
1805 W. Broadway
Van Horn, TX 79855
Phone: (915) 283-2992

Pet Restrictions: None
Exercise Area for Pets: Yes
Rates: $24 to $32

VICTORIA
Holiday Inn
2705 E. Houston Highway
Victoria, TX 77901
Phone: (512) 575-0251

Pet Restrictions: None
Exercise Area for Pets: Yes
Rates: $50 to $70

VETERINARIANS

Hillcrest Animal Hospital
4001 Johnstockbauer
(512) 573-6131

Cochran, Sandra L.
P.O. Box 256
(512) 578-9050

WACO

Best Western Classic Inn
6624 Hwy 84 W.
Waco TX 76712
Phone: (817) 776-3194,
(800) 346-1581
Pet Restrictions: Small pets
Exercise Area for Pets: Yes
Rates: $41 to $75

Holiday Inn-Waco I-35
1001 Lake Brazos Dr.
Waco, TX 76704
Phone: (817) 753-0261
Pet Restrictions: None
Pet left unattended in room: Yes
Exercise Area for Pets: Yes
Rates: $59 to $65

Ramada Inn
4201 Franklin Ave.
Waco, TX 76701
Phone: (817) 772-9440,
(800) 228-2828
Pet Restrictions: None
Pet left unattended in room: Yes
Exercise Area for Pets: Yes
Rates: $39 to $52

Sandman Motel
3820 Franklin
Waco, TX 76710
Phone: (817) 756-3781
Pet Restrictions: $20
Pet left unattended in room: Yes
Exercise Area for Pets: Yes
Rates: $21.95 to $28.25

VETERINARIANS

Glass, Billy R.
1209 S. Robinson Dr.
(817) 662-4681

Kleypas, Jackie
340 Catalina
(817) 776-7653

Stewart, Jerald F.
2801 MacArthur Dr.
(817) 753-0155

WICHITA FALLS

Days Inn
1211 Central Expressway
Wichita Falls, TX 76304
Phone: (817) 723-5541,
(800) 325-2525
Pet Restrictions: $5, small pets
Pet left unattended in room: Yes, do
not disturb sign
Exercise Area for Pets: Yes
Rates: $42 to $48

Sheraton Wichita Falls Hotel
100 Central Freeway
Wichita Falls, TX 76305
Phone: (817) 761-6000,
(800) 325-3535
Pet Restrictions: $5
Pet left unattended in room: Yes, no
maid service
Exercise Area for Pets: Yes
Rates: $64 to $235

UTAH — HOTELS

BEAVER

Country Inn
1450 N. 300 West, P.O. Box 1037
Beaver, UT 84713
Phone: (801) 438-2484

Pet Restrictions: None
Exercise Area for Pets: Yes
Rates: $32 to $36

De Lano Motel
480 N. Main St., P.O. Box 1088
Beaver, UT 84713
Phone: (801) 438-2418

Pet Restrictions: None
Exercise Area for Pets: Yes
Rates: $28 to $50

Paradise Inn
1451 North 300 West
Beaver, UT 84713
Phone: (801) 438-2455

Pet Restrictions: None
Exercise Area for Pets: Yes
Rates: $36 to $57

BLANDING

Best Western Gateway Motel
88 E. Center
Blanding, UT 84511
Phone: (801) 678-2278,
    (800) 523-1234

Pet Restrictions: None
Pet left unattended in room: Yes
Exercise Area for Pets: Yes
Rates: $40 to $64

BLUFF

Recapture Lodge
US 191
Bluff, UT 84512
Phone: (801) 672-2281

Pet Restrictions: None
Exercise Area for Pets: Yes
Rates: $30 to $45

CEDAR CITY

Comfort Inn
250 N. 1100 West
Cedar City, UT 84720
Phone: (801) 586-2082,
    (800) 627-0374

Pet Restrictions: $50 cash deposit
    or credit card imprint
Exercise Area for Pets: Nearby
Rates: $38 to $95

Economy Hotel
443 S. Main
Cedar City, UT 84720
Phone: (801) 586-4461

Pet Restrictions: None
Exercise Area for Pets: Yes
Rates: $21 to $42

Rodeway Inn
281 S. Main St.
Cedar City, UT 84720
Phone: (801) 586-9916,
    (800) 424-4777

Pet Restrictions: None
Exercise Area for Pets: Nearby
Rates: $35 to $70

EPHRAIM

Travel Inn Motel
330 N. Main St.
Ephraim, UT 84627
Phone: (801) 283-4071

Pet Restrictions: None
Exercise Area for Pets: Yes
Rates: $27 and up

FILLMORE

Fillmore Motel
61 N. Main St.
Fillmore, UT 84631
Phone: (801) 743-5454

Pet Restrictions: Small pets only,
    must be house trained
Exercise Area for Pets: Yes
Rates: $20 to $38

Spinning Wheel Motel
65 S. Main St.
Fillmore, UT 84631
Phone: (801) 743-6260

Pet Restrictions: None
Pet left unattended in room: Yes
Exercise Area for Pets: Yes
Rates: $25.07 and up

GREEN RIVER

Bookcliff Lodge
395 E. Main, P.O. Box 545
Green River, UT 84525
Phone: (801) 564-3406

Pet Restrictions: $5.50/night,
    designated rooms
Exercise Area for Pets: Nearby
Rates: $35 to $50

HURRICANE

Best Western Weston Lamplighter
280 W. State St.
Hurricane, UT 84737
Phone: (801) 635-4647,
    (800) 523-1234
Pet Restrictions: Confirm in advance
Exercise Area for Pets: Yes
Rates: $45 to $75

Park Villa
650 W. State St.
Hurricane, UT 84737
Phone: (801) 635-4010,
    (800) 682-6336
Pet Restrictions: Pets stay in certain
    rooms
Pet left unattended in room: Yes if
    well trained
Exercise Area for Pets: Yes
Rates: $34 to $60

KANAB

Shilo Inn
296 West 100 North
Kanab, UT 84741
Phone: (801) 644-2562
Pet Restrictions: $6/day
Exercise Area for Pets: Nearby
Rates: $60 to $75

Treasure Trail Motel
150 W. Center St.
Kanab, UT 84741
Phone: (801) 644-2687
Pet Restrictions: Small dogs only,
    no cats
Exercise Area for Pets: Nearby
Rates: $35 to $56

MANILA

Vacation Inn
P.O. Box 306
Manila, UT 84046
Phone: (801) 784-3259
Pet Restrictions: None
Exercise Area for Pets: Yes
Rates: $40 to $52

MOAB

Bowen Motel
169 N. Main St.
Moab, UT 84532
Phone: (801) 259-7132,
    (800) 874-5439
Pet Restrictions: $3/pet/night
Exercise Area for Pets: Yes
Rates: $40 and up

Kokopelli Lodge
72 South 100 East
Moab, UT 84532
Phone: (801) 259-7615
Pet Restrictions: None
Exercise Area for Pets: Yes
Rates: $40 to $50

Red Rock Motel
51 North 1st West
Moab, UT 84532
Phone: (801) 259-5431
Pet Restrictions: In smoking rooms
    only
Exercise Area for Pets: Nearby
Rates: $38 to $56

Virginian
70 E. 2nd St. South
Moab, UT 84532
Phone: (801) 259-5951
Pet Restrictions: $1/pet/day
Exercise Area for Pets: Yes
Rates: $32 to $50

MT. CARMEL JUNC.

Best Western Thunderbird Motel
US Hwy 89, State Rt. 9
Mt. Carmel Junc., UT 84755
Phone: (801) 648-2262,
    (800) 528-1234
Pet Restrictions: None
Exercise Area for Pets: Yes
Rates: $56 to $62

OGDEN

Best Western Flying J
1206 W. 21st St.
Ogden, UT 84404
Phone: (801) 393-8644,
    (800) 343-8644
Pet Restrictions: None
Exercise Area for Pets: Yes
Rates: $40 and up

Best West. High Country Inn
1335 W. 12th St.
Ogden, UT 84404
Phone: (801) 394-9474,
   (800) 594-8979
Pet Restrictions: None
Pet left unattended in room: Yes
Rates: $45 to $56

Big Z Motel
23 W. 2100 South
Ogden, UT 84401
Phone: (801) 394-6632
Pet Restrictions: None
Exercise Area for Pets: Yes
Rates: $27 to $40

Motel 6
1500 W. Riverdale Rd.
Ogden, UT 84405
Phone: (801) 627-2880
Pet Restrictions: 1 small pet per
   room
Exercise Area for Pets: Yes
Rates: $32.99 to $38.99

Ogden Park Hotel
247 24th St.
Ogden, UT 84401
Phone: (801) 627-1190,
   (800) 421-7599
Pet Restrictions: $25 for small pets,
   $50 for large
Pet left unattended in room: Yes
Exercise Area for Pets: Nearby
Rates: $69 to $91

VETERINARIANS

Brookside Animal Hospital
138 West 12th St.
Phone: (801) 399-5897

North Ogden Animal Hospital
1580 N. Washington Blvd.
Phone: (801) 782-4401

Borrett, Katherine B.
4840 South 1050 West
Phone: (801) 394-4208

PANGUITCH

Horizon Motel
730 N. Main
Panguitch, UT 84759
Phone: (801) 676-2651,
   (800) 776-2651
Pet Restrictions: $5
Exercise Area for Pets: Yes
Rates: $45 to $75

PAYSON

Comfort Inn
830 N. Main
Payson, UT 84651
Phone: (801) 465-4861
Pet Restrictions: Yes
Pet left unattended in room: Yes
Exercise Area for Pets: Nearby
Rates: $35 to $99

PROVO

Best Western Cotton Tree Inn
2230 N. University Pkwy
Provo, UT 84604
Phone: (801) 373-7044,
   (800) 528-1234
Pet Restrictions: $20 deposit or
   credit card imprint, in smoking
   rooms only
Exercise Area for Pets: Yes
Rates: $55 to $60

Colony Inn Suites
1380 S. University Ave.
Provo, UT 84601
Phone: (801) 374-6800,
   (800) 524-9999
Pet Restrictions: $15 deposit,
   $5/pet/night
Rates: $24 to $68

SALINA

Howard Johnson Inn
60 N. State St.
Salina, UT 84654
Phone: (801) 529-7467
Pet Restrictions: $20 deposit
Pet left unattended in room: Yes
Exercise Area for Pets: Nearby
Rates: $36 to $55

SAINT GEORGE

Regency Inn
770 E. St. George Blvd.
St. George, UT 84770
Phone: (801) 673-6119
Pet Restrictions: $5/pet
Exercise Area for Pets: Nearby
Rates: $36.95 and up

Travelodge - East Motel
175 N. 1000 East
St. George, UT 84770
Phone: (801) 673-4621
Pet Restrictions: Med. size & smaller
Exercise Area for Pets: Yes
Rates: $40 and up

Western Safari
310 W. St. George Blvd.
St. George, UT 84770
Phone: (801) 673-5238
Pet Restrictions: 15 lbs. or under
Exercise Area for Pets: Nearby
Rates: $20 and up

VETERINARIANS

Sheets, Lo
857 E. Tabernacle
Phone: (801) 673-9696

SALT LAKE CITY
Best Western Cotton Tree
1030 North 400 East
North Salt Lake City, UT 84054
Phone: (801) 292-7666,
   (800) 528-1234
Pet Restrictions: $25 deposit, pet
   must be left in kennel
Exercise Area for Pets: Yes
Rates: $63 to $142

Comfort Inn
200 N. Admiral Byrd Rd.
Salt Lake City, UT 84116
Phone: (801) 537-7444,
   (800) 531-8742
Pet Restrictions: Ground floor only
Exercise Area for Pets: Nearby
Rates: $40 to $85

Days Inn Airport
1900 W. North Temple Rd.
Salt Lake City, UT 84116
Phone: (801) 539-8538,
   (800) 325-2525
Pet Restrictions: Specific rooms
Exercise Area for Pets: Nearby
Rates: $40 to $77

Econo Lodge
715 W. N. Temple
Salt Lake City, UT 84116
Phone: (801) 363-0062,
   (800) 424-4777
Pet Restrictions: 25 lbs. or less, $20
   deposit or credit card imprint
Exercise Area for Pets: Yes
Rates: $44 to $65

Hilton Airport
5151 Wiley Post Place
Salt Lake City, UT 84116
Phone: (801) 539-1515,
   (800) 999-3736
Pet Restrictions: Small pets only
Exercise Area for Pets: Yes
Rates: $69 to $225

Holiday Inn - Downtown
999 S. Main St.
Salt Lake City, UT 84111
Phone: (801) 532-7000,
   (800) 933-9688
Pet Restrictions: $100 cash deposit
   or credit card imprint
Pet left unattended in room: Yes
Exercise Area for Pets: Yes
Rates: $79 to $129

Howard Johnson Hotel
122 W S Temple
Salt Lake City, UT 84104
Phone: (801) 521-0130,
   (800) 366-3684
Pet Restrictions: $10/pet
Exercise Area for Pets: Yes
Rates: $49 to $165

La Quinta Motor Inn
530 Chealpa Rd.
Salt Lake City, UT 84047
Phone: (801) 566-3291,
   (800) 531-5900
Pet Restrictions: Small pets
Exercise Area for Pets: Yes
Rates: $49 to $54

Quality Inn
4465 Century Dr.
Salt Lake City, UT 84123
Phone: (801) 268-2533,
   (800) 221-2222
Pet Restrictions: $5/pet
Exercise Area for Pets: Yes
Rates: $37 to $79

Quality Inn City Ctr.
154 W. 600 South
Salt Lake City, UT 84101
Phone: (801) 521-2930,
   (800) 521-9997
Pet Restrictions: None
Pet left unattended in room: Yes
Exercise Area for Pets: Yes
Rates: $49 to $89

Regency Inn
770 E. Saint Georgia Blvd.
Salt Lake City, UT 84770
Phone: (801) 673-6119,
   (800) 626-5810
Pet Restrictions: $5
Pet left unattended in room: Yes
Exercise Area for Pets: Nearby
Rates: $28.95 to $36.95

Reston Hotel
5335 College Dr.
Salt Lake City, UT 84123
Phone: (801) 264-1054,
    (800) 231-9710
Pet Restrictions: $30
Exercise Area for Pets: Yes
Rates: $53 to $68

Road Runner
315 W. 3300 South
Salt Lake City, UT 84115
Phone: (801) 486-8780
Pet Restrictions: Small pets, $30
    deposit
Exercise Area for Pets: Nearby
Rates: $39.50 to $95.50

Shilo Inn
206 SW Temple
Salt Lake City, UT 84101
Phone: (801) 521-9500,
    (800) 222-2244
Pet Restrictions: $6/pet, must be
    small
Exercise Area for Pets: Yes
Rates: $59 to $67

Travelodge-East Motel
175 North 1000 East
Salt Lake City, UT 84770
Phone: (801) 673-4621,
    (800) 578-7878
Pet Restrictions: Small pets only
Exercise Area for Pets: Yes
Rates: $35 to $75

Western Safari
310 W.Saint Georgia Blvd.
Salt Lake City, UT 84770
Phone: (801) 673-5238
Pet Restrictions: Small pets, ground
    floor only
Exercise Area for Pets: Yes
Rates: $20 to $35

VETERINARIANS

Central Valley Veterinary Hosp.
55 E. Miller Ave.
Phone: (801) 487-1321

Cottonwood Animal Hospl.
6360 S. Highland Dr.
Phone: (801) 378-0505

Sugarhouse Veterinary Hosp.
2206 McClelland St.
Phone: (801) 487-9981

VERNAL

Best Western Dinosaur Inn
251 E. Main St.
Vernal, UT 84078
Phone: (801) 789-2660
Pet Restrictions: Must be in cage at
    all times
Pet left unattended in room: Yes
Exercise Area for Pets: Nearby
Rates: $60 to $75

VETERINARIANS
Oscarson, Ed W.
85 East 650 North
Phone: (801) 789-3022

VERMONT — HOTELS

ARLINGTON

Hill Farm Inn
RR #2, Box 2D15, Rt. 7A
Arlington, VT 05250
Phone: (802) 375-2269,
      (800) 882-2545
Pet Restrictions: Cabins only;
      $5/pet/day
Exercise Area for Pets: Yes
Rates: $70 to $85

VETERINARIANS

Tschon, Reginald R.
RR #1, Box 54
Phone: (802) 375-9491

BENNINGTON

Bennington Motor Inn
143 W. Main St.
Bennington, VT 05201
Phone: (802) 442-5479,
      (800) 359-9900
Pet Restrictions: $10/pet; limited
      number of pets admitted on any
      given night
Exercise Area for Pets: Yes
Rates: $52 and up

Fife-n-Drum Motel
Rt. 75, RR 1, Box 4340
Bennington, VT 05201
Phone: (802) 442-4074
Pet Restrictions: $5; designated
      rooms; let desk know
Exercise Area for Pets: Yes
Rates: $37 to $52

Knotty Pine Motel
130 Northside Dr.
Bennington, VT 05201
Phone: (802) 442-5487
Pet Restrictions: None
Exercise Area for Pets: Yes
Rates: $38 to $62

Ramada Inn
1½ mi. N on US 7 at Kocher Dr.
Phone: (802) 442-8145,
      (800) 2-RAMADA
Pet Restrictions: None
Exercise Area for Pets: Yes
Rates: $69 to $85

South Gate Motel
1½ mi. S on US 7, PO Box 1073
Bennington, VT 05201
Phone: (802) 447-7525
Pet Restrictions: None
Exercise Area for Pets: Yes
Rates: $30 to $60

Vermonter Motor Lodge
Rte 9 West Rd., Box 2377
Bennington, VT 05201
Phone: (802) 442-2529,
      (800) 382-3175
Pet Restrictions: $5/night for pre-
      approved pets
Exercise Area for Pets: Yes
Rates: $40 to $70

BRANDON

Brandon Motor Lodge
US Rt. 7
Brandon, VT 05733
Phone: (802) 247-9594
Pet Restrictions: None
Exercise Area for Pets: Yes
Rates: $38 to $70

BRATTLEBORO

Quality Inn
Putney Rd.
Brattleboro, VT 05301
Phone: (802) 254-8701
Pet Restrictions: None
Pet left unattended in room: Yes,
      quiet
Exercise Area for Pets: Yes
Rates: $65 to $70

BRISTOL

Bristol Commons Inn
Junction 17 and 116
Bristol, VT 05443
Phone: (802) 453-2326
Pet Restrictions: 2 rooms only
Exercise Area for Pets: Yes
Rates: $39 to $68

BURLINGTON

Econo Lodge
1076 Williston Rd.
S. Burlington, VT 05403
Phone: (802) 863-1125,
      (800) 553-2666
Pet Restrictions: None
Exercise Area for Pets: Yes
Rates: $49 to $85

VERMONT — HOTELS (continued)

Harbor Sunset Motel
1700 Shelburn Rd.
S. Burlington, VT 05403
Phone: (802) 864-5080
Pet Restrictions: $3/day/pet
Pet left unattended in room: Yes, quiet
Exercise Area for Pets: Yes
Rates: $25 to $45.50

Ho Hum Motel - Rte. 2
1660 Williston Rd.
S. Burlington, VT 05401
Phone: (802) 863-4551
Pet Restrictions: None
Pet left unattended in room: Yes, in crate
Exercise Area for Pets: Yes
Rates: $32 to $96

Ho Hum Motel Rte. 7
1200 Shelburn Rd.
S. Burlington, VT 05403
Phone: (802) 658-1314
Pet Restrictions: Only dogs
Exercise Area for Pets: Yes
Rates: $32 to $80

Holiday Inn
1068 Williston Rd.
S. Burlington, VT 05403
Phone: (802) 863-6361,
(800) 465-4329
Pet Restrictions:None
Exercise Area for Pets: Yes
Rates: $65 to $122

Howard Johnson Motor Lodge
7 Dorsett St.
S. Burlington, VT 05403
Phone: (802) 863-5541,
(800) 446-4656
Pet Restrictions: None
Pet left unattended in room: Yes, in crate
Exercise Area for Pets: Yes
Rates: $49 to $90

Radisson Hotel Burlington
60 Battery St.
Burlington, VT 05401
Phone: (802) 658-6500,
(800) 333-3333
Pet Restrictions: None
Exercise Area for Pets: Yes
Rates: $95 to $115

Ramada Inn
1117 Williston Rd.
S. Burlington, VT 05403
Phone: (802) 658-0250,
(800) 2-RAMADA
Pet Restrictions: None
Pet left unattended in room: Yes
Exercise Area for Pets: Yes
Rates: $59 to $135

Sheraton-Burlington
870 Williston Rd.
S. Burlington, VT 05403
Phone: (802) 862-6576,
(800) 325-3535
Pet Restrictions: None
Exercise Area for Pets: Yes
Rates: $79 to $137

Town & Country Motel
490 Shelburne Rd.
S. Burlington, VT 05401
Phone: (802) 862-5786
Pet Restrictions: $4/pet; No cats
Exercise Area for Pets: Yes
Rates: $28 to $75

VETERINARIANS

Green Mountain Animal Hosp.
1693 Williston Rd.
Phone: (802) 862-7021

Brown, Harold P.
3017 Williston Rd.
Phone: (802) 862-6471

CRAFTSBURY COMMON

The Inn on the Common
Main St.
Craftsbury Common, VT 05827
Phone: (802) 586-9619,
(800) 521-2233
Pet Restrictions: Advance notice; $15 charge
Pet left unattended in room: Yes
Exercise Area for Pets: Yes
Rates: $190 to $260

DERBY

The Border Motel
135 N. Main
Phone: (802) 766-2213,
(800) 255-1559
Pet Restrictions: None
Pet left unattended in room: Yes, trained/caged
Exercise Area for Pets: Yes
Rates: $42 to $49

DORSETT

Barrows House
On SR 30
Dorsett, VT 05251
Phone: (802) 867-4455,
(800) 639-1620
Pet Restrictions: 3 rooms; $10/day;
$5 each add'l day
Pet left unattended in room: Yes
Exercise Area for Pets: Yes
Rates: $160 to $210

JEFFERSONVILLE

The Highlander Motel
Rte 108 S
Jeffersonville, VT 05464
Phone: (802) 644-2725,
(800) 367-6471
Pet Restrictions: None
Exercise Area for Pets: Yes
Rates: $48 to $69

KILLINGTON

The Cascades Lodge
Killington Village, RRI Box 2848
Killington, VT 05751
Phone: (800) 345-0113
Fax: (802) 422-3351
Pet Restrictions: Limited # of
rooms, from May to Nov only.
Pet left unattended in room: No
Exercise Area for Pets: Yes
Other Areas: Hiking trails, mountain
biking
Rates: $50 to $199

Cedarbrook Motor Inn/Suites
Jct. US4 & SR 100 S
Killington, VT 05751
Phone: (802) 422-9666,
(800) 446-1088
Pet Restrictions: Clean, quiet
Pet left unattended in room: Yes
Exercise Area for Pets: Yes
Rates: $38 to $99

Val Roc Motel
US Rte. 4
Killington, VT 05751
Phone: (802) 422-3881,
(800) 238-8762
Pet Restrictions: None
Pet left unattended in room: Yes, if
quiet
Exercise Area for Pets: Yes
Rates: $39 to $88

LUDLOW

The Combes Family Inn
RFD #1, Box 275
Ludlow, VT 05149
Phone: (802) 228-8799
Pet Restrictions: Certain units
Pet left unattended in room: Yes
Exercise Area for Pets: Yes
Rates: $74 to $90

Timber Inn Motel
103 S, Box 1003
Ludlow, VT 05149
Phone: (802) 228-8666
Pet Restrictions: Only dogs; 4 rooms
Exercise Area for Pets: Yes
Rates: $35 to $75

LYNDONVILLE

Lynburke Motel
Junction Rte 5, 114
Lyndonville, VT 05851
Phone: (802) 626-3346
Pet Restrictions: $5/pet/night
Pet left unattended in room: Yes
Exercise Area for Pets: Yes
Rates: $33 and up

MANCHESTER

Brittany Inn Motel
Rt. 7A-S, P.O. Box 760
Manchester, VT 05255
Phone: (802) 362-1033
Pet Restrictions: Well trained
Exercise Area for Pets: Yes
Rates: $45 to $65

Stamford Motel
Rt. 7A
Manchester, VT 05255
Phone: (802) 362-2342
Pet Restrictions: Certain rooms;
must be on leash
Exercise Area for Pets: Yes
Rates: $48 to $60

VETERINARIANS

Treat, Robert E.
RR #1, Box 1030
Phone: (802) 362-2620

MIDDLEBURY

The Middlebury Inn
14 Courthouse Sq., Rt. 7
Middlebury, VT 05753
Phone: (802) 388-4961

Pet Restrictions: Motel section only;
$8/night
Pet left unattended in room: Yes
Exercise Area for Pets: Yes
Rates: $75 to $150

VETERINARIANS

Middlebury Animal Hospital
RD 1, Box 256
Phone: (802) 388-2691

Pedie, Donald E.
RD 2, Box 530
Phone: (802) 462-2345

PERKINSVILLE

The Inn at Weathersfield
Rt. 106, P.O. Box 165
Perkinsville, VT 05151
Phone: (802) 263-9217

Pet Restrictions: Manager's
discretion; no puppies
Pet left unattended in room: Yes, if
caged
Exercise Area for Pets: Yes
Rates: $175 to $205

PUTNEY

Putney Inn
P.O. Box 181
Putney, VT 05346
Phone: (802) 387-5517

Pet Restrictions: $10 fee
Exercise Area for Pets: Yes
Rates: $58 to $78

VETERINARIANS

Veenema, Ronald
RD #2 Box 568
Phone: (802) 254-5422

QUECHEE

Quality Inn Quechee Gorge
P.O. Box Q
Quechee, VT 05059
Phone: (802) 295-7600

Pet Restrictions: None
Exercise Area for Pets: Yes, no
housekeeping
Exercise Area for Pets: Yes
Rates: $57 to $103

RUTLAND

Edelweiss Motel & Chalets
SR 34, P.O. Box 2309
Rutland, VT 05701
Phone: (802) 775-5577

Pet Restrictions: No cats
Pet left unattended in room: Yes
Exercise Area for Pets: Yes
Rates: $38 to $90

Holiday Inn
Rt. 7, S. Main St.
Rutland, VT 05701
Phone: (802) 775-1911,
(800) HOLIDAY

Pet Restrictions: None
Exercise Area for Pets: Yes
Rates: $74 to $79

Royal Motel
115 Woodstock Ave.
Rutland, VT 05701
Phone: (802) 773-9176

Pet Restrictions: $5/night
Pet left unattended in room: Yes, no
housekeeping
Exercise Area for Pets: Yes
Rates: $37 to $89

VETERINARIANS

Eastwood Animal Clinic
Rt. #4
Phone: (802) 773-7711

Rutland Veterinary Clinic
North Main St.
Phone: (802) 773-2779

SHAFTSBURY

Bayberry Motel
Historic Route 7A, Box 137
Shaftsbury, VT 05262
Phone: (802) 447-7180

Pet Restrictions: None
Exercise Area for Pets: Yes
Rates: $34 to $60

VETERINARIANS

West Mountain Animal Hospital
Route 7A, Box 120
(802) 447-7723

SOUTH HERO
Sandbar Motor Inn
2 mi. S on US Rt. 2
South Hero, VT 05486
Phone: (802) 372-6911

Pet Restrictions: $20 dog deposit
Pet left unattended in room: Yes
Exercise Area for Pets: Yes
Rates: $48 to $85

SPRINGFIELD
Howard Johnson Lodge
I-91 Exit 7, 818 Charlestown Rd.
Springfield, VT 05156
Phone: (802) 885-4516

Pet Restrictions: None
Pet left unattended in room: Yes
Rates: $53 to $91

Pa-Lo-Mar Motel
2 Linhale Dr.
Springfield, VT 05156
Phone: (802) 885-4142

Pet Restrictions: None
Exercise Area for Pets: Yes
Rates: $37 to $56

The Abby Lyn Motel
Junction 106 & Kennan
N. Springfield, VT 05150
Phone: (802) 886-2223

Pet Restrictions: None
Pet left unattended in room: Yes
Exercise Area for Pets: Yes
Rates: $38 to $55

STOWE
Anderson Lodge - An Austrian Inn
3430 Mountain Road
Stowe, VT 05672
Phone: (802) 253-7336

Pet Restrictions: None
Exercise Area for Pets: Yes
Rates: $58 to $72

Commodore's Inn
P.O. Box 970
Stowe, VT 05672
Phone: (802) 253-7131

Pet Restrictions: $10
Pet left unattended in room: Yes, briefly
Exercise Area for Pets: Yes
Rates: $68 to $168

Green Mountain Inn
P.O. Box 60
Stowe, VT 05672
Phone: (802) 253-7301

Pet Restrictions: None
Pet left unattended in room: Yes
Exercise Area for Pets: Yes
Rates: $79 to $164

The Mountain Road at Stowe
P.O. Box 8
Stowe, VT 05672
Phone: (802) 253-4566

Pet Restrictions: $10-$15 fee; sign waiver
Pet left unattended in room: Yes
Exercise Area for Pets: Yes
Rates: $60 to $375

Notch Brook Resort
1229 Notch Brook Rd.
Stowe, VT 05672-4913
Phone: (802) 253-4882

Pet Restrictions: None
Pet left unattended in room: Yes
Exercise Area for Pets: Yes
Rates: $69 to $250

The Salzburg Inn
Mountain Rd., Route 108
Stowe, VT 05672
Phone: (802) 253-8541,
(800) 448-4554

Pet Restrictions: $5
Pet left unattended in room: Yes
Exercise Area for Pets: Yes
Rates: $58 to $78

The Snowdrift Motel
2135 Mountain Rd.
Stowe, VT 05672
Phone: (802) 253-7305,
(800) 346-2702

Pet Restrictions: Small pets only; $5/night
Exercise Area for Pets: Yes
Rates: $44 to $90

Ten Acres Lodge
14 Barrows Rd.
Stowe, VT 05672
Phone: (802) 253-7638,
(800) 327-7357

Pet Restrictions: Only in 2 guest cottages
Pet left unattended in room: Yes, prefer caged
Exercise Area for Pets: Yes
Rates: $225 to $250

WATERBURY
Holiday Inn
Blush Hill Rd., P.O. Box 149
Waterbury, VT 05676
Phone: (802) 244-7822,
   (800) HOLIDAY

Pet Restrictions: $30 deposit or
   credit card; smoking rooms only;
   no housekeeping until after
   checkout
Exercise Area for Pets: Yes
Rates: $78 to $90

WHITE RIVER JCT.
Howard Johnson Lodge
US 5 I 91 & 89
White River, Junction, VT 05001
Phone: (802) 295-3015,
   (800) 370-HOJO

Pet Restrictions: None
Exercise Area for Pets: Yes
Rates: $65 to $99

WOODSTOCK
Kedron Valley Inn
Rt. 106
S. Woodstock, VT 05071
Phone: (802) 457-1473

Pet Restrictions: None
Pet left unattended in room: Yes
Exercise Area for Pets: Yes
Rates: $120 to $195

VIRGINIA — HOTELS

ALEXANDRIA

Comfort Inn
P.O. Box 10729
Alexandria, VA 24506
Phone: (804) 847-9041

Pet Restrictions: None
Pet left unattended in room: Yes if
   quiet
Exercise Area for Pets: Yes
Rates: $35 to $79

Days Inn-Alexandria
110 S. Bragg St.
Alexandria, VA 22312
Phone: (703) 354-4950,
   (800) 325-2525

Pet Restrictions: None
Pet left unattended in room: Yes
Rates: $39.95 to $57.95

Guest Quarters Suite Hotel
100 S. Reynold St.
Alexandria, VA 22304
Phone: (703) 370-9600,
   (800) 424-2900

Pet Restrictions: $10 fee/night,
   $200 max per month
Pet left unattended in room: Yes
Exercise Area for Pets: Nearby
Rates: $99 to $174

Howard Johnson Hotel
5821 Richmond Highway
Alexandria, VA 32303
Phone: (703) 329-1400,
   (800) 644-2000

Pet Restrictions: Small pets only
Pet left unattended in room: Yes
Exercise Area for Pets: Yes
Rates: $68 to $80

Ramada Hotel Old Town
901 N. Fairfax St.
Alexandria, VA 22314
Phone: (703) 683-6000
Fax: (703) 683-7597

Pet Restrictions: Smaller than 50 lbs.
Pet left unattended in room: Yes
Exercise Area for Pets: Nearby
Rates: $59 to $135

Ramada Inn - Seminary Plaza
4641 Kenmore Ave.
Alexandria, VA 22304
Phone: (703) 751-4510

Pet Restrictions: None
Exercise Area for Pets: Yes
Rates: $65 to $104

Red Roof Inn - Alexandria
5975 Richmond Highway
Alexandria, VA 22303
Phone: (703) 960-5200,
   (800) 848-7878

Pet Restrictions: None
Exercise Area for Pets: Yes
Rates: $49 to $55

VETERINARIANS

El Paw Veterinary Clinic
33 South Pickett St.
Phone: (703) 751-3707

Hayfield Animal Hospital
7724 Telegraph Rd.
Phone: (703) 971-2127

Old Town Veterinary Hosp.
425 N. Henry St.
Phone: (703) 549-3647

ARLINGTON

Holiday Inn - Key Bridge
1850 N. Fort Myer Dr.
Arlington, VA 22202
Phone: (703) 522-0400

Pet Restrictions: Small pets
Pet left unattended in room: Yes
Exercise Area for Pets: Yes
Rates: $69 to $99

Howard Johnson Hotel
2650 Jefferson Davis Hwy
Arlington, VA 22202
Phone: (703) 684-7200

Pet Restrictions: Small, well-behaved
Exercise Area for Pets: Nearby
Rates: $98 to $106

Marriott Crystal Gateway Hotel
1700 Jefferson Davis Hwy
Arlington, VA 22202
Phone: (703) 684-7200

Pet Restrictions: Sign waiver
Pet left unattended in room: Yes
Exercise Area for Pets: Nearby
Rates: $105 to $195

Marriott Key Bridge
1401 Lee Hwy
Arlington, VA 22209
Phone: (703) 524-6400

Pet Restrictions: None
Exercise Area for Pets: Yes
Rates: $164 to $184

VETERINARIANS

Carter, Julia L.
813 N. Monroe St.
Phone: (703) 528-2776

Kimble, Vernon W.
2624 Columbia Pike
Phone: (703) 920-5300

Olson, Candace
4038 Lee Highway
Phone: (703) 528-9001

BEDFORD
Best West. Terrace House Inn
921 Blue Ridge Ave.
Bedford, VA 24523
Phone: (703) 586-8286,
(800) 528-1234
Pet Restrictions: 1 small pet per room
Exercise Area for Pets: Yes
Rates: $37 to $39

VETERINARIANS
Noe, Leslie S.
Route 7, Box 220
Phone: (703) 586-0372

BLUEFIELD
Holiday Inn - Bluefield
US 460
Bluefield, VA 24701
Phone: (304) 325-6170,
(800) HOLIDAY
Pet Restrictions: None
Pet left unattended in room: Yes
Exercise Area for Pets: Yes
Rates: $61 to $66

VETERINARIANS
Bailey, Lucian P.
Route 2, Box 204A
Phone: (703) 326-1484

BRISTOL
Shyland Motel
4748 Lee Hwy
Bristol, VA 24201
Phone: (703) 669-0166
Pet Restrictions: None
Pet left unattended in room: Yes
Exercise Area for Pets: Yes
Rates: $24 to $32

VETERINARIANS
Bristol Animal Clinic
930 Commonwealth Avenue
Phone: (703) 466-4113

BUCHANAN
Natural Bridge Wattsfield Inn
81 Exit, Rt. 1
Buchanan, VA 24066
Phone: (703) 254-1551
Pet Restrictions: Small pets
Pet left unattended in room: Yes
Exercise Area for Pets: Nearby
Rates: $43 to $48

CAPE CHARLES
Holiday Motel
29106 Lankford Hwy
Cape Charles, VA 23310
Phone: (804) 331-1000
Pet Restrictions: None
Pet left unattended in room: Yes
Exercise Area for Pets: Yes
Rates: $40 to $60

CEN. SHENANDOAH VALLEY
Quality Inn
Rt. 1, Box 438
Central Shenandoah Valley, VA 24472
Phone: (703) 377-2604
Pet Restrictions: $8/pet
Pet left unattended in room: Yes
Exercise Area for Pets: Yes
Rates: $30 to $60

CHANTILLY
Marriott Wash. Dulles Airport
333 W. Service Rd.
Chantilly, VA 22021
Phone: (703) 471-9500
Pet Restrictions: Small pets
Pet left unattended in room: Yes
Exercise Area for Pets: Yes
Rates: $90 to $120

CHARLOTTESVILLE
Best Western Cavalier Inn
105 Emmett St., P.O. Box 5647
Charlottesville, VA 22903
Phone: (804) 296-8111,
(800) 528-1234
Pet Restrictions: Up to 25 lbs.
Exercise Area for Pets: Yes
Rates: $60 to $125

Best Western Mt. Vernon
1613 Emmit St.
Charlottesville, VA 22901
Phone: (804) 296-5501

Pet Restrictions: Small pets
Exercise Area for Pets: Yes
Rates: $48 to $56

Boarshead Inn
Rt. 250
Charlottesville, VA 22903
Phone: (804) 296-2181

Pet Restrictions: $15/night
Pet left unattended in room: Yes,
     notify desk
Exercise Area for Pets: Yes
Rates: $89 to $129

Knights Inn
1300 Seminole Trail
Charlottesville, VA 22501
Phone: (804) 973-8133

Pet Restrictions: None
Exercise Area for Pets: Yes
Rates: $39 to $55

Albemarle Veterinary Hospital
445 Westfield Rd.
Phone: (804) 973-6146

Georgetown Veterinary Hosp.
Georgetown Rd.
Phone: (804) 977-4600

Village Animal Hospital
3050 Berkmar Dr.
Phone: (804) 973-4341

CHESAPEAKE

Motel 6
701 Woodlake Dr.
Chesapeake, VA 23320
Phone: (804) 420-2976

Pet Restrictions: None
Exercise Area for Pets: Yes
Rates: $31 to $39

Red Roof Inn
724 Woodlake Dr.
Chesapeake, VA 23320
Phone: (804) 523-0123,
     (800) 843-7663

Pet Restrictions: House pets only
Pet left unattended in room: Yes
Exercise Area for Pets: Yes
Rates: $29.99 to $36.99

Brooks IV, Alfred A.
1025E Eden Way North
Phone: (804) 547-5100

Bucher, Glenn A.
1229 Benefit Rd.
Phone: (804) 420-2277

Gilliland, Carolyn Ann
1721-C Birch Trail Circle
Phone: (804) 487-2531

CHESTER

Comfort Inn
2100 W. Hundred Rd.
Chester, VA 23831
Phone: (804) 751-0000,
     (800) 221-2222

Pet Restrictions: Under 25 lbs.
Exercise Area for Pets: Yes
Rates: $57 to $105

Days Inn
2410 W. Hundred Rd.
Chester, VA 23831
Phone: (804) 748-5871,
     (800) 325-2525

Pet Restrictions: $5, small pets
Pet left unattended in room: Yes
Exercise Area for Pets: Yes
Rates: $31 to $50

CHRISTIANSBURG

Arborgate Inn
100 Bristol Dr.
Christiansburg, VA 24073
Phone: (703) 381-0150

Pet Restrictions: Small pets only
Exercise Area for Pets: Yes
Rates: $35 to $49

Days Inn
I-81 & US 11 Roanoke St.
Christiansburg, VA 24073
Phone: (703) 382-0261,
     (800) 325-2525

Pet Restrictions: $5
Pet left unattended in room: Yes
Exercise Area for Pets: Yes
Rates: $42 to $47

Econo Lodge
2430 Roanoke St.
Christiansburg, VA 24073
Phone: (703) 382-6161

Pet Restrictions: None
Exercise Area for Pets: Yes
Rates: $31 to $47

Hampton Inn
50 Hampton Boulevard
Christianburg, VA 24073
Phone: (703) 382-2055

Pet Restrictions: No pets in room
but kennels
Exercise Area for Pets: Yes
Rates: $44 to $63

VETERINARIANS
Tobias, Lynnette
Road 3, box 125 4
Phone: (703) 961-1506

COLINSVILLE
Dutch Inn
633 Virginia Ave.
Colinsville, VA 24078
Phone: (703) 647-3721

Pet Restrictions: Advance notice
Pet left unattended in room: Yes,
kennelled/caged, no housekeeping
Exercise Area for Pets: Yes
Rates: $45 to $100

VETERINARIANS
May, Joseph A.
207 Lester Rd.
Phone: (703) 647-3714

COVINGTON
Comfort Inn
Rt. 5 Mallow Rd.
Covington, VA 24426
Phone: (703) 962-2141

Pet Restrictions: $10
Pet left unattended in room: Yes
Exercise Area for Pets: Yes
Rates: $45 to $64

Holiday Inn
Rt. 60 & 220, Exit 16 I-64
Covington, VA 24426
Phone: (703) 962-4951,
(800) HOLIDAY

Pet Restrictions: None
Pet left unattended in room: Yes
Exercise Area for Pets: Yes
Rates: $50 to $58

DUMFRIES
Quality Inn
17133 Dumfries Rd.
Dumpries, VA 22026
Phone: (703) 221-1141,
(800) 221-2222

Pet Restrictions: Under 25 lbs.
Exercise Area for Pets: Yes
Rates: $49 to $57

EMPORIA
Comfort Inn
1411 Skippers Rd.
Emporia, VA 23847
Phone: (804) 348-3282,
(800) 221-2222

Pet Restrictions: None
Exercise Area for Pets: Yes
Rates: $40.95 to $44.95

Econolodge
3173 Sussex Dr.
Emporia, VA 23847
Phone: (804) 535-8535

Pet Restrictions: Smoking rooms
Pet left unattended in room: Yes,
notify desk
Exercise Area for Pets: Yes
Rates: $27 to $32

Hampton Inn
Hwy 58 W. Exit 11
Emporia, VA 23847
Phone: (804) 634-9200

Pet Restrictions: None
Pet left unattended in room: Yes
Exercise Area for Pets: Yes
Rates: $38 to $48

Holiday Inn
311 Florida Ave.
Emporia, VA 23847
Phone: (804) 634-4191

Pet Restrictions: None
Pet left unattended in room: Yes
Exercise Area for Pets: Yes
Rates: $36 to $56

Red Carpet Inn
1586 Skippers Rd.
Emporia, VA 23847
Phone: (804) 634-4181,
(800) 251-1962

Pet Restrictions: None
Pet left unattended in room: Yes
Exercise Area for Pets: Yes
Rates: $28.95 to $36.95

FAIRFAX
Holiday Inn Fairfax City
3535 Chain Bridge Rd.
Fairfax, VA 22030
Phone: (703) 591-5500,
(800) HOLIDAY

Pet Restrictions: None
Pet left unattended in room: Yes
Exercise Area for Pets: Yes
Rates: $59 to $72

Wellesley Inn
10327 Lee Highway
Fairfax, VA 22030
Phone: (703) 359-2888

Pet Restrictions: None
Pet left unattended in room: Yes
Exercise Area for Pets: Yes
Rates: $45 to $65

VETERINARIANS
Blue Cross Animal Hospital
8429 Lee Highway
Phone: (703) 560-1881

Commonwealth Animal Hosp.
10860 Main St.
Phone: (703) 273-8183

Montrose Animal Health Ctr
3883 Pickett Rd.
Phone: (703) 425-5020

FALLS CHURCH
Ramada - Tysons Corner
7801 Leesburg Pike
Falls Church, VA 22043
Phone: (703) 893-1340

Pet Restrictions: None
Pet left unattended in room: Yes
Exercise Area for Pets: Yes
Rates: $79 to $109

VETERINARIANS
Falls Church Animal Hospital
1249 W. Broad St.
Phone: (703) 532-6121

Doria, Diane
3400 Carlin Springs Rd. #201
Phone: (703) 379-2136

Methvin, Janet C.
2907 Montauk Court
Phone: (703) 573-7464

FANCY GAP
Cascade Mt. Inn
Rt. 2, Box 36
Fancy Gap, VA 24328
Phone: (703) 728-2300

Pet Restrictions: $5/pet
Pet left unattended in room: Yes
Exercise Area for Pets: Yes
Rates: $42 to $45

FREDERICKSBURG
Best Western Fredericksburg
2205 Williams St.
Fredericksburg, VA 22401
Phone: (703) 371-5050,
   (800) 528-1234

Pet Restrictions: None
Exercise Area for Pets: Yes
Rates: $49.95

Best West. Johnny Appleseed
543 Warrenton Rd.
Fredericksburg, VA 22406
Phone: (703) 373-0000

Pet Restrictions: None
Exercise Area for Pets: Yes
Rates: $37 to $70

Best West. Thunderbird Inn
3000 Plank Rd.
Fredericksburg, VA 22401
Phone: (703) 786-7404

Pet Restrictions: Small pets,
   housebroken
Exercise Area for Pets: Yes
Rates: $40 to $55

Days Inn - North
14 Simpson Rd.
Fredericksburg, VA 22406
Phone: (703) 373-5340

Pet Restrictions: $5
Exercise Area for Pets: Yes
Rates: $37 to $49

Days Inn - South
5316 Jefferson Davis Hwy
Fredericksburg, VA 22401
Phone: (703) 898-6800

Pet Restrictions: $5
Exercise Area for Pets: Yes
Rates: $46 to $50

Holiday Inn-North
564 Warrenton Rd.
Fredericksburg, VA 22405
Phone: (703) 371-5550

Pet Restrictions: None
Pet left unattended in room: Yes
Exercise Area for Pets: Yes
Rates: $37 to $54

Howard Johnson Hotel
5327 Jefferson Davis Hwy
Fredericksburg, VA 22408
Phone: (703) 898-1800,
   (800) 654-2000

Pet Restrictions: None
Pet left unattended in room: Yes
Exercise Area for Pets: Yes
Rates: $19 to $50

Ramada Inn
P.O. Box 36, I-95 & Rt. 3 W.
Fredericksburg, VA 22401
Phone: (703) 786-8361,
   (800) 228-2828

Pet Restrictions: $25 deposit
Pet left unattended in room: Yes, if
   caged
Exercise Area for Pets: Yes
Rates: $38 to $59

VETERINARIANS

Chancellor Animal Clinic
5316 Plank Rd.
Phone: (703) 786-2282

Ferry Farm Animal Clinic
386 Kings Highway
Phone: (703) 371-5090

Wagner, Franklin G.
1525 William St.
Phone: (703) 373-6512

GLADE SPRINGS
Glade Economy Inn
I-81 Exit 29
Glade Springs, VA 24340
Phone: (703) 429-5131

Pet Restrictions: None
Pet left unattended in room: Yes
Exercise Area for Pets: Yes
Rates: $26 to $46

HAMPTON
Days Inn-Hampton
1918 Coliseum Dr.
Hampton, VA 23666
Phone: (804) 826-4810,
   (800) 325-2525

Pet Restrictions: $4/night
Pet left unattended in room: Yes
Exercise Area for Pets: Yes
Rates: $43 to $55

Hampton Inn
1813 West Mercury Blvd.
Hampton, VA 23666
Phone: (804) 838-8484,
   (800) HAMPTON

Pet Restrictions: Small dogs only
Rates: $52 to $75

La Quinta Motor Inn
2138 West Mercury Blvd.
Hampton, VA 23666
Phone: (804) 827-8680

Pet Restrictions: Sign waiver
Pet left unattended in room: Yes
Exercise Area for Pets: Yes
Rates: $43 to $70

Red Roof Inn
1925 Coliseum Dr.
Hampton, VA 23666
Phone: (804) 838-1870

Pet Restrictions: None
Pet left unattended in room: Yes
Exercise Area for Pets: Yes
Rates: $26.99 to $44.99

VETERINARIANS

Freed, John D.
1248 N. King St.
(804) 723-6049

Silkey, Beverly J.
531 N. Armistead Ave.
(804) 723-8571

HARRISONBURG
Belle Meade Red Carpet Inn
3210 S. Main St.
Harrisonburg, VA 22801
Phone: (703) 434-6704

Pet Restrictions: None
Pet left unattended in room: Yes
Exercise Area for Pets: Yes
Rates: $25 to $38

Comfort Inn
1440 E. Market St.
Harrisonburg, VA 22801
Phone: (703) 433-6066,
   (800) 221-2222

Pet Restrictions: None
Pet left unattended in room: Yes
Exercise Area for Pets: Yes
Rates: $40 to $55

VIRGINIA — HOTELS (continued)

Days Inn
1131 Forest Hill Rd.
Harrisonburg, VA 22801
Phone: (703) 433-9353

Pet Restrictions: Only certain rooms
Pet left unattended in room: Yes
Exercise Area for Pets: Yes
Rates: $40 to $65

Howard Johnson Lodge
605 Port Republic Rd.
Harrisonburg, VA 22801
Phone: (703) 434-6771

Pet Restrictions: None
Exercise Area for Pets: Yes
Rates: $39 to $50

Motel 6
10 Linda Lane
Harrisonburg, VA 22801
Phone: (703) 433-6939

Pet Restrictions: None
Pet left unattended in room: Yes
Exercise Area for Pets: Yes
Rates: $27 to $33

Sheraton Harisonburg Inn
1400 E. Market St.
Harrisonburg, VA 22801
Phone: (703) 433-2521,
    (800) 325-3535

Pet Restrictions: None
Pet left unattended in room: Yes
Exercise Area for Pets: Nearby
Rates: $62 to $95

VETERINARIANS

Valley Veterinary Hospital
3015 S. Main St.
Phone: (703) 434-0166

HERNDON
Holiday Inn Express
485 Elden St.
Herndon, VA 22070
Phone: (703) 478-9777,
    (800) HOLIDAY

Pet Restrictions: None
Pet left unattended in room: Yes
Exercise Area for Pets: Yes
Rates: $49 to $70

Residence Inn by Marriott
315 Elden St.
Herndon, VA 22070
Phone: (703) 435-0044

Pet Restrictions: $100 cleaning fee,
    $6/day
Pet left unattended in room: Yes
Exercise Area for Pets: Yes
Rates: $110 to $140

VETERINARIANS

Dominion Animal Hospital
795 Station St.
Phone: (703) 437-6900

Herndon Animal Medical Ctr.
720 Jackson St.
Phone: (703) 435-8777

Herndon-Reston Animal Hosp.
500 Elden Street
Phone: (703) 437-5655

IRVINGTON
The Tides Inn
King Carter Dr.
Irvington, VA 22480
Phone: (804) 438-5000,
    (800) 843-3746

Pet Restrictions: Small pets only,
    $3/day
Exercise Area for Pets: Yes
Rates: $122 to $140

KEYSVILLE
Sheldon's Motel
Rt. 2, Box 189
Keysville, VA 23947
Phone: (804) 736-8434

Pet Restrictions: None
Pet left unattended in room: Yes
Exercise Area for Pets: Yes
Rates: $31.30 to $46.97

LEESBURG
Best Western Leesburg
726 E. Market St.
Leesburg, VA 22075
Phone: (703) 777-9400,
    (800) 528-1234

Pet Restrictions: $25, 2 pets per
    room
Pet left unattended in room: Yes
Rates: $55 and up

LEXINGTON

Comfort Inn
Rt. 11 N. and I-64
Lexington, VA 24450
Phone: (703) 463-7311

Pet Restrictions: None
Exercise Area for Pets: Yes
Rates: $59 to $74

Econo Lodge
I-54 US 11 Rt. 7, Box 81
Lexington, VA 24450
Phone: (703) 463-7371,
    (800) 424-4777

Pet Restrictions: None
Pet left unattended in room: Yes
Exercise Area for Pets: Yes
Rates: $42.55 to $56

Holiday Inn
Rt. 11 North I-64, Box 1108
Lexington, VA 24450
Phone: (703) 463-7351,
    (800) HOLIDAY

Pet Restrictions: None
Pet left unattended in room: Yes
Exercise Area for Pets: Nearby
Rates: $50 to $63

Howard Johnson Lodge
Rt. 5, Box 381A
Lexington, VA 24450
Phone: (703) 463-9181,
    (800) 654-2000

Pet Restrictions: None
Pet left unattended in room: Yes
Rates: $45 to $63

Blue Ridge Animal Clinic
Rt. #5, Box 80
Phone: (703) 463-7799

Lexington Animal Hospital
Route 6, Box 214
Phone: (703) 463-2715

LURAY

Intown Motel
410 W. Main St.
Luray, VA 22835
Phone: (703) 743-6511

Pet Restrictions: Need mgr's
    approval on large pets,
    $10/pet/night
Pet left unattended in room: Yes
Exercise Area for Pets: Nearby
Rates: $32.50 to $79

Luray Caverns Motel - East
831 W. Main St., Box 748
Luray, VA 22835
Phone: (703) 743-4531

Pet Restrictions: None
Pet left unattended in room: Yes
Exercise Area for Pets: Yes
Rates: $52 to $62

Ramada Inn
P.O. Box 389
Luray, VA 22835
Phone: (703) 743-4521,
    (800) 2-RAMADA

Pet Restrictions: $10
Exercise Area for Pets: Yes
Rates: $55 to $225

LYNCHBURG

Holiday Inn
Rt. 29 Odd Fellows Rd.
Lynchburg, VA 24501
Phone: (804) 847-4424,
    (800) HOLIDAY

Pet Restrictions: Pets on ground
    floor only
Pet left unattended in room: Yes
Exercise Area for Pets: Yes
Rates: $40 to $82

The Animal Hospital
1705 Memorial Avenue
Phone: (804) 845-7021

MANASSAS

Red Roof Inn
10610 Automotive Dr.
Manassas, VA 22110
Phone: (703) 335-9333

Pet Restrictions: None
Pet left unattended in room: Yes
Exercise Area for Pets: Yes
Rates: $31.99 to $44.99

Morganna Animal Clinic
9050 Liberia Ave.
(703) 361-4196

Powers, David
10822 Moore Dr.
(703) 368-8284

Todd, John
9205 Main St.
(703) 368-9241

MARTINSVILLE

Best Western Martinsville Inn
US 220 N., P.O. Box 1183
Martinsville, VA 24114
Phone: (703) 632-5611,
   (800) 528-1234
Pet Restrictions: Small pets only
Pet left unattended in room: Yes,
   housetrained, no maid service
Exercise Area for Pets: Yes
Rates: $40 to $58

VETERINARIANS

Lackey Animal Hospital
P.O. Box 909
Phone: (703) 632-3736

Price, Richard L.
1112 Memorial Blvd.
Phone: (703) 632-5262

McLEAN

Best Western Tyson's Westpark Hotel
8401 Westpark Dr.
McLean, VA 22103
Phone: (703) 734-2800,
   (800) 528-1234
Pet Restrictions: Sign pet waiver
Pet left unattended in room: Yes
Exercise Area for Pets: Nearby
Rates: $69 to $125

VETERINARIANS

Old Dominion Animal Hospital
6705 Whittier Avenue
Phone: (703) 356-5582

Patton, Charles B.
1330 Old Chin Bridge
Phone: (703) 356-5000

Murnan, George E.
6830 Elm St.
Phone: (703) 821-3838

MT. JACKSON

Best Western Mt. Jackson
250 Conicville Rd.
Mt. Jackson, VA 22842
Phone: (703) 477-2911,
   (800) 528-1234
Pet Restrictions: None
Pet left unattended in room: Yes
Exercise Area for Pets: Yes
Rates: $35 to $50

NEW MARKET

Battlefield Motel
Rt. 1 US 11
New Market, VA 22844
Phone: (703) 740-3105
   (800) 296-6835
Pet Restrictions: $3, less than 10
   lbs.
Pet left unattended in room: Yes
Rates: $30, $35, $48

NEWPORT NEWS

Best Western King James Motor Hotel
6045 Jeff Ave.
Newport News, VA 23605
Phone: (804) 245-2801,
   (800) 345-3567
Pet Restrictions: None
Pet left unattended in room: Yes
Exercise Area for Pets: Yes
Rates: $27.75 to $42.75

Motel 6
797 J. Clyde Morris Blvd.
Newport News, VA 23601
Phone: (804) 595-6336,
   (505) 891-6161 (central res.)
Pet Restrictions: None
Exercise Area for Pets: Yes
Rates: $23.06 to $34.71

Regency Inn Motel
13700 Warwick Blvd.
Newport News, VA 23602
Phone: (804) 874-4100
Pet Restrictions: $4/day
Pet left unattended in room: Yes, no
   maid service
Rates: $29.95 to $36.95

Tudor Inn
15540 Warwick Blvd.
Newport News, VA 23602
Phone: (804) 887-0180
Pet Restrictions: $30 deposit
Pet left unattended in room: Yes
Rates: $38.95 to $42.95

VETERINARIANS

Animal Med. Ctr. of the Peninsula
2816 Route 17
Phone: (804) 867-8808

Boulevard Veterinary Hosp.
12620 Nettles Dr.
Phone: (804) 874-3200

Warwick Animal Hospital
11117 Jefferson Avenue
Phone: (804) 595-3337

NORFOLK
Days Inn Military Circle
5701 Chambers St.
Norfolk, VA 23502
Phone: (804) 461-0100,
    (800) 325-2525
Pet Restrictions: $50 deposit
Pet left unattended in room: Yes
Rates: $38 to $69

Econo Lodge Airport
3343 North Military Highway
Norfolk, VA 23518
Phone: (804) 855-3116,
    (800) 296-6969
Pet Restrictions: $25 deposit
Pet left unattended in room: Yes
Exercise Area for Pets: Yes
Rates: $48.95 to $78

Econo Lodge Little Circle Rd.
1850 E. Little Creek Rd.
Norfolk, VA 23518
Phone: (804) 583-1561,
    (800) 424-4777
Pet Restrictions: $25 deposit
Pet left unattended in room: Yes
Rates: $38.95 to $48.95

Econo Lodge Military Circle
865 N. Military Highway
Norfolk, VA 23502
Phone: (804) 461-4865,
    (800) 424-4777
Pet Restrictions: Domestic pets
Pet left unattended in room: Yes
Exercise Area for Pets: Nearby
Rates: $32.99 to $50.99

Econo Lodge West Ocean View Blvd.
9601 4th View St.
Norfolk, VA 23503
Phone: (804) 480-9611,
    (800) 768-5425
Pet Restrictions: $50 deposit
Pet left unattended in room: Yes
Exercise Area for Pets: Yes
Rates: $38.95 to $56.95

Howard Johnson Inn
700 Monticello Ave.
Norfolk, VA 23501
Phone: (804) 627-5555,
    (800) 682-7678
Pet Restrictions: None
Pet left unattended in room: Yes
Exercise Area for Pets: Yes
Rates: $59 to $69

Quality Inn - Lake Wright
6280 Northampton Blvd.
Norfolk, VA 23502
Phone: (804) 461-6251,
    (800) 228-5157
Pet Restrictions: Free 1st night, $25
    fee for add'l visit
Pet left unattended in room: Yes,
    notify maid
Exercise Area for Pets: Yes
Rates: $45 to $66

VETERINARIANS
Animal Care Center
1228 W. Little Creek Rd.
Phone: (804) 423-3900

Dog and Cat Hospital
238 West 21st St.
Phone: (804) 622-1788

West's Animal Hospital
830 West 21st St.
Phone: (804) 622-4551

PETERSBURG
Comfort Inn
11974 S. Crater Rd.
Petersburg, VA 23805
Phone: (804) 732-2900
Pet Restrictions: Only cats & dogs

VETERINARIANS
Petersburg, Animal Hospital
2901 South Crater Rd.
Phone: (804) 732-4905

Metry, Margaret W.
464 S. Crater Rd.
Phone: (804) 733-8202

RICHMOND

Days Inn
1600 Robin Hood Rd.
Richmond, VA 23220
Phone: (804) 353-1287,
(800) 325-2525

Pet Restrictions: $2/night
Pet left unattended in room: Yes
Exercise Area for Pets: Yes
Rates: $43.80 to $49

Econo Lodge
5221 Brook Rd.
Richmond, VA 23227
Phone: (804) 266-7603,
(800) 637-3297

Pet Restrictions: $5/night
Pet left unattended in room: Yes
Exercise Area for Pets: Yes
Rates: $40 to $45

Holiday Inn South
301 W. Franklin St. at Madison
Richmond, VA 23220
Phone: (804) 644-9871,
(800) 289-9491

Pet Restrictions: None
Pet left unattended in room: Yes
Exercise Area for Pets: Nearby
Rates: $54 and up

Knights Inn Richmond Airport
5252 Airport Square
Richmond, VA 23150
Phone: (804) 226-4519,
(800) 638-2332

Pet Restrictions: None
Pet left unattended in room: Yes
Exercise Area for Pets: Yes
Rates: $29.95 and up

La Quinta Motor Inn
6910 Midlothian Pike
Richmond, VA 23225
Phone: (804) 745-7100

Pet Restrictions: None
Pet left unattended in room: Yes
Exercise Area for Pets: Yes
Rates: $44 and up

Red Roof Inn
4350 Commerce Rd.
Richmond, VA 23234
Phone: (804) 271-7240

Pet Restrictions: None
Pet left unattended in room: Yes
Exercise Area for Pets: Yes
Rates: $30 to $45

Red Roof Inn
100 Gresham Wood Palace
Richmond, VA 23225
Phone: (804) 745-0600

Pet Restrictions: None
Pet left unattended in room: Yes, no
housekeeping
Exercise Area for Pets: Yes
Rates: $29.99 to $50.99

Richmond Marriott Hotel
500 E. Broad St.
Richmond, VA 23219
Phone: (804) 643-3400,
(800) 228-9220

Pet Restrictions: Under 25 lbs.
Pet left unattended in room: Yes
Exercise Area for Pets: Yes
Rates: $99 to $109

VETERINARIANS

Broad St. Veterinary Hosp.
3320 W. Broad St.
Phone: (804) 353-4491

Iron Bridge Animal Hosp.
7540 Iron Bridge Rd.
Phone: (804) 743-1704

Lakeside Animal Hospital
5206 Lakeside Avenue
Phone: (804) 262-8697

ROANOKE

Holiday Inn Civic Center
501 Orange Ave.
Roanoke, VA 24012
Phone: (703) 342-8961

Pet Restrictions: None
Pet left unattended in room: Yes
Exercise Area for Pets: Yes
Rates: $60 to $46

Holiday Inn - South
1927 Franklin Rd. SW
Roanoke, VA 24014
Phone: (703) 343-0121,
(800) HOLIDAY

Pet Restrictions: None
Pet left unattended in room: Yes
Exercise Area for Pets: Yes
Rates: $48 to $58

Sheraton Airport Inn
2727 Ferndale Dr. NW
Roanoke, VA 24017
Phone: (703) 362-4500,
    (800) 325-3535
Pet Restrictions: $25 deposit, 1st
    floor
Pet left unattended in room: Yes
Exercise Area for Pets: Yes
Rates: $83 to $73

VETERINARIANS
Harris Animal Hospital
6805 Peters Creek NW
Phone: (703) 362-3753

Roanoke Animal Hospital
2814 Franklin Rd. SW
Phone: (703) 343-8021

Rosolowsky, William M.
4538 Old Cave Spring Rd.
Phone: (703) 989-8582

RUTTEN GLEN
Comfort Inn
P.O. Box 105
Rutten Glen, VA 22546
Phone: (804) 448-2828
Pet Restrictions: None
Pet left unattended in room: Yes
Exercise Area for Pets: Yes
Rates: $56 to $62

Days Inn - Carmel Church
P.O. Box 70
Rutten Glen, VA 22546
Phone: (804) 448-2011,
    (800) 325-2525
Pet Restrictions: $5/night
Pet left unattended in room: Yes
Exercise Area for Pets: Yes
Rates: $50 to $63

SALEM
Arborgate Inn
301 Wildwood Rd.
Salem, VA 24153
Phone: (703) 389-0280,
    (800) 843-5644
Pet Restrictions: None
Pet left unattended in room: Yes
Exercise Area for Pets: Yes
Rates: $32.95 and up

Holiday Inn
1671 Skyview Rd.
Salem, VA 24153
Phone: (703) 389-7061
Pet Restrictions: None
Pet left unattended in room: Yes
Exercise Area for Pets: Yes
Rates: $44 and up

VETERINARIANS
DuVall Jr., Allen C.
1035 Electric Rd.
Phone: (703) 389-0219

SANDSTON
Econo Lodge Airport
5408 Williamsburg Rd.
Sandston, VA 23150
Phone: (804) 222-1020,
    (800) 424-4777
Pet Restrictions: None
Pet left unattended in room: Yes
Exercise Area for Pets: Yes
Rates: $39.99 to $32.99

Econo Lodge South
2125 Wille's Rd.
Sandston, VA 23237
Phone: (804) 271-6031,
    (800) 424-4777
Pet Restrictions: None
Pet left unattended in room: Yes
Exercise Area for Pets: Yes
Rates: $35.93 and up

Hampton Inn
5300 Airport Sq.
Sandston, VA 23150
Phone: (804) 222-8200,
    (800) HAMPTON
Pet Restrictions: Small pets, $25
    deposit
Pet left unattended in room: Yes
Exercise Area for Pets: Yes
Rates: $58 and up

Holiday Inn
5203 Williamsburg Rd.
Sandston, VA 23150
Phone: (804) 222-6450,
    (800) HOLIDAY
Pet Restrictions: None
Exercise Area for Pets: Yes
Rates: $65 to $75

Holiday Inn Cross Roads
2000 Staple Mill Rd.
Sandston, VA 23230
Phone: (804) 359-6061

Pet Restrictions: Small pets
Pet left unattended in room: Yes
Exercise Area for Pets: Yes
Rates: $66 and up

SKIPPERS
Econo Lodge
1200 Moore's Ferry Rd.
Skippers, VA 23879
Phone: (804) 634-6124

Pet Restrictions: None
Pet left unattended in room: Yes
Exercise Area for Pets: Yes
Rates: $34.95 to $44.95

STANTON
Comfort Inn
1302 Richmond Ave.
Stanton, VA 24407
Phone: (703) 886-5000

Pet Restrictions: Smoking rooms only
Pet left unattended in room: Yes
Exercise Area for Pets: Yes
Rates: $79.95 to $53.95

Econo Lodge Stanton
1031 Richmond Rd.
Stanton, VA 24401
Phone: (703) 885-5158,
    (800) 532-2014

Pet Restrictions: None
Pet left unattended in room: Yes
Exercise Area for Pets: Yes
Rates: $31 to $36

Hessian Econo Lodge
Rt. 2, Box 364
Stanton, VA 24401
Phone: (703) 337-1231,
    (800) 55-ECONO

Pet Restrictions: $4/night, smoking room only
Pet left unattended in room: Yes
Exercise Area for Pets: Yes
Rates: $35.95 to $49.95

Holiday Inn
P.O. Box 2526
Stanton, VA 24401
Phone: (703) 248-5111,
    (800) HOLIDAY

Pet Restrictions: None
Pet left unattended in room: Yes
Exercise Area for Pets: Yes
Rates: $42 to $48

STAFFORD
Stafford Days Inn
2868 Jeff. Davis Hwy
Stafford, VA 22554
Phone: (703) 659-0022,
    (800) 325-2525

Pet Restrictions: $5/night
Pet left unattended in room: Yes
Exercise Area for Pets: Yes
Rates: $55 to $44

STERLING
Holiday Inn Washington Dulles
1000 Sully Rd.
Sterling, VA 22170
Phone: (703) 471-7411,
    (800) HOLIDAY

Pet Restrictions: None
Exercise Area for Pets: Yes
Rates: $81 to $95

SOUTH HILL
Econo Lodge
623E Atlantic St.
South Hill, VA 23970
Phone: (804) 447-7116,
    (800) 424-4777

Pet Restrictions: None
Pet left unattended in room: Yes
Exercise Area for Pets: Yes
Rates: $38 to $48

Holiday Inn
85 US 58
South Hill, VA 23970
Phone: (804) 447-3123

Pet Restrictions: None
Pet left unattended in room: Yes
Exercise Area for Pets: Yes
Rates: $52 to $59

VETERINARIANS
Nature Veterinary Center
1333 W. Danville St.
Phone: (804) 447-3553

TRIANGLE
US Inn
4202 Inn St.
Triangle, VA 22172
Phone: (703) 221-1115

Pet Restrictions: None
Pet left unattended in room: Yes
Exercise Area for Pets: Yes
Rates: $42 to $58

TROUTVILLE

Travelodge
Rt. 4, 2444 Lee Hwy South
Troutville, VA 24175
Phone: (703) 992-6700,
    (800) 578-7878
Pet Restrictions: $6
Exercise Area for Pets: Yes
Rates: $32.95 to $45

VIENNA

Residence Inn by Marriott-Tyson
8616 Westwood Center Dr.
Vienna, VA 22180
Phone: (703) 893-0120,
    (800) 331-3131
Pet Restrictions: One time deposit of
    $85, $5/day
Pet left unattended in room: Yes
Exercise Area for Pets: Yes
Rates: $103.29 to $166

VETERINARIANS

Emergency Vetny Clinic of N. VA
416 Maple Avenue West
Phone: (703) 442-0642

Vienna Animal Hospital
531 Maple Avenue West
Phone: (703) 938-2121

Draper, Douglas J.
1203 Downey Dr.
Phone: (703) 759-4500

VIRGINIA BEACH

Econo Lodge Expressway
3637 Bonney Rd.
Virginia Beach, VA 23452
Phone: (804) 486-5711,
    (800) 424-4777
Pet Restrictions: None
Pet left unattended in room: Yes, no
    made service
Exercise Area for Pets: Yes
Rates: $49.95 to $53.99

La Quinta Motor Inn
192 Newton Road
Virginia Beach, VA 23462
Phone: (804) 497-6620,
    (800) 531-5900
Pet Restrictions: 1 small pet per
    room
Exercise Area for Pets: Nearby
Rates: $52 to $71

Ocean Holiday Motel
2417 Atlantic Ave.
Virginia Beach, VA 23451
Phone: (804) 425-6920,
    (800) 345-7263
Pet Restrictions: $5/pet/night
Exercise Area for Pets: Nearby
Rates: $30 to $180

Red Roof Inn
196 Ballard Ct.
Virginia Beach, VA 23225
Phone: (804) 490-0225
Pet Restrictions: Small pets
Pet left unattended in room: Yes
Exercise Area for Pets: Yes
Rates: $51.99 to $61.99

Travelodge
4600 Bonney Rd.
Virginia Beach, VA 23462
Phone: (804) 473-9745,
    (800) 578-7878
Pet Restrictions: None
Exercise Area for Pets: Yes
Rates: $29.95 to $49

Thunderbird Motor Lodge
35th & Oceanfront
Virginia Beach, VA 23451
Phone: (804) 428-3024,
    (800) 633-6669
Pet Restrictions: 40 lbs. or less
Pet left unattended in room: Yes,
    must be quiet
Exercise Area for Pets: Yes, clean
    up after
Rates: $30 to $100

VETERINARIANS

Bay Beach Vetny Medical Clinic
4340 Virginia Beach Blvd.
Phone: (804) 340-3913

Pembroke Veterinary Clinic
4548 Wishart Rd.
Phone: (804) 464-0169

Pet Care Veterinary Hospital
4201-A Virginia Beach Blvd.
Phone: (804) 473-0111

WARRENTON

Howard Johnson Motor Lodge
6 Broadview Ave.
Warrenton, VA 22186
Phone: (703) 347-4141,
    (800) 446-4656
Pet Restrictions: Bottom floor
Exercise Area for Pets: Yes
Rates: $43.95 to $45.95

VETERINARIANS
Gilman, Arnold Robert
657 Falmouth St.
Phone: (703) 347-7788

WAYNESBORO
Days Inn
2060 Rosset Ave.
Waynesboro, VA 22960
Phone: (703) 943-1101,
(800) 325-2525
Pet Restrictions: $4
Pet left unattended in room: Yes
Exercise Area for Pets: Yes
Rates: $50 to $85

VETERINARIANS
Bowman, Bruce M.
Route 2
Phone: (703) 942-9777

Woodworth, Daniel M.
East Rockfish Rd.
Phone: (703) 942-5163

WEYTHEVILLE
Econo Lodge
1190 E. Main St.
Weytheville, VA 24382
Phone: (703) 228-5517,
(800) 424-4777
Pet Restrictions: None
Pet left unattended in room: Yes
Exercise Area for Pets: Yes
Rates: $33.99 to $50.99

Howard Johnson Lodge
Lee Hwy Exit 73 I-81
Weytheville, VA 24382
Phone: (703) 228-3188,
(800) 446-4656
Pet Restrictions: $5/pet
Pet left unattended in room: Yes,
owner responsible
Exercise Area for Pets: Yes
Rates: $41.99 and up

Johnsons Motel
1750 West Lee Hwy
Weytheville, VA 24382
Phone: (703) 228-4812,
(800) 776-4812
Pet Restrictions: Charge varies with
size
Pet left unattended in room: Yes
Exercise Area for Pets: Yes
Rates: $24 to $33

MacWeyth Inn
2040 E. Main St
Weytheville, VA 24382
Phone: (703) 228-5525
Pet Restrictions: None
Pet left unattended in room: Yes if
small
Exercise Area for Pets: Yes
Rates: $24.95 to $48.95

Motel 6
2020 E. Main St.
Weytheville, VA 24382
Phone: (703) 228-7988
Pet Restrictions: Yes
Pet left unattended in room: Yes
Rates: $22.99 to $37.99

Ramada Inn
955 Peppers Ferry Rd.
Weytheville, VA 24382
Phone: (703) 228-6000,
(800) 2-RAMADA
Pet Restrictions: None
Pet left unattended in room: Yes
Exercise Area for Pets: Yes
Rates: $30 to $65

WILLIAMSBURG
Best Western Virginia Inn
900 Capital Landing Rd.
Williamsburg, VA 23187
Phone: (804) 229-1655,
(800) 528-1234
Pet Restrictions: $5, certain rooms
Pet left unattended in room: Yes, no
maid service
Exercise Area for Pets: Yes
Rates: $39 to $69

Best West. Williamsburg West Park
1600 Richmond Rd.
Williamsburg, VA 23185
Phone: (804) 229-1134,
(800) 446-1062
Pet Restrictions: Small pets, must
have their own container
Pet left unattended in room: Yes, no
maid service
Exercise Area for Pets: Nearby
Rates: $35 to $69

Commonwealth Inn
1233 Richmond Rd.
Williamsburg, VA 23185
Phone: (804) 253-8728,
  (800) 344-0046

Pet Restrictions: $40 deposit
Pet left unattended in room: Yes
Exercise Area for Pets: Nearby
Rates: $35 to $59

Days Inn Downtown
902 Richmond Rd.
Williamsburg, VA 23185
Phone: (804) 229-5060,
  (800) 325-2525

Pet Restrictions: $5, small pets
Pet left unattended in room: Yes
Exercise Area for Pets: Yes
Rates: $45 to $85 plus

George Washington Inn
500 Merrimac Trail
Williamsburg, VA 23185
Phone: (804) 220-1410,
  (800) 666-8888

Pet Restrictions: $10/pet/night
Pet left unattended in room: Yes,
  must remove pet for cleaning
Exercise Area for Pets: Yes
Rates: $39 to $154

Heritage Inn
1324 Richmond Road
Williamsburg, VA 23185
Phone: (804) 229-6220,
  (800) 782-3800

Pet Restrictions: None
Pet left unattended in room: Yes, no
  maid service
Exercise Area for Pets: Yes
Rates: $32 to $66

Holiday Inn Patriot
3032 Richmond Rd.
Williamsburg, VA 23145
Phone: (804) 565-2600,
  (800) 446-6001

Pet Restrictions: $45 refund. deposit
  if no damage, $5/day
Pet left unattended in room: Yes
Exercise Area for Pets: Yes
Rates: $81 to $99

Quality Inn Williamsburg Conference Center
6483 Richmond Rd.
Williamsburg, VA 23187
Phone: (804) 565-1000,
  (800) 922-9277

Pet Restrictions: $10/night, $50
  deposit, 20 lbs. or less
Pet left unattended in room: Yes, no
  maid service
Exercise Area for Pets: Yes
Rates: $39 to $189

Quarter Path Inn
620 York St.
Williamsburg, VA 23185
Phone: (804) 220-0960,
  (800) 446-9222

Pet Restrictions: Yes
Pet left unattended in room: Yes
Exercise Area for Pets: Nearby
Rates: $39 to $69

Ramada Inn East
351 York St.
Williamsburg, VA 23185
Phone: (804) 229-4100,
  (800) 962-4743

Pet Restrictions: $10
Exercise Area for Pets: Yes
Rates: $69 to $97

Ramada Inn West
5351 Richmond Rd.
Williamsburg, VA 23185
Phone: (804) 565-2000,
  (800) 446-9200

Pet Restrictions: Small pets, $10
Pet left unattended in room: Yes,
  must be secured
Exercise Area for Pets: Nearby
Rates: $39 to $79

Super 8 Motel
304 2nd St.
Williamsburg, VA 23185
Phone: (804) 229-0500,
  (800) 336-0500

Pet Restrictions: None
Rates: $39 to $69

York St. Hotel Suites
351 York St.
Williamsburg, VA 23187
Phone: (804) 229-4155,
  (800) 962-4743

Pet Restrictions: 1 time $10 fee
Pet left unattended in room: Yes, if
  caged
Exercise Area for Pets: Yes
Rates: $69 to $105

VIRGINIA — HOTELS (continued)

VETERINARIANS
Animal Clinic of Williamsburg
7316 Merrimac Trail
Phone: (804) 253-0812

James City Veterinary Clinic
104 Oak Ridge Court
Phone: (804) 229-0815

WINCHESTER
Apple Blossom Motor Lodge
2951 Valley Ave.
Winchester, VA 22601
Phone: (703) 667-1200,
    (800) 468-8837

Pet Restrictions: None
Pet left unattended in room: Yes
Exercise Area for Pets: Yes
Rates: $29 to $47

Best. West. Lee-Jackson Motor Lodge
711 Millwood Avenue
Winchester, VA 22601
Phone: (703) 662-4154,
    (800) 528-1234

Pet Restrictions: None
Pet left unattended in room: Yes
Exercise Area for Pets: Yes
Rates: $44.50 plus $5 each add'l
    person

Mohawk Hotel
2754 Northwestern Pike
Winchester, VA 22601
Phone: (703) 667-1410

Pet Restrictions: None
Pet left unattended in room: Yes
Exercise Area for Pets: Yes
Rates: $26 to $32

Quality Inn East
603 Milwood Ave.
Winchester, VA 22601
Phone: (703) 667-2250,
    (800) 221-2222

Pet Restrictions: $5
Pet left unattended in room: Yes
Exercise Area for Pets: Yes
Rates: $36 to $51

Tourist City Motel
214 Milwood Ave.
Winchester, VA 22601
Phone: (703) 662-9011

Pet Restrictions: $2
Pet left unattended in room: Yes
Exercise Area for Pets: Yes
Rates: $28 to $44

Travel Lodge
160 Front Royal Hike
Winchester, VA 22602
Phone: (703) 665-0685,
    (800) 255-3050

Pet Restrictions: None
Pet left unattended in room: Yes
Exercise Area for Pets: Yes
Rates: $39 to $56

VETERINARIANS
Linden Heights Animal Hosp.
274 Linden Drive
Phone: (703) 667-4290

WOODSTOCK
Budget Host Inn
Rt. 2, US 11, Box 78
Woodstock, VA 22664
Phone: (703) 459-4086,
    (800) BUD-HOST

Pet Restrictions: None
Exercise Area for Pets: Yes
Rates: $29 to $50

YORKTOWN
Yorktown Motor Lodge
8829 G. Washington Hwy
Yorktown, VA 23692
Phone: (804) 898-5454

Pet Restrictions: $10 deposit,
    $4.26/day
Pet left unattended in room: Yes
Exercise Area for Pets: Yes
Rates: $44.95 to $80.00

WASHINGTON — HOTELS

ABERDEEN

Red Lion Motel
521 W. Wishkah
Aberdeen, WA 98520
Phone: (206) 532-5210

Pet Restrictions: In smoking rooms
only, under 30 lbs.
Exercise Area for Pets: Nearby
Rates: $48 to $58

VETERINARIANS

Uhler, Stephen P.
1001 E. Wishkah
Phone: (206) 532-9390

BELLEVUE

Best West. Greenwood Hotel
625 116th Ave. NE
Bellevue, WA 98004
Phone: (206) 455-9444

Pet Restrictions: None
Exercise Area for Pets: Nearby
Rates: $66 to $85

Holiday Inn Bellevue
11211 Main St.
Bellevue, WA 98004
Phone: (206) 455-5240

Pet Restrictions: $30 nonrefund.
Pet left unattended in room: Yes
Exercise Area for Pets: Nearby
Rates: $65

Red Lion Inn
300 112th Ave. SE
Bellevue, WA 98004
Phone: (206) 455-1300

Pet Restrictions: $50 deposit; 1st fl.
only
Pet left unattended in room: Yes
Exercise Area for Pets: Nearby
Rates: $124 to $144

Resid. Inn by Marriott Seattle
14455 NE 29th Pl.
Bellevue, WA 98007
Phone: (206) 882-1222

Pet Restrictions: $50 fee 1-5 ngts.
Pet left unattended in room: Yes
Exercise Area for Pets: Nearby
Rates: $132 to $189

VETERINARIANS

Lake Hills Veterinary Hosp.
840 140th Southeast
Phone: (206) 746-3344

Kelly, John C.
2845 93rd NE
Phone: (206) 285-7387

Toole, Roy C.
10415 Main St.
Phone: (206) 454-1246

BELLINGHAM

Val-U-Inn
805 Lakeway Dr.
Bellingham, WA 98226
Phone: (206) 671-9600

Pet Restrictions: $5 per day
Exercise Area for Pets: Nearby
Rates: $51 to $65

VETERINARIANS

Ebright Animal Hospital
1901 N. State St.
Phone: (206) 734-0720

BREMERTON

Dunes Motel
3400 11th St.
Bremerton, WA 98312
Phone: (206) 377-0093

Pet Restrictions: $10-$25 flat
Exercise Area for Pets: Nearby
Rates: $48 to $55

Nendel's Suites
4303 Kitsap Way
Bremerton, WA 98312
Phone: (206) 377-4402

Pet Restrictions: $25 deposit
Pet left unattended in room: Yes
Exercise Area for Pets: Nearby
Rates: $49.55 to $79.50

VETERINARIANS

Beecher, Eileen L.
4214 Kitsap Way
Phone: (206) 373-1465

CENTRALIA

Ferryman's Inn
1003 Eckerson Rd.
Centralia, WA 98531
Phone: (206) 330-2094

Pet Restrictions: $5 day
Pet left unattended in room: Yes
Exercise Area for Pets: Nearby
Rates: $43 to $46

Peppertree West Motor Inn
1208 Alder St.
Centralia, WA 98531
Phone: (206) 736-9362

Pet Restrictions: $5 day
Exercise Area for Pets: Yes
Rates: $35 to $38

CHELAN
Kelly's Resort
Rt. 1, Box 119
Chelan, WA 98816
Phone: (509) 687-3220

Pet Restrictions: $10 wk (small pets only)
Exercise Area for Pets: Nearby
Rates: $75 to $120

CLE ELUM
Cedars Motel
1001 E. 1st St.
Cle Elum, WA 98922
Phone: (509) 674-5535

Pet Restrictions: None
Exercise Area for Pets: Yes
Rates: $36 to $38

COUPEVILLE
The Coupeville Inn
200 NW Coveland St., PO Box 370
Coupeville, WA 98239
Phone: (206) 678-6668

Pet Restrictions: Winters only
Pet left unattended in room: Yes
Exercise Area for Pets: Nearby
Rates: $49.50 to $85

EVERETT
Apple Inn Motel
8421 Evergreen Way
Everett, WA 98204
Phone: (206) 347-1100

Pet Restrictions: $5 charge under 20 lbs.
Pet left unattended in room: Yes
Exercise Area for Pets: Nearby
Rates: $38 to $40

Nendel's Inn
2800 Pacific Ave.
Everett, WA 98201
Phone: (206) 258-4141

Pet Restrictions: $25 deposit
Exercise Area for Pets: Nearby, scooper needed
Rates: $59 to $63

Royal Motor Inn
952 N. Broadway
Everett, WA 98201
Phone: (206) 259-5177

Pet Restrictions: $5 day
Exercise Area for Pets: Yes
Rates: $38 to $40

VETERINARIANS
Diamond Veterinary Hospital
3625 Rucker Avenue
Phone: (206) 252-1106

DeMaris, Paul R.
10726 Bothell Highway SE
Phone: (206) 337-1500

GOLDENDALE
Ponderosa Motel
775 E. Broadway
Goldendale, WA 98620
Phone: (509) 773-5842

Pet Restrictions: Credit Card # needed
Exercise Area for Pets: Nearby
Rates: $38

VETERINARIANS
Alpine Animal Hospital
21800 Southeast 56th St.
Phone: (206) 392-8888

Smith, Candice Katherine
P.O. Box 1284
Phone: (206) 641-8414

KENNEWICK
Shaniko Inn Motel
321 N. Johnson St.
Kennewick, WA 99336
Phone: (509) 735-6385

Pet Restrictions: $4 per day/pet
Pet left unattended in room: Yes
Exercise Area for Pets: Nearby
Rates: $43 to $48

VETERINARIANS
Vista Veterinary Hospital
5603 West Canal Dr.
Phone: (509) 783-2131

KENT

Ascot Inn
1711 W. Meeker St.
Kent, WA 98032
Phone: (206) 854-1950
Pet Restrictions: $20 dep. ($10 non-refund.)
Exercise Area for Pets: Nearby
Rates: $55 to $65

Best Western Pony Soldier Motor Inn
1233 N. Central
Kent, WA 98032
Phone: (206) 852-7224
Pet Restrictions: $20 dep. (refund.)
Exercise Area for Pets: Yes
Rates: $57 to $65.50

VETERINARIANS
Moffat-Minnick Animal Hosp.
10834 Kent-Kangley Rd.
Phone: (206) 852-8460

KIRKLAND

La Quinta Inn - Bellevue
10530 NE Northup Way
Kirkland, WA 98033
Phone: (206) 828-6585
Pet Restrictions: None
Pet left unattended in room: Yes
Exercise Area for Pets: Nearby
Rates: $57 to $70

VETERINARIANS
Shelts, Robert L.
13603 100th Avenue
Phone: (206) 821-1105

LEAVENWORTH

River's Edge Lodge
Along Wewatchee River
Leavenworth, WA 98826
Phone: (509) 548-7612
Pet Restrictions: None
Exercise Area for Pets: Nearby
Rates: $55 to $70

LONG BEACH

The Breakers
P.O. Box 428
95th & Highway 103
Long Beach, WA 98631
Phone: (800) 288-8890
Fax: (360) 642-8772
Contact: Krissy Wyngarden
Vacation Villages (503) 246-5405
Pet Restrictions: $7 per pet per day
Pet left unattended in room: No
Exercise Area for Pets: Nearby
Rates: $54 to $160

Nendel's Edwater Inn Motel
409 10th St. SW, PO Box 793
Long Beach, WA 98631
Phone: (206) 642-2311
Pet Restrictions: Ground floor $3 day
Pet left unattended in room: Yes
Exercise Area for Pets: Nearby
Rates: $55 to $73

LONGVIEW

Lewis & Clark Motor Inn
838 15th Ave.
Longview, WA 98632
Phone: (206) 423-6460
Pet Restrictions: $5 charge
Pet left unattended in room: Yes
Exercise Area for Pets: Nearby
Rates: $36 to $40

Town Chalet Motel
1822 Washington Way
Longview, WA 98632
Phone: (206) 423-2020
Pet Restrictions: $3 day (small pet only)
Exercise Area for Pets: Nearby
Rates: $30 to $32

VETERINARIANS
Cowlitz Animal Clinic
763 Commerce
Phone: (206) 425-6440

Ocean Beach Veterinary Clinic
4011 Ocean Beach Highway
Phone: (206) 425-0850

LYNNWOOD

The Residence Inn - Seattle N
18200 Alderwood Mall Blvd.
Lynnwood, WA 98037
Phone: (206) 771-1100
Pet Restrictions: $10 day
Pet left unattended in room: Yes
Exercise Area for Pets: Nearby
Rates: $120 to $160

VETERINARIANS
Alderwood Veterinary Clinic
3819 196th Southwest
Phone: (206) 776-0121

Lynnwood Veterinary Hospital
4425 164th St. Southwest
Phone: (206) 743-0511

McGill, James A.
19011 36th Avenue West Suite C
Phone: (206) 775-7655

MOCLIPS

Hi Tide Ocean Beach Resort
P.O. Box 308
Moclips, WA 98562
Phone: (206) 276-4142

Pet Restrictions: $10 day
Exercise Area for Pets: Nearby
Rates: $79 to $84

MOSES LAKE

El Rancho Motel
1214 S. Pioneer Way
Moses Lake, WA 98837
Phone: (509) 765-9173

Pet Restrictions: Small pets only
Exercise Area for Pets: Yes
Rates: $31 to $33

Lake Shore Motel
3206 W. Lakeshore Dr.
Moses Lake, WA 98837
Phone: (509) 765-9201

Pet Restrictions: $5 day/pet
Pet left unattended in room: Yes
Exercise Area for Pets: Nearby
Rates: $33.95

Shilo Inn Moses Lake
1819 E. Kittleson
Moses Lake, WA 98837
Phone: (509) 765-9317,
    (800) 222-2244

Pet Restrictions: $6/pet/day; 40 lbs.
    & under
Pet left unattended in room: Yes
Exercise Area for Pets: Yes
Rates: $65 to $78

VETERINARIANS

Broadway Animal Hospital
890 E Broadway Extension
Phone: (509) 765-3481

OAK HARBOR

Acorn Motor Inn
8066 80th NW
Oak Harbor, WA 98277
Phone: (206) 675-6646

Pet Restrictions: $5 charge (small
    pets only)
Exercise Area for Pets: Nearby
Rates: $48 to $54

VETERINARIANS

Oak Harbor Animal Hospital
5733 N. State Highway 20
Phone: (206) 675-0737

OCEAN SHORES

Grey Gull Condo Motel
651 Ocean Shore Blvd., NW
Ocean Shores, WA 98569
Phone: (206) 289-3381

Pet Restrictions: Small pets only
Exercise Area for Pets: Nearby
Rates: $98 to $315

Nautilus Hotel
P.O. Box 1174
Ocean Shores, WA 98569
Phone: (206) 289-2722

Pet Restrictions: $10 day
    under 25 lbs.
Exercise Area for Pets: Nearby
Rates: $100 to $140

OCEAN PARK

Ocean Park Resort
Hwy 259 & R St., PO Box 339
Ocean Park, WA 98640
Phone: (206) 665-4585

Pet Restrictions: $5 day/pet (small
    pet only)
Exercise Area for Pets: Nearby,
    scooper law
Rates: $32 to $42

OLYMPIA

Olympia's West Water Inn
2300 Evergreen Pk Dr.
Olympia, WA 98502
Phone: (206) 943-4000

Pet Restrictions: $25
Pet left unattended in room: Yes,
Exercise Area for Pets: Nearby
Rates: $79 to $89

VETERINARIANS

Olympia Veterinary Hospital
155 Division NW
Phone: (206) 352-7561

Smith, John L.
7248 Capitol Blvd.
Phone: (206) 943-8144

PASCO
Val-U-Inn
1800 W. Lewis St.
Pasco, WA 98361
Phone: (509) 547-0791

Pet Restrictions: $5 day
Pet left unattended in room: Yes
Exercise Area for Pets: Nearby
Rates: $44

VETERINARIANS
Ferguson, DE
1912 N. Fourth St.
Phone: (509) 547-1781

Watson, Sharon A.
4420 Road 108
Phone: (509) 545-9949

POULSBO
Evergreen Motel
18680 Hwy 305
Poulsbo, WA 98370
Phone: (206) 779-3921

Pet Restrictions: $5 charge
Pet left unattended in room: Yes
Exercise Area for Pets: Yes,
    scooper law
Rates: $50 to $85

VETERINARIANS
Poulsbo Marine Vetny Clinic
P.O. Box 1687
Phone: (206) 779-4166

O'Donnell, Douglas
10310 Central Valley Rd. NE
Phone: (206) 692-6162

PULLMAN
Cougar Land Motel
120 W. Main St.
Pullman, WA 99163
Phone: (509) 334-3535

Pet Restrictions: $10 dep. (refund.)
Exercise Area for Pets: Nearby
Rates: $32.25

**Quality Inn Paradise Creek
    Motor Inn**
SE 1050 Johnson Ave.
Pullman, WA 99163
Phone: (509) 332-0500

Pet Restrictions: None
Pet left unattended in room: Yes
Exercise Area for Pets: Nearby
Rates: $50 to $65

VETERINARIANS
Washington State University
Phone: (509) 335-0711

Robinette, Linda R.
Route 1, Box 609
Phone: (509) 332-6575

PUYALLUP
Northwest Motor Inn
1409 S. Meridian St.
Puyallup, WA 98271
Phone: (206) 841-2600

Pet Restrictions: $5 day/pet (small
    pets only)
Exercise Area for Pets: Nearby
Rates: $43 to $47

VETERINARIANS
South Hill Veterinary Clinic
9602 112th Street East
Phone: (206) 848-1503

Leahy, Suzanne C.
11504 89th Avenue Court East
Phone: (206) 841-5924

Shirley, Susan M.
14816 S. Meridian
Phone: (206) 848-1563

QUINAULT
Lake Quinault Lodge
South Shore Rd., Box 7
Quinault, WA 98575
Phone: (206) 288-2571

Pet Restrictions: $10 day/pet
Pet left unattended in room: Yes
Exercise Area for Pets: Nearby,
    leash required
Rates: $90 to $110

RICHLAND
Bali Hi Motel
1201 George Washington Way
Richland, WA 99352
Phone: (509) 943-3101

Pet Restrictions: $10 charge
Exercise Area for Pets: Nearby
Rates: $39 to $44

Columbia Center Dunes Motel
1751 Towler Ave.
Richland, WA 99352
Phone: (509) 783-8181

Pet Restrictions: None
Exercise Area for Pets: Nearby
Rates: $34 to $37

Nendel's Valu Inn
615 Jadwin
Richland, WA 99352
Phone: (509) 943-4611

Pet Restrictions: $5/day/pet
Exercise Area for Pets: Nearby
Rates: $44.20

Richland Towers
1515 George Washington Way
Richland, WA 99352
Phone: (509) 946-4121

Pet Restrictions: Small pets only
(waiver)
Exercise Area for Pets: Nearby
Rates: $80

Shilo Inn Richland Rivershore
50 Comstock St.
Richland, WA 99352
Phone: (509) 946-4661,
(800) 222-2244

Pet Restrictions: $6/pet/day
Exercise Area for Pets: Yes
Rates: $48 to $80

VETERINARIANS

Animal Medical Center
1530 Jadwin Avenue
Phone: (509) 943-5671

Desert Veterinary Clinic
42 Goethals Dr.
Phone: (509) 946-4138

Richland Animal Hospital
2666 Van Griesen
Phone: (509) 946-7877

RIMROCK
Game Ridge Motel
27350 Hwy. 12
Rimrock, WA 98937
Phone: (509) 672-2212

Pet Restrictions: $2/pet/day
Exercise Area for Pets: Yes
Rates: $38 to $79.50

RITZVILLE
Best Western Heritage Inn
1405 Smithy's Blvd.
Ritzville, WA 99169
Phone: (509) 659-1007

Pet Restrictions: Smoking rooms only
Pet left unattended in room: Yes
Exercise Area for Pets: Yes
Rates: $58 to $63

Colwell Motor Inn
501 W. 1st Ave.
Ritzville, WA 99169
Phone: (509) 659-1620

Pet Restrictions: $2 day/pet (small
pets only)
Pet left unattended in room: Yes
Exercise Area for Pets: Nearby
Rates: $38 to $44

SAN JUAN ISLAND
Wharfside B&B
P.O. Box 1212
San Juan Island, WA 98250
Phone: (206) 378-5661

Pet Restrictions: Small pets only
Exercise Area for Pets: Nearby
Rates: $80 to $85

SEATTLE
The Alexis Hotel
1007 First Ave.
Seattle, WA 98104
Phone: (206) 624-4844

Pet Restrictions: None
Pet left unattended in room: Yes
Exercise Area for Pets: Nearby
Rates: $110 to $120

Best Western Exec. Inn
200 Taylor Ave. N
Seattle, WA 98109
Phone: (206) 448-9444

Pet Restrictions: $25 charge (small
pets only)
Exercise Area for Pets: Nearby
Rates: $103 to $126

Days Inn - Town Center
2205 7th Ave.
Seattle, WA 98121
Phone: (206) 448-3434

Pet Restrictions: $3 charge (small
pets only)
Pet left unattended in room: Yes
Exercise Area for Pets: Nearby
Rates: $85

Doubletree Inn
205 Strander Blvd.
Seattle, WA 98188
Phone: (206) 246-8220
Pet Restrictions: $20 charge/pet
    (small pets only)
Exercise Area for Pets: Nearby
Rats: $69 to $128

Howard Johnson
17108 Pacific Hwy S.
Seattle, WA 98188
Phone: (206) 244-1230
Pet Restrictions: $10 charge
Pet left unattended in room: Yes
Exercise Area for Pets: Nearby
Rates: $55 to $60

La Quinta Motor Inn
2824 S. 188th St.
Seattle, WA 98188
Phone: (206) 241-5211
Pet Restrictions: None
Exercise Area for Pets: Nearby
Rates: $70 to $77

The Marriott Resid. Inn Seattle S
16201 W. Valley Hwy, PO Box 88904
Seattle, WA 98188
Phone: (206) 226-5500
Pet Restrictions: $10/pet
Pet left unattended in room: Yes
Exercise Area for Pets: Nearby
Rates: $89 to $120

Ramada Inn
2140 N. Northgate Way
Seattle, WA 98133
Phone: (206) 365-0700
Pet Restrictions: Ground floor only
Exercise Area for Pets: Nearby
Rates: $72 to $86

Rodeside Lodge
12501 Aurora Ave. N.
Seattle, WA 98133
Phone: (206) 364-7771
Pet Restrictions: $3 (small pets only)
Exercise Area for Pets: Nearby
Rates: $48 to $50

Town & Country Suites
14800 Interurban Ave. S.
Seattle, WA 98168
Phone: (206) 246-2323
Pet Restrictions: $8.66/day, under
    40 lbs.
Pet left unattended in room: Yes
Exercise Area for Pets: Nearby
Rates: $47 to $49

Warwick
4th Ave. & Lenora St.
Seattle, WA 98121
Phone: (206) 443-4300
Pet Restrictions: Waiver (small pets
    only)
Pet left unattended in room: Yes
Exercise Area for Pets: Nearby
Rates: $118 to $185

VETERINARIANS

Aurora Veterinary Hosp.
8821 Aurora Avenue North
Phone: (206) 525-6666

Five Corners Vetny Hospital
112 SW 157th St.
Phone: (206) 243-2982

Greentree Animal Hospital
4440 California Avenue SW
Phone: (206) 932-5593

SPOKANE

Broadway Motel
6317 E. Broadway
Spokane, WA 99212
Phone: (509) 535-2442
Pet Restrictions: Small pets only
Exercise Area for Pets: Nearby
Rates: $66 to $74

Cavanaugh's River Inn
N 700 Division St.
Spokane, WA 99202
Phone: (509) 326-5577
Pet Restrictions: Small pets only
Pet left unattended in room: Yes
Exercise Area for Pets: Nearby
Rates: $74 to $99

Comfort Inn
6309 E. Broadway
Spokane, WA 99212
Phone: (509) 535-7185
Pet Restrictions: None
Exercise Area for Pets: Nearby
Rates: $65 to $74

Days Inn
1919 N. Hutchinson Rd.
Spokane, WA 99212
Phone: (509) 926-5399

Pet Restrictions: Small pets only
Pet left unattended in room: Yes
Exercise Area for Pets: Nearby
Rates: $45 to $55

Friendship Inn
4301 W. Sunset Highway
Spokane, WA 99210
Phone: (509) 838-1471

Pet Restrictions: $15 day, 1st fl. only
Exercise Area for Pets: Nearby
Rates: $49 to $55

Liberty Motel
6801 N. Division
Spokane, WA 99208
Phone: (509) 467-6000

Pet Restrictions: Small pets only
Exercise Area for Pets: Nearby
Rates: $38 to $60

Quality Inn - Valley
905 Sullivan Rd. N, PO Box 141152
Spokane, WA 99214
Phone: (509) 924-3838

Pet Restrictions: $15; 2 rooms only
Exercise Area for Pets: Nearby
Rates: $60

Ramada Inn Spokane Intl Airpt.
P.O. Box 19228
Spokane, WA 99219
Phone: (509) 838-5211

Pet Restrictions: None
Exercise Area for Pets: Nearby
Rates: $69

Red Lion Motor Inn
1100 Sullivan Rd. N, P.O. Box 3385
Spokane, WA 99220
Phone: (509) 924-9000

Pet Restrictions: Small pets only
Exercise Area for Pets: Nearby
Rates: $79

Shangri La Motel
2922 W. Govt. Way
Spokane, WA 99204
Phone: (509) 747-2066

Pet Restrictions: Small pets only
Exercise Area for Pets: Nearby
Rate: $42

Shilo Inn Spokane
E 923 Third Ave.
Spokane, WA 99202
Phone: (509) 535-9000,
     (800) 222-2244

Pet Restrictions: $6/pet/day
Pet left unattended in room: Yes
Exercise Area for Pets: Nearby
Rates: $45 to $59

Super 8 Motel
N 2020 Argonne Rd.
Spokane, WA 99212
Phone: (509) 928-4888

Pet Restrictions: $25 dep. (refund.)
Pet left unattended in room: Yes
Exercise Area for Pets: Nearby
Rates: $54 to $69

Travelodge Motor Inn
827 W. First Ave.
Spokane, WA 99204
Phone: (509) 456-8040

Pet Restrictions: $25 dep./pet
Exercise Area for Pets: Yes
Rates: $38 to $49

VETERINARIANS

Animal Clinic Spokane
6322 North Wall St.
Phone: (509) 467-7100

Brown, Terry John
East 21 Mission
Phone: (509) 326-6670

Streeter, Ronald J.
N6825 Country Homes Rd.
Phone: (509) 326-3465

SUNNYSIDE
Nendel's Motor Inn
408 Yakima Valley Hwy
Sunnyside, WA 98944
Phone: (509) 837-7878

Pet Restrictions: None
Pet left unattended in room: Yes
Exercise Area for Pets: Nearby,
     scooper law
Rates: $41.50 to $43

Town House Motel
509 Yakima Valley Hwy
Sunnyside, WA 98944
Phone: (509) 837-5500

Pet Restrictions: None
Exercise Area for Pets: Nearby
Rates: $35 to $50

TACOMA

Best Western Exec. Inn
5700 Pacific Hwy E.
Tacoma, WA 98424
Phone: (206) 922-0080

Pet Restrictions: Waiver & $25 dep.
   $10 refund
Exercise Area for Pets: Nearby
Rates: $69

Nendel's Motor Inn
8702 S. Hosmer St.
Tacoma, WA 98444
Phone: (206) 535-3100

Pet Restrictions: Small pets only,
   $4/day/pet ($50 refundable dep.)
Pet left unattended in room: Yes
Exercise Area for Pets: Nearby
Rates: $64 to $69

Royal Coachman Motor Inn
5805 Pacific Hwy E.
Tacoma, WA 98424
Phone: (206) 922-2500

Pet Restrictions: $25 dep. (refund.)
Pet left unattended in room: Yes
Exercise Area for Pets: Nearby
Rates: $58

Sheraton-Tacoma Hotel
1320 Broadway Plaza
Tacoma, WA 98402
Phone: (206) 572-3200

Pet Restrictions: Small pets only,
   $50 dep. (refundable)
Pet left unattended in room: Yes
Exercise Area for Pets: Nearby,
   leash required
Rates: $112 to $115

Sherwood Inn
8402 S. Hosmer St.
Tacoma, WA 98444
Phone: (206) 535-2800

Pet Restrictions: $6 days,
   small pets only
Pet left unattended in room: Yes
Exercise Area for Pets: Nearby
Rates: $44 to $54

Shilo Inn
7414 S. Hosmer
Tacoma, WA 98408
Phone: (206) 475-4020

Pet Restrictions: $6/day/pet
Pet left unattended in room: Yes
Exercise Area for Pets: Nearby
Rates: $70

VETERINARIANS

Bridgeport Way Vetny Hosp.
11419 Bridgeport Way SW
Phone: (206) 588-1851

Chambers Creek Vetny Hosp.
7521 Bridgeport Way West
Phone: (206) 475-7831

Nash, Pamela J.
8862 Tacoma Avenue South
Phone: (206) 537-0241

TUMWATER

Tyee Hotel
500 Tyee Dr.
Tumwater, WA 98502
Phone: (206) 352-0511

Pet Restrictions: $6 day/pet
Pet left unattended in room: Yes
Exercise Area for Pets: Nearby
Rates: $73 to $78

VETERINARIANS

Collins, Robert L.
7248 Capitol Blvd.
Phone: (206) 943-8144

TWISP

Idle-A-While Motel
505 N. Hwy. 20
Twisp, WA 98856
Phone: (509) 997-3222

Pet Restrictions: Just dogs,
   $1/day/pet
Pet left unattended in room: Yes
Exercise Area for Pets: Yes
Rates: $34 to $60

VANCOUVER

Shilo Inn Downtown Vancouver
401 E. 13th St.
Vancouver, WA 98660
Phone: (206) 696-0411,
   (800) 222-2244

Pet Restrictions: $6/pet/day
Exercise Area for Pets: Yes
Rates: $65 to $80

Shilo Inn - Haze Dell
13206 Hwy 99
Vancouver, WA 98686
Phone: (206) 573-0511,
   (800) 222-2244

Pet Restrictions: $6.46/pet/day
Exercise Area for Pets: Yes
Rates: $59 to $75

Vancouver Travelodge
601 Broadway
Vancouver, WA 98660
Phone: (206) 693-3668
Pet Restrictions: Small dogs only,
$5/pet/day
Exercise Area for Pets: Nearby
Rates: $38 to $65

VETERINARIANS

Columbia Veterinary Center
5106 NE 78th Street
Phone: (206) 694-9514

Feline Medical Clinic
10461 NE Fourth Plain Rd.
Phone: (206) 892-0224

Mountain View Vetny Hosp.
13914 NE 16th Avenue
Phone: (206) 574-7290

WALLA WALLA
Capri Motel
2003 Melrose St.
Walla Walla, WA 99362
Phone: (509) 525-1130
Pet Restrictions: $5/pet
Exercise Area for Pets: Yes
Rates: $42 to $46

Econo Lodge
305 N. 2nd Ave.
Walla Walla, WA 99362
Phone: (509) 529-4410,
(800) 446-6900
Pet Restrictions: $5 p.p. flat fee
Exercise Area for Pets: Yes
Rates: $39 to $43

VETERINARIANS

Associated Veterinary Clinic
208 Wildwood
Phone: (509) 525-2502

WENATCHEE
Econo Lodge
700 N. Wenatchee Ave.
Wenatchee, WA 98801
Phone: (509) 663-8133,
(800) 424-4777
Pet Restrictions: $5/pet/day
Exercise Area for Pets: Nearby
Rates: $35 to $45

Red Lion Motor Inn
1225 N. Wenatchee Ave.
Wenatchee, WA 98801
Phone: (509) 663-0711,
(800) 547-8010
Pet Restrictions: Yes
Pet left unattended in room: Yes
Rates: $69 to $150

VETERINARIANS

Cascade Veterinary Clinic
2127 N. Wenatchee Avenue
Phone: (509) 663-0793

WOODLAND
Scandia Motel
1123 Hoffman St.
Woodland, WA 98674
Phone: (206) 225-8006
Pet Restrictions: $5/pet
Exercise Area for Pets: Yes
Rates: $40 to $50

YAKIMA
Colonial Motor Inn
1405 N. First St.
Yakima, WA 98901
Phone: (509) 453-8981
Pet Restrictions: Small pets,
$5/pet/day
Exercise Area for Pets: Yes
Rates: $39 to $71

Huntley Inn
12 Valley Mall Blvd.
Yakima, WA 98903
Phone: (509) 248-6924,
(800) 448-5544 X-5
Pet Restrictions: None
Rates: $49 to $71.21

Red Lion Motel
818 N. 1st St.
Yakima, WA 98901
Phone: (509) 453-0391
Pet Restrictions: Small pets
Pet left unattended in room: Yes
Exercise Area for Pets: Yes

VETERINARIANS

Ruark, Stephen A.
3901 Tieton Dr.
Phone: (509) 966-4000

WEST VIRGINIA — HOTELS

BECKLEY

Beckley Hotel
1940 Harper Rd.
Beckley, WV 25801
Phone: (304) 252-8661,
(800) 274-6010

Pet Restrictions: None
Exercise Area for Pets: Nearby
Rates: $55 to $200

Comfort Inn
1909 Harper Rd.
Beckley, WV 25801
Phone: (304) 255-2161,
(800) 228-5150

Pet Restrictions: $10 deposit
Pet left unattended in room: Yes, no
maid service
Exercise Area for Pets: Nearby
Rates: $43 to $68

BLUEFIELD

Econo Lodge
3400 Cumberland Rd.
Bluefield, WV 24701
Phone: (304) 327-8171

Pet Restrictions: $5
Pet left unattended in room: Yes
Exercise Area for Pets: Yes
Rates: $38 to $45

Ramada Inn
US 52N
Bluefield, WV 24701
Phone: (304) 325-5421

Pet Restrictions: Small pets only
Exercise Area for Pets: Yes
Rates: $49 to $62

BRIDGEPORT

Knights Inn
1235 W. Main St.
Bridgeport, WV 26330
Phone: (304) 842-7115,
(800) 843-5644

Pet Restrictions: None
Pet left unattended in room: Yes
Exercise Area for Pets: Yes
Rates: $36.95 to $46.95

VETERINARIANS
Eisen, Sharon J.
Route 1, Box 5Q
Phone: (304) 842-4836

BUCKHANNON

Baxa Hotel
21 N. Kanawha St.
Buckhannon, WV 26201
Phone: (304) 472-2500

Pet Restrictions: Notify desk
Pet left unattended in room: Yes,
notify housekeeper
Exercise Area for Pets: Yes
Rates: $29 to $38

BURNSVILLE

Burnsville Motel 79
5th Ave. & Main St.
Burnsville, WV 26335
Phone: (304) 853-2918

Pet Restrictions: 1 room, $4 extra
Pet left unattended in room: Yes
Exercise Area for Pets: Yes
Rates: $26 to $31

CHARLESTON

Holiday Inn Charleston House
600 Kanawha Blvd. E.
Charleston, WV 25301
Phone: (304) 344-4092,
(800) HOLIDAY

Pet Restrictions: None
Pet left unattended in room: Yes
Exercise Area for Pets: Nearby
Rates: $65 to $84

Holiday Inn Heart O Town
1000 Washington St.
Charleston, WV 25301
Phone: (304) 343-4661,
(800) HOLIDAY

Pet Restrictions: None
Pet left unattended in room: Yes, if
quiet
Exercise Area for Pets: Yes
Rates: $51 to $68

Knights Inn
6401 MacCorkle Ave SE
Charleston E, WV
Phone: (304) 925-0451,
(800) 843-5644

Pet Restrictions: None
Pet left unattended in room: Yes,
well behaved
Exercise Area for Pets: Yes
Rates: $34.95 to $62.95

VETERINARIANS
Kanawha City Vetny Hosp.
5405 MacCorkle Ave. SE
Phone: (304) 925-4974

Pfost, John J.
1246 Greenbrier St.
Phone: (304) 342-1731

CROSS LANES
Motel 6
330 Goff Mt. Rd.
Cross Lanes, WV 25313
Phone: (304) 776-5911

Pet Restrictions: 1 small pet
Exercise Area for Pets: Yes
Rates: $28.95 to $40.95

VETERINARIANS
Warner Jr., Charles C.
524 Goff Mountain Road
Phone: (304) 776-4501

DAVIS
Highlander Village
on SR 32, P.O. Box 656
Davis, WV 26260
Phone: (304) 259-5551

Pet Restrictions: $10
Pet left unattended in room: Yes
Exercise Area for Pets: Yes
Rates: $32 to $39

ELKINS
Best Western of Elkins
Rt. 250, 219 S
Elkins, WV 26241
Phone: (304) 636-7711,
    (800) 528-1234

Pet Restrictions: $5/night
Pet left unattended in room: Yes, no
    maid service
Exercise Area for Pets: Yes
Rates: $37 to $56

Econo Lodge
Rt. 33 E
Elkins, WV 26241
Phone: (304) 636-5311,
    (800) 424-4777

Pet Restrictions: None
Pet left unattended in room: Yes
Exercise Area for Pets: Nearby
Rates: $34.34 to $38.15

Elkins Motor Lodge
830 Harrison Ave.
Elkins, WV 26241
Phone: (304) 636-1400

Pet Restrictions: Notify management
Pet left unattended in room: Yes,
    notify management
Exercise Area for Pets: Yes
Rates: $33 to $42

FAIRMONT
Fairmont Holiday Inn
East Grafton Rd.
Fairmont, WV 26554
Phone: (304) 366-5500,
    (800) HOLIDAY

Pet Restrictions: None
Pet left unattended in room: Yes
Exercise Area for Pets: Yes
Rates: $42 to $75

Red Roof Inn
Rt. 1
Fairmont, WV 26554
Phone: (304) 366-6800,
    (800) 843-7663

Pet Restrictions: None
Pet left unattended in room: Yes
Exercise Area for Pets: Yes
Rates: $28.99 to $43.99

VETERINARIANS
Middletown Animal Clinic
Route 5
Phone: (304) 366-6130

Moore, Dennis J.
1313 Fairmont Ave.
Phone: (304) 363-0930

FAYETTEVILLE
Comfort Inn - New River
Laurel Creek Rd.
Fayetteville, WV 25840
Phone: (304) 574-3443

Pet Restrictions: None
Pet left unattended in room: Yes
Exercise Area for Pets: Yes
Rates: $44 to $59

HARPERS FERRY
Cliffside Inn & Conf. Ctr.
US Rt 340
Harpers Ferry, WV 25425
Phone: (304) 535-6302,
    (800) 786-9437

Pet Restrictions: $5/pet/night, annex
    building only
Pet left unattended in room: Yes
Exercise Area for Pets: Yes
Rates: $45 to $71

HUNTINGTON

Econolodge
3325 Hwy 60E
Huntington, WV 25705
Phone: (304) 529-1331,
    (800) 4-CHOICE

Pet Restrictions: None
Pet left unattended in room: Yes, if
    behaved
Exercise Area for Pets: Yes
Rates: $36.95 to $53.95

Red Roof Inn
5190 US Rt 60 E
Huntington, WV 25705
Phone: (304) 733-3737

Pet Restrictions: None
Pet left unattended in room: Yes
Exercise Area for Pets: Yes
Rates: $36.99 to $51.99

VETERINARIANS

Ayers Animal Hospital
1514 Norway Ave.
Phone: (304) 529-6049

Huntington Dog and Cat Hosp.
200 5th Street West
Phone: (304) 525-5121

Crow, Don G.
313 3rd Ave.
Phone: (304) 525-7629

HURRICANE

Smiley's Hotel
419 Hurricane St.
Hurricane, WV 25526
Phone: (304) 562-3346,
    (800) 726-7016

Pet Restrictions: Only 1 night
Exercise Area for Pets: Yes
Rates: $33.50 and up

VETERINARIANS

Ward, Sharon
155 Green Acres
Phone: (304) 776-1000

JANE LEW

**Wilderness Plantation Inn &
Restaurant**
Rt. 7, Berlin Rd.
Jane Lew, WV 26378
Phone: (304) 884-7806

Pet Restrictions: $5/night
Pet left unattended in room: Yes, in
    cage
Exercise Area for Pets: Yes
Rates: $40.85 to $75.85

KANAWHA

Red Roof Inn
6305 MacCorkle Ave. SE
Kanawha, WV 25304
Phone: (304) 925-6953

Pet Restrictions: Small pets
Pet left unattended in room: Yes
Exercise Area for Pets: Yes
Rates: $37.99 to $50.99

LEWISBURG

Brier Inn
Rt. 219
Lewisburg, WV 24901
Phone: (304) 645-7722

Pet Restrictions: $10 deposit,
    certain rooms
Pet left unattended in room: Yes
Exercise Area for Pets: Yes
Rates: $42 to $75

Budget Host Fort Savannah Inn
204 N. Jeff St.
Lewisburg, WV 24901
Phone: (304) 645-3055,
    (800) 678-3055

Pet Restrictions: None
Exercise Area for Pets: Nearby
Rates: $45 and up

General Lewis Inn
301 E. Washington Rd.
Lewisburg, WV 24901
Phone: (304) 645-2600,
    (800) 628-4454

Pet Restrictions: $5/night, 1st floor
    only
Pet left unattended in room: Yes,
    well behaved
Exercise Area for Pets: Yes
Rates: $49.05 and up

Old Colony Days Inn
635 N. Jeff St.
Lewisburg, WV 24901
Phone: (304) 645-2345,
    (800) 325-2525

Pet Restrictions: $7/night
Exercise Area for Pets: Yes
Rates: $48 and up

VETERINARIANS

Lewisburg Vetny Hospital
US Route 60 West
Phone: (304) 645-1434

Shapira, John F.
Route 6
Phone: (304) 645-1476

Wilson, John R.
Route 4
Phone: (304) 645-1476

MARLINTON
Marlinton Motor Inn
US 219 N
Marlinton, WV 24954
Phone: (304) 799-4711

Pet Restrictions: $5/night
Pet left unattended in room: Yes
Exercise Area for Pets: Yes
Rates: $37.95 plus $6 extra per
    person

MARTINSBURG
Krista Lite Motel
Rt. 1
Martinsburg WV 25401
Phone: (304) 263-0906

Pet Restrictions: No cats
Exercise Area for Pets: Yes
Rates: $34.88 to $39.25

Martinsburg Arborgate Inn
1599 Edwin Miller Blvd.
Martinsburg, WV 25401
Phone: (304) 267-2211,
    (800) 843-5644

Pet Restrictions: None
Pet left unattended in room: Yes, no
    maid service
Exercise Area for Pets: Yes
Rates: $38.95 to $45.95

VETERINARIANS
Gilpin, Kay W.
P.O. Box 466
Phone: (304) 263-2112

PARKERSBURG
Parkersburg Best Western Inn
US 50 & I 77
Parkersburg, WV 26101
Phone: (304) 485-6551,
    (800) 528-1234

Pet Restrictions: Small dogs at
    manager's discretion
Exercise Area for Pets: Yes
Rates: $32 to $48

Red Roof Inn
3714 7th St.
Parkersburg, WV 26101
Phone: (304) 485-1741,
    (800) 843-7663

Pet Restrictions: None
Pet left unattended in room: Yes
Exercise Area for Pets: Yes
Rates: $32.99 to $53.99

VETERINARIANS
Dudley Ave. Small Animal Clinic
3200 Dudley Ave.
Phone: (304) 485-5541

Parkersburg Animal Hospital
46 Campbell Dr. Suite 6
Phone: (304) 422-6971

Rhodes, Michael D.
1504 36th Street
Phone: (304) 422-6972

PRINCETON
Days Inn
Rt. 460, I-77
Princeton, WV 24740
Phone: (304) 425-8100,
    (800) 325-2525

Pet Restrictions: $5/day/pet
Pet left unattended in room: Yes,
    owner responsible
Exercise Area for Pets: Yes
Rates: $50 to $60

Econo Lodge
901 Oakvale Rd.
Princeton, WV 24740
Phone: (304) 487-6161

Pet Restrictions: $5/day
Exercise Area for Pets: Yes
Rates: $31 to $38

Town-N-Country Motel
805 Oakvale Rd.
Princetown, WV 24740
Phone: (304) 425-8156

Pet Restrictions: $5/day, small pets
    only
Pet left unattended in room: Yes if
    behaved and quiet
Exercise Area for Pets: Yes
Rates: $33 to $45

S. CHARLESTON

Red Roof Inn
4006 MacCorkle Ave. SW
S. Charleston, WV 25309
Phone: (304) 744-1500,
(800) 843-7663

Pet Restrictions: None
Pet left unattended in room: Yes,
notify office
Exercise Area for Pets: Yes
Rates: $36 to $54.99

VETERINARIANS
Gunnoe, Paul G.
1113 D Jefferson Rd.
Phone: (304) 744-2214

ST. ALBANS

Days Inn
6210 MacCorble Ave. SW
St. Albans, WV 25177
Phone: (304) 766-6231,
(800) 669-7815

Pet Restrictions: Small pets only
Pet left unattended in room: Yes
Exercise Area for Pets: Yes
Rates: $36.50 to $48.50

WEIRTON

Best Western
350 Three Springs Dr.
Weirton, WV 26062
Phone: (304) 723-5522,
(800) 528-1234

Pet Restrictions: None
Pet left unattended in room: Yes if
quiet, no maid service, owner
responsible for damage
Exercise Area for Pets: Yes
Rates: $50 to $70

WESTON

Comfort Inn
Exit 99 I-79
Weston, WV 26452
Phone: (304) 269-7000,
(800) 221-2222

Pet Restrictions: $5/pet
Pet left unattended in room: Yes
Exercise Area for Pets: Yes
Rates: $36 to $48

WHEELING

Wheeling Days Inn
I-70 Dallas Pike
Wheeling, WV 26059
Phone: (304) 547-0610,
(800) 325-2525

Pet Restrictions: Smoking rooms
only
Exercise Area for Pets: Yes
Rates: $39 to $47

Wilson Lodge at Oglebay
SR 88 N
Wheeling, WV 26003
Phone: (304) 242-3000,
(800) 624-6988

Pet Restrictions: Cabins only
Pet left unattended in room: Yes
Exercise Area for Pets: Yes, on leash
Rates: $88 to $124

WHITE SULPHER SPRINGS

Colonial Court Motel
830 E. Main St.
White Sulpher Springs, WV 24986
Phone: (304) 536-2121

Pet Restrictions: Small pets only
Exercise Area for Pets: Nearby
Rates: $35 to $46

WINFIELD

Days Inn
Putnam Village Drive
Winfield, WV 25569
Phone: (304) 757-8721,
(800) 325-2525

Pet Restrictions: None
Pet left unattended in room: Yes
Exercise Area for Pets: Yes
Rates: $32.94 to $40

Red Roof Inn
P.O. Box 468 Hurricane
Winfield, WV 25526
Phone: (304) 757-6392,
(800) THE ROOF

Pet Restrictions: Small pets only
Exercise Area for Pets: Yes, notify
desk
Exercise Area for Pets: Yes
Rates: $30.99 to $44.99

WISCONSIN — HOTELS

APPLETON

Best West. Midway Motor Lodge
3033 W. College Ave.
Appleton, WI 54914
Phone: (414) 731-4141

Pet Restrictions: $10/per/night
Exercise Area for Pets: Yes
Rates: $65 to $80

Budgetel Inn
3920 W. College Ave.
Appleton, WI 54914
Phone: (414) 734-6070

Pet Restrictions: 1 pet room
Exercise Area for Pets: Yes
Rates: $49

Woodfield Suites
3730 W. College
Appleton, WI 54914
Phone: (414) 734-9231

Pet Restrictions: 2 pet rooms
Pet left unattended in room: Yes
Exercise Area for Pets: Nearby
Rates: $56

Chuchel, Dennis P.
1001 W. Northland Ave.
Phone: (414) 739-7816

Mikula, Wayne M.
210 S. Bluemound Dr.
Phone: (414) 739-2396

BEAVER DAM

Grand View Motel
1510 N. Center St.
Beaver Dam, WI 53916
Phone: (414) 885-9208

Pet Restrictions: None
Pet left unattended in room: Yes
Exercise Area for Pets: Yes
Rates: $26.40 to $38.50

Super 8 Motel
711 Park Ave.
Beaver Dam, WI 53916
Phone: (414) 887-8880

Pet Restrictions: $50 deposit
Exercise Area for Pets: Yes
Rates: $40 to $51

Fredericks, Jacquelyn M.
N8363 Schultz Rd.
Phone: (414) 887-8476

Siegfried, Wayne D.
1206 Declark
Phone: (414) 885-4148

BLACK RIVER FALLS

Best West. Arrowhead Lodge
I-94 & Hwy 54 RR4
Black River Falls, WI 54615
Phone: (715) 284-9471

Pet Restrictions: Medium size
Exercise Area for Pets: Yes
Rates: $40 to $130

Pines Motor Lodge
Rt. 4, Box 297
Black River Falls, WI 54615
Phone: (715) 284-5311

Pet Restrictions: None
Exercise Area for Pets: Yes
Rates: $34 to $39

BRANTWOOD

Palmquist's "The Farm"
River Rd., Rt. 1, Box 134
Brantwod, WI 54513
Phone: (715) 564-2558

Pet Restrictions: Well-behaved
Pet left unattended in room: Yes
Exercise Area for Pets: Yes
Rates: $49 to $59

BROOKFIELD

Milwaukee Marriott
375 S. Moorland Rd.
Brookfield, WI 53005
Phone: (414) 786-1100

Pet Restrictions: $20 deposit
Pet left unattended in room: Yes, if
    caged
Exercise Area for Pets: Yes
Rates: $94 to $119

Animal Emergency Center
14335 Beechwood Ave.
Phone: (414) 466-3621

Brook Falls Vetny Hospital
14885 W. Lisbon Rd.
Phone: (414) 781-5277

Burleigh Road Animal Hosp.
13725 W. Burleigh Rd.
Phone: (414) 781-4400

BARABOO

Thunderbird Motor Inn
1013 8th St.
Baraboo, WI 53913
Phone: (608) 356-7757

Pet Restrictions: None
Pet left unattended in room: No
Exercise Area for Pets: Yes
Rates: $36 to $75

CABLE

Lakewoods Resort
Rt. 2, Box 715
Cable, WI 54821
Phone: (715) 794-2561

Pet Restrictions: $25 fee per week
Pet left unattended in room: Yes
Exercise Area for Pets: Yes
Rates: $69

DUNBAR

Richard Motel
On US 8
Dunbar, WI 54119
Phone: (715) 324-5444

Pet Restrictions: 2 pets, $5 fee
Pet left unattended in room: Yes
Exercise Area for Pets: Yes
Rates: $27 to $44

EAU CLAIRE

Days Inn
2704 Craig Rd.
Eau Claire, WI 54701
Phone: (715) 835-2211

Pet Restrictions: None
Exercise Area for Pets: Yes
Rates: $49 to $57

Exel Inn
2305 Craig Rd.
Eau Claire, WI 54701
Phone: (715) 834-3193

Pet Restrictions: None
Exercise Area for Pets: Yes
Rates: $33 to $43

Heartland Inn
4075 Commonwealth
Eau Claire, WI 54701
Phone: (715) 839-7100

Pet Restrictions: None
Exercise Area for Pets: Yes
Rates: $38 to $52

Holiday Inn
1202 W. Clairemont Ave.
Eau Claire, WI 54701
Phone: (715) 834-3181

Pet Restrictions: None
Exercise Area for Pets: Yes
Rates: $58 to $79

Howard Johnson Motor Lodge
809 W. Clairemont Ave.
Eau Claire, WI 54701
Phone: (715) 834-6611

Pet Restrictions: None
Exercise Area for Pets: Yes
Rates: $62 to $66

VETERINARIANS

Menard, David G.
1025 N. Hastings Way
Phone: (715) 835-0761

FENIMORE

Fenimore Hills Motel
5814 Hwy 18 W
Fenimore, WI 53809
Phone: (608) 822-3281

Pet Restrictions: None
Pet left unattended in room: Yes,
    kennelled
Exercise Area for Pets: Yes
Rates: $49 to $105

FLORENCE

Sunset Dog Boarding Kennels
HCI Box 569
Florence, WI 54121
Phone: (715) 589-2157
Fax: (906) 774-1008

Pet Restrictions: None
Exercise Area for Pets: Yes
Other Areas: Most of our motels do
    not allow pets. Best Western,
    A-1 Cabins, Downtowner do
    allow pets.
Rates: $7 per day

FOND DU LAC

Budgetel Inn
77 Holiday La.
Fond du Lac, WI 54935
Phone: (414) 921-4000

Pet Restrictions: Designated rooms
    only
Exercise Area for Pets: Yes
Rates: $39.95 to $71.95

WISCONSIN — HOTELS (continued)

Traveler's Inn
1325 S. Main St.
Fond du Lac, WI 54935
Phone: (414) 923-0223,
    (800) 585-3010 South only
Pet Restrictions: None
Pet left unattended in room: Yes,
in cage
Exercise Area for Pets: Yes
Rates: $32 to $50

VETERINARIANS

Town & Country Vetny Clinic
961 S. Main St.
Phone: (414) 922-3133

Jung, Joseph S.
161 N. Rolling Meadows Dr.
Phone: (414) 923-6608

GREEN BAY

Best West. Downtowner Motel
321 S. Wash. St.
Green Bay, WI 54301
Phone: (414) 437-8771,
    (800) 252-2952
Pet Restrictions: Small pets only
Exercise Area for Pets: Nearby
Rates: $31.95 to $79.95

Days Inn - Green Bay
406 N. Wash. St.
Green Bay, WI 54301
Phone: (414) 435-4484,
    (800) 325-2525
Pet Restrictions: None
Pet left unattended in room: Yes
Exercise Area for Pets: Yes
Rates: $50 to $63

Exel Inn
2870 Ramada Way
Green Bay, WI 54304
Phone: (414) 499-3599,
    (800) 356-8013
Pet Restrictions: None
Exercise Area for Pets: Yes
Rates: $34.99 and up

Green Bay Airport Holiday Inn
2580 S. Ashland Ave.
Green Bay, WI 54304
Phone: (414) 499-5121
Pet Restrictions: Small pets only;
    outside rooms only
Pet left unattended in room: Yes,
    quiet
Exercise Area for Pets: Yes
Rates: $71 to $78

Holiday Inn - City Center
200 Main St.
Green Bay, WI 54301
Phone: (414) 437-5900,
    (800) 465-4329
Pet Restrictions: None
Exercise Area for Pets: Yes, leashed
Rates: $66 to $68

Ramada Inn
2750 Ramada Way
Green Bay, WI 54304
Phone: (414) 499-0631,
    (800) 228-2828
Pet Restrictions: Yes, small pets
    w/some restrictions
Exercise Area for Pets: Yes
Rates: $53 to $85

Sky Lit Motel
2120 S. Ashland Ave.
Green Bay, WI 54304
Phone: (414) 494-5641
Pet Restrictions: Yes, leashed
Exercise Area for Pets: Yes
Rates: $28.50 to $40.00

Valley Motel
116 N. Military Ave.
Green Bay, WI 54303
Phone: (414) 494-3455
Pet Restrictions: None
Pet left unattended in room: Yes,
    in cage
Exercise Area for Pets: Yes
Rates: $36.30 to $50.60

VETERINARIANS

Bay East Animal Hospital
1475 Lime Kiln Rd.
Phone: (414) 468-5800

Roningen-Nyren Animal Hosp.
1030 Willard Dr.
Phone: (414) 499-0805

Green Bay Animal Hosp.
1518 W. Mason St.
Phone: (414) 494-2221

HAYWOOD

Ross' Teal Lake Lodge
Rt. 7A
Haywood, WI 54843
Phone: (715) 462-3631
Pet Restrictions: $3 fee/day
Pet left unattended in room: Yes
Exercise Area for Pets: Yes, with
    supervision
Rates: $95 to $280

WISCONSIN — HOTELS (continued)

HURLEY

Holiday Inn
1000 10th Ave.
Hurley, WI 54534
Phone: (715) 561-3030

Pet Restrictions: None
Exercise Area for Pets: Yes
Rates: $39 to $62

IRON RIVER

Lumbermens Inn
P.O. Box 723
Iron River, WI 54847
Phone: (715) 372-4515,
  (800) 569-4169

Pet Restrictions: $5/night
  housebroken
Pet left unattended in room: Yes,
  quiet
Exercise Area for Pets: Yes
Rates: $31.95 and up

JOHNSON CREEK

Howard Johnson Motor Lodge
just W of I-94 SR 50 exit
Johnson Creek, WI 53142
Phone: (414) 857-2311

Pet Restrictions: None
Exercise Area for Pets: Yes
Rates: $64 to $69

LA CROSSE

Exel Inn
2150 Rose St.
La Crosse, WI 54601
Phone: (608) 781-0400

Pet Restrictions: None
Exercise Area for Pets: Yes
Rates: $31.99 to $45.99

Roadstar Inn
2622 Rose St.
La Crosse, WI 54601
Phone: (608) 781-3070

Pet Restrictions: $25 deposit
Exercise Area for Pets: Yes
Rates: $34 to $42

VETERINARIANS

Lindesmith, Lisa A.
3812 South 33rd St.
Phone: (608) 788-8820

Spencer, Robert R.
W-5706 Highway 33 State Rd.
Phone: (608) 788-3425

Thompson, Jean
4540 Morman Coulee Rd.
Phone: (608) 788-8820

LADYSMITH

Best West. El Rancho Motel
W 8500 Flambeau Ave.
Ladysmith, WI 54848
Phone: (715) 532-6666

Pet Restrictions: None
Exercise Area for Pets: Yes
Rates: $40 to $44

Evergreen Motel
1201 W. Lake Ave.
Ladysmith, WI 54848
Phone: (715) 532-5611

Pet Restrictions: None
Exercise Area for Pets: Yes
Rates: $33 to $49

LUCK

Luck Country Inn
at jct. SR 35N & SR 48, PO Box 179
Luck, WI
Phone: (715) 472-2000

Pet Restrictions: None
Pet left unattended in room: Yes
Exercise Area for Pets: Yes
Rates: $45 to $48

MADISON

Best West. Midway Motor Lodge
3710 E. Wash. Ave
Madison, WI 53704
Phone: (608) 244-2424

Pet Restrictions: None
Pet left unattended in room: Yes, if
  caged
Exercise Area for Pets: Yes
Rates: $56 to $64

The Collings House
704 E. Gorham St.
Madison, WI 53703
Phone: (608) 255-4230

Pet Restrictions: None
Exercise Area for Pets: Yes
Rates: $65 to $125

Exel Inn
4202 E. Towne Blvd.
Madison, WI 53704
Phone: (608) 241-3861

Pet Restrictions: None
Exercise Area for Pets: Yes
Rates: $35.99 to $47.99

Holiday Inn East Towne
4402 E. Wash. Ave.
Madison, WI 53704
Phone: (608) 244-4703

Pet Restrictions: None
Pet left unattended in room: Yes,
    notify desk
Exercise Area for Pets: Nearby
Rates: $90 to $99

Quality Inn South
4916 E. Broadway
Madison, WI 53716
Phone: (608) 222-5501

Pet Restrictions: None
Pet left unattended in room: Yes,
    in kennel
Exercise Area for Pets: Yes
Rates: $49 to $59

Red Roof Inn
4830 Hayes Rd.
Madison, WI 53704
Phone: (608) 241-1787

Pet Restrictions: None
Pet left unattended in room: Yes
Exercise Area for Pets: Yes
Rates: $43 to $54

VETERINARIANS
University of Wisconsin
2015 Linden Dr.
Phone: (608) 263-7600

Flannigan, Kelly M.
911 Atlas Avenue
Phone: (608) 221-1870

Valenta, Joseph C.
7530 Mineral Point Rd.
Phone: (608) 833-6585

MARSHFIELD
Marshfield Innkeeper
2700 S. Roddis Ave.
Marshfield, WI 54449
Phone: (715) 387-1761

Pet Restrictions: None
Pet left unattended in room: Yes
Exercise Area for Pets: Yes
Rates: $50

VETERINARIANS
Marshfield Veterinary Svc.
512A S. Walnut Ave.
Phone: (715) 387-1119

Krogstad, Roger E.
217 West 14th Street
Phone: (715) 387-1225

MEDFORD
Kramer Motel
321 N. 8th St.
Medford, WI 54451
Phone: (715) 748-4420

Pet Restrictions: None
Exercise Area for Pets: Yes
Rates: $38.50

MILWAUKEE
Budgetel Inn
7141 S. 13th St.
Milwaukee, WI 53154
Phone: (414) 762-2266

Pet Restrictions: Only 2 pet rooms
Pet left unattended in room: Yes
Exercise Area for Pets: Yes
Rates: $45 to $46

Exel Inn - Milwaukee South
1201 W. College Ave.
Milwaukee, WI 53221
Phone: (414) 764-1776

Pet Restrictions: None
Rates: $34.99 to $39

Exel Inn - Milwaukee West
115 N. Mayfair Rd.
Milwaukee, WI 53226
Phone: (414) 257-0140

Pet Restrictions: None
Exercise Area for Pets: Yes
Rates: $36 to $51

Holiday Inn - South
6331 S. 13th St.
Milwaukee, WI 53221
Phone: (414) 764-1500
Pet Restrictions: None
Pet left unattended in room: Yes
Exercise Area for Pets: Yes
Rates: $73 to $80

Ramada Inn - Conv. Ctr.
6401 S. 13th St.
Milwaukee, WI 53221
Phone: (414) 764-5300
Pet Restrictions: None
Pet left unattended in room: Yes
Exercise Area for Pets: Yes
Rates: $68

Residence Inn by Marriott
7275 N. Port Wash. Rd.
Milwaukee, WI 53217
Phone: (414) 352-0070
Pet Restrictions: $175 cleaning fee;
    $6 per day
Pet left unattended in room: Yes
Exercise Area for Pets: Yes
Rates: $91 to $156

VETERINARIANS
Greenfield Veterinary Clinic
5981 South 27th St.
Phone: (414) 282-5230

Lakeside Animal Hospital
211 W. Bender Rd.
Phone: (414) 962-8040

Park Pet Hospital
7378 N. Teutonia Avenue
Phone: (414) 352-1470

MINOCQUA
Northwoods Inn
Jct. US 51 & SR 70 W, PO Box 325
Minocqua, WI 54568
Phone: (715) 356-9541
Pet Restrictions: None
Exercise Area for Pets: Yes
Rates: $42 to $57

NEW GLARUS
Swiss-Aire Motel
1200 SR 69, P.O. Box 253
New Glarus, WI 53574
Phone: (608) 527-2138
Pet Restrictions: $2 fee per pet
Exercise Area for Pets: Yes
Rates: $44 to $65

NEW LISBON
Edge O' The Wood Motel
W 7396 Frontage Rd.
New Lisbon, WI 53950
Phone: (608) 562-3705
Pet Restrictions: Yes
Exercise Area for Pets: Yes
Rates: $25 to $37

OAK CREEK
Knights Inn
9420 S. 20th St.
Oak Creek, WI 53154
Phone: (414) 761-3807
Pet Restrictions: $25 deposit
Pet left unattended in room: Yes,
    if caged
Exercise Area for Pets: Yes
Rates: $37.50 to $51.50

Red Roof Inn
6360 S. 13th St.
Oak Cree, WI 53154
Phone: (414) 764-3500
Pet Restrictions: None
Pet left unattended in room: Yes
Exercise Area for Pets: Yes
Rates: $32.99 to $55.99

OSHKOSH
Holiday Inn Holidome & Meeting Center
500 S. Koeller Rd.
Oshkosh, WI 54901
Phone: (414) 233-1511
Pet Restrictions: Outside room
Pet left unattended in room: Yes
Exercise Area for Pets: Yes
Rates: $60 to $70

Howard Johnson Lodge
1919 Omro Rd.
Oshkosh, WI 54901
Phone: (414) 233-1200

Pet Restrictions: Small pets only
Pet left unattended in room: Yes
Exercise Area for Pets: Yes
Rates: $32.95 to $70

Oshkosh Hilton & Conv. Ctr.
1 N. Main St.
Oshkosh, WI 54901
Phone: (414) 231-5000,
(808) HIL-TONS

Pet Restrictions: Under 20 lbs.
Exercise Area for Pets: Yes, quiet
Rates: $55 to $85

VETERINARIANS
Lakeside Animal Hospital
1834 Algoma Blvd.
Phone: (414) 426-2647

Lorfeld, John H.
2321 Jackson
Phone: (414) 233-8081

OSSEO
Friendship Inn
P.O. Box 7
Osseo, WI 54758
Phone: (715) 597-3175,
(800) 424-4777

Pet Restrictions: $10 deposit -
refundable
Pet left unattended in room: Yes
Exercise Area for Pets: Yes
Rates: $36.75 to $56.70

PLATTEVILLE
Mound View Motel
1455 E. Hwy 151
Platteville, WI 53818
Phone: (608) 348-9518

Pet Restrictions: Yes, small, $20 fee
Pet left unattended in room: Yes
Exercise Area for Pets: Yes
Rates: $35 to $43

PLOVER
Day Stop
5253 Harding Ave., P.O. Box 4
Plover, WI 54467
Phone: (715) 341-7300,
(800) 325-2525

Pet Restrictions: None
Pet left unattended in room: Yes
Exercise Area for Pets: Yes
Rates: $30.66 to $48.18

Elizabeth Inn & Conv. Ctr.
5246 Harding Ave.
Plover, WI 54467
Phone: (715) 341-3131,
(800) 472-8322 WI only

Pet Restrictions: Small pets only
Exercise Area for Pets: Yes
Rates: $33 and up

POYNETTE
Jamieson House
407 N. Franklin St.
Poynette, WI 53955
Phone: (608) 635-4100

Pet Restrictions: With prior approval
Exercise Area for Pets: Yes
Rates: $55 to $100

PRAIRIE DU CHIEN
Best Western Quiet House
Hwy 18135 S
Prairie Du Chien, WI 53821
Phone: (608) 326-4777,
(800) 528-1234

Pet Restrictions: $7/night;
2 rooms only
Exercise Area for Pets: Yes
Rates: $65 to $135

Prairie Motel
1616 Marquette Rd.
Prairie Du Chien, WI 53821
Phone: (608) 326-6461,
(800) 526-3776

Pet Restrictions: None
Pet left unattended in room: Yes
Exercise Area for Pets: Yes
Rates: $32 to $55

RACINE

Holiday Inn
3700 Northwestern Ave.
Racine, WI 53405
Phone: (414) 637-9311,
   (800) HOLIDAY

Pet Restrictions: None
Pet left unattended in room: Yes, no
   maid service
Exercise Area for Pets: Yes
Rates: $56 to $82

VETERINARIANS
**North Shore Animal Hosp. of
   Racine**
4630 Douglas Ave.
Phone: (414) 639-7500

Perry, Curtis A.
4701 Spring St.
Phone: (414) 637-8308

RHINELANDER

Holiday Inn
P.O. Box 675
Rhinelander, WI 54501
Phone: (715) 369-3600,
   (800) HOLIDAY

Pet Restrictions: None
Exercise Area for Pets: Yes
Rates: $53 to $75

RICE LAKE

Curriers Lakeview Resort Motel
on Rice Lake, Rt. 4, Box 464
Rice Lake, WI
Phone: (715) 234-7474,
   (800) 433-5253

Pet Restrictions: None
Exercise Area for Pets: Yes
Rates: $31 to $130

RIPON

Best Western Welcome Inn
240 E. Ford Du Lac St.
Ripon, WI 54971
Phone: (414) 748-2821,
   (800) 241-2821

Pet Restrictions: $10/stay
Exercise Area for Pets: Yes
Rates: $39.50 to $52

SPARTA

Heritage Motel
704 W. Wisconsin Ave.
Sparta, WI 54656
Phone: (608) 269-6991

Pet Restrictions: None
Pet left unattended in room: Yes,
   housebroken
Exercise Area for Pets: Yes, pick up
   after your dogs
Rates: $29 to $39

SPOONER

Green Acres Motel
1 mi. S on US 63, P.O. Box 28
Spooner, WI 54801
Phone: (715) 635-2177

Pet Restrictions: $5 charge
Exercise Area for Pets: Yes
Rates: $35 to $65

ST. CROIX FALLS

Dallas House Motel
P.O. Box 664
St. Croix Falls, WI 54024
Phone: (715) 483-3206,
   (800) 341-8000

Pet Restrictions: None
Exercise Area for Pets: Yes
Rates: $37 to $66

STEVENS POINT

Holiday Inn
1501 N. Point Dr., P.O. Box C
Stevens Point, WI 54481
Phone: (715) 341-1340,
   (800) 922-7880 WI only

Pet Restrictions: Small pets only, if
   not behaved they will have to leave
Exercise Area for Pets: Yes
Rates: $69.95 to $130

Point Motel
209 Division St.
Stevens Point, WI 54481
Phone: (715) 344-8312,
   (800) 344-3093

Pet Restrictions: $3/night
Pet left unattended in room: Yes,
   behaved
Exercise Area for Pets: Yes
Rates: $31 to $44

VETERINARIANS

Community Animal Hospital
3133 Church St.
Phone: (715) 341-1723

STURGEON BAY

Chal-A-Motel
3910 SR 42 & 57
Phone: (414) 743-6788

Pet Restrictions: Non-shedding
   dogs only
Exercise Area for Pets: Yes
Rates: $19 to $44

Holiday Motel
Business R. 42 & 57
Sturgeon Bay, WI 54235
Phone: (414) 743-5571

Pet Restrictions: $5/night
Pet left unattended in room: Yes,
   small periods of time
Exercise Area for Pets: Yes
Rates: $24 to $72

VETERINARIANS

Peninsula Veterinary Service
5654 County T
Phone: (414) 743-7789

SUPERIOR

**Best West. Bridgeview Motor
   Inn**
415 Hammond Ave.
Superior, WI 54880
Phone: (715) 392-8174,
   (800) 777-5572

Pet Restrictions: None
Exercise Area for Pets: Yes
Rates: $49 to $140

Days Inn Bayfront
110 E. 2nd St.
Superior, WI 54880
Phone: (715) 392-4783,
   (800) 325-2525

Pet Restrictions: None
Exercise Area for Pets: Yes
Rates: $38 to $97

VETERINARIANS

Superior Veterinary Clinic
3027 E. Second St.
Phone: (715) 398-6655

TOMAH

Budget Host Day Break Motel
Hwys 12 & 16
Tomah, WI 54660
Phone: (608) 372-5946,
   (800) 999-7088

Pet Restrictions: $4/pet/night
Exercise Area for Pets: Yes
Rates: $32 to $53

Econo Lodge
20050 N. Superior Ave.
Tomah, WI 54660
Phone: (608) 372-9100,
   (800) 424-4777

Pet Restrictions: $5 charge
Exercise Area for Pets: Yes
Rates: $41.95 to $57.95

Lark Inn
229 N. Superior Ave.
Tomah, WI 54660
Phone: (608) 372-5981,
   (800) 477-LARK

Pet Restrictions: $3/pet/night
Exercise Area for Pets: Yes
Rates: $35 to $76

WASHBURN

Super 8 Motel
Harborview Dr., P.O. Box 626
Washburn, WI 54891
Phone: (715) 373-5671,
   (800) 800-8000

Pet Restrictions: Small pets,
   $25 deposit
Exercise Area for Pets: Yes, on leash
Rates: $44.98 and up

Redwood Motel & Chalets
26 W. Bayfield St., P.O. Box 385
Washburn, WI 54891
Phone: (715) 373-5512

Pet Restrictions: None
Exercise Area for Pets: Yes
Rates: $29.95 to $65.95

WAVIVATOSA

Exel Inn - West
115 N. Mayfair Rd.
Wavivatosa, WI 53226
Phone: (414) 257-0140,
   (800) 356-8013

Pet Restrictions: None
Exercise Area for Pets: Yes
Rates: $36.99 to $51.99

Sheraton Mayfair
2303 N. Mayfair
Wavivatosa, WI 53226
Phone: (414) 257-3400,
    (800) 325-3535

Pet Restrictions: None
Exercise Area for Pets: Nearby
Rates: $69 to $120

WAUSAU
Exel Inn
116 S. 17th Ave.
Wausau, WI 54401
Phone: (715) 842-0641,
    (800) 356-8013

Pet Restrictions: None
Exercise Area for Pets: Yes
Rates: $35.99 to $48.99

Super 8 Motel
2006 Steward Ave.
Wausau, WI 54401
Phone: (715) 848-2888,
    (800) 800-8000

Pet Restrictions: $50 deposit -
    refundable
Exercise Area for Pets: Yes
Rates: $44 to $68

Wausau Inn & Conf. Ctr.
2001 N. Mt. Rd.
Wausau, WI 54401
Phone: (715) 842-0711,
    (800) 928-7281

Pet Restrictions: Smoking rooms only
Pet left unattended in room: Yes
Exercise Area for Pets: Yes
Rates: $45

VETERINARIANS
Marathon Animal Hospital
1025 South 17th Ave.
Phone: (715) 845-1919

Wausau Animal Hospital
1006 Townline Rd.
Phone: (715) 845-9637

WISCONSIN FALLS
Holiday Inn
P.O. Box 236
Wisconsin Falls, WI 53965
Phone: (608) 254-8306,
    (800) HOLIDAY

Pet Restrictions: Small pets only
Exercise Area for Pets: Nearby
Rates: $52 to $92

WISCONSIN RAPIDS
Mead Inn
451 E. Grand Ave.
Wisconsin Rapids, WI 54494
Phone: (715) 423-1500

Pet Restrictions: $15 fee
Pet left unattended in room: Yes
Exercise Area for Pets: Yes
Rates: $44 to $81

WYOMING — HOTELS

AFTON

Mountain Inn
Hwy 89 Rt. 1
Afton, WY 83110
Phone: (307) 886-3156,
(800) 682-5356
Pet Restrictions: No cats, under 20
lbs.
Exercise Area for Pets: Yes
Rates: $47 to $65

BUFFALO

Arrowhead Motel
749 Fort St.
Buffalo, WY 82834
Phone: (307) 684-9453,
(800) 824-1719
Pet Restrictions: $5/pet/night
Exercise Area for Pets: Yes
Rates: $32 and up

CASPER

Casper Inn
123 West E St.
Casper, WY 82602
Phone: (307) 235-5713
Pet Restrictions: None
Pet left unattended in room: Yes, no
maid service
Exercise Area for Pets: Yes
Rates: $39.95 and up

Holiday Inn
300 West F St.
Casper, WY 82602
Phone: (307) 235-2531,
(800) HOLIDAY
Pet Restrictions: Quiet
Exercise Area for Pets: Yes
Rates: $48 to $64

Shilo Inn
Curtis Rd.
Casper, WY 82636
Phone: (307) 237-1335,
(800) 222-2244
Pet Restrictions: $6/pet/night
Exercise Area for Pets: Nearby
Rates: $33 to $49

Animal Clinic
2060 Fairgrounds Rd.
Phone: (307) 266-1660

CHEYENNE

La Quinta Motor Inn
2410 W. Lincolnway
Cheyenne, WY 82003
Phone: (307) 632-7117,
(800) 531-5900
Pet Restrictions: None
Exercise Area for Pets: Yes
Rates: $41 to $59

Rodeway Inn
3839 E. Lincolnway
Cheyenne, WY 82001
Phone: (307) 634-2171
Pet Restrictions: Designated rooms
Exercise Area for Pets: Yes
Rates: $32.95 and up

Cheyenne Pet Clinic
3740 E. Lincolnway
Phone: (307) 635-4121

CODY

Mt. View Lodge
2776 N. Fork
Cody, WY 82414
Phone: (307) 587-2081
Pet Restrictions: Small pets only
Exercise Area for Pets: Yes
Rates: $45 to $100

Wise Choice Inn
14 & 16 & 20 - North Fork Hwy
Cody, WY 82414
Phone: (307) 587-5004
Pet Restrictions: $3/pet/night
Exercise Area for Pets: Yes
Rates: $39 to $49

DOUGLAS

Holiday Inn
1450 Riverbend Dr.
Douglas, WY 82633
Phone: (307) 358-9790,
(800) HOLIDAY
Pet Restrictions: None
Exercise Area for Pets: Yes
Rates: $49 to $67

DUBOIS

Black Bear Country Inn Budget Hotel
505 N. Ramshorn
Dubois, WY 82513
Phone: (307) 455-2344,
(800) 873-BEAR
Pet Restrictions: Only dogs
Exercise Area for Pets: Yes
Rates: $32 to $40

Pinnacle Motor Lodge
3577 US 26
Dubois, WY 82513
Phone: (307) 455-2506
Pet Restrictions: $2/pet
Exercise Area for Pets: Yes
Rates: $35 and up

Rendezvous on the Wind River
1349 W. Ramshorn, P.O. Box 597
Dubois, WY 82513
Phone: (307) 455-2844,
(800) 682-9323
Pet Restrictions: $5 for small/night,
$10 large/night
Exercise Area for Pets: Yes
Rates: $42 to $80

Stagecoach Motor Inn
103 Ramshorn
Dubois, WY 82513
Phone: (307) 455-2303
Pet Restrictions: $2/pet/night, under
20 lbs.
Exercise Area for Pets: Yes
Rates: $30 to $55

EVANSTON

Best Western Dunmar Inn
1601 Harrison Dr.
Evanston, WY 82930
Phone: (307) 789-3770,
(800) 654-6509
Pet Restrictions: None
Exercise Area for Pets: Yes
Rates: $64 to $88

Weston Lamplighter
1983 Harrison Dr.
Evanston, WY 82930
Phone: (307) 789-0783,
(800) 255-9840
Pet Restrictions: Designated rooms
only
Pet left unattended in room: Yes, if
well behaved
Exercise Area for Pets: Yes
Rates: $39 to $49.95

GILLETTE

Days Inn Gillette
910 E. Box Elder
Gillette, WY 82716
Phone: (307) 682-3999,
(800) 325-2525
Pet Restrictions: $5
Pet left unattended in room: Yes, no
maid service
Exercise Area for Pets: Yes
Rates: $32 to $55

GRAND TETON NATIONAL PARK

Signal Mt. Lodge
Hwy 89
Grand Teton Natl Pk, WY 83013
Phone: (307) 543-2831,
(800) 672-6012
Pet Restrictions: None
Exercise Area for Pets: Yes
Rates: $62 to $140

GREEN RIVER

Western Motel
890 W. Flaming Gorge Way
Green River, WY 82935
Phone: (307) 875-2840
Pet Restrictions: Smoking rooms
only, $20 deposit
Exercise Area for Pets: Nearby
Rates: $30 to $40

JACKSON

The 49er Inn
330 W. Pearl
Jackson, WY 83001
Phone: (307) 733-7550,
(800) 451-2980
Pet Restrictions: Certain rooms
Exercise Area for Pets: Yes
Rates: $56 to $110

VETERINARIANS

Jackson Hole Veterinary Clinic
2905 Big Trail Dr.
Phone: (307) 733-4279

LARAMIE

Holiday Inn of Laramie
2313 Soldier Springs
Laramie, WY 82070
Phone: (307) 742-6611,
(800) HOLIDAY
Pet Restrictions: None
Rates: $58 and up

VETERINARIANS

Burton, Vicki A.
1171 Baker St. #5
Phone: (307) 742-4627

Johnson, Bruce
1759 N. 3rd
Phone: (307) 742-5590

LOVELL
Horseshoe Bend Motel
375 E. Main
Lovell, WY 82431
Phone: (307) 548-2221

Pet Restrictions: None
Exercise Area for Pets: Yes
Rates: $28 to $44

PORRINGTON
Maverick Motel
West Hwy 26
Porrington, WY 82240
Phone: (307) 532-4064

Pet Restrictions: None
Exercise Area for Pets: Yes
Rates: $26 to $36

RAWLINS
Key Motel
1806 E. Cedar St.
Rawlins, WY 82301
Phone: (307) 324-2728

Pet Restrictions: Under 20 lbs., $10
    deposit
Exercise Area for Pets: Yes
Rates: $32 and up

Rawlins Motel
905 W. Spruce St.
Rawlins, WY 82301
Phone: (307) 324-3456

Pet Restrictions: None
Exercise Area for Pets: Yes
Rates: $32 to $48

RIVERTON
Holiday Inn
N. Federal Blvd. at Sunset
Riverton, WY 82501
Phone: (307) 856-8100,
    (800) 465-4329

Pet Restrictions: None
Exercise Area for Pets: Yes
Rates: $45 to $60

Thunderbird Motel
302 E. Tremont
Riverton, WY 82501
Phone: (307) 856-9201

Pet Restrictions: None
Pet left unattended in room: Yes
Exercise Area for Pets: Yes
Rates: $25 to $40

ROCK SPRINGS
Holiday Inn
1675 Sunset Dr.
Rock Springs, WY 82901
Phone: (307) 382-9200,
    (800) HOLIDAY

Pet Restrictions: Designated rooms,
    $2/night
Exercise Area for Pets: Yes
Rates: $60.80 to $74.80

Inn at Rock Springs
2518 Foothill Blvd.
Rock Springs, WY 82901
Phone: (307) 362-9600,
    (800) 442-9692

Pet Restrictions: None
Pet left unattended in room: Yes
Exercise Area for Pets: Yes
Rates: $48.80 and up

SARATOGA
Hacienda Motel
P.O. Box 82331
Saratoga, WY, 82331
Phone: (307) 326-5751

Pet Restrictions: Smoking rooms only
Exercise Area for Pets: Yes
Rates: $29 to $52

SHERIDAN
Holiday Inn
1809 Sugarland Dr.
Sheridan, WY 82801
Phone: (307) 672-8931,
    (800) HOLIDAY

Pet Restrictions: None
Pet left unattended in room: Yes,
    quiet
Exercise Area for Pets: Yes
Rates: $66 and up

VETERINARIANS
Moxey, Lance T.
Box 6529
Phone: (307) 672-5533

TETON VILLAGE

Crystal Springs Inn
3285 McCollister Dr.
Teton Village, WY 83025
Phone: (307) 733-4423

Pet Restrictions: None
Exercise Area for Pets: Yes
Rates: $52 to $89

THERMOPOLIS

Best West. Moonlighter Motel
600 Broadway
Thermopolis, WY 82443
Phone: (307) 864-2321

Pet Restrictions: None
Exercise Area for Pets: Nearby
Rates: $50 and up

Holiday Inn by the Waters
115 East Park
Thermopolis, WY 82443
Phone: (307) 864-3131,
    (800) HOLIDAY

Pet Restrictions: None
Exercise Area for Pets: Yes
Rates: $76 to $64

WAPITI

Absaroka Mt. Lodge
1231 E. Yellowstone Hwy
Wapiti, WY 82450
Phone: (307) 587-3963

Pet Restrictions: $25 deposit, house
    trained
Exercise Area for Pets: Nearby
Rates: $46 to $94

WORLAND

Sun Valley Motel
500 N. 10th St.
Worland, WY 82401
Phone: (307) 347-4251

Pet Restrictions: Small pets only,
    house trained
Exercise Area for Pets: Yes
Rates: $24 to $48

YELLOWSTONE NATIONAL PARK

Lake Lodge & Cabins
1½ mi. S. of lake jct.
Yellowstone, WY 82190
Phone: (307) 344-7311

Pet Restrictions: Only in cabins,
    must be on leash, not on trails
Exercise Area for Pets: Yes
Rates: $42.80 to $72.80

Lake Yellowstone Hotel & Cabins
1 mi. S. of lake jct.
Yellowstone, WY 82190
Phone: (307) 344-7311 / 344-7901

Pet Restrictions: Only cabins, no
    trails, must be on leash
Rates: $77.04 to $278.20

Mammoth Hot Springs Hotel & Cabins
Mammoth Hot Springs
Yellowstone, WY 82190
Phone: (307) 344-7311

Pet Restrictions: Only in cabins, on
    leash, not on trails
Rates: $53 to $116

Notes:

Notes:

Notes:

Notes: